Themes in the
Historical Geography
of France

Themes in the Historical Geography of France

Edited by

HUGH D. CLOUT

Department of Geography,
University College London,
England

1977

ACADEMIC PRESS · London   New York   San Francisco

A Subsidiary of Harcourt Brace Jovanovich, Publishers

ACADEMIC PRESS INC. (LONDON) LTD.
24/28 Oval Road
London NW1

U.S. Edition published by
ACADEMIC PRESS INC.
111 Fifth Avenue
New York, New York 10003
Copyright © 1977 By
ACADEMIC PRESS INC. (LONDON) LTD.

Library of Congress Catalog Card Number: 76–54375
ISBN: 0–12–175850–8

Printed in Great Britain by
W & J Mackay Limited, Chatham
by Photo-litho

List of Contributors

Pierre Bonnaud   Université de Clermont-Ferrand.
Hugh D. Clout   University College London.
André Fel   Université de Clermont-Ferrand.
Pierre Flatrès   Université de Haute-Bretagne, Rennes.
Gwyn I. Meirion-Jones   City of London Polytechnic.
Hugh Prince   University College London.
Keith Sutton   University of Manchester.

Preface

The recognition and status of historical geography in various 'national schools' of geography displays many profound contrasts. These are particularly striking as one examines conditions on either side of the English Channel (Baker, 1972). Until recently, French geographers have incorporated the consideration of past conditions in much of their writing, often using study of the past as a key to understanding the present. By virtue of such an approach, 'historical geography' was not identified as a distinct subsection of the discipline. None the less, a rich harvest of research dealing with the human geography of France in past times was published in regional monographs and specialized articles in learned journals. In recent years, however, many French geographers have turned their interests in other directions and have lessened their commitment to what would be recognized across the Channel— and across the Atlantic—as 'historical geography'. By contrast, historical geography displays considerable identity and strength in Great Britain and the English-speaking world, as the volume of publication and the appearance of the Journal of Historical Geography have shown. Recent publications in English by geographers (e.g. Smith, 1967) and by historians (e.g. Cameron, 1970; Price, 1975) provide much valuable material for students who are interested in the historical geography of France but whose library resources or linguistic abilities are limited and thereby exclude examining literature in French. The present volume has been compiled with the objective of bringing together a number of selected themes in the historical geography of France and to present them to a wider audience. In no way does it strive to provide a 'complete' view, nor does it claim to exemplify any particular or unified methodology. As editor, I have been encouraged by the willingness of geographers on both sides of the English Channel to write for this volume but I must confess that the finished product contains much more from my own typewriter than was intended when the book was first envisaged. I extend my thanks to each of the contributors for his kindness in agreeing to co-operate in preparing this book and for his patience during the editorial process (Steel and Wreford Watson, 1972, p. 144). In particular, I should like to express my gratitude to Monsieur Bonnaud, Professor Fel and Professor Flatrès for presenting their detailed knowledge to a rather different audience.

With customary speed and efficiency, members of the secretarial and cartographic staff in the Department of Geography at University College London have produced the greater part of the typescript and most of the illustrations. The hard work of Trevor Allen, Ros Bushell, Val Cawley, Richard Davidson, Alick Newman, Claudette John, Annabel Swindell, Margaret Thomas, Ken Wass and especially Tina Hill is greatly appreciated, as are the artistic skills of Miss M. Teed at the City of London Polytechnic who drew the illustrations for chapter 10. I must thank those who kindled my initial interest in the historical geography of France; the geographers, archivists, librarians and mayors' secretaries who have introduced me to some of the documentary sources relating to their particular regions; and the various organizations—including the Centre National de la Recherche Scientifique and University College London—that have generously contributed financial support to enable me to undertake research in France. Last, but not least, I appreciate the good company of colleagues and students as we have gained first-hand experience of the French way of life in conditions much more comfortable than those endured between 1812 and 1814 by the future occupant of the first Chair of Geography at University College London (Barry, 1958).

HUGH D. CLOUT

Baker, A. R. H. (ed.), *Progress in Historical Geography*, Newton Abbot (1972).
Barry, J., *Alexander Maconochie of Norfolk Island*, Melbourne (1958).
Cameron, R. E. (ed.) *Essays in French Economic History*, Homewood, Illinois (1970).

Price, R., *The Economic Modernization of France, 1730–1880*, London (1975).

Smith, C. T., *An Historical Geography of Western Europe before 1800*, London (1967).

Steel, R. W. and Wreford Watson, J., Geography in the United Kingdom 1968–72, *Geographical Journal*, 138, (1972), 139–153.

Acknowledgements

Librairie Armand Colin 3.5, 5.5, 6.1, 6.2, 6.4, 12.2, 12.9;

Librairie Armand Colin & Annales, Economies, Sociétés, Civilisations 3.6, 11.1, 12.8;

Association de Géographes Français figure 8 in appendix;

Professor Jacqueline Beaujeu-Garnier 12.13, 13.13;

Professor Maurice Beresford 3.8;

Professor Roger Béteille 7.6;

Professor Pierre Bruyelle 13.21, 13.22;

M. J. Chauvel & the Société Géologique et Minéralogique de Bretagne 6.3;

Professor Raymond Chevallier 3.4;

Professor Roger Dion 12.10;

Professor Max Derruau 5.6, 5.7;

Professor Robert Dickinson & Routledge and Kegan Paul 3.11;

La Documentation Française 13.14;

Dr. Jacques Dupâquier 7.1;

Ecole des Hautes Etudes en Sciences Sociales 4.1, 4.2, 4.3;

M. Georges Hahn and Editions Privat 12.7, 13.4, 13.12;

Professor Charles Higounet 13.3;

Institut National d'Etudes Démographiques 7.5, 13.8, 13.9, 13.10, 13.11;

Institut National de la Statistique et des Etudes Economiques 13.25;

Professor René Lebeau 5.5;

Professor Serge Lerat 3.12;

Martinus Nijhoff 6.5;

Madame G. Pinchemel 13.22, 13.23;

Professor P. Pinchemel 13.18, 13.20;

Professor Abel Poitrineau 7.7;

Presses Universitaires de France 12.3, 12.4, figure 3 in appendix;

Professor Jean Robert & Norois 9.5; 9.6;

Société Royale de Géographie d'Anvers figures 1 & 4 in appendix;

Professor Ian Thompson 13.24;

Professor Fernand Verger 6.8.

Contents

1
The Practice of Historical Geography in France   1
Hugh D. Clout

2
Peopling and the Origins of Settlement   21
Pierre Bonnaud

3
Early Urban Development   73
Hugh D. Clout

Appendix II
Additional Reading on Themes in the Historical
Geography of France   565
Hugh D. Clout

List of Illustrations

Peopling and Origins of Settlement

Early Urban Development

Retreat of Rural Settlement

Regional Contrasts in Agrarian Structure

Reclamation of Coastal marshland

La Petite Culture 1750–1850

Reclamation of Wasteland

Western France

Vernacular Architecture and the Peasant House

Agricultural Change

Industrial Development

Urban Growth, 1500–1900

Appendix I

List of Tables

1
The Practice of Historical Geography in France

HUGH D. CLOUT

Historical Geography and Geographical History

'Historical geographers' acknowledging that particular title above all others are a rare academic breed in France.[1] It is true that Auguste Longnon occupied a Chair of Historical Geography at the Collège de France as early as 1892–1911 but his work was concerned primarily with the evolution of territorial divisions in France. This approach investigated neither the inter-relationship between cultural and physical systems nor the temporal evolution of spatial patterns that have been subsequently at the heart of much French geographical writing (Cholley, 1946). According to Roger Dion (1957), its most eminent practitioner:

'. . . historical geography is a retrospective form of human geography that . . . searches back into the past as far as is necessary to explain the variety of features created by human effort on the face of the land' (p. 183).

Thus it is more than a branch of archaeology or history. Historical geographers need also to examine varying perceptions of physical resources for settlement, cultivation, and other purposes, and study changing spatial distributions through time (Dion, 1947–8, 1949). They should not be

'disinterested in the modern world or ignore it, for the aim of historical geography is simply to explain what we see around us' (Dion, 1949, p. 26).

This type of definition of historical geography has been accepted widely by French geographers who have examined aspects of human geography in an historic context. But Dion himself in recent writings, and some other authors, have occasionally investigated themes that have no direct relevance to understanding the present.

Although much French human geography contains an important historical aspect, few French geographers have fully accepted historical geography as a distinct sub-branch of the discipline and have focused their work on the study of the past. Now perhaps only Dion, occupying the Chair at the Collège de France many decades after Longnon, would see himself as an historical geographer above all else (Gulley, 1961; de Planhol, 1972a). But this is not to suggest that little historical geography has been written, indeed the situation is just the opposite. In de Planhol's words:

'. . . historical geography in France is . . . both everywhere and nowhere' (1972a, p. 40).

The answer to this apparent contradiction is found in the fact that in the French educational system

'. . . history and geography live together harmoniously to their mutual profit' (Duby, 1968, p. 6).

Thus university undergraduates specializing in either discipline have been required to take courses in the other (Meynier, 1969).

Given such an early training, many French geographers have looked instinctively to changing social and economic conditions in the past as an essential means of attempting to explain contemporary differences in spatial organization. Without study of the past geographers

'. . . would have to resign themselves to superficial explanations and risk slipping towards physical determinism' (Meynier, 1958, p. 5).

In his study of rural settlement in Basse-Provence Livet (1962) argued in a similar vein.

'If we wish to reach a precise and yet subtle explanation of geographical realities, accounting for the complexity that we find with every step we take in human geography, we must enrich descriptions of the present by geographical study of the past' (p. 422).

Praise for the quality of historical research by French geographers has come from the historian Georges Duby when he remarked:

'. . . we must remember that, in France at least, geographers have contributed to our knowledge of rural life at the time of Charlemagne and Saint-Louis more than have historians in the strict sense of the word' (Duby, 1968, p. xi).

Similar statements might also be appropriate for other periods.

On the other hand, French historians have made use of their geographical education in elucidating spatial patterns of historical phenomena and paying attention to variations in land resources in their analyses of social and economic processes in the past (Boutruche, 1947; Higounet, 1953). Duby's (1968) instruction issued to aspiring medieval historians reads with a very geographical ring.

'Proceed to a searching scrutiny of the landscape as it is today, and the natural conditions which govern peasant activity, climatic features and soil fertility; tramp the countryside and gradually acquire a familiarity and intimacy with it until those hitherto unnoticed features which were so often deeply implanted upon it by the toil of an earlier generation are at last revealed beneath the outward appearance; then tackle the medieval documents and systematically despoil them; reconstruct from them a society with all its ramifications, and attempt to isolate the relationships which bound hamlet and village to market town and peasant household to lord's residence' (p. xii).

Many French historians have practised such an approach, which was summarized by Lucien Febvre as '. . . historians . . . be geographers' (quoted in Dupâquier, 1969). It is a telling fact that Baulig (1945), a geographer, wrote an appreciation of the life and work of the historian Marc Bloch and entitled it 'Marc Bloch—geographer'.

Study of the past flourished with exceptional brilliance in
France during the 1930s under the guidance of Bloch and Febvre,
as the pages of the *Annales: Economies, Sociétés, Civilisations*,
which they founded in 1929, testify (Prince, 1958). The thoughts
and findings of archaeologists, ethnographers, geographers,
historians, linguists, psychologists, sociologists and others sparked
off controversy but also led to agreement in an 'alliance of
disciplines' throughout the decade (Baulig, 1945). Bloch and his
school of human scientists were eminently aware of the significance
of the physical environment as a resource base for human evaluation and use and recognized the importance of examining distributions of phenomena in space. They prepared maps of many kinds,
displaying variations in agricultural techniques, place names, and a
host of other features. In addition, Bloch (1929, 1932, 1933, 1935,
1943) wrote a number of articles illustrating the importance of
cartographic sources in historical research.

In short, French geographical writing is imbued with history,
just as French historical research contains much geography.
Whilst recognizing that the substance of historical geography has
been written by practitioners of both disciplines, and indeed of
several others, the following paragraphs will be concerned primarily with geographical contributions.

Geographical Contributions to the Historical Geography of France

The usual vehicles whereby French geographers, historians, and
other academics expressed their research findings have been
doctorat d'état theses, published in their authors' academic prime
or maturity, and the scholarly papers written prior to the submission of the theses. Historians cast their research in fairly
closely-defined frameworks both in time and space, adopting the
approach articulated by Duby (1968), when he argued that it was
necessary to bring together

'. . . landscape, nature and man, and relate all the social groups
who . . . combined to exploit the soil. For, in the crucial phases
of all worthwhile research it is always necessary to come back
to regional studies' (p. xii).

Geographers, writing in the first half of the twentieth century, adopted a rather similar approach following the model of Albert Demangeon's (1905) study of Picardy. But usually they covered a wider timespan than their historian colleagues, starting from the remote past, which was necessary to describe the evolution of the physical environment, and working through the human geography of past centuries up to the period in which they were writing or to the past immediately prior to that time. Study of the past was an end in itself for historians, but was simply a means to understanding the present for geographers. This particular approach to the past surely accounts to some extent for the small number of French geographers who have concentrated on studying the past for its own sake.

Regional monographs written by geographers prior to World War II contained almost predictable descriptions of themes such as land clearance and the foundation of monastic houses in medieval times, agricultural production in the eighteenth and nineteenth centuries, domestic craft manufacturing, and a host of other processes. Discussions of social and economic conditions were normally graded in length for successive historical periods, with greater numbers of pages being devoted as the story moved towards the present century. Thus Gallo-Roman settlement and medieval colonization were dismissed with greater brevity in these studies than, for example, farming techniques in the nineteenth century. Most monographs were organized chronologically working from the remote past progressively towards the present. This arrangement was correct logically and respected rules of historical training. However, the kind of retrogressive approach that was outlined by Bloch (1931) might have been more appropriate, working from the known to the unknown, from the best known to the less well known. This may have been the mental approach used by geographers during their research but only the work of Pierre Deffontaines (1932) on the Middle Garonne adopted something of a retrogressive presentation (Baker, 1968; Jäger, 1965). Very few of these pre-war studies were problem orientated. Rather they were concerned with categorizing every significant aspect of the physical and human geography within chosen study areas. Dion's (1934a) study of the Val de Loire was a notable exception, being focused on the history of human struggle against flooding by the Loire and on the various patterns of settlements and fields found in the region.

Many post-war theses also diverged from the traditional framework for regional monographs, either by adopting a novel arrangement of material, for example discussing physical resources after presenting spatial differences in the contemporary scene (P. Brunet, 1960), or by concentrating on distinct problems in the study region instead of attempting encyclopaedic description. Such problem-orientation included peasant traditions (Fel, 1962), urban growth (Rochefort, 1960), ownership of rural lands by city dwellers (Brunet, 1965; Dugrand, 1963; Elhaï, 1965), the influence of an international boundary on patterns of human activity (Daveau, 1959), the social geography of a region (Juillard, 1953a), among many others. Such monographs, both old and new, certainly contain much of the substance of French historical geography, but their authors would simply view their writing as 'geography', exemplifying a method whereby they sought to comprehend the present through study of the past.

It is true that some research articles by geographers have concentrated on past conditions without explicit reference to the present, but examples of such work are relatively rare (Gay, 1958b; Lerat, 1957). However many of the recent historico-geographical publications by Roger Dion have not attempted to illuminate an understanding of the present.[2]

Regional monographs and research articles of great number and academic respectability present the student with indispensable but fragmented historical evidence for many parts of France. The task of sifting information in order to generalize for the whole country or even to propose wider explanations than those valid at a purely local level is certainly formidable. It would seem that historians, such as Bloch (1931, 1956, 1966) and Duby (1962, 1968), have been rather more willing to make the attempt than have geographers. Thus Bloch (1931), in an early and masterly interpretation of field patterns, recognized the fundamental difference between enclosed areas and openfields, with the second type comprising elongated parcels in northern France and irregular plots in the South. Enclosures were interpreted as occupying areas of poor soil, with openfields in more favourable environments. The distinction between the two openfield types was attributed to cultural factors. Simple 'racial' distinctions were rejected as a mode of explanation, but instead Bloch favoured a broader concept of 'agrarian civilization' (Juillard, *et al.*, 1957) (see Chapter 5).

This seminal historical work was soon followed by a geographical synthesis from Roger Dion (1934b) who recognized a somewhat different distribution of field patterns but also argued for the importance of cultural differences in explaining variations in rural economy. Using evidence from the late-eighteenth-century writings of Arthur Young and from many other sources, Dion noted that communal agricultural traditions had been strong in the area north of the river Loire, but to the south freedom to enclose one's land had been greater and there had been more individuality in farming practices. Thus in his explanation he combined the importance of cultural variables with a sophisticated appraisal of spatial differences in physical resources, contrasting the broad *limon* covered plains of the North, with the much more broken relief and diverse soil conditions of central and southern France. As in many of his other writings, Dion (1934b) rejected physical determinism stressing that

'. . . the geographer will realise that enclosures do not derive of necessity from granites, nor are openfields only found on calcareous rocks' (p. 2).

Yet in spite of a few syntheses and a vast amount of research, information on major cultural processes at work in forming French rural landscapes, such as clearing wood, draining marsh, and reclaiming heath, still has to be gleaned from disparate sources. Indeed, in view of the fact that almost all French geographers studied history it is surprising that so few specialized studies of processes in historical geography have been made (Harrison-Church, 1951). It is true that some collations were attempted by non-geographers in the last century but recent systematic works are few and far between (Brown, 1876; de Dienne, 1891). Masterly syntheses of silvicultural activities by the historian Devèze (1961) and the history of viticulture by Dion (1943, 1948–9, 1950, 1952, 1959) form the most impressive examples. In the latter collection of publications Dion argued that the vine was perhaps the best-conserved Roman relic in France. He showed that in post-medieval times the great vineyards of France were

located near navigable waterways which facilitated distribution and
that the quality of the wine produced reflected the wealth of the
owner and the skill with which the soil had been fertilized and
improved. Thus the best wines did not derive from vineyards
with the best 'natural' soils, but from those near episcopal seats
and centres of commerce where great amounts of capital, labour
and expertise had been devoted to viticulture.

In addition to writing regional monographs, French geographers have devoted a great, perhaps even a disproportionate,
amount of attention to classifying and analysing the evolution of
features in the rural landscape, again using study of the past to aid
understanding of the present. Juillard (1964) claims that this
rural bias

> '. . . should not be surprising, since no other *milieu* allows one to
> study so well the interaction of physical and human factors
> whose internal logic geographers try to explain' (p. 46).

Variations in the structure and dynamism of landscapes, in his
opinion, form '. . . the proper domain of geographical research'
(p. 47). As a result of this orientation, rural-landscape studies are
not only numerous but also diverse. However, five fairly distinct
realms of research may be determined and each of these will be
examined in turn.

The first involves the description of 'settlement patterns',
viewing that term in a narrow sense as involving distributions of
inhabited points and variations in their spatial arrangement
through time. Such an approach was pioneered by Demangeon
(1920, 1939) who devised indices of nucleation and dispersion to
classify patterns of settlement that might be derived from topographical maps or adduced from census statistics. This method of
investigation has been applied to Berry (Gay, 1958a), the Jura
(Lebeau, 1955), Nivernais (Chiffre, 1969) and other regions. It
is essentially a static approach, involving some period in the past
or indeed the present, or occasionally comparing past with present. But even when diachronic comparisons are attempted this
approach cannot provide explanations of change but simply offers
numerical statements describing its net results. Explanations of
the variations in distribution through time may only be found by

detailed analysis of morphological changes and the various social and economic processes that produced them.

This broader approach forms the second and probably most important realm of French rural geography. 'Settlement patterns' are considered to include villages, hamlets, farmsteads, with their surrounding fields and landholdings. Early interpretations of rural landscapes offered by Bloch (1931) and Dion (1934b) four decades ago have been questioned and refined as a result of many detailed regional enquiries by geographers. Perhaps the best-known examples derive from investigations of the evolution of field patterns, and village and hamlet types in north-western France that have been undertaken by geographers based at the University of Rennes (Flatrès, 1957, 1958; Meynier, 1962, 1966, 1969).[3] Important work has also been completed in Aquitaine (R. Brunet, 1960), Languedoc (Sion, 1937, 1940), the Massif Central (Derruau, 1949; Fel, 1962), Normandy (P. Brunet, 1955, 1968), the northern part of the Paris Basin (P. Brunet, 1960), Provence (Livet, 1962), and Lorraine. Research in the latter region has been particularly stimulating, comprising analyses of the metrology of field patterns, and the remodelling of fields and rebuilding of villages after destruction in the Thirty Years' War (de Martin, 1971; Peltre, 1966, 1968, 1971; de Planhol et al., 1965; Reitel, 1966). Commentaries on earlier examples of the regional interpretations in this particularly important branch of French geographical study are provided by Champier (1956), Juillard et al. (1957) and Meynier (1958).

The third realm of investigation is concerned with the evolution of micro-features in rural landscapes. Variations in the distribution and evolution of house types have attracted much attention (Bouhier et al., 1969; Coque, 1956; de Planhol, 1968, 1971; Robert, 1939).[4] In Demangeon's (1936) words the peasant house is

'. . . the concrete and visual image of rural culture. It is the product both of preceding traditions and the requirements of farm management' (p. 512).

In addition, the study of rural house types provides a range of particularly intriguing interactions between cultural and physical factors. Other investigations of rural micro-features have concerned rural roads (Chaumeil, 1949; Gautier, 1971; Meynier, 1949), headland ridges (Juillard, 1953b), terraces (Despois, 1957), and lynchets (Aufrère, 1929; Fénelon, 1956).

The fourth approach focuses on historical aspects of agrarian organization, and is best exemplified by the early writings of Roger Dion (1946). In an eminently geographical essay he outlined detailed variations in physical conditions in the Paris Basin in some areas, such as calcareous, *limon*-topped plateaux, offered 'attractive' environments to early settlers but in others presented distinctly 'hostile' areas of clay and other impermeable soils that could not be managed effectively using the implements of early technology. As one would expect, Dion's interpretation of subsequent forms of agrarian organization was far from deterministic, since he went on to stress variations in land ownership, communal organization, and capital investment in farming from early times through to the modern period to elucidate spatial variations and differential dynamism in rural landscapes. Two additional aspects of this approach have involved critical examination of the supposed 'agricultural revolution' in the eighteenth and nineteenth centuries (Faucher, 1962); and regional differences in agricultural rotations (Faucher, 1961), paying particular attention to northeastern France (Colin and Blanc, 1966; Juillard, 1952).

The final branch of geographical investigation into past rural conditions has involved the detailed analysis of land-use patterns. An initial sample study in the Limousin region was extended by the late Aimé Perpillou (1935, 1940, 1961) to the whole of France with the aim of producing a complete series of handsome coloured maps which display land use for the early nineteenth century, the early twentieth century, and the post-war period at both national and regional scales.[5]

By contrast with the wealth of information that has been presented by French geographers on the historical evolution of rural landscapes and the social and economic processes that have formed them, other aspects of enquiry remain relatively untouched. An appreciation of urban historical geography in France, for example, may only be attempted by reference to the research of architects, town planners and historians. For two generations of French geography before World War II it was almost as if, in Buttimer's (1971) words:

'. . . cities were somehow anathema, unwelcome intrusions in the neatly ordered agricultural landscape' (p. 118).

Urban growth has, of course, been examined by many French geographers but, almost without exception, their method has been to describe isolated case studies, treating the morphological evolution of individual towns along with their contemporary social and economic functioning. The end result of this kind of approach has been no more than a collection of disparate case studies which almost defy generalization. Detailed geographical analyses of distinctive types of industrial housing (Pinchemel, 1954), impact of differential land ownership on urban expansion (Prêcheur, 1953), chronology of urban street patterns (Rouleau, 1968), and suburban growth (Bastié, 1964) are relatively few and far between. Fortunately architects and city planners have produced valuable historical studies (Lavedan, 1952, 1953, 1959) and now historians are devoting greater attention to urban matters.

Geographical interest in the history of population has focussed largely on the spatial patterns of rural depopulation and the economic implications of population loss in the countryside (Bravard, 1961; Pinchemel, 1957; Pitié, 1971). Studies of this kind are complemented by the work of the distinguished French school of historical demographers, headed by Louis Henry (1972), which has pioneered a number of new analytical approaches, including family reconstitution from the contents of parish registers. Some of the published works by members of this school are eminently geographical in character, being perhaps best characterized by Pierre Goubert's (1960) regional study of the historical demography and economy of the Beauvaisis.

It would be correct to acknowledge that in France, if not in Britain, historical geography is 'less appreciated in some quarters than it was' (Steel and Wreford Watson, 1972, p. 144). This state of affairs may be seen as a response to three main trends.

First, and in a general sense, French geographers no longer regard the comprehensive regional monograph as the pinnacle of academic achievement. Emphasis has shifted towards detailed, and increasingly quantitative, investigation of a wide variety of both human and physical themes. Such systematic enquiries are still pursued within regional frameworks but, on the human side at least, are little concerned with historical antecedence. Urban and economic studies are orientated increasingly from the present towards the future for purposes of planning and prediction, rather than into the past for reasons of explanation. The only real growth points in retrospective study by modern French geographers involve the history of geographic thought (Claval, 1964, 1972; Claval and Nardy, 1968; Mollat and Pinchemel, 1972) and past perceptions of the environment (Broc, 1965, 1969).

Second, in a similar way but in a specific context, there has been a notable change in research emphasis among French agrarian geographers who in previous decades were responsible for producing the bulk of historico-geographical work. Analysis of the content of papers presented at successive symposia on European rural landscapes and of the work of individual rural specialists suggests that by comparison with the 1950s and 1960s fewer French geographers are now concerned with examining the evolution of rural landscapes and explaining relict features that are contained in the modern scene (Dussart, 1971; Flatrès, 1972; Géographie et Histoire Agraires, 1959; Jäger et al,. 1968). Instead, a prospective approach is being increasingly adopted which concentrates on processes whereby rural landscapes are being remodelled to accommodate modern agricultural activities and meet new demands from commuters and tourists (Juillard, 1964). After having been historical geographers in part, many French agrarian specialists have moved over the years from being concerned with regional description, the classification of settlement patterns, and explanation of their evolution, to acting as applied geographers (Fel, 1957). Only Roger Dion, in his isolated post at the Collège de France aside from the mass of French research students, would employ the title of 'historical geographer' (de Planhol, 1972a).

Finally, the strong and expanding school of French economic history is colonizing academic territory that was once held in condominium with geographers. Historians naturally view the study of the past as their own realm of investigation and many are now turning to landscape studies (Juillard, 1964). As a result of their geographical training and the general strength of the discipline, French historians are now probably the main producers of what might be recognized as 'historical geography' (Juillard, 1957).

Nevertheless, the scope for historico-geographical studies remains great and is indeed enhanced by the possibility of employing modern numerical techniques for data-handling, analysis, and display. Three broad areas are worthy of attention, albeit likely that the work may not be done by geographers. Additional detailed investigations of the historical realities of economic and social life are needed. Once the necessary data for such enquiries have been transcribed, new prospects of analysis await researchers through computerization. Second, the task of synthesizing still largely remains to be done in both historical geography and economic history. Systematic themes have been investigated scrupulously in regional or local contexts but have rarely been pursued nationwide. However, for the recent past at least, valuable statistical sources are available which provide a body of information that may be manipulated to allow local case studies to be measured against broader spatial and temporal patterns. Finally, the task of mapping historical phenomena on a national scale has, as yet, made little progress, although a very suggestive re-interpretation of the supposed 'agricultural revolution' in eighteenth-century France has been assisted by mapping information on cereal yields derived from the 1840 estimates (Morineau, 1968). In addition, a series of regional historical atlases is being produced (Baratier et al., 1969; de Planhol, 1972a).[6] Maps and statistical manipulation cannot of course replace detailed archival investigation but they do provide suggestive displays of data at levels above the local or regional scales that have been employed almost exclusively in the past.

1. Notes

1. This discussion is complemented by the review by de Planhol (1972a and b) of historical geography in France and allied research by French historians.
2. For a list of these see de Planhol (1972a).
3. This work is summarized by Flatrès in Chapter 9.
4. For a more detailed discussion see Chapter 10 by Meirion-Jones.
5. Some of these land-use maps have been included in the series of regional atlases being prepared for most parts of France: e.g. *Atlas de Paris et de la Région Parisienne* (1967), *Atlas du Languedoc-Roussillon* (1969), *Atlas Midi-Pyrénées* (1970), *Atlas des Pays de la Loire* (1973).
6. In addition, many of the historical studies of French provinces in the *Univers*

de France series edited by Professor P. Wolff contain material that might be embraced by the heading 'historical geography'.

1. References

Aufrère, L., 'Les rideaux: étude topographique', *Annales de Géographie*, 38, (1929), 529–30.

Baker, A. R. H., 'A note on the retrogressive and retrospective approaches in historical geography', *Erdkunde*, 25, (1968), 243–44.

Baratier, E., Duby, G., and Hildesheimer, F., *Atlas Historique, Provence, Comtat, Orange, Nice, Monaco*, Paris (1969).

Bastié, J., *La Croissance de la banlieue parisienne*, Paris (1964).

Baulig, H., 'Marc Bloch, géographe', *Annales d'Histoire Sociale*, 8, (1945), 5–12.

Bloch, M., 'Les plans parcellaires', *Annales d'Histoire Economique et Sociale*, 1, (1929), 392–98.

Bloch, M., *Les Caractères originaux de l'histoire rurale française*, Paris (1931).

Bloch, M., 'Une bonne nouvelle: l'enquête sur les plans cadastraux français', *Annales d'Histoire Economique et Sociale*, 2, (1932), 370–71.

Bloch, M., 'Le cadastre par nature de cultures', *Annales d'Histoire Economique et Sociale*, 5, (1933), 152.

Bloch, M., 'Une nouvelle image de nos terroirs: la mise à jour du cadastre', *Annales d'Histoire Economique et Sociale*, 7, (1935), 156–59.

Bloch, M., 'Les plans cadastraux de l'ancien régime', *Melanges d'Histoire Sociale*, 3, (1943), 55–70.

Bloch, M., *Les Caractères originaux de l'histoire rurale française: tome deuxième*, Paris (1956).

Bloch, M., *French Rural History*, trans. J. Sondheimer, London (1966).

Bouhier, A., 'Actes du colloque sur la maison rurale, Poitiers', *Norois*, 63, (1969), 1–336.

Boutruche, R. *La Crise d'une Société: Seigneurs et paysans du Bordelais pendant la guerre de cent ans*, Paris and Strasbourg (1947).

Bravard, Y., 'Le dépeuplement des hautes vallées des Alpes-Maritimes', *Revue de Géographie Alpine*, 49, (1961), 5–127.

Broc, N. 'Aspects de la connaissance géographique des Pyrénées en 18e siècle', *Bulletin de la Société Languedocienne de Géographie*, (1965), 355–386.

Broc, N., *Les Montagnes vues par les géographes et les naturalistes de langue française au 18e siècle*, Paris (1969).

Brown, J. C., *Reboisement in France*, London (1876).

Brunet, P., 'Problèmes relatifs aux structures agraires de la Basse-Normandie', *Annales de Normandie*, (1955), 115–34.

Brunet, P., *Structure agraire et économie rurale des plateaux tertiaires entre la Seine et l'Oise*, Caen (1960).

Brunet, P., 'Evolution des bocages herbagers en Basse-Normandie', in Jäger, H. *et al.* (eds) (1968).

Brunet, R., 'Les paysages ruraux de l'Aquitaine du sud-est', *Revue Géographique des Pyrénées et du Sud-Ouest*, 31, (1960), 233–76.

Brunet, R., *Les Campagnes toulousaines: étude géographique*, Toulouse (1965).

Buttimer, A., *Society and Milieu in the French Geographic Tradition*, Chicago (1971).

Champier, L., 'La recherche française en matière d'histoire et de géographie agraires depuis un quart de siècle', *Revue de Géographie de Lyon*, 31, (1956), 319–27.

Chaumeil, L., 'Les chemins creux de Bretagne', *Annales de Géographie*, 58, (1949), 55–8.

Chiffre, J., 'Une nouvelle formule de dispersion de l'habitat rural: son application en Nivernais', *Revue Géographique de l'Est*, 9, (1969), 149–175.

Cholley, A., 'Problèmes de structure agraire et d'économie rurale', *Annales de Géographie*, 55, (1946), 81–101.

Claval, P., Essai sur l'évolution de la géographie humaine, *Cahiers de Géographie de Besançon*, 12, (1964), 1–162.

Claval, P., *La Pensée géographique*, Paris (1972).

Claval, P. and Nardy, J-P., 'Pour le cinquantenaire de la mort de Paul Vidal de la Blache', *Cahiers de Géographie de Besançon*, 16, (1968), 1–130.

Colin, G. and Blanc, A. 'Extension et déclin de l'assolement triennal au 19e siècle: l'évolution sociale d'une communauté lorraine', *Revue Géographique de l'Est*, 1–2, (1966), 89–95.

Coque, R., 'L'évolution de la maison rurale en Amiénois', *Annales de Géographie*, 65, (1956), 401–17.

Daveau, S., *Les Régions frontalières de la montagne jurasienne*, Lyons (1959).

Deffontaines, P., *Les Hommes et leurs travaux dans les pays de la moyenne Garonne*, Lille, (1932).

Demangeon, A., *La Picardie*, Paris (1905).

Demangeon, A., 'L'habitation rurale en France: essai de classification des principaux types', *Annales de Géographie*, 29, (1920), 352–75.

Demangeon, A., 'Trois questionnaires et trois enquêtes de géographie humaine', *Annales de Géographie*, 45, (1936), 512–18.

Demangeon, A., 'Types de peuplement rural en France', *Annales de Géographie*, 48, (1939), 1–21.

Derruau, M., *La Grande Limagne auvergnate et bourbonnaise*, Clermont-Ferrand (1949).

Devèze, M., *La Vie de la forêt française au 16e siècle*, 2 vols., Paris (1961).

Despois, J., 'Pour une étude de la culture en terrasses dans les pays méditerranéens', in *Géographie et histoire agraires*, 105–17 (1957).

de Dienne, M. le Comte, *Histoire du dessèchement des lacs et marais en France avant 1789,* Paris (1891).

Dion, R., *Le Val de Loire,* Tours (1934a).

Dion, R., *Essai sur la formation du paysage rural français,* Tours (1934b).

Dion, R., 'Grands traits d'une géographie viticole de la France', *Publications de la Société de Géographie de Lille,* 5–69 (1943) ; 6–45 (1948–9).

Dion, R., 'La part de la géographie et celle de l'histoire dans l'explication de l'habitat rural du bassin parisien,' *Publications de la Société de Géographie de Lille,* (1946), 6–80.

Dion, R., 'Leçon d'ouverture du cours de géographie historique de la France', *Publications de la Société de Géographie de Lille,* (1947–8), 9–27.

Dion, R., 'La géographie humaine rétrospective', *Cahiers Internationaux de Sociologie,* 6, (1949), 3–27.

Dion, R., 'Les origines du vignoble bourguignon', *Annales, Economies, Sociétés, Civilisations,* 5, (1950), 433–39.

Dion, R., 'Métropoles et vignobles en Gaule romaine : l'exemple bourguignon', *Annales, Economies, Sociétés, Civilisations,* 7, (1952), 1–12.

Dion, R., 'La géographie historique', in Chabot, G. *et al.* (eds) *La Géographie française au milieu du 20e siècle,* Paris (1957), 183–86.

Dion, R., *Histoire de la vigne et du vin en France des origines au 19e siècle,* Paris (1959).

Duby, G. *L'Economie rurale et la vie des campagnes dans l'Occident medieval,* 2 vols., Paris (1962) in translation as *Rural Economy and Country Life in the Medieval West,* trans. C. Postan, London (1968).

Dugrand, R., *Villes et campagnes en Bas-Languedoc : le réseau urbain du Bas-Languedoc méditerranéen,* Paris (1963).

Dupâquier, J., 'Essai de cartographie historique : le peuplement du bassin parisien en 1711', *Annales, Economies, Sociétés, Civilisations,* 24, (1969), 976–98.

Dussart, F., (ed.) *L'Habitat et les paysages ruraux d'Europe,* Liège (1971).

Elhaï, H., *Recherches sur la propriété foncière des citadins en Haute-Normandie,* Paris (1965).

Faucher, D., 'L'assolement triennal en France', *Etudes Rurales,* 1, (1961), 7–18.

Faucher, D., La Vie rurale vue par un géographe, Toulouse (1962).

Fel, A., 'Un questionnaire d'enquête géographique dans une exploitation agricole', *Revue d'Auvergne,* 71, (1957), 3–15.

Fel, A., *Les Hautes terres du Massif Central ; tradition paysanne et économie rurale,* Paris and Clermont-Ferrand (1962).

Fénelon, P., Les rideaux de Picardie et de la péninsule ibérique, *Bulletin de l'Association de Géographes Français,* 255 (1956), 2–9.

Flatrès, P., 'La structure rurale du Sud-Finistère d'après les anciens cadastres', *Norois,* 4 (1957), 353–67, 425–53.

Flatrès, P., 'L'étendue des finages villageois en Bretagne', *Norois,* 5 (1958), 181–189.

Flatrès, P., 'Géographie agraire et aménagement rural: réflexions sur une évolution', in *La Pensée géographique française contemporaine*, St. Brieuc, (1972), 431–42.

Gautier, M., *Chemins et véhicules de nos campagnes*, St. Brieuc (1971).

Gay, F., 'Habitat groupé et dispersé dans le département du Cher', *Norois*, 5 (1958a), 66–71.

Gay, F., 'Aspects de l'agriculture berrichonne au moyen âge d'après les textes des inventaires des établissements réligieux', *Norois*, 5 (1958b), 191–201.

'Géographie et Histoire Agraires', *Annales de l'Est*, 21 (1959).

Goubert, P., *Beauvais et le Beauvaisis de 1600 à 1730*, Paris (1960).

Gulley, J. L. M., 'The practice of historical geography: a study of the writings of Professor Roger Dion', *Tijdschrift voor Economische en Sociale Geografie*, 52 (1961), 169–83.

Harrison-Church, R. J., 'The French school of geography', in Taylor, G. (ed.) *Geography in the Twentieth Century*, London (1951), 70–90.

Henry, L., 'Historical demography', in Glass, D. V. and Revelle R., *Population and Social Change*, London (1972), 43–54.

Higounet, C., 'Mouvements de population dans le Midi de la France du IIe au 15e siècle, d'après les noms de personne et de lieu', *Annales, Economies, Sociétés, Civilisations*, 8 (1953), 1–24.

Jäger, H., 'Reduktive und progressive Methoden in der deutschen Geographie', *Erdkunde*, 22 (1965), 245–6.

Jäger, H., *et al.* (eds), 'Beiträge zur Genese der Siedlungs—und Agrarlandschaft in Europa', *Geographische Zeitschrift, Beihefte*, 18 (1968).

Juillard, E., 'L'assolement biennal dans l'agriculture septentrionale. Le cas particulier de la Basse-Alsace', *Annales de Géographie*, 61 (1952), 34–45.

Juillard, E., *La Vie rurale dans la plaine de Basse-Alsace*, Paris and Strasbourg (1953a).

Juillard, E., 'Formes de structure parcellaire dans la plaine d'Alsace. Un indice de l'ancienneté des limites agraires, les crêtes de labour', *Bulletin de l'Association de Géographes Français*, 232–33 (1953b), 72–77.

Juillard, E., 'La géographie agraire', in Chabot, G. *et al.* (ed.), *La Géographie française au milieu du 20e siècle*, Paris (1957), 159–166.

Juillard, E., 'Géographie rurale française: travaux récents (1957–63) et tendances nouvelles', *Etudes Rurales*, 13 (1964), 46–70.

Juillard, E., Meynier, A., de Planhol, X. and Sautter, G. 'Structures agraires et paysages ruraux', *Annales de l'Est*, 17 (1957), 1–188.

Lavedan, P., *Histoire de l'urbanisme: époque contemporaine*, Paris (1952).

Lavedan, P., 'Le nouveau Paris', *La Vie Urbaine* (1953), 180–240, 302–17.

Lavedan, P., *Histoire de l'urbanisme: renaissance et temps modernes*, Paris (1959).

Lebeau, R., *La Vie rurale dans les montagnes du Jura méridional: étude de géographie humaine*, Lyons (1955).

Lerat, S., 'Les pays de l'Adour à la fin du 18e siècle, d'après la carte de Cassini', *Revue Géographique des Pyrénées et du Sud-Ouest*, 28 (1957), 373–87.

Livet, R., *Habitat rural et structures agraires en Basse-Provence*, Gap (1962).

Martin, P., de, 'Matériaux pour la géographie historique et agraire de la Lorraine, VII: sur la genèse des champs courbes en Lorraine', *Revue Géographique de l'Est*, 11 (1971), 37–8.

Meynier, A., 'A propos des chemins creux de Bretagne', *Annales de Géographie*, 58 (1949), 345–47.

Meynier, A., *Les Paysages agraires*, Paris (1958).

Meynier, A., 'Les études de géographie agraire au Laboratoire de Géographie de Rennes', *Norois*, 9 (1962), 127–47.

Meynier, A., 'La genèse du parcellaire breton', *Norois*, 13 (1966), 595–610.

Meynier, A., *Histoire de la pensée géographique en France*, Paris (1969).

Mollat, M. & Pinchemel, P., 'Rencontres de la géographie et de l'histoire', in Comité National Français de Géographie, *Recherches Géographiques en France*, Paris (1972), 13–18.

Morineau, M., 'Y a-t-il eu une révolution agricole en France au 18e siècle?' *Revue Historique*, 486 (1968), 299–326.

Peltre, J., 'Du 16e au 18e siècle: une génération de nouveaux villages en Lorraine', *Revue Géographique de l'Est*, 6 (1966), 3–27.

Peltre, J., 'L'évolution des méthodes d'arpentage en Lorraine du 16e au 18e siècles et ses conséquences sur la structure agraire', in: Jäger, H. *et al.* (eds) *op. cit.* (1968), 138–144.

Peltre, J., 'Les faits d'orientation dans la structure agraire en Lorraine', in Dussart, F. (ed.) *op. cit.* (1971), 333–40.

Perpillou, A., 'Les plans cadastraux, sources d'information géographique', *Annales de Géographie*, 44 (1935), 194–98.

Perpillou, A., *Cartographie du paysage rural limousin*, Chartres (1940).

Perpillou, A., 'L'utilisation agricole du sol en France et les transformations des paysages ruraux', *Acta Geographica*, 38 (1961), 9–21.

Pinchemel, G., 'Cours et courettes lilloises', *La Vie Urbaine* (1954), 9–37.

Pinchemel, P., *Structures sociales et dépopulation rurale dans les campagnes picardes de 1836 à 1936*, Paris (1957).

Pitié, J., *Exode rural et migrations intérieures en France*, Poitiers (1971).

de Planhol, X., 'Observations statistiques sur les champs courbes en Lorraine', *Revue Géographique de l'Est*, 6 (1966), 97–100.

de Planhol, X., 'Les limites septentrionales de l'habitat rural de type lorrain', in Jäger, H. et al. (eds) *op. cit.* (1968), 145–163.

de Planhol, X., 'Aux origines de l'habitat rural lorrain', in Dussart, F. (ed), *op. cit.* (1971), 69–91.

de Planhol, X., 'Historical geography in France', in Baker, A. R. H. (ed), *Progress in Historical Geography*, Newton-Abbot (1972a), 29–44.

de Planhol, X., 'Structures universitaires et problématique scientifique: la géographie historique française', in *La pensée géographique française contemporaine* (1972b), 155–165.

de Planhol, X., Peltre, J., and Thouvenin, M., 'L'orientation des villages-rues en Lorraine', *Revue Géographique de l'Est*, 5 (1965), 345–47.

Prêcheur, C., 'Nancy: rapports de l'actuelle structure urbain et de l'ancienne structure agraire', *Bulletin de l'Association de Géographes Français*, 235–6 (1953), 106–16.

Prince, H. C., 'Historical geography in France', *Geographical Journal*, 124 (1958), 137–39.

Reitel, F., 'A propos de l'openfield lorrain', *Revue Géographique de l'Est*, 6 (1966), 29–51.

Robert, J., *La Maison rurale permanente dans les Alpes françaises du Nord*, 2 vols., Tours (1939).

Rochefort, M., *L'Organisation urbaine de l'Alsace*, Paris (1960).

Rouleau, B., *Le Tracé des rues de Paris*, Paris (1968).

Sion, J., 'Sur la structure agraire de la France méditerranéenne', *Bulletin de la Société Languedocienne de Géographie* (1937), 109–31.

Sion, J., 'Sur la civilisation agraire méditerranéenne', *Bulletin de la Société Languedocienne de Géographie* (1940), 16–40.

Steel, R. W. and Watson, J. W., 'Geography in the United Kingdom 1968–72', *Geographical Journal*, 138 (1972), 139–53.

2
Peopling and Origins of Settlement

PIERRE BONNAUD *

Introduction

Changes in rural landscapes in the modern world are the material results of changing socio-economic conditions, but this was not the case in the remote past when natural landscapes were modified following the arrival of mankind and the beginning of land clearance for settlement. Changes in population density through time have had important repercussions on rural landscapes, as have the arrival of new groups of settlers living different ways of life and practising different techniques of subsistence from the existing population.

The creation of early cultural landscapes in France was inextricably linked to the history of peopling. As we explore this relationship two fundamental problems demand our attention. The first of these is the problem of number. Population growth formed the stimulus for improving agriculture and extending man modified landscapes during the long period of primitive and traditional farming which preceded the modern 'agricultural revolution'. By contrast, decline or stagnation in population numbers was synonymous with economic stagnation. It is thus vitally important to investigate changing pressures of population on French rural resources in the past.

The second problem is the need to determine the 'ethnic' origins

* Translated by the editor.

of early settlers in each part of France, since it would be equally improper to treat the country as a uniform area in the prehistoric period as at the present time. The problem of the origin of settlers in France is significant in at least two ways. First, the chronology of settlement followed the arrival of waves of migrants who supplied the basic source of population in each part of the country. The ratio of successive migrant groups to the existing population in each area would be extremely important. Second, differences in the spatial origin of migrant groups are significant in tracing how distinctive types of farming, settlement, and rural landscape developed, even though each has been modified in many ways by later socio-economic changes (Bonnaud, 1971a). In spite of this fact, fundamental contrasts in French landscapes appear and re-appear with varying degrees of clarity across an enormous span of time. Similarly, many of the regional units that may be recognized in modern France were created in the remote past, as a result of goods being exchanged between neighbouring, complementary environments. Sometimes these patterns of interaction were later formalized as hinterlands around market towns and local trading centres.

The following pages will show that it is necessary to appreciate these permanent or recurrent regional themes in any study of the historical geography of rural France.

New Methods, Ideas and Findings

New research methods and new ideas provide help in testing hypotheses that were generated in the past to make up for a lack of information.

It is becoming increasingly clear from anthropological evidence that the population of Europe evolved on the continent from an ancient prehistoric stock and thereafter acquired its modern characteristics (Marquer, 1967).[1] Important research problems still remain; for example, the relations between Neanderthal man and *homo sapiens* (Nestourkh, 1960), the origin of the Nordic race, and the demographic dynamism of the invading groups.[2]

Modern studies in linguistics have started to reveal the existence of a vast and only slightly-differentiated Eurasian substratum during the Mesolithic, from which Indo-European, Finno-Ugrian and other great modern linguistic groups gradually developed.[3] This revelation spares us the ultra-hypothetical migration flows and land bridges that were proposed in the past. It also simplifies the irritating problem of the origins of Basque and its links with Caucasian, Finno-Ugrian and even Hamitic languages; clears place-name evidence of apparently insoluble contradictions (such as the extension of 'Ligurian' place names far from where this group lived); and opens very broad perspectives for investigating the formation of dialect groups in modern languages. We will try to show that dialects have great geographical importance (Bonnaud, 1970, 1971a).[4]

However, problems still remain since the current trend is to think that Indo-European languages crystallized relatively late. To us this opinion appears to be open to debate if, for example, one accepts that 'no traces of earlier languages than the Scandinavian tongues are recognizable' in northern Europe even though the region was occupied from deglaciation onwards (Musset, 1970). This fact interests us, since it was on this idea of the late crystallization of Celtic languages that the most critical historians have based their arguments for diminishing the role of the Celts in peopling and settling France (Harmand, 1970). Later we shall consider the problem in its historical and geographical contexts but even from a linguistic point of view these arguments are difficult to sustain if one accepts that Celtic strongly influenced the Germanic languages, and, as many British linguists have argued, brought an important imprint of non-Aryan syntax.[5] This could have been acquired by a long process of contact with other linguistic groups or might, alternatively, represent the remains of a great Eurasian, pre-Indo-European substrate. But the geographer is also concerned with sources of population. From this point of view, as we bear in mind the origin and direction of migration currents, it seems improbable to consider the Tumulus folk and the Urnfield people as other than Proto-Celts derived from a common human stock.

It seems to us that a large 'gap' exists in the methods used to investigate the peopling process and its regional variations. This 'gap' might be filled by the findings of ethnography. This is a relatively underdeveloped science in France but information gleaned from a wide range of writing suggests the type of result that can be derived from ethnographic enquiries.[6]

By contrast, historical demography has made great progress. At best its results go back only to the medieval period, but the findings of this discipline, if treated with caution, help suggest what the situation may have been like at earlier periods. Three main types of population change and agricultural evolution may be distinguished in the traditional rural environment.

The first involved the persistence of high population densities, supported by agricultural systems that were improved continuously by the addition of new forms of arable farming. The crucial question is to determine when this type of peopling started in regions such as Normandy, Picardy, Alsace, the Limagnes, and the eastern mountains of the Massif Central. According to region, the answer might be any point in time from the prehistoric period through to the end of the early Middle Ages.[7]

The second type involved a range of physical environments that traditional farming proved unable to master. Simple applications of manure were insufficient to fertilize soils in these areas where improvement was to come only after adding mineral fertilizers (for example, in Limousin and the Armorican Massif) or providing protection against erosion (as in the southern Alps).

The third type involved sudden changes or 'demographic explosions', following the exploitation of new agricultural resources. This was exemplified by agricultural changes in Basse-Normandie, and so it would seem in Gascony in the early Middle Ages. Sudden changes might also follow particular events, such as the great plague in southern France, and general disruption in central and south-western France at the end of the Middle Ages. Changes in landownership and the reconstruction of the countryside after the Hundred Years' War, together with other socio-economic changes also produced important demographic results.

The following conclusions from research in historical demography are relevant to the present discussion.
(i) From early times France seems to have been a zone of high demographic pressure, which easily supplied replacements to fill local gaps as they occurred in the pattern of settlement.
(ii) There were, however, important regional differences in population pressure. Some areas provided almost continuous supplies of outmigrants. Others functioned almost exclusively as reception areas. Finally a third group of regions experienced dramatic

fluctuations through time. Many changes in ownership and occupation of land may be elucidated by an analysis of differing population
pressures.

Pollen analysis has provided two groups of important results
which help investigations of the rural landscape. Quaternary
changes in climate and vegetation undoubtedly affected the processes of peopling and land settlement in early periods when man
was still intimately dependent on the natural environment. It is
possible to argue that conditions during the glacial periods had the
effect of stimulating man to improve his technology as he was
obliged to adapt to harsher environments. He was thus better
equipped in the post-glacial period of climatic improvement than
in the early Quaternary and could benefit from his improved condition to increase his numbers and thereby impart a human imprint on larger areas of land. For a long time man reacted in a
'negative' way during periods of climatic deterioration which were
marked by high death rates, migration, and a return to simpler
ways of life. Eventually, man managed to react to harsh conditions
in a 'positive' way, for example by extending the area of land under
cultivation to compensate for falling yields. But to try to arrange
these two types of response into a well-defined chronological
sequence would be both a fruitless and a dangerous exercise. Much
modern research has shown that both might co-exist in neighbouring areas which supported human groups at different stages
of cultural development and, as a result, displayed very different
reactions to environmental change. But it would seem that during
the first millennium A.D. a stage had been reached when population densities had risen to such an extent that to return to more
extensive systems of production would not have been feasible.
Instead, agricultural technology had to become progressively
more advanced.

Second, the results of pollen analysis seem to have destroyed the
old loess-steppe theory to show that woodland still covered virtually the whole range of soil-types when man became able to leave
his imprint on the landscape. However, in some areas the woodland was undoubtedly open and vulnerable. It is thus impossible
to accept the argument that

> 'from its origin early agriculture had to confront the renaissance
> of the forest' (Nougier, 1959).

The woodland cover had already existed for a long time. By contrast, it is reasonable to think that early areas of cultivation were not established in clearances in dense woodland but rather on patches of land where the vegetation had already been degraded by more primitive activities, ranging from burning that was undertaken by hunters to maintain a suitable environment for their game, to the ecological effects of rearing semi-domesticated animals.

Comparisons might be made with primitive ways of life in the modern world. Parallel trends in human evolution may certainly be recognized and these help us move from the excessively 'Europe-centred' type of scholarship that flourished in the past. Cross-cultural investigations also reveal similarities in early economic development. It is now known that loose groupings of population existed everywhere in the remote past, even in Mediterranean Europe, and thus the later diversification of settlement needs to be explained by reference to historic events and changing socio-economic conditions. From the very earliest times, 'ethnic' groups did not possess all their distinctive characteristics. These were acquired progressively in specific historic and geographic environments. Acceptance of this fact allows information on 'ethnic' differences to be re-incorporated into explanations of the evolution of settlement, after such material had been denied almost as brusquely as it had been presented. We are gradually beginning to appreciate that each agrarian culture does not 'float in the air' but originated in a particular geographic environment, is capable of improvement within that environment, and while still bearing the indelible imprint of its earlier history, may be distorted or fall into decline if transferred to another environment (Bonnaud, 1971a).

In the past, archaeology was concerned almost exclusively with the study of ancient monuments, but in recent years this discipline has started to investigate humbler buildings and has thus provided valuable information for geographers. Aerial photography has revealed features of ancient settlement patterns that are quite different from the modern network, for example, in Picardy and some other regions. But the results of archaeology from the air are still fragmentary. They convey important new information for geographers but they have not yet permitted past settlement patterns to be recognized over wide areas or the chronology of various settlement features to be obtained.

Archaeology has not provided a broad view of past cultural landscapes, but place-name studies have presented clearer ideas which result from manipulating existing evidence and testing new concepts. In spite of undoubted merits, classical studies of place names in France produced by Longnon (1929), Dauzat (1932, 1939, 1945) and their followers contain faults and deficiencies (Dauzat and Rostaing, 1963; Vincent, 1937).[8] Place names were studied almost exclusively from a linguistic point of view without reference to the character of the geographical environment.[9] Phonetic features were overstressed. The role of personal names in French toponomy was underestimated. Many experts specialized in Germanic and Latin studies but there were few who investigated Celtic names. This bias, of course, over-emphasized certain aspects of research to the detriment of others. Dialects, minority languages, and the place names derived from them have not received the attention they deserve even though they can be particularly revealing. Our understanding of place names that do not derive from French or from *langue d'oïl* dialects close to French has undoubtedly lagged. Place-name studies have made little progress in Corsica or Brittany, or throughout the *langue d'oc* region covering some 200,000 km^2 of southern France.

At present a healthy reaction to the classical approach to place-name study is taking place as researchers such as Roblin (1951), Falc'hun (1966, 1970), and Trepos (1957) stress the significance of the natural environment in trying to explain place names. Recent articles demonstrate the impact of this new emphasis in interpretation.[10] Past generations of scholars experienced the excesses of 'Celtomania' and reacted by mistrusting any explanations which involved Celtic origins of place names. Renewed interest in dialects and minority languages, has brought dialect place names solidly back into the field of enquiry (Nègre, 1963).

For all of these reasons, as well as the failure of earlier experiments (De Felice, 1907) French geographers either shunned place-name studies or else criticized them severely. However, we believe that the time has come for geographers to make use of the results of place-name enquiries and dialect studies in their own research (Bonnaud, 1969a and 1969b).[11]

Now that the ground has been cleared of preliminary comments on methodology, we must make use of the information obtained from the various human sciences to elucidate some of the many problems that stem from the early phases of human occupation and settlement in France.

Prehistory and Protohistory

From the Aurignacian period onwards, square or rectangular huts were built against the limestone cliffs of Périgord where maximum insolation could be enjoyed. But Palæolithic man had little possibility of modifying the natural environment since his numbers were too small (perhaps 1 person/10 km^2) and his technology and way of life remained at the primitive level of hunting and fishing (Nougier, 1959). By contrast, Mesolithic man had started to make his impact on the French landscape when pine and birch were established as pioneer species and hazel had become more frequent preceding the invasion of mixed oak woodland which would replace them in the seventh millennium. From this time onwards sheep seem to have been domesticated, for example at Château-neuf de Martigues in the lower Rhône valley with its loosely-developed villages of round huts occupied by hunters and fishermen. Cave deposits further to the north at Meaudre-en-Vercors suggest that seasonal hunting expeditions were taking place, forming the predecessors of transhumance movements of flocks and herds (Nougier, 1970). These Mediterranean or sub-Mediterranean sites were not being occupied simply as a matter of chance.[12] The margins of the Mediterranean Sea had formed a refuge zone during the glacial periods, and a 'hearth' from which mixed ways of life involving stock-rearing and seed-gathering could be diffused (Nougier, 1959) (Fig. 2.1). Population increased, settlement features multiplied, and the dry, open forest of the Mediterranean region experienced damage from fire. Man's impact on the forest was clearly in evidence.

This fact could help explain the spectacular 'spatial inversion' that was to take place in the Neolithic. Cereals were first grown in the Mediterranean region but it was in Central Europe that vigorous forest clearance was taking place and the 'peasant continent' was established, capable of supporting high densities of population. Early deforestation and soil erosion have been shown

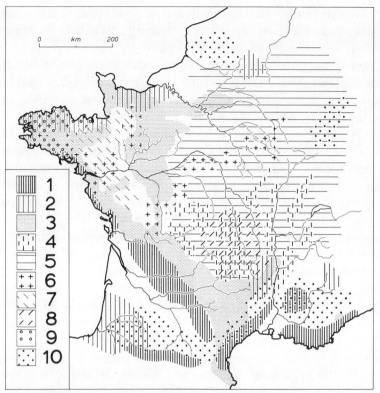

FIG. 2.1. Peopling of France until the end of the tenth century A.D.

1. Main refuge zones for man during the glacial periods.
2. Anthropological evidence of the northward expansion of western Archaeo-Mediterranean folk. (Relatively great importance of blood group O.)
3. Areas with high densities of Megalithic remains.
4. Protohistoric expansion of settlement from southern France.
5. Expansion of settlement of Proto-Celts and Celts from central Europe.
6. Regions characterized by alternate expansion and contraction of settlement in antiquity.
7. Lowland regions undergoing agricultural colonization during the early Middle Ages, settled by migrants from neighbouring regions.
8. Upland regions undergoing agricultural colonization during the early Middle Ages.
9. Settlement of Celtic refugees from Britain between the third and sixth centuries A.D.
10. Other refuge zones.

to have taken place in Italy from prehistoric times onwards and it is probable that parts of Mediterranean France suffered in a similar way. Early cultivation came up against sharp limitations in the dry Mediterranean environment and it is likely that advances in animal domestication and stock rearing retarded the further development of cultivation in this region.

Beyond the Mediterranean region, the borderlands between Aquitaine and the Pyrenees and the Massif Central, supported hunter-gatherer economies from the Neolithic period onwards, with hunting still prevailing elsewhere. The new ways of life centred on hunting and gathering were fairly stable and allowed population to increase. All was prepared for focal areas of hunting and gathering to become established from which many components of agrarian life in southern France developed. Conditions improved as a mixed way of life developed, involving cereal cultivation and rearing small livestock. One or other of these components predominated, varying in response to place and time, but it is clear that stock rearing with demands for large areas of land was the most important element in changing the landscape and directing essential aspects of development for the future.

The southern culture (or rather group of cultures, since there were important regional nuances) showed a great ability for expansion. In the Neolithic period it spread into the southern part of the Massif Central through the Grands Causses, the Gardonnenque, and the calcareous 'isthmus' of Rouergue to advance northwards into Velay, central and eastern parts of Basse-Auvergne, and into the Vienne basin (Bonnaud, 1969a) (Fig. 2.2). Southern cultures also reached the Armorican Massif where land was cleared for pasturing c. 4500–3500 B.C. which led to an increase in grass pollen in the peat bogs of Finistère and Basse-Normandie. This expansion involved a northwards spread of population. There are many places along the Atlantic coastline from the Pays Basque to Basse-Normandie which demonstrate strong concentrations of blood group O which is considered to be characteristic of the Archaeo-Mediterranean folk in western France (Bourdieu, 1967, pp. 366–7). The spread of Megalithic folk formed a link from the southern Massif Central to Brittany, and from there into the British Isles. The Atlantic coast might have functioned as a routeway along which bell-shaped beakers were diffused from Iberia, but this source is still open to dispute. Ancient historians attributed the origins of some of the peoples of Brittany, and even the Silurians of Wales, to Iberia (Dion, 1953). The Atlantic migration

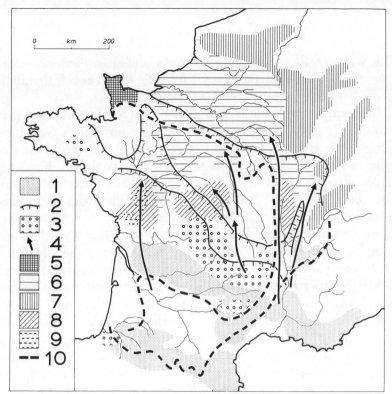

FIG. 2.2. Trends of Peopling and Settlement from the Neolithic Period to the end of the tenth century A.D.

1. Regions where gathering and stock rearing (with some shifting cultivation) replaced hunting and gathering from the Mesolithic period onwards.
2. Stages in the northward expansion of the Southern agricultural culture in Neolithic times, involving the predominance of pastoral activities, but with some cultivation.
3. 'Parkland' landscapes which developed as residual forms of the primitive Southern agricultural system.
4. Northwards spread of components of the intensive agricultural system of southern France, from the Roman period onwards. Vines, fruit trees, and other such plants left important legacies in rural landscapes.
5. Core area for the development of enclosed landscapes.
6. Regions where cereal-producing cultures developed, from the third millennium onwards.
7. Other areas with cereal-producing cultures which originated in Central Europe.
8. Areas of *plaine* which form transitional landscapes in Middle France.
9. Expansion of openfield areas in west-central France during the medieval and modern periods.
10. Regions in northern, eastern and south-western France with small parishes (and *commune* areas) which indicate that colonization was active and farming became more intensive at the end of the early Middle Ages and in the medieval period proper.

route was not forgotten in later times and was also used in the reverse direction, for example when Celtic refugees left Britain for Galicia between the fourth and sixth centuries A.D.

The southern agricultural system displayed certain distinctive features. Firstly, the size of its village territories which, on average, varied between 1800 ha and 4000 ha in western and southern France.[13] These village territories could not have been derived directly from the hunting spaces of Palæolithic tribes, since it has been estimated that at least 10,000 ha would have been necessary to support a tribe of thirty to fifty people. Southern village territories stand in clear contrast with much smaller units of 500 ha to 1000 ha which derived from the cereal-based cultures of Central Europe and are dominant in northern and eastern France. Southern settlements are frequently sited on elevated ground away from water-courses, and are often served by ridge-ways.[14] Such settlements show considerable variety of detail, ranging from truly Mediterranean nucleated villages to total dispersion in parts of Aquitaine, but elevated sites predominate throughout. These are inconvenient in terms of water supply but are useful for keeping an eye on livestock, and command access to a variety of types of pasture and cultivable soils at different altitudes.[15] A wide range of ethnographic features, including styles of house construction, rural tools and dress, cover an approximately similar area of the South.

This broad zone of southern and western France could be distinguished at a very early period of land clearance and occupation. It stretched as far north as the Central Jura, Maconnais, Auvergne, Touraine and Basse-Normandie, and has also demonstrated remarkable resilience so as to remain recognizable through the centuries in spite of numerous social and economic changes. The zone acquired local nuances in differing geographical and socio-political *milieux*, but managed to resist the diffusion of openfields from Central Europe. This type of agricultural organization had the potential to spread well south of its classic limit (from Caux, through Beauce to Châlonnais), bearing in mind the nature of geographical conditions south and west of the line and the superiority of the openfield system in providing foodstuffs in the traditional agricultural economy where self-sufficiency predominated. It is certainly possible to recognize with Dion (1934) the existence of a 'gap' in the peopling of middle France which served as a buffer zone where mixed forms of landscape developed, such as the *plaines* of Poitou and Berry.[16] Fragments of openfield are still found in the Limagnes, northern Poitou and the Charentes which suggest the kind of dimensions that this buffer zone may once have possessed. The reasons behind the contrast between openfields and enclosed landscapes are undoubtedly very complicated. We may also note that evidence from archæological excavations shows that cattle seemed to have been important in north-west Europe from the prehistoric period onwards. This was not the case in the Armorican massif and the western parts of the Massif Central where sheep dominated until a recent period in spite of the fact that soils and other geographical conditions of these areas were more favourable for cattle than for sheep.

Southern cultures demonstrated stability but also a capacity to adapt. This was partly because the Mediterranean zone was one of the cradles of plant domestication but also because climatic conditions in France south of the Loire permit a wide range of agricultural activities. Archæologists have recognized a regional-ization of economic activities which seem to reflect underlying geo-graphical characteristics, being orientated towards stock-rearing in the Causses but with more emphasis on cereal farming in the Cortaillod Jura which was perhaps already influenced by important contacts with central Europe.[17] Later on two fundamental types emerged in southern France which could, of course, be subdivided by the degree of local agricultural intensification. One might be called the 'Atlantic' type and the other the 'northern sub-Mediter-ranean' which was just part of a broad zone stretching from Galicia, through Aquitaine, the Saône-Rhône corridor, northern Italy, and Pannonia to Romania. The embryo of rural landscapes in these areas may be traced back to the early Middle Ages and many primitive aspects survived until the period of agricultural im-provement in the nineteenth century.[18] Residual features of earlier landscapes may be recognized in the 'parkland landscapes' of the high plateaux of Limousin and the western Auvergne (southern Combrailles and Artense) where moorland, copses, and arable fields mixed with pastures, are all scattered together, with hay meadows and damp valley bottoms being the only common fea-tures. This kind of landscape seems quite incoherent when viewed at a *commune* level, but it is more intelligible when considered by *section*, involving the land around individual villages, hamlets and small groups of farms. The *sections* formed the basic units of rural life in the past which coincided with the small groups of human beings that the extensive agro-pastoral system of these plateaux could support. The larger and more recent *communes* each regroup a number of *sections* derived from parishes that were set up at the end of the early Middle Ages to group small settlements together for ecclesiastical purposes.

One might claim that the early phases of the southern agro-pastoral cultures displayed few differences from those that flourished in other parts of Europe. That opinion is partly correct. Modern research has demonstrated similar conditions elsewhere, involving the existence of small settlement foci surrounded by small patches of land that were cultivated intensively close to the dwellings, but were worked more extensively as one moved outward into more recently-cleared land. This fact is confirmed by studying place names from maps of forest areas in Franche-Comté, Lorraine, Burgundy and Champagne, which bear witness to woodland degradation around nuclei of cultivation.[19] But modern research has also done justice to the contrast between round, primitive Mediterranean dwellings and Nordic rectangular houses. These distinct types recur consistently from the earliest phases of settlement, being modified of course in detail by local ways of life and the availability of building materials. This evidence all confirms the principle of parallelism in the evolution of human groups, especially in their more elementary stages. This is scarcely surprising, considering the evidence of Mesolithic people spreading northwards in milder post-glacial conditions away from their southern refuges.[20]

However important differences started to appear from pre-historic times (5000–3000 B.C.). Terraces and valley sites formed favoured points for settlement creation in central and north-western Europe. Only at later stages were settlements founded on higher plateau sites.[21] Northern forests were more dense than those in the South or perhaps there was less need to clear them. But, once introduced, arable cultivation flourished on areas of good soil which could be cultivated easily using rudimentary tools.[22] The importance of cattle and pigs in north-west Europe has already been mentioned. These livestock could make use of grazing re-sources in woodland areas more easily than sheep, as was to be clearly in evidence in the Middle Ages. The medieval peasant in the Munster basin was still a *Waldbauer* combining work on his patch of arable land with employment in the forest. There is no doubt that this type of cultivator was also found in many parts of northern and north-eastern France. Poor environments supported either this kind of semi-tamed woodland or else more truly 'natural' vegetation which remained virtually untouched until the beginning of the Christian era. Sandy soils and other areas from which timber was easily cleared supported a way of life that was quite similar to that in the South, but involved cattle and smaller stock grazing areas of rough moorland. The cultures of the Paris Basin flourished in more favourable environments with rich soils and land that might be worked easily. This way of life derived from a mixed economy based on hunting, and the rearing of dogs, cattle and pigs. It had been transformed during the fourth and especially the third millennium B.C. into a stable form of cereal cultivation that was influenced by techniques diffused from the Danubian lands to the east. Cereal cultivation became stabilized, partly as a result of the migration of folk from the already over-populated agricultural lands of central Europe. Protohistory saw the establishment of foci of permanent cultivation, with distinctive lynchets. Such foci were later to expand and develop into open-fields (Millotte, 1970). Some areas of cultivation were totally cleared of their forest cover and ploughing instruments were developed that were more effective than the light southern ploughs that had also been used in the North. As a result, heavier ploughs came into use in northern regions from the end of the Iron Age onwards. It was also necessary for the population to be regrouped and organized effectively so that mutual help for long and difficult agricultural tasks would be possible. Archaeological evidence demonstrates changes in settlement location that were often in response to climatic reasons or followed particular historical events. But the abandoned sites did not represent parts of a former network of intercalated settlement between villages which have survived to the present day. It seems that there was a trend to-wards settlement concentration which ran parallel with the develop-ment of cereal cultivation and that this type of expansion of village settlements occurred from quite remote periods in protohistory. At least, place-name evidence would suggest this kind of interpretation, since village names in northern and north-eastern France are frequently pre-Latin in origin but this is not the case for names of smaller settlements and names of places in the country-side (*lieux-dits*).[23] Finally some village types were foreshadowed in the remote past. For example, Danubian settlements in Alsace took acquired forms rather similar to later *Haufendörfer* (Juillard, 1953). Settlement sites were undoubtedly more stable and agricultural systems more productive in northern and north-eastern France than in western and southern regions.[24]

Now it is necessary to consider if a link existed between the landscape and the original peopling of northern and eastern France. Agricultural techniques in these regions were derived largely from Central Europe but was this true for population as well as for material influences? The question is still a matter of debate. After having thought for a long time that the peopling of Europe was the result of three great westward movements by Nordic, Alpine and Mediterranean groups, modern research points increasingly to the importance of an indigenous population being transformed in response to work, ways of life, interbreeding, and different geographical environments. The indigenous stock was itself varied from prehistory onwards, and hence the question remains to discover whether the protohistoric melting pot of people in Central Europe spilled over into the territory that was to become France. The backwardness of French anthropology does not help the search for an answer.[25] Past research showed that human body heights were, on average, greater to the north-east of a line from Avranches through Orléans to Geneva (Derruau, 1949). The presence of tall Alpine brachycephalic types with blond hair and blue eyes (sometimes called the 'Lorraine' type) in north-eastern France, and other more diverse human forms in western Auvergne and other regions of the Massif Central, is an important fact. These folk might be the direct descendants of similar folk in the remote past (since the Lorraine type seems to have been found from the Bronze Age onwards) or else they might be the result of a mixture with Nordic dolichocephalic elements. But after the era of the Urnfield folk in eastern France and notably during the Tène period in the Massif Central, the proportion of dolichoce-

phalic types in excavated skeletons became greater. Later on, it is
true that the same phenomenon could be observed at the period of
the Germanic invasions, but it was more limited in proportion and
geographical extent.[26] It is clear that the essential part of the
human stock of north-eastern and central-eastern France and part
of the Massif Central, resulted from migrations during the Bronze
and Iron Ages. These migrations all derived from the same geographical source and this fact is confirmed by archaeological
evidence on the proximity of groups of Unětice, middle-Bronze-
Age tumuli, and Hallstatt and La Tène urn fields. The 'racial'
diversity of these migrants was a consequence of the conditions
under which the Alpine type, itself a mixed human group, was
formed. This mass of humanity which spread westwards and
southwards from a common region of origin cannot be other than
Celtic in origin. Reasons proposed for dividing this mass into
smaller isolated groups are simply quibbles, of which the background has been discussed in the first section of this essay. Moreover, reading the most critical of historians who defend the
concept of small groups of independent conquerors we note that they
considered at least half of the population of the various regions of
'France' (excluding Aquitaine) to be of Celtic origin before the
Roman conquest (Harmand, 1970).[27]

During a long period of domination, the Celts must have linguistically assimilated part of the indigenous population.[28] That
is obvious. But remembering that the Celts did not have a struc-
tured administrative organization, or a written culture, or massive
superiority in terms of culture. 'Celticization' could only have
resulted from frequent and repeated contacts between folk who
lived closely together and continually interacted one with another.
This would have been particularly significant at this time since
small, inward-looking groups lived in an almost 'closed' economy.
The number of migrants could not have been insignificant since
they continued to arrive for 1000 years or so.[29]

The Celtic occupation of Gaul was characterized by apparently
contradictory features. On the one hand, increasing density of
valley settlement, especially in the Paris Basin, might have been
either a feature of inherited culture or a functional aspect of the
cultivators' way of life back on the terraces and light soils of
Central Europe. But on the other hand, settlements were also

being established in higher areas. It might have been that these villages or groups of houses in the Paris Basin were created by people who had been driven back, or else they represented 'anchor points' established by the conquerors as they increased their hold on the country. But this could not have been so everywhere, for example, where the proportion of newcomers was clearly high in the anthropological stock (as in the mountains of the Auvergne), or where elevated settlements seem to have been too small to have any military value, as in Bresse. We must therefore recognize among at least some of the Celts and for a certain period of time the existence of a way of life in elevated areas in which stock-rearing was important. This is not surprising if one thinks of the analogy with the Germanic invaders of later times who proved to be poor farmers of the land they conquered, even though respectable agricultural cultures had existed in their homeland from the Neolithic period onwards. These apparent failures resulted from changed ways of life among the migrant peoples, who failed to immediately discover new 'anchoring points' and settle into the environments they had conquered. It remains to be seen whether this upland economy was practised by backward groups bringing with them the mass of Celtic population that had already developed improved forms of cultivation; or whether it was simply the result of a temporary change in ways of life linked to migration. In favour of this hypothesis we must recall the facts that have been discovered in the Massif Central, namely the penetration into the eastern mountains of an agricultural system based on cultivation and involving relatively little forest clearance from La Tène times onwards; and the importance of clearing alders from the valleys of the region from the days of independent Gaul through to the early Middle Ages (Bonnaud, 1971a). This seems to indicate a return to intensive forms of agriculture that were already known, or rather a stabilization and return to traditions of settlement, bearing in mind the fact that the valleys of the Massif Central were rarely suitable for cereal cultivation.

The Celtic era, especially La Tène period, is also often considered to have been characterized by a fresh dispersion of settlement in the form of aristocratic domains established near lakes or watercourses or on forest margins. Such settlements were certainly created but one must challenge the use of the term 'dispersed settle-

ment' since the great domains supported village-sized populations. It
would be better to save the term to refer to the small groups of Celtic
farms that were established in higher areas where ploughing was
difficult and stock rearing predominated, for example in Bresse.

Invasion by the Celts added new features to the settlement
pattern and enlarged the cultivated area. But it was also responsible
for the judicious organization of France into territorial units which
have survived in broad terms through to the modern period, in
spite of a multitude of intervening economic and political changes.

Regional divisions appeared from the Neolithic period onwards
that were to be recognizable in recent times: for example, the
complementarity between the Pyrenees and Aquitaine to the south
of the river Garonne; the contrast between southern and south-
western parts of the Massif Central and areas to the north and
north-east; the 'attractive' nature of the coastlands of Brittany
which contrasted with the interior of the peninsula; and the
emergence of a great Centre-Est region, covering the Jura,
northern Alps, the middle section of the Saône-Rhône corridor,
and the western parts of the Swiss plateau.[30]

But the key feature was the spatial arrangement of Gaulish
tribes in La Tène period. This demonstrated two types of territory.
On the one hand, there were homogeneous areas. Some came into
existence because they were too broad to allow a single tribe to
extend beyond them, for example the Lémovices simply occupied
and gave their name to the Limousin. Such regions might also
result from the fact that several tribes might be installed in
discrete areas of a larger territory, such as the Armorican Massif.
Finally, an homogeneous area might develop because the geographical environment allowed a range of diverse but complementary economic activities to flourish within it, for example in the
territory occupied by the Nitiobroges which covered calcareous
areas and stretches of *molasse* dissected by great alluvial valleys in
Agenais, southern Périgord, and eastern Bordelais. Local nuances
of complementarity and adaptation to geographical conditions
were not excluded. The same was true for the tribes of Brittany
(Armorica) who divided up the peninsula by 'permanent' geographical features, such as coastal areas, patches of loess and other
favourable soils, and the less attractive interior which served as a
buffer zone. A final example is provided by the close links which

existed between the Lémovices of Limousin and the Petrocorii who inhabited the complementary calcareous plateaux of Périgord.

On the other hand, heterogeneous regions contained clear features of internal complementarity, with sharply differing areas being bound together by trade. In the Auvergne, for example, the Arveni not only made use of the Allier plain but also the surrounding hillslopes and mountains with very different economic potential. The Aedui exploited the resources of both plateaux and upland areas along the Saône axis. In lower regions, with rather more uniform characteristics, local differences in soil conditions became extremely important. Thus the foci of activity for the Bituriges, Pictones and Santones were on calcareous plains and plateaux, with surrounding sands and clays being used for more extensive activities and also serving as strategic buffer zones.

Physical factors were clearly very important in defining peripheral areas. The poorest 'negative' areas were patches of 'no man's land' or marchlands. Thus the Montagne Limousine formed the division between the Lémovices and the Arveni (Lanly, 1962), and a long band of limestone with poor dry soils, practically devoid of pre-Latin place names divided the Pictones of Poitou from the Santones of Saintonge (Dauzat, 1939).

Trading settlements appeared from the beginning of the Celtic period onwards and later domination by Rome overthrew neither the territorial units that had been established nor the way of life of the inhabitants. After the period of Gaulish independence, local and regional networks of trade and exchange were reinforced by the construction of Roman roads and the trend for town development. Distinct rural hinterlands became articulated around particular towns and the territorial division of Gaul remained in operation. It was perfectly suited to a traditional economy characterized by the preponderance of subsistence agriculture with some local exchange of goods, and for this reason the ancient territorial divisions survived to relatively recent times. In a country like France, the potential for agricultural development is very high and the rate of investment in farming is closely linked to environmental capacity, but the recognition of functional regions around a small number of major cities remains a rather dubious affair. For these reasons the geographer might ask whether the traditional 'regions' inherited from the remote past retain an operational value in the modern world and might even be more useful in the future than the large, city-based regions that have been recognized by planners.

In summarizing the impact of peopling and land occupation at the end of the protohistoric period we may accept the estimate of 10–15 persons/km^2 proposed by Harmand (1970). But in mountain areas, the Armorican massif, much of Gascony and the western section of modern Belgium, densities were lower, probably in the order of 5–10 persons/km.^{2} From the early Neolithic onward, patterns of density seem to have been inverted, with the cereal producers of north-eastern France becoming more numerous than the inhabitants of southern and western France, where mixed economies flourished, being more orientated to stock farming than to arable cultivation. Important contrasts in density at both regional and local scales existed between attractive, well-peopled areas and 'negative' environments. Loess-covered plateaux, limestone areas (provided that they had soil cover), river terraces, and hillslope areas provided a great variety of resources over a small area and supported large numbers of people.[31] 'Negative' areas included the heavy soils of Bresse and the Limagnes des Terres Noires, very dry plateau areas, high areas with leached soils that were too poor for either pasture or cultivation (as in the Montagne Limousine), and wooded upland areas with little agricultural land (as in the Pre-Alps and the Haut-Jura). Some areas experienced very distinctive types of occupation, for example sandy areas which had been settled early but from which population moved away as light soils became gradually depleted.[32] The peopling of upland areas of old hard rocks varied greatly, as a function of both general and local conditions. In general terms, the Ardennes, Vosges and Morvan in north-eastern France were virtually deserted, since they were of little interest to cereal growers of the surrounding plains. By contrast, upland areas of western and southern France were used more intensively for pastoral purposes. At a local level, settlement expanded from overpopulated hillslopes bordering the Limagnes on to the surrounding uplands of the Auvergne. But problems still remain in tracing peopling and settlement up to the end of the protohistoric period. Not least of these is the evolution of Beauce which formed the focus of the powerful Carnutes. It is difficult to accept the interpretation proposed by Dauzat (1939) that the area was only cleared and exploited in the Merovingian period.

The Gallo-Roman Period and the Early Middle Ages to A.D. 1000

The Roman domination of Gaul did not involve much immigration. Traditionally the period has been characterized as one comprising demographic growth under the *Pax Romana* and clearance of extensive parts of the countryside for human occupation. The frequent occurrence of place names of Gallo-Roman origins (*-anum*, *-anicum*, and especially *-acum*) has been used as evidence to back up this view.[33] Modern research does not suggest that such an interpretation should be rejected but rather that a few qualifications should be added.

1) Towards the end of his career A. Dauzat noted that the *-acum* place-name element also related to the Merovingian era, and thereby involved Germanic personal names. Quite a lot of evidence indicates the survival of the language of the Gauls into the eighth century and even the ninth century in some isolated areas. Some eminent linguists would extend it further.[34] The *-acum* element was linguistically of Celtic origin and clearly survived over many centuries.

2) In a similar way, place names supposedly derived from personal names need to be viewed more critically. Place names ending in *-acum* may also be linked to dialect words or words of Celtic origin. Nothing guarantees that they had not already appeared during the period of independent Gaul since the existence of domains during La Tène period (from which personal names might also derive) is no longer denied.

3) Place names ending *-anum* cannot be other than Gallo-Roman, since this form is a Latin ending. However *-anicum*, which has traditionally been seen as a cross between *-anum* and *-acum*, has recently received a purely Celtic explanation (Falc'hun, 1966 and 1970). The result is that many place names that were once interpreted as Gallo-Roman may in fact have appeared over a very much longer period from La Tène times through to the early Middle Ages.

In addition, we must note that areas with high densities of 'Gallo-Roman' place names often coincided with regions that were densely peopled at earlier periods. The plateaux of the central Jura provide a particularly clear example of this situation.

Two conclusions emerge from all these points. First, new place names often resulted from the reorganization of areas of land that had been occupied in the past, rather than from clearance and colonization of virgin land. Roman domination favoured the development of a system of domains at the expense of independent peasant farmers. The Roman power structure stressed the role of the aristocracy. Roman Law concepts of private property and early cadastral surveying favoured the 'usurpation' of land by powerful groups in society. Second, apparently new place names might simply be 'rebaptisms' of old settlements or relate to new settlements that had been founded as the result of reorganized land-ownership. In either case they denoted the re-use of areas that had already been occupied.

However, it would be absurd to deny the expansion of the settled area of Roman Gaul. In the absence of radical methods of agricultural intensification, and even if some improvement took place, population increase in Roman Gaul must have been paralleled by an extension of the cultivated surface. In addition, archaeological evidence reveals a trend of settlement dispersion around existing villages and trading points during the Roman peace (for example, around Lézoux in the Auvergne), but also a wider scattering of population, as in the Lembronnais area of the southern Limagnes where Gallo-Roman place names are too numerous to correspond with large *villæ*. This evidence suggests the existence of two types of agricultural development.

First, there were areas which had been neglected previously but were now being used for agricultural purposes. Thus, land clearance operated in areas with clay soils and settlement spread into some damp valley bottoms. In addition, population moved from overpopulated areas into poorer land nearby that had not been occupied previously. By way of example, Gallo-Roman settlement spread on to the western plateaux of the Auvergne up to 20 km from the western hillslopes of the Limagnes. Similarly, population densities increased significantly in areas of the Armorican massif in Haut-Maine (Beszard, 1910; Dornic, 1960; Musset, 1917). However the era of large migrations and important exploration of the resources of Gaul seemed to have drawn to a close, for a while at least.

Second, redistribution of settlement was linked to increased trade and exchange of all kinds of goods over greater distances. In the most savage parts of Gaul, the Roman roads were essentially strategic in character and had few links with the settlement pattern, but in more hospitable regions settlement flourished alongside the highways. Increased commercial activity followed aspects of agricultural advance. These were certainly not 'revolutionary' but were significant nonetheless.

The Gallo-Roman period really marked the beginning of a new phase in the continuing dialogue between North and South on the 'isthmus of Gaul' (Bonnaud, 1971b). After the importance of the South during the Mesolithic period and part of the Neolithic era, and the northern development of cereal cultivation in middle Europe, the South again became important in terms of agricultural advance and the extension of the cultural landscape. These southern changes were linked to the more widespread cultivation of tree crops, including almonds, fruit and especially the vine. This latter crop gained great importance and by the early Middle Ages had become widespread throughout the southern half of Gaul. Many texts indicate the existence of the vine in the Saône-Rhône corridor, in Aquitaine, Auvergne, and as far north-west as the Plaine de Neuville in Poitou (documentary evidence of A.D. 876). Thus the key elements were established for a sub-Mediterranean zone of agricultural development, which rarely extended beyond the middle Loire but in the rich environment of certain plains and basins was to incorporate maize and an even wider range of southern crops in the future (Lot, 1933, 1945; Salin, 1949–59).

In general terms however, the Gallo-Roman period was a time of stabilization rather than one of radical change. From the third century onwards, Gaul entered into a new phase of mobility, but little is known about this period which may have been very important in the formation of the French rural landscape (along with the reconstruction period at the end of the Middle Ages). Controversy and supposition surround our knowledge of both settlement and farming in these nebulous phases of French history.

In terms of peopling it is now due time that the numerical importance of the Germanic invasion be reduced to its real proportions, which were slight in all areas south of a line from the Somme through Paris to the Belfort Gap, and only modest to the north of the line, with the exception of a few small areas on the

margins of the present territory of France which were 'Germanized'. Place names ending -court, -ville, -villers, and -villiers, which
have been interpreted traditionally as Germanic foundations that
were 'Romanized' at a later date, need critical consideration.[35]
Their density is so great in some regions that one can hardly
imagine that so many folk who held political power and social
supremacy would allow themselves to be absorbed by the population they had conquered. However it is now known that not all
apparently Germanic personal names related to Germans, but
often referred to members of the indigenous population who had
taken on Germanic names.[36]

In fact, place names ending -court, -ville, -villers, -villiers are
even more useful than Gallo-Roman ones in demonstrating a redistribution of already occupied land among the invaders. The
mechanism of this operation, involving brutal dispossession of
established landowners or imposed division of land, has been
known for such a long time that it is surprising that notions about
fresh colonization of new areas at the behest of new Germanic
masters are still retailed in some books. The peddling of such ideas
is especially alarming since the assumed colonization involved
areas which were occupied by the most barbarous invaders,
namely the Franks, whose migration involved continuing warfare
with the resident population being reduced in number by massacre,
epidemics and flight in the face of invasion. The place names in
question are dense in areas where the Frankish aristocracy established its power most solidly, and which were later to become the
hard core of feudalism.[37] If such place names were abundant in
Beauce, Caux, Picardy, and the north-central part of the Paris
Basin, it was not because of an advance in farming by the invaders
who themselves were agriculturally less sophisticated than the
indigenous population. Rather it was because these rich and well-
settled areas provided a large enough financial return to meet the
needs of their masters and their soldier-servants. The creation of
the system of new domains has been elucidated recently by
'archaeology from the air', with aerial photographs for almost all
parts of the Paris Basin revealing Gallo-Roman villa sites which
would have been abandoned by this time (Chevallier, 1965). As
with the Gallo-Roman redistribution of land, some short-distance
shifts in settlement occurred as land was divided in new ways.

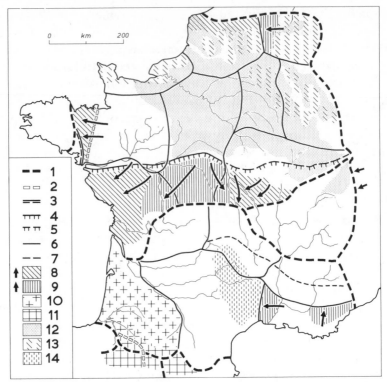

F IG. 2.3. Place-Name and Dialect Evidence in the History of Peopling and
Settlement.

1. Present boundaries between the three Gallo-Roman tongues (*langue d'oïl,
   langue d'oc* and Franco-Provençal).
2. Boundaries between the three Gallo-Roman tongues and other linguistic
   groups at the end of the early Middle Ages, where such boundaries differ
   from those found in the present century.
3. Eastern boundary of Breton speech until the seventeenth–nineteenth
   centuries (varying according to locality).
4. Approximate southern boundary of the *langue d'oïl* in the ninth century.
5. Less certain southern boundary of the *langue d'oïl* for the same period.
6. Dialect boundaries of the three Gallo-Roman tongues.
7. Major divisions within dialects.
8. Expansion of a dialect zone as a result of agricultural colonization, among
   other processes.
9. Expansion of a dialect zone as a result of trading activities. (Other examples
   probably occurred in the Massif Central during the medieval period but
   little is known of these changes.)
10. Retreat of the Basque tongue, mainly during the sixth century A.D.
11. Retreat of the Basque tongue in the pre-Pyrenean area between the sixth
    century and the end of the tenth century A.D.

12. Regions where place-name evidence indicates an important redistribution of land ownership following the Germanic invasions during the early Middle Ages.
13. Regions where many examples of Germanic place names are found, for example derived from personal names.
14. Zone in Bas-Languedoc and in the Massif Central with place names ending *-argues* and *-ergues* derived from *-anicum*. (Because of their very wide distribution it is not possible to map place names derived from *-acum* endings.)

Some sites that changed hands were 'rebaptized' even though they continued to be occupied in a stable way as they had been for a long period in the past. Much archaeological evidence indicates continuous occupation since the protohistoric and even prehistoric era of sites that are now contained by modern villages (Durvin, 1972a and b). Linguistic and place-name evidence demonstrates important Germanic influence only in Lorraine, Picardy, some parts of Normandy, and Wallonia which was then part of Gaul (Verlinden, 1955).[38] Some concentrations of *-ville* names in Charente-Toulousain simply indicate a reorganization of landholding in strategic and economic foci of the Visigoth aristocracy. This was rather similar to what happened in northern France. Arguments are still being raised in favour of a similar origin for *-ens* place names in Languedoc. Such an explanation for Pyrenean place names with *-ein* endings derived, according to Dauzat from *-ing* (*en*), seems very unlikely. These names are more probably linked to the Aquitaine tongue (*paléobasque*). It is high time that the *-inge*, *-in* and *-ing* features in Franco-Provençal endings are recognized as derivatives of *-anicum* or *-ianus* but not of *-ingen*. In addition, the classical explanation that names in Franche-Comté ending *-ans* derived from *-ingen* has also to be seriously questioned.

The installation of Breton refugees in Armorica, fleeing from Irish pillagers and then from the Anglo-Saxons, involved a small area but was nonetheless important in terms of settlement history (Fig. 2.3). The arrival of the Bretons was not of great significance to the agricultural landscape of Brittany, which seems to have scarcely changed, but was of great significance in rural life, which thereafter was organized in the framework of large primitive parishes (*plou*). The numerical importance of the newcomers has been debated at length and depends on which of the two main theories one adopts to explain the development of the Breton tongue. The classic theory of Loth (1883) was that the Bretons re-converted a Romanized country back to the Celtic tradition after the Romanized population had been decimated or put to flight following the Saxon raids in the third and fourth centuries. A more recent theory, proposed by Falc'hun (1962) adopts some of the earlier ideas. According to this the newcomers found an important substrate that continued to speak the language of the Gauls and which in turn influenced their own language to which it approximated. This was particularly so in the densely-populated Vannetais area. These two approaches are totally different from each other, and have deep implications which may not be discussed further at this point because of the complexity of the debate and the subjectivity of interpretation.[39] But whether it involved the total or partial repeopling of a deserted land or the superimposition of immigrants on to an unknown number of indigenous people, the general pattern of peopling was not greatly changed. The sparsely-populated interior of Brittany still contained important areas for later clearance and occupation.

Giot (1972) presents a vigorous discussion of the anthropological problems of Brittany. First, he demonstrates the distinction between northern and eastern coastal areas and the rest of the peninsula, and then examines historical difficulties of interpreting this distinction. The region experienced progressive 'brachycephalization' during the historic period. This might be linked to the development of endogamy among groups of rural settlers which became progressively more stable and self-sufficient. By contrast, 'debrachycephalization' is in evidence in the contemporary period, which might correspond to a greater mixing of the inhabitants of Brittany with folk from other regions. But the evidence put forward by the author could be interpreted in other ways. Giot's conclusions are purely 'speculative', as is his statement that future research will demonstrate that the Breton immigration played an important part in the formation of the current anthropological stock of the peninsula. As Falc'hun has clearly shown, one must not forget that political convictions, either overt or concealed, have all too frequently encroached in the interpretation of scientific findings regarding the immigration of refugees to Brittany.

Finally, bearing in mind the demographic dynamism of conquering groups and pioneers, the decline of population during the troubled period of the Middle Ages seems to have been a temporary event, coming at the end of the Bas-Empire and during the Merovingian period. It was limited to the central part of the Paris Basin, and northern and eastern France, which formed the epicentre of bloody struggles by the Frankish aristocracy, even if important but periodic massacres followed conquering raids and pillage in other parts of France, especially in Aquitaine. The main place names relating to settlements in northern France were established by the early Middle Ages, except on the massifs of old hard rocks. Sometimes the number of settlement units might contract but widespread regional abandonment did not result, apart from in the Basse-Seine area at the time of the Norman attacks.[40] The density of rural population in 'France' was probably greater than in any other part of Europe and was also extremely stable.[41] This claim cannot be accepted without posing more problems. For example, does the rarity of Gallo-Roman place names in Caux and much of Picardy indicate that the removal of land from the hands of the Gallo-Roman aristocracy was particularly radical, following a powerful Germanic invasion? We must remember that many *villa* sites have been discovered by aerial photography. Or perhaps it means that the domain regime had only been implanted to a modest extent alongside a large peasant population during the Roman domination and that the Germanic invaders were responsible for the triumph of the domain and the reduction of the population to servitude? We must remember the importance and the continuity of prehistoric and protohistoric features in these regions, but also that they were marginal to the great commercial axes and economic foci of the Roman Empire whence innovations were diffused. Also we must be reminded of the old but still valuable comment of Marc Bloch (1931) that the village was the symbol of peasant servitude in eastern Europe but of emancipation in the west.[42] But village settlements in many western regions dated from prehistoric times and this would help explain a lengthy resistance to the domain system.

Certain parts of rural France supported great demographic reserves at the end of the early Middle Ages when conditions were more peaceful and great colonization movements started in parts of northern France which previously had been only lightly settled. The conquest of the Vosges massif had already been started on the

Alsace slopes by Gallo-Roman refugees, but began vigorously from the slopes of Lorraine which were only sparsely settled (Levy, 1929). Population densities were high in Anjou and Maine and a wave of settlers moved from this region into eastern Brittany, taking the Latin language with them. The gradual spread of place names with -*ville* endings from east to west, followed by -*ière* and -*ais* endings demonstrates this well (Souillet, 1947).[43] It is possible that this movement of population also converted the southern part of the Armorican massif, lying south of the Loire, to the *langue d'oïl* to replace a more southern *langue d'oc* type of dialect that had been spoken until the tenth century.[44] Once the Norman raids were over, devastated areas of Basse-Normandie were re-occupied. This is shown by the existence of numerous place names ending in -*vast* (waste or fallow) which date from the end of the early Middle Ages. In a similar fashion, colonization spread further westwards into western Normandy. Demographic growth was so great that it was necessary for this region to operate a new type of economy, involving the creation of enclosed landscapes with small intensively-cultivated parcels of land being planted with cider-apple trees. The development of rural craft activities and the rise of outward migration both represented adjustments between growing population numbers and the region's resources.

Regions lying south of the Loire were more sheltered from disruption than those in northern France, but they too witnessed an expansion of settlement and land clearance. Four examples will be used to show the diversity of these processes.

In the Auvergne Fournier (1962) has shown an important extension of human activity from the Merovingian period onwards. The incursion of pillaging warriors into the rich plain of the Limagnes did not prevent marshland being drained and the cultivated surface being extended. At the same time settlements became much more nucleated than they had been in the past, with examples of perched villages being created. This trend contrasted with the relatively dispersed settlement pattern of the earlier Gallo-Roman era. New settlements were also founded on the surrounding plateaux and in the mountains, but the density of human settlement in these areas remained slight.

The lowlands of Provence suffered from the decline of Mediterranean trade, invasion by the Saracens, and subsequent population loss. But, by contrast, population increased in the mountains of Provence where important rural communities developed and started land clearance in this harsh environment. By the end of the early Middle Ages Haute-Provence was richer and more populous than Basse-Provence (Baratier, 1961; Sclafert, 1959).

In the Cévennes a line of small village territories stretched through the piedmont and the dissected hilly land. This contrasted with the large village territories on the surrounding calcareous plateaux of les Gras and in the mountains of Vivarais. Normally size of village territory is inversely related to population density and this suggests that these small village territories had experienced an important increase in their population before A.D.1000.[45] There is no doubt that this was associated with the settlement of the Châtaigneraie region, since mention of dues being paid in chestnuts appeared in early documents. The local economy also included other tree crops, together with the grazing of sheep on high summer pastures in the mountains of Mézenc, Lozère and Tanargue (Fel, 1962). In similar fashion a dense network of small parishes also indicates that population densities were once high in the *garrigues* and *soubergues* of Bas-Languedoc.

Finally, one region poses particularly difficult and challenging problems, and that is Gascony, which is taken to include the whole area where the Gascon dialect was spoken, involving the complementary regions of the Pyrenean mountains and the hills and plains which stretch northwards to the river Garonne. Widespread evidence exists of important population growth during the early Middle Ages in the Pyrenean valleys and the *molasse* hillslopes. The pattern of village territories is very dense and was even more so in the past. Part of the place-name evidence is in dialect form, but this is no longer understood easily by modern Gascons. Historical fact and the evidence of personal names indicate the important part played by Gascon emigrants in the Spanish *Reconquista* (Moll, 1959). This also suggests that population pressures were high in Gascony.[46] Moreover it is likely that an important number of Christian refugees fleeing from the Saracen invaders settled in Gascony.[47] A new means of subsistence was developed to sustain such population growth. In the Pyrenean valleys and on the terraces of Béarn this was achieved by developing a cereal-based economy which involved nucleating settlement into village

groups, creating more regularly-shaped parcels of land, and clearing more land. Conditions were different on the *molasse* hillslopes
where heavy land and fragmented terrain could not be used to
support the same kind of economic solution. The modern pattern
of dispersed settlement is not the result of secondary dispersion
between villages, since the individual houses and small groups of
dwellings with the surrounding cultivated land are closely inter-
woven with the remnants of the ancient woodland cover. There is
no evidence that in the past villages existed in areas where the
focus (*chef-lieu*) of a modern *commune* may involve five houses or
less. It is likely that increased population and land occupation
resulted from the settlement of refugees and partially itinerant
stock-rearers who became arable farmers, working the hillslope
soils with their spades to produce vegetables, fruit, and vines as
well as cereals. Similar kinds of change may have affected the
molasse regions of eastern Languedoc, Bas-Quercy, and Agenais
where village territories remained small or certainly were so before
the Albigensian crusade.

A final important feature of the rural geography of France during the early Middle Ages was the delimitation of 'ethnic' regions
across the former territory of Gaul. The territory of the *langue
d'oïl* was found to the north of a line running approximately from
the mouth of the Loire, north of Nivernais, through Burgundy to
the gate of Alsace. To the south was the *pays d'oc*, with the realm
of Franco-Provençal covering the south-eastern section of France.
In later centuries the dividing line was to shift southwards to the
Charente, the margins of the Massif Central, the Bresse and the
middle Jura, as larger areas spoke the *langue d'oïl*. But the main
aspects of the pattern were already in place by the tenth century.
Why should these linguistic features be of interest to geographers?
Without going into a long discussion of methodology, two important remarks must be made.[48]

First, the main reasons for this 'ethnic' pattern are not really
ethnic at all, but economic. The palatilizations which characterize
the *langue d'oïl* are of Celtic origin, but so too are those of northern
dialects of the *langue d'oc*, especially the Auvergnat dialect. Indeed, it is known that Celtic influence was important in these
regions. Thus the early history of peopling and settlement certainly
has a place in explanations of the character of the *langue d'oïl* and

the *langue d'oc* but it has no significance in explaining their relative distributions. The impact of the Germanic invasion seems to have played a role in establishing certain features of the Norman-Picard dialects and even those used in Wallonia and Lorraine, but elsewhere Germanic influence was less important than has been claimed. New interpretations are much more stimulating. Müller (1971), remembering that 'frontiers of communication lie at the origin of linguistic frontiers', has shown the importance of currents of exchange during the Romanization of Gaul which continued through the early Middle Ages. In a similar way Falc'hun has shown that the Franco-Provençal dialect zone corresponded with the zone of influence of the great commercial and cultural centre of Lugdunum (Lyons). We must add that the Auvergne and other regions of the Massif Central which had been affected by strong Celtic influence belonged to the *langue d'oc* because they functioned as parts of the 'southern' trading sphere during the early Middle Ages which was the formative period for Gallo-Roman dialects. This 'southern' sphere of activity was more important than is usually proposed in conventional interpretations of French history which tend to focus on Paris (Imberdis, 1967).[49]

Second, the economy was almost entirely agricultural and society almost entirely rural during the early Middle Ages, hence the division of France into two parts was also reflected by differing types of farming system and degrees of agricultural development. The North was to develop a strictly-organized openfield system, especially in regions such as the Paris Basin which were well suited to cereal cultivation. Thus openfields were already quite well established in Alsace by the early Middle Ages. By contrast, backward agrarian systems continued to operate in the Armorican West and in surrounding areas of poor sands, except for areas such as Basse-Normandie which, as we have seen, developed their own special systems of agricultural intensification. But agricultural backwardness did not restrict population growth in parts of Brittany and Maine where non-agricultural resources could also be exploited. In southern France, the distinctive 'southern' agricultural system that had existed in the Gallo-Roman period was developed even further, with the vine, tree crops and other non-cereal products becoming even more important.[50] This kind of farming involved different techniques from those in the North and

produced a distinctive agricultural landscape. Later on, the southern farming system was to become even more intensive as a result,
for example, of maize production. Between these two systems a
sparsely-peopled 'buffer zone' stretched to the south of the Paris
Basin. This relative lack of population stemmed from the fact that
the zone was located on the margins of two great currents of prehistoric peopling and also reflected the existence of unattractive
sandy areas (*gâtines*) within it. In addition, the buffer zone contained a range of agrarian conditions resulting from climatic
diversity and the varied origins of the folk who cleared its wasteland.

Thus environmental differences became reinforced by variations
in dialect and by 'ethnic' contrasts. Higounet (1953) has shown
that '*oc* and *oïl* did not interact' during the numerous migrations of
the early Middle Ages and there is much evidence to confirm this
statement.[51] It was not until the end of the Middle Ages that rural
migrations started to distort the boundary between *oc* and *oïl*, for
example when migrants from Poitou and Saintonge moved into
Aquitaine. For a very long time it was almost as if two countries
existed within France. Political and economic unification since the
Revolution of 1789 has tended to hide this fact from us today but it
was still clear to nineteenth-century writers such as Michelet who
wrote of 'the real France, that is to say northern France'

Further Aspects of the Peopling of France after A.D. 1000

By comparison with other European countries, France was well
populated at the beginning of the medieval period proper but it
still displayed important variations in population density. Densities changed, of course, with the passage of time, in response to
historical events, intensification of traditional types of agriculture,
and the appearance of rural industries, towns and other new
economic factors which were unevenly distributed throughout the
land. But by the time that traditional farming reached its peak in
the eighteenth and early nineteenth centuries, variations in density
were much less pronounced than they had been in earlier centuries.
This was the result of historic migrations, which have been largely
neglected. It is necessary to consider the role of these movements

in renewing or replacing the population of declining areas, for example the unhealthy regions along the coastal plain of Langue-doc (Derruau, 1953). Very little research has been undertaken on this topic, with only one pioneer study existing on migration between *communes* in rural areas (Chabot, 1953). However useful information may be derived from studies in historical demography, from detailed reports drawn up by local experts, and from linguistic studies. But unfortunately lists of anthroponyms that would permit the analysis of problems relating to the geographical origin of family names have not been prepared.[52]

One of the main problems of investigation is the evolution of the buffer zone of middle France, between the Loire, the Gironde, and the northern part of the Massif Central. Did the replacement of *oc* speakers by *oïl* speakers during the course of the medieval and modern periods represent a simple linguistic change following particular political and economic events, or was it linked to a transfer of population? No simple answer to this question is emerging. In the west, after north-western Poitou had been conquered by *oïl*-speakers, probably because of an influx of land clearers from Anjou, population moved southwards from these poor areas which might easily become overpopulated. The foundation of La Rochelle introduced more northern migrants from Normandy and Brittany, and the southwards spread of *oïl*-speakers has continued almost without interruption to the present day. After the terrible devastations of the Franco-English wars (especially the Hundred Years' War), the population of Saintonge and western Angoumois changed almost completely. But in the marginal areas of the Massif Central (Montmorillonais, Civraisien, and eastern Angoumois) and in the Pays Gabay north of the Gironde, the *langue d'oc* retreated between the seventeenth century and the end of the nineteenth century. In the sixteenth century the Gavaches or 'northerners', from Poitou and Saintonge, had spread across the *oc/oïl* linguistic division and had established the Petite Gavacherie de Montségur in the eastern part of Entre-Deux-Mers. In the modern period *oïl*-speakers have become increasingly numerous in Aquitaine and because they live in less compact groups than their predecessors have been assimilated into the local population.

Much evidence from place names, family names and dialect features indicates the southwards spread of colonization from

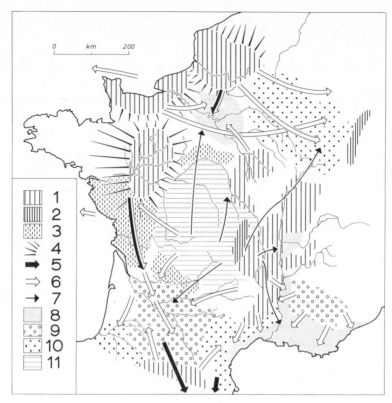

F IG. 2.4. Density of Peopling and Migration Patterns in France, between the
tenth and eighteenth centuries.

1. Regions with consistently high densities of population and constant outmigration. Agricultural systems in such regions were able to support large
   population numbers with the help of a range of rural industries.
2. Regions with a similar history of peopling, but with the addition of
   temporary inmigration absorbing migrants from poorer neighbouring
   regions.
3. Regions supporting high densities of population and permitting outmigration, but only in recent centuries.
4. Important zones of colonization involving migrants from the preceding
   regions who either repeopled abandoned areas or cleared new land from the
   waste.
5. Consistent but weaker migration movements dating from before the end
   of the Hundred Years' War (1450).
6. Consistent but weaker migration movements dating from after the end of
   the Hundred Years' War.
7. Main trends of temporary migration, involving some permanent settlement
   of migrants in the reception zone.

8. Regions of 'demographic depression', forming *zones de passage* and characterized by high mortality conditions and consistent inmigration.
9. Regions where demographic conditions became 'depressed' after an earlier period of vigorous population growth during the early Middle Ages and the medieval period proper.
10. Regions where 'demographic depression' alternated with over-population. Rapid growth of population characterized the final centuries of the *ancien régime*.
11. Regions in Middle France displaying low densities of population in all periods.

Nivernais to convert northern Bourbonnais into a region of *langue d'oïl*. A similar development occurred in Charolais, involving migration from the Morvan and Châlonnais. The situation is less clear in Berry and Nivernais. Certainly there is evidence of southern linguistic forms having been used in the past but these were probably closer to French than were other southern linguistic forms and it is well known that the influence of the Capetians was precocious in this area.[53] Politico-economic origins for this particular linguistic change are suggested by the importance of southern (*oc*) place names in the southern part of Indre *département* to the south of the Bresse and the forests around Châteauroux. These poor areas were set aside from the commercial influence of Paris, Orléans and other great markets in the Paris Basin and thus managed to conserve their original identity rather longer.

These problems of middle France lead to broader issues since there have always been important variations in population density in the French countryside in the past. Densely-populated regions, with either an over-abundance of population or only limited resources with which to support their inhabitants, dispatched migrants to other areas (Fig. 2.4). These reception areas were not the poorest regions in France but those which had been affected by catastrophes or by early demographic and socio-economic changes which led to population decline.

Differences in population density were particularly marked in northern France. Picardy, Normandy, Maine, Anjou and the valleys around Tours have always formed a region of high population pressure and this also characterized Bas-Poitou and Saintonge. Gaps in the distribution of population were rapidly filled when they occurred for example, as a result of the Franco-English wars in Haute-Normandie and Angoumois-Saintonge. We have already noted the activities of settlers from Anjou and Maine moving into the eastern part of the Armorican massif, and the migrations of folk from Poitou and Saintonge into Aquitaine. Normandy, especially Basse-Normandie, supplied population to the Paris Basin, and even to the eastern provinces. Migrants from Picardy were also numerous in Paris from the early years of the medieval period. After having divided up the Forest of Arrouaise, they went on to 'Romanize' Boulonnais and parts of Flanders. The presence of Picard place names on the Plain of Flanders from the Middle Ages onwards indicates that 'Romanization' was not the consequence of French domination in part of the formerly Flemish-speaking zone but rather the result of much earlier rural colonization. The Picards also repeopled Petit-Caux, between Bray and the river Bresle, which had been devastated during the medieval wars (Loriot, 1967) and later played a fundamental role in resettling certain parts of northern Champagne and Lorraine which were sacked during the seventeenth century. Picards were particularly important in introducing French-speaking folk into a large depopulation area to the north and east of Château-Salins where German had been spoken formerly (Levy, 1929). Further examples of this kind of repeopling by both Picards and Normans may be found as far east as Burgundy and Franche-Comté.

In practical terms Alsace was virtually beyond the French realm, but the Morvan and lower Burgundy supplied population to the Paris region.[54] By contrast, Lorraine and Champagne often contained very low population densities and therefore needed to attract migrants from elsewhere. The attraction of the capital city and the acquisition of rural land by the urban bourgeoisie in the inner parts of the Paris Basin promoted mobility among the rural population. These were *régions de passage* which absorbed population from more distant areas but also dispatched migrants elsewhere.

Thus there existed a contrast within northern France between the western areas of high population pressure and the central and eastern zone of low population densities. Brittany was rather a special case, which is not surprising since this region long survived as a separate nation. After a period of prosperity and agricultural expansion in the Middle Ages when migrants were attracted to Brittany from Normandy, Maine and Anjou, the north-western peninsula experienced economic crisis from the fifteenth century onwards and became a region of outmigration.

Many unhealthy areas of sands and clays in middle France, such as the Sologne and the Brenne, attracted migrants in search of land but often they found it impossible to prosper if, indeed, they managed to survive. Such areas never achieved high population densities. Population pressure was also low on plateaulands with oceanic climates in the north-western parts of the Massif Central, such as Limousin, the Bocage Bourbonnais, and part of Combrailles. Nevertheless, these were regions of outmigration, for example from Limousin to Périgord, Poitou and Charentes, and from Marche and Combrailles to Berry. However such movements involved relatively small numbers of people, since population densities were low and mortality rates were high in the 'exporting' areas. Later on rural industries and temporary outmigration provided additional resources to help retain folk in their home areas.

Southern parts of middle France also comprised some areas with high population densities. These included the fertile areas of Bresse, the Limagne, Grésivaudan, and the hillslopes of Dauphiné. Intensive agriculture in the southern fashion (involving vines, mulberries, tree crops, and sometimes maize) permitted these areas to sustain growing population numbers and even to accommodate migrants from poorer surrounding regions. These fertile areas contained population with roots firmly implanted in solid rural communities, which were supported by productive agricultural systems and gave them great facility for assimilating migrants.[55] In addition, the eastern parts of the Massif Central supported high population densities, linked to rural industries and farming systems based on cereals, tree crops, and stock-rearing. These areas dispatched their surplus populations to destinations both near and far. In the latter case, permanent outmigration often followed temporary movements, for example, folk who moved from Auvergne and Forez to Burgundy and Lorraine after the sixteenth century.

In southern France there was much greater variability. Few regions functioned consistently as reception areas or as 'reservoirs of humanity' dispatching migrants to other parts of France throughout the medieval and modern periods. Southern agriculture was less strictly linked to subsistence but was sensitive to competition and disruption, such as the Albigensian crusade in Languedoc and the Black Death of 1348 which was followed by epidemics for almost two centuries. However, losses of population which followed these disasters were less serious than in central and northern France. Only the Pyrenean mountains and the southern Massif Central tended to escape the ravages of epidemics and functioned as quasi-permanent regions of outmigration, with movements from the Pyrenees towards Gascony and Spain, and from the southern Massif-Central to Bas-Languedoc, Albigeois and the lower Rhône valley.[56] Some parts of the South repeatedly required inmigration to maintain their population numbers. These areas included the western section of Basse-Provence, parts of the Rhône Plain, marshy areas of Bas-Languedoc and Bordelais. However, these areas were to achieve relatively important densities after the seventeenth century.

From the Middle Ages onwards Bordelais functioned as a reception area for migrants, but its dense pattern of small *communes* indicates that it had supported large population numbers in the remote past, with these declining later. A variety of other types of population inversion may be noted elsewhere. Languedoc, for example, received refugees when Spain was conquered by the Moors in the early Middle Ages but later dispatched population back in the reverse direction when Spain was reconquered. Le Roy Ladurie (1966) has shown the later phases for Bas-Languedoc in detail: medieval population pressure, dramatic decline in the fourteenth and fifteenth centuries, gradual recovery, then an excess of population in the seventeenth century, leading to a new equilibrium with new resources being utilised in the eighteenth century. Quercy, which had been a settled area from time immemorial, was depopulated during the Hundred Years' War and then partially repopulated by folk from the Massif Central (Rouergue, Limousin, and even Velay). The hillslopes of Gascony experienced a parallel history to that of Bas-Languedoc until the seventeenth century, with even a stronger tendency towards outmigration, especially to Spain. However, the Franco-English wars and then the Wars of Religion of the sixteenth century greatly disturbed the demography of the hillslopes. From the seventeenth century onwards the region started to stagnate and even to decline, for reasons as yet imperfectly understood. Demographic decline remained a permanent feature through to the present day, so that Gascony and other parts of Aquitaine south of the Dordogne functioned as reception areas for northerners before receiving migrants from Italy and Spain in the present century.

Finally, we should like to return to a question of methodology. The crisis of regional geography in France has partially resulted from the fact that the country is less clearly organized around major cities than is the case in some other European countries which were more strongly urbanized at an earlier period. The crisis is perhaps also linked to the fact that classical regional geography in France has dealt with small areas, provinces and large physico-geographical regions but has not perceived the existence of regions at other scales. In the past rural France was largely concerned with subsistence farming, but trade took place nonetheless, sometimes involving long distances but more often involving short- and medium-distance transactions. Economic activities were organized around towns and smaller central places. It was around these centres that the real territorial units of daily life were defined. So far we have gained only a partial and sporadic view of these units but documentary and anthroponymic material might be used; however this would be a mammoth and lengthy task. We believe that there is a more direct way of investigating these territorial units, namely through the study of dialects. Variations in dialect and accent corresponded with spatial units within which it was necessary to make oneself understood for purposes of trade. Eventually a more or less common dialect would develop in response to the frequency and continuity of exchange. Classical studies in regional geography failed to recognize the existence of spatial units that resulted in this way. For example, many small areas of the Pyrenees combined with the hillslopes and plains of Gascony to form a single linguistic area. Limousin and Périgord, right through to the middle Dordogne, spoke the same dialect which once extended into the Charentes. Velay and Vivarais belonged to the province of Languedoc but, for ethnic and economic reasons going right back to the origins of the *langue d'oc*, their dialect was a northern form of *oc*, very far removed from *langue-docien*. However, this dialect on the eastern edges of the Massif Central displays certain common traits with Provençal, largely due to later trading links with the Rhône region from Velay and Vivarais. Current research in central-western France and in the Massif Central indicates how geography and dialectology may help each other, and points to the need to establish a real linguistic geography which would study both language and the hierarchy of economic 'cells' in the rural world which stood the test of time and therefore merit much more attention than they have received so far.[57] In fact one might wonder if the recognition of such spatial units might not be of importance for translating planning schemes into operational terms. Such studies would highlight spatial complementarities that are far from being dead. They would also assist an understanding of the history of trade links, place their operation into the framework of the real world, and thus rescue them from the realm of abstract reasoning. Thus the retreat of *langue d'oc* speakers from the Alpine region in the face of advancing Provençal speech from the southern Alps was probably not linked to the historic transhumance northwards of Mediterranean flocks and herds into the mountains, as has been claimed in the past. It was in fact a more recent change which might well express the inverted importance of Haute- and Basse-Provence at the end of the Middle Ages, when low-country settlements became more important than those in the uplands. A recent study has sought to show the advance of southern linguistic forms (*langue d'oc*) into Dauphiné and Forez which are characterized by Franco-Provençal speech forms (Horiot, 1972). If this surprising trend could be confirmed, it would reinforce the contacts that one must recognize between these regions and the Midi. Research into the causes of such a situation would demand a 'southward' orientation of enquiry in a country dominated by the continuous strengthening of political and economic power in the Paris Basin.

This provides yet more evidence of the enormous problems in the geography of settlement and the rural environment of France that still await research.

2. Notes

1. Bourdier (1967) stresses the possibility of Europe being *one* of the cradles of mankind.
2. The main interpretation in Western Europe is that two different strains once existed, with Neanderthal man somehow becoming extinct. The whole

matter is extremely dubious, as is the supposed distribution of Neanderthal man on the face of the earth. It is hard to accept, for example, that relict groups should not be found. Therefore, we tend to follow the ideas of Soviet anthropologists, such as Nestourkh (1960), who see Neanderthal man as an ancestor of *homo sapiens*. The facts of 'juvenism' and 'neotenism' (namely the appearance and stabilization of new characteristics in young people) invoked by Bourdier (1967) give support to this interpretation.

It seems to us that if certain physical characteristics of the Nordic race are due to depigmentation in a cold environment, this must have taken a long time and could scarcely have occurred in northern Europe which was ice-covered until relatively recent times. Only in northern Asia were vast areas free of an ice cover during the glacial periods and only in these areas could these physical characteristics have developed. In support of this hypothesis, one can invoke certain analogous physical traits among the Palaeo-Siberians who are widely recognized as a residual but autochtonous racial group resulting from interbreeding of yellow- and white-skinned peoples.

It has been proved that the conquering groups derived from the Nordic racial stock were never very numerous, but nevertheless they left strong physical traits in the population of France, and indeed in northern Italy. This fact might be linked to greater survival chances of the conquerors who more easily withstood famines and other disasters. But in historic times the blond group has become less significant in the total population of France.

3. Bosch-Gimpera (1961) provides valuable information but many useful articles have appeared in the *Revue Internationale d'Onomastique*.

4. On the one hand, because the study of dialect place-names can provide useful insights into the processes of land clearance and occupation; but on the other, because dialects provide crucial evidence in understanding the formation of 'regions'. Dialects were the means of communication for individual units of territoriality within which agricultural goods and other commodities were exchanged.

5. British linguists, such as J. Rhys and J. Morris-Jones, see Hamitic features in Celtic syntax, basing their view on the contacts between Iberia and the British Isles in the prehistoric and protohistoric periods. This interpretation however is open to debate. It is possible that there was simply a convergence, since the Hamitic language must have been a branch of the great Eurasian substrate during the Mesolithic. But it is difficult to accept that the language of the Gauls was distinct, since close similarities with the Celtic languages of Britain have been shown by Falc'hun (1963, 1970).

6. For example, the *Bulletin de la Société Folklorique du Centre-Ouest* (1972) contains mention of the survival until recent times of the southern tradition of treading out grain (*dépiquage*) in the plain of Poitou far to the north. This kind of information might be used to help elucidate past patterns of

peopling. Studies of spatial variations in traditional dress in Brittany suggest that these corresponded with ancient trading areas.

7. 'Haut-Moyen-Age' has been translated as 'early Middle Ages', referring to the period A.D. 400–1000.

8. Publications in *Onomastica* and later in the *Revue Internationale d'Ono-mastique* reflect almost exclusively the same 'ideology' which still has strong support from some quarters.

9. In this way the place names 'Montagny' or 'Montagnac' would have been explained by a Latin personal name (Montanius), even if the sites in question were on high ground, hilltops or in mountainous terrain (*mont*).

10. In particular Taverdet (1971), who has queried the explanation of such place names as 'Ruffey', 'Savigny' and 'Flagey' by reference to the Latin personal names Rufus, Sabinus, and Flavius.

11. This belief has guided work on place names which has already been published by the author and also forthcoming studies on the role of dialect in defining small regions within which traditional rural life and trading activities were articulated (Bonnaud, 1972 and 1974). More attention will be paid to the geographical importance of personal names which has received little emphasis in France, unlike neighbouring countries, for example Switzerland.

12. Interesting maps of prehistoric remains in the Alps are included in Nougier (1959). These show very strong concentrations of artefacts in the south-western Pre-Alps (especially in Diois) at each phase of the prehistoric and suggest that the mountain massif was peopled by folk from this core area, or refuge, which was in a relatively favoured location during cold periods.

13. With the exception of some parts of the South (such as sub-Pyrenean Gascony, the south-eastern and eastern border of the Massif Central, the hillslopes surrounding the Limagne, and Basse-Normandie) where population densities increased in response to agricultural intensification which, in turn, fragmented village territories even more when the network of parishes was established later.

14. To our way of thinking, this proves that hunting must have lost all importance in the way of life of these people from very early times. Watercourses formed the gathering places for game where they came to drink. Later on terraces would be vital for cereal cultivation, and the valley bottoms provide valuable meadowland for cattle.

15. Demographic pressure, which might have led to conflict, was experienced early in the Mediterranean zone but there are four reasons why it would not seem appropriate to invoke defensive motives to explain the development of elevated settlement sites. First, because the most ancient forms of grouped, fortified settlement seem to have been more recent than the post-glacial spread of mankind further to the north. Second, because until the end

of the Neolithic period population densities in France seem to have been sufficiently low for 'peaceful co-existence' by human groups to have been the rule. Third, because elevated sites outside the Mediterranean region *stricto sensu* were rarely in the best positions for defence. Finally, because many of these sites were much too small to have been able to 'dissuade' the enemy. This was particularly so in central, south-western and central-western France.

16. We are using the term *plaine* in the same way as the peasant farmers of middle France, namely to mean an open landscape with massive parcels of farmland, but sometimes with a few stone walls and supporting a few vines. *Communes* are large, and settlement nucleated, with a secondary dispersion of farms or small groups of dwellings between the villages.

17. In spite of the preponderance of stock-rearing, Maury (1967) notes that cereal growing was important and that the precise relationship between the two activities varied through the prehistoric period.

18. Dion (1934) includes useful extracts from old maps and Thabault (1952) uses historic documents in reconstructing the landscape of the *gâtine* of Poitou in the eighteenth and early nineteenth centuries. In particular he describes the landscape of Mazières-en-Gâtine.

19. Many of these modern woodlands of oak, beech and hornbeam have dialect names which recall pioneer tree species in the vegetation succession (such as the hazel) but also other trees (alder, ash) that no longer cover large woodland areas. Some names even indicate the past existence of broad expanses of open land with no tree cover. These features all relate to ancient names and may not be attributed to the devastation of the forests after the medieval period when fuel was sought for glassworks and forges. They confirm that the balance between cultivated areas and woodland is a relatively recent feature, linked to the triumph of the openfields for cereal cultivation. That is not to deny that woodland remained more stable for a longer period in the North than in the South of France, but this evidence invites fresh thought about the classic image of north-eastern France as being clothed by a vast mantle of woodland studded by cultivated clearings.

20. This does not prevent the ancient refuge points remaining more densely peopled until at least the third millennium. Stock rearing and cultivation allowed densities to increase from quite an early period and also permitted the formation of sedentary groups alongside groups of nomads.

21. This was perhaps linked to insecurity but perhaps also to the infiltration of tribes from the South who raised small livestock. The Seine-Oise-Marne culture of the inner Paris Basin is generally considered to have derived from earlier cultures which practised cultivation and land-clearance, but some authors have recognized archaeological evidence of influences derived from cultures in the Centre-Est of France (Bourdier, 1967).

22. Not only are there areas of loess and broad river terraces on these plains and low plateaulands, but the soil cover of the calcareous plateaux was thicker and more continuous in Quaternary paleoclimatic conditions before man-induced erosion was triggered off by woodland clearance.

23. We are not underestimating the known fact that names of small places (*lieux-dits*) disappear more readily than names of villages, mountains and rivers. But nevertheless, many more pre-Latin place names relating to settled points have survived among the *lieux-dits* of southern and western France than in the North and North-east (defined as east of Maine and north of a line through Orléans, Nivernais and the central Jura).

24. A systematic study of changes in settlement as revealed by archaeology and by place-name study in different geographical environments of the two great agrarian cultures of France would undoubtedly be very rewarding.

25. Let us recall the background to this situation. Reactions against German racism, from the end of the nineteenth century through to the Hitler regime, discredited the whole notion of 'race' and created a mental climate which was suspicious of any investigation into 'racial' characteristics.

26. The Seine formed the extreme limit in this case. Moreover the Goths who occupied a great part of southern Gaul were very 'mixed' racially following their lengthy peregrinations. Indeed, traces of Mongoloid features attributed to intermixture with the Huns have been noted in the Burgundians (Musset, 1965).

27. These estimates are open to debate. They are based on the volume of supply of armed forces coming to the aid of Vercingetorix at Alesia and convey a reasonable impression for parts of Gaul located close to the conflict zone, which supplied the most numerous contingents of warriors. But they probably underestimate the importance of population in more distant areas from which warriors could not travel easily.

28. We must remember that Celtic was still spoken throughout much of Gaul (excepting areas south of the Garonne) after Caesar's conquests, in spite of the survival of more or less important residual groups in the West, Centre and South of the country. Attempts to consider all of the Belgians as having become 'Germans' come up against serious objections, and one must continue to accept that only certain Belgian tribes in the north-east were 'Germanized' or received an important proportion of Germanic elements. How else could one explain either the prolonged resistance to 'Germanization' of the population around Trier, Prüm and in the lower Moselle, or the evidence from the end of the Roman Empire which indicates partial and incomplete 'Romanization' of the Belgians?

29. Many of the general findings of modern research (rather than the details) find links with earlier ideas, such as those of Hubert (1939). The same is true of the origins of different types of rural landscape, even though some

of the ideas of Dion (1934) and Deléage (1941), for example of the unchanging character of the openfields through time, must be rejected.

30. In some privileged areas, such as the Pyrenees and Aquitaine, clear regional divisions were apparent even from the Mesolithic.

31. The idea that the Grands Causses were densely populated in prehistoric times is simply legend, as is the belief in catastrophic soil erosion following deforestation by man (Maury, 1967). But that does not mean that there was erosion or that the Causses escaped prolonged environmental deterioration as the result of grazing.

32. The temporary nature of land clearance and the frequent abandonment of farmland form recurrent themes in the history of sandy regions such as the Brandes of Poitou (Debien, 1952) and the Puisaye areas of the Paris Basin (Moreau, 1958).

33. Very few detailed studies of important place-name elements are in existence. One can, however, mention the work of Dauzat (1939) on the Auvergne, Hamlin (1971–2) in Hérault, and Boudet (1970) in Cher. A few other studies have been undertaken but over half of the *départements* of France lack *Dictionnaires Topographiques* which would provide some information.

34. For example, R. Sindou who, from the evidence of Souvigny in Allier *département*, argues the use of this place-name feature right through into the medieval period.

35. This interpretation was honestly accepted by some German scholars, but nevertheless was linked in the minds of some with retrospective claims to support expansionist policies.

36. The proportion of Germanic personal names increased continually during the early Middle Ages to reach 50–80 per cent of names contained in documents of the Carolingian period (even including evidence from southern France), before declining during the medieval period.

37. It is well known that the rigour of the French feudal system rapidly declined to the west of Paris and to the south of Orléans, due to the lack of an aristocracy as aggressive, powerful, and cohesive as that of the Frankish warrior lords.

38. See Pope (1952) on dialect features indicating an important Germanic influence, and Musset (1965) and Guinet (1967) on place names.

39. See Bonnaud (1969a) and Fleuriot (1958).

40. Demographic growth and the advance of traditional agriculture were linked intimately. Population grew in areas where densities were already important and this in turn fostered agricultural intensification. These early foci developed in favourable geographic environments which permitted highly-productive agricultural systems to operate.

41. Let us remember that in spite of numerous wars and disturbances (Franco-

English wars in the Middle Ages in the West and South-West; the Albigensian crusade in Languedoc; civil wars in the sixteenth century; wars in the seventeenth century, especially in northern and north-western France) the French countryside did not experience very lengthy or important periods of desertion. 'Gaps' in the pattern of peopling were rapidly filled by migrants from areas of high demographic pressure. See, for example, Boutruche (1935), Higounet (1953), and Le Roy Ladurie (1966).

42. One can think that sheer strength of numbers, especially in areas of nucleated settlement, allowed the French peasantry to resist the efforts of aristocrats and bourgeoisie to engross and enclose land at the end of the Middle Ages and in the modern period. The French peasantry were certainly more resistant than their counterparts in England, Scandinavia and northern Germany. The difference was certainly not linked to variations in the availability of capital.

43. The first examples date from the ninth century in Maine and then multiplied in Haute-Bretagne from the eleventh century onwards. We think it is possible that this place-name element (-ville) influenced the Breton form -ker, with the same meaning and semantic evolution.

44. The hypothesis was put forward in Bonnaud (1969b). We believe that it is strengthened by the growing importance which modern linguistic research has brought to the oc substratum in the northern (oïl) dialect of Poitou and Saintonge. See also Chaussée (1966) on the Vendée region.

45. The parish was the ancestor of the modern commune. The parish system was devised in the Carolingian period as the means of organizing the rural population for political and religious purposes. In order to be efficient the parishes covered smaller areas of land in densely-peopled regions than in sparsely-inhabited ones.

46. Migration to areas beyond the Pyrenees was a solution taken easily by folk from Gascony and Languedoc when overpopulation built up (Nadal and Giralt, 1960).

47. This must have contributed to the retreat of the Basque language (paléo-basque-aquitain) which, according to recent research, survived for a long time in parts of Aquitaine and the central Pyrenees (Rohlfs, 1955, 1970).

48. With the exception of the Paris Basin north of the Loire, the majority of French place names are derived from dialects. Hence it is necessary to study dialects and minority languages in order to make use of place-name evidence. In the past, inadequate attention was paid to provincial problems by excessively-centralized research.

49. This study shows that the commercial exchanges of the Auvergne were orientated predominantly to the South and especially towards the Rhône corridor until the fourteenth century and that this direction remained important right through to the late eighteenth century. Not until the

transport 'revolution' of the nineteenth century was this traditional orientation changed substantially.

50. The first great commercial vineyards were in northern France (Dion, 1959) but many declined very rapidly (for example, those in Lorraine) and others became limited to very specialized forms of production. By contrast, the vine became an intimate component of landscapes throughout the South.

51. The only notable exception, and an urban one at that, is provided by the attraction of Paris. Auvergnats migrated to the capital from the medieval period onwards but this was not their habitual destination.

52. By comparison with Switzerland where the origin of family names has been studied over a long period which allows migrations to be investigated with great precision.

53. We must remember that ancient French and old forms of the *langue d'oc* were much less different than their modern forms. The distinction increased from the fourteenth century onwards, in response to an acceleration of the influence of northern French linked to innovations stemming from the Paris region.

54. But in the seventeenth century devastated parts of Alsace were repeopled by folk from Switzerland and from southern Germany.

55. For example, the spread of *oïl* stopped on the northern edge of the Grande Limagne around Gannat, even though northerners migrated into areas of rich agricultural land further south. But they were absorbed by southern culture and the *langue d'oc* continued to predominate, albeit with some northern influence.

56. However the Ossau valley that was devastated in the fifteenth century was repeopled by folk from the plain of Béarn.

57. By a 'real linguistic geography' we mean a discipline which would involve the whole of geography, not just a study that introduces random geographical facts to try to explain linguistic features, as has been the case in some studies in the past.

2. References

Baratier, E., '*La Démographie provençale du XIIIe au XVIe siècle*', Paris (1961).

Beszard, L., '*Origine des noms de lieux habités du Maine*', Paris (1910).

Bloch, M., '*Les Caractères originaux de l'histoire rurale française*', Paris (1931).

Bonnaud, P., 'Les problèmes du peuplement du Massif Central vus par un géographe', *Revue d'Auvergne*, 83 (1969a), 1–38.

Bonnaud, P., 'Les problèmes du peuplement du Centre de la France', *Norois*, 61 (1969b), 31–46.

Bonnaud, P., 'La haie et le hameau, les mots et les choses', *Revue d'Auvergne*, 84 (1970), 1–28.

Bonnaud, P., 'Les toponymes relatifs à la végétation et aux défrichements et à l'évolution du paysage rural en Auvergne, Bourbonnais et Velay', *Revue d'Auvergne*, 85 (1971a), 199–230.

Bonnaud, P., 'Du relief aux hommes', in *Le Sud et le Nord, dialectique de la France*, ed. R. Lafont, Toulouse (1971b), 13–72.

Bonnaud, P., 'Correspondances phonétiques, lexicales et morphologiques entre le poitevain-santongeais et l'occitan', *Revue de Recherches Ethnographiques* (1972).

Bonnaud, P., 'Toponymes dialectaux de type occitan et 'méridional' dans les Charentes', *Revue Internationale d'Onomastique*, 26 (1974), 17–49.

Bosch-Gimpera, P., *Les Indo-Européens*, Paris (1961).

Boudet, R., 'Recherches sur les noms de lieux en -acus du département du Cher', *Cahiers de la Société d'Archéologie et d'Histoire du Berry*, 21 (1970), 2–83.

Bourdier, F., *Préhistoire de la France*, Paris (1967).

Boutruche, R., 'Les courants de peuplement dans l'Entre-Deux-Mers', *Annales d'Histoire Economique et Sociale*, 31 (1935), 13–36 and 124–155.

Chabot, G., 'Les migrations intérieures de population provoquée par les mariages: l'exemple de Villette (Ain) depuis trois siècles', in *Mélanges Arbos*, vol. I, Paris (1953), 215–227.

Chaussée, F., *Les parlers du centre-ouest de la Vendée*, Paris (1966).

Chevallier, R., 'Photographie aérienne et villages désertés', in *Villages désertés et histoire économique*, Paris (1965), 63–81.

Dauzat, A., *Les noms de lieux*, Paris (1932).

Dauzat, A., *La toponymie française*, Paris (1939).

Dauzat, A., *Traité d'anthroponymie française*, Paris (1945).

Dauzat, A. and Rostaing, C., *Dictionnaire des noms de lieux de France*, Paris (1963).

Debien, G., *En Haut-Poitou, defricheurs au travail, XVe–XVIIe siècle*, Paris (1952).

Deléage, A., *La Vie rurale en Bourgogne jusqu'au début du XIe siècle*, Macon (1941).

Derruau, M., *La Grande Limagne auvergnate et bourbonnaise*, Grenoble (1949).

Derruau, M., 'Un village-tombeau dans le Bas-Languedoc: Capestang', *Revue de Géographie Alpine*, 41 (1953), 99–115.

Dion, R., *Le Val de Loire*, Tours (1934).

Dion, R., 'Le problème des Cassiterides', in *Mélanges Arbos*, vol. II, Paris (1953), 23–29.

Dion, R., *Histoire de la vigne et du vin en France: des origines au XIXe siècle*, Paris (1959).

Dornic, F., *Histoire du Maine*, Paris (1960).

Durvin, P., 'Les églises carolinginnes de la région de Beauvais', *Eklitra tradition picarde*, 6 (1972a), 31–37.

Durvin, P., *Essai sur l'économie gallo-romaine dans la région de Creil*, Amiens (1972b).

Falc'hun, F., 'Le Breton, forme moderne du gaulois', *Annales de Bretagne*, 62 (1962), 202–213.

Falc'hun, F., *Histoire de la langue bretonne d'après la géographie linguistique*, 2nd Ed., Paris (1963).

Falc'hun, F., *Les noms de lieux celtiques; vallées et plaines*, Rennes (1966).

Falc'hun, F., *Les noms de lieux celtiques; problèmes de doctrine et de méthode, noms de hauteurs*, Rennes (1970).

Fel, A., *Les Hautes terres du Massif Central*, Clermont-Ferrand (1962).

Felice, R. De., *Les Noms de nos rivières*, Paris (1907).

Fleuriot, J. L., 'Recherche sur les enclaves romaines anciennes en territoire bretonnant', *Etudes Celtiques*, 8 (1958), 164–178.

Fournier, G., *Le Peuplement rural en Basse-Auvergne durant le Haut-Moyen-Age*, Paris (1962).

Giot, P. R., 'Armoricains et Bretons, vingt ans après', *Annales de Bretagne*, 79 (1972), 103–118.

Guinet, L., *Contribution à l'étude des établissements saxons en Normandie*, Caen (1967).

Hamlin, F. R., 'Les noms de domaines en -anum dans le département de l'Hérault', *Revue Internationale d'Onomastique*, 23 (1971), 241–256 and 24 (1972), 15–32, 81–97.

Harmand, J., *Les Celtes*, Paris (1970).

Higounet, C., 'Mouvement de population dans le Midi de la France du XIe au XVe siècle', *Annales, Economies, Sociétés, Civilisations*, 8 (1953), 1–24.

Horiot, B., 'Recherches sur la morphologie de l'ancien franco-provençal', *Revue de Linguistique Romaine*, 36 (1972), 1–74.

Hubert, H., *Les Celtes*, Paris (1939).

Imberdis, F., *Le Reseau routier de l'Auvergne au XVIIIe siècle*, Paris (1967).

Juillard, E., *La Vie rurale en Basse-Alsace*, Paris and Strasbourg (1953).

Lanly, A., *Enquête linguistique sur le plateau d'Ussel*, Paris (1962).

Le Roy Ladurie, E., *Les Paysans de Languedoc*, Paris (1966).

Levy, P., *Histoire linguistique d'Alsace et de Lorraine, des origines à la Révolution française*, Strasbourg (1929).

Lognon, A., *Les Noms de lieux de la France*, Paris (1929).

Loriot, R., *La Frontière dialectale moderne en Haute-Normandie*, Amiens (1967).

Lot, F., 'Les noms de lieux en -ville et en -court', *Romania*, 59 (1933), 199–246.

Lot, F., 'Ce que nous apprennent sur le peuplement germanique de la France les recents travaux de toponymie', *Comptes Rendus de l'Académie de l'Inscription* (1945), 289–298.

Loth, J., *L'Emigration bretonne en Armorique*, Paris (1883).

Marquer, P., *Morphologie des races humaines*, Paris (1967).

Maury, J., *Les Etapes du peuplement sur les Grandes Causses*, Millau (1967).

Millotte, J. P., *Races de protohistoire européenne*, Paris (1970).

Moll, De B. F., *Els llinatges catalans*, Palma de Mallorca (1959).

Moreau, J. P., *La Vie rurale dans le sud-est du bassin parisien*, Paris (1958).

Müller, B., 'La bi-partition linguistique de la France, mise au point de l'état de recherches', *Revue de Linguistique Romane*, 35 (1971), 17–30.

Musset, L., *Les Invasions : les vagues germaniques*, Paris (1965).

Musset, L., 'Germains', in *Encyclopaedia Universalis*, vol. VII, Paris (1970), 692–695.

Musset, R., *Le Bas-Maine*, Paris (1917).

Nadal, J. and Giralt, E., *La Population catalane de 1553 à 1717*, Paris (1960).

Nègre, E., *Le Noms de lieux en France*, Paris (1963).

Nestourkh, M., *L'Origine de l'homme*, Moscow (1960).

Nestourkh, M., *Les Races humaines*, Moscow (n.d.).

Nougier, L. R., *La Géographie humaine préhistorique*, Paris (1959).

Nougier, L. R., *L'Economie préhistorique*, Paris (1970).

Pope, M. K., *From Latin to Modern French*, Manchester (1952).

Roblin, M., *Le Terroir de Paris aux époques gallo-romaine et franque*, Paris (1951).

Rohlfs, G., 'Couches de colonisation romaine et préromaine en Gascogne et en Aragon', *Revue International d'Onomastique*, 7 (1955), 1–12.

Rohlfs, G., *Le Gascon*, 2nd Ed. Tübingen and Pau (1970).

Salin, E., *La Civilisation merovingienne d'après les sépultures, les textes et le laboratoire*, 4 vols., Paris (1949–59).

Sclafert, T., *Culture en Haute-Provence, déboisement et pâturages au Moyen-Age*, Paris (1959).

Souillet, G., 'Chronologie et repartition des noms de lieux habités en -ière et -ais dans la Haute-Bretagne', *Annales de Bretagne*, 50 (1947), 90–98.

Taverdet, G., Hypothèses toponymiques, *Revue Internationale d'Onomastique*, 23 (1971), 219–232.

Thabault, R., *L'Ascension d'un peuple : mon village*, Paris (1952).

Trepos, P., *Le Pluriel breton*, Brest (1957).

Verlinden, C., *Les origines de la frontière linguistique en Belgique et la colonisation franque*, Brussels (1955).

Vincent, A., *Toponymie de la France*, Brussels (1937).

3
Early Urban Development

HUGH D. CLOUT

Introduction

France, like other countries of Western Europe, experienced a rich town-based civilization in classical times, the Middle Ages, and the Renaissance era. However, the nineteenth-century phase of industrial urbanization which was expressed so harshly in the landscapes of Britain and Germany was confined to relatively few localities in France. Three distinctive features emerge from an examination of the modern form and functioning of French urban settlements. First, there is the unrivalled supremacy of Paris with more than nine million inhabitants towering above the fifteen major provincial cities with between 250,000 and one million residents apiece. Second, and much lower in the urban hierarchy, comes the endowment of an extraordinary number and variety of small market towns with less than 20,000 residents each. Finally, the landscapes of French urban settlements, both large and small, display a rich legacy of historic features. Sometimes this endowment is expressed directly in the survival of *châteaux*, historic houses, cathedrals, and other ancient buildings. But it is also demonstrated in indirect ways. For example, ancient settlement sites are still in use after centuries of occupation, even though their original *raisons d'être* are no longer relevant. In a similar vein ancient street plans have been retained or modified only slightly by generations of city builders. The key to these and to many other important features of French urbanism lies in its historical development. It is the purpose of this chapter to examine the earlier phases of that development, namely the first two generations of French urban settlement, dating from classical and medieval times.[1]

One of the initial problems in such a discussion is the definition of what should be considered as 'urban settlement'. Precise statements relating to medieval towns were proposed by Pirenne (1925) and these will be examined later in the present chapter. But a broader interpretation seems more appropriate to this discussion. In Smith's words (1967):

> '. . . Economic functions in trade, crafts, industry or marketing have generally been regarded as fundamental components of town life and it could be argued that agricultural occupations should be in a minority . . . For our purpose it could be enough . . . to regard a town as a concentration of population larger than the neighbouring agricultural settlements in which there is a substantial non-agricultural population which may be concerned with defence, administration, religion, commerce, and/or industry' (p. 299).

First Generation: The Classical Legacy

The arrival of Asiatic Greeks from Phocaea at a Mediterranean roadstead which they named Lacydon introduced the first generation of towns in France, with the settlement of Massalia (Marseilles) being constructed on this site. Greek traders in Massalia organized commerce in the western Mediterranean between Carthage, Corsica, Italy, Sardinia, Sicily, and Spain. Further Greek trading posts were set up at Arles, Avignon, and Cavaillon in the fifth century B.C. and these were complemented by a chain of ports in sheltered coves and other appropriate sites on the Mediterranean littoral, including Antipolis (Antibes), Olbia (near Hyères), and Niké (Monaco). To the west, the 'colony of good fortune' (Agde) was planted on the coast of Languedoc, which was less favoured than Provence in respect of natural shelters.

Roman annexation of southern Gaul (Gallia Narboniensis) did not follow until 121 B.C. following requests from the inhabitants of Marseilles for protection against pirates operating along the Ligurian coast. The subsequent presence of Roman troops between the Alps, Cévennes and Pyrenees ensured that trade routes along the Rhône valley should be guarded against attacks from Celtic folk in the Massif Central or from Germanic newcomers in the eastern Alps. Effective control of land movement was a key component in the establishment and maintenance of Roman power in Gaul, and to guarantee this a network of roads and settlements needed to be constructed (Desjardins, 1876–93).

The building of Roman roads began in southern Gaul long before the conquests of Caesar, with the Via Domitia between the Alps and the Pyrenees being the oldest of these (Fig. 3.1). In the interior of Gaul, construction of the road network began c. 20 B.C.,

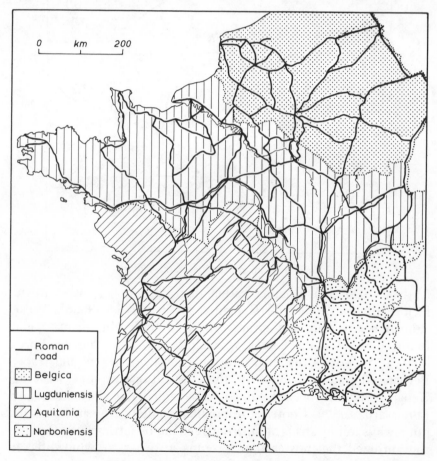

FIG. 3.1. Roman Roads and Provinces.

in association with the operation of the imperial land survey. Lugdunum (Lyons), newly-founded capital of Roman Gaul, formed
the focal point not only for the three provinces of Gaul (Belgica,
Lugduniensis, and Aquitania) but also for the network of main
roads, on to which secondary roads were grafted later (Fig. 3.2)

FIG. 3.2. Roman Provinces and *Civitates*.

(Mirot, 1947–50). Rheims, rather than Paris or any other town,
formed the focal point for Roman roads in northern Gaul. These
Roman roads were not entirely new in their alignment. Some
followed earlier Gallic routes, which in turn were the legacy of prehistoric trackways that had long been used for travel and trade.
Perhaps the most famous of these traditional routes was the
Tenarez running between the Pyrenees and the Garonne valley
(Boussard, 1957). Contrary to popular opinion, Roman roads did
not always follow straight lines between major settlements. Rather,
they utilized the most rational routes in order to avoid difficult
topography, with many being located along ridgeways.

Pre-Roman Gaul had contained native 'towns' (*oppida*) which became increasingly numerous during the second century B.C. so that Caesar could quote thirty or so (Duval, 1952). *Oppida* were essentially fortresses and many occupied defensive hill-top sites or were surrounded by rivers or marshland. Initially they might have only been occupied on a temporary basis but gradually they became permanent refuge centres, acquiring new functions related to administration, manufacturing, religion and trade. Troedsson (1959) maintained that it was only in what was to become the Provincia Narboniensis that the Romans found a truly urban culture in Gaul.

> 'Narbonne was thriving, so was Toulouse, the sacred Toloasa where the Gallic state treasure was kept, so was Bazas, . . . so was Cahors. These cities had sought, or arisen due to, natural protective locations—Cahors in the bend of a river, Bazas on a hill top whose triangular shape is repeated in the market place. Because the towns were originally Gallic they show none of the geometric pattern of the Roman town' (p. 24).

Undoubtedly there had been stone constructions in the *oppida* of the Midi, as had been the case in the old Greek colonies along the coast in earlier centuries. For example, at Ensérune, between the sites of Béziers and Narbonne, early dwelling huts were made of wickerwork plastered with mud. However, by the end of the fifth century B.C. the inhabitants of the town were occupying stone houses. By contrast, *oppida* in the interior of Gaul were still composed of fragile huts. Beyond the Midi, the *grande ville* with its public monuments, solid streets, and stone houses was not to appear until after the Roman conquest.

The indigenous population of Gaul lived in fifty to sixty tribes (*civitates*), each forming a sort of moral and political organization bound together by social contact (Schmittlein, 1970). Many of these *civitas* groupings were subsequently to give their names to urban settlements.[2] Areas commanded by *civitates* were divided for administrative purposes into *pagi*, based on sub- or client tribes, and these in turn were divided into *vici*. Thus a relatively well-developed hierarchy of administration and settlement was in existence in Roman times. Many of the 44 capitals of *civitates* depicted on the thirteenth-century Peutinger map have retained their importance as administrative centres (Desjardins, 1869). Twenty six are modern *préfectures*, seven are *sous-préfectures*, and the remainder are minor settlements (Pinchemel, 1969).

Three categories of Gallo-Roman town were established. The first of these was made up of Roman colonies which were founded for veterans. These colonies included Béziers, Narbonne, Orange, and above all Arles which was the earliest Roman foundation in Gaul. The town was carved from territory which had been commanded from Marseilles and in 46 B.C. was set up as a colony for veterans of the Sixth Legion. Roman colonies were laid out on chequer-board grids and were equipped with amphitheatres, baths, theatres, and the other material trappings of Roman civilization. Colonies of this type did not normally exceed 6000 ex-servicemen with their respective families and some native residents.

Latin colonies formed the second type of urban creation. These were established to resettle impoverished and under-employed dwellers from rural Italy. Aix, Avignon, Carcassonne, Nîmes and Vienne exemplified this kind of settlement in which indigenous people usually predominated. Latin colonies were much larger than the preceding type, reaching perhaps as many as 60,000 inhabitants apiece. Thus Nîmes and Vienne were much larger than the nearby Roman colonies of Arles and Orange. Latin civilian colonies were also laid out according to the regular plans and were provided with urban equipment. Thus at Nîmes the 55 m-high Pont du Gard aqueduct was constructed at Agrippa's command to bring water some 50 km from the river Gard to thereby provide 400 litres of water per person per day.

Finally, there were purely indigenous centres, such as Rheims and Tours, which were re-established as Roman capitals by Augustus.

'Before the Romans, Gallic *oppida* had been shabby and disorganized: the donkey was their city planner. Now the Romans encouraged those they set up as the Gallic ruling class to emulate Italian cities' (MacKendrick, 1971, p. 60).

New building materials included bricks, mortar, quarried and shaped stone, and tiles which together afforded a new dimension in city construction. The speed of Roman urbanization was amazing, with towns mushrooming up, being embellished with monuments and fitted with new pieces of practical equipment that construction in stone would allow.[3] Thus water was supplied to Lyons by a series of lengthy aqueducts, of which two were 60 km and 75 km. Shorter but nonetheless impressive aqueducts supplied many other towns.

Roman towns were not usually fortified, excepting military colonies in Gallia Narboniensis, the Rhône valley, and the Rhinelands (Lot, 1945). Towns grew without the constraint of walls as the *Pax Romana* extended throughout Gaul, but many of them followed well-practised Roman traditions. Gentle hillslopes with protective rivers and areas of lowland at the base formed ideal sites for city building. Thus the hillslope of Fourvière was chosen as the nucleus for Lyons, Saint-Eutrope for Orange, and Mont Capron for Beauvais. Sometimes river-bank sites were selected for their command of fluvial routes, as at Amiens, Narbonne, and Orléans. But the first type of site was preferred and was utilized wherever feasible. Thus the Romanized settlement of Lutetia Parisiorum occupied ground which rose southwards from marshland in the Montmartre meander above islands where the Seine might be crossed easily (Dion, 1961; Duval, 1961) (Fig. 3.3). Grid plans, orientated along a north/south *cardo* and an east/west *decumanus* were employed in building the larger Roman settlements wherever topography would permit. But this kind of chequer board, with its *forum* located at the intersection of the two main arteries, was not found in every small urban settlement. Neither was it so very regular that all urban blocks had exactly the same dimensions. The largest and most populous urban settlements of Gaul were of modest spatial extent, with the circumference of Nîmes at the time of its peak prosperity being no more than 6 km.

Estimating the population of Roman towns and cities is a delicate matter in the absence of written records. Suffice it to say that recent researchers have revised estimates downwards, so that where past calculations might have been presented in tens of thousands, modern ones are expressed in thousands. Most urban settlements in Gaul contained less than 15,000 inhabitants apiece at the peak of their development. However, there were some exceptions. For example, maximum figures in the order of 60,000 have already been quoted for the Latin colonies, and a recent estimate for Lyons (Lugdunum) was 50–80,000 souls at the city's prime (Mac-Kendrick, 1971). Roman Paris failed to achieve such numerical importance, reaching its greatest size in the second century A.D. when it contained some 20,000 souls (Troedsson, 1959).

Moving beyond the towns of ancient Gaul, pre-Roman nucleated settlement existed in the countryside of the lower Rhône and in Provence. But hamlets and scattered settlements were normal in northern Gaul where there were few traces of nucleation (Jullian, 1908–26). Roman *villas*, involving not only residences and farm buildings but also workshops, were inserted into such a diverse rural environment. *Villa* sites were particularly numerous around Lyons, in the Rhinelands, along routeways through Burgundy leading to the Seine or to Rheims, in Aquitaine, south-eastern Gaul, and parts of the West where land and sea routes were juxtaposed.

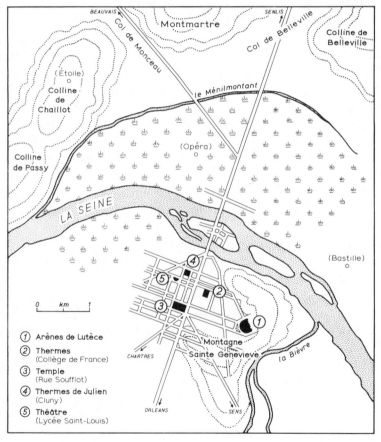

FIG. 3.3. Lutetia Parisiorum, second century A.D.

Regular grid patterns of centuriation were traced out in parts of Roman Gaul where veterans were settled or colonists were installed in frontier districts, as indeed was the practice elsewhere in the Roman world (Chevallier, 1960). Each century was divided into 100 lots that together provided land for an equivalent number of veterans. Provence, Alsace, and several other regions of Gaul were surveyed and divided up in this fashion (Chevallier, 1962). The great squares of centuriation may still be distinguished from aerial photographs of the modern rural landscape of southern France (Fig. 3.4).

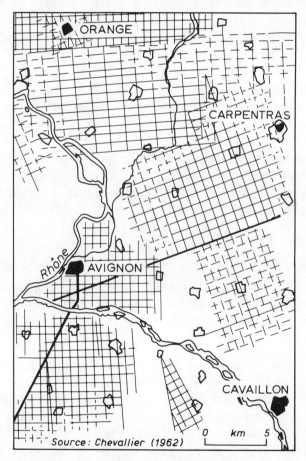

FIG. 3.4. Centuriation around Avignon.

The Dark Ages

The confused, lengthy but little-known period of the Germanic invasions followed the flourishing town life of Roman Gaul. Unfortunately it would seem that '. . . no aspect of early medieval civilization has received so little attention from social and economic historians as town life' (Dopsch, 1969, p. 303). As early as A.D. 257 Gaul was ravaged by invaders, and its towns were devastated. The Gallo-Romans rebuilt their ruined settlements and modified their ways of life. Thus in place of open, wall-less towns, and opulent *villas* that had been built in the first century A.D., much smaller towns were reconstructed from the debris of temples, public monuments, and other buildings. These settlements were surrounded by defensive walls and some amphitheatres were even transformed into fortresses, as at Arles and Tours. Urban folk, always in fear of fresh invasion, lived a precarious existence in these shrunken, over-populated towns. At the end of the third century and in the fourth century the Barbarians entered Gaul, sometimes infiltrating in small groups but also invading in massive hordes. In 406 the Vandals, Suevi and Alains crossed the Rhine and ravaged Gaul *en route* for Spain.[4] The Roman Empire disaggregated as Visigoths, Franks, and Huns made their conquests. It is very clear that towns in the fifth century A.D. appeared very differently from those of the Imperial heyday. Nevertheless these settlements which had shrunk within their ramparts were to form nuclei from which medieval towns were to grow in later centuries. But, as Smith (1967) has observed:

'. . . one of the major problems in a historical geography of towns in Western Europe is to establish the ways in which this continuity was achieved from Roman to medieval times' (p. 297).

At the same time as towns and cities contracted, the broad economy of the Roman world fragmented into a series of local or regional economic units, which were paralleled by a flight of population into the countryside. Pirenne (1925) argued that urban settlement survived in spite of the fall of Rome.[5] The continued existence of and functioning of the Christian Church contributed to this survival, with Mediterranean trade, so long as it operated,

supporting Marseilles and other Mediterranean cities such as
Arles, Avignon, Fos, Toulon, Valence and Vienne. Trading links
operated through the Rhône valley and also more widely along the
traces of Roman roads.[6]

Invasions by Muslim bands along the Mediterranean littoral in
the ninth century brought further devastation to the shrunken
urban settlements of the Midi, especially in eastern Provence
where Fréjus and Toulon were destroyed. At the same time the
Muslim advance caused the trade of Marseilles to wane. But perhaps the main result of this disruptive period was to convert
shrunken towns into fulfilling defensive functions. Thus walled
towns in the Midi contained the wealth and possessions of
ecclesiastics and the lesser nobility and functioned in a roughly
similar way to castles that were found further north. Whilst many
towns subsisted in material terms, they lost much of their population of artisans and traders, and with them whatever municipal
organization had survived from Roman times (Pirenne, 1941).
Features of Roman urbanism were erased rather more substantially from northern France than from the Midi. But some northern
traces still remained, with *civitates* being adopted as noble residences or functioning as the centres of bishoprics. This, in Pirenne's
words (1955), was because:

> '. . . in the territory of the ancient Roman Empire the episcopal
> "cities" were built at the most favourably situated points, since
> the diocesan centres were established from the beginning in the
> principal towns and these owed their importance to the advan-
> tages of their position' (pp. 215–6).

Decaying walls around these *civitates* were repaired hastily when
fresh troubles threatened, as at the time of the Scandinavian
invasion. New town walls and castles were built by feudal lords.
Such fortified places formed new types of pre-urban core besides
the ancient Roman settlements, many of which were soon to be
built upon in the medieval expansion phase.

But in A.D. 1000 only a few carcasses of Roman amphitheatres,
aqueducts, baths, gateways and other monuments remained in
France (Duby and Mandrou, 1958). Most ancient towns were depopulated and almost empty, with just a handful of vinegrowers,
stockmen, and priests living inside the walls and defences that had

been built at the time of the Germanic and later invasions. Sometimes folk lived around the ruins of religious buildings or public
monuments that had been converted into strongholds or used as
animal shelters. An urban landscape invaded by scrub symbolized
the remains of urban civilization. For many folk urban life was
completely forgotten, since population had returned to the land
and after two or three generations the culture and manners of the
towns had been forgotten completely.

Second Generation : Medieval Urbanization

After the contraction of cities and other manifestations of economic
life in France, the later Middle Ages represented a period of re-
vitalization, characterized by land clearance, agricultural settlement, and a new and important phase of urban development. In
Smith's words (1967) :

'. . . the central feature of the historical geography of Western
Europe in the later Middle Ages is undoubtedly the expansion,
at a quickening pace of population and economic activity from
about 1050 to about 1300' (p. 163).

Urban life was renewed at nodes of transit, particularly in the
trading regions of Provence (and northern Italy) and in Flanders.
By the fact that they had outstripped the rest of Europe in the
history of commerce, the first medieval manifestations of urban life
occurred in these two regions (Pirenne, 1955). As trade flourished
so did many of these towns and cities. Thus Count Philippe of
Alsace, who succeeded to Flanders in 1157, vigorously promoted
the growth of towns such as Douai and Lille, and others including
Bruges, Ghent and Ypres which are beyond the boundaries of
modern France (Troedsson, 1959). Some medieval towns were
created by deliberate foundation, but the majority acquired their
rights gradually as privileges were extended to existing villages
and semi-rural communities (Dickinson, 1951).
    According to Pirenne (1955) :

'. . . In spite of innumerable differences in detail, the towns of
the Middle Ages presented everywhere the same essential
features, and the same definition may be applied to one and all.

We may formulate this definition by saying that the medieval city was a fortified agglomeration engaged in trade and industry, possessing a special law and provided with more or less highly developed jurisdiction and communal autonomy. The city enjoyed immunities which did not exist in the surrounding countryside; which amounts to saying that it had a morally privileged personality. It was constituted, indeed on the basis of privilege . . . Juridically . . . the town was another world. Directly one entered the gates one became subject to a different law, just as one does today on passing from one state to another' (p. 221).

Villeins who succeeded in finding protection for a year and a day inside city walls shed the hated classmarks that otherwise would have adhered to them and to their descendants as long as they had remained on the land of their feudal lord, for example, the inability to inherit, and the extra tax that was imposed on every villein who married outside his lord's domain.

Medieval trading cities flourished on the coast of the Midi and in the Flemish North, with each region linked to a series of inland manufacturing towns. Major cities of the interior flourished on important trade routes, such as Lyons on the Rhône, and small towns also developed along these trading links.[7] Formerly the traveller had passed from monastery to monastery; now he journeyed from town to town as they proliferated at intervals of a few leagues on all main routeways, constituting a transition between the great cities '. . . like the little beads of a rosary between the *dizaines*' (Pirenne, 1955, p. 230).

Most towns in medieval France were small by modern standards, with their population being counted in hundreds and only occasionally reaching 4–5000 in particularly dynamic centres around great abbeys and bishoprics. In some respects urban settlements were visually similar to villages. They sheltered farmers and often contained fields and meadows inside their walls. Urban streets were muddy and cluttered with livestock. Harvest time remained an important event in the yearly round of many medieval townsfolk. However, in formal terms, medieval towns were separated from the countryside by their surrounding walls that were equipped with guarded gates that were closed for security at night. But by virtue of their liberties and privileges medieval towns were quite distinct from rural areas.

Many urban settlements were under divided jurisdiction, with several lords controlling different parts of the town. Thus at Arles there were four 'towns': the *cité* under the archbishop; the *vieux bourg* divided into three fiefs held by the archbishop, the Count of Provence, and the family of Porcellet; the *marché* depending on the archbishop but held by two vassals; and the *bourg neuf* belonging to the Seigneur des Baux (Evans, 1956). Similar examples might be found throughout medieval France.[8]

The growth of trade in Western Europe throughout the twelfth century favoured the growth of a number of large cities, including Avignon, Lyons, and the urban centres of Flanders and Languedoc. But:

> '. . . one single city in the interior of France developed until it was the peer of the greatest, but this was for political reasons; Paris. It was the only city of the kind in Europe, a true capital, growing larger with every forward movement of the monarchy' (Pierenne, 1955, p. 228).

By the middle years of the thirteenth century the city contained at least 80,000 souls and perhaps even twice as many. 'Paris was a monster in France and in the whole of the Christian world' (Duby and Mandrou, 1958, p. 145).

The site of the ancient Gallo-Roman town of Lutetia Parisiorum had been on the hillslopes of Sainte-Geneviève on the left bank of the Seine commanding a bridging point across the river (Fig. 3.3). This left-bank settlement was completely destroyed by fire by Teutonic invaders in A.D. 280 and, as with many other Roman towns, contracted to a small defensive site, in this case on an island in the Seine. A rampart was constructed around this settlement by César-Julien. Portions of the left-bank city were rebuilt, but only to be destroyed again. Under Merovingian rule buildings were constructed on both banks of the Seine and at times Paris functioned as the residence of royalty. But during the Carolingian era Paris lost the little political importance it had enjoyed and was ravaged once again by Viking raiders in the ninth century. For centuries Paris was confined to the Ile-de-la-Cité, inside the walls of the *castrum* and clustered around the cathedral on the eastern part of the island, with the original site of the palace of the Capetian kings in the western half. Small settlements were found on the river banks both north and south of the island in order to protect the bridges, each of which was under the command of a *châtelet*.

In the eleventh century Paris was still a small city among many others in France. Its fortunes date from the twelfth century, and for three main reasons: first, the development of trade along the Seine valley, linked to the growth of the fairs of Champagne; second, the success of teachers and professors in Paris drawing students from the whole of Europe; and finally, the choice of the Capetian kings to make their favoured residence in Paris.[9] By the thirteenth century Paris had become five or six times more populous than any other city of France, combining administrative, economic, and intellectual functions for the whole nation. It was indeed a *ville triple* in a formal as well as a functional sense.

Paris had become the undisputed capital of the Capetian kingdom. During the twelfth century the great abandoned meander of Montmartre was drained and the city that grew to the south of it comprised three clearly-defined parts, separated by the river Seine (Fig. 3.5). The first component was the Ile-de-la-Cité which formed the administrative nucleus of the city, containing the royal palace, court, cathedral, and bishop's palace. The island had accommodated the commercial activities of the city around the *rues* Draperie and Juiverie, and had also sheltered scholastic life in the cloisters of the cathedral. But these two functions were dispersed to different banks of the Seine in the second half of the twelfth century. Jews were expelled from the island by Philippe Auguste in 1180 and they re-established themselves on the right bank where the new trading quarter became the *ville*.

Markets had already been transferred by Louis VI in 1137 to a right-bank site which was close to the port facilities of Paris, for the northern arm of the Seine was the wider of the two that flowed around the islands and afforded better facilities for shipping. Philippe Auguste had the first market halls constructed in which goods might be left in safety at night (Fig. 3.6). The right-bank quarter was traversed by two major routes along the *rues* Saint-Martin and Saint-Denis, and linked to the Ile-de-la-Cité by a great six-arched stone bridge under the protection of the guard of

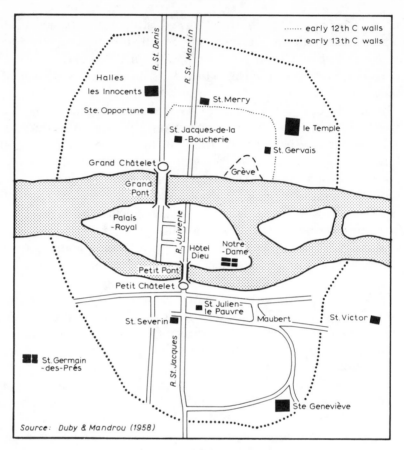

FIG. 3.5. Paris, early thirteenth century.

the *Grand Châtelet*. This bridge formed the most secure part of the city and it was there that money changers established their booths. But the greatest activity was at the Grève a little upstream from the bridge where grain, wine, wood and other commodities were unloaded from the upper Seine and the fairs of Champagne. By contrast, fish and salt were brought upstream from Rouen and landed at the Châtelet.

Between the abbeys of Saint-Germain-des-Prés and Saint-Victor on the left bank stood the educational quarter on the slopes leading up to the hill of Sainte-Geneviève (Fleury, 1961). Teachers and students received a statute from the Pope in 1215, thus instituting the University of Paris. The university:

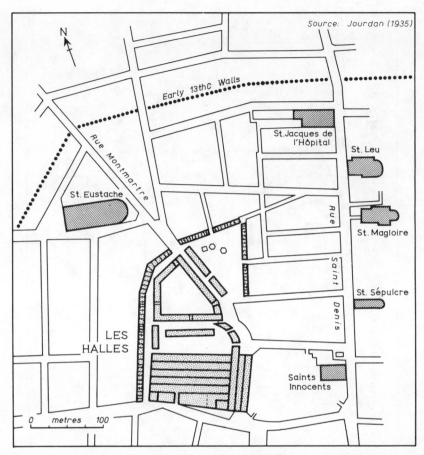

FIG. 3.6. The Medieval Halles.

'. . . meant a community of colleges, schools, monasteries and churches, and the living quarters of numerous students and those who catered for their spiritual and worldly needs' (Dickinson, 1951, p. 227).

Between 1190 and 1210 the northern bank of the city had been enclosed by a wall and in the following decade the right bank was also defended. The complete encircling wall was equipped with 67 towers and 13 gates. Philippe Auguste added to these defences in 1204 by building the stone stronghold of the Louvre just beyond the western limits of the new city wall (Fig. 3.7). Thereafter, the city was to grow unequally, developing more rapidly on the right

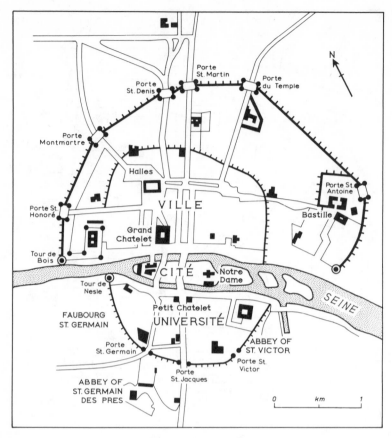

FIG. 3.7. Paris, fourteenth century.

bank than on the left. By the middle years of the fourteenth
century, Paris had grown considerably and yet a further city wall
was built.

With fewer than 15 million inhabitants in the early fourteenth
century, France was a relatively over-populated country, soon to
suffer the onslaught of warfare, and plague as well as periodic
famine. Cities as well as rural settlements were to decline during
the course of the century. Thus for example, the population of
Toulouse contracted from 40,000 *c.* 1300 to only half that number
100 years later. However, Avignon and Paris continued to grow
during the fourteenth century. As well as being the Papal city,
Avignon participated in the flourishing commerce of Italy with
supplies coming from the port of Marseilles and by overland trade

routes along the valley of the Durance. But above all, it was Paris
that continued to expand, reaching 200,000 inhabitants and perhaps even more *c*. 1400. As well as housing the royal court, Paris
had by that time replaced the Champagne fairs as the major centre
for trade and finance between the Alps and the Netherlands.

Planned Medieval New Towns

In addition to a prodigious expansion of ancient towns and cities,
new urban settlements were established in France from the eleventh
century to the mid-fourteenth century.

> 'So many were the new towns that came into being out of no-
> where, so dynamic was urban construction . . . that the eleventh
> century came to mark a dividing line in the way one spoke
> about cities in France—there were the "old" towns, generally
> with roots in antiquity . . . and the "new" towns, the *villeneuves*
> of the eleventh and twelfth centuries' (Troedsson, 1959, p. 23).

Three categories of medieval new towns together formed the
second generation of French urban centres. The first involved
settlements which grew almost spontaneously at crossroads,
bridging points, along highways, near mills, or in other favoured
points. The second type grew in the shadow of monasteries or outside the walls of castles. Such castle-towns fulfilled the dual function
of being strongholds for territorial lords and refuges for surrounding countryfolk at times of unrest. Once their urban charters had
been granted, outlining the rights and privileges of their citizens,
examples of these two types of new town evolved in a gradual,
highly individualistic, and unplanned fashion.[10] Such was not the
case for the third type of medieval new town. These settlements
were created deliberately by powerful landowners at specific
points in time. They were towns which possessed birth certificates
(Pinchemel, 1969). Charters were drawn up, ground plans prepared, and settlers attracted to the new towns by the privileges and
liberties that were offered.

Creation of planned medieval new towns affected many parts of
France.[11] *Villeneuves* in Flanders, Normandy, the Ile-de-France,
and Burgundy complemented *bourgs* in the West and *bastides* in the
South-West (Gutkind, 1970). Indeed Gascony experienced the

greatest proliferation of medieval planned towns of any part of France, with the foundation of *bastides* perhaps representing the major event in the history of the South-West (De Saint-Blanquat, 1949). The remainder of this chapter will examine new towns in that region, however, town foundations in Brie (1150–1225) and in many other regions of France should not be forgotten (Brunet, 1960). Neither should the new agricultural villages (*sauvetés*) of the eleventh and twelfth centuries which were created in Aquitaine a little earlier than the *bastides*.[12] Many of these *sauvetés* were established by lay lords and ecclesiastical owners who co-operated to create colonization centres from which unoccupied land might be cleared, or re-cleared, and cultivated. Lords of the manor in the South-West saw the *sauvetés* as a useful means of augmenting their revenues from agriculture, providing both security and provisions for pilgrims who travelled along routes to the shrine of Saint James of Compostella, and stabilizing the turbulent population of their region. Most *sauvetés* were created deliberately as small agglomerations of agricultural workers, but others were spontaneous nucleations of peasants seeking refuge close to castles and strong-points that proliferated in Gascony during the eleventh and twelfth centuries.

At a basic level, *bastides* were instruments in the complicated processes of colonization and occupation of territory on behalf of various power groups. The Middle Garonne, for example, was a disputed area that had been fought over and the resultant pattern of new towns reflected the struggle for power. Thus French territory lay to the north and east, English possessions were in the west, and the land of the Counts of Toulouse in the south and east (Deffontaines, 1932). In the so-called Albigensian crusade the Pope and the King of France had allied to destroy the heretics and the Counts of Toulouse who had supported them. After an abject peace had been achieved, the Counts of Toulouse sought to re-colonize their land and restore its fortunes by establishing *bastides*. However in 1248 the brother of the King of France became Count of Toulouse and thereafter *bastide* creation aimed at meeting two objectives (Fig. 3.8). The first was the need to occupy effectively on behalf of the kings of France land that was held by former allies of the Counts of Toulouse who had not been brought into total submission. Thus in the middle years of the thirteenth century

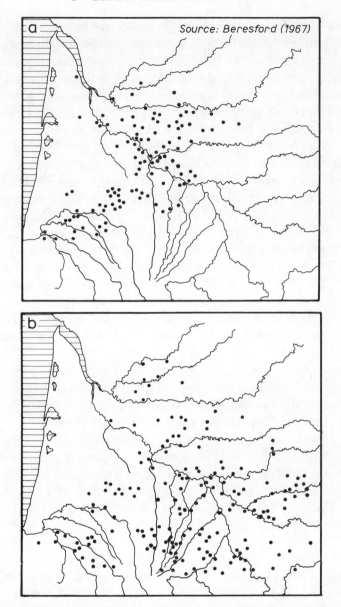

F IG. 3.8. Medieval New Towns in Gascony. (a) English and Anglo-French *bastides*: (b) French *bastides*.

Alphonse de Poitiers established new settlements in the territories of Armagnac, Astarac, Comminges and Foix. Thereafter relatively few *bastides* were built on the territories of the Count of Toulouse since these lands had been brought under royal administration by 1250. The foundation of new towns permitted the distant French monarchy to take a firm hold of the land it had recently acquired, and allowed the region's profits to be directed to the Crown.

The second objective was for the rival kings of France and England to consolidate their occupation of Aquitaine. Thus in the last four decades of the thirteenth century the English established over 70 *bastides* in that part of the South-West that owed allegiance to Henry III and to his son Edward II. In some cases new towns were built in pairs, with an English creation facing a French one a short distance away. For example, Valence-d'Agen was constructed in 1283 in response to Donzac (1265) and Dunes (1269) that had been built by Alphonse de Poitiers. Similarly, Fourcis faced the French settlement of Montréal-en-Condomois. Frequently new towns were created through partnerships (*paréages*) between the Church, providing the land, and the kings of England or France, who provided power. Sometimes agreements were made between local lords of the manor and a variety of other partners, but seigneurial *bastides* were much less important than royal ones.

Whether *bastides* in south-western France were planned to establish networks of fortified settlements or not formed an important point of academic debate.[13] Higounet (1948, 1948–9) argued that a grand design existed to provide the *bastides* with defences, and De Saint-Blanquat (1949) likened the *bastides* to frontier fortifications built by Vauban in the seventeenth century. Earlier commentators also stressed defence factors. Tout (1917) had written '. . . in the humble beginnings of the new towns of the middle ages military considerations were always paramount' (p. 9). In a similar way, Dickinson (1951) detected Provençal origins for the word *bastide* meaning 'fortress'.

Trabut-Cussac (1954) challenged this kind of military interpretation. Only one third of the Gascon *bastides* were provided with defences. Many new towns created by the English in that region were completely undefended until warfare in the fourteenth century forced Edward II and Edward III into installing defences that had not been envisaged by Edward I. Similarly, charters of French *bastides* established by Alphonse de Poitiers prior to 1265 contained no mention of ramparts. Incidentally, other authorities attribute the origin of the word *bastide* to a southern form of the verb 'to build' (*bâtir* in modern French). The sites of some new towns were certainly far from defensive in character. *Bastides* established on river banks, at level sites along highways, or at vulnerable points overlooked by adjacent hills must have been set up for other purposes than those of defence.

Some *bastides* in the Middle Garonne did perform defensive functions, but Deffontaines (1932) insisted that '. . . whilst bastides were grouped settlements they performed agricultural functions' (p. 153). Many charters stressed the need for new-town settlers to undertake land clearance, cultivation and trade. Thus in the Middle Garonne, Monpazier and Villefranche-du-Périgord were established near the Bois de Belves; Villeréal in the forest of Montlabour; and Verfeil in the woodlands of Bouissas. The *bastides* were not unproductive garrisons, rather they sheltered communities of peasant landowners and traders (Brunet, 1965). Many new towns appear to have been created primarily for economic reasons rather than to meet military or political ends.

Certainly most *bastides* in the Adour valley were colonization centres (Lerat, 1963). New settlements established by lay lords in southern Béarn played a vital role in organizing the clearance and cultivation of this region which supported a very sparse population and still contained many areas of moor, rough pasture, and woodland during the medieval period. Other *bastides* in south-western France were created on land belonging to monastic orders which the monks had been unable to clear and cultivate. The Cistercian order was particularly important in encouraging the creation of *bastides* for agricultural purposes (Beresford, 1967, Higounet, 1950). Some 44 French new towns were established by *paréages* on land belonging to Cistercian abbeys in the Garonne valley, often at the sites of granges. In English Gascony a further 24 monastic *bastides* were developed, nearly all of which were Cistercian in origin. Many new towns were similar in function to the agricultural *sauvetés* established in the tenth and eleventh centuries. In Beresford's words (1967):

'. . . The affinity between colonizing villages and new towns is indicated elsewhere in France by the indifferent use of the place names *sauveterre* and *villeneuve* for new colonizing settlements, whether urban or village; and sometimes the very name of a colonists' village in the tenth or eleventh century reads like the name of a thirteenth-century *bastide*' (p. 77).

But there were, of course, juridical differences between new towns with their charters and feudal villages.

In addition to encouraging occupation, clearance, and cultivation of land some *bastides* in the South-West had more specific agricultural and commercial functions. In 1224 the English had been expelled from the vine-producing Angevin lands of northern France and at the same time the Albigensian crusade was drawing to a close in the South. English demands for wine from alternative sources were growing and Gascony contained stretches of poor, sparsely-settled land that could be converted to viticulture to supply the English market. The vine had the great advantage of flourishing in many soils that were not suited to cereal cultivation. Unlike the *sauvetés*, *bastide* settlements were endowed with rights for holding fairs and markets and thus played an important role in the dispatch of wine to England as well as in local commerce. One might argue that *bastides* were distributed too widely in the South-West to conform to any political or strategic frontiers, but many were sited on or close to trade routes leading to the wine ports of Bayonne and Bordeaux.

Of 226 new-town plantations in medieval France excluding English Gascony, that have been examined by Beresford (1967), 63 were established between 1040 and 1260 (Fig. 3.9) but in many of these intervening decades the number of creations was small. Henry I planted Nonecourt and Pont-Orson in Normandy as early as 1100–1135. William, Duke of Aquitaine, established La Rochelle (1130–50), with Richard I creating Saint-Rémy (1184) and Petit-Andelys (1197) before the end of the twelfth century. Town creation greatly increased in volume in the 1260s when 43 settlements were started, representing 19 per cent of the total. Fifty-five more were created in the next two decades, but thereafter the number of new-town foundations fell dramatically, with only two additional plantations being made after 1350.

The chronology of 124 plantations in Gascony was roughly similar (Fig. 3.10), with the graph rising vigorously after 1250 to reach a peak in the 1280s, when 26 settlements were established.

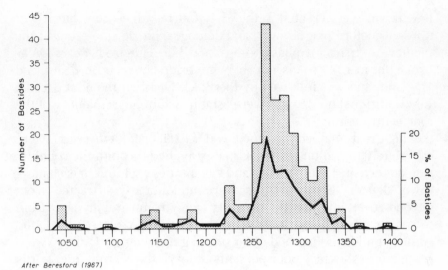

After Beresford (1967)

FIG. 3.9. Medieval Town Foundations in France, excluding English Gascony.

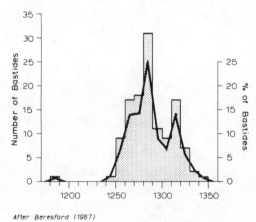

After Beresford (1967)

FIG. 3.10. Foundation of *Bastides* in Gascony.

Marmande, the first English new town in Gascony had been planted as early as 1182. The creation of Gascon *bastides* was initially most important in the County of Toulouse in the mid-thirteenth century but then spread to other parts of the South-West. The 1290s registered a check in this process, since England and France were at war between 1294 and 1297, with fighting spreading to Gascony in 1295–96. No new English *bastide* of any importance was established until full peace was achieved in 1303. A few more new towns were created in the early fourteenth century but it was not long before plague, war, and demographic decline brought the medieval expansion phase to an end. The Hundred Years' War broke out in 1337 to disrupt the wine trade between Bordeaux and England, and was followed by the Black Death in the next decade. Few additional new towns were established in the remainder of the fourteenth century.

The great majority of medieval *bastides* and *villeneuves* were completely new foundations. Criers travelled through the countryside advertising the liberties and advantages spelt out in each new-town charter. Some settlers were undoubtedly attracted from beyond Aquitaine, but the majority came from rural areas or from towns that had been pillaged in the region. A plot of land, the right to build a house, and other privileges of being a 'citizen' were adequate to convince poor peasants to leave the countryside. Lords of the manor complained repeatedly that their vassals were migrating to nearby *bastides*. The only way to prevent their departure from seigneurial land was for these lords to create their own *bastides* offering equal or more attractive privileges than those already available.

New-town charters typically included the following range of contents (Beresford, 1967). Settlers were declared free from arbitrary taxation and other feudal obligations. Property of burgesses was protected against seizure, save by due course of law. Townsfolk were free to dispose of property as they wished. Details of the jurisdiction of each of the partners who shared in town foundation were enumerated. Penalties for crimes, together with rules for operating fairs, markets, mills, and ovens were spelled out. Military services and the organization of municipal government were defined. Thus the new inhabitants of *bastides* enjoyed the privilege of having left behind their villein status and having received their liberty. The old German saying that 'town air sets a man free' was fully applicable to the citizens of *bastides*.

In addition to completely new *bastides*, some existing settlements were 'bastidized' by the granting of urban charters. For example, the settlements of Saint-Livrande, Saint-Sardos, and Sérignac in the Middle Garonne valley were converted into *bastides* and extra streets and houses were constructed (Deffontaines, 1932). Septfonds developed around an abbey built in 1130 and was 'bastidized' in 1273. The small villages of Le Fossat and Lunas were united in 1301 to form the new town of Aiguillon. Similarly the *bastide* of Valence-d'Agen (1283) occupied the site of an earlier village. Some *bastides* were simply suburbs (*faubourgs*) tacked on to existing towns and known by the term *barry* (Barry d'Islemade). Many other variants on the *bastide* theme were encountered beyond the Middle Garonne. Carcassonne developed as a twin city, with the *ville basse* (the *bastide*) being joined to the old *cité*. Villefranche-de-Rouergue was founded for the novel purpose of decongesting the neighbouring town of La Peyrade. In 1264 Villeneuve-sur-Lot was rebuilt as a *bastide* on the site of the early medieval town of Gajac that had been destroyed during the Albigensian crusade (Gutkind, 1970).

Bastides were remarkable for their place names which were sometimes devised to attract settlers to the new towns. At least six categories of new town name may be recognized (Tout, 1917). At the simplest level the novelty of the experiment was recorded, with a crop of new towns named *Villeneuve* springing up in many parts of France. *Bastides* offered liberties to their inhabitants, as Villefranche recalled. The security of new towns was advertised (La Garde, Montségur, Le Salvetat, La Sauve, Sauveterre), and if distinctive sites were occupied this fact might also be recorded in the toponymy (Aigues-Mortes, Beaumont, Mirabel, Miramont, Mirande, Montjoie). Famous names of well-established European cities were sometimes borrowed as an added inducement to settlers (Barcelone, Cordes, Fleurance, Grenade, Londres, Plaisance, Pampelonne, Valence). Finally, some new-town names identified their founders. Thus Libourne was named after Roger of Leybourne; Feltone after Felton the English seneschal; Nicole after Henry of Lacy, Earl of Lincoln; and Beaumarchès after Beaumarchais, seneschal of Philip III. The name Castelnau-Montratier demonstrated a more complex variation on the final theme. This *bastide* was built in 1250 by the lord of the manor Ratier on the site of Castelnau-des-Vaux which had been destroyed by Simon de Montfort (Deffontaines, 1932).

The morphology of many *bastides* and *villeneuves* was as distinctive as their names. A large number were laid out on more or less geometrical ground plans, be they rectangular, as was most commonly the case, lozenge-shaped (Sauveterre-de-Guyenne), roughly circular (Sainte-Livrande, Villeréal), or even square (Damazan, Valence-d'Agen). However such ideal shapes might be modified by topographical conditions since some *bastides* were situated on plateau spurs, on isolated hills, or on sloping terrain. Beaumont-du-Périgord, founded in the name of Edward I on a long and narrow plateau, formed a fine example of a hill-top *bastide* (Fig. 3.11). A regular ground plan was adapted to the elevated site, with four principal streets running the whole length of the town, being crossed by short side streets. The town plan of Cordes, with its hill-top market place, was even more distorted. Some *bastides* followed the direction of a valley or an existing

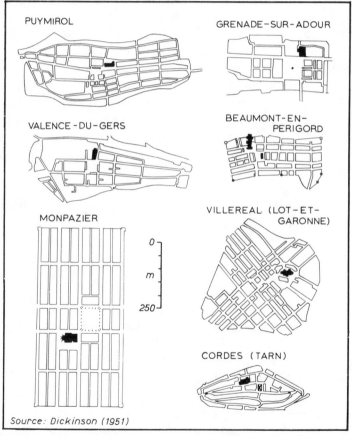

FIG. 3.11. Morphology of Seven *Bastides*.

routeway, as in the Adour valley (Fig. 3.12) where street-*bastides* were surrounded by defensive hollow ways (Lerat, 1963). Regular settlement plans were rare among the *villeneuves* of Brie (Brunet, 1960).

But other new towns did follow strictly regular grid-iron plans, with streets crossing one another at right angles. Monpazier has been said to be the ideal *bastide*, fulfilling all expectations of regularity, repetition, and uniformity (Fig. 3.11). The town was laid out in 1284, enclosing a long rectangle 400 m $\times$ 220 m, with a regular chequer-board street system, a large square with surrounding *couverts* (or *cornières*) that were wide enough for

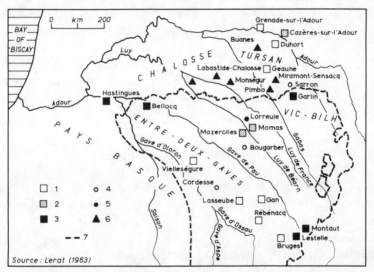

F IG. 3.12. *Bastides* founded in the Pays de l'Adour during the thirteenth and fourteenth centuries. (1) grid plan settlement not on a defensive site; (2) grid plan settlement founded on land belonging to the Church; (3) grid plan settlement on a defensive site; (4) street settlement not on a defensive site; (5) street settlement founded on land belonging to the Church; (6) street settlement on a defensive site; (7) frontier of Béarn.

vehicular traffic to circulate beneath them, and uniformly laid-out rows of houses (Gutkind, 1970). Almost all *bastides* had central public squares that might serve as places of refuge. Castles were absent from *bastides*, since their presence would have conflicted with one of the main characteristics of the new towns, namely the freedom of the inhabitants from feudal power.

The formal chequer plan was more prevalent in Gascony than among plantations in England and Wales where the grid plan had been in use long before the first English *bastide* was established in Gascony in 1182 (Beresford, 1967). Widespread acceptance of the grid plan in south-western France may be attributed to the fact that town foundation was undertaken by relatively few people, across a span of not much more than a century. Thus 71 per cent of Gascon *bastides* were founded by English kings, either alone or in *paréage* with other landowners. A further 15 per cent were established by the Counts of Toulouse, either alone or in *paréage*. The grid plan had been tested and found to be successful elsewhere. It was easily emulated.

Medieval new towns in France were astonishing in their number, but few prospered.

'. . . Every founder of a town had to be a prophet, hoping to discern existing and future opportunities of success; yet prophecies could fail . . . and the very names of towns pass into oblivion' (Beresford, 1967, p. 290).

Some of the towns that failed were simply 'abortive'.[12] All the preparations for creation went ahead but no settlers arrived. The second type of failure related to settlements which were inhabited for a while but then decayed and were reduced to miserable collections of buildings or were abandoned completely. Of 125 *bastides* in Gascony, 44 (35 per cent) were failures, including at least 11 'abortive' attempts and 25 settlements which decayed. The peak period for *bastide* failures in this part of France corresponded fairly closely with that for town creation, with approximately half of all new settlements established in the 1270s, 1280s, and 1300s proving unsuccessful (Fig. 3.13).

The new town of Aigues-Mortes set out by Louis IX in 1246 far on the west bank of the delta land of the Rhône provides a fine example of a stagnant *bastide*. The walled town was built on a grid plan and a harbour constructed for the embarkation of the Crusades in 1248 and 1270. This site represented the eastern-most point of French territory on the Mediterranean coast since the left bank of the Rhône was not yet in French control. But Aigues-Mortes was condemned to decline as the vital channels of the port silted up,

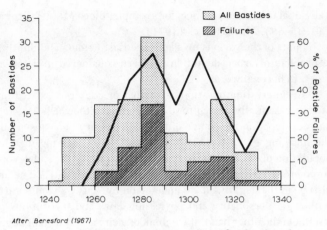

After Beresford (1967)

FIG. 3.13. Failure of Gascon *Bastides*, by decade.

stranding the town well away from the navigable waters of the the Gulf of Lions. Much of its medieval appearance remains.

Few *bastide* towns were to grow to any great size in future centuries. Carcassonne, Libourne and Montauban experienced perhaps the most important expansion (Pinchemel, 1969). The majority of surviving *bastides* function simply as agricultural centres or as small market towns. Most *canton* service centres in the South-West are of *bastide* origin (De Saint Blanquat, 1949). The proliferation of such settlements in the Toulouse region not only over-provided the area with small service centres but created a class of small peasant landowners, since *bastide* dwellers were also smallholders. The *bastides* were to attract impoverished migrants from upland areas to the plains and valleys of Gascony in later centuries, but by the middle years of the fourteenth century the second phase of urban creation had drawn to a close in the South-West, as elsewhere in France.

3. Notes

1. Later phases of urban development in France are discussed in Chapter 13.
2. Examples of cities with names derived from *civitates* include: Amiens (Ambiani), Arras (Atrebates), Bourges (Biturges), Chartres (Carnutes), Langres (Lignons), Metz (Mediomatrici), Paris (Parisii), Rheims (Remes), and Soissons (Suessiones) (Gutkind, 1970).
3. Many studies of Roman Gaul contain descriptive sections on the morphology

of individual urban centres. See, for example, Bloch (1900), Brogan (1953), Lot (1945–53), MacKendrick (1971).

4. For accounts of the various invasions see East (1956) and Smith (1967).

5. The problem of urban definition has been considered in detail by Pirenne (1925). In his own words

'... An interesting question is whether or not cities existed in the midst of that essentially agricultural civilization into which Western Europe had developed in the course of the ninth century. The answer depends on the meaning given to the word "city". If by it is meant a locality the population of which, instead of living by working the soil devotes itself to commercial activity, the answer will have to be "No". The answer will also be in the negative if we understand by "city" a community endowed with legal personality and possessing laws and institutions peculiar to itself. On the other hand, if we think of a city as a centre of administration and as a fortress, it is clear that the Carolingian period knew nearly as many cities as the centuries which followed it must have known. That is merely another way of saying that the cities which were then to be found were without two of the fundamental attributes of the cities of the Middle Ages and of modern times—a middle-class population and a communal organization' (p. 56).

6. See Havinghurst (1969) for a critical discussion of the ideas and writings of Pirenne.

7. A controversial study of the medieval city regions of Dijon, Montpellier, Paris and Toulouse, amongst others, is presented by Russell (1972).

8. Examples of internal morphology of medieval towns and cities are presented by Dickinson (1951), Fleure (1920), and Gutkind (1970).

9. The fairs of Champagne, Châlons, Flanders and Lyons are discussed by Verlinden (1963).

10. A valuable series of case studies of medieval urban growth in France is presented by Dickinson (1951) summarizing much material from the journal *Urbanisme* during the 1930s and from other sources. Similarly a 140-page survey of the morphological history of many French cities is presented by Gutkind (1970), together with an extended bibliography (pp. 471–79).

11. The foundation of medieval new towns in England, Wales and France is analysed in detail by Beresford (1967).

12. The establishment of *sauvetés* in Aquitaine is discussed in detail by Bousquet (1963), Higounet (1963), and Ourliac (1949).

13. Brunet (1965, pp. 694–5) provides a valuable bibliography on *bastides* relating to the Toulouse region which lists many of the dispersed articles by Professor C. Higounet.

3. References

Beresford, M. W., *New Towns of the Middle Ages: town plantation in England, Wales and Gascony*, London (1967).

Bloch, G., *Histoire de France: les origines, la Gaule indépendente, la conquête romaine*, Paris (1900).

Bousquet, J., 'La fondation de Villeneuve d'Aveyron et l'expansion de l'abbaye de Moissac en Rouergue', *Annales du Midi*, 75 (1963), 517–537.

Boussard, J., *Atlas historique et culturel de la France*, Paris (1957).

Brogan, O., *Roman Gaul*, London (1953).

Brunet, P., *Structure agraire et économie rurale des plateaux tertiares entre la Seine et l'Oise*, Caen (1960).

Brunet, R., *Les Campagnes toulousaines: étude géographique*, Toulouse (1965).

Chevallier, R., 'Un document fondamental pour l'histoire et la géographie agraires: la photographie aérienne', *Etudes Rurales*, 1 (1960), 70–80.

Chevallier, R., 'La centuriation et les problèmes de la colonisation romaine', *Etudes Rurales*, 3 (1962), 54–80.

Deffontaines, P., *Les Hommes et leurs travaux dans les pays de la moyenne Garonne*, Lille (1932).

Desjardins, E., *Géographie de la Gaule d'après la Table de Peutinger*, Paris (1869).

Desjardins, E., *Géographie historique et administrative de la Gaule romaine*, Paris, 4 vols (1876–93).

Dickinson, R. E., *The West European City*, London (1951).

Dion, R., 'Le site de Paris', in Michaud, G., ed. *Paris: croissance d'une capitale*, Paris, (1961), 17–39.

Dopsch, A., *The Economic and Social Foundations of European Civilization*, New York (1969).

Duby, G. and Mandrou, H., *Histoire de la Civilisation Française*, Paris (1958).

Duval, P. M., *La Vie quotidienne en Gaule pendant la Paix Romaine*, Paris (1952).

Duval, P. M., 'Lutèce gauloise et gallo-romaine', in Michaud, G., ed. *Paris: croissance d'une capitale*, Paris (1961), 41–72.

East, W. G., *An Historical Geography of Europe*, London (1956).

Evans, J., *Life in Medieval France*, London (1956).

Fleure, H. J., 'Some types of cities in temperate Europe', *Geographical Review*, 10 (1920), 357–74.

Fleury, M., 'Paris du bas-empire au début du XIII siècle', in Michaud, G., ed. *Paris: croissance d'une capitale*, Paris (1961), 73–96.

Gutkind, E. A., *International History of City Development: Volume V, Urban Development in Western Europe: France and Belgium*, New York (1970).

Havinghurst, A. F. ed., *The Pirenne Thesis: analysis, criticism, revision*, London (1969).

Higounet, C., 'Bastides et frontières', *Le Moyen Age*, 54 (1948), 113–121.

Higounet, C., 'La frange orientale des bastides', *Annales du Midi*, 61 (1948–9), 359–367.

Higounet, C., 'Cisterciens et bastides', *Le Moyen Age*, 56 (1950), 69–84.

Higounet, C., 'Les sauvetés de Moissac', *Annales du Midi*, 75 (1963), 505–513.

Jourdan, M., 'La ville étudiée dans ses quartiers: autour des Halles de Paris au moyen âge', *Annales d'Histoire Economique et Sociale*, 7 (1935), 285–301.

Jullian, C., *La Gaule romaine*, Paris, 8 vols (1908–26).

Lerat, S., *Les Pays de l'Adour: structures agraires et économie agricole*, Bordeaux (1963).

Lot, F., *Recherches sur la population et la superficie des cités remontant à la période gallo-romaine*, Paris, 3 vols (1945–53).

MacKendrick, P., *Roman France*, London (1971).

Mirot, L., *Manuel de géographie historique de la France*, Paris, 2 vols (1947–50).

Ourliac, P., 'Les villages de la région toulousaine au XIIᵉ siècle', *Annales, Economies, Sociétés, Civilisations*, 4 (1949), 268–277.

Pinchemel, P., *France: a geographical survey*, London (1969).

Pirenne, H., *Medieval Cities*, Princeton (1925).

Pirenne, H., *La Civilisation occidentale au moyen âge du XIᵉ au XVᵉ siècle*, Paris (1941).

Pirenne, H., *A History of Europe: from the invasions to the sixteenth century*, New York (1955).

Russell, J. C., *Medieval Regions and their Cities*, Newton Abbot (1972).

Saint-Blanquat, De O., 'Comment se sont créés les bastides?' *Annales, Economies, Sociétés, Civilisations*, 4 (1949), 278–289.

Schmittlein, R., *Avec César en Gaule*, Paris (1970).

Smith, C. T., *An Historical Geography of Western Europe before 1800*, London (1967).

Tout, T. F., 'Medieval town planning', *Bulletin of the John Rylands Library*, 4 (1917), 1–34.

Trabut-Cussac, J.-P., 'Bastides ou forteresses', *Le Moyen Age*, 60 (1954), 81–135.

Troedsson, C. B., 'The growth of the western city during the Middle Ages', *Transactions of the Chalmers University of Technology: Gothenburg*, 217 (1959), 1–60.

Verlinden, O., 'Markets and fairs', *Cambridge Economic History of Europe*, 3 (1963), 119–153.

4

Retreat of Rural Settlement

HUGH D. CLOUT

Introduction

As has been shown in Chapter 2, the clearance and occupation of land in France was not a simple, uninterrupted process through time. Periods of advance in various parts of the country were followed by important phases of retreat when population numbers declined, settlements contracted in size or were totally deserted, and stretches of agricultural land became idle or reverted to waste, with perhaps just tiny nuclei of cultivation remaining close to the few houses that might remain inhabited. This kind of complicated pulsation process has operated, albeit at varying scales, from the early Middle Ages through to the modern day.

Previous chapters have outlined progress in land clearance and settlement establishment in the medieval period, hence this discussion will emphasize aspects of recession. Particular stress will be placed on changes occurring during the Middle Ages since this forms the only documented period in European history during which a large decline in population followed a prolonged expansion phase. This is not to deny, of course, that contraction has continued in parts of the French countryside right through to the present day, with perhaps a larger number of rural dwellings and small settlements being abandoned since 1900 than during any other equal span of French history (Duby, 1965).

Varying degrees of settlement contraction will be investigated, together with changes in population numbers and in the areal extent of agricultural land. The discussion will include a consideration of 'deserted villages' but will not be restricted to this extreme expression of settlement contraction. Temporary abandonment of villages and hamlets and the permanent desertion of small hamlets form far more frequent features in French rural history than the totally 'deserted villages' that have been studied in England and in other European countries. Such aspects of contraction fit into a prolonged modification of the rural habitat in France which continues to the present. Small settlements containing fifty households or less have always been particularly susceptible to decline (Pesez and Le Roy Ladurie, 1965). In Alsace this kind of adjustment process has operated from the twelfth century to the modern day, with the trend being accentuated in periods of demographic decline or during other crises resulting from famine, war or a host of other causes (Juillard, 1953). It does not seem unrealistic to accept this regional argument, involving the contraction and disappearance of small clusters of settlement to the benefit of larger villages and towns, and to apply it to other parts of France.

In the present chapter the 'contraction' or 'retreat' of settlement will be considered in a broad sense to encompass changes involving hamlets and small rural settlements as well as large nucleations ('villages'). Temporary abandonment will be included as well as permanent desertion, together with a consideration of historic variations in the density of rural peopling, and in the organization and intensity of agricultural land use.

Two separate but complementary methods of investigation may be employed to help elucidate fluctuations in rural settlement through time. The first approach involves ground investigation. Traces of abandoned settlements may be identified from aerial photographs (Chevallier, 1965). Archaeological excavation at selected sites may then be employed to reveal details of the sequence of occupance up to the desertion phase (Courbin, 1965; Demains d'Archimbaud, 1965; Hensel 1965a and b). The second group of methods involves analyzing contemporary or near-contemporary documents in order to identify depopulation and settlement contraction and also to investigate the causes of retreat. Records which specifically mention the abandonment of settlement in France are rare (Pesez, 1965). Enquiries were never undertaken of a magnitude comparable to those in Sardinia or in

sixteenth-century England. Such an absence of direct documentation in France may be interpreted in two ways. It may be taken to
suggest that settlement contraction did not occur, or else that it
was so frequent and of such relative insignificance that it merited
neither investigation nor recording in official documents. Indirect
information from many parts of France indicates that the first
interpretation should be discarded in favour of the second.

However, written sources which contain indirect information
suggesting settlement contraction require very cautious analysis
and interpretation. Listings of ecclesiastical parishes at various
periods provide a useful starting point for study but also raise
enormous problems. In a nation-wide investigation 32,500 parishes
were identified as being in existence in 1328 (Lot, 1929). The
total had decreased by only 900 (−2.8 per cent) five centuries
later. But fifteen dioceses in the Paris Basin, for example, are
known to have experienced increases in parish numbers between
the fourteenth century and the mid-eighteenth century (Pesez and
Le Roy Ladurie, 1965). Such net increases followed the disappearance of some old-established parishes and the creation of
more than an equal number of new ones. By contrast, other regions
experienced net decreases in parish numbers, with apparent losses
from nine sample areas ranging from 3 to 22 per cent over the same
four centuries (Table 4.1).

This ostensibly clear evidence cannot be accepted at its face
value. The apparent 'disappearance' of a parish, as suggested by its
omission from a list of place names, may signify various forms of

Table 4.1

Net Loss of 'Parishes' for Selected Areas, c. 1370–c. 1750

Area	Percentage Loss	Area	Percentage Loss
Avranches diocese	22	Nîmes-Carcassonne region	10
Bayeux diocese	10	Paris Diocese	8
Bourges diocese	10	North-west of Paris	3
Eastern Languedoc	6	Rouen diocese	10
Nevers diocese	10		

Source: Pesez, J. M. & E. Le Roy Ladurie. (1965): 'Les villages désertés en
France: vue d'ensemble', op. cit., 258–260.

modification in the settlement pattern, the system of local administration, or both (Moufrin, 1965). First, the parish (or village) may have been deserted, but alternatively it may simply have shrunk in size and importance to become a hamlet or even an isolated farm and as a result have lost its parish status. Second, there may have been a change in the organization of settlements, with one village becoming the dependant of another. Hence only one name might be recorded for what would still be recognizable on the ground as two distinct settlement units. Depopulation and settlement shrinkage of at least one of those units need not have accompanied such an administrative modification. The 22 per cent decline in parish names in Avranches diocese, for example, is highly deceptive (Table 4.1). The majority of these apparently 'deserted villages' survived even though they had been demoted in ecclesiastical status between the mid-fourteenth century and the mid-eighteenth century. Third, evidence relating to 'parishes' in western France and some other parts of the country may always have involved more than one nucleation per parish unit. Broad patterns of change may be recognizable under such circumstances but detailed modifications for individual villages escape detection. Fourth, there may simply have been clerical errors leading to the omission of place names from ecclesiastical lists, taxation records, or other written source material.

Despite many ambiguities and imperfections in documentary evidence, it is clear that four broad groups of causes led to settlement contraction in France. Each of these will be considered in general terms before discussing detailed examples of contraction.

Causes of Settlement Contraction

Catastrophic causes of settlement desertion survive in the folk memory but also represent frequent components in local mythology. Natural disasters, in the form of flooding, invasion by shifting sand dunes along the coast, marine erosion in western France, and many other processes, played their role in the physical destruction of rural settlements. But such occurrences were rare. More frequently famine and disease decimated population numbers and further disruption resulted from man-made catastrophes such as fires, brigandage, and the devastations of war. In many cases, however, these disasters simply produced interruptions in the sequence of land occupation and were soon followed by phases of repeopling and resettlement.

A second group of causes relates to the mobility of the rural population, especially during the medieval period when new towns and villages were planned and laid out. Attractive inducements were offered for peasant farmers to move from other agricultural areas in order to settle them. Under such circumstances the desertion or contraction of old-established settlements might result. The general tendency for hamlets and other small settlements to shrink to the advantage of larger villages and towns also resulted from the mobility of the peasant population.

Technological and organizational changes in farming caused rural settlers to revaluate the physical resources of the land that their predecessors had cleared and occupied. Such revaluations form the third group of causes of settlement contraction. Early agricultural occupation in many parts of France took place on light soils that could be cultivated by farmers using simple ploughs (Roncayolo, 1965). Rendzinas and other permeable soils on the borders of the Paris Basin were thus particularly appreciated. Other areas of light soils included in the Champagne crayeuse, the plateaux of Burgundy and Lorraine, Mâconnais, the southern Jura and Bas-Quercy. However, the agricultural potential of heavier soils was realized between the ninth and the twelfth centuries following the introduction of powerful, wheeled, mould-board ploughs. New techniques for harnessing draught animals into six- or eight-ox gangs enabled heavy ploughs to turn the soils of loess-covered plateaux and clay vales. As a result, such areas were preferred to some of the lighter soils that had been occupied at earlier stages. But agricultural adjustment to soil resources worked in different ways according to local environmental conditions. Thus the density of settlement in areas of excessively damp soil in Hurepoix was reduced and the occupation of less humid areas nearby was intensified (Tulippe, 1934). Further spatial adjustments of settlement involved movements downslope from upland terrain to more inviting lowlands, or from remote areas to others close to major routeways. 'Negative' areas of poor sandy soils, such as the *brandes* and *brennes* of western France experienced a complicated pulsation of settlement and land clearance, with periods of advance alternating with phases of retreat in response to changes in population pressure (Debien, 1952). Duby (1965) has suggested that the majority of desertions for which place-name evidence may be detected were located in areas of France where soil and other environmental conditions were so poor that the land was occupied only when population pressures were particularly high.

A final range of causes involved the 'clearance' of agricultural landscapes by powerful landowners who were able to exert their will over a sparse and weakened peasantry at times of demographic contraction and economic decline. The establishment of monastic granges and sheepwalks, construction of *châteaux*, creation of landscaped gardens and parks, and the engrossing of property provide examples of clearance operations. Desertion resulted but in many cases affected only the smaller units in the settlement hierarchy.

Broad causes such as these may be identified from the findings of archaeologists, demographers, geographers, historians and other human scientists who have considered the evolution of rural settlement in many parts of France but usually stressed phases of expansion rather than recession. No attempt has been made by French scholars to produce a map showing deserted settlements throughout the country or to devise regional desertion quotients. Methods of enquiry and subsequent results varied enormously between researchers, and from one part of France to another (Ponsot, 1968). Thus the evolution of settlement in Alsace and in parts of the Paris Basin is relatively well known but this is far from being the case in central, southern and western France (Humm, 1971). The tendency for hamlets rather than nucleated villages to dominate the settlement pattern of the last-mentioned region makes the detection of settlement contraction particularly difficult since individual hamlets were rarely identified in historical documentation.

Settlement Retreat Prior to the Fourteenth Century

Vigorous demographic growth occurred in Western Europe from the eleventh century to the early fourteenth century. This contrasted with the stagnation and decline that followed later in the fourteenth century and in the fifteenth century. It is therefore surprising that settlement retreat and agricultural contraction operated in some parts of France between A.D. 1000 and 1320 contrary to the general trend of expansion.

Three facts help to explain this apparently anomalous situation. First, the twelfth and thirteenth centuries formed an important period of peasant migration as many areas of woodland and scrub were cleared and brought into cultivation. Second, this tendency for rural mobility was reinforced by the fact that new settlements were being planned and established which required the influx of settlers from other areas. Peasant farmers were attracted to migrate from existing villages by the privileges that they would enjoy in newly-founded settlements. Such moves operated to the detriment of old-established villages that might experience a decline of population even to the point of desertion. Unfortunately it is not easy to discover whether the villages in question were declining before the new settlements were created. Third, some newly-created settlements failed to flourish for a variety of reasons and thus joined early examples of contraction and desertion that had resulted for other reasons.

The 'attractive' powers of new towns and villages appealed to peasant farmers occupying settlements less than 50–70 km away (Glénisson and Misralli, 1965). For this reason the *bastides* and *villeneuves* were a cause of complaint in many parts of France. Landlords objected to the publicity that the new foundations received and they alleged that clearance and forced depopulation of already occupied stretches of country was engineered by incoming rival lords.

The establishment of Cistercian abbeys and other monastic houses in the upper Marne valley (Fig. 4.1) and in comparable wooded areas of eastern France was certainly followed by changes in the distribution of population and settlement, even to the point of desertion (Pesez and Le Roy Ladurie, 1965). There are detailed examples of Clunesians and members of similar old-established religious orders accusing Cistercians and other newcomers of deliberately clearing land and destroying parishes in the upper Marne so that the area might be used for monastic ranches and the depopulated villages and hamlets be converted into granges. But

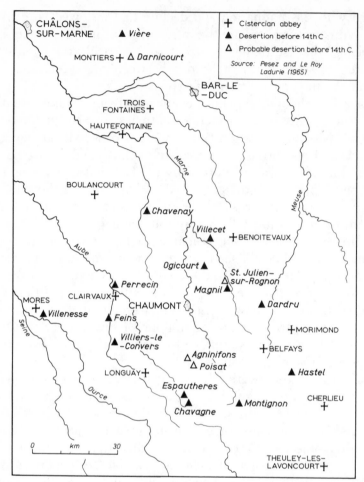

CHÂLONS-
SUR-MARNE   ▲ Vière

MONTIERS + △ Darnicourt

+ Cistercian abbey
▲ Desertion before 14th C.
△ Probable desertion before 14th C.

Source: Pesez and Le Roy
Ladurie (1965)

BAR-LE
-DUC

TROIS
FONTAINES +

HAUTEFONTAINE
+

Marne

Meuse

BOULANCOURT
+

▲ Chavenay

Aube

▲ Villecet
+ BENOITEVAUX

Ogicourt ▲

St. Julien-
sur-Rognon

Magnil ▲

▲ Perrecin
MORES   CLAIRVAUX +
+ ▲ Villenesse   CHAUMONT

▲ Feins

Seine

▲ Dardru

+ MORIMOND

+ BELFAYS

▲ Villiers-le
-Convers

LONGUAY +

△ Agninifons
△ Poisat

▲ Hastel

 Source

Ource

Espautheres
▲▲
Chavagne

▲ Montignon

CHERLIEU
+

0   km   30

THEULEY-LES-
LAVONCOURT +

FIG. 4.1. Monastic foundations and deserted settlements in the upper Marne
area.

whether changes of this type close to monastic foundations in other
parts of France resulted from the differential attractiveness of
individual settlements or from the enforcement of a clearance policy
must remain a matter for debate until more local investigations are
completed. Other powerful landowners certainly engineered
changes in the settlement pattern as in the Woëvre where examples of fields being flooded and converted into fishponds for
the local nobility are quoted by Pesez and Le Roy Ladurie (1965).
It is possible that similar changes occurred in the Dombes.

Further examples of settlement abandonment suggest that earlier colonists may have misjudged environmental conditions in some areas and thus cleared and occupied land which later proved to be unsatisfactory for cultivation. This was true of some of the early abandoned sites in the upper Marne, which had been established on the plateau de Langres and in other areas which are now largely under timber. Similarly the colonization of the marshlands of Artois involved examples of early over-optimism that were followed by settlement retreat.

A marked reduction in settled places occurred in some parts of France during the great clearance phase between the tenth century and the twelfth century (Duby, 1965). However important questions remain open to debate regarding the size and type of settlement to which such place names referred. As has already been mentioned, the omission of a place name from historic records does not signify necessarily the disappearance or desertion of a settlement. At a local scale of investigation, place names recorded in Cluny *canton* (Saône-et-Loire *département*) declined by 47 per cent from A.D. 1000 to the twentieth century but the proportion of names that related to villages and hamlets remains unknown (Deléage, 1941). Many must have referred simply to isolated farms that had functioned as the direct descendants of Roman villas.

The planning and creation of new villages and towns, known by a variety of names including *bastides*, *sauvetés* and *villeneuves*, produced failures as well as successes during the medieval period (Beresford, 1967). About 500 new settlements were projected in the Paris Basin between the early eleventh century and the late thirteenth century, with a similar number being proposed in the Basin of Aquitaine and in Languedoc over the same time span (Higounet, 1965). But whilst charters and other documents recording the foundation of such settlements are relatively abundant far less information is available on new towns that declined.

New towns appear to have experienced four types of fate. Some 'aborted settlements' failed to progress beyond the project stage and were never established on the ground. A second group passed through the foundation stage but failed to expand sufficiently to fill the ground plans that had been prepared for them. Other new settlements managed to survive and flourish. A final group went through the foundation phase successfully but disappeared later.

In some cases desertion occurred in the thirteenth century but generally it took place in the fourteenth and fifteenth centuries. More than thirty ephemeral new settlements are known to have disappeared from Aquitaine and the north-eastern section of the Paris Basin after, at most, four centuries of existence (Fig. 4.2).

These and other new foundations elsewhere in France declined

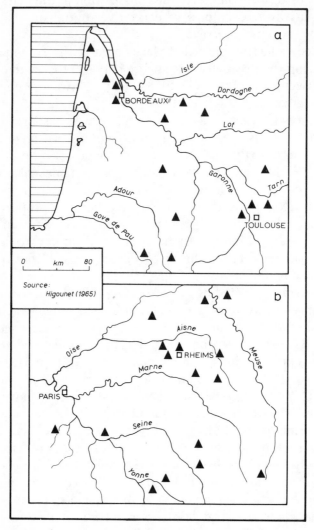

FIG. 4.2. Deserted settlements in Aquitaine and the eastern part of the Paris Basin. (a) *sauvetés* and *bastides*; (b) *villeneuves*.

for a variety of reasons, involving catastrophic events, such as fire or warfare, but also a failure on the part of their founders to perceive correctly the physical and human environment into which their settlements were to be inserted. Some new villages failed to attract the volume of population that was necessary for survival. Others were sited in areas with extremely poor terrain conditions such as the marshes and sandy areas of the Médoc at the mouth of the river Garonne. The conquest of such harsh environments posed too great an economic challenge for the peasant population of the eleventh and twelfth centuries with their fairly rudimentary agrarian techniques and the occupation of at least five new settlements in that area proved unsuccessful (Fig. 4.2a).

In the Paris Basin and in other parts of northern France *villeneuves* were established on heavy, decalcified forest soils that had been shunned by colonists during earlier phases of land occupation and settlement. Many failed to grow beyond hamlet size and a number disappeared within a few centuries. Thus the Brie area was settled late, between 1150 and 1225, but many of its *villeneuves* were soon to disappear both before and during the Hundred Years' War (Brunet, 1960). One fifth of the new settlements in nearby northern Champagne also failed (Fig. 4.2b) (Higounet, 1965). This was partly due to devastation during feudal disturbances and the Hundred Years' War but was also a response to the poor physical environment in which many of these predominantly agricultural settlements had been sited. Newly-cleared areas of very light or excessively humid soils between old-established villages lacked the quality of having been worked, fertilized and improved through centuries of human occupation. The most recent foundations were frequently the first to disappear during the subsequent recession period in the fourteenth and fifteenth centuries.

Settlement Retreat in the Fourteenth and Fifteenth Centuries

The fourteenth century and the first half of the fifteenth century formed a period of social disruption in France linked to the interaction of economic causes, brigandage, civil disturbance, epidemics, famine, and the Hundred Years' War. Documentation becomes more abundant than for the previous period and reveals numerous examples of population contraction and settlement abandonment. Chronicles and other contemporary sources provide an almost monotonous repetition of such events and describe the flight of the peasantry from the countryside in the face of invading armies. Town life offered more security but there were severe problems of disease, inadequate provisioning and poor accommodation in urban areas. Not surprisingly death rates in towns were high.

Rural depopulation in this period was often just a temporary phenomenon that prepared the way for later repopulation and re-organization of the agricultural structure. Frequently this involved changes in the distribution of villages and hamlets as well as in the size and layout of farms and fields. Reorganization of this kind resulted from the action of engrossing landlords, both ecclesiastical and lay, and from modifications in the operation of communal peasant farming. Such structural alteration, albeit not widespread at this stage, reflected a changeover from intensive arable systems involving large inputs of peasant labour to either less-intensive arable farming in sections of the Paris Basin or extensive grazing in parts of southern France.

In this period a fairly clear distinction in trends of settlement retreat may be drawn between the Paris Basin and the peripheral parts of France. In general terms, the network of rural settlement remained stable in the French 'heartland', in spite of numerous examples of temporary village desertion and the permanent dis-appearance of some small hamlets and isolated farms. Naturally there were some exceptions to this general observation, with examples of permanent retreat of both settlement and cultivation from some of the poorer soils in the Paris Basin occurring in the early fifteenth century, for example from areas of damp clay-with-flints (Dion, 1946). This might be interpreted as a continuation of the adjustment process to the physical environment that has been noted for an earlier period. Important spatial contrasts in settle-ment evolution were in evidence in the fourteenth and fifteenth centuries. The pattern of occupance remained fairly constant on the fertile plateau lands of lower Burgundy, for example, but retreated from the marshy areas of Puisaye. Stability was usual in Valois and Soissonnais but the number of hamlets and small villages con-tinued to decline in Brie as it had done in the previous period.

The trend of settlement change was different in Alsace, Languedoc and Provence where larger villages, as well as hamlets and farms, were deserted permanently as well as temporarily. Thus two-thirds (137) of the 213 village desertions in Alsace have been dated to the fourteenth and fifteenth centuries (Pesez and Le Roy Ladurie, 1965). This retreat of settlement in the province did not conform to a recognizable geographical pattern but operated to the benefit of larger villages and towns as such nuclei functioned as reception centres for folk migrating from smaller settlements. Some town- and village-ward movements were in response to the offer of security which larger nuclei could afford but many appear to be linked to a fundamental change in the scale of rural organization involving the creation of large, nucleated villages, surrounded by open arable fields and areas of common pasturage, which took the place of smaller agricultural settlements. Such a movement was not due to the action of engrossing landlords but involved the whole of the rural community. It displayed certain similarities to processes operating in the German lands that contributed to the creation of *Haufendörfer* with surrounding *Gewannfluren* (Thirsk, 1964). Settlement contraction in Alsace at this period might thus be viewed as a westerly extension of agrarian processes operating east of the Rhine. These have been attributed to a decline in the price of food grains resulting from a reduction in the number of city dwellers which, in turn, destroyed the basis of the old cereal-based rural economy and encouraged a further drift of population to the towns (Abel, 1965). Rural outmigration of this kind operated to the detriment of hamlets and small villages but to the benefit of large nucleations. Settlements were abandoned not only in infertile areas, such as the Sundgau, but also in some of the very fertile parts of Alsace with rich loess soils.

A series of interlinked processes promoted settlement desertion in Languedoc and Provence at this time. Deforestation of upland areas, following the clearance of land for intensive agricultural use, provoked soil impoverishment and erosion in some parts of Haute-Provence (Sclafert, 1959). The peasant population responded by moving downslope to more fertile areas (Baratier, 1961). One-third of the settlements of the Mercantour massif experienced desertion. Serious losses also were recorded in the Esterel and Maures uplands. Similar adjustments took place in Languedoc with the agricultural population shunning villages on

the unhealthy marshlands and in the infertile *garrigues* and mountains. But in Provence place-name evidence suggests that rural
retreat in the fourteenth and fifteenth centuries only affected small
villages, hamlets and isolated farms which were abandoned and
their fields allowed to revert to woodland or rough pastureland
(Duby, 1965). Large villages, with their surrounding nuclei of
arable land that had been fertilized for centuries, survived as foci
of cultivation in contrast with areas of 'marginal' land from which
cultivation retreated. Other landscape modifications resulted from
reductions in population pressure and subsequent changes in
agricultural systems in the uplands of the South. Large estates were
established in areas where arable farming continued to operate but
with perhaps just one isolated farmstead where a small village or
hamlet had been previously. In some upland areas in the Midi
cereal production was abandoned and replaced by the grazing of
transhumant cattle and sheep which were tended from isolated
granges. In spite of local changes in the settlement pattern, the
network of parishes in the South remained largely unchanged as
was the case in other parts of France.

Many examples of desertion at this time were temporary and
were erased as a result of later repeopling by migrants from other
parts of the country. In Quercy, for example, 78 villages were
abandoned during the 1380s but 76 of these were in existence
again in the seventeenth century after being repopulated by migrants from the Massif Central who moved downslope to more
fertile lands in the Garonne valley (Pesez and Le Roy Ladurie,
1965). Similarly during the Hundred Years' War the Entre-
Deux-Mers region at the mouth of the Garonne attracted migrants
from areas of high population pressure such as Brittany, Poitou,
Saintonge and Spain.

Regions that were devastated as a result of warfare might lose
their remaining population to the benefit of surrounding areas.
This was certainly the case in Southern Champagne whence
peasant farmers migrated to Burgundy and to Lorraine. As Bonnaud has shown in Chapter 2, migration flows generally operated
away from demographically dynamic regions where land resources
were inadequate to support a continuing expansion of population.
Thus prolonged phases of outmigration from Rouergue, other
parts of the Massif Central and from western France did not induce

settlement desertion in the departure zones. Basse-Normandie performed a similar supply role for the Paris Basin by providing migrants to repeople villages that had been temporarily abandoned. Again virtually no changes took place in the settlement structure of the departure zone.

Many researchers have emphasized the general recovery of the settlement pattern of the Paris Basin after phases of disruption. Moreau (1958), working to the south-east of the capital, noted that there was a remarkable continuity in the occupation of the plateaux throughout the wars and crises of the fourteenth and fifteenth centuries. In spite of devastation and temporary abandonment, the agricultural landscape assumed almost the same features as before. Similarly, Tulippe (1934) had traced damage to the area immediately west of Paris during the Hundred Years' War. He too found that many settled areas returned almost completely to their previous condition. There was, however, a rather greater emphasis on the occupation of areas of fertile soil than had previously been the case. Tulippe interpreted this as a reaction against indiscriminate occupation of land of varying qualities by earlier settlers. Serious destruction occurred in the northern part of the Paris Basin during the 1460s but after 100 years this too had been replaced by resettlement and reconstruction (Brunet, 1960).

Important changes in the scale of settlement were, however, being implemented in some sections of the Paris Basin as large landowners reorganized estates that had been devastated and temporarily depopulated. Small villages, hamlets, tiny tenant farms and highly fragmented openfields were, to use Roncayolo's word, 'digested' (1965, p. 29). They were replaced by large consolidated farms, arranged in an 'openfield-mosaic' with blocks of land that were much larger than the previous peasant strips. The new enterprises were operated from large isolated farmsteads which were served by simpler networks of rural roads than had existed previously. Such modifications heralded greater changes in agrarian structure that were to follow in the modern period.

Settlement Retreat after the Fifteenth Century

A further phase of land clearance and settlement expansion occurred in many parts of France between 1450 and 1550 but of course there were localized exceptions to this trend. For example, settlements were destroyed and abandoned temporarily in the Paris Basin as a result of warfare in the sixteenth century and the Frondes of the seventeenth century. The long-recognized process of settlement adjustment continued to operate in Alsace and presumably elsewhere in France to the advantage of larger inhabited places.

The seventeenth century represented a period of serious devastation with many settled sites throughout France being temporarily or permanently lost. The first type of abandonment was by far the more general. Figure 4.3 illustrates such a contraction of settle-

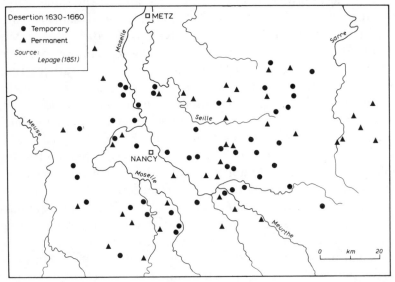

FIG. 4.3. Desertion of settlement in central Lorraine as a result of the Thirty Years' War.

ment in central Lorraine following the impact of famine, plague and the ravages of the Thirty Years' War (1618–48). Settlements of all sizes that were considered to have been abandoned permanently or temporarily between 1630 and 1660 have been plotted from Lepage's (1851) analysis for the former *département* of Meurthe. It is likely that Lepage overestimated the number of permanent desertions and underestimated temporary losses. In spite of radical short-term disruptions, the number of permanently deserted villages in Lorraine that may be dated to the seventeenth century was small. Similarly in Burgundy, war, plague, failed harvests and famine combined to ruin the countryside. Fields reverted to scrub, marshes reformed in valley bottoms, and villages were reduced to ruins. Survivors subsisted on wild fruit and game from the forests, or fled to nearby towns where food supplies were also short. Dijonnais were reduced to eating dogs, cats, rats, and worse (Roupnel, 1955). But, as elsewhere in eastern France, few village sites were abandoned permanently.

The Thirty Years' War was also traumatic in neighbouring Alsace where military invasion combined with famine and other disasters. The province's population fell by almost 50 per cent during the first half of the seventeenth century but numbers recovered quickly through inmigration as well as natural increase so that many abandoned villages were soon repeopled (Kintz, 1970). However, some did disappear as, for example, Gibert (1930) has shown for the Porte d'Alsace area (Fig. 4.4). In addition, the

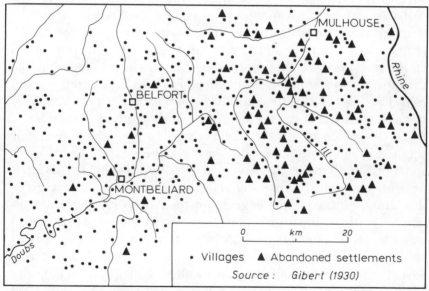

FIG. 4.4. Abandoned settlements in the Porte d'Alsace area.

number of hamlets and tiny nucleations continued to decline as it had done in previous crisis periods.

Northern Champagne presented an image of war-torn countryside when the Peace of the Pyrenees brought the Franco-Spanish

war to a halt in 1660. Peasants had left many villages in favour of
the towns as they attempted to escape rural poverty and distress.
This was described in graphic terms by a contemporary observer
who noted that between Rheims and Retel

'. . . with our own eyes we have seen flocks of men and women,
not livestock, foraging in the soil like swine in search of roots'
(Desailly, 1867, p. 121).

At least fifteen villages failed to recover from the onslaught of war
and distress in northern Champagne. Many more experienced
contraction or temporary abandonment. The readjustment process
that followed was not solely in response to the impact of war.
Some areas of light soil, such as the Champagne pouilleuse, which
might have been suitable for earlier occupation and cultivation
with the use of light ploughs, were abandoned at this time in
favour of heavier and more fertile soils that could be tilled more
effectively with heavier implements. Rural poverty, *vis-à-vis* the
real and imaginary advantages of town life, also contributed to the
outmigration process from the countryside during the seventeenth
century as it was to do in more recent times. Thus the population
of Rheims grew at the expense of surrounding villages in the
Champagne area at mid-century. In addition to the reasons already
considered, local variations in levels of taxation help explain why
some settlements in the region declined while others flourished.

The seventeenth century represented a period of economic
stagnation and demographic decline not only for Alsace, Champagne
and Lorraine but for the whole of the Paris Basin. Large landowners, bourgeois, noble and religious alike, took advantage of
this situation to continue engrossing their property and remodelling the settlement pattern. Thus the monastic house of Port-Royal
was one of the pioneers of large-scale farming, replacing peasant
holdings by large enterprises managed from isolated farmsteads.
Seventeen of the 28 hamlets of the locality of Magny-les-Hameaux
(Seine-et-Oise *département*) disappeared between 1550 and 1702
for kindred reasons (Tulippe, 1934). Similarly in Hurepoix farmhouses were demolished when holdings were amalgamated
(Venard, 1957).

Sometimes the work of the engrossers was swift but it might
equally well be protracted. In the second instance structural

modifications resulted gradually following the contraction of the local agricultural population or the failure of an adequate number of migrants to repeople the land after wartime devastation. In some places large landowners failed to attract a sufficient number of peasant tenants to operate their properties and responded by re-grouping tiny plots and small farms into larger holdings with massive parcels of land. At the same time villages and hamlets were replaced by isolated farmsteads. Maps from the seventeenth and eighteenth centuries show that large farms of this nature were being established by Cistercians, Praemonstratensians and other religious orders in Multien, Soissonais and Valois, not as the result of clearing new land for cultivation but by radically reorganizing existing properties (Brunet, 1960). Nevertheless the new rural structure that was emerging in some parts of the Paris Basin was still orientated to the production of wheat and oats with a period of fallow.

Châteaux and parklands were inserted in the rural landscapes of France at this time, not only by royalty but by members of the ranks of the nobility as well. The creation of Saint-Cloud, for example, involved the destruction of the settlements of Le Marché and Trianon (Pesez and Le Roy Ladurie, 1965). Similarly the planned landscapes of Versailles erased the villages of Choisy-aux-Boeufs and Versailles and the hamlet of Muscelone. The handiwork of Louis XIV's landscape gardeners did not represent isolated examples of change since they were emulated on a more modest scale by many other landowners throughout France.

The second half of the sixteenth century and the whole of the seventeenth century witnessed the spread of the system of share cropping on large estates held by the nobility in Poitou and in other parts of western France where rural population had declined. Villages and hamlets in these areas were gradually replaced by isolated sharecroppers' farmsteads (Merle, 1958). Stretches of openfield were divided into blocks that were separated by hedgerows. Such an invasion of *bocage* removed traces of openfield, rough-grazing land and copses from several parts of western France. The agricultural system of such newly-enclosed western areas remained firmly based on cereal production but it was far from being as advanced as the capitalist enterprises on the large farms that were emerging in some parts of the Paris Basin.

Changes also took place in the settlement pattern of southern France during this period as a result of three distinct processes. First, military operations against the Camisards of the Cévennes and against other rebellious groups in the South involved the 'clearance' and systematic devastation of some areas. Second, population retreated from the malaria-infested marshlands of the Languedoc coast; and third, engrossing by large landowners operated in parts of the South as elsewhere in the country.

The Continuum of Settlement Adjustment

In the present chapter emphasis has been placed on settlement retreat but the proportion of 'deserted villages' to the total number of nucleations inhabited at some time in the past is probably much smaller in France than in England or in Germany. The rural settlement network of France, at the village scale at least, has remained impressively vital and resilient to the numerous misfortunes that have befallen it through the centuries (Hilton, 1968). Thus the impression of stability conveyed by the nationwide analysis of parish numbers between 1328 and the present century is probably a fairly realistic statement of change at the village level. However, numerous subtle modifications operated in the lower ranks of the settlement hierarchy.

Settlement contraction in France appears to have been more complicated than was the case in neighbouring west European countries. Nevertheless a protracted pruning operation has taken place whereby small nucleations that were once inhabited by peasant farmers have disappeared. This opened the way for the creation of large capitalist farms in the Paris Basin and in southern and western France. In addition, it progressively strengthened the large nucleations of north-eastern France with their surrounding openfields and facilitated the insertion of *châteaux*, parks and other decorative features into the rural landscapes of many parts of the country.

Two major phases of settlement retreat have been depicted: namely between the eleventh and thirteenth centuries, and from 1560 to 1720, with the two being separated by the Renaissance period. But the contraction of hamlets and small villages, the retreat of cultivated land, and the depopulation of the French countryside are not simply historic phenomena. They have continued with vigour during the eighteenth, nineteenth and twentieth centuries which form the third great phase of rural decline. Such relatively recent changes must be considered as stages on a continuum of settlement adjustment that stretches from the early medieval period up to the present day. The implications of one aspect of this adjustment, namely rural/urban migration, will be considered in Chapter 13 in the context of urban growth between 1500 and 1900. In the present age of the ubiquitous automobile a reversal of rural decline is noticeable in some parts of France which underwent settlement contraction in the past. Cottages are being restored for full-time occupation or for use as second homes during weekends and vacations. A new phase of permanent or seasonal repeopling is replacing earlier periods of retreat in the complicated pulsation of rural settlement through time.

4. References

The volume entitled *Villages désertés et histoire économique*, Paris (1965), contains a most valuable collection of references relating to the retreat of rural settlement in France and in other European countries. Items quoted below relate to that volume unless otherwise identified.

Abel, W., 'Désertions rurales: bilan de recherche allemande', *op. cit.* (1965), 515–532.

Baratier, E., *La Démographie provençale du XIIIᵉ au XVIᵉ siècle*, Paris (1961).

Beresford, M. W., *New Towns of the Middle Ages: town plantation in England, Wales, and Gascony*, London (1967).

Brunet, P., *Structure agraire et économie rurale des plateaux tertiaires entre la Seine et l'Oise*, Caen (1960).

Chevallier, R., 'Photographie aérienne et villages désertés, *op. cit.* (1965), 63–81.

Courbin, P., 'Méthodologie des fouilles de villages disparus en France', *op. cit.* (1965), 49–61.

Debien, G., *En Haut-Poitou: défricheurs au travail XVᵉ–XVIIIᵉ siècles*, Paris (1952).

Deléage, A., *La Vie rurale en Bourgogne jusqu'au début du XIᵉ siècle*, Macon (1941).

Demains d'Archimbaud, G., 'Archéologie et villages désertés en Provence: resultats des fouilles', *op. cit.* (1965), 287–301.

Desailly, A., *Histoire de Witry-les-Reims et des villages détruits*, Reims (1867).

Dion, R., 'La part de la géographie et celle de l'histoire dans l'explication de l'habitat rural du bassin parisien', *Publications de la Société de Géographie de Lille* (1946), 6–80.

Duby, G., 'Démographie et villages désertés', *op. cit.* (1965), 13–24.

Gibert, A., *La Porte de Bourgogne et d'Alsace*, Paris (1930).

Glenisson, J. and Misralli, J., 'Désertions rurales dans la France médiévale', *op. cit.* (1965), 267–286.

Hensel, W., 'Le village déserté de Montaigut: rapport de fouilles', *op. cit.* (1965a), 303–326.

Hensel, W., 'Le village déserté de Saint-Jean-le-Froid: rapport de fouilles', *op. cit.* (1965b), 327–339.

Higounet, C., 'Villeneuves et bastides désertés', *op. cit.* (1965), 253–265.

Hilton, R. H., 'Villages désertés et histoire économique: recherches françaises et anglaises', *Etudes Rurales*, 32 (1968), 104–109.

Humm, A., *Villages et hameaux disparus en Basse-Alsace*, Strasbourg (1971).

Juillard, E., *La Vie rurale dans la plaine de Basse-Alsace: essai de géographie sociale*, Strasbourg and Paris (1953).

Kintz, J.-P., 'La mobilité humaine en Alsace: essai de présentation statistique 14–18e siècles', *Annales de Démographie Historique* (1970), 157–183.

Lepage, H., 'De la dépopulation de la Lorraine au XVIIe siècle, *Annuaire de la Meurthe* (1851), 11–58.

Lot, F., 'L'état des paroisses et des feux de 1328', *Bibliothèque de l'Ecole des Chartes*, 90 (1929), 51–107 and 256–315.

Merle, L., *La Métairie et l'évolution agraire de la Gâtine poitevine de la fin du Moyen Age à la Révolution*, Paris (1958).

Moreau, J.-P., *La Vie rurale dans le sud-est du bassin parisien*, Paris (1958).

Moufrin, J., 'Habitats ruinés et noms de lieux', *op. cit.* (1965), 103–124.

Pesez, J. M., 'Sources écrites et villages désertés', *op. cit.* (1965), 83–102.

Pesez, J. M. and E. Le Roy Ladurie, 'Les villages désertés en France: vue d'ensemble', *op. cit.* (1965), 127–252.

Ponsot, P., 'Villages désertés en Europe du XIe au XVIIIe siècle', *Annales, Economies, Sociétés, Civilisations*, 23 (1968), 663–69.

Roncayolo, M., 'Géographie et villages désertés', *op. cit.* (1965), 25–47.

Roupnel, G., *La Ville et la campagne au XVIIe siècle: étude sur les populations du pays dijonnais* (1955), Paris.

Sclafert, T., *Cultures en Haute-Provence: déboisements et pâturages au Moyen Age*, Paris (1959).

Thirsk, J., 'The common fields', *Past and Present*, 18 (1964), 3–25.

Tulippe, O., *L'habitat rural en Seine-et-Oise*, Paris (1934).

Venard, M., *Bourgeois et paysans au XVIIe siècle: recherche sur le rôle des bourgeois parisiens dans la vie agricole au sud de Paris au XVIIe siècle*, Paris (1957).

5

Regional Contrasts in Agrarian Structures

HUGH PRINCE

The Concept of an Agrarian Civilization

To the end of the nineteenth century no civilization was more profoundly and intensely rural than that of France. Its *pays* attained
their identity earlier in time; through the ages their distinctive
traits were cultivated more assiduously and their traditions were
cherished and safeguarded more vigilantly than in other parts of
the western world (Longnon, 1922). During the late nineteenth
century sociologists, historians and geographers turned their attention to studying regional consciousness in order to understand
what Vidal de la Blache (1903) called the personality of regions.[1]
Later geographers have examined in detail the boundaries of
regions, the ways in which inhabitants wrest their livings from the
soil, and the characteristics of civilizations rooted in the countryside.[2] In view of the long and close association between the teaching
of geography and history in France, it is hardly surprising that
great efforts should have been devoted to the study of the distinctiveness of French *pays* and to their agrarian histories. Inevitably,
research has proceeded unevenly so that some areas and some
periods are less well known than others, but by comparison with
the rest of the world France possesses an incomparable wealth of
regional studies. By implication, these studies add fresh support to
the widely held view that the *pays* in France impart a strong and
possessive sense of place and imbue their inhabitants with a deep
and lasting attachment to the homeland.

French civilization is exceptional both in its firm adherence to
its rural origins and in its persistent regional diversity. In the
Mediterranean, notably in Greece and in Italy, civilization is the
gift of cities, beyond whose jurisdiction barbarism prevails. When
cities fall civilizations collapse and strangers walk uncomprehend-
ing amid their ruins. On the steppes of the east and deep in the
forests of central and northern Europe people did not settle in
groups large enough or powerful enough, nor did they remain long
enough to create and sustain independent civilizations of their own
(Lot, 1937). They were unable to establish themselves sufficiently
securely to ensure the survival of their languages, laws and
religions. They were driven from their homes by invaders and the
wilderness took over their deserted fields. Cultures displaced one
another and features of old landscapes were erased and replaced by
new structures.[3] The essence of French civilization, setting it apart
from these others, is that elements from diverse cultural traditions
have been acquired and domesticated into its durable and intensely
local way of life.

In the history of France, more than for other European nations,
major cultural discontinuities are difficult to discern. It is true that
the results of recent studies suggest that early work repeatedly
underestimated the significance of rapid changes in agrarian
history, but the effects of these changes were technical and
administrative rather than cultural and constitutional. The ulti-
mate check on cultural displacement is that the most productive and
most highly cultivated soils are too precious to abandon. They
have supported populations large enough and cohesive enough to
absorb and assimilate invading peoples (Jullian, 1909–20). If
Gaul was transformed it was not at the behest of Rome, but by the
will of the Gauls themselves. Strangers who came to stay learned
the ways of the natives. The skills of handicrafts, the arts of
husbandry, and indigenous modes of expression in music, poetry
and the fine arts have been passed from one group to another.
From a newcomer's view, the transaction required them to adopt
local traditions as a condition of their naturalisation.

Deep respect for ancestral beliefs, for ancient practices and for
time-honoured institutions are abiding and fundamental bases of
rural life in most French *pays*. Where else in the world are such
legacies from the past celebrated as sources of distinctive rural

cultures and cohesiveness? Where else do geographers and historians attribute the special virtues of their works to the inspiration and wisdom they have received from their peasant forebears, establishing their credentials through their kinship and identity of outlook with tillers of the soil?[4] Where else are vernacular styles and peasant crafts dignified as the high achievements of civilization? In no other country are the *vins de pays*, regional cuisines and farmhouse cheeses studied with such devotion as works of art.[5] The characteristically French concept of an agrarian civilization is described by Meynier (1958) as a complex of adaptations to physical and social environments expressed through local customs and practices peculiar to the locality. Above all, it manifests itself in the appearance of the landscape, faithfully preserving the outlines of trackways, fields and homesteads dating back to remote antiquity. In other countries the contradiction implicit in the term *civilisation agraire* would call for comment and those who used it would be at pains to explain why an epithet signifying rustic simplicity should be linked with an expression signifying urbane refinement. In France no such justification is expected and none is given.

The Density of History

In addition to and reinforcing its essential rusticity, French civilization is characterized by the *density* of its history. It is not that Frenchmen have more direct access to the past or are able to approach the origins of their civilization more closely than other people. On the contrary, Americans commemorate their history more frequently and with greater solemnity than the French, recalling at a symbolic feast on Thanksgiving Day the survival of the Pilgrims after the ordeal of their first year, recalling on Independence Day the founding of their republic, and remembering on Memorial Day those who died in the Civil War. And no opportunity is lost to celebrate a centenary or to re-enact an episode in American history. The whole course of American history from its earliest beginnings is recorded in great detail in documents, in pictures and in sound recordings. No such repository of documentary evidence is available to French historians. The reconstruction of the past must proceed laboriously from reasoned inference to judicious interpretation.[6]

The beginnings of French rural history must be pieced together from fragments unearthed by archaeologists, from patient detective work on place-name elements, from the imperfect testimony of chronicles, charters and local customs. Yet everywhere the past is palpably present. It has left a bewildering variety of traces on every object in the environment. Shrines built by Neolithic peoples continue to exert an attraction upon contemporary visitors (Fleure, 1943). The ruins of Grecian temples and Roman roads are still being quarried for building stones. Terraces constructed by Iron Age cultivators and ancient irrigation channels are still being maintained and used. Dion (1949) aptly remarked that among the legacies of Roman imperialism:

'viticulture and the cultivation of Mediterranean fruits count for more in the material and spiritual life of the nation than the monumental remains of hot baths, arenas and triumphal arches' (p. 7).

The ploughman at his daily task must continually turn over the bones of his ancestors, and his wife may draw water from a well dug perhaps a thousand years ago. Fields laboriously hacked from the woods in the twelfth century must, by dint of unceasing effort, be made to yield crops of wheat in the twentieth. These things look old but are not disused. They make up the fabric of a lived-in, working environment, greatly modified, often shorn up, restored, rehabilitated to serve the needs of their possessors, past as well as present. The effects of weathering, constant wear and tear, occasional repairs, major overhauls and extensions produce surfaces that not only look aged but, because they have been altered and added to, bear witness to the repeated efforts of, successive generations of craftsmen and handymen to keep them in service. The cumulative marks of these labours add to the historical density of the landscape; their decipherment is a difficult art. In Dion's (1949) view it is:

'an archaeological study in the broadest sense of the word, a search for reasons which have determined the choice of sites for man's works' (p. 8).

Forms and Functions in Agrarian Structures

In studying French rural landscapes no theme is more crucial and none is more difficult to understand than the regional distinctiveness of agrarian structures. It takes pride of place in the study of human geography (Sorre, 1947–52). It starts by examining the basic features on the ground. First, it traces the origins of the fields carved from the waste, to be ploughed, to be grazed or to be planted with trees. Here they appear long and narrow, the strips of one farmer intermixed with those of his neighbour; there they are small and squarish, separated from one another by deep hedges. Beside the fields are the cottages, farmsteads, churches and other buildings, clustered close together in villages or hamlets, or dispersed through the countryside. Between them, connecting field to dwelling, dwelling to church, and farm to market place are paths and roadways, here narrow and winding, there broad and straight. By these lines agrarian structures are articulated and held together.[7] And separating one agrarian territory, be it farm or commune or province, from its neighbour is a boundary line or marchland tract of waste or forest, lying outside the jurisdiction of local courts (Dion, 1947).

A problem that agrarian historians and rural geographers must constantly bear in mind, although there can be no prospect of providing a conclusive solution to it, is the problem of relating morphology to function. Because, in some localities, scattered strip holdings are associated with common field husbandry, it does not follow that in other localities similar forms are to be accounted for in a similar way. In the valley of the upper Bruche in the Vosges, Marthelot (1948) describes an openfield landscape with elongated strips, grouped into furlongs, centred upon agglomerated settlements. The system is untypical in that communal grazing is excluded from the arable land. The arrangement is explained by a combination of factors: an isolated community jealously guarding its traditions; only a limited amount of land available for water meadows; the woods almost completely cleared at an early date for industrial as well as for agricultural purposes. In Normandy, Touraine, and also in the Argonne unenclosed fields of great length are to be seen stretching back from a farmstead to the edge of a wood. Like true common fields they are subject to collective regulations, but they owe their distinctive shape to the gradual advance of clearings into the woods, in the manner of *Waldhufendorf* colonization in central Europe (Bloch, 1931; Enjalbert, 1948). A source of confusion in understanding the differences between field patterns and field systems arises from the words used. It is particularly misleading to employ a morphological term 'openfield' to describe a 'system' of farming practices regulated and sustained by collective customs (Baker, 1969). Meynier's (1958) collation of evidence from several parts of the world virtually closes the prospect of reconstructing a universal chronology for the origins and development of champion land that will satisfactorily accommodate the asymmetric histories of such associated features as nucleated settlements, communal grazing arrangements and feudal obligations.

For similar reasons, it is wrong to consider *bocage* as being either uniquely related to and created by rugged individualism or simply an adjustment to poor soils (Meynier, 1952; Poirier, 1934). Many hedgerows and earth banks in the *bocage* of Brittany were planted very recently, during the great clearance of wasteland in the last century, whilst others have been dated by discoveries of coins to the ninth and tenth centuries, and some may be still older (Meyer, 1972; Meynier, 1966). These plot boundaries have been explained in various ways. Musset (1917) argues that they are residual features left after *défrichement*, and sketches a history of piecemeal encroachment in which each clearing is cut back into the fringe of wood separating it from its neighbours until only a hedge-width remains. Others stress that enclosures serve to defend cropland from livestock, offer shelter to crops and stock, and supply valuable resources of timber, firewood and perhaps also fruit. Chaumeil (1954) argues that a privilege enjoyed initially by a minority of cultivators to fence out straying cattle, to protect their growing crops, became a generally accepted practice among arable farmers, and eventually forced livestock farmers to enclose in order to save their pastures for their own exclusive use. But other hedges and banks are primarily symbolic, being too small and insignificant to perform any physical function, but clearly marking boundaries of land-ownership (Chapter 9). Delaspre (1952) observes that squatters always believe, and are often proved right by events, that once a plot of waste ground has been enclosed their claim to possession of it is securely established. 'Hedge and wall,' for them, 'are the equivalents of legal deeds' (p. 493). Patches of enclosed land of different ages, perhaps created to perform different functions, may be intermixed.

'Next to areas of recent *bocage*, whose development may be grasped, there are areas of ancient, perhaps even primeval enclosure whose origins escape us' (Champier, 1956).

To begin to understand the confused and anarchic appearance of *bocage*, we must look beneath the present forms, in an attempt to find structures that more closely 'reflect agrarian adaptations to a range of physical and social factors' (Brunet, 1968).

Southern polyculture presents too large a variety of forms to be classified intelligibly as an assemblage of component parts. It cannot be characterized as a distinctive and readily defined arrangement of fields, or as a regular and identifiable pattern of farms (Roupnel, 1932; Sion, 1937). It is more easily understood as a way of farming, partly committed to maintaining long-term enterprises such as the tending of vines and tree crops, the renovating of terraces and irrigation works, and partly exploiting short-term opportunities by inter-cropping, by planting catch crops, by breaking new ground, by abandoning areas in temporary cultivation, by expanding or reducing the size of flocks. It is a system in which some elements are extremely durable, almost permanently fixed, whilst others are highly flexible, almost subject to a passing whim (Faucher, 1934; Deffontaines, 1932; George, 1935; Marcelin, 1942). Features observed on the ground and portrayed on maps do not necessarily and invariably indicate the manner in which agrarian systems operate, nor do they reveal how they originated.

The Antiquity and Continuity of Agrarian Structures

The tracing of past changes presents other serious problems. In practice it is not always clear from available evidence whether landscape features have developed slowly over a long period of time or whether they have been constructed within a short time-span, whether they are products of gradual evolution or whether

they result from rapid innovations. The exact age of a landscape
feature is not easily determined by field examination. Rarely is an
earth bank or burial mound found to overlie an undisturbed fossil
soil whose surface may be dated with precision.[8] Occasionally,
coins or broken tools or dateable pot fragments indicate when a
structure was lived in. Much less frequently does archaeological
evidence reveal how long a site was used or occupied and it can
provide only vague clues about the continuity of occupation. It is
very difficult to discover whether places once occupied were abandoned and subsequently reoccupied. It is also difficult to trace the
beginnings of a period of occupation. The earliest material relics
of Greek penetration up the Rhône valley beyond Avignon cannot
be traced back further than the third century B.C. (Dechelette,
1908–12). But literary evidence indicates that the confluence of the
Saône had been reached and was settled well before that time
(Levêque and Claval, 1970).

In reconstructing a sequence of stages in the settlement history
of a district an examination of place-name elements may provide
valuable information. Bloch (1939) and Dauzat (1939) have
traced the steps by which the woods covering the plateau of
Beauce were cleared and their place was taken by cultivated fields.
More recently, similar reconstructions, drawing upon place-name
studies in conjunction with archaeological findings, have traced the
progress of clearing and the advance of settlement in the Jura in the
Saône basin, on the Langres plateau and also in Lorraine, where
the method has been applied to evidence from later periods (Lebeau,
1955; Millotte, 1963; Jeanton, 1934; Blache, 1937, 1938; de
Planhol and Lacroix, 1963; de Planhol and Perardel, 1969). A
longer sequence of steps in the occupation of Picardy from early
Iron Age through Gallo-Roman to medieval times has been pieced
together by Fossier (1968). For larger areas, evidence derived
from place names is simplified by literary evidence and, above all,
by inspection of early maps (de Planhol, 1972).

Unequivocal documentary evidence for landscape changes often
comes to be recorded long after the changes have occurred. The
earliest allusion to fields as *saisons*, or courses in a regular rotation,
is to be found in the ninth century Polyptique d'Irminon (Perrin,
1945). Not until 1248 may we discover an explicit reference to a
three-fold division of the cultivated land, and only in the fourteenth

century are customary regulations governing fallowing and communal grazing set down in writing (Higounet, 1956, 1965). The most difficult tasks facing a historian are to judge how far such evidence may be relied upon to throw light on earlier conditions and how far back in time such inferences may be pushed.

Interpreting the documentary record would present no difficulties if the structures being studied had remained unchanged. Problems arise because the structures change and changes occur at different speeds and in different directions in different localities. In parts of western France, for example, *bocage* has replaced openfields in recent times (see Chapter 9). In some localities, a pattern of former strips has been fossilized by newly planted hedgerows and banks. In other localities, expanses of 'neo-openfield' have been created since the second world war by the removal of hedges in connection with plot consolidation schemes. In parts of northeastern France, where openfields dominate the landscape, fragmentary evidence suggests that very different patterns of fields and settlements may have prevailed in earlier times. It is now clear that some openfield layouts in Lorraine and in Burgundy were reconstituted after villages had been destroyed in the Thirty Years War (de Planhol, 1961; de Saint Jacob, 1941–46; Peltre, 1966; Reitel, 1966; Roupnel, 1922). In those villages an ancient order, simplified and regularized in parts, was restored and given a new lease of life. In many parts of western France openfields faded away gradually. Temporary fences preceded the construction of permanent enclosures. Rough barriers of thorns and dead branches or neat lines of woven hurdles were placed around land when a crop was sown, to be taken away when the harvest was gathered and communal flocks were admitted. Permission to make temporary enclosures was granted by Brittany in the twelfth century, in the Vendée in the fourteenth, and in Normandy in the sixteenth (Meynier, 1958; de Chabot, 1943).

Dividing France into Two, Three or More Cultural Provinces

In assessing the strengths and weaknesses of different interpretations of regional contrasts in agrarian structures, three questions are of critical importance. The first asks how far it is permissible to interpret landscape features and artefacts in functional terms, seeking utilitarian and materialistic explanations, invoking the virtues of calling a spade a spade, in preference to aesthetic and symbolic explanations. Without corroborative evidence from literary sources or from oral traditions, interpretations based on morphology alone cannot escape from the realms of conjecture. The second question asks how far we are entitled to infer historical continuity for institutions and structures recorded in the muniments. Among the fullest and most illuminating accounts of functioning agrarian systems are those written in the late eighteenth century by Arthur Young, by French *agronomes* and by the compilers of the late eighteenth-century *enquêtes* (Bloch, 1930; Bourde, 1953). How far do these accounts describe accurately arrangements made in earlier centuries and how far do the field patterns depicted on large-scale maps of the sixteenth century and later represent faithfully much earlier forms? The assumption of unchange, of stasis, of continuity is tenable only as long as all evidence from earlier periods is congruent with it. The third question cannot be answered conclusively. It asks how far regional contrasts are to be considered specific, distinctive, unique or, on the other hand, how far they are to be regarded as generic, representative, interrelated. Investigators inclining to the former view will proceed to divide and disaggregate the universe until the smallest indivisible regional entities have been isolated. Those proceeding in the opposite direction will attempt to associate phenomena in one area with those in another until a network of connections has been built up, enabling the workings of different structures to be understood within the mechanism of an agrarian system as a whole. The relationships being sought may be either spatial or temporal. Or they may be evolutionary, tracing changes of a spatial order through time.

As fresh studies have added to the stock of precise local information, broad definitions of the cultural divisions of France have been modified, revised and qualified until it is no longer profitable to attempt to draw boundaries separating distinctive provinces. In the section of this chapter dealing with the division of France into two, three or more cultural provinces, we shall review the steps by which the classical view that cultural regimes are permanently geographically separate has come to be abandoned. In the section that follows, dealing with the integration of agrarian history, alternative ways of interpreting regional contrasts are discussed. Deterministic approaches, attempting to explain regional differences in terms of physical geography or in terms of the ethnic origins of the occupiers of the land, have failed in reality to account for historic changes and have failed in logic to show why the same causes do not always produce the same effects.[9] Historical studies identify the occasions and indicate the circumstances in which agrarian structures have been transformed. From these interpretations a few general statements about the processes of change have been derived, and these statements in turn have provided the bases for theories to account for the evolution of agrarian structures.

A Twofold Division: le Nord and le Midi

'No country in Europe was submitted so forcefully to the contrary influences of north and south',

wrote Camille Jullian in the introduction to his *Histoire de la Gaule* (1920, vol. I, 66). From the time of Strabo's description to that of Arthur Young's travels the nature of the contrast between le Midi and le Nord was observed and commented upon by many writers, in terms that are broadly similar. Le Midi was essentially Mediterranean in character, a land of fruit growing and garden cultivation, of acropolis-like settlements commanding small basins, separated from one another by mountains and extensive sheep-walks (Newbigin, 1924). Le Nord was devoted to grain growing, a province of openfields and of nucleated villages, where grazing and crop husbandry were regulated by village communities (Dopsch, 1937). The prototypes were distinct and easily identified, but where were the limits of the respective provinces to be drawn? Did the two provinces meet each other at a common frontier? To these questions different observers have given different answers at different periods in history, depending whether their viewpoint was that of a northerner or of a southerner.

For northerners there was little doubt that the limit of le Nord
had been reached when the *campagne*, or openfield landscape,
disappeared and a world of *bocage* was entered (Fig. 5.1). Behind
lay a treeless expanse of ploughland, divided into long narrow
strips, a land of villages. Ahead lay a land of hamlets and isolated
farms, set in a patchwork of thickly hedged, irregularly shaped
fields, some ploughed and some permanently under grass. But a
bocage landscape was not yet the true south. To be sure, it clung
traditionally to a biennial rotation, not, as practised in the north,
to a three-field course, with a fallow every third year. The separation of grazing land from cultivated areas was also characteristic

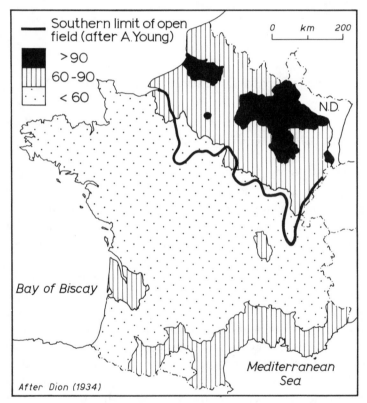

FIG. 5.1. Openfields and nucleated villages. Southern limit of openfield
cultivation, drawn by Roger Dion, from descriptions in Arthur Young's
'Travels in France in 1787, 1788 & 1789'. Values represent percentages of total
rural population in 1891 living in *chefs lieux*.

of the south. But it could not be claimed that deep hedges, isolated farms or hamlets were essential features of the southern scene, and in the absence of olives, vines and figs, the landscapes of Brittany or Limousin bore little resemblance to those of Roussillon or Provence. The distinctive feature of the agrarian regime in le Nord, distinguising that region from all others in France, was the power exercised by the village community in regulating farming activities. The key to the system was the subjection of the arable land to grazing by communal flocks and herds, to obligatory *vaine pâture*. Under that restraint a farmer had to follow a course of cropping agreed by common consent among his neighbours, to plough, to sow, to gather his harvest, to lay down his land to fallow and to throw his strips open to grazing at the same time as every other farmer in the community. Neither enclosure nor the consolidation of scattered strips could be accomplished as long as the system was rigorously adhered to. In other districts in France, those who occupied a plot of land were free to exploit it more or less as they pleased. Mediterranean polyculture in this respect stands at an opposite pole to northern *vaine pâture* where all land was open to grazing by communal flocks.

In its narrowest sense le Midi extends no further than the limit of olive growing (Fig. 5.2). 'A Valence le Midi commence', is a strictly Mediterranean view of the south, an area defined by the culture of the olive, the vine and of wheat. It is an area of prolonged summer drought where the growth of citrus fruits, almonds and peaches is sustained by irrigation, whilst extensive areas of scorched garrigue and maquis yield only the scantiest pasturage. Abiding features of the agrarian landscape are the contrasts between highland and lowland, between desert and sown, between summer and winter. In essence, the rural economy is characterized by the freedom of farmers from collective obligations, by a high degree of specialization in the techniques employed, and by the range and diversity of the agricultural produce raised. Taking a broader view, the south extends to the limits of romanization, where towns, roads, churches, farm buildings, and squarish fields bear the stamp of Mediterranean images. The legacies of Latin language, classical learning, Roman law and Catholicism have been important in holding the allegiance of southerners to the source of their traditions.

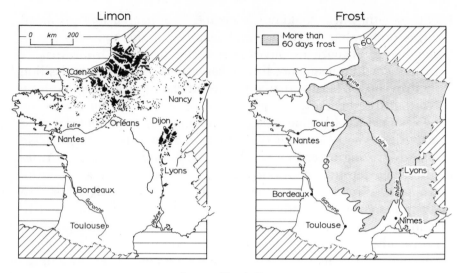

Source : Atlas de France

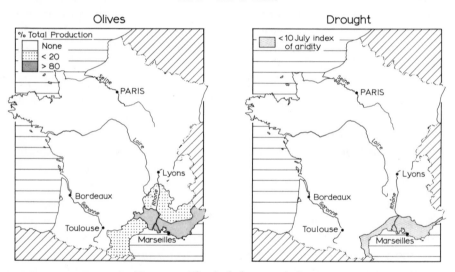

FIG. 5.2. Physical characteristics.
Top left: deposits of limon and loess; top right: stippled, more than 60 days per
year, temperatures below 0°C.; bottom left: dark tint, contributed over 80 per
cent of national production of olives, open stippled, contributed over 10 per cent;
bottom right: stippled, July index of aridity of 0–10 whose formula is $\dfrac{P \times 12}{T + 10}$
where P = precipitation in mm and T = temperature in °C.

Natural Divisions

Following in the footsteps of eighteenth-century travellers, agricultural writers and local topographers, nineteenth-century historians and geographers were also deeply impressed by the appearance of contrasts between north and south, and they set out to find natural and cultural divides corresponding with the variations they observed in the landscape. In earlier searches for fundamental causes for regional differences, Jean Bodin in the sixteenth century, and the Baron de Montesquieu and the Physiocrats in the eighteenth century, had been led to think of warmth and cold as the most basic characteristics differentiating places. These early philosophers shared the view that a study of climate afforded a most promising approach to the problem but they did not regard the debate as closed. Caution was thrown to the winds in the late nineteenth century by Victor Cousin whose *Introduction à l'histoire de la philosophie* boldly asserts:

> 'Give me the map of a country, its configuration, its climate, its waters, its winds, and all its physical geography; give me its natural productions, its flora, its zoology, and I pledge myself to tell you, *a priori*, what the man of that country will be, and what part that country will play in history, not by accident, but of necessity; not at one epoch, but in all epochs; and, moreover, the idea which it is destined to represent.' (Cited in Lucien Febvre, 1925, p. 10).

Whilst the arrogance of such a claim serves only to discredit environmental determinism, the correspondence between elements of climate and agrarian structures awaits serious investigation.

An area subject to protracted winter frosts fits roughly the area dominated by traditional common field agriculture, practising a three-year rotation, where provision has to be made for feeding livestock indoors during the winter months. The correspondence between the area subject to summer drought and Mediterranean polyculture, where conservation of water plays an important role, is also approximate (Fig. 5.2). But the incidence of drought is not simply an economic problem; it is a matter of life and death. Braudel (1972) describes it as 'the scourge of the Mediterranean' (vol. I, 238–9, 245). At this point, conscientious historical geo-graphers must be wary of the deterministic trap that lies ahead. The limits of agrarian systems and climatic phenomena rarely coincide, and the discrepancies at the margins cannot be accommo-dated by trying to set up zones of transition. This is because the directions in which different agrarian systems become inter-mingled are in no way graded according to climatic parameters.

The methods by which agriculture is adjusted to climate are related to several different demographic and technical factors. In Lorraine, for example, the archetypal three-field system employed six or eight ox plough-teams, and when the population growth reached its maximum almost all lands capable of raising crops were ploughed. Under these conditions crops from the arable land had to support not only the human population, but also had to provide winter feed for a large number of draught oxen and for breeding stock to maintain flocks to manure the soil (Bloch, 1931; Dion, 1934). But these conditions were not permanent. They might be relaxed by a decline in population, by a substitution of horses for oxen, by the introduction of root crops and artificial grasses, by a change in the practice of manuring or by a combination of such changes. Furthermore, the assumption that climate remains a fixed and unvarying element throughout history was seriously challenged by the work of Angot (1883), and has been largely demolished since then, notably by the researches of Le Roy Ladurie (1962, 1967, 1971). In the light of our present knowledge the notion that climate exerts an unchanging and dominating influence over our ways of life, and agriculture in particular, must be laid aside.

Turning to the characteristics of the ground itself, contrasts in soils and slopes correspond only very loosely with the core areas of le Nord and le Midi. For Elie de Beaumont (1841–79) the geological map provides a key to understanding the differences between north and south. He visualizes a figure eight formed by the outcrop of Jurassic rocks, whose southern loop encloses an inlier of older rocks—the Massif Central, whilst the northern loop en-circles younger rocks of the Paris basin. The Massif Central, from which not only fresh water but also life itself flows outwards to the lowlands, is characterized as *'le pôle répulsif'* of France, and the Paris basin is viewed as drawing toward itself materials and energy from surrounding regions. The poles of le Nord and le Midi stand further apart both in distance and in the range of geographical differences that separate them. Vidal de la Blache (1903) casts his eye over a much wider territory, beyond the Rhine, across the Channel, over the Pyrenees and over the Alps, to trace the sources of some features making up the personality of France. From this viewpoint the antithesis between north and south appears to be compounded from many different elements having their origins outside France. The establishment of connections with distant places in early times created paths along which ideas, people and materials have been transferred and from which different regions have acquired their distinctive traits.[10]

In several regional monographs, the regions under study are identified largely in terms of their physical attributes. Demangeon (1905) defines Picardy not in terms of its cultural characteristics but as a flat, chalk upland with few surface streams, bounded on all sides by well-watered lowlands. The region is subdivided by lithological differences in the superficial deposits, separating limon in the east from clay-with-flints in the west. No tests are made to find how far divisions based on structure, soils and drainage fit areal differences in settlement types and field systems more closely than divisions based on other criteria, nor is it proved that differences in physical phenomena are directly and invariably related to cultural features. Moreover, Demangeon's thesis largely ignores the history of the name 'Picardy' and fails to explore its changing usage through time. The meanings and derivations of *pays* names in neighbouring areas in the Paris basin are examined in a critical study by Gallois (1908). That study, based on a wealth of literary and cartographic evidence, throws light on the diverse origins of geographical names and it also indicates that the concept of natural regions has been developed only in very recent times. It prepares us to expect that areas occupied by traditional agrarian systems will change from time to time and will transgress boundaries drawn from geological maps.

Dion (1934) remarks on the coincidence between the extent of the limon-covered plateaux with their deep, easily worked soils, and the furthest limits of the medieval three-field system, (Fig. 5.2). He points out that the coincidence is far from perfect. Waterlogged lands in the Woëvre and in Thiérache as well as waterless limon-covered uplands once lay within the domain of the three-field system. Conversely, on light soils in Berry and the Causses medieval settlements were dispersed and a two-year course of cropping was followed. In the Mediterranean region, Jules Sion (1934) observes that the irregular shapes, sizes and distribution of fields are reflected in the extreme diversity of relief and soils. Fields appear to have been taken piecemeal from the edges of mountain-girt basins, leaving barren *garrigues* between them. That pattern is associated with a dispersal of settlements and a lack of cohesiveness in the arrangement of their territories. Both Sion and Dion treat these apparent coincidences with the utmost reserve, taking care to point out the tenuous nature of the connections between physical settings and man-made features in the landscape. The areas under review are too extensive and complex in their physical characteristics to permit generalization. Nor is one single explanation adequate to account for the divergences.

Cultural Divisions

Cultural relationships are much stronger and closer than relationships between culture and environment. As soon as we think of le Midi as a dialect province the horizon rises beyond the narrow confines of the Mediterranean fringe. *Langue d'oc* is spoken as far north as the Gironde, to the northern edge of the Massif Central, as far as Lyons, up the Rhône to Lake Geneva (Fig. 5.3). The difference between north and south is indicated by the way 'yes' is pronounced. A northerner says 'oui' or 'oïl', a contraction of the Latin 'hoc illud' meaning 'even this', 'even so', 'yea'; a southerner affirms briefly with the word 'oc' from the Latin 'hoc'; hence the two speech forms are called *langue d'oïl* and *langue d'oc* (see Chapter 2). The significance of the division is that it separates the deeply latinized part of France from Parisian France. It could be, although clear, confirmatory evidence is lacking, a result of territories being occupied by peoples who originally spoke different languages.

This is where a false trail begins, followed to the point of absurdity by Augustin Thierry (1853), who interpreted the whole history of France as a prolonged conflict between 'two races of men, two societies which had nothing in common but religion, united by force, and face to face in one political grouping'.[11] The

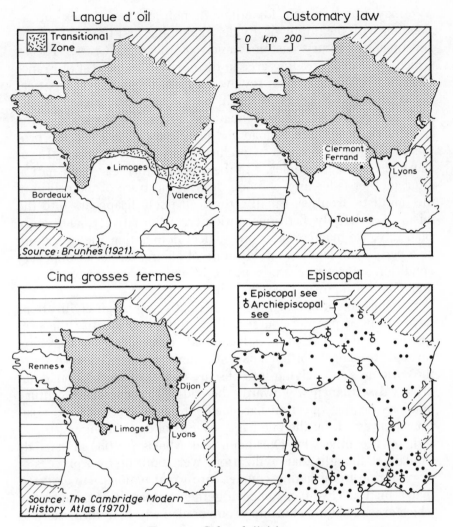

F ɪ ɢ. 5.3. Cultural divisions.
Top left: stippled, dominantly *Langue d'oïl*, granular, intermixed *Langue d'oïl*
and *Langue d'oc*; top right: stippled, customary law prevailed in 1789; bottom
left: stippled, Colbert's customs union of Cinq grosses fermes; bottom right:
sees of bishops and archbishops.

argument contains two fatal errors: first, that hostile nations ever
confronted each other across this language barrier and, secondly,
that in all later times succeeding occupants perpetuated the division by occupying exactly the same territory as their predecessors.

We may search in vain for ethnic or political boundaries corresponding with the linguistic divide, examining first the limits of the
seventeenth century customs union of the *Cinq Grosses Fermes*
which separated a trading area in the north from the rest of France
(Fig. 5.3). We may then review, in turn, the medieval frontiers
between Anglo-Normans, French, Burgundians and Flemings, the
dark age realms of Gallo-Roman and Frankish colonization, the
tribal divisions within Roman and pre-Roman Gaul, and the provinces allegedly occupied in prehistory by partly mythical Ligurian and Danubian peoples.[12] In the course of this search one nation
after another fades into oblivion, leaving no trace of the origin of
the linguistic frontier. Finally, the trail itself disappears into the
mists of a largely fictitious antiquity. Alternatively, and more
plausibly, we may consider one dialect dominating the other, not
as a permanent and immutable state of affairs, but as a temporary
condition subject to changes in the balance of demographic forces
and of political power (see Chapter 2).

Searches for ethnic origins of distinctive agrarian civilizations
have followed parallel courses. The attempt to identify the pro-
genitors of different cultures has failed repeatedly after searching
through the annals of feudalism, through fragmentary records of
the dark ages and delving into obscure depths of speculation about
primeval settlements. Towards the end of the nineteenth century
opinions on this question hardened into two irreconcilable positions expressed, on the one hand, by Fustel de Coulanges (1923)
and, on the other, by Durkheim and Mauss (1903). Fustel de
Coulanges thought that civilizations were built up by a process of
aggregation from mating couples into great nations. He asserted
that a man and woman joined together to form a nuclear family
which extended into a kinship group or clan which, in turn, merged
with other clans into a tribe which might ally itself with other
tribes to form a nation.[13] The hypothesis implies that the partners
to the first marriage belonged neither to clan, nor tribe, nor nation
and that they owed allegiance to no larger group than their own.
Both logically and empirically it fails to explain how a nation came
to speak a common language, how a tribe came to possess a continuously bounded territory, or how a formerly independent family
came to hold strips of land scattered through the fields of a commune.

Emile Durkheim, on the other hand, asserts that primeval societies were large, uniting all who spoke a common language, who held the same traditions, and who shared a sense of ethnic identity. And if, after such a primeval society had been formed, parts of it were detached or incorporated in another society, its members might at some later time reassert their identity and seek to be reunited. For Durkheim (1903), nineteenth-century nationalism and the struggle for self-determination were manifestations of this 'remembrance, an echo of an ancient sentiment which had never disappeared' (pp. 49–50). Panslavism has existed since the beginning of Slav societies, and ancient Gaul, although split into warring tribes, was instantly mobilized under Vercingetorix to resist a Roman invasion. Modern history, however, furnishes many contrary examples. Bretons abandoned their native language, Huguenots fled the country of their birth and revolution swept away a few ancestral traditions and expelled a few émigrés. Other weaknesses in the hypothesis are more fundamental. The origins of languages, traditions and ethnic identity are left unaccounted for, and also it is presumed that national consciousness does not change its modes of expression through time.

A few intrepid explorers in search of anonymous tribes who might have been responsible for organizing the earliest prototypes of modern field systems have invaded the realms of prehistory. Ignoring a warning from Bloch (1954) that

'the explanation of the very recent in terms of the remotest past has sometimes dominated our studies to the point of hypnosis' (p. 29),

they have persevered in their quest. Even such an austere critic as Jullian, whose writings are untainted by fanciful guesswork, whilst expressing surprise at the precocity of the enterprise, assigns to the early part of the first millenium B.C. the task of draining the Limagne. He concludes that newly-arrived groups of Indo-Europeans must have carried out the work,

'which transformed an immense marsh into a wonderful land, the pride of France. It was no mean or trifling work of an isolated hand, but a task undertaken by thousands of men together

on thousands of acres, a systematic attack upon the marsh'
(Jullian, 1922, 86).

In Burgundy, almost all waste lands had been cleared by Gallo-
Roman times, and there was little room for further expansion.
With few exceptions all rural settlements must have originated
at some earlier date and Deléage (1941) is drawn to prehistory
to account for the contrast between northern and southern forms.
He attributes to Neolithic and early Bronze Age dolmen builders
from Spain the founding of scattered hamlets in south west Burgundy, and to Bronze Age and Halstatt tumulus builders from
central Europe the founding of large compact villages in the north-
east. Successive invasions by societies organized on a familial
basis and on a tribal basis created, first, a land of hamlets and,
later, a land of villages. In the southern Jura Lebeau (1955)
reaches a similar conclusion from comparable evidence. In the
north of the region, in Haut-Bugey, openfields and massive villages
are considered to be the work of Hallstatt Celts, whilst in the
south, in the basin of Belley and in the Rhône valley, Bronze Age
Ligurians founded small hamlets. In all these places, we need to
know a great deal more about the vicissitudes of intervening history before we can be certain that differences in present day agrarian landscapes are related to the distribution of prehistoric
dolmens and tumuli, or before we can associate a vast programme of
land reclamation with the arrival of Bronze Age settlers.

Nougier (1950a, b, 1959) attributes the major features of the
settlement pattern of the Paris basin to the coming of a well-
equipped, well-organized group of Neolithic peoples, the Cam-
pigniens. Having followed the loess deposits bordering the
northern edges of the Hercynian forests, they entered the limon-
covered uplands of northern France between 5000 and 3000 B.C.
They cleared the lightly wooded surfaces with their advanced tools,
billhooks, axes and mattocks, the flints for which were mined and
manufactured in large quantities in the Somme valley and elsewhere. By the beginning of the third millenium B.C., vast areas of
wastes had disappeared and almost all the land north of the Loire
had been settled. The countryside, as we now see it, had been called
into existence. The origins of field systems in Burgundy, according
to Champier (1952, 1956a) may be ascribed to two formative

epochs. The first is associated with the arrival of grain-growing La Tène people, who initiated an early openfield landscape in northern Burgundy. The second is associated with Halstattian pastoralists, who settled in what are now *bocage* lands in Bresse. This latter movement is remote from the events, which in more recent history, have led directly to the planting of hedges, not only in Bresse but also in southern parts of the Paris Basin. And several advances and retreats in limits of agricultural settlement have occurred since the primeval Neolithic colonization. The making of the rural landscape is largely the work of recent times, and, for lack of positive indications in the archaeological record, we should suspend judgement on the prehistory of differences between north and south.

The Legacy From Rome

When we look for other characteristics dividing le Nord from le Midi, we find a long-standing boundary between the jurisdiction of codified Roman law, the *droit écrit*, in the south, and the juris-diction of customary law, the *droit coutumier*, in the north (Fig. 5.3). The two legal systems differ in their methods of adjudicating disputes over property interests and inheritance. In the south, the rights of individuals are more securely protected than in the north, but individuals have fewer opportunities to share in governing communal activities. In the north, the community possesses ex-tensive powers to regulate the use that private individuals may make of their property. The contrast between southern indivi-dualism and northern collectivism is reflected in many aspects of rural life and, to some extent, differing ways of holding land in the two provinces. In the north, in the thirteenth century, many cul-tivators were bond tenants and even serfs were not forbidden to occupy parcels of land. In the south, most land was owned and occu-pied by free men and most medieval slaves were landless. Mano-rial courts in the north recognized many degrees of servitude and upheld many forms of feudal obligations scarcely known in the south. Southern customs accorded much greater autonomy to heads of households, subordinating women and children to positions of inferiority.

The vital formative period of southern individuality was the long period of Roman rule. Whence it derived not only language, literature and laws but a rich heritage of institutions and material structures. Fleure (1943) claims that 'southern France is in a rather special sense Roman France' (p. 28). Among its institutions, the Roman church continued to exert a profound influence and wielded great power until the end of the eighteenth century. Its strength was much more firmly established in the south than in the north. Southern dioceses and archdioceses were smaller, less populous and their clergy were more numerous than in the north (Fig. 5.3). Opposition was repressed wherever it arose, but heresy in the south was crushed with greater ferocity than dissent in the north. In secular affairs, however, southerners enjoyed about as much or as little freedom of expression as northerners. Southern universities were more precocious in their advancement of learning, their faculties were more cosmopolitan and their students were freer to run their own lives. In northern universities students were cloistered, collegiate and conservative. In building, the south followed the style of Byzantium and developed its own sturdy form of Romanesque. Walls were built in stone and roofed with rounded Roman tiles (Fig. 5.4). Gothic architecture and high-pitched roofs entered the south belatedly and in small amounts. All the purest and most majestic gothic cathedrals were built to the north of the Loire.

Romanization was more intense in the south than in the north, but that one difference is neither sufficient to explain the diversity of past and present agrarian structures nor to account for the persistent popular expression of northern and southern provincialism. Certainly the French are not alone among Europeans in their awareness of differences between north and south (Broek and Webb, 1968). Italy, Germany, the Scandinavian nations, Britain and other countries have experienced a similar sense of being divided and, within each division, further distinctions may be drawn between north and south as, for example, in Ireland, in Wales, in Scotland and in England, or, at a still smaller scale, between north and south in the Alps, in the Jura, in the Armorican peninsula or, indeed, between the right bank and the left bank of the Seine in Paris. A district, however small, carries a potentiality for splitting. We have only to scratch the surface of local pride to observe the rapid polarization of opinion and the arousal of provincial or parochial rivalries.

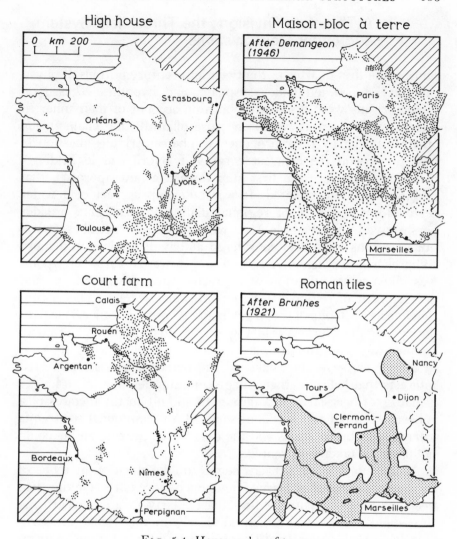

FIG. 5.4. House and roof types.
Top left: high house, living quarters above wine presses; top right: *maison bloc-à-terre*, dwelling and farm buildings under one roof, long house; bottom left: court farm, house and buildings arranged around farmyard; bottom right: Roman or hollow tiles prevalent.

A Threefold Division : the Three-field System and Other Field Systems

During the first quarter of the twentieth century notions of physical determinism fell under suspicion and hypotheses based on ethnic origins were discredited both on account of their inherent logical weaknesses as well as because of conflicting claims made on their behalf by their proponents. The underlying question of how to explain the contrast between le Nord and le Midi remain unanswered. As a first step toward a new approach, that question was reformulated. It was taken up as part of a wider search for the causes of regional distinctiveness. In a broader perspective le Nord and le Midi were viewed as special cases and other regions were also considered as having a place in a more comprehensive scheme. A second step towards a new viewpoint was taken when attention was directed towards the origins and development of regional variations in field systems. The disruptive effects of floods of cheap grain and torrents of other farm produce from the New World together with a persistent drain of people away from the land, accentuated by losses during the First World War, severely weakened the personal bonds and vested interests that held together village communities. It was no longer a matter of necessity for a farmer to submit to the dictates of a collective organization. The survival of communal restraints governing crop rotations and the exercise of grazing rights could no longer be taken for granted.

At the same time historians began to take stock of the scope of local customs and they learned how much more extensive they had been in the eighteenth century, particularly in areas where the three-field system was practised. Early in the 1930s these researches provided material for three new interpretations of agrarian civilizations. The studies had much in common. They each approached the problem from a historical point of view, tracing changes in the forms and functions of agrarian structures. They each focused attention on the three-field system as an archetypal structure in which the working of every component was finely balanced in relation to the workings of all other components. They each adopted a three-fold division of France instead of a simple two-fold division between north and south, but the three interpretations differ in the criteria they use for making their three-fold divisions.

Roger Dion's Regions of Collectivism, Individualism and Opportunism

Dion (1934) notes a basic contrast between *plaine* and the rest of France. The north is characterised as essentially the domain of openfield agriculture where triennial rotations and communal grazing practices are strictly followed. At the opposite extreme are areas where individualism prevails, where private interests are not tightly circumscribed by collective regulations, where cultivators enjoy the right to fence in land growing crops (*ager*) and where pastoralists graze their animals on the open range (*saltus*). He proceeds to show that the space between these two provinces is occupied by field systems in no way transitional in character, as Marc Bloch suggested, but differing in kind from both three-field land and *ager*-with-*saltus*. Whereas the northern province was more or less uniformly subject to a three-field system, the rest of France practised a diversity of systems, not closely related to one another. In contrast to the *grande culture* of the north and the intensively cultivated lands in the south, the intervening territories contain vast extents of poor soils and uncultivated wastes. They have more than their share of large estates, hunting forests, open heaths, marshes, moors and mountain grazings. The dispersion of settlements characteristic of these areas partly reflects their low densities of rural farm population and in some areas some dispersion may be associated with piece-meal colonization of the waste by squatters. Because its population is thinly scattered, because it pursues a variety of agricultural enterprises under a wide range of different physical conditions, the rest of France does not exhibit the social cohesiveness and identity of interest that unite farming communities in the north. The relationships between members of communities and their fields, farms and villages are nowhere as predictable or as purposeful as they are in the north.

The one common purpose to which all medieval farming systems were directed was to secure a harvest sufficient to ensure that the villagers had enough to eat through the year and to provide seed corn for the next crop. Yields expressed as quantities of grain per family or as returns on quantities of seed sown provide more relevant guides to productivity than yields per acre or returns on investment. In these terms, differences in field systems indicate differences in the capacities of different regions to produce regular and reliable harvests. As long as villages strove to maintain their self-sufficiency, traditional methods of minimizing the risks of harvest failure persisted. Field systems, in Dion's view, are devised to circumvent, as far as possible, local hazards of climate, soils and drainage.

A special characteristic differentiating the northern system from others was the vital part played by oxen or horses used as draught animals. Large teams were required to draw the heavy mould-board plough, the *charrue*, which ploughed long deep furrows and ridged up heavy soils to improve their drainage. In winter these animals had to be stall-fed on hay, oats and pulses. When almost all the land was brought under cultivation, hay was very precious and areas of meadowland were several times more valuable than arable land, but, in addition, it was necessary to devote a part of the field crops to supplement their feeding. The expansion of ploughed land at the expense of pasture could only be accomplished when essential grazing rights over the arable were strictly enforced. In the final analysis, the strength of the triennial system rested on the solidarity of village communities.

Marc Bloch's Regions of Regular Openfields, Irregular Openfields and *Bocage*

Bloch (1931) proposes a somewhat different three-fold division of France. For him, the northern openfields, *champs ouverts réguliers*, represent the most balanced arrangement of medieval fields. Openfields with squarish parcels, *champs ouverts irréguliers*, represent transitional forms and *bocage* is identified as former openfield land completely transformed by enclosure. Bloch shares with Dion the view that the primary objective of traditional farming was to produce enough bread for the villagers, enough fodder for the oxen and horses, enough seed corn for the next sowing and enough feed for the breeding flocks and herds. He reaches Dion's conclusion that they were systems for producing grain. Bloch analyses differences between systems in terms of the productivity of grains, of manure, of alternative crops and, not least, the productivity of their fallows. Such a comparison suggests how one element in a system might be substituted for another or how yields of one product might be increased at the expense of others. Ley grasses, legumes or root crops, for example, might replace bare fallows, and maize or potatoes introduced from the New World, might reduce the primacy of indigenous bread grains. Above all, the analysis suggests that divergent systems in which crops produced for sale freed communities from their dependence on home-grown grains also enabled them to dispense with communal restraints. In Provence, the vine, in Flanders, industrial crops, in Normandy, a variety of products provided commercial bases for new systems of agriculture associated with early enclosure and a struggle for individualism.

Bloch's treatment differs from that of Dion in being more historical. Bloch describes how changes have occurred in different field systems and how some systems are in the course of being transformed into others. It is not an entirely evolutionary interpretation in which all field systems may be classified as stages in a developing sequence beginning with pure openfield and culminating in *bocage*. Bloch, like Dion, acknowledges that changes may be retarded or arrested by local conditions. Systems finely adjusted to poor soils or harsh climates may be inflexible. Again, Bloch recognizes that a course of development may be deflected or reversed by a demographic catastrophe or by a technological revolution. The progress of medieval *défrichement* was interrupted at different times by foreign invasions, by local disorders, by famines and by plagues. And the development of modern agriculture has been profoundly affected by the introduction of machinery and by changing patterns of world food production and world trade. Change has proceeded fitfully by stops and starts and has frequently turned from its previous direction.

Gaston Roupnel's Division into Southern Individualism, Western *Bocage* and Northern *Campagne*

Roupnel, whose *Histoire de la campagne française* appeared in 1932,

is more concerned than either Dion or Bloch to provide a general
theory to explain the origin and development of differences in
agrarian civilizations. By contrast with this sparsely documented
treatise, the works of Dion and Bloch offer more detailed and more
realistic accounts of the ways in which land is used and of the
workings of agrarian institutions. Whereas Dion and Bloch
approach agrarian structures through the eyes of practical hus-
bandmen struggling to wrest their livings from stubborn soils
with imperfect tools, Roupnel looks for regularities in human
behaviour, seeking common patterns in response to environment.
Roupnel makes few references to primary sources, apart from
those drawn from his study of Dijonnais, citing documents in the
archives of the Côte d'Or (1922). Among authorities most frequently cited are general surveys of prehistory by Dechelette
(1908–12), Hubert (1932) and Jullian (1928). Several regional
monographs are mentioned in passing, and extensive use is made
of René Musset's *Le Bas Maine* (1917). Musset's thesis is
tightly constructed within an evolutionary framework, and Roupnel follows Musset in tracing the progressive elaboration of agrarian structures from the founding of settlements in primitive
wastes to the emergence of fully integrated field systems. The
process of *défrichement* provides a connecting link and Roupnel
regards historical discontinuities as temporary interruptions in the
process of expansion rather than as major breaks or reversals.
The forms of rural settlements are directly related to the earlier
disposition of woods, heaths and marshes. Roupnel (1932) asserts
that:

> 'clearing fashioned the village in its image, as it formed its
> utilization. The village was moulded by the shape of the clear-
> ing and constructed its ground plan on the nature of the land on
> which it was built' (p. 264).

He also considers that a field system attains its fully developed
form when the labour of clearing is completed and the limit of
cultivation has been reached. Over much of France a steady state
was achieved by the Bronze Age. Since then no further progress
has occurred but field systems have been modified or destroyed or,
in some places, restored after destruction.

Roupnel associates three types of agrarian structure with three different regions. To the south of the Massif Central, compact grouped villages are situated among fields of irregular shape and size. The layout reflects the diversity of terrain and the absence of communal restraints. To the west, in the Armorican massif and its borders, lies a country of dispersed settlements where most fields are enclosed and many are small. Across the Paris basin and throughout northern and eastern France a well-ordered system is dominant. Rural population is concentrated in villages which are surrounded on all sides by unenclosed cultivated land. The land is divided into numerous long thin parallel strips grouped in massive blocks. This arrangement of parcels is associated with the practice of triennial fallowing and *vaine pâture*.

According to Roupnel's interpretation, true *campagne* and communal organization both originated in pre-Celtic times. But the evidence he offers for such early foundations is not strong enough to allow us to disregard the disruptive effects of later population changes. Whether we consider the quantities of food that had to be produced to feed increasing numbers in the early Middle Ages or whether we turn our attention to the contraction of arable that accompanied population decline in the late Middle Ages, we observe everywhere a need to change agrarian structures. Roupnel's thesis demands evidence for stability continuing for a very long period of time. From our present knowledge of historical records, we cannot be certain whether or not a three-field system existed before the thirteenth century, nearly two thousand years after the arrival in Gaul of the Celts. On the other hand, it is clear from medieval documents and from early maps and plans that not all parts of France passed through a succession of stages from waste to *bocage* to *plaine*. In the west, *bocage* frequently succeeded *plaine* as a result of enclosure and in some areas openfields were carved directly from the waste (see Chapter 9). The best that can be said about Roupnel's history is that it presents an extremely simplified view of the processes at work and it poses a challenge to other scholars to find alternative explanations.

Agrarian Structures in Transition

The revision of agrarian history initiated in the 1930s by the essays of Dion, Bloch and Roupnel focused discussion on two topics.

First, having replaced a two-fold regional division with a three-fold regional division, there arose a question of defining three regions or of adding further regions. Secondly, having discarded the views that distinctive agrarian civilizations were generated by the nature of the soil or by the genius of different ethnic groups, speculation was set free. A fresh search for origins could range freely over time back to the Neolithic and unconfined in space across the western end of the old world (Childe, 1931; Clark, 1952). And, significantly from a historical viewpoint, relations between different types of agrarian structures could be examined with impartiality.

The idea expressed by Roupnel that agrarian structures might be arranged in an evolutionary progression advancing towards the most orderly and fully articulated three-field system is disputed by Faucher (1934). Southern polyculture, he claims, is in no way less developed and cannot be explained as an antecedent stage in the development of northern three-field arrangements. Southern land use patterns are more durable because it is difficult to transplant olive groves, vineyards, orchards and to rebuild irrigation works, terraces and walled gardens. Nor may biennial fallowing be interpreted as an indication of inferior standards of husbandry. It is a necessity imposed by the vagaries of summer drought and scorching heat. Northern farmers need take no precautions to conserve soil moisture, they may expect greater returns from winter sown grains than from spring sown grains, and they may be unable to turn their livestock to graze outdoors over the fallow land in winter time, but southern farmers must manage their land under these conditions. Farming methods are not transferable and there appears to be little likelihood that a three-field system could have evolved out of a primitive southern system.

Discussion is also focused on agrarian structures in the area lying between north and south. If northern and southern field systems are expressions of independent agrarian civilizations, the middle ground may be a transitional zone in which elements from both are intermixed. Early medieval evidence for triennial rotations and communal grazing in the *campagne* of Berry has been presented by Gay (1958, 1959), and enclaves of openfields have been traced as far south as the valleys of the Dordogne and the Lot by Fenélon (1955, 1959). In the west, André Meynier and his students have demonstrated how *bocage* may be integrated with *plaine* (see Chapter 9). Champier (1956b) notes that:

> 'in predominantly enclosed regions "islands" of openfield alternated with stretches that were defended by field boundaries. *Bocage* and *champagne* are thus not incompatible and can even co-exist in the territory of a single village' (p. 321).

Combinations of open and enclosed fields may be observed in many other parts of western and central France (Juillard *et al.*, 1957, pp. 55–97). A question that arises is how many subdivisions are required to accommodate all the variations in field systems to be found between Brittany and the Alps. On the other hand, the middle ground, as Dion suggests, may be presided over by a truly autonomous but poorly endowed agrarian civilization. The most distinctive characteristics of the area are its lack of nucleated villages, its vast tracts of waste and its constricted patches of highly productive soils such as the Val de Loire, the Limagne, and the southern Jura. North and south perhaps have more in common with each other than with the intervening territory. An inventory of a quarter of century's research, published in 1957, divides France into three parts: the openfield landscape of the north and east, the mostly *bocage* landscapes of western France, and the agrarian landscapes of the Mediterranean (Juillard, *et al.* 1957). In a search for origins, the trail leading back to the Neolithic continues to be followed resolutely by Nougier (1950a and b) and others acknowledge the formative influence of pioneer farming on the subsequent development of rural settlements. For Deléage (1941), Champier (1952), Roblin (1951) and Lebeau (1955) that beginning did not occur until late Bronze Age or Halstatt times, since when the structures erected on the earliest foundations have been altered many times. Both Bloch and Dion are cautious in drawing inferences about the remote past and Bloch's regressive method, of proceeding from evidence of the better known present through the less well known past towards obscure origins, serves to concentrate attention on modern and medieval history. To account for many present day settlements it is hardly necessary to go back as far as Gallo-Roman times. The first settlements on the plateau of Beauce were not established until the dark ages (Bloch, 1939). In upland Brie there were no villages until the eleventh

century (Brunet, 1960). In Bordelais the early pattern of settlements was almost entirely destroyed in the course of the Hundred
Years' War (Boutruche, 1947) and in Dijonnais villages were
built anew after the Thirty Years' War (Roupnel, 1932). In the
settlement history of the middle Garonne the most important
changes took place in the eighteenth and nineteenth centuries
(Deffontaines, 1932) whilst much of the rural geography of the
plain of Alsace may be explained by events occurring since 1800
(Juillard, 1953). The history, especially of recent times, of the
territory between north and south now takes on a fresh significance. On the poorest soils, little change, other than a mass exodus
of population, is possible and that may be achieved only slowly,
but on the most productive soils agrarian structures may be
changed rapidly. They are more vulnerable than in localities enjoying economic security or where traditions are deeply entrenched. Viticulture, for example, is more precarious in the Val
de Loire, in the Limagne and in the Jura than it is in either
Languedoc and Bordeaux in the south or in Alsace and Champagne
in the north. Agricultural improvements in the marginal environments of the Dombes, in the Sologne and in the Vendée were
carried out more swiftly than in other parts of France and agricultural depression struck the Limagne and the southern Jura
more forcefully than elsewhere. To understand the agrarian landscapes in these areas we cannot appeal to immemorial traditions or
to an unbroken continuity of development. Instead, we must
follow closely the history of modern times and observe the alternate strengthening and weakening of connections with the south
and the north. Lebeau (1955) has examined the vicissitudes of
agrarian change in the southern Jura (Fig. 5.5) and Derruau
(1949) has studied the Grande Limagne, a particularly illuminating area in which to trace the interplay of northern and southern
elements in the rural landscape.

Mediterranean Features in the Limagnes

If a southerner were searching France for Mediterranean habitats,
he would hardly expect to find what he was seeking in the interior
of the Massif Central, in basins drained by the north-flowing Loire
and Allier. But landscapes distinctly Mediterranean in appearance

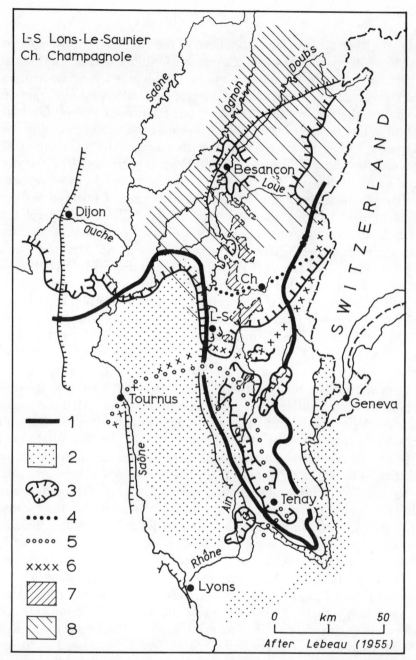

L-S Lons-Le-Saunier
Ch. Champagnole

FIG. 5.5. Cultural divides in the southern Jura. (1) southern limit of open fields; (2) *bocage* country; (3) southern limit of nucleated settlements; (4) southern limit of great farmsteads; (5) northern limit of hollow tiles; (6) northern limit of Provençal dialects; (7) place-name element—*ans* most numerous; (8) place-name element—*ans* fairly common.

survive over 300 km from the shore of the Mediterranean, reached by tortuous ways across the Cévennes. Unlike the true south these districts are more than 300 m above sea level, experience winters too severe for the growth of olives, and receive more rain in summer than in winter (Arbos, 1931; Derruau, 1949; Gachon, 1939). The basins of the upper Allier and the southern half of the Grande Limagne are crowded with monuments of prehistoric occupation and with relics of Gallo-Roman antiquity. But it is not the ruins of classical civilization so much as the form of present villages which recall the Mediterranean scene. Clustered tightly around Romanesque churches they crown hilltops and perch on ledges above miniature plains and valleys. Some, surrounded by medieval ramparts, have the acropolis form of Mediterranean cities. More like towns than villages, they are aptly styled *bourgades*. Closely huddled together are tall houses whose white walls, small windows and red roofs rise one above another to the culminating height of a church tower. The roofs are low-pitched and tiled with Mediterranean hollow tiles (Arbos, 1930). The architectonic piles of stone buildings, hewn out of grey andesite, the geometric rectitude of the vaulting and the purity of the classical motifs proclaim their Mediterranean affinities. Beyond these compact villages are fresh reminders of Mediterranean scenes. With the volcanic peaks of the Chaîne des Puys looming in the background, the terraced slopes and the minutely subdivided parcels of crop land on the plain look like parts of Provence or Attica. The sight of skiers on the snow-covered slopes of Mont Dore in April, the sombre mantle of spruce and pinewood over the lower slopes, the swift-flowing streams cascading to the plains, the freshness of summer meadows and fields of ripening maize, tobacco, potatoes and sugar beet lend an alpine aspect to the scene, but the agrarian structures are Mediterranean in their composition. The summits of the Auvergne are bare of trees, the bald-headed mountains of France, in this respect resembling the Maritime Alps more closely than either the Jura or the Vosges. The uplands are devoted exclusively to livestock husbandry, the highest pastures being used as summer grazings, winter feed being raised on lower land. The lowest slopes, facing the sun, are planted with vines, nuts, peaches, apricots, interplanted with a great variety of crops. Garden-sized plots of land tended by hand, are elaborately terraced as in le Midi. In the Grande Limagne the amount of precipitation received is scarcely sufficient to support plant growth without the aid of irrigation and other means of moisture conservation.

Ancient Links with the South Preserved

Whilst the Limagnes were not especially predisposed by virtue of their physical geography to become a home for Mediterranean culture, they were brought into cultivation at an early date by settlers who began to arrive in Neolithic times and were succeeded by pioneer farmers during the Bronze Age and early Iron Age. The district was colonized at a time when Lorraine and the country to the north of the Loire was still largely uncleared woodland (Grenier, 1931, 1934, 1958). Throughout the Gallo-Roman epoch it supported a dense and increasing population. Unlike other areas that were repeatedly devastated and depopulated, it enjoyed long periods of peace and prosperity. Villas and villages expanded in size and towns flourished. The district remained somewhat isolated and was little disturbed by the strife and turmoil following the break-up of the Roman empire. The ancient social order was preserved, the dead continued to be buried in ancestral burial grounds, and old place-names survived. Farmers continued to practise traditional methods and newcomers were absorbed into established communities without upsetting the old culture. The Roman way of life more than held its own. Christianity was well established before the fall of Rome and new land and new adherents were converted by monastic colonization. Not only was the boundary of *langue d'oc* pushed northward but the cultivation of vines advanced in the same direction and the use of hollow tiles reached Bourbonnais before the end of the fifteenth century (Dauzat, 1939; Guyot, 1868). The hollow tile, indeed, was taken beyond its useful limit into the mountains of the Auvergne. There, low-pitched roofs are unable to shed heavy loads of snow and slightly higher-pitched roofs are unable to hold hollow tiles. On some roofs the tiles have to be held in place by ropes weighted down with rocks. Here we may observe a southern artifact manifestly unsuited to these inhospitable climates (Estienne, 1953).

Throughout the Middle Ages the province of Auvergne remained steadfastly southern. The linguistic boundary of *langue*

d'oc extended to the northern edge of the Massif Central and
crossed the Limagne between St. Pourçain and Randan (Brun,
1936). Its eastward extension into Forez and between the upper
Loire and the Rhône was less well-defined, broadening into a zone
of transition where neither speech form was dominant (Fig. 5.6).

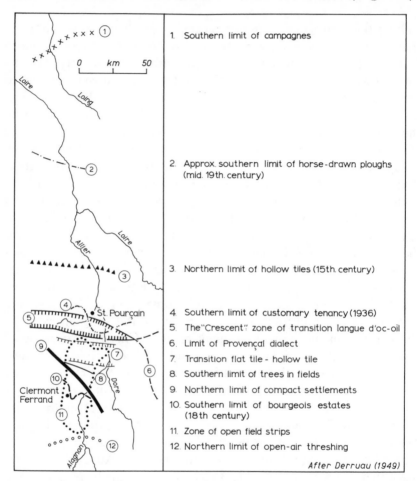

1. Southern limit of campagnes

2. Approx. southern limit of horse-drawn ploughs
    (mid. 19th. century)

3. Northern limit of hollow tiles (15th. century)

4. Southern limit of customary tenancy (1936)
5. The "Crescent" zone of transition langue d'oc-oïl
6. Limit of Provençal dialect
7. Transition flat tile - hollow tile
8. Southern limit of trees in fields
9. Northern limit of compact settlements
10. Southern limit of bourgeois estates
    (18th century)
11. Zone of open field strips
12. Northern limit of open-air threshing

After Derruau (1949)

FIG. 5.6. Cultural divides in the Limagnes of the Auvergne and Bourbonnais.

The church maintained and increased its power, unshaken by the
heresies which elsewhere weakened its authority. Neither Bogo-
mils nor Albigensians were strong enough to confront it with a
serious challenge. At the height of its ascendancy from 900 to 1200

many new churches were built. They were designed in the Roman-esque not in the Gothic style, affirming a continuing allegiance to a southern heritage. Politically, Auvergne succeeded in avoiding the grasp of an assertive French monarchy. A customs barrier on the road between Riom and Clermont separated Colbert's union of the *Cinq grosses fermes* from the territories *réputés étrangers* (Rigodon, 1944).

Independent provincial intendants imposed their own widely detested duties on salt (*gabelles*) and raised their own land and property taxes (*tailles*) (Jalenques, 1929; Mège, 1897–98). The imposition of taxes was hardly calculated to win approval for self-government but the contemplation of surrendering those powers to Parisian officials or to their agents was an infallible deterrent. Until the end of the *ancien régime*, the province enjoyed, or suffered, some measure of financial autonomy and, in resisting the centripetal power of the monarchy, it maintained friendly relations with other southern provinces.

The effect of the Revolution was to reduce the differences between the north and south.[14] The customs barrier of the *ancien régime* was removed. Regional autonomy and provincial assemblies were dissolved. The central government set up *départements* of similar area and population as units of local administration. *Langue d'oïl* was introduced as the official medium of instruction in schools. The Code Napoléon, embodying the principles of Roman law, was a concession to the south. Local customs lost their legal authority and customary weights and measures were superseded by standardized metric units. The regulation of communal grazing, the enforcement of fallowing, the prohibition of enclosure could no longer be upheld by the courts. Private property was encumbered by a minimum of communal restraints. Partible inheritance was legalised. The opportunity to reorganise ancient field arrangements was now open and the subdivision of holdings among heirs was made obligatory for northerners as well as southerners. On balance, southern institutions were changed less radically than those of the north.

The Revolution broke down the provincialism of the Auvergne and opened new channels to widening markets. With the commercialization of agriculture the south, to a greater extent than the north, and in particular formerly isolated districts within the south, enjoyed a revival of prosperity. Districts such as the Limagnes were able to sell more, grow more and feed more people. During the early years of the nineteenth century they remained largely self-sufficient in grain production whilst producing and processing increasing quantities of fruit. The vine, above all, contributed the largest share to farmers' earnings. Later in the century and for a brief period sugar beet was the most profitable cash crop grown in the northern Limagne, but all these activities ceased to be profitable in times of depression.

Northerly Field Systems in the *Plaine Marneuse*

To this picture of unity and uniformity and southern hegemony a note of reservation must be added. Whilst the mountains of Auvergne and Forez appeared more like those of the south than of the north, whilst the greater part of the Grande Limagne possesses more southern than northern features, notably in the *buttes* and in the *varennes*, the *plaine marneuse* is exceptional (Fig. 5.7). A northerner coming to it for the first time in the sixteenth century, would have observed the resemblance with the plain of Alsace (Juillard, 1953). An area of northern *campagne* landscape occupied the floor of the rift valley. Compact nucleated villages were surrounded by open arable fields. The arable land, minutely subdivided into long narrow strips, stretched without interruption from one village to the next. Trackways, ditches, lines of willows are the only boundaries marked on the ground. As in Alsace, *crêtes de labour* rise towards the headlands, clearly tracing the passage of heavy mould-board ploughs drawn by teams of oxen or horses (Imberdis, 1951; Hartke, 1954). It is not easy to account for these features as direct importations from northern regions. There are few Germanic place-name elements, as in Beauce or Poitou (Dauzat, 1939). There is no clear evidence of secondary colonization by northern people. Piecemeal intakes produced a *bocage* landscape not openfields. Nor, as happened in Burgundy after the Thirty Years' War, was the agrarian landscape reconstructed around rebuilt villages. But, whereas in surrounding districts law was administered from written codes, in this area unwritten local custom had the force of law. The origins of this peculiar distinction are obscure.

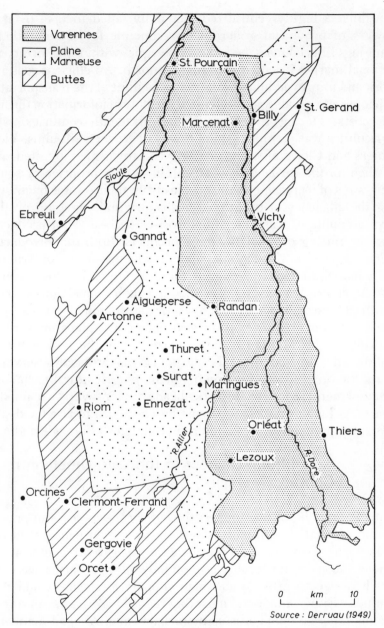

FIG. 5.7. Physiographic regions of the Grande Limagne.

Whilst a highly centralized monarchy failed to take over the powers of provincial government, economic forces succeeded in bringing Bourbonnais and the Auvergne within the orbit of a national market oriented towards the north. An efficient road network and improved inland waterways facilitated the transportation of people and goods and accelerated the flow of information through the posts. During the fifteenth and sixteenth centuries, when agriculture was stagnating, the towns of Nevers, Moulins, Vichy, Thiers and Clermont were growing and townsmen invested some of their profits in landed estates. These new proprietors sought new ways of increasing their incomes from their estates by improving the efficiency of traditional husbandry and engaging on their own accounts in commercial enterprises such as wool production and the raising of other livestock products. Both the introduction of new agricultural techniques and also the marketing of farm produce had the effect of bringing these estates into closer contact with northern France and of weakening their connections with the south. Horses displaced oxen as draught animals whilst farm buildings were rebuilt on northern open court plans or were improved by the addition of large barns or by the replacement of hollow tiles by flat tiles. These bourgeois properties served as outposts for the dissemination of northern agricultural techniques. But northernization made little headway for over two hundred years. As long as population densities continued to rise the district remained predominantly southern in character (Figs. 5.8 and 5.9).

Agricultural Distress in the Late Nineteenth Century

Until the middle of the nineteenth century the increase in population is associated with increasing dependence on wine production and on fruit growing. By 1870 the area was grossly overcrowded. Under the most favourable economic conditions farms were too small in size to provide adequate support for farmers and their families. Either numbers must be reduced or fresh sources of income must be found seasonally or part-time. A small number of people were able to supplement their incomes by taking up industrial employment. Quarrying for building stones and gravel, glass making, cutlery, carpet weaving, papermaking, and other

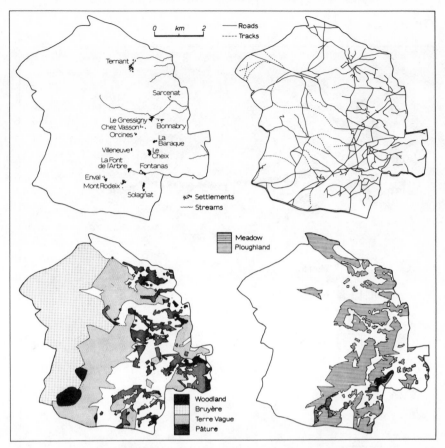

FIG. 5.8. Orcines in the mountains of the Auvergne.
Top left: settlements; top right: roads and tracks; bottom left: woods and pastures, unimproved land; bottom right: arable and meadow, cultivated land.
Source: Old cadaster (Archives Départementales du Puy-de-Dôme).

seasonal occupations relieved pressure on subsistence and also brought back money from sources outside the locality. Seasonal migration was often a prelude to long-term and permanent moves. In the last quarter of the nineteenth century migration increased in volume, in duration and in distance.

At the end of the nineteenth century the economic basis of commercial agriculture suffered a series of setbacks. After 1870 grain imported from the New World caused a disastrous fall in the prices of crops. Vineyards were spared the first outbreak of phylloxera in the 1880s but when it appeared among the vines in the closing years of the century its effect was devastating. The crisis when it came caused migration to rise to a mass exodus. In the

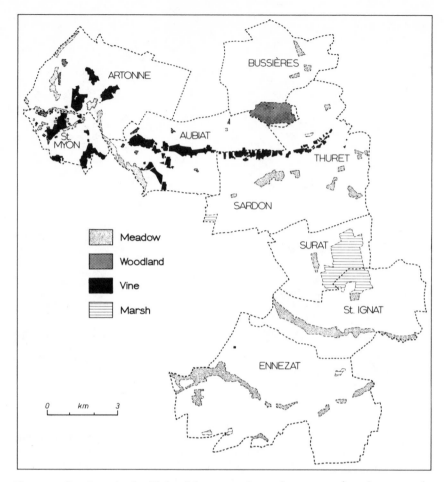

FIG. 5.9. Land use in the Plaine Marneuse. Apart from a marsh and two woods, the entire territory of these *communes* was under cultivation at the beginning of the nineteenth century. The ploughland (most of the blank area) is crossed by long ribbons of meadow and by a ridge planted with vines. *Source: Old cadaster (Archives Départementales du Puy-de-Dôme).*

interwar years farms were abandoned, land fell derelict and the population of several communes was halved between 1891 and 1936. Vineyards were overgrown with scrub; ploughed land was converted to grass or sown with fodder crops and ley grasses; new crops were introduced; potatoes and mangolds replaced sugar beet. The call was for diversification of enterprises and for amalgamation of holdings. Curiously little cooperation was achieved either in marketing farm produce or in purchasing stocks of fertilizers, and very little consolidation of scattered holdings was accomplished. A large number of absentee owners rented their farms to neighbours but this did not involve any large-scale or lasting change in field or farm boundaries.

The south became a chronically distressed area. Everywhere the margin of cultivation retreated and signs of decay appeared in every village although not to the extent of causing entire villages to be deserted. Dry stone walls and terraces crumbled for want of regular attention. Roofs fell in and the traditional hollow tiles were not replaced. Pantiles and corrugated iron were used as substitutes. The effect of the agricultural depression was to give a new value to the northern *bocage*. That is not to say that farming prospered. The polish largely went out of it. *Châteaux* fell into disrepair or stood empty, farms fell vacant, ponds and ditches were left unscoured for years. Hedges were neglected, eventually being cut down altogether with sheltering trees in the fields. But livestock numbers were maintained.

The history of agriculture in the Auvergne follows a course familiar to those acquainted with events in other parts of western Europe and in the rest of the world. The sequence of events is broadly predictable but the impact of particular events is peculiar to the locality. The peopling of the Limagne, the clearing and draining of the *plaine marneuse*, as in Provence, in the plain of Alsace or in the valley of the Somme, occurred much earlier than in surrounding districts. For over one thousand years including the whole of the Gallo-Roman period population growth and the extension of cultivation continued with few setbacks. During the ensuing dark ages the area was spared the worst ravages of invasion. Newcomers settled peacefully where there was space for them and, having fortified their *bourgades*, set about tending their vines and irrigating their meadows (Figs. 5.10 and 5.11). They were able to withstand occasional assaults by aggressive neighbours and for over a thousand years resisted insidious pressures exerted by a centralizing monarchy in Paris. The Revolution itself secured southern forms of land tenure and inheritance and ensured that southern civilization would survive as long as the vine and grain growing were able to sustain population growth. The depression of agricultural prices and the destruction of vines by

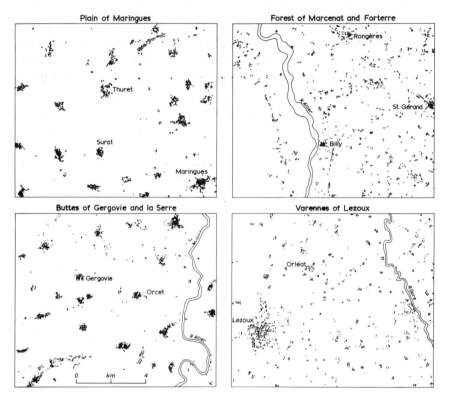

FIG. 5.10. Settlement types in the Grande Limagne.
Top left: large compact villages with no isolated farms in the *plaine marneuse*; top right: widely spaced hamlets and isolated farms in the northern forested *Varennes*; bottom left: walled hilltop *bourgades* in the *buttes* to the south of Clermont-Ferrand; bottom right: dispersed farmsteads, small hamlets and loosely agglomerated town of Lezoux in southern pastoral *Varennes*.
Source: Carte d'Etat Major.

phylloxera was followed by a mass exodus of people and a decay of southern agrarian institutions. Under these conditions livestock farming and some new types of crop husbandry were the only enterprises that remained profitable. Northern agrarian structures were more resilient than southern structures and survived in the storm.

The agrarian history of the Limagnes as recounted by Max Derruau (1949) explains how regional boundaries shift from time to time. The essence of the new approach to the study of regions is to be aware of change rather than of fixity.

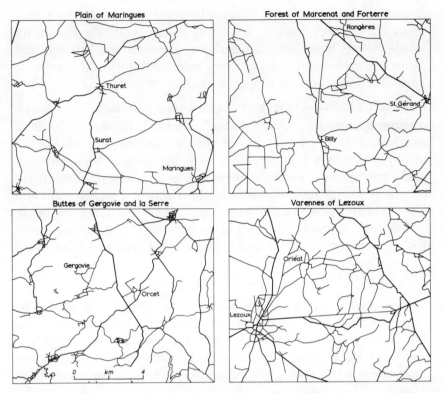

FIG. 5.11. Road networks in the Grande Limagne.
Top left: roads and tracks radiating from village centres to outlying fields;
top right: major roads cut straight through forest; minor roads linking farms;
bottom left: major roads avoiding *bourgades*; local roads centred upon *bourgades*;
bottom right: major roads cut straight through *Varennes*; minor roads connecting farms and hamlets. *Source: Carte d'Etat Major.*

Agrarian Structures as Systems

In a seminal paper, Cholley (1946) outlined the value of what
would now be recognised as a 'systemic' approach to the study of
agrarian structures. Such structures were themselves 'systems'
(*combinaisons*), operated by physical, biological and human
agencies. The relative significance of different components would,
of course, change with the passing of time, but Cholley argued
that at all times they were bound together indissolubly. Many
authors have identified such factors and have attempted to inte-
grate their actions into a dynamic account of the genesis of
agrarian structures. Dion maintains that:

'rural landscapes are not a direct legacy from a mysterious pre-historic culture; we can see them being established little by little, being born from a marriage of nature and history, and then being changed as technology and social, juridical, economic and demographic conditions also change'.[15]

Meynier's (1958) synopsis of basic themes is remarkably similar, comprising mental, social, juridical, political, natural and ethnic factors, each of which may be sub-divided and re-ordered. Hartke (1951) presents a comparable array. Interaction between such factors conditions a settler's perception and his use of physical resources including such elements as climate, water supply, soil and slope, which themselves change through time as well as being modified by human action. The net result is an amalgam of agrarian structures within which agricultural production and rural life are organized.

Meynier (1966), writing of Brittany, observes that:

'the essential feature in the whole of our province seems to be the establishment of small groups, clearing patches of moorland or woodland without any preconceived plan around farmsteads or hamlets, creating elliptical areas of cultivation varying in size according to the numerical strength of the settling group', (p. 608).

In all regions, initial phases of land occupation produce somewhat similar clearings and it is subsequent modifications that bring about differences in modern rural landscapes. Juillard *et al.* (1957) argue that when studying agrarian structures:

'none of the factors involved should be neglected; the dogma of immutability of agrarian systems cannot be upheld seriously, nor can that of the perennial nature of the cultural landscape; the physical environment should not be underestimated, nor should aspects of social evolution' (p. 165).

Such an integrated approach imposes demands on all branches of a geographer's skill. The use of a checklist of the kind suggested by Meynier (1958) might offer new coherence for further studies and allow past enquiries to be reappraised.

It is valuable to look outside the period, region and nation under scrutiny to seek new ideas and approaches. Cross-cultural and cross-temporal comparisons between rural patterns in modern tropical Africa and those in Europe in the past have proved to be highly suggestive (Sautter, 1962). Rural research in the Germanic lands has generated fresh ideas that might be employed usefully in examining French evidence (Mayhew, 1973). In particular, two lines of enquiry await further exploration (Brunet, 1954). The first is to study in detail the early phases of occupying different settlement sites and different patches of land and to examine forms of management devised to ensure the survival of settlers during their first seasons. Uhlig's (1961) comparative survey of hamlets and foci of cultivation throughout north-western Europe indicates the value of extending the inquiry to areas of France where large nucleations and openfields now prevail but where formerly very different structures may have existed. The possibility that discontinuities in agricultural history may have been much deeper than is generally acknowledged in France is also suggested by recent work in Germany and forms the second line of enquiry. Modern rural landscapes may not have developed continuously from an initial form but may have arisen from a completely fresh arrangement superimposed on previous structures at some period, or periods, in the past. Krenzlin, Niemeier and Jäger have shown that in the Germanic lands many hamlets and cultivated patches were replaced in the medieval period by large nucleations and openfields whilst much farmland was abandoned to woodland or waste (de Planhol, 1961; Meynier, 1964). Evidence for similar changes in France is not entirely lacking. Dion (1938) reported an earlier, more dispersed pattern of land occupation beneath the nucleated villages and openfields of northern France, and Aufrère (1931) has found similar traces in Beauce (see Meynier, 1958, 1964). In north-eastern France, de Planhol (1959) indicates that old enclosures and dispersed settlements preceded communal openfields. References to hedges and field boundaries continue until the thirteenth century, at which time communal shepherds are first mentioned. In that district, at least, de Planhol is confident that the thirteenth century witnessed 'a revolution in our rural landscapes'. The same term might be applied to structural changes in Burgundy after the Thirty Years' War. Whether such 'revolutions' occurred elsewhere in France remains to be discovered.

Looking ahead, a dynamic, systemic approach, seeking evidence for retreat and discontinuity as well as for progressive development in agrarian history may provide deeper insights into the vagaries of past situations and may also contribute to an appreciation of the transience of present landscapes and of those being planned for the future.

5. Notes

1. Le Play (1855), Durkheim (1895), Michelet (1835–67, Preface and Book III), Reclus (1875–94), Vidal de la Blache (1903) express different but complementary views on what they consider to be the essential characteristics of regions; Simiand (1903) and Febvre (1922, 1925) expose the fundamental weaknesses in arguments making appeal to environmental determinants.
2. For example, Demangeon (1905), Blanchard (1906), Gallois (1908), Brunhes (1921).
3. Huntington (1907, 1945), Spengler (1926–28), and Toynbee (1934–61) attempt to provide general explanations for the rise and fall of cultures as experienced in Europe and Asia.
4. Illuminating examples of dedications to peasant ancestors are to be found in the following works chosen entirely at random: Febvre (1911) commemorates his own origins as a descendant of a long line of Franche-Comtois peasants; Roupnel (1932) offers his book to his son as a reminder of his peasant forebears in Normandy, Maine and Burgundy; Faucher (1962) honours the memory of his grandmother who instilled in him a love of the fields; Fel (1962) dedicates his work in gratitude to several hundred peasants whose daily lives have been wholly occupied with simple tasks. The only book, among this random selection, not acknowledging a family connection with the land is Braudel (1949) *La Méditeranée et le monde méditerranéen à l'époque de Philippe II*. In a special way, Braudel's disclaimer expresses more eloquently than the others the force of his attachment to his region: 'I have loved the Mediterranean with passion', he declares, 'no doubt because I am a northerner like so many others in whose footsteps I have followed. I have joyfully dedicated long years of study to it —much more than all my youth' (p. ix).
5. Dion (1959) pays the most scholarly tribute to the special qualities of wines from different districts.
6. Bloch (1954) *The Historian's Craft* is a masterly exposition of the problems confronting scholars in this field.

7. A morphological approach to the study of agrarian structures is exemplified in Demangeon (1939).
8. Meynier (1958) discusses the nature of evidence for the chronology of hedges.
9. Henri Berr in Foreword to Febvre (1925, p. x).
10. Paul Vidal de la Blache (1903, pp. 7–54) portrays the geographical personality of France.
11. A. Thierry (1853, p. 14) cited in Febvre (1925, p. 9).
12. Whatmough (1970) discusses the name 'Ligurian' on pp. 78–80.
13. Fustel de Coulanges (1923, II, p. 130) claims that for long ages the Roman *gens*, or family group was the only unit of social organization, and that 'each one had its own domain, its own internal government, and its own Gods'.
14. See articles by F. Mège (1866–1876) in *Memoires de l'Académie de Clermont* cited by Derruau (1949) p. 507.
15. Quoted in Juillard *et al.* (1957) p. 31.

5. References

Angot, A. 'Etudes sur les vendanges en France', *Annales du Bureau Central Météorologique de France* (1883).

Arbos, P., 'Quelques types de maisons rurales en Limagne', *Bulletin de l'Association de Géographes Français*, 43, (1930), 63–64.

Arbos, P., *L'Auvergne*, Paris (1931).

Aufrère, L., 'L'habitation et le village en Beauce', *Comptes Rendus du Congrès International de Géographie de Paris*, III, (1931), 299–314.

Baker, A. R. H., 'Some terminological problems in studies of British field systems', *Agricultural History Review*, 17, (1969), 136–40.

Blache, J., 'De la structure parcellaire à l'habitat rural en Lorraine', *Bulletin de l'Association de Géographes Français*, 105, (1937), 58–64.

Blache, J., 'Un village de la Voge: Martinville, dans ses rapports avec le village de type lorrain', *Comptes Rendus du Congrès International de Géographie de Paris*, II, (1938), 26–31.

Blanchard, R., *La Flandre*, Lille (1906).

Bloch, M., 'La lutte pour l'individualisme agraire dans la France du 18e siècle', *Annales d'Histoire Economique et Sociale*, 2, (1930), 329–81, 511–56.

Bloch, M., *Les Caractères originaux de l'histoire rurale française*, Paris (1931).

Bloch, M., 'Le problème du peuplement beauceron', *Revue de Synthèse Historique*, 17 (1939), 62–73.

Bloch, M., *The Historian's Craft*, Manchester (1954).

Bourde, A. J., *The Influence of England on the French Agronomes*, Cambridge (1953).

Boutruche, R., *La Crise d'une société: seigneurs et paysans du Bordelais pendant la guerre de cent ans*, Paris and Strasbourg (1947).

Braudel, F., *La Méditerranée et le monde méditerranéen à l'époque de Philippe II*, Paris (1949).

Braudel, F., *The Mediterranean and the Mediterranean world in the age of Philip II*, 2 vols., London (1972).

Broek, J. O. M. and Webb, J. W., *A Geography of Mankind*, New York (1968).

Brun, A., 'Linguistique et peuplement, essai sur la limite entre les parlers d'oïl et parlers d'oc', *Revue de Linguistique Romaine*, 12, (1936), 165–251.

Brunet, P. 'Les méthodes de la géographie de l'habitat en Allemagne', *Revue du Nord*, 143(1954), 41–54.

Brunet, P., *Structure agraire et économie rurale des plateaux tertiaires entre la Seine et l'Oise*, Caen (1960).

Brunet, P., 'Evolution des bocages herbagers en Basse-Normandie', in Jäger, H. *et al.* (eds), 'Beitrage zur Genese der Siedlungs—und Agrarlandschaft in Europa', *Geographische Zeitschrift Beihefte*, 18 (1968), 12–26.

Brunhes, J., *Géographie humaine de la France*, 2 vols., Paris (1921).

Chabot, M. de, 'Le problème économique des haies en Vendée, *Bulletin du Groupe Poitevin d'Etudes Géographiques* (1943), 19–25.

Champier, L., 'Qu'est-ce qu'une civilisation agraire?' *Annales Universitatis Saraviensis*, 1 (4) (1952), 321–44.

Champier, L., 'Paysages humains de Bourgogne méridionale', *Annales de l'Académie de Macon*, 42 (1956a), 8–18.

Champier, L., 'La recherche française en matière d'histoire et de géographie agraires depuis un quart de siècle', *Revue de Géographie de Lyon*, 31 (1956b), 319–27.

Chaumeil, L., 'L'origine du bocage en Bretagne', in *L'eventail de l'histoire vivante, mélanges offerts à Lucien Febvre*, Paris, I (1954), 163–85.

Childe, V. G., *The Dawn of European Civilization*, London (1931).

Cholley, A., 'Problèmes de structure agraire et d'économie rurale', *Annales de Géographie*, 55 (1946), 81–101.

Clark, J. G. D., *Prehistoric Europe: the economic basis*, London (1952).

Coulanges, F. de, *La Cité antique: étude sur le culte, le droit, les institutions de la Grèce et de Rome*, Paris (1923).

Dauzat, A., *La Toponymie française*, Paris (1939).

Dechelette, J., *Manuel d'archéologie préhistorique celtique et gallo-romaine*, 6 vols., Paris (1908–12).

Deffontaines, P., *Les Hommes et leurs travaux dans les pays de la moyenne Garonne*, Lille (1932).

Delaspre, J., 'La naissance d'un paysage rural au 18e siècle', *Revue de Géographie Alpine*, 40 (1952), 493–99.

Deléage, A., *La Vie rurale en Bourgogne jusqu'au début du 11e siècle*, 3 vols., Macon (1941).

Demangeon, A., *La Picardie et les régions voisines: Artois, Cambrésis, Beauvaisis*, Paris (1905).

Demangeon, A., 'Types de peuplement rural en France', *Annales de Géographie* 48 (1939), 1–21.

Demangeon, A., *La France: économique et humaine*, Paris, 2 vols (1946).

Derruau, M., *La Grande Limagne auvergnate et bourbonnaise*, Clermont-Ferrand (1949).

Dion, R., *Essai sur la formation du paysage rural français*, Tours (1934).

Dion, R., 'Perspectives de recherches sur l'évolution des types d'habitat rural en France', *Comptes Rendus du Congrès International de Géographie d'Amsterdam*, 11 (1938), 62–72.

Dion, R., *Les Frontières de la France*, Paris (1947).

Dion, R., 'La géographie humaine retrospective', *Cahiers Internationaux de Sociologie*, 6 (1949), 3–27.

Dion, R., *Histoire de la vigne et du vin en France*, Paris (1959).

Dopsch, A., *The Economic and Social Foundations of European Civilization*, New York (1937).

Dufrenoy, O. P. A. P. and Elie de Beaumont, J. B. L., *Explication de la carte géologique*, Paris (1841–79).

Durkheim, E., *Les Règles de la méthode sociologique*, Paris (1895).

Durkheim, E. and Mauss, M., 'De quelques formes primitives de classification: contribution à l'étude des representations collectives', *L'Année Sociologique*, 6 (1903), 1–72.

Enjalbert, H., 'L'habitat groupé dans les pays du centre-ouest français', in *Melanges Faucher*, I (1948), 217–40.

Estienne, P., 'La neige dans le Massif Central', in *Melanges Arbos*, I (1953), 197–200.

Faucher, D., 'Polyculture ancienne et assolement biennal dans la France meridionale', *Revue Géographique des Pyrénées et du Sud-Ouest*, 5 (1934), 241–55.

Faucher, D., *La Vie rurale vue par un géographe*, Toulouse (1962).

Febvre, L., *Philippe II et la Franche-Comté*, Paris (1911).

Febvre, L., *La Terre et l'évolution humaine: introduction géographique à l'histoire*, Paris (1922).

Febvre, L., *A Geographical Introduction to History*, London (1925).

Fel, A., *Les Hautes terres du Massif Central*, Paris and Clermont-Ferrand (1962).

Fenélon, P., 'Quelques terroirs périgourdins', *Norois*, 4 (1955), 399–406.

Fenélon, P., 'Structure des finages périgourdins', in 'Géographie et Histoire Agraires', *Annales de l'Est*, 21, (1959), 168–92.

Fleure, H. J., *French Life and Its Problems*, London (1943).

Fossier, R., *La Terre et les hommes en Picardie jusqu'à la fin du 13ᵉ siècle*, Paris (1968).

Gachon, L., *Les Limagnes du sud et leurs bordures montagneuses*, Tours (1939).

Gallois, L., *Régions naturelles et noms de pays*, Paris (1908).

Gay, F., 'Finages et terroirs en Champagne berrichonne', in 'Géographie et Histoire Agraires', *Annales de l'Est*, 21 (1959), 221–32.

Gay, F., 'Aspects de l'agrigulture berrichonne au moyen âge, d'après les textes des inventaires des etablissements réligieux', *Norois*, 5, (1958), 191–201.

George, P., *La Région du Bas-Rhône*, Paris (1935).

Grenier, A., *Manuel de l'archéologie gallo-romaine*, 3 vols., Paris (1931, 1934, 1958).

Guyot, J., *Sur la viticulture et la vinification du département du Puy-de-Dôme*, Paris (1868).

Hartke, W., 'Die Heckenlandschaft', *Erdkunde*, 5 (1951), 132–52.

Hartke, W., 'A propos des crêtes de labour comme indice de l'ancienneté des limites agraires', *Bulletin de l'Association de Géographes Français*, (1954) 196–98.

Higounet, C., 'L'assolement triennal dans la plaine de France au 13ᵉ siècle', *Comptes Rendus des Séances de l'Académie des Inscriptions et Belles Lettres* (1956), 507–10.

Higounet, C., *La Grange de Vaulerent: structure et exploitation d'un terroir cistercien de la plaine de France, 12ᵉ–15ᵉ siècles*, Paris (1965).

Hubert, H., *Les Celtes*, 2 vols., Paris (1932).

Huntington, E., *The Pulse of Asia*, Boston and New York (1907).

Huntington, E., *Mainsprings of Civilization*, New York (1945).

Imberdis, F., 'Le problème des champs courbes', *Annales, Economies, Sociétés, Civilisations*, 6 (1951), 77–81.

Jalenques, L., 'Le rôle des intendants d'Auvergne à la fin de l'Ancien Regime', *Bulletin Historique et Scientifique d'Auvergne*, 49 (1929), 28–48.

Jeanton, G., *Le Pays de Macon et de Chalon avant l'an mille*, Paris (1934).

Juillard, E., *La Vie rurale dans la plaine de Basse-Alsace*, Paris and Strasbourg (1953).

Juillard, E., Meynier, A., Planhol, X. de and Sautter, G., 'Structures agraires et paysages ruraux', *Annales de l'Est*, 17 (1957), 1–188.

Jullian, C., *Histoire de la Gaule*, 6 vols., Paris (1909–1920).

Jullian, C., *De la Gaule à la France*, Paris (1922).

Jullian, C., *Au Seuil de notre histoire*, Paris (1928).

Lebeau, R., *La Vie rurale dans les montagnes du Jura méridional*, Lyons (1955).

Le Roy Ladurie, E., *Les Paysans du Languedoc*, Paris (1962).

Le Roy Ladurie, E., *Histoire de climat depuis l'an mille*, Paris (1967).

Le Roy Ladurie, E., *Times of Feast, Times of Famine*, London (1971).

Levêque, P. and Claval, P., 'La signification géographique de la colonisation grecque', *Revue de Géographie de Lyon*, 45 (1970), 179–200.

Longnon, A., *La Formation de l'unité française. Leçons professées au Collège de France en 1889–1890*, Paris (1922).

Lot, F., *Les Invasions barbares et le peuplement de l'Europe*, Paris (1937).

Marcelin, P. 'La forme des champs de la garrigue nîmoise', *Bulletin de la Société Languedocienne de Géographie*, 13 (1942), 171–96.

Marthelot, P., 'Survivances de la communauté villageoise dans la vallée de la Bruche', *Revue d'Alsace* (1948), 31–43.

Mayhew, A., *Rural Settlement and Farming in Germany*, London (1973).

Mège, F., 'Charges et contributions des habitants de l'Auvergne à la fin de l'Ancien Régime', *Revue d'Auvergne*, 14 (1897), 400–42; 15 (1898), 130–239.

Meyer, J., 'L'évolution des idées sur le bocage en Bretagne', in *La Pensée géographique française contemporaine*, Saint-Brieuc (1972), 453–67.

Meynier, A., 'Signification et évolution du bocage', *Information Géographique*, 16 (1952), 37–46.

Meynier, A., *Les Paysages agraires*, Paris (1958).

Meynier, A., 'Points de vue nouveaux sur l'évolution des paysages agraires, notamment en Europe centrale', *Information Géographique*, 28 (1964), 206–15.

Meynier, A., 'La genèse du parcellaire breton', *Norois*, 13 (1966), 595–610.

Michelet, J., *Histoire de France*, 17 vols., Paris (1835–67).

Millotte, J. P., *Le Jura et les plaines de la Saône aux âges des métaux*, Paris (1963).

Musset, R., *Le Bas Maine*, Paris (1917).

Newbigin, M., *Mediterranean Lands*, London (1924).

Nougier, L. R., *Les Civilisations campiginennes en Europe occidentale*, Le Mans (1950a).

Nougier, L. R., *Le Peuplement préhistorique, ses étapes entre Loire et Seine*, Toulouse (1950b).

Nougier, L. R., *La Géographie humaine préhistorique*, Paris (1959).

Peltre, J., 'Du 16e au 18e siècle: une génération de nouveaux villages en Lorraine', *Revue Géographique de l'Est*, 6 (1966), 3–27.

Perrin, C., 'Observations sur le manse dans la région parisienne au début du 9e siècle', *Annales d'Histoire Sociale*, 8 (1945), 39–52.

Planhol, X. de, 'Essai sur la genèse du paysage rural de champs ouverts,' in 'Géographie et Histoire Agraires', *Annales de l'Est*, 21 (1959), 414–24.

Planhol, X. de, 'La genèse des paysages agraires européens au symposium de Vadstena', *Revue Géographique de l'Est*, 1 (1961), 235–46.

Planhol, X. de, 'Historical geography in France', in Baker, A. R. H. (ed.), *Progress in Historical Geography* (1972), 29–44.

Planhol, X. de and Lacroix, J., 'Géographie et toponymie en Lorraine', *Revue Géographique de l'Est*, 3 (1963), 9–14.

Planhol, X. de and Perardel, A., 'La répartition géographique des vestiges archéologiques gallo-romains en Lorraine', *Revue Géographique de l'Est*, 9 (1969), 177–80.

Play, P. G. F. Le, *Les Ouvriers européens*, Paris (1855).

Poirier, L., 'Bocage et plaine dans le sud de l'Anjou', *Annales de Géographie'*, 43 (1934), 22–37.

Reclus, E., *Nouvelle Géographie universelle: la terre et les hommes*, 19 vols., Paris (1875–94).

Reitel, F., 'A propos de l'openfield lorrain', *Revue Géographique de l'Est*, 6 (1966), 29–51.

Rigodon, R., *Histoire de l'Auvergne*, Paris (1944).

Roblin, M. *Le Terroir de Paris aux époques gallo-romaine et franque*, Paris (1951).

Roupnel, G., *La Ville et la campagne au 17ᵉ siècle*, Paris (1922).

Roupnel, G., *Histoire de la campagne française*, Paris (1932).

Saint-Jacob, P. de, 'Etudes sur l'ancienne communauté rurale en Bourgogne', *Annales de Bourgogne* (1941–46).

Sautter, G., 'A propos de quelques terroirs d'Afrique occidentale', *Etudes Rurales*, 4 (1962), 24–86.

Simiand, F., 'Méthode historique et science sociale', *Revue de Synthèse Historique*, 6 (1903), 1–21; 129–57.

Sion, J., *La France méditerranéenne*, Paris (1934).

Sion, J., 'Sur la structure agraire de la France méditerranéenne', *Bulletin de la Société Languedocienne de Géographie*, 8 (1937), 109–131.

Sorre, M., *Les Fondements de la géographie humaine*, 3 vols., Paris (1947–52).

Spengler, O., *The Decline of the West*, 2 vols., London (1926–28).

Toynbee, A. J., *A Study of History*, 12 vols., Oxford (1934–61).

Uhlig, H., 'Old hamlets with infield and outfield systems in western and central Europe', *Geografiska Annaler*, 43 (1961), 285–313.

Vidal de la Blache, P., *Tableau de la géographie de la France*, Paris (1903).

Whatmough, J., *The Dialects of Ancient Gaul: prolegomena and records of the dialects*, Cambridge, Mass (1970).

6
Reclamation of Coastal Marshland

HUGH D. CLOUT

Introduction

Drainage and reclamation of damp, low-lying land represents an important component in the formation of the cultural landscapes of France. Major valleys and inland marshes as well as coastal areas experienced this kind of improvement through many centuries.[1] The present chapter, however, is limited to a consideration of changes in the third category of marshland, found along the coasts of the Atlantic, the Channel, and the Mediterranean. Drainage in other areas is examined elsewhere in this collection of essays.[2]

Rising sea level contemporaneous with the Flandrian transgression created broad estuaries and shallow bays along the French coasts. This phase came to an end by the early centuries A.D., judging from the discovery of Gallo-Roman coins and other objects in peat deposits overlying Flandrian marine alluvium, and from the existence of Roman routeways across what are now the damp marshlands of Aunis, Bordelais, and Saintonge (Gabet, 1966). Sedimentation proceeded vigorously along the west coast, being helped by the development of marine and estuarine vegetation, and protected in some places by off-shore islands. The onset of the Dunkirkian transgression may be dated to the end of the fifth century A.D., but important sedimentation has continued since then, creating extensive salt marshes in many areas (Wagret, 1968).[3] Settlements such as Luçon and Niort, close to the mouth of the river Sèvre, were connected to the sea and functioned as maritime ports until the twelfth century (Fig. 6.1). The sheltering effect of the Ile de Ré, detailed configuration of Aiguillon Bay, and heavier load of silt brought down by rivers during the medieval period of land clearance combined to accentuate the rate of sedimentation. Now these two towns are located 13 km and 48 km respectively from the open sea. Comparable examples of sedimentation are found in the Marais Breton inland from the Ile de

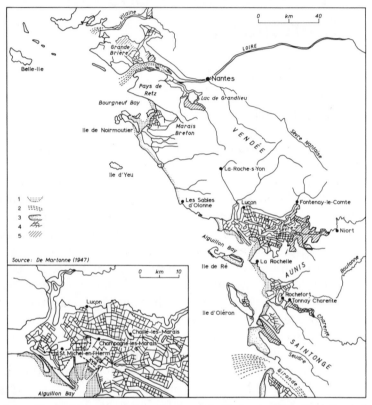

FIG. 6.1. The Western Marshes, between the Loire and the Gironde. (1) areas of sand and mud uncovered at low tide; (2) submarine delta formation; (3) coastal dunes; (4) drained marshland; (5) poorly drained marshland.

Noirmoutier, and in the estuary of the Charente. However, Gabet (1966) argues that the uninterrupted exploitation of salt pans at many points along the western coastline suggests that the sea level has remained relatively stable from the Middle Ages to the present.

The smoothed-out coastlines of northern, southern, and especially western France represent the end-products of centuries of painstaking reclamation to complement marine and estuarine deposition. Such drainage work was undertaken from Roman times through to the present century, at varying scales, and with differing degrees of success. Schemes ranged from the laborious winning of a few hectares of marshland by peasant communities to grand programmes for reclamation proposed by Dutch engineers in the first half of the seventeenth century. The first type of scheme gave rise to an irregular mosaic of dikes, ditches, and reclaimed parcels of land, while the second generally left a more distinctly geometrical imprint in the landscape (Verger, 1958).

Progress in winning back areas of marshland has been erratic. Many periods of civil calm were characterized by important drainage activities which stood in contrast with the abandonment of once-reclaimed land at times of strife and economic depression. Important advances were made in many marshland areas during the great clearance phase of the medieval period and again in the seventeenth century, but many of these achievements were lost in the recession of the fourteenth century and in the difficult period after the Revocation of the Edict of Nantes (1685) when Protestant drainage engineers from the Netherlands left France. Sometimes the abandonment of once-drained land back to marsh was a gradual process, resulting from a lack of interest or financial means, but it might equally well be sudden with, for example, devastation resulting from political decisions to cut dikes and inundate reclaimed land for strategic purposes.

Hence the story of marshland drainage along the coasts of France is long and complicated, with phases of advance being interspersed with setbacks. Ancient examples of reclamation date from Roman times when sections of the low-lying, malarial coastland of the Mediterranean were drained in Roussillon, at the mouth of the Aude, in the Camargue, and in the Arc deltaic plain (Houston, 1964). Settlers along the shores of the Mediterranean had to battle with two major hydrological problems: stagnant waters in the disease-ridden marshland, and torrential floodwaters descending from the Pyrenees, southern Massif Central, and the Alps. Early drainage achievements in the Midi were limited, both in extent and in importance.

Drainage in Medieval France

Marshland drainage during the medieval period was undertaken by two main types of organization. One involved monastic houses which were established in many desolate coastal areas and from which reclamation works were engineered. The other comprised groups of local inhabitants in drainage associations. During the seventh and eighth centuries abbeys were founded at Mont-Saint-Michel, on Noirmoutier island, at Luçon, Saint-Michel-en-l'Herm, and at other points on the Atlantic coast between the Loire and the Gironde (Fig. 6.1). These abbeys formed nuclei of settlement from which dikes were constructed and reclamation started along the bays of Aiguillon and Mont-Saint-Michel (Wagret, 1968). But the Norman invasion in the ninth century led to depopulation, destruction of monastic houses, and abandonment of drainage work. By contrast, new channels continued to be dug in the Mediterranean marshlands during that century (Houston, 1964).

Repopulation, following the triumph of the Capetians, initiated a new phase of coastal reclamation in northern and western France from the eleventh century to the early fourteenth century. Old abbeys were re-occupied and new ones were founded, for example by the Benedictines at Maillezais (1010) and Nieul-sur-Autise (1116) at the mouth of the Sèvre. These were joined by the houses of Cistercians, Praemonstratensians, and other orders. In addition, abbeys were endowed by lay landowners at 'island' sites perhaps 10 m or 20 m above the general level of the coastal marshes in the Vendée and other parts of western France. For example, landowners of the Pays de Retz founded the abbeys of la Chaume (at Machecoul in 1055), Ile Chauvet (1060), and Saint-Pierre-des-Moutiers (1092) (Talureau, 1965).

Dike construction and land drainage operated in many of the coastal marshlands around France during the eleventh and twelfth centuries. In the marais de Dol reclamation started as early as 1024. Work began in the first half of the century in the marshes of Poitou and south of the river Loire. But around Arles near the mouth of the Rhône and in the Marquenterre of Artois drainage started after 1150. Each of these schemes comprised three types of work: first, construction of dikes to protect low-lying marshland from marine invasion; second, erection of more dikes to contain rivers and prevent them discharging across the marshland that was protected from the sea; and third, digging of channels through enclosed marshland to ensure that surplus water could be removed efficiently at low tide (Demangeon, 1946). Such channels were protected by sluice gates both at their mouths, to keep out the sea, and inland, to avoid floodwater penetrating in winter. However, river water could be diverted into them to irrigate parched coastal pastures during periods of summer drought. In some cases marshland drainage simply extended the agricultural surface of existing parishes, but elsewhere new parishes were created on the reclaimed land.

Individual religious houses generally operated their drainage schemes without collaboration and the resulting pattern of ditches and dikes was piecemeal and irregular. But there was at least one example of abbeys joining together to undertake an important drainage operation (d'Hollander, 1962). This followed the action of Pierre de Chaillé in 1217 when he granted rights over the marshes on his estates at the mouth of the Sèvre to five abbeys (Absie, Maillezais, Nieul, Saint-Michel-en-l'Herm, and Saint-Maixent) on condition that the marshes between Langlée (Poiré) and Marans should be drained. As a result of this agreement, the *canal des cinq abbés* was dug from Velluire to Aiguillon Bay (Fig. 6.2) to keep out floodwaters from the river Vendée and permit the conversion of marshland into rich pastures (Dumont, 1951). Inundation by the Vendée was certainly avoided in the lower sections of the valley, but the settlement of Fontenay-le-Comte upstream was still subject to flooding. Not until 1283 were local quarrels brought to an end by the intervention of Philippe III and work completed on the King's Channel (*Achenal-le-Roi*) to take water from the Vendée river along the northern edge of the marshland to the Luçon channel, whence it was carried out to sea. This engineering programme was undertaken at the expense of the 12 parishes through which the channel passed and which benefited from the scheme.

Further north the task was not only to defend the 30,000 ha of the marais de Dol from the sea, but also to void away water from the low-lying peatlands (black marsh) which had shrunk below the level of the shore deposits of sands and comminuted shells (white marsh) (Phlipponneau, 1955). This two-fold objective was

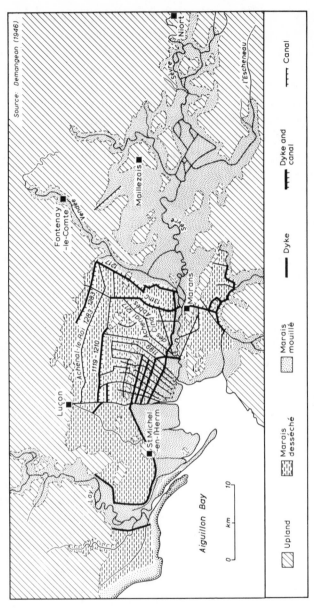

Fig. 6.2. Marshes at the mouth of the Sèvre Niortaise.

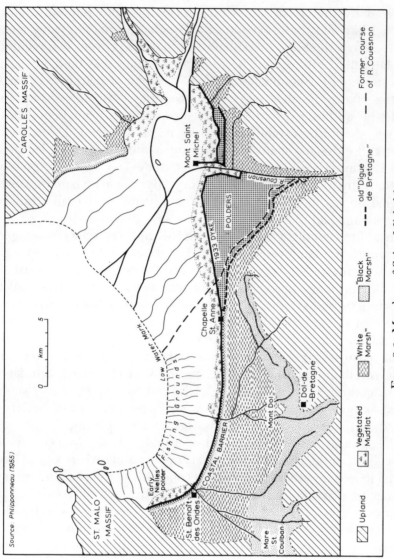

FIG. 6.3. Marshes of Saint-Michel bay.

realized by the construction of a series of dikes out into Saint-Michel bay and the provision of adequate channels to carry river water across the black marshland and thereby prevent it spreading out laterally (Fig. 6.3). The first line of dikes was built of earth and stones at the command of Alain V, Duke of Brittany, as early as the 1020s. Further work was encouraged by the bishops of Dol who authorized that new parishes, such as Saint-Bénoît-des-Ondes, should be established on the reclaimed land. Dikes were built and extended many times, being named, for example, after Duke Jean III in the fourteenth century and Queen Anne of Brittany in the late fifteenth century. But such reclamation was carried on without a coherent plan and hence an overall strategy for drainage had to be drawn up in the seventeenth century.

In addition to the work of the monastic houses, often encouraged by other large landowners, the medieval period witnessed groups or associations of villagers and peasant farmers being established to tackle drainage problems. In the marshes of Poitou fifteen such associations and syndicates were founded during the relative tranquility of the twelfth and thirteenth centuries in order to protect marshland that had already been drained, improve unreclaimed areas, ensure that channels were not obstructed by mud or vegetation, and maintain dikes in good order (Welsch, 1916). Similarly in the estuaries of the Authie, Canche and Somme on the Channel coast associations of landowners were formed to reclaim areas of mudflats that were covered by water at each high tide. The work of the associations is perhaps best exemplified in the Marquenterre area south of the river Authie. Parishioners and owners of isolated farms joined together during the second half of the twelfth century to make a start on dike construction which was to be continued in later centuries (Fig. 6.4) as polders spread northwards across the mudflats (Verger, 1968). Ten similar associations, known locally as *wateringues*, were formed during the twelfth century elsewhere in the coastlands of what are now the *départements* of Nord and Pas-de-Calais.

Associations of dike builders at the mouth of the Rhône may also be traced back to the twelfth and thirteenth centuries when Arlesians grouped together to form *corps de vuidange*. But little of lasting significance was achieved at this time (George, 1935). The inhabitants of Tarascon and Benedictine monks at Montmajour abbey

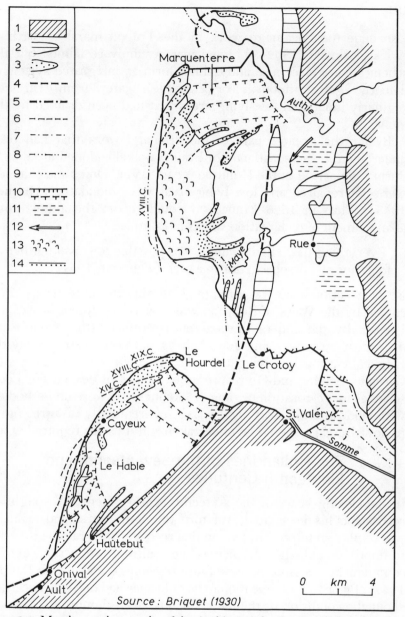

Key (legend):

1.
2.
3.
4. ----------
5. -·-·-·-
6. - - - - -
7. -·--·--·-
8. --·--·--
9. -··--··-
10. ⊤⊤⊤⊤⊤
11. ⊤- ⊤- ⊤-
12. ⟵
13. ⌐⌐⌐⌐
14. ·········

Marquenterre

Authie

Maye

Rue

XVIII.C.

XIX.C
XVIII.C
XIV.C

Le Hourdel
Le Crotoy

Cayeux

St.Valéry

Somme

Le Hable

Haûtebut

Onival
Ault

0   km   4

Source: Briquet (1930)

FIG. 6.4. Marshes at the mouths of the Authie and the Somme. (1) chalk lands; (2) Quaternary coastal formation; (3) Flandrian or more recent coastal formation; (4) recent Quaternary coast; (5) Flandrian coast; (6) medieval coast; (7) coastline 1715–18; (8) late 18th century coast; (9) coast 1835–6; (10) dikes; (11) marshes; (12) former branch of the Authie; (13) mobile dunes; (14) cliffs.

also undertook drainage work in the Trébon marshes north of Arles (Rainaud, 1892–3). Land was certainly reclaimed but the schemes were piecemeal and did not form an integrated system of defence against floods. For example, water from Tarascon regularly inundated low-lying areas that had been drained by the monks.

By far the greater part of the drainage work that had been undertaken in the coastlands of France was abandoned after 1350 during the period of the Hundred Years' War. Dikes and channels were not repaired and low-lying areas were inundated (Huguet, 1955). Thus in 1526 François I could report the almost total abandonment of reclamation works in Poitou.

> 'Everything has fallen in and it was possible to travel neither on foot, nor on horseback, nor in a cart' (Dumont, 1951).

Reconstruction work was attempted later but this in turn was interrupted by the Wars of Religion which were so violent in western France. By the end of the sixteenth century little evidence remained of earlier reclamation. Abbeys had been destroyed by the Huguenots, and low-lying areas at the mouths of the Charente, Gironde, Seudre and Sèvre presented scenes of desolation. Local schemes for restoration began c. 1580 but these were unmethodical with landowners, clergy, and peasantry frequently disagreeing as to how drainage should be undertaken and if it was required at all.

The Hollandries of the Seventeenth and Eighteenth Centuries

In the closing years of the sixteenth century Henri IV sought to reconstruct his devastated, war-torn kingdom. Marshland drainage was to play an important part in this recovery programme in order to improve public health, increase agricultural production, extend communications, and increase State revenues (Nadault de Buffon, 1852). Prior to this time monarchs of France had been unconcerned about the condition of their marshlands, even though disease was endemic in the West, and food shortages and famines were numerous. Henri IV looked unsuccessfully to his own people to undertake the task of draining and then sought the services of the Dutch—the master-drainers of Europe—and in particular those of Humphrey Bradley.

Bradley, a native of Berg-op-Zoom, had come to France in 1597 at the request of landowners to investigate the possibility of draining inland marshes at Chaumont-en-Vexin and Sacy-le-Grand. His skills were soon to be employed in many other marshland areas in France after Henri IV created the special position of 'dike-master of the kingdom' for him by edict of 5 April 1599. This edict formed the veritable charter for land drainage that was to be undertaken in many parts of France during the seventeenth century. Eight years later the *Association pour le Desséchement des Marais et Lacs de France* was created to bring together 'persons of quality, merit, industry, and great financial means' (De Dienne, 1891).

Bradley visited each of the major marshland areas in the kingdom and enlisted the help of his fellow Netherlanders, Calvinists and Roman Catholics alike, in the difficult task of reclamation. These immigrants were granted special privileges by royal edicts of 1599, 1607 and 1639 which allowed them to collect tolls and control navigation in the areas that they were to drain. Thus, for example, Bradley received a large concession of land along the Sèvre Niortaise in the Marais Poitevin. In addition, the Netherlanders were exempted from the poll tax and from other personal taxation during their stay in France.

The Dutch system of drainage involved digging ditches to carry river water to the sea by means of elevated ring canals (*ringsloot*) and to pump water up from low-lying marshland to reach the required level. Bradley and his compatriots rarely undertook drainage directly from the sea. The work of the Dutch in France formed just a small part of the Europe-wide movement of marshland drainage (Fig. 6.5) which created 'Hollandries' from the Somerset Levels to the Vistula (Van Veen, 1955).

Many schemes put forward by Bradley and his fellow Netherlanders were bitterly opposed by local inhabitants who resented intervention by foreigners and defended the traditional marshland economy of fishing, fowling, and stock-grazing which they perceived as far superior to anything that cultivation might offer (Demangeon, 1946). In some places local inhabitants destroyed newly-built dikes, as was the case at Tonnay-Charente in 1610, or else impeded progress by other means. Bradley's scheme to drain the Marais Vernier on the left bank of the lower Seine was not completely successful because of opposition from the powerful

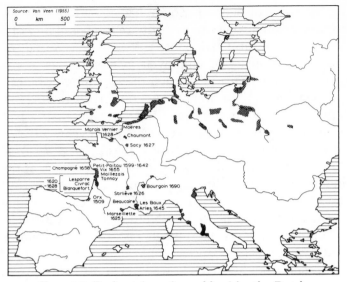

Fɪɢ. 6.5. Reclamation of marshland by the Dutch.

Abbot of Jumièges. Nevertheless, the *Digue des Hollandais* was constructed in 1633 (Fig. 6.6). Unfortunately drainage installations were not adequately maintained and the marshes soon returned to a watery state (Sion, 1909). Neither was the grand design for the Dol marshes accomplished. Work was slowed down by local hostility everywhere along the Atlantic littoral. Thus the marshes of Petit-Poitou (Sèvre) and Petite-Flandre (Charente) had been studied by Bradley in 1599 and 1609 respectively but reclamation was not complete at the time of his death in 1639. Marshland drainage at Blaye on the Gironde, at the Etang d'Orx on the lower Adour, and in parts of the Landes was similarly delayed.

The unity of the Association ended with the death of its founder, but some of Bradley's compatriots met with greater success in undertaking their own projects than their leader had done. With the encouragement of the *intendants* of Bordeaux and several large landowners, Conrad Gaussen had already drained the marshes of Blanquefort, Bordeaux and Bruges in the first decade of the seventeenth century. These marshes had been a serious health hazard, contributing to the death of one-third of the inhabitants of Bordeaux during the epidemic of 1501 (De Dienne, 1891). In the 1620s Leeghwater reclaimed the marshes of Civrac and Lesparre

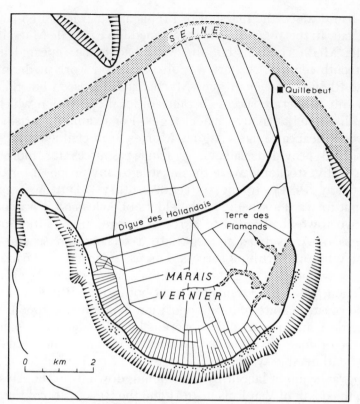

FIG. 6.6. The Marais Vernier.

which were renamed the 'Polders de Hollande'. Boutruche (1947) provides a vivid description of the conversion of mosquito-ridden marshes into rich polderland covered with pastures, market gardens and vineyards. But not all the marshlands of the Gironde remained in good condition. Some fell back into their former state during the late seventeenth century and in the eighteenth century so that drainage had to be started afresh after 1800.

In the Midi capitalists financed important draining work in Bas Languedoc from the 1590s until *c.* 1670 (Braudel, 1972). Comparable work had begun rather earlier near Narbonne where malarial pools were gradually drained, but the movement gained speed in the early years of the seventeenth century when Provençal engineers lent their assistance. These men were specialists in hydraulics and were disciples of Adam de Craponne (1519–59)

who had drained the marshes of Fréjus and had irrigated parts of
the Crau. In the 1620s Bradley reclaimed the Etang de Marseillette
on the Mediterranean, but the work had to be repeated in the
eighteenth century. A start was also made on work at the mouth
of the Rhône between Aigues-Mortes and Tarascon but this met
with only moderate success because of local opposition which had
been displayed at many earlier stages. For example, parishioners
between Beaucaire and Aigues-Mortes had claimed that their
marshland provided valuable grazing resources for more than
100,000 livestock and were thus hostile to any proposal for drainage (Sion, 1934). In the sixteenth century Adam de Craponne
had put forward a scheme to the elders of Arles and Tarascon but
the two towns had failed to agree (George, 1935). In 1600 the
citizens of Arles tried to negotiate a reclamation scheme with
Bradley but met with no success. Discussions were restarted with
Van Ems some 40 years later and were concluded positively
(Rainaud, 1892–3). Drains were cut both to the Rhône and direct
to the coast, in spite of local opposition (Gangneux, 1966). Some
riverside communities did cooperate but Braudel (1972) insists
that the drainage work undertaken in the lower Rhône would have
been unthinkable without the provision of capital by Italian
immigrants and of labour by folk coming down from the Alps. But
after the death of Van Ems in 1651 and the Revocation of the Edict
of Nantes 34 years later, drainage installations were not adequately
maintained and a particularly bad flood in 1674–5 undid much of
the good work that had been achieved. It is true that the area of
marshland in the lower Rhône had contracted and settlement had
spread on to formerly flooded areas in the Durance and Rhône
valleys, but the safety of the region was not guaranteed. Land
reclamation had failed to tame the larger marshland zones of
Anguillon, Arles, les Baux, and the Camargue.

Bradley himself completed relatively little reclamation work in
the western marshes between the Loire and the Gironde but after
his death in 1639 Louis XIII granted privileges for 20 years to
Pierre Siette from La Rochelle, who held the position of 'engineer
and geographer to the court', in order to drain marshes and
flooded land in the provinces of Aunis, Poitou, and Saintonge.
Frequently it proved necessary to redrain areas that had been reclaimed, albeit partially, in the medieval period. Thus in 1643 a

zone of 40,000 ha was drained in the marshes of Petit-Poitou (Sèvre) by means of a 24 km channel, known as the *Ceinture des Hollandais*, which followed the line of the old *Achenal-le-Roi* and replaced the piecemeal drainage operations that had been undertaken in the meanwhile by local landowners.[4] The *Société du Marais du Petit-Poitou* was founded in 1646 and grouped together farmers and landowners for reclamation. The statute of this society served as a model for later syndicates that were to be established in the region (Miaud, 1961). To the north of the Sèvre, the canal de Vix was dug between 1643 and 1662, and south of the river the Canal de la Bauche was excavated in 1656 to drain the marshes of Boëre and Taugou. Supplementary channels to the Sèvre were provided in the following decade (Welsch, 1916).

Land drainage between the *Ceinture des Hollandais*, the Sèvre, canal de Luçon, and the Bot de l'Anglée was declared to be a 'perfect success' at the end of the seventeenth century (d'Hollander, 1962). Excess water was voided seawards when sluices were opened at low tide. Other sluices on the *Ceinture des Hollandais* controlled water that could be directed through the reclaimed marshland to irrigate parched meadows in times of summer drought. Similar schemes operated in other sections of the Marais Poitevin. The work of the Netherlanders left a very distinctive imprint on the rural landscape in the form of geometrical patchworks of ditches and dikes surrounding rectangular parcels of land between 3 ha and 10 ha apiece. Yet in spite of progress in the improved marshes on the coast of western France during the seventeenth century, 14,000 ha of damp marshland remained inland and suffered serious inundation in winter and at times of exceptionally heavy rainfall.

Perhaps the most striking, but regrettably short-lived, example of land drainage undertaken by the Netherlanders in the territory that is now France, is provided by the *moëres* depression in Flanders which covers a 4–5000 ha behind the dune-fringed Channel coast and contained two reed-covered lakes known as the *grande* and *petite moëres* where extensive peat cutting had been undertaken in the Middle Ages (Verhulst, 1966). The base of the depression was 4 m 50 below high-tide level in the Channel and hence pumping would be necessary to expel water (Blanchard, 1906). Unlike the coastal marshes, where remarkable progress had been made as a result of gradual reclamation work by the wateringues administration through building dikes and ditches (*watergands*), a master-plan was required for draining the *moëres*. This was furnished in 1617 by a Fleming from Antwerp, named Wenceslas Cobergher (1550–1634), who received letters patent authorizing drainage (de Saint-Leger, 1900). He devised a *ringsloot* to the north and west of the *moëres* at a level above the depression which was criss-crossed by drainage ditches (Fig. 6.7). The whole scheme was ringed by a circular dike to exclude floodwater from

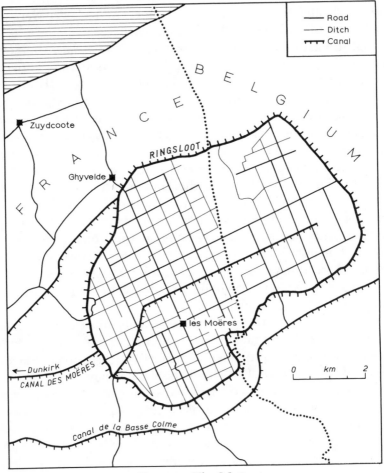

FIG. 6.7. The Moëres.

the surrounding land. A score of windmills was built to drive pumps for raising water from the *moëres* into the *ringsloot* which carried it out to sea at Dunkirk. The lakes of the *grande* (3150 ha) and *petite* (176 ha) *moëres* were drained between 1622 and 1626 after Cobergher had invested the funds of the Monts-de-Piété of Antwerp in his scheme. One hundred and forty new farms were built on the former marshland and by 1630 the polder, with its rectangular pattern of ditches and roads, was transformed into fine pastures and fields of colza.

However, the success of Cobergher's undertaking was short-lived. In 1646 the *moëres* were flooded purposely by the governor of Dunkirk, the Marquis de Léde, to protect his town during the Thirty Years' War. Twenty years later the inhabitants of Dunkirk petitioned that the unhealthy marshland should be drained once again, and Louis XIV made a gift of the submerged land to Colbert and Louvois, on condition that reclamation be undertaken. Unfortunately they were unable to achieve this objective and the *moëres* remained in their watery state. The Treaty of Utrecht (1713) altered the political boundary of northern France, dividing the *moëres* between France and the Austrian Netherlands, closing the port of Dunkirk, and thereby preventing water from the *ringsloot* draining through the sluices of that town. Louis XIV ordered that an alternative outlet channel should be dug to Mardyck. This was completed in 1717 but drainage was inefficient (Quarré-Reybourbon, 1893). Further flooding and serious outbreaks of disease occurred in the 1740s. Antoine de Ricouart, Comte d' Hérouville, took up the challenge of improving conditions and draining started seriously after the Peace of Aix-la-Chapelle (1748). By 1759 work was complete and fine crops were harvested in the following decade. But floodwater broke the dikes in 1770 and the Comte d'Hérouville and his fellow drainers were ruined. Another drainage society was set up by Vandermey, a lawyer from The Hague. A dozen windmills were built by Dutch workers and reclamation recommenced. But landowners with property alongside the *ringsloot* feared that it would burst its banks and they petitioned the *intendant* to take action to prevent further draining. In spite of this, the *petite moëre* was completely dry and under crops by 1788 but the larger part of the *grande moëre* remained under water and was soon to be completely so when the basin was inundated purposely in 1793 as a defensive measure to protect Dunkirk.

Associations of landowners continued their valuable reclamation work in the estuaries of the Authie, Canche and Somme during the seventeenth and eighteenth centuries, as tidal mudflats were empoldered. The area south of the mouth of the Somme had been subject to serious inundation in the late sixteenth century (Fig. 6.4). Immediate repairs were inadequate and the sea broke through shingle defences to invade Le Hable d'Ault again in the eighteenth century (Demangeon, 1905). This event formed the stimulus for new dikes to be built and the mouth of the Authie was completely converted into fertile polders (Fig. 6.8). Similar reclamation was

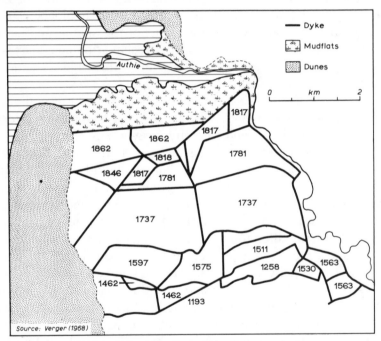

FIG. 6.8. Reclamation of the Marquenterre.

achieved on the right bank of the Somme where each estuarine parish had access to a stretch of mudflats. Efforts by Chauvelin and other *intendants* between 1740 and the 1770s resulted in a series of dikes being constructed, including one 4 km long which was erected for the Comte d'Artois. Further to the north, marshland on the right bank of the Authie had been drained in 1729 by Sieur de Halloy for the use of the inhabitants of Berck and Grof- fliers, while the reclamation of the Marquenterre continued on the left bank. Encouragement from the royal administration in the second half of the eighteenth century enabled new lines of dikes to be built. In addition, a syndicate was established to drain marsh- land between the Somme and the Authie. This was financed by a group of Parisian investors in 1784. As a result of the Revolution the good offices of the Comte d'Artois were removed, but in- habitants on the banks of the Somme and the Authie continued to support reclamation associations in the nineteenth century as they had done at earlier times. In addition, planting of marram grass to stabilize shifting coastal dunes was encouraged by the general council of Pas-de-Calais *département*.

Turning from these northern examples to drainage undertaken in other parts of France, it would be correct to observe that coastal marshes had enjoyed a period of prosperity during the reign of Louis XIV and the régime of Colbert. But following the Revoca- tion of the Edict of Nantes Protestant Netherlanders left France, having returned concessions of land either to the individual com- munities where the land was found or to the State, which in turn gave it back to local inhabitants. Many draining schemes were abandoned and the return of property to the local population gave rise to some of the commonlands found along the coast of western France (Bouhier, 1966; Talureau, 1965).

However in 1764, a royal declaration expressed new recognition of landowners' rights to drain marshland and in return to obtain exemption from dues and taxes (Braudel and Labrousse, 1970). The ideas of the physiocrats on agricultural improvement en- couraged large landowners to empolder areas of marine warpland on the islands of Noirmoutier, Oléron and Ré, and along Aiguillon and Bourgneuf Bays.[5] Rich merchants and landowners from Nantes and La Rochelle were prominent in undertaking these improve- ments which were accomplished with the help of technicians from the Low Countries. Thus, for example, a Fleming named Jacobs reclaimed stretches of saltmarsh along the coast of Bourgneuf Bay in the third quarter of the century. But the Revolutionary decades formed yet another phase of disturbance when dikes and channels again suffered the fate of temporary abandonment.

Drainage in the Nineteenth Century

Reclamation of coastal marshland experienced a new phase of activity during the nineteenth century. Napoleon I was interested in drainage and in September 1807 a law was promulgated establishing conditions for diking and draining. Further legislation in 1854, 1858 and 1860 fixed conditions for flood protection, land drainage, and the improvement of drained soils, and in 1865 a mass of earlier laws on drainage associations and syndicates was revised, abbreviated, and placed on the statute books.

Memoranda by the national hydraulic service (*Ponts et Chaussées*) show that not only were many patches of coastal marsh drained during the first three decades of the century but also that many drainage companies drew up grand designs for reclamation on a regional or even a national scale (A.N. F^{14} 6390; F^{14} 11167).[6] Thus in 1828 the *Compagnie générale de desséchement des marais, lacs, étangs, lais et relais de la mer* estimated that 600,000 ha of coastal and inland marsh needed drainage in 1680 *communes* in 69 *départements* of France and then sought permission to tackle this enormous task (A.N. F^{10} 1631). Such organizations often failed to obtain the concessions of land and rights for drainage that they requested and, as a result, achieved little or nothing.

Estimates of the areas of interior and coastal marshland remaining in France varied greatly. By contrast with the figures from the *Compagnie générale*, a report by the Ministry of Public Works in 1839 listed only 185,460 ha of coastal marsh (A.N. F^{10}

Table 6.1

Départements with Large Areas of Coastal Marsh, 1839

Bouches-du-Rhône	15,270 ha
Charente-Inférieure	30,531
Gard	11,325
Gironde	10,584
Landes	13,742
Loire-Inférieure	19,498
Total	100,950
National Total	185,460

Source: A.N. F^{10} 3371 *Ministère des Travaux Publics, Contenance des Marais*

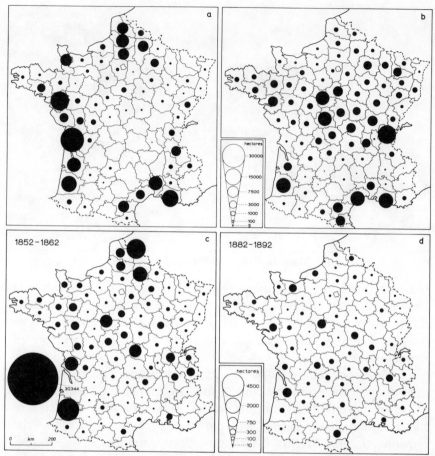

F IG. 6.9. Marshland in the nineteenth century. (a) Estimated distribution of lakes and (b) of marshland in 1839; (c) Marshland drained 1852–62 and (d) 1882–92.

3371) (Fig. 6.9). More than half of this total was located in six *départements* on the Atlantic and Mediterranean coasts (Table 6.1). In addition, large areas of interior marsh surrounded lakes in the Sologne, the Landes and Dombes. A survey of marshland in the Gironde *département* had been undertaken in 1820 (A.N. F[10] 1624). Details of this enquiry, conducted at *commune* level, help account for variations in marshland estimates (Fig. 6.10). Some 36,981 ha of marsh were itemized, with drainage work in progress on 7364 ha. An area of 19,378 ha had previously been improved

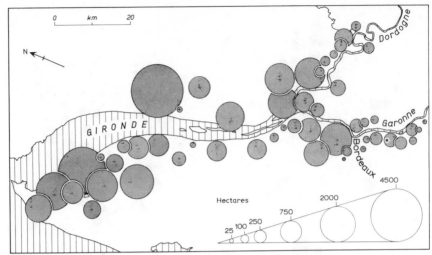

FIG. 6.10. Marshland in the Gironde *département*, 1820.

but was in need of re-drainage. Finally, it was stated that 9239 ha had never been improved and required reclamation. This third figure corresponds fairly closely with the 1839 estimate (Table 6.1) which may have related simply to the worst category of marshland.

Important drainage work was achieved in many parts of France during the nineteenth century, using steam-driven pumps in the place of unreliable windmills which relied on the vagaries of the weather. Reclamation was particularly significant along the Gironde, in the Marais Charentais, at the mouths of the Loire, Rhône and Seine, and around Aiguillon and Bourgneuf bays. Statistical sources are not available to chart the progress of drainage for more than a few periods, for example between 1852 and 1862 when an astonishingly high figure of more than 30,000 ha of coastal and inland marsh was reported to be improved in the Gironde *département*, with a total of 58,026 ha being drained throughout France (Fig. 6.9). Large areas of inland marsh were also drained at this time in the Sologne and in some northern valleys.[7]

To the north of Aiguillon bay the landscape of Saint-Michel-en-l'Herm *commune* exemplified the progress of recent reclamation, with successive dikes and polders being extended into the bay (Fig. 6.11). The clustered village settlement on an 'island' of dry

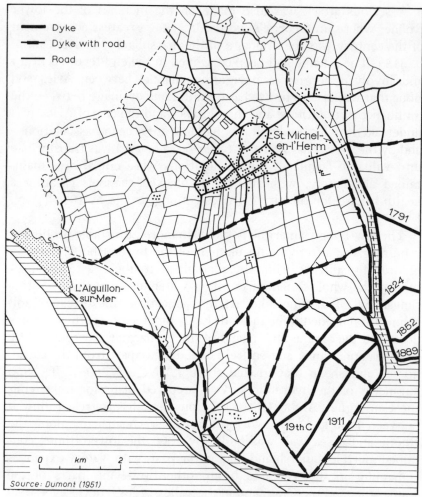

Fig. 6.11. Coastal reclamation at Saint-Michel-en-l'Herm.

land was fringed to the north by old-reclaimed parcels of land which stood in contrast with the rectangular fields that had been established at numerous stages since the Middle Ages (Dumont, 1951). In the Seine estuary, where epidemics had been reported in the early part of the century, more than 10,000 ha of marsh and low-lying ground were drained on both banks of the river (De- mangeon, 1946; Sion, 1909). Excellent hay meadows were pro- duced, but the reclamation of the Marais Vernier was not a complete success until after World War II (Wagret, 1968).

A serious attack was also made on the marshes of the lower Rhône, where, in George's words, '. . . the greatest achievement of the century was the drainage of the marshland of Arles' (1935, p. 318). The scheme had been conceived in the eighteenth century and involved digging a navigation channel between Arles and Bouc that was also to be used as outfall. Land drainage between the confluence of the Rhône and the Durance and the city of Arles was undertaken by local inhabitants banding together in associations, and by the *Service des Ponts-et-Chaussées*. The area was transformed into valuable farmland, but installations were not always maintained adequately, with reports of blocked channels creating a health hazard for the city of Arles coming as late as 1873 (A.N. F^{10} 3771).

The low-lying Camargue posed even more intractable problems, requiring the effective embankment of the lower Rhône, digging of drainage ditches from the marshland to the coast, and protecting the whole scheme from high-water levels in the Mediterranean by a maritime dike. At the same time, the threat of soil salinization needed to be tackled. Early nineteenth-century reports described the area as the 'island of the Camargue', surrounded by marshes and water, and entirely abandoned apart from the cattle, horses and sheep that grazed there (A.N. F^{10} 209^A). In 1850 engineers of the hydraulic service prepared plans for improving the Camargue (A.N. F^{10} 1631). Considerable progress followed between 1855 and 1870 when dikes were reconstructed along the Rhône and a sea wall was built. By 1900 the lower Rhône contained much less marshland than in the past, with watery expanses remaining in the Vaccarès basin, other low-lying parts of the Camargue, and the Crau, and in the valley of les Baux. Fevers had almost completely disappeared and 30,000 ha were reclaimed during the century (George, 1935). But perhaps an equal amount of marshland still awaited improvement.

After 1800 new schemes were also put into operation in the marshlands of Picardy, for example in the Authie valley where drainage had been planned by the Comte d'Artois in the eighteenth century. Work was continued by the Marquis d'Aullep so that in 1827 the projected network of channels and dikes was complete. Three years later a syndicate of landowners was formed to ensure that the installations should be maintained in the future. In the place of inundated marshes, which had formed '. . . des terrains sauvages, domaines de pêche et chasse, perdus pour l'homme', neighbouring farmers enjoyed access to 2500 ha of well-drained meadow-land (Demangeon, 1905, p. 138).

The task of re-draining the *moëres* was undertaken in 1802 by a new company headed by M. Jean-Louis Debuyser, at which time the prefect of Nord *département* reported that the basin was submerged for the greater part of the year and formed only a vast area of marsh (Dieudonné, 1804). Once again the land was drained, but in 1814 France was invaded by allied troops and inundation threatened the *moëres* for strategic purposes. Debuyser managed to avoid this and only a small area of low-lying land was flooded. Under his careful supervision the *moëres* were converted to dry land by 1826 and a syndicate was set up to control future water management. But the drainage works could not cope with very heavy rainfall and thus the *Annuaire du Nord* for 1830 reported:

'. . . as a result of continuous rain during the summer of 1829 the *wateringues* and *moëres* have been totally inundated; and very considerable damage has resulted' (p. 284).

Nevertheless, under normal precipitation conditions the drainage of the *moëres* could be ensured by the use of steam-driven pumps.

In spite of so much activity large areas of poorly-drained land remained along the coasts of France and in the interior. In 1877 the General Inspector of the *Ponts et Chaussées* service estimated that almost 200,000 ha needed reclamation in the five main river basins and their associated coastal marshes (A.N. F[14] 6391). He considered that improvement would cost 36 million *francs*, and that the value added would total 123 million *francs* (Table 6.2). But it seems that the volume of reclamation slowed down between 1882 and 1892 by comparison with the 1850s, with only 10,000 ha being drained. As before, important inland schemes complemented the ongoing task of coastal improvement (Fig. 6.9d).

Even in the present century sections of the western marshlands still experienced drainage problems. Improvements were certainly made in the second half of the nineteenth century, for example over 14,000 ha of saltmarsh in four western *départements* that had been declared to be in a state of abandonment in 1860.[7] In the

Table 6.2

Estimated Marshland by River Basin, 1877

River Basin	Surface (ha.)	Estimated Cost of Drainage (francs)	Estimated Added Value (francs)
Nord	46,831	5,329,300	20,217,000
Seine	11,495	1,549,050	6,485,000
Loire	50,745	5,702,100	20,933,500
Garonne	16,810	3,605,200	7,006,300
Rhône	73,061	19,931,900	68,402,000
	198,942	36,117,550	123,043,800

Source: A.N. F¹⁴ 6391, Rapport de M. de Fourcy, Inspecteur Général des Ponts et Chaussées, 31 Mars, 1877

following decade associations of local landowners were established to ensure that drainage channels were maintained adequately (A.N. F¹⁰ 4885). Even so, large areas of poorly-drained land still remain to either side of the Loire estuary (Fig. 6.1). The 6500 ha of the Grande Brière, owned by 21 neighbouring *communes*, are in need of effective water management, as is the shallow Lac de Grandlieu to the south of the Loire, which grows from 3500 ha in summer to double that size in winter (Maître, 1912–14). In addition, during exceptionally dry summers the grass of the Lac de Grandlieu turns yellow, the Grande Brière is covered by clouds of smoke rising from burning reeds and peat fires, and the pastures of Bourgneuf Bay become like the pampas (Vince, 1962). Under such conditions irrigation is sorely needed. Drainage systems in the inland sections of peatland ('damp marsh') of the Marais Niortais (Fig. 6.2) are still incapable of dealing effectively with winter floods as water flows westward but is prevented from reaching the sea by the drained marshes which form a kind of 'natural' barrier, being at a slightly higher level than the peatlands which are only of use for summer grazing (Jambu and Nijs, 1966). Almost identical problems are encountered in the damp marshes between Longeville and Aiguillon Bay where 25,000 ha are flooded each winter.

Thus the contrast remains between the improved marsh along the coast, which in many places have been drained spasmodically since the medieval period, and the inner peatlands where really effective water management still has to be achieved. Great scope exists for implementing schemes for summer irrigation and winter drainage, and continuing the empoldering of areas of saltings beyond the sea walls along several parts of the western littoral. In the hands of the associations and the society for improving the *Marais de l'Ouest*, land reclamation, drainage, and coastal defence continue with financial support from the State as they have done in the past, but certain sections of marshland have been safeguarded for their biological interest and amenity value, as in the Grande Brière regional nature park. Cultural appraisals of the worth of marshland are changing once again.[8]

6. Notes

1. The view of marshland drainage as 'improvement' was not, of course, held by all observers. Inhabitants of marshy areas perceived the fish, fowl, and pastures of their watery lands as valuable resources. But to outsiders the same areas appeared as inhospitable, disease-ridden wastelands. Such a difference in perception emerges from many case studies of marshland reclamation, both along the coast and inland.

2. Drainage of wasteland as a component of land clearance is examined by Sutton in Chapter 8 and piped underdrainage is considered by Clout in Chapter 11.

3. The physical geography of the French coastline has been studied in great detail by Briquet (1930), Papy (1941), Ters (1961), and in particular by Verger (1968). A brief summary is contained in De Martonne (1947). Information on the historical geography of coastal reclamation has been collated in Demangeon (1946), de Dienne (1891), and Wagret (1968). The present author acknowledges his indebtedness to the last three sources.

4. The role of French landowners in draining the Marais Poitevin during the seventeenth century has been stressed by Huguet (1955) who argues that it was their initiative and finance which permitted the operation of the *Société du Marais du Petit-Poitou*. However, part of the labour and certainly the techniques used were of Dutch or Flemish origin.

5. The physiocratic movement is examined in great detail by Bourde (1967).

6. The prefix A.N. indicates documents in the *archives nationales*. Other large drainage projects were proposed by Dupuis (1806), Desorgues (1817), Daudrillon and Bocquet (1818), and the *Société industrielle agricole pour les défrichemens, desséchemens et canalisation* (1829).

7. Loire-Inférieure (2088 ha), Charente-Inférieure (8400 ha), Morbihan (920 ha) and Vendée (2592 ha).
8. The continuing story of the reclamation of coastal marshland in western France in the twentieth century is presented by Talureau (1965).

6. References

Blanchard, R., *La Flandre*, Dunkirk (1906).

Bouhier, A., 'Les communaux de la partie orientale du marais poitevin', *Norois*, 13, (1966), 5–52.

Bourde, A. J., *Agronomie et agronomes en France au XVIIIe siècle*, Paris (1967).

Boutruche, R., *La Crise d'une société: seigneurs et paysans du Bordelais pendant la guerre de cent ans*, Paris and Strasbourg (1947).

Braudel, F., *The Mediterranean and the Mediterranean World in the Age of Philip II*, 2nd edition, London (1972).

Braudel, F. and Labrousse, E. (1970): *Histoire économique et sociale de la France*, II, Paris (1970).

Briquet, A., *Le Littoral du nord de la France et son évolution morphologique*, Paris (1930).

Demangeon, A., *La Picardie*, Paris (1905).

Demangeon, A., *La France: économique et humaine*, Paris (1946).

de Dienne, C., *Histoire du desséchement des lacs et marais en France avant 1789*, Paris (1891).

Dieudonné, M., *Statistique du départment du Nord*, Douai (1804).

Dumont, R., *Voyages d'un agronome en France*, Paris (1951).

Gabet, C., 'Le Dunkerquien sur le littoral d'Aunis et Saintonge', *Norois*, 13, (1966), 215–219.

Gangneux, G., 'Un grand domaine au XVIIe siècle: la Commanderie de Saliers en Camargue', *Etudes Rurales*, 21 (1966), 110–121.

George, P., *La Région du Bas-Rhône*, Paris (1935).

Hollander, D' R., 'Le marais poitevin', *Etudes Rurales*, 3 (1962), 80–90.

Houston, J. M., *The Western Mediterranean World*, London (1964).

Huguet, J., 'Un polder du marais poitevin', *Norois*, 2 (1955), 19–39.

Jambu, P. and Nijs, R., 'Contribution à l'étude des sols de la partie orientale du marais poitevin', *Norois*, 13 (1966), 565–593.

Maître, L., 'Etudes sur le lac de Grandlieu', *Annales de Bretagne*, 28 (1912), 62–75; 29 (1913), 138–151, 679–707; and 30 (1914), 82–107.

de Martonne, E., *La France: physique*, Paris (1947).

Miaud, G., 'Le canton de Chaillé-les-Marais: Vendée', *Norois* (1961).

Nadault de Buffon, M., 'Des marais de la France', *Journal d'Agriculture Pratique*, 4 (1852), 5–10, 92–97, 140–47.

Papy, L., *L'Homme et la mer sur la côte atlantique d'entre Loire et Gironde*, Bordeaux (1941).

Phlipponneau, M., 'La baie de Mont-Saint-Michel: étude de morphologie littorale', *Memoires de la Société Géologique et Minéralogique de Rennes* (1955), 1–215.

Quarré-Reybourbon, L., *Desséchement des wateringues et moëres de l'arrondissement de Dunkerque*, Lille (1893).

Rainaud, A., 'Le Crau,' *Annales de Géographie*, 2 (1892–3), 189–211.

de Saint-Leger, A., *La Flandre maritime et Dunkerque sous la domination française, 1659–1789*, Paris (1900).

Sion, J., *Les Paysans de la Normandie orientale*, Paris (1909).

Sion, J., *La France méditerranéenne*, Paris (1934).

Talureau, R., *Marais de l'Ouest*, Paris (1965)

Ters, M., *La Vendée littorale: étude de géomorphologie*, Paris (1961).

Van Veen, J., *Dredge, Drain, Reclaim*, The Hague (1955).

Verger, F., 'Le paysage rural des polders littoraux vendéens', *Norois*, 5 (1958), 51–59.

Verger, F., *Marais et wadden du littoral français: étude de géomorphologie*, Bordeaux (1968).

Verhulst, A., *Histoire du paysage rural en Flandre de l'époque romaine au XVIIIe siècle*, Brussels (1966).

Vince, A., 'L'aménagement des marais du lac de Grandlieu et de la baie de Bourgneuf', *Norois*, 9 (1962), 174–178.

Wagret, P., *Polderlands*, London (1968).

Welsch, J., 'Le marais poitevin', *Annales de Géographie*, 25 (1916), 328–346.

7

Petite Culture 1750-1850

ANDRÉ FEL*

'At all times the number of small farmers and proprietors in France was great: and though such a state of things is by no means unfavourable to the clear surplus produce or disposable wealth of a nation; yet sometimes it is not unfavourable to the absolute produce, and it has always a strong tendency to encourage population.' Malthus, T. R. *An Essay on the Principle of Population*, London (1803).

This chapter analyses agricultural changes in regions of France where land was cultivated by systems of *petite culture*, involving the use of neither horses nor heavy ploughs. Small peasant landowners, sharecroppers and landless labourers were found in great numbers in many areas. This side of rural France was largely forgotten by the eighteenth-century physiocrats even though it involved the greater part of the country, from the western *bocage*, through the poor soils (*gâtines*) of central France, to the main mountain masses, and the southern plains from Béarn to Provence.

Population and Resources

The century under consideration encompasses the last great wave of demographic growth in the French countryside, with the agricultural population reaching its peak in 1846. But of course the earlier part of this evolution is not known clearly since real censuses were not conducted before the Premier Empire. Eighteenth-century estimates derived from the number of households recorded in fiscal documents are open to criticism, for example because of uncertainties about average family size. Other estimates,

*Translated by the editor.

based on the numbers of births recorded, allow crude birth rates to be calculated. In spite of these imperfections it is obvious that the rural population of France increased during the first half of the eighteenth century following the crises at the end of the reign of Louis XIV (Fig. 7.1).

Fertility rates were high. Poitrineau (1965) noted an average of five children being baptized following each marriage in the Auvergne. The number was slightly higher in Perche but a little lower in Quercy. The crude birth rate of rural France rarely fell much below 40 per thousand at this time, thus Le Roy Ladurie (1966) recorded 38 per thousand in Languedoc on the eve of the Revolution. Other researches have shown a tendency for fertility rates to decline towards the end of the eighteenth century. Women in the villages of Quercy were marrying later (mean age 27 years) than at previous periods (Valmary, 1965). In addition, intervals between births were longer than before. Several authors have suggested that the 'deadly secrets' of birth control were beginning to be known in rural parts of southern France. The results of such practices were very limited at this time but this was no longer to be the case in the second half of the nineteenth century.

Death rates were frighteningly high in the early eighteenth century, with deaths greatly exceeding the number of births in some years. Vauban, Mirabeau, and others believed that the villages of France were being depopulated. In fact more time was needed before natural decline was established firmly in many parts of the countryside. Infant mortality, covering the first twelve months after birth, killed off one child in five in the middle years of the eighteenth century (Thézel-en-Quercy 19 per cent, Crulai-en-Perche 17 per cent, Sotteville near Rouen 24 per cent). Scarcely two-thirds of the rural population survived beyond the age of ten. In addition, death rates rose terribly when harvests were poor. Thus a cycle of disaster occurred, involving food shortages, high cereal prices, epidemics, and high death rates. Crude death rates in Quercy surpassed the appalling figure of 50 per thousand in ten years during the second half of the eighteenth century. Such shocking conditions were not to be erased rapidly.

However, if decennial periods rather than individual years are considered, it is clear that survival rates improved during the course of the eighteenth century. Natural increase in rural Langue-

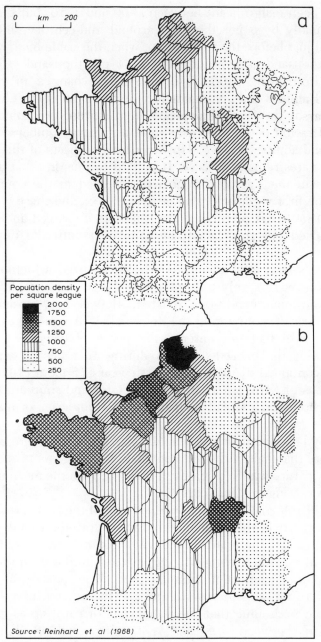

Fig. 7.1. Estimated density of population in (a) 1700; (b) 1789.

doc had been insignificant between 1700 and 1710, but thereafter rose annually by 6 per thousand around mid-century, and 8 per thousand just before the Revolution, when the crude birth rate was 39 per thousand and the death rate 31 per thousand (Collomp, 1972). Poitrineau (1965) noted similar changes in the Auvergne. Famines and epidemics became rarer than before with the exception of the disastrous years immediately preceding 1789. Mean duration of life increased, and a greater number of young people and adults survived. However many aspects of this decline in death rates remain obscure. It is hard to imagine that any real progress in medical conditions was achieved in the countryside before the first vaccinations against smallpox, and these were still rare in 1850! It is possible that rural diets improved and became more varied but this cannot be confirmed until the nineteenth century.

Progress was slow and those who recognized a 'demographic revolution' were surely too optimistic. Great regional differences in demographic conditions existed. Between 1778 and 1788 western France, comprising the Loire valley, Anjou and especially Brittany, still had not entered the phase of consistent natural growth. Deaths exceeded births during that decade which, of course, contained a number of harsh years (Soboul, 1970). But most areas of *petite culture* in the mountains and southern parts of the kingdom were already functioning as 'nurseries of mankind'. Densities increased and age pyramids in these regions were distorted by large numbers of people under 20 years of age who formed more than half of the total population of the countryside. This striking feature was to change only slowly, with the mean duration of life increasing in later years.

It is difficult to discover the precise role of the rural areas in the general growth of the population of France during the study period. The number of inhabitants in the whole country increased from 20 millions in the mid-eighteenth century to 25 millions on the eve of the Revolution, and 35 millions in 1846. A proportion of this increase of 15 millions involved Paris and the other towns, but it is reasonable to assume that the population of rural areas grew by 10 millions between 1750 and 1850, almost all of whom were peasants.

Did agricultural progress follow these demographic improvements? This is a highly controversial question. An 'agricultural revolution' during the eighteenth century has been recognized in France, with Bloch (1930), Faucher (1934) and other eminent historians and geographers demonstrating that some improvements took place. But the reverse interpretation has been put forward recently by Morineau (1970) who argued that French farming did not experience substantial advance at this time. A similar pessimistic opinion had been expressed by Arthur Young in his travels in France in 1787, 1788 and 1789.

The criticisms from Arthur Young and the scepticism of Michel Morineau seem to have been well founded. Large landowners certainly conducted experiments, agricultural societies were established, and much information was published but, as the English traveller noted, all this was of little consequence since the peasants were unable to read. Efforts by the kings of France and their *intendants* to promote a 'new agriculture' were real enough, but many serious obstacles were encountered. Bloch (1930) noted that edicts from Paris ordering the suppression of rights of stubble grazing and the division of commonlands had little or no effect in the heart of the country. The diffusion of new ideas from the royal court to the *intendants* thence to the local officials and finally to individual parishes was a far from simple process. Agricultural 'progress' was greatly retarded for this reason and old traditions often remained in use. Undoubtedly those in high places attempted to do away with the customs and traditions of French farming in too radical and too rapid a fashion. A little-known example from the cattle-rearing mountains of the Auvergne illustrates this point. In 1730 the local *intendant* sought to encourage the manufacture of new kinds of cheese (*façon gruyère* and *façon hollande*) but his efforts met with no success. A little later, a great landowner, the Abbé de Pradt, introduced a new breed of Swiss bull on his estate near Allanche. No-one emulated his example. Old traditions lived on. Improvements in cheese making and breeding local strains of cattle came much later, without any kind of 'revolution'.

Morineau (1970) demonstrated painstakingly that cereal yields scarcely increased between 1750 and 1840. But it is difficult to compare the rare estimates and records of the mid-eighteenth century with the so-called official estimates collected 100 years later. However, one must agree with Morineau that the term 'revolution' is excessive when applied in an agricultural context. In southern France, which was backward by comparison with the North, cereal yields five or six times greater than the volume of seed were still being recorded in 1850 as they had been in the mid-eighteenth century. It is also true that cultivation of artificial grasses made little impact over the same period. If areas of *grande culture* (from Nord to Loiret, and from Seine-Inférieure to Marne) are excluded, only the Mediterranean fringe of France (Gard, Hérault, Aude, Drôme, Var) obtained the greater part of its fodder supplies from artificial grasses (Statistique Agricole, 1840). The pessimism of Arthur Young's interpretation in the 1780s must be extended into the first half of the nineteenth century, as one searches in vain for an agricultural revolution *à l'anglaise* involving regular rotations of improved cereals and cultivated fodder crops. But agricultural progress took place in other less 'revolutionary' ways. Cereals were not only harvested from old-established fields, subject to biennial or triennial rotations. They were also produced as a result of temporary cultivation. Rough pasture and land that had reverted to scrub for 20 years or more was cleared using picks and light ploughs. Paring and burning provided an effective but only temporary means of fertilization for the soil. Temporary cultivation operated in the mountains of southern and central France and in areas of *bocage* and *gâtine* as it had since time immemorial. By reducing the fallow period between phases of temporary cultivation a considerably greater amount of grain might be produced.

Areas of woodland, waste and moor declined progressively between 1750 and 1850 (Fig. 7.2). Royal decrees of 1761, 1764 and 1766 encouraged land clearance, for example by exempting harvests gathered on newly-cleared land from payment of the tithe. *Bocage* spread over large areas of cleared moorland in Brittany (Meyer, 1966). Similarly in Burgundy the cultivated surface increased by 8 per cent (de Saint-Jacob, 1960). The story of land clearance at this period remains largely unknown, however studies of the detailed archives of a few rural communities allow the achievements of local, anonymous land clearers to be recounted. Thus at Azéreix, near Tarbes, 180 ha of moorland were cleared and converted to arable and meadows between 1767 and 1818 (Zink, 1960). So long as enough rough pastureland was

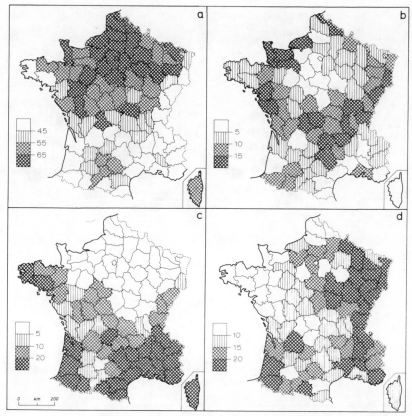

FIG. 7.2. Major aspects of land use at the time of the old cadaster (a) arable land as a proportion of the total surface; (b) permanent grass; (c) wasteland; (d) woodland.

left to meet the needs of local flocks and herds, the moors and heathlands of France provided an important reserve of land that might be used for periodic cultivation of grain.

The model of agricultural improvement that was being perfected in lowland England at this time suited only one region in France, namely the central part of the Paris Basin. English methods were not easily adapted to conditions in other regions of France where real progress was, however, being achieved through *cultures diverses* and polyculture (Fig. 7.3). The role of potatoes, maize, the vine, and mulberry bushes in French peasant farming has never been discussed adequately, but Faucher (1934) alluded to it when he outlined the originality of southern polyculture. This

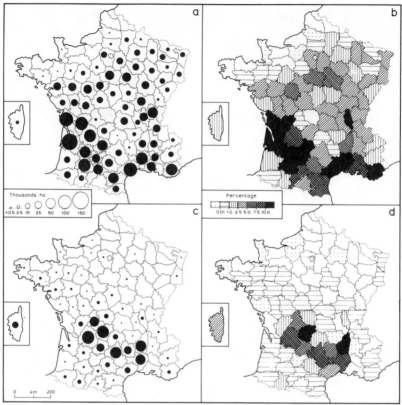

FIG. 7.3. Vines and chestnut trees at the time of the old cadaster. (a) hectares under vines; (b) vines as a proportion of total surface; (c) hectares covered by chestnut trees; (d) chestnut groves as a proportion of total surface.

involved a great variety of resources that were completely unknown on the plains of northern France. Bread, wine, olive oil, chestnuts, vegetables and dried fruits ensured well-balanced diets south of the Loire (Fig. 7.4). Middle mountain areas, hills and valleys in southern France supported fine, abundant farming landscapes more reminiscent of Tuscany than Norfolk. Mixed farming, with vines and fruit trees mingled with cereal crops, was far more suited to manual labour, involving the use of hoe and spade rather than the plough. It would certainly be wrong to talk of overpopulation in southern and central France without analysing the potential of intensive polyculture to support a dense agrarian population.

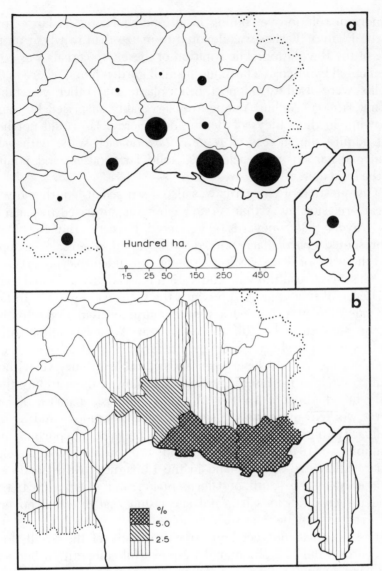

FIG. 7.4. Almonds, olives and mulberries at the time of the old cadaster. (a) hectares; and (b) proportion of total surface devoted to these crops.

Parisian observers generally underestimated the importance of maize in southern farming. This crop had been known around Bayonne at the end of the sixteenth century and 100 years later was being cultivated in many parts of Aquitaine where it played an important role in overcoming local food shortages. A larger part of the Plain of Tarbes was devoted to maize than to wheat on the eve of the Revolution. The rotation of these two cereals was complemented by intensive farming in small garden plots, where maize stalks were used to support bean plants and other vegetables (Zink, 1960). Arthur Young was agreeably surprised by maize growing in the valleys of Béarn and Quercy. He could not help but admire the success of *petite culture* on rich soils, with well-managed gardens and enclosures, solid farmhouses, and poultry in the local diet.

The question of vineyards was also discussed at length and with great precision by Arthur Young who was surprised to learn on his travels that vineyards engendered poverty. But the 1780s represented a particularly unfavourable period, when sales dropped and the price of wine was low. Young concluded that poverty was not the direct result of vine cultivation but rather was linked to the existence of tiny holdings on which the vines were grown. In fact, the sale of wine produced a very favourable circulation of money in the Limagne, the Rhône valley near Andance, and in other southern areas. Many small peasant farmers in Bas-Vivarais and the Cévennes would have been scarcely able to survive without profits obtained from selling wine that allowed them to buy their daily bread (Bozon, 1961). Tiny, vine-covered patches of land were worked intensively using hoes and spades, and extraordinarily high densities of population were supported. For example, in 1840 between 150 and 175 people lived on each square kilometre of hilly land in the Limagne, to the north and especially to the south of Clermont-Ferrand (Derruau, 1949). Under such conditions it is not surprising that extreme poverty occurred when wine sales were poor.

The time had not yet arrived when many of the small, local vineyards would be eliminated by powerful competition between the large wine-producing regions of France. The agricultural enquiry of 1840 showed that vines were grown widely throughout central and southern France, where very few areas needed to bring in wine from other regions. Vines were even grown in mountain areas wherever climatic conditions would allow. Richeprey (1784) noted that the vine was the only commercial crop produced on the steep slopes of the Lot valley at Entraygues in Aveyron, and this was purely for local sales in Aubrac and the highlands of Lozère which were cut off from the outside world by poor communications.

The potato made its appearance in the peasant economy rather late and played a different, more direct, and more effective role than the vine. Potato growing was well established in eastern France as far south as Vivarais during the eighteenth century and was adopted in other regions such as Auvergne, Limousin, and Rouergue at about the time of the Revolution. The potato provided an extremely valuable addition to the diet of the poor. Observers such as Barbut in Lozère, Dupin in Morvan, and Texier-Olivier in Limousin were agreed on this point. A little later, Marel described conditions in the uplands of Livradois.

> '. . . The potato has become the essential foodstuff for the poor in this region . . . whole cauldrons of potatoes are cooked . . . in years when cereal prices are high, potato soup forms the main part of the diet to compensate for the shortage of bread.'

Cultivation and consumption of the potato allowed many landless labourers and their families to survive. But potatoes also provided food for pigs so that, whilst pig rearing had previously been too expensive in Limousin, by 1801 '. . . even the poorest household could fatten a pig' (Fel, 1962).

Early agricultural statistics contain little information on the various other intensive crops grown in France but if the production of vines is added to potatoes, buckwheat, garden vegetables, hemp, flax, tobacco, madder, mulberries and chestnuts more than 30 per cent of the value of the country's agriculture production in 1840 was accounted for. Collectively, these crops were certainly less important than cereals (48 per cent) but were well in advance of animal products (18 per cent) which were probably underestimated.

The Problem of Poverty

How can the poverty of the peasants be measured and changes in their living conditions appreciated? Dues and taxes levied by royalty and the nobility during the *ancien régime* plunged much of the population of the French countryside into poverty, but unfortunately it is only possible to describe conditions in a very

226

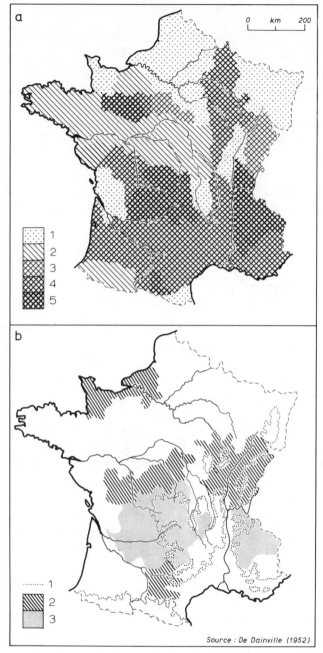

FIG. 7.5. Poverty and population, on the basis of Orry's enquiry, 1745. (a) Les facultés des peuples: (1) 'à l'aise'; (b) 'vivent'; (c) 'les uns vivent, les autres sont pauvres'; (4) pauvreté; (5) misère; (b) Population: (1) land above 500 metres; (2) over-populated areas; (3) areas of outmigration.

general way and make broad regional comparisons (Fig. 7.5).

The burden on the agricultural population of the royal poll tax and the tithe (which became the *vingtième* in 1741) was enormous, when compared with the total income as estimated by rural communities and by the *intendants*. But reports of the profitability of farming are of dubious validity since only a small proportion of the land had been surveyed accurately and hence the relationship between land, labour, and financial yield was poorly understood. Schnerb (1933) showed that the poll tax was particularly harsh in isolated country areas far away from the towns. Poitrineau (1965) estimated that poll tax payments consumed 60 per cent of the total agricultural yield in the district of Clermont. But there were extraordinary variations from parish to parish and anomalies were so great that it is hard to know what conclusions to reach. By contrast conditions were less burdensome in Bas-Dauphiné where only 15 per cent of the yield was absorbed by the poll tax in 1762.

Collection of feudal dues varied considerably between regions. The *cens* was rarely very harsh, but dues levied on crops from areas of temporary cultivation and the various labour duties greatly inflated the total. The tithe that was payable to the clergy might be less than one-tenth of the value of agricultural production and was not paid on new crops such as maize and various garden crops. In Haute-Auvergne the nobles and clergy together collected dues accounting for about one-fifth of the total value of farm production. But in Brittany, where a multitude of small nobles was found in the early eighteenth century, peasant farmers were much more oppressed. By contrast, conditions were less burdensome in the Rhône valley and in Provence, where the power of the nobility had already undergone a slow decline well before the Revolution.

Because of this uncertainty regarding the quality of peasant life during the *ancien régime* it is virtually impossible to determine the precise impact of the Revolution in the various regions of France. But it is clear that the sale of property (*biens nationaux*) formerly held by the clergy and émigré nobles did little to improve the condition of the peasantry. Little land was transferred and bids for property often rose very high. Traders, merchants, lawyers, and other members of the bourgeoisie replaced the clergy and nobles as landowners. In the Aubrac region of the Massif Central the vast highland pastures formerly held by the Hôpital d'Aubrac passed into the hands of cattle dealers (Bardy, 1971). At Chaponost in the Monts du Lyonnais members of the urban bourgeoisie divided up the few estates that were sold (Léon, 1966). However, the burden of dues and taxes that fell on the peasantry was undoubtedly lightened after the Revolution. Former seigneurial rights of hunting, operating mills, and using forests and uncultivated land were abolished, after having been criticized vigorously by rural inhabitants in the *cahiers de doléances* of 1789. These seigneurial privileges had seriously affected the daily lives of most French countrymen. The illusion of a really egalitarian revolution that had been held by the *brassiers* and the *travailleurs* in 1793 turned out to be shortlived, but it is clear that existing landowners both large and small saw their rights consolidated and their general condition improved after 1789.

However the real peasant farmer still had to be created. Social inequality remained strong, even in rural areas where there were few bourgeois landowners and other privileged folk. Many types of rural dweller, from rich to poor, were differentiated in the everyday language of rural France.

The rich peasant, who owned enough land to feed his family and to cultivate a range of crops, was known as a *ménager* in Provence, Languedoc and Vivarais. Elsewhere this type of cultivator was described as a *laboureur*. Relatively rich peasants cultivated the land that they owned and also made use of hired labour to help them (Goubert, 1973; Lefebvre, 1973). Poorer peasants were known by a range of special names. In western France and Limousin they were *bordiers*, who owned their own houses and enclosures, and used cattle for ploughing their land. The vine growers, as we have seen, often combined the roles of small landowner, wine seller, and occasional day labourer. The share-cropper was quite distinct and we shall discuss his condition is some detail. He often worked a fairly large holding but owned neither the house he lived in, the livestock he used, nor the land he farmed. He was poor, but was sheltered from hardship since he did not have to purchase food from other producers. He had little or no hope of improving his social status, since there was no chance of purchasing land on the estate that he worked, even after many years of saving. He lived in a median position between the peasant who owned his own land and the pauper. The final group in the rural population was made up of very poor folk, craftsmen, labourers, workers hired by the day, and those who were described as 'paupers' and 'beggars'. How many were there? We shall never know.

Recent research in historical demography and social anthropology, based on family reconstruction from parish records, has confirmed the hypothesis formulated by Meuvret (1946) regarding the dual character of rural population at the end of the *ancien régime*. On the one hand, there were 'stable' families which inherited land and other property. Such people knew how to write and to sign documents. They were the real peasant farmers and records relating to them provide the raw material for family reconstruction. They formed the social backbone in areas of *petite culture*. On the other hand, there existed a far more 'fluid' population, migrating from one region to another, and working as small craftsmen or being simple vagabonds. They were 'the poor' and little is known about them. Such families migrated frequently, with children often leaving home at 15 years of age. As a result of these movements whole families disappeared from parish records. Hypotheses of migration or extinction would explain such 'disappearances' but unfortunately they cannot be tested.

This two-fold model of peasant society clarifies some of the ambiguities and contradictions encountered in past judgements on the French 'peasantry'. The period between 1750 and 1850 may be considered as a long phase of rising agricultural prices. Labrousse (1970) has shown that price increases in the order of 60–70 per cent were recorded for cereals, meat, and wood. Short-term fluctuations certainly occurred but the general upward trend continued during the nineteenth century. The 'peasantry' may be divided into two economic categories: the *ménagers, laboureurs* and small vine growers who sold farm products and benefited from rising prices; and the poor tenant farmers and day labourers who had to purchase their food from others and for whom years with poor harvests were always catastrophic.

Statistics on the number of beggars arrested on the highways, and variations in the number of internal passports issued to migrants combine to tell an eloquent story. These figures increased dramatically during crisis years when the price of rye was high. Certainly this was the case in the Auvergne region during the final years of the *ancien régime* (Liris, 1965). As a result, poverty varied enormously in both time and space, and it is hardly surprising that appraisals of the quality of peasant life were very different from year to year and from region to region. Even more variation stemmed from whether peasant groups producing crops for sale or relying on goods purchased from others were being investigated.

Let us begin by considering the most impoverished groups and the forms of economic support available for them. The village community, rural craftwork, and temporary outmigration each provided some assistance to the rural poor.

The village community formed the essential framework within which peasant life took place. Each community controlled a distinct block of territory, covering both privately-owned holdings and commonland. The community governed the peasants' rights to grow crops, put livestock out to graze, and make use of timber resources. The opinion of the village population was expressed in the 'general assembly' which in theory at least, allowed the views of all the inhabitants to be aired. The community might play an important role in sustaining the poor. But what exactly would that involve? During the *ancien régime*, the village community could not operate without reference to the local lord and many regional differences resulted from variations in this relationship. The local lord or 'the first among the inhabitants', could levy dues. In 1732 the parliament of Brittany, which governed a region of strong seigneurial power, decided that commonlands would be restored to the local lords. Similarly, it was declared just before the Revolution that the commonland at Devesset in Haut-Vivarais belonged to the local lord. When moorland was cleared for cultivation in the Auvergne and Gévaudan one quarter of the harvest had to be paid to the local lord who was recognized as being virtually the owner of the commonland. But of course there were exceptions, and many villages made use of their commonland as if the local lords did not exist.

Variety was the general rule. In Haute-Auvergne, Limousin and Gévaudan, where the settlement pattern was fragmented into hamlets, rural communities were often extremely small. Some parishes, such as Sainte-Geneviève in Aubrac and Aydat near to Clermont-Ferrand, included up to ten individual communities. They were apparently very weak organizations and the documents tell us little about their powers. But, on the other hand, some villages were influential and well-organized communities. Reading the archives of the community and parish of Azéreix near Tarbes conveys the impression that real local power existed whereby elected consuls and the assembly of inhabitants decided in full sovereignty how the life of the village should be organized (Zink, 1960).

But the real debate revolves around the problem of who formed part of the village community and who possessed common rights. This issue was not even concluded when the feudal and seigneurial regime came to an end in 1789. Were all inhabitants who had their own hearth members of the community? Did that include the very poorest peasants? Was it enough to have just a miserable dwelling, as was the case of the day labourers, to qualify as a member of the community? Conditions were often not very liberal and only owners of land enjoyed community rights. This was certainly so at Fraisse-sur-Agout in the uplands of Espinousse. The same ambiguity existed when rights to make use of commonlands were investigated. Should the very poor have the right to send as many stock as they wished to graze on the common moorland and rough pasture? The most usual solution was found in compromise. On the one hand, the old custom of 'hay and straw' was evoked whereby everyone might make use of the communal rough grazing in summer to pasture stock that had wintered on his own private pasture. This tradition favoured those peasants with land of their own for winter grazing. But on the other hand, the rule might be modified to the benefit of the poorest inhabitants, with each individual having the right to graze a minimum number of stock, say five or six sheep, even if he owned no pasture of his own. Sometimes eyes were closed to what went on, but once the custom of 'hay and straw' had been broken many abuses might occur. How could one prevent certain inhabitants with rights of pasture, and often the most affluent villagers at that, from exploiting the high summer pastures for their own profit by bringing in extra stock from surrounding areas? This kind of conflict was frequent in the Alps, Massif Central, Pyrenees and all mountain areas during the eighteenth and nineteenth centuries. The poorer peasantry might thus be excluded from making use of common grazing lands. Some disputes of this kind dragged on for decades, as was the case at Séderon in the southern Alps (Vigier, 1963).

Sometimes village communities were favourably disposed towards the poor, with first-comers and squatters being allowed to work the land that they had occupied. Temporary clearances encroached on the margins of common moorland and these areas were then transformed into peasant plots, clearly bounded by dry-stone walls or hedgerows. Steep slopes and stony soils were used for farming and 'improved' in this way as population pressures grew and squatting became more widespread. Village communities allowed this kind of encroachment to occur but they were not in favour of the systematic division of commonland, especially if proposals were made for this to be done in an absolutely egalitarian fashion. For this reason it is possible to understand the failure of schemes for division that were put forward by the Crown and especially by the Revolutionaries (who proposed the principle of dividing commonland on a *per capita* basis in 1792 and 1793). Even the most democratic communities and municipal councils avoided putting these new regulations into operation. During the Empire attempts were soon made to return to the old order and seek out those who had 'usurped' land (laws of 1804 and 1819). But the old order was not always restored and local demographic and political conditions often permitted the poor to acquire portions of land. Commonlands were 'nibbled away' between 1750 and 1850 in Livradois, which was one of the most densely-peopled mountain areas in the Auvergne. Gachon (1939) recounted the adventure of the small peasants and craftsmen as they brought the remaining moorland of the region into cultivation.

Somewhere between these two extremes, many mountain regions contained a balance of between small properties and common moorland. This has been demonstrated clearly in a study of landholding in the Alps which revealed the co-existence of small blocks of private property and vast areas of commonland in the Maurienne, Queyras and Ubaye (Vigier, 1963). Mountain villages in these areas were strongly nucleated and were intensely involved in the collective organization of daily life. Large landowners were almost unknown and old traditions of stubble grazing, use of summer grazing land by communal flocks, and communal cheese-making still remained in operation in 1850, and sometimes persisted longer. Similar features were found in the mountains of Ariège and in certain isolated parts of the Massif,

Central (Chevalier, 1956; Fel, 1962). In Margeride, for example, the peasant farming system was organized around the village regulations, with rye growing alternating with fallow on tiny fields, and communal flocks of sheep grazing fallow and moorland in turn. Very detailed regulations controlled nocturnal sheep folding so that all members of the community benefited from the dung left by the flocks that were herded into movable pens at night. The poor might find adequate means for survival in the isolated, tradition-bound conditions of such highland communities.

But without the existence of craft activities and manufacturing many of the poor in other parts of France would not have been able to eke out a living in the countryside. Just before the Revolution the 'real peasants' of Aubrac contrasted with the craftsmen in a striking way. Grazing land formed the sole resource of the affluent inhabitants of the region, but the poor made cloth. During the eighteenth century clog-makers were so numerous in Perche that they represented 20 per cent of all married men in the region. Even in the plain of Languedoc, it would have been impossible to support the rural population without craft industries. Priests and consuls complained when work for the poor was short, since manufacturing kept them from begging.

Workers and craftsmen in woodland regions were undoubtedly the least integrated into peasant life. Woodcutters, plank-sawyers, clog-makers, and charcoal burners lived on the edge of the great forests of western and central France and in Périgord. Their work was very seasonal in character and each year saw the arrival of new groups of poor folk 'hardened by the most wretched forms of work'. Villagers were suspicious of the forest workers who lived on the edge of their settlements. However many of them were poor peasants who migrated downslope from the Auvergne and Limousin to work in the forests in winter and then moved back to the mountains once their seasonal jobs were over.

Craftwork provided a useful complement to the agricultural work of many poor peasant families. This was certainly the case in Velay, where village life involved rye-cultivation by the men and lace-making by the women. The extra money gained from craftwork was not great but was quite indispensable. The employment of tens of thousands of peasant women in the domestic lace industry depended on the goodwill of the middlemen and a few.

wholesalers at Le Puy who sold their goods to distant markets. Not far away, woollen cloths that had been woven by the peasants of Livradois were collected at the town of Ambert. This industry was favoured by the existence of a highway from the Auvergne into Lyonnais, that had been recently constructed at the behest of the *intendant*. Cloth-making continued to flourish into the nineteenth century but eventually foundered because of strong competition from urban manufacturers.

Finally, there were some regions where craft activities employed not only the poor but formed the focus for the whole of rural life. In the countryside of Maine the making of canvas and linen involved a host of farmers who grew the plants, women who spun yarn, and weavers who made the cloth. Musset (1917) noted that cloth-making complemented agricultural work throughout the *bocage* of Maine. At the end of the eighteenth century the weaver-peasants divided their time between craftwork and farming. But all of these activities failed to survive the loss of markets and growing competition from urban mills which occurred in the early years of the nineteenth century. In 1811 the prefect of Mayenne *département* noted that farming was then the sole occupation of the peasantry in his area.

The last phase of population growth among the peasantry had been sustained in many parts of France by the persistence of craft activities. The decline of rural manufacturing was an undoubted cause of mass outmigration as Pinchemel (1957) discovered in the villages of Picardy. However some new industries were being set up in the countryside at the same time as traditional crafts were dying out. Many types of worker-peasant and miner-peasant were created as farmers combined working the land with employment in new factories and mines. Thus miner-peasants flourished around the collieries of Decazeville and La Machine where each miner cultivated his own plots of land. Similarly, Le Play (1866) described the way of life of lead miners near Pontgibaud who still farmed patches of land. In Nièvre:

> 'the forges employed workers who still lived in surrounding villages, with the same trade being passed down from father to son. The workers could combine work at the forge with agricultural tasks such as planting potatoes or sowing corn' (Vidalenc, 1970).

The time had not yet arrived for industry to completely uproot small peasant landowners.

Temporary outmigration provided another source of assistance for the poorest members of the peasant population and in the most impoverished regions of France. By the end of the eighteenth century these movements had taken on a really proletarian character, involving beggars and vagabonds. This phenomenon did not disappear in the early nineteenth century but continued during the Empire and haunted prefects in many parts of France who investigated the employment, habits, and morality of these poor folk (Fig. 7.6). 'Professional beggars' were trained in some villages, such as Saint-Jean-des-Ollières in Livradois. Conditions gradually improved but work was still short and wages were low in winter time. Seasonal migrants left their homes in the Massif Central and the Alps in winter to work as woodcutters and labourers in other parts of France. Up to one-tenth of the population, usually involving able-bodied men, left Saint-Amand-Roche-Savine, Viverols and other villages in Haut-Livradois.

In addition to these winter migrations, agricultural workers were involved in a range of other seasonal movements during part of the summer. Large numbers of harvesters migrated to the plains of southern France from the Pyrenees, Cévennes, and southern Alps in search of supplementary wages and better food. The grape harvest stimulated yet another distinctive form of seasonal migration. Similarly in Drôme and the lowland parts of Ardèche mountain folk were needed to tend silk worms. All these types of migration flourished before the age of agricultural mechanization. They involved not only landless labourers but also small landowners who managed to find additional temporary work in areas near to their own homes where harvesting occurred at a slightly different time of the year. A proportion of these agricultural migrants remained in the areas where they had found seasonal work. Thus many mountain folk settled as small vine-growers or sharecroppers in the more agreeable climate of the lowlands of Languedoc and Provence and in the valley of the Rhône. This kind of renewal of the lowland population by migrations of mountain folk has been exemplified by Derruau (1953) in his study of Capestang near Béziers.

Temporary out-migration might take on even more original

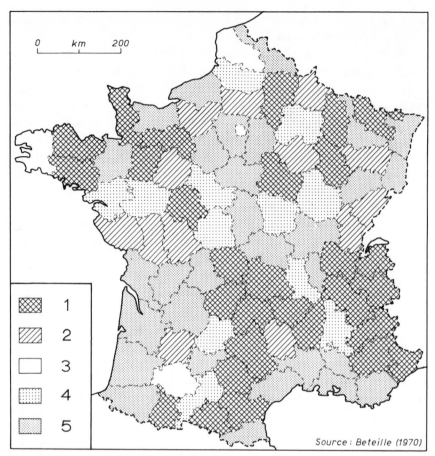

FIG. 7.6. Seasonal migration during the *Premier Empire*. (1) strong and very strong net outmigration: R>2; (2) predominance of outmigration: R>1; (3) approximate balance between in- and outmigration; (4) predominance of inmigration: R<1; (5) strong and very strong net inmigration: R<2. (R calculated as outmigration ÷ inmigration).

characteristics. Sellers of tracts and copperware and dealers in second-hand goods from the Cantal no longer worked the land. Instead they operated as peddlers and traders along the highways of France and in its towns and cities (Fig. 7.7). This kind of migration marked the beginning of a real break from farming. But it was slow in coming since members of the traders' families remained on the farmland that they had inherited and wished to enlarge. Seasonal building workers left Creuse *département* each

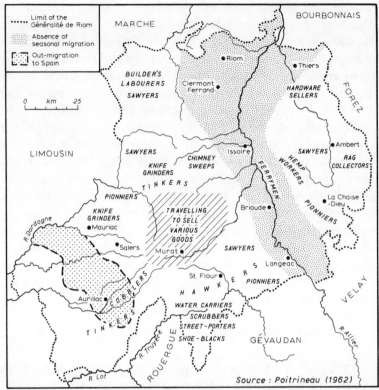

FIG. 7.7. Types of employment of temporary migrants from the Auvergne, in the late eighteenth century.

summer, leaving their womenfolk behind to work in the fields. Some 6000 migrants left each year in the early eighteenth century, but by the 1780s the number had risen to 15,000 and increased to 35,000 by 1850. At the end of the century even more seasonal migrants were leaving Creuse each year. The monetary rewards of migration increased with the passage of time. A summer's building work had brought in 50 *livres* in 1763, but wages rose to 200–300 *francs* in the early nineteenth century, and 500 *francs* at the beginning of the Second Empire (Carron, 1965). Attachment to one's birthplace was still strong and most migrants returned to their family for part of the year. However after 1860 seasonal migration was gradually replaced by permanent outmigration.

It is not easy to understand how temporary migrations developed in detail. Blanchard (1938–50) noted a contrast in migratory behaviour between villages in the northern Alps and those in the south. Migrants from the latter region obtained seasonal farm-work, harvesting cereals and grapes in Provence, but their main role was still in Alpine farming. Only from the Forcalquier region were more complicated types of seasonal outmigration in opera-tion, with hawkers leaving each winter with their mules loaded with herbs to be sold in other parts of France. But this was an exception in the southern Alps. By contrast, a wide range of trades was practised by migrants from the northern Alps. These folk included the travelling merchants of Chablais, traders from the Thônes region, water-carriers and chimney-sweeps from Mauri-enne, not to forget the travelling 'teachers' from the Oisans mountains who taught the plainsmen how to read. Yet surprisingly, the rural population of the southern Alps started to decline after 1836, some 15 years or so earlier than in the northern Alps. This example provides additional proof that temporary out-migration was an effective way of retaining a large resident population in mountain areas.

Sharecropping and the Rise of Smallholdings

In the 1780s Arthur Young had reported the main obstacles hinder-ing the advance of farming in France: the excessive fragmentation of the land into tiny holdings, and the sharecropping system.

> Sharecropping particularly roused his irritation as he remarked:
> '. . . this subject may be rapidly discussed since there is not a single word to be said in its favour, yet a thousand objections might be raised . . . The system may only be excused as a harsh necessity. The poverty of the sharecroppers is so great that landowners must provide the livestock or else the farmer would have none. . . .'

Sharecropping was found in many parts of France where *petite culture* was practised: Sologne, Berry, Marche, Limousin, Anjou, Burgundy, Bourbonnais, Auvergne, Brittany, Maine, Provence, and throughout the South. Young found the poorest sharecroppers in central France (Poitou, Berry, Nivernais) where sharecropping formed part of the system of *fermage-général*. Rich landowners 'hired out great stretches of land, after sub-dividing these into smaller holdings to lease to the sharecroppers'. All this, in Young's opinion, was symptomatic of poverty and 'the principles of an arbitrary government.' However, sharecropping was to persist in France for a long time during the nineteenth century and continue beyond 1900.

The *gâtine* of Poitou, in the extreme south-western corner of the Armorican massif, provides a useful example of an area with cold damp soils suitable for cattle-rearing but only capable of growing rye and buckwheat. This area supported sharecropping for many centuries and has been studied in detail by Merle (1958). A share-cropper's holding of 40 ha, like that at Sanay, yielded a mere 440 *francs* during an average year in the mid-eighteenth century. That sum was divided between the noble landowner and the share-cropper who owned nothing. Many sharecroppers left their holdings when their leases still had some time to run. Thus at La Baudrière, near Secondigny-en-Gâtine, six families of share-croppers occupied the same holding in succession between 1734 and 1756. Social and economic change was slow in this kind of environment. Paring and burning of moorland continued to be practised in the early nineteenth century and artificial grasses were completely unknown in the region. Lease stipulations scarcely encouraged progress. Gradually leases were drawn up for longer periods and cash payments replaced payments in kind. Share-cropping appeared to be an immutable system, at least in the short term.

Living conditions of sharecroppers at Bourbon-l'Archambault in Bourbonnais during the mid-nineteenth century have been described in graphic detail by Guillaumin (1904). Tenants had little security. From an early age sons of sharecropping families helped look after the cattle and were thus prevented from attending school. They, in their turn, became sharecroppers in the neighbourhood. The over-riding impression was that the landlords and bailiffs dominated rural life. They could always find someone else in need of a sharecrop farm: '. . . you or someone else . . . tenants are not difficult to find.' Early examples of agricultural advance, involving the use of threshing machines and the sale of milk, were always accompanied by strengthened lease conditions imposed by the landowners. Bourbonnais appeared to be a 'closed' environment, where there was little hope of progress being made. 'If we had not agreed to take on the holding ten others were ready to do so.'

But one final point regarding sharecropping needs to be made. The sharecropper's family often formed a kind of 'family community', with each sharecropper being surrounded by his brothers (who were often married and with children of their own) and other relatives 'whom we supported partly through charity but also because they could be of help and were not expensive' (Guillaumin, 1904). Everyone worked in together and managed to survive somehow, since a large family provided more labour for the farm. An attitude of paternalism from the landowner combined with the sharecropper's submissiveness to allow the system to survive.

Certain qualifications must be added to the many pessimistic observations on small peasant farming in France. Arthur Young deplored the division of inheritances into very tiny holdings and expressed a desire that a law should be passed to prevent further fragmentation of landownership. In fact, the Napoleonic civil code produced just the opposite result. But local customs of land inheritance differed greatly throughout France and the civil code did not unify in some magical way the traditions of transmitting land from one generation of peasant farmers to the next. According to Yver (1966) conditions in Anjou and Brittany approximated most closely to the type of land division that had been criticized by Arthur Young. But in the mountain areas of the Alpine interior and in Velay holdings and even parcels of land were also broken up in an attempt to distribute the inheritance in a completely equal way between all of the heirs. By contrast, the reverse situation which involved the system of the favoured heir, was widely practised in southern France (Béarn, Languedoc, Provence). In these areas it was considered desirable to keep each inheritance intact if possible. In the Castellane region, half of the marriage contracts in the eighteenth century indicated the existence of large families with two generations living under the same roof. The favoured son, who would eventually inherit the family land, might marry but would continue to live in the parental house where his father remained master of hearth and farm alike. Stem-families of this kind which kept their holdings intact were not as exceptional in the mountains of Béarn as once had been believed (Le Play,

1866). Family communities like this certainly became rarer with the passage of time, but they were still numerous in Nivernais and in the eastern Auvergne at the end of the eighteenth century. Thus the family communities of the Jault and the Garriaux in Morvan, and the Guittard-Pinon near Thiers gradually broke up, but some new fraternities were established in the early nineteenth century.

As the pressure of population grew in the French countryside, small peasant holdings occupied an increasing proportion of the land surface. Sometimes this trend had been well established before the Revolution. In Bas-Dauphiné, where land was of poor quality and the local lords were weak, land clearance had operated throughout the eighteenth century and small farmers, vine-growers, and day-labourers purchased small pieces of land. Half of the land surface at Saint-Hilaire-le-Côte had been owned by the peasantry in the early eighteenth century but its share increased to two-thirds in 1776, and 90 per cent in 1834 when the old cadaster was drawn up (Léon et al., 1966).

Such an increase in the number and importance of small peasant holdings became more widespread during the course of the nine-teenth century. An analysis of the contents of cadastral registers in south-eastern France has shown the growing importance of small landowners (Vigier, 1963). To take the example of Isère *départe-ment*, properties of less than 3 ha increased in number by 53 per cent between 1820 and 1870 and occupied 43 per cent more land at the end of the period than at the beginning. Similarly, properties between 3 ha and 5 ha increased by more than one-fifth. By contrast, properties of more than 10 ha became less important. Small proper-ties acquired increasing significance in both mountain and low-land areas of *départements* around the Isère. Sometimes large and medium-sized properties were fragmented by banking houses 'which bought up estates wholesale in order to sell them retail'. A cadastral expert in Basses-Alpes *département* remarked in 1839 that:

> '*petite culture* continued to increase in importance because it was easier to fertilize, improve and cultivate a small parcel of 30–40 *ares* than a larger stretch of land' (Vigier, 1963).

Such land-hunger among the peasantry is quite understandable but it is surprising that so many parcels of land were acquired when prices were high. A day's agricultural work yielded little more than one *franc*'s pay but a hectare of ploughland, meadow or vineyard could cost 1000 or 2000 *francs* or even more. Only owner-occupiers could make the necessary sacrifices to raise such sums. Large landowners were amazed by such expensive land sales. Thus in 1831 the Comte de Chambray declared 'I have witnessed the sale of a farm which would not yield 1200 *francs* in rent for the sum of 100,000 *francs*' (Vidalenc, 1970). The trend was exactly the same in the Auvergne where observers analysed changes with great precision. Many estates were broken up into tiny parcels. Former day-labourers and other humble peasants purchased many of these miniscule plots at great expense, and thus became tenants and eventually landowners in their own right. Thus tenant farmers who had previously helped as labourers on the large farms of the region found it more advantageous to undertake *la petite culture* for themselves. A similar process was taking place in the Livradois uplands east of the vineyards of the Limagne. Hoes and picks wielded by small peasant proprietors brought more and more of the land into cultivation that had been so poorly managed when it was held in large estates. The tiny plots owned by the peasantry were intensively worked and sharecropping estates were nibbled away piece by piece, just as the commonlands had been split up in the past. Densities of up to 100 persons /km² were supported on the granitic hillslopes of Livradois where all the savings of the farm labourers and rural craftsmen were consumed in the purchase of land (Gachon, 1939).

But the growth of *petite culture* would remain inexplicable without mentioning one other factor. In the middle years of the nineteenth century France was still composed of a series of local, isolated economies. The country was still not unified in economic terms and competition between regions was slight. Neither had international competition made a serious impact at this time. A fascinating study might be undertaken of the geography of agricultural prices in France just before the coming of the railway. A few examples indicated the range of prices encountered. In 1840 a *hectolitre* of wheat was worth 11 *francs* in Lorraine but 23 *francs* in Var. Wine cost 6 *francs* in Hérault but reached more than double that amount in *départements* on or beyond the northern margins of vine cultivation, for example 13 *francs* in Sarthe. Great regional price variations were in evidence for all commodities. This situation explains the persistence and even strengthening of *petite culture* in areas where it would appear to have been badly placed and scarcely economic from a 'rational' or modern point of view. Local producers still enjoyed the privilege of being sheltered from competition before the railways were built when agricultural prices started to level off throughout the country. *Petite culture* took the opportunity to flourish under such conditions.

Nevertheless, *petite culture* was vulnerable and was soon to face serious competition. The years from 1846 to 1848 formed a period of agricultural poverty and as a result the censuses of 1846 and 1851 recorded the maximum population in many parts of the French countryside. Depopulation was produced by rural out-migration, as in the Cantal where seasonal movements hardened into permanent losses, or by natural decrease. The economist Frédéric Bastiat understood the social and economic problems of the Chalosse region in the mid-nineteenth century as he wrote:

'. . . the land no longer gives the same return . . . now farmers need to contemplate their chances of economic success before they decide to marry . . . fathers understand that family farms can no longer support as many people as they did in the past.'

In the second half of the nineteenth century fewer observers were willing to defend the system of *petite culture* and critics urged radical changes in the name of 'modernization'.

7. References

Bardy, E., *Vente des biens nationaux en Aubrac lozérien*, in *L'Aubrac: étude ethnologique*, vol. II, Paris (1971).

Bastiat, F., *De la répartition de la contribution foncière dans le département des Landes*, in 'Oeuvres complètes', Paris (1862).

Blanchard, R., *Les Alpes occidentales*, 9 vols., Grenoble (1938–50).

Bloch, M., 'La lutte pour l'individualisme agraire dans la France du XVIIIe siècle', *Annales, Histoire Economique et Sociale*, 2 (1930), 329–381, 510–556.

Bozon, P., *La Vie rurale en Vivarais*, Valence (1961).

Chevalier, M., *La Vie humaine dans les Pyrénées ariégeoises*. Paris (1956).

Carron, M. A., 'Les migrations anciennes des travailleurs creusois, *Revue d'Histoire Economique et Sociale*', 53, (1965), 289–320.

Collomp, A., 'Famille nucléaire et famille élargie en Haute-Provence au XVIIIᵉ siècle', *Annales Economies, Sociétés, Civilisations*, 27 (1972), 969–975.

Dainville, F. De, 'Un dénombrement inédit au XVIIIᵉ siècle: l'enquête du contrôleur-général Orry 1745, *Population*, 7 (1952), 49–68.

Derruau, M., *La Grande Limagne auvergnate et bourbonnaise*, Grenoble (1949).

Derruau, M., 'Un village-tombeau du Languedoc: Capestang', *Revue de Géographie Alpine*, 41, 1953, 99–115.

Faucher, D., 'Polyculture ancienne et assolement biennal dans la France méridionale', *Revue Géographique des Pyrénées et du Sud-Ouest*, 5 (1934), 241–255.

Fel, A. *Les Hautes terres du Massif Central*, Clermont-Ferrand (1962).

Gachon, L., *Brousse-Montboissier: une commune d'Auvergne du XVIIIᵉ au XIXᵉ siècle*, Clermont-Ferrand (1939).

Goubert, P., *The Ancien Regime: French society, 1600–1750*, London (1973).

Guillaumin, E., *La Vie d'un simple: mémoires d'un métayer*, Paris (1904).

Labrousse, E., 'Les "bons prix" agricoles du XVIIIe siècle', in Braudel, F. and Labrousse, E. (eds.) *Histoire économique et sociale de la France*, vol. II, Paris (1970), 367–416.

Lefebvre, G., *The Great Fear of 1789*, London (1973).

Léon, P., *Structures économiques et problèmes sociaux du monde rural dans la France du Sud-Est*, Paris (1966).

Le Play, F., *La Réforme sociale en France*, Paris (1866).

Le Roy Ladurie, E., *Les Paysans du Languedoc*, Paris (1966).

Liris, R., 'Mendicité et vagabondage en Basse-Auvergne à la fin du XVIIIᵉ siècle', *Revue d'Auvergne*, 79 (1965), 48–64.

Meuvret, J., 'Les crises de subsistance et la démographie de la France d'ancien régime', *Population*, 1 (1946), 643–650.

Merle, L., *La Mètairie et l'èvolution agraire de la Gâtine poitevine*, Paris (1958).

Meyer, J., *La Noblesse bretonne au XVIIIᵉ siècle*, Paris (1966).

Morineau, M., *Les faux-semblants d'un démarrage économique: agriculture et démographie en France au XVIIIᵉ siècle*, Paris (1970).

Musset, R., *Le Bas-Maine*, Paris (1917).

Pinchemel, P., *Structures sociales et dépopulation dans les campagnes picardes*, Paris (1957).

Poitrineau, A., *La Vie rurale en Basse-Auvergne au XVIIIᵉ siècle*, Paris (1965).

Reinhard, M., Armengaud, A., and Dupâquier, J., *Histoire générale de la population mondiale*, Paris (1968).

Richeprey, F., *Description des diverses qualités de sol de la Haute-Guyenne*, Montauban (1784).

Saint-Jacob, De. P., *Les Paysans de la Bourgogne du Nord au dernier siècle de l'ancien régime*, Paris (1960).

Schnerb, R., *Les Contributions directes à l'époque de la Révolution dans le département du Puy-de-Dôme*, Paris (1933).

Soboul, A., *La Civilisation et la révolution française: la crise de l'ancien régime*, vol. I, Paris (1970).

Statistique agricole de la France, Paris, (1840).

Valmary, P., *Familles paysannes au XVIIIᵉ siècle en Bas-Quercy*, Paris (1965).

Vidalenc, J. *Le Peuple des campagnes: la société française de 1815 à 1845*, Paris (1970).

Vigier, P., *Essai sur la répartition de la propriété foncière dans la région alpine*, Paris (1963).

Young, A., *Voyages en France en 1787, 1788 et 1789*, trans. H. Sée, Paris (1931).

Yver, J., *Essai de géographie coutumière*, Paris (1966).

Zink, A., *Azéreix: la vie d'une communauté rurale*, Paris (1960).

8

Reclamation of Wasteland During the Eighteenth and Nineteenth Centuries

KEITH SUTTON

'France has her deserts, dare to cultivate them: change her frightful reed-covered marshes into golden cornfields and rich pastures'. Voltaire, *Sur l'agriculture*, Paris, 1761.

The Study of Land Clearance

'There are few aspects of agrarian history that are more difficult and complex than the retreat of wasteland' according to Debien (1952, p. 1) who regarded the fluctuation in the extent of wasteland as being linked to many other aspects; the role of stock-rearing, the strength and area of communal pasturage, the extension of the road network, the type of crop rotation being practised, etc. However, Debien was only looking at the wasteland of one estate in Haut-Poitou. The problem becomes immeasurably greater when considering land clearance for a whole region or for the whole country.

Studies of the 'clearing of the waste' have a small but distinguished place in historical geography. Orwin's (1929; 1970) classic study of reclamation on Exmoor, Hoskins' (1943; 1952) work in Devon, and Darby's (1940) on the Fens are now standard to any methodological treatise on the epistemology of historical geography. Wider national themes of wasteland clearance were pursued by East (1936) for England in the eighteenth century and through a longer time span by Hoskins (1955), while Monk-house (1949) assessed heathland clearance in the nineteenth-century landscape changes of the Belgian Kempenland. The theme has been taken up again by Williams (1970) in an attempt to quantify regional disparities in the enclosure and reclamation of wasteland in England and Wales particularly in the nineteenth century. Data limitations are stressed and a plea is made for more detailed local research which Williams (1972) goes on to supply in a study of the enclosure of wasteland in Somerset.

This essay attempts to treat the clearance of wasteland as more than landscape change; rather it attempts to use it as a regional index of the progress of the agricultural revolution in France. Perpillou (1940) in his study of Limousin draws attention to the radical changes in economic and legal conditions which have to take place before widespread clearance can be pursued. The system of long fallowing must be replaced by new crops which themselves render the wastes less vital for the agricultural economy. Sheep must become less important in the livestock economy freeing areas of wasteland from an extensive pastoral function. Legal restrictions on the subdivision, private ownership, and enclosure of the wastes have to be terminated. In summary, 'a complete revolution in the use of land resources is necessary' (Perpillou, 1940, p. 26). The reduction in wasteland thus offers a possible index of agricultural progress during the eighteenth and nineteenth centuries, a quantitative land use indicator of that complex and multi-faceted collection of changes involved in the term 'agricultural revolution'. Strong doubts have been expressed on whether much progress was in fact made by French agriculture in the eighteenth century. Morineau's (1970) work on cereal crop yields tends to

'confirm and verify the striking constancy of agricultural pro-ductivity between the first half of the eighteenth century and 1840, sometimes from the beginning of the seventeenth century or even the Middle Ages' (p. 182).

He criticizes earlier studies as placing too much emphasis on qualitative changes i.e. the mere appearance of maize and fodder crops, or on legal changes limiting the rights of commoning, which could take many decades to fully realize their effect. A recent exhaustive study of eighteenth century clearance by Castang

(1967) while in part supporting Morineau's thesis and finding only limited evidence of wasteland reduction, does re-emphasize the undoubted contribution of the late *ancien régime* period in establishing the legal bases of subsequent land clearance.

Obviously less doubt exists over the designation of the nineteenth century as a period of considerable agricultural transformation. From 1821 to 1911 French agricultural output is estimated to have grown at an average rate of 0.9 per cent per annum with growth being interrupted in the late 1870s and in the 1880s. More importantly, productivity per member of the agricultural population (at 1905–1914 prices) rose from 275 *francs* in the late 1810s to 774 *francs* in the last decade prior to World War I, though half the increase came in the last two decades. Within this growing output the share of animal products is estimated to have increased from 30 to 35 per cent over the 90 year period. Further qualitative evidence, concerning improved diets in rural areas, confirms this slow but real growth and progress attained during the nineteenth century (Hohenberg, 1972; Toutain, 1961). The series of maps in this chapter showing the relative areas under wasteland throughout France at four dates through the century, together with other maps of changes in the proportion under wasteland between the cross-sections illustrate this progress through time and space of the agricultural revolution.

Land clearance offers an alternative index of change to measures of the introduction of new crops or techniques, or of the use of fertilizers, etc.

The problem of explaining the temporal and spatial patterns which emerge remain extremely complex.

'When efforts are made to establish relationships between changes in agriculture and those in other sectors of the economy still further difficulties arise and causal statements can only be made with caution'.

wrote Kemp (1971, p. 227) when discussing the agricultural depression of the 1880s. The divergent and, at times, decidedly opposing trends in the area of wasteland in the various regions of France reflect the complexity and multiplicity of causes involved. Some attempt at explanation is made on a partial and regional basis in so far as present studies allow.

Wasteland Clearance in the Early Eighteenth Century

The term 'wasteland' is used fairly widely in this essay to encompass that range of uncultivated land variously known as
bruyères, chômes, pâturages, friches, brandes, landes, and so on.
Perpillou (1940) discusses the details of equating the varying
land-use rubric between the old cadaster and the 1908 revision
including even certain categories of *pacages* in his maps of early
nineteenth-century wasteland in Limousin. The clearing and converting of this land into more intensive economic use, be it arable,
pastoral or forestry, is covered by the term *défrichement,* literally
the 'taming of the wasteland'. Although the land-use statistics do
not always differentiate between clearance and drainage of land,
and in some areas the distinction in practice would not always have
been too clear, it is not proposed to make more than passing reference in this essay to the reclamation of coastal and inland marshes
and the draining of bodies of water.

Uncultivated though they were, the wastelands were far from
being totally outside the contemporary agricultural economy.
Wasteland may have been an apt description but functionally they
had a role in the semi-subsistence-level peasant economy providing
open pasture, firewood, turf, peat and stable litter. The communal
nature of ownership or of rights of use of these wastelands kept
them as a reserve for the whole rural community and in part
explained their perpetuation. An eighteenth-century parish register
summarizes the way in which they were indispensable to rural life:

> 'without wasteland there would be no sheep, without sheep
> there would be no manure for the farms, and without manure
> there would be no corn in the fields' (Perpillou, 1940, p. 23).

Sheep-rearing interests were particularly noted in Alsace as being
opposed to early attempts to clear and improve the extensive
wastelands there. As communal pasture land the waste was 'the
inhabitants' most precious resource on which they grazed livestock almost without expense' (Leuillot, 1957, p. 57). Consequently, partial clearance there resulted in a decline in sheep
numbers in the Haut-Rhin *département* from 99,000 in 1812 to
50,000 in 1829.

Obviously the vegetation and the type and frequency of this occasional use varied from one area of wasteland to another, but an interesting and fairly basic threefold division of the wastes of Haut-Poitou is given by Debien (1952). Firstly there were small areas of privately-owned wasteland adjacent to and occasionally used by the farm. Secondly, the small and large commonlands were used by all members of the rural community. Finally, the improved land and the village common lands were set in the vastness of the great wastelands extending from the periphery of one village's economic area to the next. As relics of centuries of neglect they 'remain a real desert for mankind, a vast reserve of rough pastures, a land for hunting, characterized by poverty' (Debien, 1952, p. 8).

A nineteenth-century description evokes the wasteland landscapes of the Landes of Gascony,

'acid sands, heather, furze, clumps of pines, and occasional flocks of sheep with shepherds on stilts. In summer these areas display drought and nakedness reminiscent of the deserts of Africa, but in winter they make a cold picture like the marshes of Siberia' (Dorgan, 1846, p. 292).

A similar scene of desolation was described by Gaugiran (1857) in the Sologne region:

'. . . at our feet a hollow filled with water and reeds. The water does not seem to flow, and spreads out in marshy pools over the immense stretch of wasteland, with a few wretched woodlands scattered here and there. The stagnant vapours arising from these pools await the arrival of strong westerly winds to carry them away' (p. 12).

Although lacking in precise land-use statistics, the eighteenth century did see many estimates made of the extent of wasteland in France.

'Even if differences exist between the figures and the percentages quoted, opinion is unanimous that uncultivated land occupied great stretches of territory in France' (Castang, 1967, p. 43).

Vauban, in the first decade of the century, estimated that wasteland represented 30 per cent of the then territory of France, that is about 14·8 million ha. A later estimate by Espilly in 1780 gave a figure of 12·8 million ha. At a regional level evidence exists in both words and statistics. In the South-West, La Maillardière comments on an uncultivated expanse, 50 leagues long by 20 leagues wide stretching from Bayonne to the borders of Roussillon, while north-wards between Bayonne and the Gironde the immense 'wastelands of Bordeaux were more extensive than several sovereign states' (Castang, 1967, p. 44). More precise figures for Brittany serve as a reminder of the regularity of wasteland in the landscapes of western France, not just in immense and notorious blocks but repeatedly in significant amounts in various bishoprics throughout the province (see Table 8.1). Furthermore this vast area of waste-land appeared to have increased during the seventeenth century when wars ravaged important agricultural areas like Burgundy, Alsace and Roussillon. It is doubted whether the first half of the eighteenth century saw any reductions: 'far from declining during the eighteenth century, on the contrary areas of wasteland in-creased' (Castang, 1967, p. 43). Nevertheless certain agronomic, commercial, and legal beginnings of later land-clearance policies could be detected.

Regional examples do exist of land clearance in the first half of the eighteenth century, largely to the north of a line from the Bordelais to Franche-Comté. Limited clearance and reclamation is recorded on riverside areas along the Somme and in Picardy (Demangeon, 1905), in the Pays de Bray (Clout, 1969), in Brit-tany, Poitou, and the *généralité* of Riom. Viticultural expansion, prompted by rising wine prices, accounted for some limited land clearance in Bordelais (Castang 1967). Certain significant innova-tors in this period included the short-lived success of the *Compagnie des Rizières de France*, established in 1740 which rented land in the Forez, on the edge of the Loire and the Lignon, in Dauphiné, Bourbonnais, near Valence, and at Thiers, with the aim of convert-ing sterile, marshy terrain into rice fields. An epidemic in 1741 at Thiers was attributed to the stagnant water of the rice fields and the projects here and elsewhere were soon abandoned (Castang, 1967). An important innovator, because he was also a writer, was the Marquis de Turbilly who practised a policy of systematic land clearance on his estates from 1737. Having cleared by plough and by fire, and having added manure to the soil, Turbilly's planting

Table 8.1

Cultivated and Uncultivated Land in Brittany in 1733

	Areas in arpents		
Bishoprics	Uncultivated land	Cultivated land	Total
Rennes	119,200	252,379	371,579
Nantes	273,645	357,662	631,307
Saint-Malo	153,605	223,755	377,360
Dol	20,681	13,804	34,485
Saint-Brieuc	96,344	108,055	204,399
Tréguier	89,888	87,035	176,923
St. Pol de Léon	80,343	149,000	229,343
Quimper	140,497	151,758	292,255
Vannes	242,098	286,919	529,017
	1,216,301	1,630,367	2,846,668

Source: Sée, 1906, pp. 371–373.

included flax, hemp, mulberry bushes, pasture grassland as well as cereals (Turbilly, 1760; Castang, 1967). The forestry possibilities of cleared land were explored in the 1730s by Buffon, the director of the Jardin des Plantes, who went on to establish the royal nursery gardens.

Contemporary government enquiries also stressed the possibilities offered by land clearance. An enquiry in 1731 specifically asked the provincial *intendant* to evaluate the possibilities of reclaiming uncultivated or abandoned land. The *intendant* of the *généralité* of Paris adjudged wasteland to be fairly extensive but of importance for pasturage and suggested tax exemptions for the reclaimers (Castang, 1967). A later enquiry in 1745 to evaluate the economic and demographic situation came to similar conclusions. The 1740s also saw the accession to government power of individuals interested in agricultural progress and open to physiocratic ideas, culminating in the appointment of Bertin to the post of *Contrôleur Général des Finances* in 1759. Influential publications included Duhamel du Monceau's *Traité de la culture des terres d'après les principes de M. Tull, anglais* (1750) propagating English agronomic experience, to be followed in 1762 by his *Elements d'agriculture*. Other popularisers of new methods included Pattullo with his *Essai sur l'amélioration des terres* (1758) and Turbilly's *Mémoire sur les défrichements* (1760) (Bourde, 1953). More general economic philosophy was being influenced by Quesnay and other physiocratic writers advocating that 'land is the only source of wealth and it is agriculture that increases wealth' (Quesnay, 1758, Augé-Laribé, 1955, p. 62.) As well as a ministerial representative in the form of Turgot, the physiocrats were able to directly influence Louis XV as Quesnay was personal physician both to him and to Madame de Pompadour.

'Thus in the mid-eighteenth century, enlightened opinion clearly posed the problem of the "priority of priorities", namely agriculture' (Castang, 1967, p. 148).

Certain economic and demographic factors also strengthened the case of those advocating clearance. Cereal prices were rising in the second half of the eighteenth century, a stimulus to production. However rents were rising even faster, in this case benefiting the landowner and prompting him to contemplate the development of new tenant farms on the waste areas of his estates. Debien (1952) has graphed the declarations of land clearance in Haut-Poitou and the price of wheat in western France, 1766–1790, and sees a parallel. When wheat prices were lower from 1775 to 1781, land clearance was measurably less important.

Increased market demand for agricultural products can be postulated from Toutain's (1963) evidence of strong population growth 1755–1776 (0·8 per cent per annum) and average growth 1776–1801 (0·4 per cent per annum), compared with the 1700–1755 period of low growth (0·2 per cent per annum). Consequently by the 1760s one can detect the use of land clearance as part of the state's agricultural policy. However to encourage the extension of the agriculturally utilizable area, two related policies had to be promoted; firstly to free inter-provincial trade within France, and secondly to remove the hold of collective rights over wasteland areas. The 1760s saw several enactments to legalize such policies. Following suggestions from the newly-founded *Société d'Agriculture de Paris*, Bertin produced a decree in 1761 exempting from taxes for ten years lands improved by reclamation. More precisely, taxes were only levied at the pre-clearance levels for these first ten years and this exemption only applied initially to the following *généralités*; Paris, Amiens, Soissons, Orléans, Bourges, Moulins, Lyons, Riom, Poitiers, La Rochelle, Limoges, Bordeaux, Tours, Auch, Champagne, Rouen, Caen, and Alençon (Castang, 1967). Later, the *généralités* of Bresse, Bugey, Valromey and pays de Gex were added. Further edicts in 1763–64 freed internal trade in France of cereals, vegetables and flour from certain provincial taxes, representing progress towards the free circulation of goods. Government officials then went on to question the system of common rights, 1764–1770, in an attempt to permit easier enclosure and greater freedom in individual cultivation practices. Regionally there was some effect; in 1767 the *intendant* of Limousin was given authority for enclosing properties and other edicts attacked common rights in Béarn (1767), Franche-Comté (1768), Champagne (1769), Bourgogne (1770), and Bourbonnais (1777). Considerable progress was made in restricting the effects of open pasture in Languedoc and Roussillon but elsewhere reaction was stronger (Castang, 1967). The question arose of whether owners of wasteland in the process of reclamation should also be exempt for several years from tithes and poll tax. This was enacted by the Declaration of 13th August, 1766.

The Results of Land-Clearance Legislation of the 1760s

The French government authorities appear to have watched quite closely the results of their land-clearance legislation though many of the documentary records of their national enquiries have been lost. A 1768 circular sent to each provincial by d'Ormesson of the *Ministère des Finances* evaluated a national clearance between 1766 and 1770, of 400,000 *arpents* (1 *arpent ordinaire* = 0·4220 ha). A later circular sent round in 1780 by Necker, attempting to see if the fifteen years of tax exemptions granted by the 1766 edict were sufficient to promote clearance concluded that some 950,000 *arpents* had been cleared, 1766–1780 (Necker, 1784, p. 233). Necker admitted that these were declarations of clearance which must precede the actual work of reclamation in order to obtain tax and tithe concessions.

'One can understand that a change of opinion or failure to achieve land clearance must have led to great differences between

the areas of land where clearance was intended and those that
were actually reclaimed' (Necker, 1784, p. 231).

Most extensive clearing was suggested in Provence while Lorraine and Alsace appeared least interested in reclamation. Based on
regional sample studies and on contemporary suggestions that
only about five eighths of the declarations were actually cleared,
Castang concludes that the trend of clearance grew from 1766 and
reached an apogee in the year 1770–1773. In all about 750,000
arpents or 316,500 ha were in fact cleared plus, locally further
reclamation of polders through drainage (Castang, 1967). While
representing an important addition these 300–350,000 extra ha
must be put into perspective, namely that Quesnay's estimate of
the contemporary area of arable land in France was of the order of
21 million ha and that Turbilly estimated the wastelands to cover
an area of nearly half of that of the arable.

Table 8.2 has been drawn up from Castang's researches. Given
that it reflects only a sample of the provinces of France and that its
accuracy depends on the survival of local surveys in departmental
archives, this regional evidence does help to substantiate Necker's
claims though suggesting also that declarations of intent to clear
land were frequently never carried out. Set against the total area
of wasteland and against the total French agricultural production,
the addition of 300–350,000 ha could only represent a very limited
success for the government policy of land clearance. In Limousin,
while certain cropping patterns and agronomic practices were
being improved, Perpillou (1940) concludes that the ordinance of
1766 had very limited results for the whole of the country. Debien's
(1952) detailed study in Haut-Poitou does detect positive and
permanent gains after the 1766 declaration, but in examining the
land use of the newly-cleared land he considers that 'one is still far
from the beginnings of the agricultural revolution' (p. 86).
Furthermore it must be admitted that many of the clearances were
only ephemeral, soon being neglected and abandoned. Land in
Languedoc having been cleared despite protests from pastoral
interests was recorded as later being abandoned. Arthur Young
remarked on a farm near Nantes returning to the wild and commented on the failure of clearance attempts in the Landes district
of Gascony (Young, 1969, p. 54 and p. 95). In Narbonne the

Table 8.2

Regional Aspects of Land Clearance, 1766–1789

Locality	Dates	Area cleared	Comments
Provence	1767–1782	65,000 ha	More than 61 per cent in seneschalships of Aix and Arles.
Languedoc	1779–1788	18,925 ha	Much reaction; the Parliament of Toulouse only registered the 1766 declaration in 1770.
Roussillon	—	3,800 ha	Fairly significant addition to the estimated 51,000 ha of arable.
Brittany	1766–1780	44,447 ha	Impetus lost and results declined after 1768–70 spurt.
Normandy	1766–1783	9,525 ha	Decline in clearance rate after 1773.
Généralité of Tours	1766–1784	20,000 ha	Annual rate decreases after 1775.
Généralité of Orléans	1766–1784	19,000 ha	Mainly in Sologne as little waste remaining in Beauce.
Généralité of Bourgogne	1766–1781	10,000–12,500 ha	
Généralité of Picardie	1763–1772	above 840 ha	Includes land drainage.
Généralité of Auvergne	1779–1789	3,010 ha	

Source: Castang, 1967, pp. 286–326.

intendant complained of the difficulty of assessing the extent of clearance because of the rapid abandonment of cleared land. The intendant of Roussillon even locally forbade further clearance as it so often led to soil erosion and abandonment (Castang, 1967).

Throughout the period there were many opponents of the land-clearance policy. To the intendant of Burgundy in 1780 it was 'a false attraction, as one moved from one field to clear another and enjoy tax exemption' (Castang, 1967, p. 354). Common-land and pastoral interests consistently opposed clearance as a threat to their economic well-being. The Church was unwilling to lose

tithes on land being cleared. The continuing low technical ability
of French agriculture coupled with the absence or paucity of
fertilizers limited progress as did the heavy capital outlays required. Rozier in his *Cours d'Agriculture* (1783) doubted the
profitability of land clearance in view of its high initial investment.
Duhamel du Monceau (1762) considered it better to 'improve
land that the farmer already made use of rather than undertaking
clearance of new land' (p. 112). The essential problem was not to
cultivate more but to cultivate better. Eighteenth-century land
clearance was criticized because it often merely extended traditional cereal-based agriculture rather than introducing more intensive and varied 'modern' systems of agriculture. Thus the intensive
legislative activity, 1761–1780, should not obscure the weakness
of the results. The limited additional cultivation of marginal wasteland could reflect

> 'not the dynamism of agrarian capitalism or the enthusiasm of a
> youthful agronomy, but simply the anxious necessities of a
> burgeoning and ill-nourished population' (Morineau, 1970, p.
> 172).

Mere demographic increase could account for the extension of the
cultivated area, but that would mean the dominance of smallholders in piecemeal clearance of land. The surveys instigated by
d'Ormesson and Necker would appear to have recorded more
often the limited results of better capitalized large and medium
landowners taking advantage of the tax and tithe exemptions.
While not heralding any widespread agronomic revolution,
eighteenth-century attempts at land clearance established the legal
bases and requirements for which the state was called on to free
potential improvers from common rights over the wastelands.
Some of these were to be embodied in the rural code of 1791. Subsequent legislation in 1793, which gave each village the option of
dividing up its communal lands for cultivation, has been designated as a legal turning point for the Pays de Bray so that by 1830
the bulk of the region's waste had been cleared (Clout, 1969).
Also some of the techniques of land clearance had been tried and in
part perfected, and it was upon these that the infrastructural
developments and commercial possibilities of the nineteenth

century were able to base a more fundamental addition to the agricultural area of France.

Wasteland in the Early Nineteenth Century

The continued presence of vast expanses of wasteland were graphically recorded by Arthur Young in the course of his travels in France, in 1787, 1788 and 1789. He made a particular effort to see the wastelands of Bordeaux observing that 'they reach almost to the gates of Bayonne; but broken by cultivated spots for a league or two' (Young, 1969, p. 54). The wastes of Brittany especially made an impression.

> 'The country to Châteaulin more mountainous; one third waste . . . no exertion, nor any marks of intelligence, yet all near to the great navigation and market of Brest water, and the soil good' (Young, 1969, pp. 91–92). 'To Auray, the eighteen poorest miles I have yet seen in Brittany . . . To Vannes, the country varied but *landes* the more permanent feature' (Young, 1969, p. 93).

The region of Sologne came in for criticism of a social as well as an agronomic nature as Young crossed it southward from Orléans to La Ferté-Saint-Aubin, describing the terrain as:

> 'a dead flat of hungry, sandy gravels, with much heath . . . Yet all this country highly improvable . . . the property, perhaps, of some of those glittering beings who figured in the procession the other day at Versailles' (Young, 1969, p. 16).

While observing some enclosure and land clearance in the Pyrenees where he recorded that the parish communities were selling common land free of pastoral or fuel-gathering rights, elsewhere, as in the waste plains of Brittany, Anjou, Maine, and Guienne the large landowners would only lease out the wastes, being restricted by continuing rights of commonage (Young, 1969, p. 299). As well as regional and local observations, Young also gave an estimate of the areas under various land uses for France as a whole (Table 8.3). Although amalgamated with pastures the wasteland category amounted to one third of the area under arable.

Table 8.3

France—Land Use in 1789, After Arthur Young

	Acres	Percentage
Arable land	70,000,000	53·4
Vines	5,000,000	3·8
Woods	24,000,000	18·3
Meadows and rich pasturage	4,000,000	3·0
Lucerne	5,000,000	3·8
Pastures and wastes	23,000,000	17·7
Total	131,000,000	100·0

Source: Young, 1969, p. 360.

Attempts to provide more accurate and more detailed land use statistics were made during the revolutionary and Napoleonic periods and locally figures and maps did result. The major survey which produced the documents of the old cadaster was eventually to follow the law of September 15th, 1807, and the results of this together with revisions during the nineteenth century are to form the principal data sources for the rest of this essay (Clout and Sutton, 1969). Certain problems attend the use of these cadastral data, a major one being the timespan involved in the compilation of the old cadaster. Maps based on it, while usually referred to as 'early nineteenth century' can in fact cover 40 years or more between the earliest and latest surveyed sections of the map (Sutton, 1969). Also areas of France which were only tardily added to the national territory, such as Nice and Savoy, were not completely surveyed until 1877 in the case of Nice, and well into the twentieth century for Savoy. Their old cadastral statistics thus are more contemporaneous with the second re-evaluation of 1879. This lengthy timespan limits the usefulness of Fig. 8.1 as a cross-sectional view of wasteland. Also, being land-tax documents, certain of the land-use categories are legal definitions and are thus open to redefinition in the course of time. Apparent land-use changes may be nothing more than reappraisal by the taxation authorities. Also certain categories of land use were excluded from taxation and hence from the surveys. A major instance is that of state or royal forests which locally were quite important. This omission from the earlier surveys can be projected back from the 1908 new cadaster when

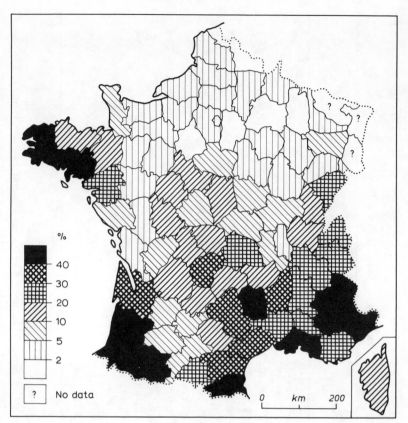

FIG. 8.1. Wasteland in the early nineteenth century. *Source*: Ministère des Finances, 1884.

state forests totalled 1,013,651 ha (Ministère des Finances, 1913, Vol. 2). On the other hand, the completeness, fiscal impartiality, and field-survey approaches of the direct-taxation authorities carrying out the cadastral surveys have produced an invaluable source of land-use data. This essay will employ them on both national and local scales.

Given the problem of the varying dates of survey within and between *départements* the statistics of the old cadaster give a detailed picture of the prevalence of wasteland in France in the early part of the nineteenth century. The results for the cadaster and later evaluations are given in Table 8.4. Some 8,108,306 ha of waste were recorded at the time of the old cadaster covering 16·2

Table 8.4

Evolution of Major Land Uses During The Nineteenth Century

	Old Cadaster ha	%	1850* ha	%	1879 ha	%	1908 ha	%
High quality land	1,415,993	2·8	1,337,947 (1,423,487)	2·8 (2·8)	1,398,758	2·8	1,140,218	2·3
Arable land	25,452,452	50·9	25,009,762 (25,803,377)	52·1 (51·6)	26,173,657	52·3	24,508,057	49·1
Meadows	4,804,440	9·6	4,603,418 (4,783,459)	9·6 (9·6)	4,998,280	10·0	6,912,508	13·8
Vineyards	2,109,250	4·2	2,142,811 (2,178,194)	4·5 (4·4)	2,320,533	4·6	1,499,048	3·0
Woodland	8,144,718	16·3	7,672,757 (8,123,916)	16·0 (16·2)	8,397,131	16·8	8,703,264	17·4
Wasteland	8,108,306	16·2	7,188,634 (7,705,481)	15·0 (15·4)	6,746,800	13·5	7,205,648	14·4
Total	50,035,159	100·0	47,955,329 (50,017,914)	100·0 (100·0)	50,035,159	100·0	49,968,743	100·0

Sources: Cadaster: *Ministère des Finances*, 1884.

1850, 1879, 1908: *Ministère des Finances*, 1913.

* The 1850 totals do not include the *départements* of Alpes-Maritimes, Corse, Savoie, and Savoie (Haute). The lower figures in brackets in the 1850 column are adjusted by adding the cadastral values for the four *départements* concerned.

per cent of the area surveyed. Proportionally this bears some relation to Arthur Young's 1789 estimate which considered that 17·7
per cent of France's area was under pasture and waste. Considerable regional variation in this proportion existed (Fig. 8.1).
Whereas most of the *départements* of the Paris Basin, northern, and
eastern France were practically devoid of wasteland, all having
less than 4 per cent, and some less than 2 per cent of their area
under waste, the *départements* of central, southern, and western
France generally had above 10 per cent and often above 30 per cent
of their area so categorized. Vast expanses of waste must have
dominated the landscapes of Brittany, Gascony, the Massif Central,
Languedoc, and Provence, as well as the more mountainous regions
of the Alps, Pyrenees, and Cévennes. Similar, though in detail far
from identical, north-south contrasts were found for the 1840
cereal yields per unit area or as a ratio to seed (Morineau, 1970,
pp. 178–180). Morineau posed the hypothesis that these north-
south discrepancies were the result of the incomplete diffusion of
new agronomic techniques into France, particularly from England
and the Low Countries. Such innovations hardly ever entered
French agriculture from the south, except perhaps in sheep raising.
He admitted the possibility of northern innovation centres but to
this must be added permanent differences in geology, soil quality,
and climate. After all, he points out:

'the areas of high productivity in 1840 are also those of 1967 . . .
The absolute figures as well as their geographical distribution
fit easily into a structural explanation with a possible exception
for the Flemish area' (Morineau, 1970, p. 180).

Regional variations in agricultural productivity per unit area
and per man have also been studied by Pautard (1965). The visual
correlations between Fig. 8.1 and Pautard's maps of the value of
crops per ha in agricultural use 1852 and per worker in 1862 are
particularly strong, though there is some lack of fit in the Mediterranean coastlands. The interesting group of *départements* with
low wasteland percentages in the Garonne Basin can also be identified as an area of higher productivity on Pautard's maps, and indeed earlier Young had included them with Flanders and Alsace
as the three most prosperous and advanced regions. Comparing the
mid-nineteenth with the mid-twentieth-century regional variations

in agricultural productivity Pautard is struck by the permanency of regional patterns. '*Départements* were ranked almost in the same order as a hundred years earlier' (Pautard, 1965, p. 51). Only Brittany and the Mediterranean region appear to have improved their relative position in terms of productivity. Inherent environmental constraints account for the continued agricultural backwardness of many of the *départements* which stand out on Figure 8.1 as having high proportions of their surface area covered with wasteland. Potentially less permanent factors would have been backward agricultural techniques, especially those associated with land reclamation, a low degree of integration into national and regional commercial circuits, a high degree of isolation, restrictive communal-grazing practices, and a relatively low population density resulting in a widespread under-use of the land resources. Certainly, through the nineteenth century one can suggest links between improvements in these restrictive factors and the occurrence of land clearance.

Some of the *départements* with only moderate proportions of their areas under waste in fact showed considerable internal variations if one examines the cadastral statistics in more detail. Thus the Sologne section of the *départements* of Loiret and Loir-et-Cher, to the south of the river Loire, stands out. The *arrondissement* of Romorantin alone accounts for 45,341 ha of the 63,688 ha of waste recorded in Loir-et-Cher's three *arrondissements*. In Loiret the southern *arrondissements* of Orléans, 22,389 ha under waste and Gien, 18,242 ha, contrast with Montargis and Pithiviers to the north with 2,665 ha and 970 ha of waste respectively. (A. D. Blois, Série P.; A. D. Orléans, G. F. 414.) In Deux-Sèvres the departmental proportion of 3·9 per cent under waste obscures a north–south contrast; the *arrondissement* of Bressuire (6·7 per cent of its area under wasteland) and Parthenay (6·7 per cent) to the north incorporate most of the wasteland compared with Niort (0·6 per cent) and Melle (0·5 per cent) in the south (A. D. Niort, Série continue No. 3243). Thus those areas apparently containing little waste could possibly have that wasteland concentrated in a few less well-endowed and more isolated regions. The finer details of the distribution of wasteland have been mapped by Perpillou (1963) and his colleagues at the Laboratoire de Géographie Rurale of the Institut de Géographie, Paris.

The desirability of turning some of these wastelands into agri-culturally-productive land was not lost on the French governments of the early nineteenth century. The shortage of bread grain in 1816 prompted a government enquiry in 1817 to establish where and how much of the wasteland of each *département* was capable of being reclaimed (Sée, 1927, p. 23; A. N. F^{10} 1624). Although fragmentary the results are interesting in that they reflect con-temporary opinion over clearance possibilities. Corsica reported 11,858 ha of unused land, a low figure compared with the 120,956 ha recorded in the old cadaster carried out much later in the cen-tury. Côte d'Or, in which 32,832 ha of wasteland were recorded in the cadaster, was designated by its prefect as containing no waste-land which could immediately be reclaimed. Often the details were divided according to ownership hinting at the continued restrictive influence of the common-grazing interests. Indeed in the *départe-ment* of Yonne, of the area admitted as being uncultivated wasteland, the vast bulk was declared to be maintained as pastureland. Cer-tainly, given the limited techniques of clearance early in the nine-teenth century, the idea of widespread conversion to agricultural use of many areas of waste must have seemed quite impracticable.

Before going on to consider the progress of land clearance during the nineteenth century, it is worth briefly considering the tech-niques employed. Undoubtedly these varied from region to region. In the Sologne, even where the use of marl was uneconomic, the act of land clearance still afforded a powerful means of improvement and in the higher parts, where the heath vegetation was short, it was relatively inexpensive and gave quick results. Land could be sown after a few ploughings following its initial clearance using the plough. In lower areas a more vigorous type of vegetation, which stood about one metre high, required greater investment to clear. Repeated ploughings and manurings were necessary, taking up to two years, before the land could be sown with wheat (Sutton, 1971; Deloynes de Gautray, 1826). A more detailed rotation of leading to clearance involved the sowing of rye for two years, followed by a year in pasture or fallow; then rye or potatoes and turnips were cultivated, and again a year of fallow. This rotation con-tinued for ten or even fifteen years. After mid-century experimen-tal rotations leading to clearance in the Sologne employed marl and phosphatic fertilizers.

In Limousin Perpillou (1940) found a basic approach to clearance plus a modified technique for more difficult, wetter areas. Generally clearing involved cutting down brushwood, bracken, grasses, etc., which were piled up and then fired. A winter crop of oats was sown on the ashes. After its harvesting the work of grubbing up the roots ensued and only then could a first ploughing take place. Rye was sown, followed by turnips. In wetter wasteland areas sheep were pastured while ditches and later stone or brick channels drained the terrain. When ferns entered the modified vegetation it was judged time to deep plough the area and sow it in buckwheat for a year or two. Only then could a rye–forage crop rotation be established.

The Process of Land Clearance through the Nineteenth Century

Land-use developments through the nineteenth century can be derived from two sets of data, the censuses of the *Ministère de l'Agriculture* and the two re-evaluations of the old cadaster carried out in 1850 and 1879 together with the new cadaster of 1908. It is proposed to concentrate on the latter data source in the study (Clout and Sutton, 1969). The general trends through the century in the various main categories of land use can be traced from Table 8.4. As the total 'cadastral' area varies around the 50 million ha more attention should be given to the percentage values. A particular problem concerned the 1850 figures as the *départements* of Alpes-Maritimes, Savoie, and Haute-Savoie were not then part of France, and the figures for Corsica were not available. To render the official 1850 total of 47,955,329 ha more readily comparable the old cadastral values for the four *départements*, all of which were surveyed later than 1850, have been added to give an adjusted set of values indicated on Table 8.4 within brackets. A similar exercise was carried out by the *Direction Générale des Contributions Directes* in its 1913 report (*Ministère des Finances*, 1913, p. 265, footnote) allowing them to remark on a reduction in the area of wasteland 1850–1879 of 956,065 ha, which bears comparison with an adjusted value arrived at from Table 8.4 of 958,681 ha (*Ministère des Finances*, 1913, p. 91).

The changes in the absolute and relative area of waste is summarized in Table 8.5. Two salient points emerge; firstly the decrease in area through the nineteenth century according to the early cadaster, 1850, and 1879 surveys, but then a reversal represented by an increase in area according to the 1908 survey. Secondly, there appears to have been a major period of clearance between

Table 8.5

Changes in The Wasteland Area, Old Cadaster—1908

	Wasteland (ha)	% of total area	Absolute change (ha)	% change	% change in %
Old Cadaster	8,108,306	16·2			
1850					
(adjusted figures)	7,705,481	15·4	−402,825	− 5·0	− 4·9
1879	6,746,800	13·5	−958,681	−12·4	−12·3
1908	7,205,648	14·4	+458,848	+6·8	+6·7

Source: Table 8.4.

1850 and 1879 during which nearly one million ha of wasteland were reclaimed, representing as 12·3 per cent decrease in the proportion of land under waste. In absolute terms this represented three times the area of clearance estimated for the period 1766–1789. It amounted to an enlargement of the agricultural and woodland area of France of 2·3 per cent in slightly under 30 years. Because of the varying date of the old cadaster it is difficult to make comparisons between the periods before and after the new evaluation of 1850 but an increasing pace of clearance through the century up until the 1880s can certainly be postulated, and locally can be more definitively demonstrated (Sutton, 1971).

The 1850 distribution of waste (Fig. 8.2) shows relatively little change compared with the situation at the time of the old cadaster. Outside the Paris Basin and north-eastern France where the number of *départements* with less than 2 per cent of their area under waste had increased, the established patterns were maintained. Figure 8.5 shows that significant decreases, i.e. above 5 per cent, mainly occurred to the north of a line delimiting the areas of relatively extensive wasteland in western, central, and southern France. Exceptions occurred on the margins of Brittany, i.e. Loire Atlantique (old cadaster 20 per cent under waste, 1850 15

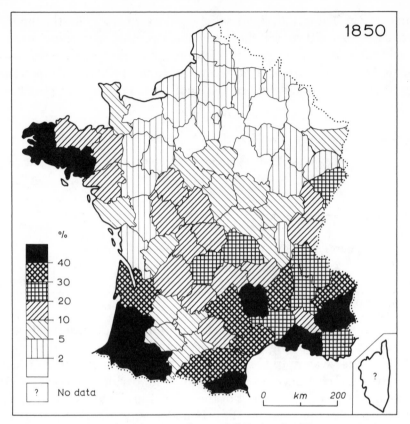

F I G. 8.2. Wasteland in 1850. *Source:* Ministère des Finances, 1913.

per cent), and Vendée (old cadaster 9 per cent, 1850 5 per cent)
in the central regions, i.e. Indre-et-Loire (old cadaster 13 per cent,
1850 11 per cent) in a southern belt of *départements* running westwards from Bouches-du-Rhône to Lot-et-Garonne.

Some of the regional results of the 1850–1879 period of land
clearance are discernible on Fig. 8.3. By 1879 the bulk of the
northern *départements* have quite insignificant proportions of waste,
usually well below 2 per cent, and they have been joined by many
central *départements* such as Loiret, Loir-et-Cher, Cher, Nièvre,
and Allier, which all now had less than 5 per cent of their area
under waste. Brittany and the Aquitaine Basin also show significant decreases in their wasteland components. By 1879 the results
were becoming apparent of the first successful large-scale reclamation of the Landes region of Gascony. Wasteland in Gironde

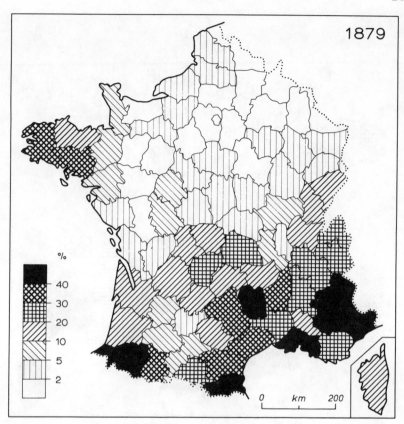

FIG. 8.3. Wasteland in 1879. *Source:* Ministère des Finances, 1913.

département had decreased from 32 per cent in 1850 to 17 per cent in 1879, and in Landes *département* from 47 per cent to 19 per cent (Fig. 8.4). The 1913 report of the *Ministre des Finances* remarked on the variety of trends in the area under waste. It showed continuous increase from 1850 in 10 *départements*, decrease until 1879 and then increase in 43 others, while two *départements* increased 1850–1879 and then decreased (Fig. 8.5). Twenty-eight *départements* displayed continuous decrease in wasteland 1850–1908 (*Ministère des Finances*, 1913).

Figure 8.6 emphasizes some of the 1850–1879 regional trends. If one ignores the fluctuations in northern France where wasteland is of minor importance, significantly large decreases stand out in the aforementioned regions of the Centre, Brittany, and Aquitaine. Slower rates of decrease prevailed in the upland regions

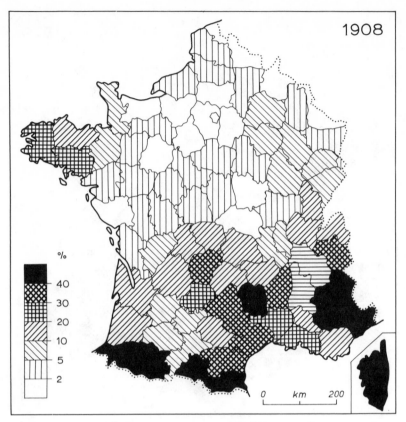

F IG. 8.4. Wasteland in 1908. *Source:* Ministère des Finances, 1913.

though in absolute terms these were sometimes quite large, i.e.
Ariège, 136,650 ha of waste in 1850, 120,084 ha in 1879, and
Isère, 162,163 ha in 1850, 155,973 ha in 1879. Generally, though,
land clearance had made most impact on the lowland areas of
western and central France. One significant lowland exception consisted of the *départements* of Languedoc and the lower Rhône
Valley where increases in wasteland area were the rule, 1850–1879.
Here decreases in the areas of vineyards corresponded fairly closely
to this expansion of wasteland, representing viticultural abandonment following the devastations of phylloxera. In Gard the vineyard area slumped from 78,319 ha in 1850 to 7,485 ha in 1879
while the waste increased by 30,649 ha, most of the rest remaining
as arable land.

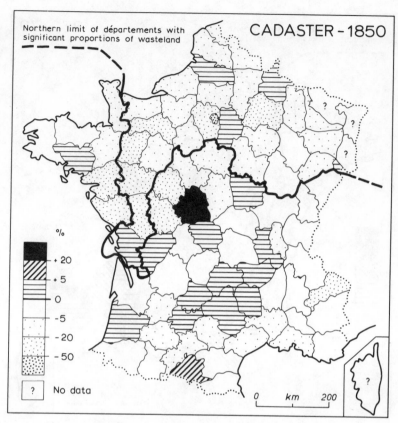

Fig. 8.5. Change in the percentage under wasteland between the Cadaster and 1850. *Source:* Ministère des Finances, 1884 and 1913.

By the time of the 1908 re-evaluation the nineteenth-century trend of land clearance had ceased and a reversal had resulted in a 6·8 per cent increase in the area of waste, an addition of 458,848 ha or approximately one third of the area cleared from the old cadaster up until 1879. Only detailed local studies would reveal whether this was the abandonment of recently cleared land or not. A close examination of the 1908 distribution of wasteland on Figure 8.4 can pick out certain of these increases in wasteland particularly in the eastern Paris Basin, Lorraine, and Champagne together with certain Alpine and Pyrenean *départements*. Brittany, Gascony, northern Limousin, and Touraine, though, continued to show a decrease in their wasteland proportion. In Finistère and Morbihan quite considerable areas were cleared, 70,990 ha and 80,729

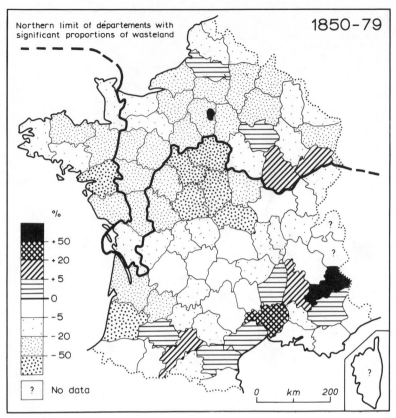

FIG. 8.6. Change in the percentage under wasteland between 1850 and 1879.
Source: Ministère des Finances, 1913.

ha respectively. The resulting map of change 1879–1908 is thus
fairly complex. Again concentrating on the central, southern, and
western parts of France, where wasteland was a significant land-
use feature, Fig. 8.7 reveals the considerable increases in the wasteland proportions of many *départements* especially in the upland and
western regions excluding Brittany, Gascony, parts of the Mediterranean littoral and a belt of central *départements* stretching eastwards from Vienne to the Jura mountains. Some of the possible
factors behind this late nineteenth–early twentieth century land
abandonment will be discussed later. For the moment, the 1908
picture serves to focus attention on the importance of the 1850–
1879 period as encompassing a major effort to land clearance the

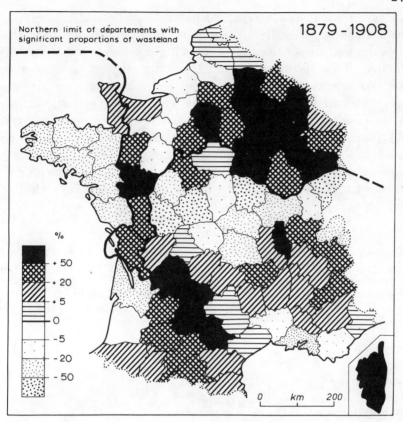

FIG. 8.7. Change in the percentage under wasteland between 1879 and 1908.
Source: Ministère des Finances, 1913.

effects of which were considerable on the land-use patterns of
certain regions, while in others it was more ephemeral.

Mention must be made of other data sources which serve to
substantiate the national and regional trends in clearance which
have emerged from the above study of the cadastral land-use
statistics and their periodic re-evaluations. Of the nineteenth-
century decennial agricultural enquiries that of 1852 nearly coincides in date with the first revision of the early land survey in 1850
(Statistique de la France, 1855). Considering that one concerned
an agricultural definition of land use and the other a taxation
definition, there is an encouragingly close correspondence between
the areas recorded as waste in the two surveys. When the two

values for each *département* are plotted against each other on a graph there is generally a close linear relationship, with the 1850 re-evaluation values usually slightly higher than those of the 1852 enquiry. This results probably from the slightly divergent definitions of 'waste', the 1852 enquiry including some 'uncultivated land' in a category of 'diverse uses' including woods and forests. In the case of ten *départements* the discrepancy between the 1850 and 1852 values for waste was more considerable and these are listed in Table 8.6 to allow adjustments to be made to any impressions gained from the maps. The writer puts more reliance on the thoroughness and impartiality of the cadastral statistics (Sutton, 1967).

Table 8.6

Departements Where a Large Discrepancy Exists Between The Areas of Waste According to The 1850 New Evaluation And The 1852 Agricultural Enquiry

Départements	Area under wasteland (ha)	
	New Evaluation 1850	Agricultural Enquiry 1852
Allier	60,421	19,125
Aveyron	276,154	172,963
Cher	60,170	15,850
Haute-Garonne	46,813	23,644
Loiret	43,626	26,568
Lot-et-Garonne	42,846	26,335
Nièvre	33,973	11,339
Rhône	6,757	15,129
Saône-et-Loire	51,957	19,978
Deux-Sèvres	15,474	2,116

Sources: 1850: *Ministère des Finances*, 1913.
1852: *Statistique de la France*, 1855.

Two of the subsequent decennial agricultural enquiries, those of 1862 and 1892, also provide additional evidence of regional disparities in clearance. They both sought information on areas affected by various agricultural improvements including clearance, irrigation, drainage, marling, etc., during the previous decade. The areas of waste cleared between 1852 and 1862 are mapped on Fig. 8.8. If one ignores those *départements* of northern France where wastelands are relatively insignificant in area, the patterns

of concentration on Fig. 8.8 bear comparison with those on Fig.
8.6, despite the different time-spans involved. High absolute
amounts of wasteland were cleared between 1852 and 1862 in the
central parts of France, in Limousin, Sologne, as well as in
Brittany, Vendée, and Gascony (*Statistique de la France*, 1868).
Obviously this data sourse gives no indication of areas which relapsed back into wasteland. The 1882–1892 recorded results of

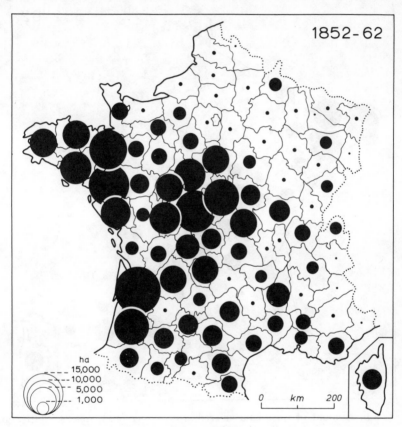

FIG. 8.8. Amount of wasteland cleared, 1852–1862 (ha). *Source:* Statistique de
la France, 1868.

land clearance totalled 130,942 ha compared with the 235,963 ha
cleared 1852–1862 (*Statistique Agricole de la France*, 1897). This
accords with the trend observed in the cadastral data which indicated a lessening of the pace of clearance and indeed an over-com-
pensating relapse of land back into waste. Regionally, land

clearance was fairly extensive, 1882–1892, in Brittany, the middle
Loire, Limousin, northern and western parts of the Massif Central,
and Languedoc and the Rhône delta, the latter two areas perhaps
reflecting a recovery after the phylloxera crisis in the viticultural
regions. Outside of Brittany, Gascony, and parts of the northern
Massif Central, Fig. 8.9 shows many anomalies with the patterns

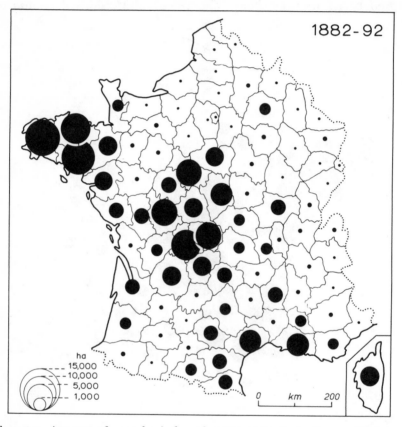

FIG. 8.9. Amount of wasteland cleared, 1882–1892 (ha). *Source:* Statistique
Agricole de la France, 1897.

observable on Fig. 8.7 of the changes in the area of waste 1879–
1908. This does not necessarily refute the validity of the 1882–
1892 statistics but rather demonstrates the complex, fluctuating
situation of wasteland, constantly being reclaimed or added to as
local agricultural economies prosper or stagnate.

Land Clearance as an Indicator of Agricultural Change

Within these fluctuations certain regional and temporal trends in land clearance have emerged and these can be compared with other indicators of the regional progress of the agricultural revolution in France. Initially, however, the valid questions raised by Morineau and others over whether there in fact was an agricultural revolution in France during the nineteenth century must be considered. Although concentrating on the preceding century, Morineau's evidence, based on yields per unit area or per quantity of seed sown, extends well into the nineteenth century. He concludes that, prior to 1840:

> 'on the basis of the national average . . . there was no agricultural revolution in France, but a long period of stagnation of yields.' Furthermore 'the yields ratio to seed improved little during the nineteenth century, contrary to output per ha, since the 1930–1939 average was still 7·5:1 for an output of 15·4 quintals of wheat per ha.'

Morineau admitted that geographic contrasts in yields postponed judgement over this apparent nineteenth century stagnation. A further valid point made by Morineau (1970) was that the use of qualitative data, such as the appearance of a new crop or technique, was 'merely evidence of potential not an index of change' in French agriculture (p. 172). The quantification of one of these hitherto qualitative indices namely under-drainage, supports this argument (Phillips and Clout, 1970). In spite of contemporary opinion that between 17 per cent and 23 per cent of France's area required draining in the 1850s, it is estimated that less than 2 per cent of the area, that is less than 3 per cent of the cultivated land, in fact benefited from under-draining in the rest of the century. Thus despite much government support this particular improvement simply failed to get accepted in the 1850s and 1860s, certainly outside of a few *départements* in northern France and the Paris Basin. 'If a definition were based on draining alone, it would be hard to say that a "revolution" had occurred' in French agriculture (Phillips and Clout, 1970, p. 91).

However other recent writers remain convinced of the contribution of the nineteenth century to the agricultural transformation of France. Dumont (1951) equates the agricultural revolution with the period of the Second Empire. Kindleberger (1964) lists several bodies of information supporting the case for an agricultural revolution in the second half of the nineteenth century. Except for the crisis of 1848, the countryside was prosperous from 1840 to 1870; fertilizer was introduced and, with the spread of the railways, so was liming; wheat yields rose 50 per cent between 1850 and 1880; technical efficiency, in the form of the Brabant plough, reapers, and combines, improved especially after 1860; and the area supplying the Paris market spread from a 50 km to a 250 km radius between 1830 and 1855. Moreover farm income in this period was rising rapidly. It is estimated that it rose 1·8 per cent a year from 1850 to 1880, following a rise of only 1 per cent a year from 1788 to 1850. Thereafter no rise ensued to the end of the century (Kindleberger, 1964, pp. 212–213; *Institut de Science Économique Appliquée*, 1952, p. 60). This 1850–1880 acceleration of farm incomes followed by stagnation ties in remarkably closely to the trends in land-clearance activity. A similar time-scale is suggested by Sirol's index which Kindleberger considered as the best evaluation of real-output in agriculture despite the omittance of meat and fresh vegetables which results in an understatement of the total output.

'A moving average suggests that the index ran from 65 in the early 1840s and 70 in the early 1850s to 90 in the middle 1870s before slumping in the late 1880s to 70.' (Kindleberger, 1964, p. 213; Sirol, 1942, appendix 4).

Similar conclusions were reached by Pautard (1965) after a review of many contemporary and later sources. His graph of French agricultural production demonstrates that 'the rhythm of growth is poorly known before 1840, very rapid between 1840 and 1892, and then there is a flattening out of the curve with the rate of growth increasing again after 1948' (p. 39). Although this ties in chronologically with the 1850–1879 period of maximum clearance the proportionate increase in agricultural production is far greater than the contemporaneous extension of the utilisable agricultural area. Pautard's index, in constant *francs* with a base of 100 in 1892, increased from 27 in 1840 to 93 in 1882, a threefold increase compared with the slight enlargement of agricultural land (woodland excluded) from 68·4 per cent of the total area of France in 1850 to 69·7 per cent in 1879 (Fig. 8.10). This discrepancy suggests an intensification of agricultural production, a feature unsuccessfully sought after by Morineau in his eighteenth-century study.

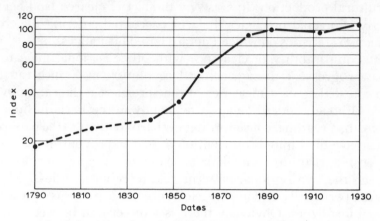

FIG. 8.10. Growth of French agricultural production, 1790–1830, Index 100 = 1892. *Source:* Pautard, 1965, 40–41.

The 1840–1892 progress in French agriculture displayed marked regional contrasts. Through the calculation of indices of crop production using the agricultural enquiries for 1852 and 1892 Pautard (1965) has regionalized the patterns of agricultural growth. The resulting map shows that, between 1852 and 1892, practically all the *départements* north of a line from Saint-Malo to the Jura progressed at a slower rate than elsewhere. Most progress was registered in the *départements* of the West, the Centre and Languedoc. Despite data deficiencies the appearance of regional blocks with a fairly high degree of similarity between adjoining *départements* satisfies Pautard of the validity of the broad regional pattern. If one concentrates on those *départements* in which wasteland was a significant land use, there is some agreement between the above regional pattern and that of 1850–1879 clearance on Fig. 8.6. Considerable clearance of land in Brittany, northern parts of the Massif Central, and the middle Loire Valley 1850–1879, certainly equates with above-average increases in agricultural production. Further south in the Massif Central and in

Languedoc clearance was relatively less important in percentage terms, but as Fig. 8.3 shows, these were the *départements* with the highest areas under waste and so even slight decreases in areas under waste could significantly expand the useful agricultural area. In Languedoc the fluctuating fortunes of viticulture interfere with direct comparisons between clearance and increases in agricultural production. In Gascony the fact of cleared land being directly afforested precludes the area concerned entering the crop production statistics on which Pautard based his indices.

The comparability of clearance with other regional indicators of the progress of the agricultural revolution in France can be further tested against measures of the spread of technical innovations. Although underdrainage was mainly in the Paris Basin and the North, a regional concentration in sharp contrast to the patterns of clearance the limited contribution of that improvement measure to French agriculture as a whole probably makes any comparisons between the two regional patterns relatively meaningless. More relevant perhaps is to compare clearance with patterns of use of mineral fertilizers. Obviously there is a direct link between these two improvement techniques. the availability of marl and other fertilizers making clearance an economic proposition. Clout and Phillips (1972) have studied the use of mineral fertilizers 1852–1862 and in 1876. As in the case of underdraining the areas affected and the amount of fertilizer used was less than anticipated even allowing for the fact that marl and lime were only periodically applied to the land. The use of marl, 1852–1862, showed a strong geographical concentration in the Paris Basin which alone accounted for 75 per cent of the area marled. A second focal region of marling centred on southern Gascony. By 1876 these two regions had been joined by a concentration of marling in north-west France with Ille-et-Vilaine and Manche now accounting for 15 per cent of all the marl used. Elsewhere there was much evidence of the wish to practice marling but costs were too high due to excessive distance from appropriate marl deposits or to inaccessibility in both distance and cost terms. The lowest costs prevailed in the central Paris Basin though even there complaints were registered. Locally in the West and especially in Brittany fertilizers and marls of marine origin were utilized, and even the interior of Finistère benefited from this source via the canal between Nantes and Brest.

In the course of the nineteenth century the use of lime was added to that of marl. Obviously lime was more limited in its areas of origin being restricted to regions of calcareous deposits. By 1876 it formed 17·5 per cent by volume of the fertilizers then used. The regional patterns of the use of lime, 1852–1862, show an interesting spatial complement to those of the use of marl (Clout and Phillips, 1972). Liming was more important in the zone between the Paris Basin and Brittany, and to the north of the Massif Central. Forty per cent of the total liming occurred in 11 *départements* in the West of France on the margins of peninsular Brittany. It can be argued that the use of lime was still something of an innovation in the 1860s and early 1870s and its widespread use required further improvement of local transport infrastructures. In Brittany, for example, its use in the interior only became generally possible after the construction of narrow-gauge railways after 1885. The agricultural enquiry of 1867 revealed the widespread desire in most regions for improved transport facilities and subsidies to make the use of lime and other fertilizers more economic for the agriculturalist.

The extensions south and west of the Paris Basin of the use of lime does correspond to a degree with the patterns of progress suggested by land clearance, 1850–1879. But generally there is only limited correspondence between clearance and other indicators of the regional progress of the agricultural revolution. The spatial coincidence of several measures only really occurs in the Centre, North-Western, and Gascony regions. The very small proportion of land still in waste in the Paris Basin renders land clearance a poor indicator there, though of course other measures do reinforce this region's position as the advanced and often innovating centre of French agriculture. Also as underdraining and the use of fertilizers are associated primarily with arable land improvement, clearance for other than arable extension will obviously not spatially correspond. Consequently one must attempt to look at the land-use changes associated with the reduction of wasteland before fully assessing clearance as an index of the agricultural revolution.

To some extent the question of what became of the wastelands after clearance, and indeed the reasons for clearing, can be answered by looking at the related changes in the proportions of the other land uses. Several regional examples can illustrate this, focussing on the 1850–1879 period of greatest land clearance. In the five *départements* of peninsular Brittany the 1850–1879 clearing of waste was closely paralleled by an extension of the arable area. In Finistère an almost identical area was involved in both land-use categories; in Loire-Atlantique the dramatic clearance of waste-land resulted in increased meadowland as well as 60,371 ha extra arable. By contrast in Gascony the substantial 1850–1879 reductions in wasteland appeared to equate with expanded woodland areas in Gironde and Landes. In neighbouring Lot-et-Garonne a more complex situation involved a decline in wasteland and arable together with an increase in woodland and vineyards. The three Languedoc *départements* of Aude, Hérault, and Gard all had increases in their already substantial wasteland areas 1850–1879. Hérault and Gard both suffered drastic reductions in their vine-yards areas over the same period, the result of phylloxera outbreaks. Although most of these former vineyards appear to have been added to the arable-land category by 1879, it can be presumed that some relapsed into wasteland, as other land use categories appeared to have remained static. A final regional example covers the block of five *départements* between the Paris Basin and the Massif Central which stand out on Fig.8.6 as all having decreases of more than 50 per cent in their wasteland areas, 1850–1879. Table 8.7 compares these substantial reductions in waste with changes in the other major land-use categories. Generally reclamation for an expanded arable area is suggested except for the

Table 8.7

Absolute Change in Major Land-use Categories, 1850–1879

Departements	Gains (+) and losses (−) of major land use categories (ha)				
	Wasteland	Arable	Meadow	Woodland	Vineyards
Allier	−41,180	+52,938	+2,672	−12,977	− 1,542
Cher	−33,783	+30,893	−3,549	+ 4,341	+ 1,682
Indre	−74,266	+66,614	+8,503	+ 1,795	+ 7,322
Loir-et-Cher	−39,947	+13,189	−700	+16,950	+10,383
Loiret	−28,511	+42,490	−63	+ 3,883	− 7,243

Source: Ministère des Finances, 1913.

Loir-et-Cher where woodland and vineyard areas have also shown significant extensions.

These regional examples have reflected a variety of land use changes associated with clearance other than merely an expanded arable area. Unfortunately the crude statistics only suggest associations between the fluctuations of waste as against other categories; the actual mechanics of change might be more complex. In a study of land use changes in the Sologne during the nineteenth century this complexity was revealed when the detailed statistics of the 1850 and 1879 revisions were examined (Sutton, 1967). In addition to absolute areas in each land-use category, the revisions gave details of additions from and losses to all other categories since the old cadaster. Thus in the *arrondissement* of Romorantin the decline in the wasteland area of 32,362 ha between the old cadaster and 1879 was in fact composed of the clearance of 32,365 ha for arable, 3428 ha for woodland, 16 ha for vineyards, and 5 ha for meadows, while 26 ha of meadows and 3426 ha of woodland deteriorated into wasteland during the same period. Thus, although land clearance and afforestation in the western Sologne superficially appeared to be reciprocal processes, they were in fact both related to the arable land, a category undergoing great changes in location if not in quantity.

This kind of detailed regional study is necessary before attempting anything other than the broadest generalizations concerning the explanation of patterns of land clearance. However, a pilot survey has suggested that the survival of the manuscript base statistics of the 1850 and 1879 revisions is only fragmentary (see Appendix pp. 551–58). Five surviving bodies of data do allow a very restricted glimpse of the mechanics of land-use change in four regions (Table 8.8). In the adjoining *départements* of Loiret and Loir-et-Cher a similar process has emerged involving clearance for arable land, with only a relatively small area of waste being directly afforested. Indeed, 3426 ha of woodland were downgraded to the wasteland category in Loir-et-Cher. In sharp contrast clearance in the Landes *département* and undoubtedly in adjoining Gironde too, meant the conversion of waste into woodland with much smaller areas being cleared for arable, meadows and vineyards. Here the clearance took place after the 1850 revision and indeed can be directly related to legislation in 1857 compelling the improvement

Table 8.8

Details of Land Clearance Between the Old Cadaster and 1879

Département	Wasteland (ha) Old cadaster	1879	Details of change, including land use from which gained (+) or lost (−)
Loiret	51,688	12,115	+ 22 arable: + 30 meadow: + 6 wood: + 77 other; − 35,257 arable: − 96 meadow: − 9 vineyard: − 4337 wood
Loir-et-Cher	63,687	16,099	+ 19 arable: + 26 meadow: + 5 vineyard: + 3426 wood: + 5 other: − 1 garden: − 43,496 arable: − 10 meadow: − 613 vineyard: − 6949 wood
Landes	405,480	170,356	+ 182 arable: + 55 meadow: + 104 vineyard: + 968 wood: + 575 other: − 152 garden: − 4,150 arable: − 1,786 meadow: − 994 vineyard: − 229,738 wood: − 188 other
Deux-Sèvres	22,280	9,211	+ 180 meadow: + 15 vineyard: − 12,733 arable: − 97 meadow: − 124 vineyard: − 310 wood
Seine-Maritime	20,729	13,345	+ 7 garden: + 17 arable: + 5 meadow: + 160 wood: + 35 other: − 765 garden: − 4274 arable: − 1339 meadow: − 1230 wood

Source: A.D. Loiret (Orléans)—G.F. 423
A.D. Loir-et-Cher (Blois)—Série P. Evaluation des propriétés foncières. Instructions, Récapitulation, Rapport du Directeur, Contributions Directes, 1879.
A.D. Landes (Mont-de-Marsan)—PS 322
A.D. Deux-Sèvres (Niort)—3P22
A.D. Seine-Maritime (Rouen)—2PP 246

of common wasteland through afforestation. By 1878 it was estimated that less than one tenth of the area so affected still awaited improvement (Fourcade, 1909). In Deux-Sèvres land clearance was similar to that for Loiret and Loir-et-Cher being primarily for arable land. Further north in Seine-Maritime a third variation appears in that, although of less importance in areal terms, clearance here was for much more varied aims with waste being converted into meadowland, woodland, and 'gardens', that is a more intensive form of cultivation, as well as into arable land (Clout, 1969). Despite being a small sample, these detailed statistics contained in the manuscript revision of 1879 have suggested three types of clearance according to the mechanics of land-use change: namely land clearance for arable, for afforestation, and for mixed land improvement. These regional contrasts reflect the fact that land clearance can be a consequence of several demands on land. Thus in one land-use indicator, the area under wasteland, are combined the effects of several factors influencing the reclamation or abandonment of land. Detailed local research does not yet allow the drawing together of these factors in a complete explanation of the regional and temporal variations in land clearance which have emerged in this essay. Furthermore, the variety of causes suggested by this complexity limits the usefulness of wasteland as an indicator of the progress of the agricultural revolution. Some of these factors must be considered briefly before returning to this central theme.

Factors Behind Nineteenth-Century Land Clearance

A major factor influencing the extension of the agricultural area together with its intensification would be an increase in the general demand for agricultural and forestry products. Qualitative evidence certainly supports an improvement in the diet of the rural population. A probably more important source of growth in demand was the provision of food to towns.

'The urban population rose from some 7 million in 1821 to 17·5 million in 1911, and the rise in urban incomes perhaps doubled the increase in the markets for food due to numbers of people' (Hohenberg, 1972, p. 224).

The towns themselves were also ceasing to be 'agrotowns' and were coming to depend increasingly on full-time commercial farmers rather than on local, informal food sources. Hohenberg goes on to postulate that this increased demand for agricultural produce, which runs through the whole nineteenth century, showed an acceleration after 1850. As 'urban demand was noted for the period between 1850 and 1880' (Hohenberg, 1972, p. 235). One can suggest that clearance partly reflects the response of French agriculture to this stimulus.

However the commercially-minded farmer anxious to meet this market demand might well find his plans to intensify production or to extend his arable area frustrated by restrictive common rights which in many parts of France had survived both the limited and often localized legislation of the eighteenth century and the more fundamental changes during the revolutionary period. Thus in the Landes region by the mid-nineteenth century common rights interests still affected more than half of the area. The elective assemblies controlling these commons in the Landes were dominated by pastoral interests advocating free and open pasture. They even considered that improved rearing would eventually assure the region's development (Larroquette, 1935). Bremontier's dune-fixation experiments, 1787–1793, and Chambrelent's successful reclamation experiments in 1849 provided the silvicultural techniques but widespread clearance had to await the Law of the 19th June 1857 which enacted that the common interests had to improve their land through afforestation or else allow the state to take over (Fourcade, 1909). Many regional studies include the weakening of the communal rights and the associated development of forage crops to replace wasteland pastures, as a significant factor in local progress in land clearance (Musset, 1917; Perpillou, 1940). Nevertheless a report in 1860 could still bemoan the restrictive influence of common rights which, it estimated, still covered 4,720,000 ha (A.N.F.[10] 3771). Of this 2,790,000 ha were classified as marshes, wasteland, heaths, and pastures. Allowing for the continuation of major pastoral interests, the signatories requested an extension of the 1857 law from the *départements* of Gironde and Landes to cover the whole of France. A consequent law of 28th July, 1860 sought to improve the nation's commonlands but an 1880 report suggested only limited progress (A.N.F.[10] 2314).

Only 239,050 ha were considered susceptible of such improvement, and only 29,751 ha had apparently been so improved, with a further 40,800 ha projected, and 7159 ha underway. Thus it would seem that the legal restrictions on land clearance were ceasing to be an obstruction by the late nineteenth century.

By the mid-nineteenth century a third factor had ceased to place limitations on clearance at least in theoretical terms, namely the development of appropriate techniques of reclamation together with the introduction of new crops for the reclaimed areas. In addition to the standard treatises on agricultural techniques by Duhamel du Monceau, Pattullo, Turbilly, etc. there had been developed many regional approaches to land clearance which had entered the literature. In the Sologne local efforts at improvement were to some extent co-ordinated by the *Société Royale d'Agriculture d'Orléans*, whose Bulletin formed a medium for information on agrarian matters. In 1786 the Société had organized a competition for a general scheme of improvement. The agricultural improvements suggested by the two major contributors included the planting of pine, birch, and chestnut trees, artificial meadows, land draining, and viticulture. The system of fallowing was sharply attacked, the answer to diminishing grain yields being to alternate crops rather than to leave the fields to rest for several years (Autroche, 1787).

> 'One has not stopped repeating that there was no cultivation without manures, no manure without animals, no animals without fodder crops. : that the very secret of agriculture lay in the true proportion of these means' (Froberville, 1788, p. 43).

Practical experimentation included the use of lucerne, sainfoin, and clover with the associated spreading of gypsum powder by Lockhart prior to 1810 (Lockhart, 1810). Also in the northern fringe of the Sologne, the Count of Tristan achieved improved rye yields after starting to use marl in 1780 (Tristan, 1819). Lasteyrie Dusaillant's (1823) land-improvement approach included the digging of numerous ditches and the clearance of sections of wasteland.

By mid-century these and other documented experiments provided the regional basis for a more systematic policy of improvement for the Sologne. On a national level clearance and land-improvement techniques were advanced during the century. Thus during the early 1850s the use of new systems of draining and of pipes and tiles were introduced into French agriculture from England (Phillips and Clout, 1970). The practice of marling, which Arthur Young had reported relatively infrequently, had become sufficiently widespread by 1862 that only 12 *départements* did not make reference to it in the agricultural enquiry. To this traditional fertilizer were also added lime and later guano and phosphates (Clout and Phillips, 1972).

However, even if the above three factors had been implemented, that is the stimulus of a growing market, the removal of restrictive common rights, and the availability of crops and techniques for improvement, there was little possibility of widespread clearance without the provision of adequate communications links to both suppliers and market. 'Poor communications, lack of markets, deprived agriculture of the vital outside stimulus which it needed' (Kemp, 1971, p. 20). Until railways broke their isolation many rural areas had only very restricted markets. Indeed, evidence contained in the 1850 revision for Loir-et-Cher illustrates this autarchy. Each *commune* report states to which markets agricultural products were taken. The fact that several Sologne *communes* reported that produce had to be sold locally reflects their continued position outside the market circuits (Sutton, 1967). Generally though, by mid-century communications were improving. The length of railway track, which was only 600 km in 1842, had tripled by 1848. Augé-Laribé (1955) considered this transport improvement as the decisive factor describing it as 'more important and promising for agricultural improvement than the introduction of turnips and other root crops into rotations' (p. 145). The increased commercialization of agriculture engendered by the development of railways included the expansion of widespread viticulture in Languedoc in the 1860s and the extension of the area supplying the Paris food market from a 50 km to a 250 km radius between 1830 and 1855 (Kindleberger, 1964). As well as transporting produce out, the railways allowed marl to be carried in to formerly isolated regions. Often this transport of marl had to be subsidized as in the Sologne, where the Orléans–Vierzon railway line benefited from a state subsidy on marl from 1853 to 1873 (Sutton 1967). Locally marl to be used in conjunction with land clearance and for general improvement was carried by canals such as that from Nantes to Brest and on the Canal de la Sauldre in the Sologne (Sutton, 1973). More generally rural communications benefited considerably from the improvement of established roads and the addition of a network of local roads. Kemp (1971) argues that 'the improvement of local roads from 1836 no doubt had more effect on the peasantry than the main line railways' (p. 113). This was certainly the case in the Sologne where between 1861 and 1874 more than 500 km of agricultural track were constructed. Local roads were also an integral part of the post-1857 improvement of the Landes region.

However backwardness and a low level of commercialization could still prevail despite the presence of the above factors. The self-sufficiency of the peasant household could remain high. Furthermore, 'this sovereignty of habit which resisted both technical innovation and reforms in agrarian law, operated at all levels of society' (Bloch, 1966, p. 223). Through the century the restraints of the village community on individual enterprise were only slowly undermined by the corroding forces of individualism. Hohenberg argues the strength of 'counter-forces' working to limit growth and technical change in the rural economy. For example, the return of an aristocratic rural elite to its landed estates following the July Revolution in 1830 failed to give an adequate economic leadership to the traditional peasantry.

'Though agriculture in the west benefited from the return and concerned presence of aristocratic landowners, the effect was neither widespread nor notably strong' (Hohenberg, 1972, p. 225).

Later additions to the rural elite were often seeking to secure fortunes made in trading ventures by investing in land, so giving rural capital an anti-innovational bias. Locally though improving landowners did propagate new methods of clearance as well as new crops and techniques. Sometimes their efforts were combined in improvement societies or were supplemented by companies promoting agricultural developments. One such was the *Compagnie Générale de desséchement des marais, lacs, étangs, lais, et relais de la mer* which was established in 1828 with the aim of reclaiming some

74,000 ha of marshes and ponds scattered over twenty *départements* in what were termed 'rich regions' which promised greater commercial success. (A.N.F^{10} 1631). Of more localized interest was the *Compagnie agricole et industrielle d'Arcachon* in the Landes region. Established in 1837 with a capital backing of 8,000,000 *francs*, this company purchased 13,000 ha of waste which in parts were marshy. After draining, most of the area was planted with pines but 3000 ha were converted to irrigated meadow and some was developed as arable with the introduction of maize, potatoes, colza, rice and fruit trees. Results were encouraging and the opening in 1841 of the first railway in the region from Bordeaux to La Teste prompted the company to supplement its agricultural and forestry interests with dependent industrial projects involving the distillation of resin, metallurgy, silk-worm breeding, starch, and glass manufacturing. This attempt at industrialization overstretched the profitability of what had commenced as a successful reclamation project and the company was liquidated in 1845 (Larroquette, 1935). A more successful reclamation project, perhaps because of its more limited objectives, was carried out by the *Compagnie des chemins de fer de la Dombes*. Numerous petitions were sent to the Minister of Agriculture, 1830–1850, requesting state aid and subsidies to rectify the unhealthy and uneconomic state of the Dombes region. Comparisons were drawn between the lack of help for the region and the provision of studies and even funds for the Sologne. Action was eventually taken in 1863, and between then and 1878 the company was responsible for reclaiming some 550 ponds amounting to 6000 ha most of which became arable land, possibly prior to a later conversion to meadow (A.N.F^{10} 2332). An important pressure group behind the eventual granting of state assistance to the Dombes was the *Comité d'amélioration agricole et sanitaire de la Dombes et de la Bresse insalubres*. A similar regional improvement society was the *Comité Central Agricole de la Sologne* which was created in 1859 to coordinate the activities of those landowners interested in improvement. Despite its limitations in implementing its views and its internal disagreements over whether to concentrate on cereals or afforestation and whether to promote the use of marl or lime, the *Comité* did provide an impetus to government action in improving the area's communications. Although limited in their effect, such improvement societies could coordinate demands for state action and moreover could operate on a more realistic regional basis cutting across administrative boundaries.

Several of these factors encouraging clearance have emerged as being particularly active during the 1815–1870 period of authoritarian rule represented by the Second Empire, certainly where they involved state action. Indeed, as Kemp (1971) has observed, 'there is no doubt that the economic life of France in this period cannot be understood apart from the policies applied by the state' (p. 159). The major period of reclamation 1850–1879, coincides with this burgeoning of state aid to communications and to improvement companies. Commercial treaties in the 1850s and 1860s made international trade freer favouring an increasingly commercialized agriculture, while legislation in 1857 and 1860 has already been discussed as furthering the erosion of restrictive common rights.

'For an authoritarian regime brought to power as a result of a conspiracy . . . the Second Empire has come to possess a reasonably good historical image' (Kemp, 1971, p. 200).

From the rather restricted viewpoint of the progress of land clearance, the Second Empire with its widespread interest in public works was a significant two decades (Girard, 1952).

Certain factors inducing the abandonment of land to waste must also be briefly mentioned. Locally land abandonment had been present throughout the nineteenth century but only in the 1879–1908 period was it to become a generalized feature (Fig. 8.7). Some connection must be invoked between this land-use trend and the wider economic events involved in the great depression, 1880–1900, with the return of France to a stricter adherence to a protectionist trade policy. Certainly by 1880 agriculture was still too prominent in the French economy and along with other sectors of that economy, it can be criticized as still containing large areas of under development. There were still too many small peasant units at a semi-subsistence level which combined inefficiency in agricultural production with inadequacy in their consumption of manufactured products. However, in gauging the impact of the general downward trend in the prices of agricultural products during the depression period, the difference between crop and livestock farming is significant.

'Too much emphasis is usually laid on the fall in grain prices and
on the unfavourable consequences for arable farmers; not enough
attention has been paid to the much less difficult situation of livestock producers' (Tracy, 1964, p. 26).

Kemp argues that there is evidence that the extent of the agricultural crisis was exaggerated by large landowners together with
industrialists to obtain the protection embodied in successive
tariffs in 1881, 1885, 1887 and culminating in the Méline Tariff of
1892.

'While the family farmers had more to gain from free trade and
cheap grain than from the Méline system, the large-scale wheat
producers spoke for agriculture' (Hohenberg, 1972, p. 237).

Livestock farmers, while suffering from the reduced value of their
produce, benefited from the greater fall in the price of their feed
grain inputs. Thus the best policy would have been to carry out a
shift from crop-production to livestock as was the case in Denmark
and the Netherlands. However, cushioned behind its protective
barriers, French agriculture missed this opportunity for developing a profitable export trade with the other industrial countries.

To what extent did the agricultural depression force land out of
cultivation to revert in part to wasteland? Tracy (1964) has
suggested that with reduced imports of wheat, France's cultivated
area tended to rise up to 1890, falling slightly afterwards, though
production levels were maintained by increased yields. Augé-
Laribé (1955) has specified Languedoc and Provence as regions
especially badly hit as falling agricultural prices only compounded
earlier natural disasters which had hit viticulture and silkworm
raising. But by 1908, many other regions of France must have also
seen a reduction in their arable land area, according to the figures
in Table 8.4, though not necessarily involving total land abandonment, often being converted to meadow or woodland. Certainly
this period involved a substantial increase in the numbers of cattle
in France, especially after 1892 when cattle imports were prohibited for health reasons. On the other hand wool was left free
from import duty, reflecting the interest of manufacturers, and so
sheep numbers fell from 24 million in 1852 to 17 million in 1910
(Tracy, 1964).

This conflicting pattern of trends experienced by the various sectors of French agriculture during the period of the great depression renders a monocausal explanation of the 1879–1908 expansion of wasteland impossible. Two other factors adding to wasteland areas were also involved. Firstly, there was a general trend of increased efficiency, given the continued presence of great 'pools of traditional backwardness'. One result of this was the greater use of the fallow land. With the reduction of these areas of idle land agricultural production could be maintained on a smaller cultivated area than hitherto. A second, more localized factor, for which there is more specific evidence of land abandonment to waste, concerns those areas badly affected by phylloxera from the 1860s onwards and by other natural blights on specialized crops. In the Bas-Pays de Brive in southern Limousin, two such maladies contributed to an extension of wasteland. Early in the nineteenth century vineyards covered 20–25 per cent of the area but phylloxera nearly completely destroyed them, much land being left as waste. Then later, between 1900 and 1910, another blight ravaged the chestnut-tree groves of the region. Their extent declined from about 37 per cent of the total area to less than 15 per cent (Perpillou, 1940). Other instances of wasteland extension through the ravages of phylloxera could be quoted, particularly from Languedoc.

The preceding few pages have reviewed a variety of factors contributing to the clearance of wasteland during the nineteenth century as well as a few which could be invoked in an explanation of the reversal of this trend of clearance delimited by the statistics of 1879 and 1908. The complexity of regional trends suggests a local as well as a national component to any explanatory model. If a generalized statement beyond the above guidelines cannot yet be elaborated in view of the limited evidence available at present at least certain regions stand out as having benefited considerably from land clearance by the date of the last cadastral survey used in this study, 1908. Brittany, the middle Loire regions, Gascony, and Limousin in particular saw a significant reduction in their wasteland areas, while many *départements* of the Paris Basin saw its total disappearance. In Limousin the steady progress of clearance was such as to give rise to itinerant groups of specialist land clearers often Auvergnats by origin, who travelled around in teams of five or six carrying out the initial work of cutting down and clearing of vegetation and then burning it. During the 1890–1910 period in the Montagne part of south-east Limousin, they even bought several ha of wasteland, cleared, improved, and subdivided them into farms complete with buildings, prior to moving on, as a team, a few km into unimproved waste, there to recommence the operation (Perpillou, 1940).

Such positive examples of regional agricultural and forestry development through the clearance of wasteland suggest its use as an indicator of the regional and temporal progress of the agricultural revolution through France as a whole. This possibility has been shown in this chapter through a comparison of the patterns of land clearance with those of increased crop production after Pautard, and of the use of underdrainage and fertilizers. However, the role of wasteland as an indicator of agricultural change is far from proven. Indeed can any one index be that sensitive, especially as the 'agricultural revolution' was a multi-faceted development? Furthermore, Morineau's idea, that such a revolution must involve considerable increases in productivity both per man employed and per unit area, could well result in an extension of wasteland rather than in a reduction as agriculture became more efficient.

Perhaps the active presence of clearance rather than any actual decline of wateland area is a better measure. The breakdown of static, traditional land-use systems; the removal of common-rights restrictions; the reassessment of the agricultural potential of various soil types; all of these would indicate change, momentum, even revolution in agrarian practice and structure. Land clearance could well be an index of this overturning of a static system without necessarily resulting in widespread reductions in the area under waste. As wasteland entered the agricultural system in some localities, it could well be added to by land abandonment elsewhere. Crude land use statistics would not reflect these more subtle changes which would only be revealed by detailed regional studies, especially of areas for which 1850 and 1879 data remains. Only then can the wider index of land clearance be evaluated. At present on a national scale the necessary use of crude statistics renders the fluctuations in wasteland area a limited though interesting indicator of deeper agricultural changes. In this as in other aspects of change in rural France one must re-echo Hohenberg's (1972) plea:

'We must await many more local studies, focussing on a

manageable and homogeneous area yet informed by the major trends and question of the French case' (p. 240).

Archival Sources

A.   The principal data sources used were the land use statistics by *départements* contained in the fiscal records produced by the old cadaster and its revisions in 1850, 1879 and 1908. These were consulted in the offices and the archives of the Sous-Direction du Cadastre et de la Publicité Foncière, 1 rue des Mathurins, Paris 9e, where they were found under the following three headings.

1. Ministère des Finances—Direction Générale des Contributions Directes— *Nouvelle Evaluation du Revenu Foncier des Propriétés Non-Bâties de la France.* Faite par l'Administration des Contributions Directes en exécution de l'article ler de la loi du 9 aôut 1879—*Tableaux Graphiques*, Paris Imprimerie Nationale, 1884—an accompanying *Atlas Statistique* presented some of the data visually.

This gave the land-use figures by *départements* for the old cadaster and for 1879.

2. Evaluations des propriétés non-bâties—Loi du 31 décembre 1907, art. 3. Récapitulation des résultats généraux de l'évaluation. Direction générale des contributions directes.

This consists of several bound volumes, each of one or two *départements*, containing the manuscript reports of the 1908 revision. Data are at all levels; *département, arrondissement, canton,* and *commune.*

3. Ministère des Finances. Direction Générale des Contributions Directes. Evaluation des Propriétés Non-Bâties—préscrite par l'article 3 de la loi du 31 décembre, 1908. Rapport de M. Charles Dumont, Ministère des Finances, sur l'ensemble des opérations (3 novembre, 1913). Tome Premier, Paris. Imprimerie Nationale, 1913.

This volume contains the land use statistics by *départements* for the 1850, 1879, and 1908 revisions. A second volume, entitled *Graphique et Cartes,* visually presents some of the data.

B.   Certain regional statistics of the old cadaster and its three revisions were used to obtain data on an *arrondissement* and a *commune* level. The details of their location and reference number are included in the accompanying appendix.

C.   Archives Nationales, Paris.

A.N. F^{10} 1624—Renseignements fournis en réponse à la circulaire du Ministre de l'Intérieur du 6 novembre 1817, classés par départements, 1817–1842.

A.N. F¹⁰ 1631—Desséchements et assainissements, Dombes.

A.N. F¹⁰ 2314—La mise en valeur des communaux—Exécution dès la loi du
28 juillet 1860 pour la mise en valeur des biens communaux. Relevé sur les
comptes de fin arrêtés au 31.12.1880 des résultats obtenus par l'application
de cette loi.

A.N. F¹⁰ 2332—Ponts-et-Chaussées, Département de l'Ain, Arrondissement
de l'Ouest, Amélioration des Dombes.

A.N. F¹⁰ 2333—Ponts-et-Chaussées, Département de l'Ain, Dombes, Situation
des travaux de desséchement des Etangs par la Compagnie de la Dombes.

A.N. F¹⁰ 3771—Rapport à Sa Majesté l'Empereur, 17.1.1860: includes an
inventory of marshes, ponds, and waste land and the extent of them owned by
the *communes*.

Appendix

Table 8.9

A Sample Survey of The Survival Rate of The 1850 and 1879 Revisions and
Their Place of Storage.

Département	Details
Allier	A.D. (Moulins) Série P (unclassified)—a few *communes* only survive for 1850 and 1879.
Cher	None surviving.
Côtes-du-Nord	None surviving.
Eure	None surviving.
Finistère	None surviving.
Garonne (Haute)	None surviving.
Gironde	Direction des Services Fiscaux de la Gironde, Bordeaux— a few *communes* survive for 1850 only.
Ille-et-Vilaine	None surviving.
Landes	A.D. (Mont-de-Marsan) PS 322—1850 and 1779 revisions survive.
Loire-Atlantique	None surviving.
Loiret	A.D. (Orléans) G.F. 414 and G.F. 423—1850 and 1879 revisions survive.
Loir-et-Cher	A.D. (Blois) Serie P.—1850 and 1879 revisions survive.
Lot-et-Garonne	None surviving.
Maine-et-Loire	Direction des Services Fiscaux, Angers—1850 and 1879 revisions survive.
Manche	None surviving.
Mayenne	None surviving.
Oise	None surviving.
Pas de Calais	A.D. (Arras) P 999 and P 1037—1850 revisions only survive.

Seine-Maritime	A.D. (Rouen) 2PP 99, 132–134, 181, 184, 205, 217, 224, 246, 248.—1850 and 1879 revisions survive.
Sèvres (Deux)	A.D. (Niort) Série continue No. 3243 and 3 P 22.—1850 and 1879 revisions survive.
Tarn	None surviving.
Vaucluse	None surviving.
Vienne	Services Fiscaux de la Vienne, Poitiers. 1850 revisions survive but only a few *communes* remain of the 1879 revisions.
Vienne (Haute)	None surviving.
Vendée	None surviving.

A.D. = Archives départementales.

It is hoped to extend this survey to the rest of the *départements* of France. The above sample was chosen on the basis of being *départements* which experienced the reclamation of above-average proportions of their wasteland during the nineteenth century. This selection was in order to plan a short research visit to several of the surviving bodies of data in the summer of 1972.

Acknowledgements

The author would like to acknowledge the kind assistance of Messieurs Breton, Leccia, and Lamartinie of the Sous-Direction du Cadastre et de la Publicité Foncière, 1 rue des Mathurins, Paris, 9e, who allowed him ready access to their archives during a visit at Easter, 1971. Gratitude is also due to M. Charles Castang for making available a copy of his unpublished doctorate thesis entitled *La Politique de mise en culture des terres à la fin de l'Ancien Régime* which afforded much original material for the first part of this chapter.

8. References

Augé-Laribé, M., *La Révolution agricole*, Paris (1955).

Autroche, L. d', *Mémoire sur l'amélioration de la Sologne*, Orléans (1787).

Bloch, M., *French Rural History*, London (1966).

Bourde, A. J., *The Influence of England on the French Agronomes, 1750–1789*, Cambridge (1953).

Castang, C., *La Politique de mise en culture des terres à la fin de l'ancien régime*, Unpublished thesis for Doctorat en Droit, Paris (1967).

Clout, H. D., 'The retreat of the wasteland of the Pays de Bray', *Transactions of the Institute of British Geographers*, 47 (1969), 171–189.

Clout, H. D. and Phillips, A. D. M., 'Fertilisants minéraux en France au XIXe siècle', *Etudes Rurales*, 45 (1972), 9–28.

Clout, H. D. and Sutton, K., 'The Cadastre as a source for French rural studies', *Agricultural History*, 43 (1969) (2), 215–223.

Darby, H. C., *The Draining of the Fens*, Cambridge (1940).

Debien, G., *En Haut-Poitou défricheurs au travail XVe–XVIIIe siècles*, Paris (1952).

Deloynes de Gautry, *Eloge de la Sologne*, Orléans (1826).

Demangeon, A., *La Picardie*, Paris (1905).

Dorgan, P. H., *Histoire politique, réligieuse et littéraire des Landes*, Auch (1846).

Duhamel du Monceau, *Eléments d'agriculture*, Paris, 2 vols. (1762).

Dumont, R., *Voyages en France d'un agronome*, Paris (1951).

East, W. G., 'England in the Eighteenth Century', in *An Historical Geography of England before A.D. 1800* (H. C. Darby, ed.), Chapter 13, Cambridge (1936).

Fourcade, A., *De la mise en valeur des Landes de Gascogne. Résultats économiques de la loi du 19 juin 1857*, Doctorate thesis, Bordeaux (1909).

Froberville, H. de., *Vues générales sur l'état de l'agriculture dans la Sologne et sur les moyens d'améliorer*, Orléans (1788).

Gaugiran, E., *Vues de Sologne. Sa renaissance*, Paris (1857).

Girard, L., *La Politique des travaux publics du Second Empire*, Paris (1952).

Hohenberg, P., 'Change in rural France in the period of industrialization, 1830–1914', *Journal of Economic History*, 32 (1972), 219–240.

Hoskins, W. G., 'The reclamation of the waste in Devon, 1550–1800', *Economic History Review*, 13, (1943), 80–92.

Hoskins, W. G., 'The making of the agrarian landscape', in *Devonshire Studies* (W. G. Hoskins and H. P. R. Finberg, eds.) pp. 289–33, London (1952).

Hoskins, W. G., *The Making of the English Landscape*, London (1955).

Institut de Science Economique Appliquée, 'La croissance du revenu national français depuis 1870', *Cahiers de l'Institut de Science Appliquée*, Series D, 7 (1952).

Kemp, T., *Economic Forces in French History*, London (1971).

Kindleberger, C. P., *Economic Growth in France and Britain 1851–1950*, Cambridge, Mass. and London (1964).

Larroquette, A., *Les Landes de Gascogne et la forêt landaise*, 2nd Edition, Mont-de-Marsan (1935).

Lasteyrie Dusaillant, 'Extrait d'un mémoire sur quelques améliorations faites en Sologne', *Mémoires de la Société d'Agriculture, Sciences, Belles-Lettres et Arts d'Orléans*, 6 (1823), 281–287.

Leuillot, P., *L'Alsace au début du XIXe siècle. Essais d'histoire politique, économique et réligieuse (1815–1830)*, Vol. 2, Paris (1957).

Lockhart, C., 'Mémoire sur l'introduction de la culture des prairies artificielles dans la Sologne', *Mémoires de la Société d'Agriculture, Sciences, Belles-Lettres et Arts d'Orléans*, 2 (1810), 90–98.

Ministère des Finances, Direction Générale des Contributions Directes. *Evaluation des propriétés non-bâties prescrite par l'article 3 de la loi du 31 décembre 1908. Rapport de M. Charles Dumont, Ministre des Finances, sur l'ensemble des opérations*, Paris (1913).

Monkhouse, F. J., *The Belgian Kempenland*, Liverpool (1949).

Morineau, M., 'Was there an agricultural revolution in 18th. century France?', in *Essays in French Economic History* (R. Cameron, ed.), Homewood, Ill. (1970), pp. 170–182.

Morineau, M., *Les Faux-semblants d'un démarrage économique: agriculture et démographie en France au XVIIIe siècle*, Paris (1971).

Musset, R., *Le Bas-Maine*, Paris (1917).

Necker, M., *De l'administration des Finances de la France*, Paris, Vol. 3 (1784).

Orwin, C. S., *The Reclamation of Exmoor Forest*, London (1929).

Orwin, C. S. and Sellick, R. J., *The Reclamation of Exmoor Forest*, Second Edition, Newton Abbot (1970).

Pautard, J., *Les Disparités régionales dans la croissance de l'agriculture française*, Paris (1965).

Perpillou, A., *Cartographie du paysage rural limousin*, Chartres (1940).

Perpillou, A., 'Construction de la carte de l'utilisation du sol en France', *Acta Geographica (Paris)* (1963), Nos. 46–47, 35–37.

Philips, A. D. M. and Clout, H. D., 'Underdrainage in France during the second half of the nineteenth century', *Transactions of the Institute of British Geographers*, 51 (1970), 71–94.

Quesnay, F., *Tableau Economique* (1758).

Rozier, Abbé, 'Défrichement', in *Cours d'agriculture*, Paris, 1781–1800, 12 vols (1783).

Sée, H., *Les Classes rurales en Bretagne du XVIe siècle à la Révolution*, Paris (1906).

Sée, H., *La Vie économique de la France sous la monarchie censitaire* (1815–1848), Paris (1927).

Sirol, J., *Le Rôle de l'agriculture dans les fluctuations économiques*, Paris (1942).

Statistique Agricole de la France, publiée par le Ministère de l'Agriculture, *Résultats Généraux de l'Enquête de 1892*, Paris (1897).

Statistique de la France, *Statistique Agricole, 1852*, Deuxième Série, Paris (1855).

Statistique de la France, publiée par le Ministère de l'Agriculture, *Résultats Généraux de l'Enquête décennale de 1862*, Strasbourg (1868).

Sutton, K., *The Changing Land Use of the Sologne in the nineteenth century*, Unpublished M.A. Thesis, University of London (1967).

Sutton, K., 'La Triste Sologne. L'utilisation du sol dans une région française à l'abandon au début du XIXe siècle', *Norois*, 61 (1969), 7–30.

Sutton, K., 'The reduction of wasteland in the Sologne: nineteenth-century French regional improvement', *Transactions of the Institute of British Geographers*, 52 (1971), 129–144.

Sutton, K., 'A French agricultural canal—the Canal de la Sauldre and the nineteenth-century improvement of the Sologne', *Agricultural History Review*, 21, (1973), 51–56.

Toutain, J. C., 'Le produit de l'agriculture française de 1700 à 1958', *Cahiers de l'Institut de Science Economique Appliquée*, 115 (1961), 1–224 and Supplement, 1–287.

Toutain, J. C., 'La population de la France de 1700 à 1959', *Cahiers de l'Institut de Science Economique Appliquée*, 133 (1963), Supplement, 1–254.

Tracy, M. A., *Agriculture in Western Europe. Crisis and adaptation since 1880*, London (1964).

de Tristan, J., 'Note sur l'effet du marnage des terres en Sologne', *Mémoires de la Société d'Agriculture, Sciences, Belles-Lettres et Arts d'Orléans*, 2 (1819), 43–46.

de Turbilly, H., Marquis, *Mémoire sur les défrichements*, Paris (1760).

Williams, M., 'The enclosure and reclamation of waste land in England and Wales in the eighteenth and nineteenth centuries', *Transactions of the Institute of British Geographers*, 51 (1970), 55–70.

Williams, M., 'The enclosure of waste land in Somerset, 1700–1900', *Transactions of the Institute of British Geographers*, 57 (1972), 99–124.

Young, A., *Travels in France during the years 1787, 1788, and 1789*. Edited by Jeffry Kaplow, New York (1969).

9
Historical Geography of Western France

PIERRE FLATRÈS*

The Concept of Western France

Western France, which covers the ancient Gaulish territory of Aremorica, corresponds with the great peninsula located between the mouths of the Loire and the Seine and stretches westwards to the Iroise sea, where the English Channel and the Gulf of Gascony meet.

The physical basis of the region is quite clearly determined, since it corresponds with the Primary massif of Armorica and the sedimentary rocks on its margins (Fig. 9.1). To the north of the river Loire, the precise limit of the West is the outer fringe of Cretaceous rocks which, beyond a girdle of champion country (*champagnes*) on Jurassic rocks, encircles the massif. This border zone is composed of a belt of uneven terrain, involving damp clays and sands, which contrasts markedly with the open, loam-covered plains in the centre of the Paris Basin. South of the river Loire, where the geological pattern is different and the Jurassic belt is broader, one may consider the physical boundary of western France to coincide with the boundary of the Primary massif.[1]

Although gradually decreasing towards the east, the classic 'oceanic' climate strengthens the unity of this region, as does the presence of certain Atlantic plants, notably heathland vegetation in the form of gorse (*Ulex europaeus, Ulex gallii, Ulex minor*) and

*Translated by the author and the editor.

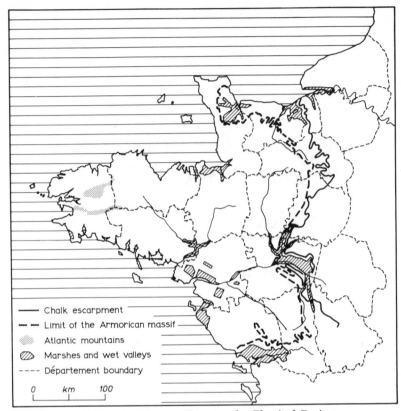

FIG. 9.1. Western France: the Physical Basis.

heather (*Erica cinerea, Erica ciliaris, Erica tetralix, Calluna vulgaris*). Most of this territory may be cultivated, the principal exceptions being the Atlantic 'mountains' where farming and settlement are practically impossible. But such conditions prevail in only a small area, namely the Montagnes d'Arrée.

In addition, the West contains a range of distinctive cultural landscapes which may be characterized by the word *bocage*. This term originated in Basse-Normandie, probably from the district of Villers-Bocage to the south of Caen, and has been accepted and used by geographers to describe wooded, enclosed landscapes, whose appearance in Auge, Perche and the southern boundary of the Vendée massif heralds a traveller's arrival in the West.

Dispersed agricultural settlement goes hand in hand with the *bocage*. Moreover a whole series of religious, political and economic factors combine to distinguish the West from the other major parts of France. But this does not exclude the existence of important local differences within western France, for example, there are many exceptions to the general rule of *bocage* with dispersed farms. These nuances, which depart from the classical pattern, represent specific cases which diverge from analogous forms found in the interior.

Regional Divisions

The West, like the rest of France, displays several levels of regional division, ranging from the small *pays*, held dear in classical geographical studies, up to much larger units covering, for example, the whole region currently under discussion.

The Pays

Some people have seen the *pays* as the basic divisions of France, representing an expression both of physical geography and human adaptation to it. (One dare not call these divisions *circonscriptions*, since the word evokes something far too official.) But unlike the other major regions of France, the West is not richly endowed with clearly individualized *pays*. They are only found in certain areas and have only been really significant during certain periods. There have always been serious difficulties in determining their precise limits (Couffon, 1944; Longnon, 1890).

The old Breton texts (lives of the saints, charters) mention a whole series of *pagi* (*pou* in Breton) of varying sizes and very different in character. In northern Brittany, medium sized *pou* served as the framework for bishoprics and archdeaconries (Treger, Trégor, Trégorrois; Ach and Léon, Goelo and Penthièvre) (Fig. 9.2). In central Brittany some of the very large *pou* became counties (Poher, Poutrecoet or Porhoët). In southern Brittany, the *pou* were very small, rather like modern *cantons* (Cap Sizun and Cap Caval); some were hardly bigger than modern *communes* (Foenant, Fouesnant, Tregunc, Belz). The *pou* of Treger was notable since it was a division brought over from Cornwall (hundred of Trigger, pagus Tricurius).

The pays de Retz to the south of the river Loire has remained

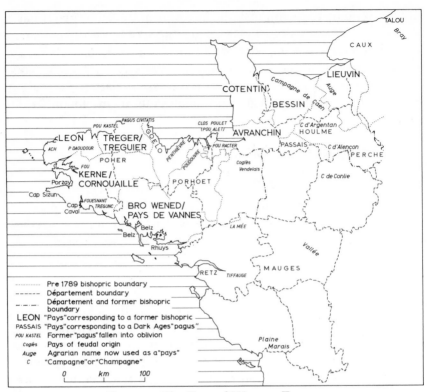

FIG. 9.2. The Pays of Western France.

very distinctive, but its neighbours, Tiffauges and Herbauges were less successful. Further east, the *pagus* Mauges in Anjou is still recognized. The origins of these *pays* are very different. The pays de Retz (*pagus ratiatensis*) dates back to a branch of the Gaulish people, the Lemovices, who became separated from the main body of the tribe and settled along the Loire estuary. By contrast, the names Tiffauges, Herbauges and Mauges are of Teutonic origin.

The *pays* of Normandy that are quoted in many textbooks belong to two very different types of division. Bessin, Cotentin, Lieuvin and Avranchin date back through medieval dioceses to ancient Gallo-Roman *civitates* which we can still trace in the administrative framework of the country. But others, such as Auge, Bray, and the *campagnes* of Alençon, Argentan and Caen are agrarian terms which originally described areas of marsh or forest and, in the case of the final three, cultivated land. Only Perche and the rather elusive Talou (*pagus tellaus*) and Houlme (*pagus oximensis*) correspond to the traditional concept of the *pays*.[2] Next to the present boundary of Normandy, the Passais area is a fraction of Maine which came under Norman domination at an early date. It remained part of the diocese of Le Mans up to the 1789 Revolution, and retained some legal and customary characteristics up to that time.

Elsewhere one would search in vain for ancient *pays* in the West. In the Vendée massif, some geographers distinguish the *Bocage* and the *Gâtine*. *Bocage* is not a native word in that area, but on the other hand, *gâtine* is an old name in the Loire country and in Poitou, meaning wasteland or an area with extensive uncultivated territory. The distinction between *bocage* and *gâtine* does not appear to have a popular basis.

Some authorities recently thought of resuscitating the *pays* as units for planning. In Brittany the divisions referred to by this name have no links with the ancient traditional *pays* and are simply based on employment hinterlands.[3]

From the Gaulish Tribes to the Creation of Départements

Territorial divisions in the next highest order are much more significant. They made their appearance with the Gauls and remain the basis of administration and local life. However, they have undergone profound modifications in northern Brittany (Delumeau, 1969; De Bouard, 1970; Dubois, 1965; Merlet, 1950–51).

The Gaulish tribes were politically autonomous and had their own coinage and collective organization. To what extent their territories were separated from those of their neighbours we do not know. However there is certainty about the location of the core areas that each of the tribes settled, using evidence from the texts of Caesar and the studies of past geographers. The study of coin hoards, undertaken by Colbert de Beaulieu (1952–66), provides some interesting information, such as the fact that Jersey belonged to the Curiosolitae, and the proof of the existence of the Lemovices in the pays de Retz. Place names allow certain frontiers to be located, such as the place name 'Ingrandes', from Equoranda, which probably mean 'the frontier on the water' (Fig. 9.3.) On the river Loire the Ingrandes which separated the Namnetes from

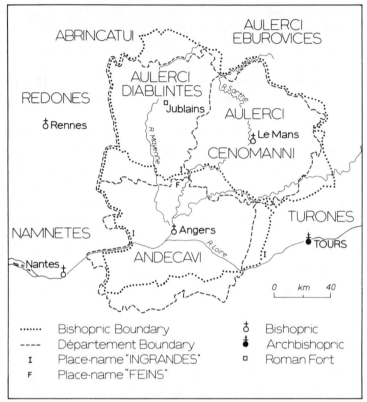

F I G. 9.3. Second-level divisions from the Gaulish tribes to modern *départements*:
the example of Maine and Anjou.

the Audecavi is located exactly at the boundary between the
départements of Loire-Atlantique and Maine-et-Loire. Another
Ingrandes, 13 Km from the present *département* boundary between
Maine-et-Loire and Indre-et-Loire, marked the boundary between
the Audecavi and the Turones. By contrast, however, there is great
uncertainty about the territories occupied by some Gaulish tribes,
especially those that occupied what is now known as Brittany. The
Curiosolitae, in particular, have given rise to many different
hypotheses. A notable feature of the Gaulish era was the great
diversity in the size of the *civitates*. The *civitas* of the Pictones,
stretching from the Massif Central to the Atlantic Ocean, was
immense. Further north, the territory of the Aulerci was also very
large, but was divided between three groups (the Aulerci Eburovices, Cenomanni and Diablintes) who from an early date behaved

as if they were separate tribes. Other *civitates* were very small. The Abrincatui, for example, had a small and well delimited territory, of which the southern and eastern boundaries have survived through to the present day.

The Gaulish tribes, in turn, provided the territorial framework for *civitates* during the Roman Empire. Little is known about the transition period or of changes during the old imperial era. Sources from the Bas-Empire, namely the Notitia Dignitatum and the Notitia Galliarum, provide a few glimpses. In addition, Gallo-Roman placenames add a few more hints. For example, the place name Fins, Feins, comes from *fines* meaning limit or boundary. Above all, the *civitates* of the Bas-Empire provided the framework for Christian dioceses which have perpetuated their names and, one must presume, have preserved their boundaries quite well.

These diocesan units remained very important features in regional life right through to the Revolution. Some, such as the diocese of Angers, survived almost without change. By contrast, further to the north, the diocese of Le Mans was extended further to the West to include the former *civitas* of the Diablintes, whilst the western part of the immense diocese of Poitiers was sub-divided to form the new medieval diocese of Maillezais and Luçon. A new group, called the Saii or Sagii which appeared during the Bas-Empire on the territory of the Aulerci, gave rise to the diocese of Sées. On the other hand, the *civitas* of the Viducasses only gave its name to the *commune* of Vieux and never became a diocese. It is remarkable that in Normandy, in spite of the disruption of the Norman invasions, all the former dioceses were maintained or were re-established to correspond with the old Gallo-Roman *civitates*. The *civitas* of the Caletes (Lillebonne) formed the only exception, being absorbed into the metropolis of Rouen.

By contrast, profound transformations took place in Brittany. Already during the Bas-Empire the military headquarters in certain *civitates* had been transferred from earlier settlements in the interior to points along the coast. Thus, for example, the chief settlement of the Curiosolitae at Fanum Martis (Corseul) was replaced by Alet (Saint Servan). Similarly, Vorgium (Carhaix) ceased to be the capital of the Osismii. Following the Breton invasions and especially the arrival of the Celtic saints the whole ecclesiastical organization that had been inherited from Roman times was modified and was, in fact, swept away in the northern part of the peninsula right from Pointe Saint Mathieu to the Couesnon river. The much less organized system of the Celtic church prevailed. It was only under King Nominoe during the ninth century that regular territorial bishoprics were re-established but without any links to the former pattern of organization, save for the see of Alet at Saint Malo. The bishoprics of Saint Pol, Tréguier, Saint Brieuc and Dol, by their very location remind one of Welsh or Irish bishoprics. Right through to the Revolution the diocese of Dol retained numerous enclaves scattered from the Seine estuary to the ria of Morlaix. The boundary between the dioceses of Saint Malo and Rennes probably roughly follows the line of the border between the *civitates* of the Redones and the Curiosolitae, but it may also have been corrected to correspond to the linguistic boundary between Breton- and Romance-speakers. By contrast in southern and eastern Brittany vast dioceses perpetuated the Roman *civitates*, including Quimper (Osismii), Vannes (Venetes), Nantes (Namnetes), and Rennes (Redones). However, Quimper had to give up some of its territory to the new bishoprics of northern Brittany.

When the *départements* were established in 1789, the diocescan division was again, if not the main, at least an important basis for dividing up the territory of France. The diocese of Angers may be recognized in the *département* of Maine-et-Loire, deprived of a few *cantons* to the north, south and east. The diocese of Poitiers and its subdivisions gave rise to three new *départements* (Deux-Sèvres, Vendée, and Vienne); and the diocese of Le Mans was divided in two (Sarthe and Mayenne, with the latter reconstituting the *civitas* of the Diablintes). By contrast, in Normandy, the smallest bishoprics were regrouped in pairs to create the *départements* of Manche (Avranches and Coutances) and Calvados (Bayeux and Lisieux, with part of the diocese of Sées). In south-eastern Normandy, however, the *département* of Orne bears no relation to the former dioceses. In Brittany, the diocese of Nantes gave rise to the *département* of Loire-Inférieure (now called Loire-Atlantique). The diocese of Rennes became the core of Ille-et-Vilaine *département*, and the diocese of Vannes became the core of the Morbihan. But the reorganization of the territory of the small Breton bishoprics on the northern coast gave rise to many problems. Eventually, these areas were either given to Finistère or Ille-et-Vilaine or united in a new *département* known as Côtes-du-Nord, the territory of which included Corseul, the former capital of the Curiosolitae, but did not cover the whole extent of that ancient *civitas*. Certainly attention was paid to local interests and detailed aspects of economic life when the precise delimitation of the *départements* was made, and this led to further modifications of the traditional limits.[4] But some boundaries were, however, left untouched. These related to provinces, which formed divisions of a third level of importance, with each including several *civitates*.

Provinces and Regions

Several traditional 'provinces' in Western France, such as Anjou, Maine and Poitou, simply correspond to former Gallo-Roman *civitates*. By contrast, the provinces of Brittany and Normandy group together a number of ancient *civitates*. It is these provinces, moreover, that are recognized the most readily and which had the most considerable privileges before the Revolution. Both owe their origins to invasions, with the Norse (or Norman) invasions dating from the ninth century, and the Breton invasions being between the fifth and seventh centuries.

As Giot *et al.* (1962) have shown, the spatial extent of certain civilizations and cultures from as early as prehistoric times seemed to anticipate the existence of the future province of Brittany, or, more precisely, its western part (Daniel, 1960). The primary Neolithic passage graves (of the late fourth and early third millenia B.C.) are distributed west of a line from Pornic to the south of the river Loire to the area of Lamballe in the north. The boundary passes a little to the west of what was the Breton linguistic boundary during the Dark Ages. Bronze-Age 'Armorican' barrows have an even more striking distribution, with their boundary being a little further west than the preceding one but only a few kilometres away from the modern boundary of the Breton language. During the Gaulish period, the distribution of stelae and of souterrains formed roughly the same pattern. The factors behind the distinctiveness of western Brittany are linked to maritime connections, but the reasons for the establishment of the various boundaries that distinguish the western end of the peninsula remain shrouded in mystery.

The great administrative reorganizations of the Roman Bas-
Empire increased the number of 'provinces' and defined their
limits by regrouping a number of *civitates.* Three 'provinces'
involved parts of western France. Lugdunensis secunda, with
Rouen as its capital, grouped together the Baiocasses, Abrincatui,
Ebroici (or Eburovices), Saii, Lexovii and the *civitas* of Con-
stantia (Coutances, the tribe of the Unelli). Lugdunensis tertia,
with its capital at Tours, embraced the Cenomanni, Redones,
Audecavi, Namnetes, Curiosolitae, Venetes, Osismii, Diablintes,
as well as the Turones. The Pictones were dependant on Aquitania
secunda with its metropolis at Bordeaux. This provincial framework continued to be that of the archbishoprics or ecclesiastical
provinces.

   In fact, it was only after the Breton invasions from the fifth to
the seventh centuries A.D. that the name 'Brittany' appeared in the
form of Brittania in Latin or Breiz in Breton (from the Celtic
Brittia) which was brought in by immigrants from Great Britain,
the Britannia of the Latin-speakers. Opinions differ on the importance and consequences of these invasions, with Loth (1883a and b)
and Falc'hun (1963, 1966) arguing opposing points of view.
According to Loth, the weakened and entirely Romanized peoples
of Armorica were overwhelmed by the invaders who re-introduced
a Celtic language into the peninsula. But according to Falc'hun the
Armorican population was quite numerous and had retained the
use of Celtic, in spite of Roman influence, so that modern Breton
developed as a fusion of Gaulish dialects and imported forms of
speech from Great Britain. Undoubtedly it is necessary to make a
clearer distinction between lay immigrants, on the one hand, who
came mostly from Cornwall and Devon, and the missionaries or
religious leaders, including the Celtic saints, on the other hand,
who came mainly from south Wales.

   A geographical balance sheet of these invasions may be drawn
up on the basis of regional divisions.
1. From linguistic evidence one may distinguish the eastern part
of the Armorican peninsula, which remains Romance-speaking, from
the Breton West. Place-name evidence allows an earlier linguistic
boundary to be reconstructed rather further to the east, between
the mouth of the Couesnon and Saint Nazaire, leaving Rennes and
its region and the Nantes district as Romance-speaking. During

the course of the Middle Ages Breton retreated westward and the modern linguistic boundary was established from Plouha to Rhuys, with an enclave which survived until the beginning of the twentieth century in the Guérande area (Fig. 9.4). This boundary divides the Breton-speaking part of Brittany (Basse-Bretagne) from Romance-speaking Brittany (Haute-Bretagne, or Bretagne gallo) to the east. It is remarkable that this east-west contrast is at variance with the north-south distinction based on ecclesiastic divisions which sets the Celtic north in contrast with the Romanized south.

2. Thus established, Brittany at first experienced great fluctuations in its territorial extent. However, limits became fixed a little before the year 1000 A.D. and remained stable for centuries. The Breton chiefs took a long time to conquer Vannes, and then Rennes and Nantes. They made raids and short-lived conquests in Avranchin and in Maine. Eventually it was not until after the Norse invasions and the reconquest carried on by the Breton princes who had taken refuge in England (curiously enough at the court of the Anglo-Saxon King Athelstan, the conqueror of Celtic Cornwall) that the boundaries of the feudal principality of Brittany seem to have become fixed along the eastern limits of the *civitates* of Rennes and Nantes. Feudal Brittany thus included as its capitals two non-Breton speaking towns and embraced territory that has always been Romance speaking. The only area where the boundaries were vague and disputed is the sector bordering on Poitou which involved the territory of the small and extinct *civitas* of the Lemovices. It was there that a series of complicated compromises led to the establishment of a mixed zone of 'separating marchlands'.

The Norse invasions, after a long period of plundering, destruction and colonization, also ended in the creation of a new feudal principality which was one of the best organized and most dynamic in Europe.

The three most important areas of settlement for the 'Northmen' were the Lower Seine, the Cotentin peninsula, and the Lower Loire. The sector of Normandy that comprised the Lower Loire was completely eliminated by the Breton reconquest. Cotentin Normandy left its traces in physical anthropology and place names but was subjected to the descendants of Rollon, the Norse chieftain of the Lower Seine who, by the Treaty of Saint-Clair-sur-Epte in

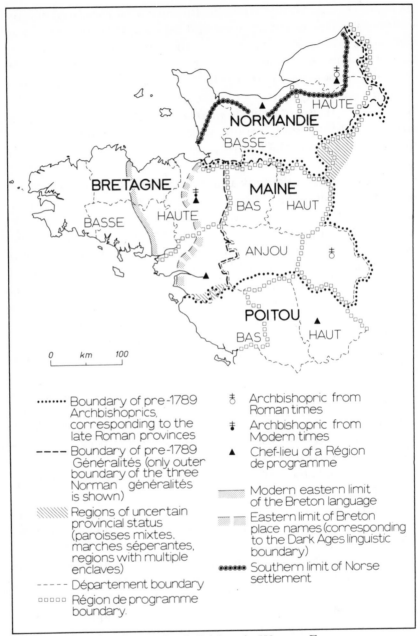

F IG. 9.4. Third-level divisions in Western France.

911, took possession of the *civitates* that were to give rise to feudal Normandy. It seems that it was on the advice of the clerics of Rouen, keepers of the Roman tradition, that the dukes of Normandy extended their dominion to the borders of the ecclesiastical province of Rouen, the former Lugdunensis secunda (Boussard, 1951). Indeed, they extended it beyond that border in the south-east when they conquered the lands occupied by the ambitious and unruly house of Bellême and the castles that they had founded on the margins of Normandy and Maine.

The Scandinavian speech forms of the invaders disappeared within a century or two, leaving traces in personal names and place names in belt of territory to the north of the latitude of Granville (Adigard des Gautries, 1954). But the administrative organization and the regional system of laws imposed by the dukes imparted great coherence to Normandy and gave the Normans a remarkable sense of distictiveness.

Normandy was conquered by the Capetians in 1204, and Brittany was united with the Crown of France in 1532. However the two provinces retained great individuality until the Revolution of 1789 in terms of their local administration (as *pays d'état*), law (having *parlements*, courts which applied provincial laws), and even economic affairs, with Brittany being outside the territory where salt tax was imposed.

A curious feature of several former provinces in the West (Normandy, Brittany, Maine, Poitou) was a division between a 'higher' (*haut, haute*) and a 'lower' (*bas, basse*) part. As it happens, the 'higher' part is always the eastern one and the 'lower' to the west. But it seems that the origin of these terms goes back to the provincial capitals (Rouen, Rennes, Le Mans, Poitiers) which were always in the 'higher' part.

The 1789 Revolution, which set up the *départements*, suppressed the old provinces. But these recovered some sense of official reality again under the Napoleonic reorganization with respect to the law (courts of appeal), the university world (*académies*), and the church (archbishoprics). Even so, Brittany founded part of the ecclesiastical province of Tours until the archbishopric of Rennes was created under Napoleon III in 1858. Yet that archdiocese did not have Nantes as a suffragant. As in Roman times, that see remains part of the ecclesiastical province of Tours.

These regional divisions have been partially resuscitated in recent times. The revival started in the economic field, involving chambers of commerce. Rivalries between chambers of commerce in large towns partly explain some of the spatial peculiarities that resulted, such as the division of Normandy into Haute-Normandie (Rouen) and Basse-Normandie (Caen), and the separation of Nantes and Loire-Atlantique from the four other Breton *départements* which were centred around Rennes. The other western *départements* have been regrouped in quite an artificial fashion around Nantes and have made up the so-called Pays-de-la-Loire region, for which there are no antecedents in history. However, it seems that this system is here to stay, since it served as the basis for the new regional institutions set up in 1973–74. Some people, however, envisage changes such as joining the two Normandies together and perhaps linking the regions of Bretagne and the Pays-de-la-Loire.

Armorica

At certain periods in the past the whole of Western France bore a single name even if it was not under one administration. The term Aremorica, which was used in Caesar, indicates a maritime region (*are* meaning close to, and *mori*, the sea). According to the researches of Loth (1883b) the spatial extent of Aremorica varied through time.[5] In his opinion, Caesar's Aremorica included the territories of the Caletes, Esuvii, Ambibarii, Unelli, Aulerci Diablintes, Redones, Curiosolitae, Osismii, Venetes and Namnetes. One must probably add the Lemovices of the Lower Loire which are quoted by Caesar. Aremorica thus extended from the Pays de Caux to the mouth of the Loire.

During the administrative and military reorganizations of the Bas-Empire the area to which this term related (now written Armorica) was altered. The *tractus armoricanus* extended from the river Seine to the Garonne.

Later on, the term became only a literary form. In the modern period it was taken up first by historians and writers to mean the province of Brittany, and then in the nineteenth century was used by geologists to relate to an area that was rather similar to that defined by Caesar. But it never reappeared in official administrative use.

However, after the Liberation (1944) a military command and then an administrative organization under an Inspecteur Général de l'Administration en Mission Extraordinaire (IGAME) assembled around Rennes the *départements* of the three future 'regions' of Bretagne, Basse-Normandie, and the Pays-de-la-Loire. But this broad administrative definition of the whole of western France has only survived in the context of military affairs.

Rural Settlement

The preceding discussion allows us to locate more clearly the subtle changes which, against an apparent uniformity of settlement dispersion, distinguish many types of provinces, regions and *pays*.

Studying the genesis and evolution of settlement in western France is difficult. Conservation of sites and their revelation is far less favourable than in the loamy champion country of the Paris Basin, where aerial photography has, for example, revealed the entire network of Gallo-Roman villas (Agache, 1970). Moreover, and perhaps because of the large number and importance of medieval religious monuments and prehistoric funerary monuments, the remains of dwelling houses have not encouraged extensive excavations comparable to those undertaken in Cornwall, for example.

Therefore it is necessary to start from the present and then, by judicious use of scarce documentary and archaeological evidence, to work back into the past in order to determine the origins of the various components of the modern settlement pattern.

Analysis of the Modern Settlement Pattern

The modern settlement pattern is one of widespread but complicated dispersion. Settlements meeting different needs and fulfilling different types of economic function do not display the same kinds of distribution. Farms are often isolated, but sometimes two or three are grouped together. In some places more important groups of farms are found, which would be known to British geographers as clachans. However, the people of the West use the term *village* to designate even the smallest grouping of farms. Isolated farmhouses and clachans are usually located in response to differences in soil type and relief, and have not been established along roads.

Along major and minor roads alike and on some valley sides, one finds small houses that are abandoned or are in the process of being abandoned. These are, or were, subsidiary agricultural dwellings occupied by farmworkers or by retired people. In Breton they are known as *penti*; in English they would be called cottages.

Non-agricultural dwellings are usually concentrated around the parish church in the chief nucleation of the *commune*. Such centres, which support tertiary services and perhaps a little manufacturing industry, are called *villages* by Parisians and by people from eastern France, but for the inhabitants of the West they are *bourgs* which are quite different from the agricultural *villages* found in the heart of the country. The *bourg* of western France would correspond to the Cornish *churchtown* or *treveglos*, the Welsh *treflan*, or the Scottish *kirktun*. However, non-agricultural dwellings are not all found in *bourgs*. Small groups are found around chapels in the countryside, and linear settlements have developed along some main roads. Some *bourgs* are flourishing, but others are in decline. The same is true for roadside settlements. In addition, the complexity of the settlement pattern varies from region to region. It is fairly simple on the margins of Armorica, where each *commune* includes its *bourg* plus a scatter of isolated farms, but becomes very complex in western Brittany.

Evolution of Agricultural Settlements

Cadastral documents drawn up in the first half of the nineteenth century give a precise picture of rural settlement. They were prepared at or about the period of maximum population in the countryside or in some cases a few decades before the peak was reached. At that time, some farmsteads were isolated but more often they were arranged in small groups of two or three. Clachans of five or six farmhouses were not rare and some overgrown clachans evoked the types of small village that are found in some areas of nucleated settlement. Large clachans were especially numerous on the islands, along the coast, and in the interior uplands (the so-called *montagnes*). But detailed investigations show that these clachans involved areas of only about 50 ha and rarely more than 100 ha (Flatrès, 1958). They represented overgrown groups of farms in a period of relative over-population, which were sometimes supported by ancillary resources in the form of fishing, quarrying and pastoral activities. Many clachans at the beginning of the nineteenth century were composed of one or several rows or terraces of houses, especially along the coast and in the poor regions of the interior. Others had no visible organized pattern, the only common feature being the frequent orientation of houses towards the south.

Older documents are either very general and summary in form, such as the Cassini maps, or, like estate maps and plans showing fortifications around Brest, are detailed but give only localized information. From an examination of these documents it seems certain that the main features of agricultural settlement in the West were already well established by the seventeenth century. Relatively few farms were created in more recent times except where areas of moorland had been cleared for cultivation. The great majority of *villages* and farms shown on the cadastral maps of the nineteenth century had been mentioned already in earlier centuries. However some of the clusters shown on these maps came into being from the subdivision of single farms that had been in existence in the eighteenth century. Isolated farms were probably more numerous but clachans less important in Brittany before the phase of population increase which began in the eighteenth century. By contrast, in the Gâtine poitevine Merle (1958) has shown that clachans and clusters were more numerous and important in the sixteenth century than in the following periods. In the Gâtine the seventeenth century is characterized by a struggle among bourgeois landowners to reorganize agricultural holdings in the same spirit that was to stimulate the English enclosure movement in the eighteenth century. These landowners replace former family clachans, composed of small tenancies that were subject to traditional dues, by large isolated farms that were held by sharecroppers. One cannot yet know to what extent a similar evolution affected other parts of the West, but it is likely that such a change affected the whole of the marchlands of Brittany which long remained sharecropping areas.

Uncertainties are even greater for the medieval period. A great number of farms and villages that are found in the modern landscape were mentioned in ancient deeds and charters. The survey of the rights of the archbishop of Dol, ordered by King Henry II of England, provides the names of farms and groups of farms in the twelfth century, and especially mentions thirteen *métairies* at La Fresnaye (Allenou, 1917). But it is often difficult to tell if the Latin term *villa*, that was normally used in the charters, relates to isolated farms or to groups of farms. However placenames some-times evoke the existence of families and other groups of land clearers. The *Mesnil* names in Normandy indicate groups of people who were obedient to their seigneurs and who, in turn, gave their names to the resultant settlements. By contrast, place names pre-ceded by the definite article (*les*) and such names as 'La Ville-ès . . .', which are frequent in northeastern Brittany indicate appar-ently independent family groups. It is difficult to know under what conditions villages with names ending in *-ière*, *-erie*, or *-ais* were created. Those ending *-ais* appear to be later than the others, but their establishment probably extended over several centuries.

The series of charters of Redon abbey gives us even more in-teresting information for the Dark Ages since they apply to settlements in both Frankish and Breton parts of the peninsula. These documents reveal a very clear contrast between the Frankish country, where the Roman estate structure was still preserved, and the Breton areas where landownership was very divided, and corresponded with a large number of apparently isolated farm-steads (Flatrès, 1971). (The generic Breton name for 'estate' in these charters is *ran* which means part, or fraction.) This study must put one on ones' guard against interpreting place-name evidence too rapidly. The Breton parishes described in the Redon charters are located, with only one exception, in the *pays gallo* where Breton has been extinct for several centuries. In these areas as a rule the *commune* name is Breton, as are names of castles and hamlets. But most farmsteads have Romance names, often with the suffix *-ière* or *-erie*. It should not be thought that these farms were created as a result of secondary dispersion following the disappearance of Breton. The charters of Redon are proof that already in the tenth century, when these areas were Breton-speaking, the agricultural settlement was dispersed. This con-trast between Breton and Frankish territory in the tenth century is all the more curious since it relates to vast areas which border the *civitates* of Vannes, Rennes and Nantes, all of which appear to have been equally subject to Roman influence. Should one believe that their apparent Roman influence failed to remove fundamental differences between eastern, Romanized Armorica and western Armorica which remained more 'native' in character? Or should one conclude that the Breton invaders had reorganized the region that they occupied so profoundly that the structures they established were strongly different from those in Frankish territory? In either case, the Redon charters prove that there has been a tendency to make settlement structures more uniform since the Dark Ages. The pattern of estate settlements in eastern Armorica has been broken up and added to by the foundation of numerous farms and clachans during the great clearing period, to make the end product increasingly similar to the more ancient dispersed forms of the far west.

The recent discovery of a buried *village* under the sand dunes at Guidel (Morbihan), which must date back to the first Breton period, has revealed houses with an oval plan which represent a transition between circular huts and rectangular houses. The partition of the houses into two rooms suggests the classical elongated plan that characterises most old farms in the West. About six houses have been excavated and these suggest the existence of a well-developed clachan which shows that the tradition of important groups of farmsteads on the coast—large *villages* as one would call them in Brittany—dates back to at least the immediate post-Roman period (Bertrand, 1973; Delumeau, 1971).

The Roman period represented a phase set apart in the whole of Western Europe, when social structures (based on estates worked by slaves), hierarchical political arrangements, and an advanced but uniform type of architecture were imposed on native populations with often widely different traditions. But in spite of numerous finds of coins, statuettes, tiles and Roman foundations to buildings, this period is still poorly understood. The agrarian structure makes investigations such as those by Agache (1970) in Picardy very difficult in the West and one must be content with fragmentary evidence from place names and a few archaeological excavations. It is certain that the whole of the Armorican peninsula came under Roman influence in material terms. This is borne out by Roman roads, towns, *villas* (that is to say agricultural holdings) and nowhere more clearly than in coastal settlements for commercial or military use. But one does not know if the whole of the cultivated land was held under the *villa* estate system or whether native holdings survived beyond the *villas*. In addition, it is very difficult to make any statement on the average size of the *villa*. Those that have been excavated vary greatly in size. Some were very small, for example the site excavated at Sizun in the Montagnes d'Arrée, but others, such as 'les Bosseno' at Carnac, were quite considerable. However the distribution of remains and place name evidence allow one to think that in most parts of Armorica, even in the eastern areas, *villas* were smaller and distributed more closely than across the plains of the central Paris Basin (Delumeau, 1971). But more detailed study is necessary on this topic.

One knows virtually nothing about agricultural settlement before the Roman period. Most sites that are known and have been excavated are groups of huts in cliff-, promontory- or hillforts which date back especially to the Gaulish period and functioned as tribal defensive points rather than as agricultural settlements. However the numerous excavated souterrains of Gaulish times, most probably linked with surface settlements, bear witness to a very scattered but yet relatively densely distributed pattern of settlement. It is probable that the Breton West followed the same kind of evolution as the islands and peninsulas of western Britain, where dispersion of agricultural settlement from Neolithic times onwards has been shown.

Subsidiary Agricultural Settlements

The history of these settlements is much briefer than that of the farmsteads in the West. Cadastral maps prepared *c.* 1930 show them at their peak periods. At that time, the countryside of the West contained not only a scatter of farmsteads but also an almost equal number of cottages (*penti*). These were located along roads, on former areas of wasteland, and especially on steep slopes that once had been communal land. Often these cottages were isolated, but sometimes they were clustered in groups of five or six. In areas where clachans were numerous the distinction between farms and cottages was less clear, and in upland areas and zones of marshland the cottages were often constructed in the clachans.

Most of these subsidiary agricultural settlements are of recent origin. Cadastral maps dating from the 1840s show hardly any at all. In the past the majority of agricultural labourers 'lived in' on the farms, and really were domestic servants. One suspects that small holdings with very little land and no plough teams were in existence in earlier times. They depended on larger farms for their ploughing activities, but very little is known about them.

The density of these subsidiary settlements depends on the phases of growth of the agricultural population. Construction of workers' housing was quite limited in areas such as eastern Brittany, where the peak population was reached at the period of the domestic servants who 'lived in', that is to say towards the middle of the nineteenth century. But where the demographic peak came later, as in western Brittany, the settled points sometimes doubled in number between 1840 and 1940.

The Territorial Framework of Non-Agricultural Settlements:
Trèves, Parishes, and Communes

The essentially dispersed nature of agricultural settlement in the West has not directly given rise to territorial units of any size. But it is true that the clachans sometimes possessed sectional or common land, in the form of moorland, rough grazing, and small greens which belonged in common to all the inhabitants.

A special kind of unofficial, local unit has been recognized between the clachan, the village and the isolated farm, on the one hand, and the civil *commune* on the other. In western Brittany this unit is known as the *trève* (*treo* in Breton) which comes from an old Celtic word derived from the root *treb*, meaning 'settlement'. The *trève* was indeed the settlement unit *par excellence*. A similar type of division exists in Cornwall (*trev*) and in Wales (*tref*). The *trève* comprises a number of villages and served especially as a unit for certain communal activities, such as ecclesiastical collections and fund raising. But the *trève* also commanded a certain loyalty and feeling of belonging and often contained its own chapel where a *pardon* was held each year and brought the local people together from the surrounding area.

Outside western Brittany things are not so clear. The *frairies* of eastern Brittany display some comparable features but they served especially for the organization of mutual help in farming and covered smaller areas than the Breton *trèves*.

The *commune* in western France, unlike its namesake in the East does not form an economic community. Communal land is mostly owned by the *clachans* but rarely by the *communes*. It is only along the coast that the *communes* have an economic function to fulfil, and that has been only since Colbert's ordinances in the seventeenth century regulating rights of collection of seaweed.

The present *communes* of western France are essentially ecclesiastical in origin and often correspond to the parishes that existed before 1789. Most parishes, and modern *communes*, are very large throughout the greater part of the West. However there are certain striking contrasts, with, for example, coastal *communes* being smaller than those in the interior. The plateau of northern Brittany has both large and very small *communes* side by side, and the triangle between Rennes, Angers and Le Mans has quite small ones. Above all, the whole of Basse-Normandie is remarkable for the small size of its *communes*, with the exception of hilly areas in the forest belt of the southern *bocage*.

These contrasts are partially explained by physical conditions, with the more fertile coastal areas being more densely populated and supporting a large number of parishes more readily than the moorlands of the interior. But historical circumstances are perhaps even more important. The parish had to be large enough to support a parish priest, and so the size of parish was linked to its agricultural wealth.

The origins of the parish system in western Brittany have been reconstructed by Largillière (1925) and have been studied in Normandy by local historians, but are understood imperfectly in other regions (Meynier, 1945b).[6] Western Brittany bears the imprint of the original Celtic church. The Celtic saints established a random distribution of settlements. As in Cornwall and Wales, the earliest examples received *Lan* names followed by a saint's name (for example, Laniltud = Llanilltyd in Wales) or some other qualification (for example, Lanmeur = Llanfor in Wales). Later foundations received *Loc* names, derived from *locus*, meaning 'the place of'. However this prefix was unknown in Britain. During the ecclesiastical reorganization of Nominoe, a number of sanctuaries were chosen as foci for parishes and others simply received chapels. These new parishes were called *plebs* or *plebem* in Latin, and *ploue* or *plou* in Breton, which was an ecclesiastical term borrowed from the Latin *plebem* (Welsh *plwyf*) to indicate the community of the faithful. But this term was never used as a place name in Britain. The creation of parishes in Wales and probably in Cornwall is later than in Brittany. The primitive *plou* were often subdivided and new parishes were created around sanctuaries to receive *Lan* or *Loc* names, or else they were established around lay settlements and received *Tré* names. These new parishes sometimes remained dependant on other units and were called *trèves*. Such ecclesiastical *trèves* are not to be confused with the civil or agrarian *trèves* that have been discussed already.

Delimitation of the early *plou* poses difficult problems. With very few exceptions, such as Le Tuch near Douarnenez, civil and feudal units seem to have had no influence on the formation of rural parishes. Medieval manor houses, which represented the old foci of seigneurial power and bore place names with the *Les* prefix, were always located away from parish churches. But more ancient territorial units, dating from Gallo-Roman times, may have provided the framework for some of the more ancient *plou*. This hypothesis perhaps explains differences in the pattern of *communes* between the north and far-west of Brittany (from Dol to Penmarch), and the south and centre on the other. In the latter areas a number of large parishes have Gallo-Roman names with -*ac* endings, but this is rare in the north. The pattern of parishes is often regular and compact in the south and centre, but in the north and far-west there are many sanctuaries and parishes that seem to have been divided and sub-divided quite freely and from early times. In the far-west, a parish with an enclave (Saint Jean Trolimon) and another parish made up of several villages inside another *commune* (Lababan in Pouldreuzic) carry ancient Celtic ecclesiastical traditions through to the present day (Flatrès, 1956). In the central-western part of the peninsula, the example of two parishes with focal points in close proximity perhaps bears witness to a compromise division between an old Gallo-Roman unit and a newer Celtic religious foundation. Thus Brieuc, formerly Brithiac, is Gallo-Roman in origin while Edern bears the name of a Celtic saint.

In non-Breton parts of the West, the movement of the Celtic saints had no impact, and the Gallo-Roman framework has been the basis for creating parish territories. *Villa* units were too small and were rarely selected for this purpose, but larger units, called *vicaria* in Carolingian deeds, were selected. Several *communes* in the West contain localities bearing Gallo-Roman elements in their place names. These western parishes were larger than the parishes (now *communes*) of the Paris Basin which, as a rule, retained the name and territory of Roman *villas* even though they were sometimes subdivided during the Middle Ages. Study of place names and *commune* territories, according to the method initiated by Largillière in Brittany, allows the story to be unfolded. Land clearance by peasant families and seigneurs in medieval times is certainly one of the causes of these subdivisions. Attribution of parish status to the numerous *Mesnil* settlements in Normandy, is the origin of the small Norman parishes. In most parts of the West and in Breton country, the seigneuries were normally based in hamlets or isolated manorhouses.

Non-Agricultural Rural Settlement

The parish church was the first focal point for secondary and tertiary activities. With the exception of Normandy, there are few isolated parish churches or *communes* without a central settlement. Such central places are always known as *bourgs* in western France, by contrast with the agricultural *villages* in the countryside. These *bourgs* vary greatly in size, with the most important factors explaining these variations being the size of territory involved and the number of people living outside the central point of the *commune*. In addition, the existence of lines of communication and the role of individual initiative have played their part. At present, most large *bourgs* are flourishing and some contain populations in excess of 2000 which makes them 'towns' according to official criteria in France. Smaller *bourgs* are usually stagnant or on the decline. Many small or medium-sized *bourgs* experienced their peak development in the first third of the present century, after having undergone accelerated growth after the end of the nineteenth century. The large *bourgs* were already in existence in the eighteenth and seventeenth centuries, but the smaller ones were made up of only a handful of thatched houses. There is very little information on the *bourgs* in medieval times, but it is probable that they originated during that period when the first inns were established near churches. In as much as they are medieval or modern developments, the *bourgs* owe their existence to the location of parish churches.[7]

Parish *bourgs* do not contain all the non-agricultural settlement in the West. Small settlements (which are really *bourgs tréviaux*) are found around some chapels in Brittany. Rather more frequent are roadside settlements, which increase in importance from east to west across the peninsula. Sometimes they have grown around inns or isolated workshops, but more often near small groups of houses. Some of these roadside settlements have enjoyed considerable development and challenge the old *bourgs* that are located away from main roads. Sometimes the old *bourgs* were abandoned during the nineteenth century and became known as *vieux bourgs*, each with the ruins of a church and a few houses, whilst new central places complete with churches, schools and town halls were built along the main roads.

Cultivated Land and Waste

Agriculture had certainly been introduced right to the far west of the peninsula by the fourth millenium B.C. The first patches of land to be cleared and cultivated being of modest size and, in Brittany, were mainly coastal in location. But very soon virtually the whole of the Armorican peninsula became involved in farming.

The idea of a vast woodland in central Brittany which was not cleared substantially until the Middle Ages is apparently more of a romantic myth than anything else (Couffon, 1946). The first maps of Brittany of any precision date from the late sixteenth and early seventeenth centuries and show quite distinct woodland areas which had almost the same limits as those in the modern landscape. Gallo-Roman place names, discovery of *villa* remains, and the lines of Roman roads indicate a region that undoubtedly supported a relatively low density of population but which had been largely penetrated by settlers. Discoveries of prehistoric evidence, from and including the 'secondary Neolithic' period, indicate widespread human settlement.

Breton place names provide useful information on this topic. Early *plou* are rare and cover large areas but their foci are nevertheless located right in the central part of Brittany. One of these was Plélan, which was the favourite seat of King Nominoe. In the eastern part of the Breton peninsula, ancient Breton place names indicate the existence of small settled points in these ancient *plou*. Place names relating to woodland (such as Koad or Coat, Killi or Quilly) indicate the proximity of tree cover or the clearance of woodland, but they also prove that places with such names were already in existence by the beginning of the Middle Ages. Most of these woodlands seem to have been disconnected, irregular patches, rather than vast compact stretches. Doubtless it would be nearer the truth to depict central Brittany in the Dark Ages as an area of low population density, but nevertheless widely penetrated by settlement, where patches of woodland remained as 'islands' surrounded by fields and moorland, rather than as a large forest interrupted only by a few clearings.

Another idea that is worthy of discussion is that of the 'frontier-forests'. It seems to correspond quite well to reality on the eastern margins of Armorica, in Haute-Normandie, Anjou and perhaps in Haut-Maine. But in the heart of the Armorican massif if does not seem that the boundaries of the old *civitates* were marked by forest belts. The archdeaconry of Le Désert was found on the border between the bishoprics of Rennes, Avranches and Le Mans in medieval times. But this ecclesiastical term related to an eremitic way of life and did not necessarily suppose the existence of vast forested areas. Parish names in Le Désert are, indeed, very ancient, with La Bazouge dating back to the Dark Ages and Louvigné to Gallo-Roman times. The southern frontier of Normandy is to the south of the forest belt which follows the quartzite crest of the southern hills of the Bocage from Domfront to Avalois. It is indeed difficult to understand the contrast between the Paris Basin with its wooded marchlands and the Armorican massif which appears to lack them. Perhaps the relatively uniform physical environment of Armorica avoided this kind of specialization on forest activities, even in marchland areas. Most of the large woodlands that survive are the remnants of ancient seigneurial forests, sometimes close to towns or castles (for example, Rennes or Fougères) or else once belonged to abbeys, but woodlands of the latter type are rarer and less extensive.[8]

Woodland represented only a small proportion of the uncultivated land surface. Moorland was more important and more extensive. Like north-western Iberia and western Britain, western France supported a veritable moorland civilization, involving communal pasture for livestock, gathering stable-litter and kindling material, and the periodic clearance of land for cultivation. Now only a few areas of moorland survive along the coast and in the mountains of the Atlantic West. These are nibbled away by fresh clearances each year and considerable areas are being re-afforested. The last extensive land-clearance operations date back to the 1920s and involve the moorlands of Lanvaux. The whole of the nineteenth century was characterized by numerous and repeated attacks on the moors.[9] The picture that one can reconstruct from the first cadastral survey of the nineteenth century, together with the evidence of travellers in the eighteenth century and the Cassini maps, shows a considerable extent of open moorland. The further westward one moved the more extensive the moors became. They were less important in the east where woodland was more extensive. It is very hard to reconstruct the history of the moorlands before the eighteenth century. Notarial deeds make mention of *terres froides*, but it is difficult to distinguish between real waste and some types of outfield with very long periods of fallow.

Field Patterns

We are beginning to unravel the complex range of field patterns in Armorica, especially in Brittany and Normandy (Brunet, 1955; Flatrès, 1957; Gautier, 1971; Meynier, 1943, 1944a, 1944b, 1945a, 1966). There are two essential facts. First, *bocage* has never been the only type of agrarian structure; and second, the formation of *bocage* has been a very long and gradual process. The traditional landscapes that are being erased by modern land-consolidation schemes are in fact a patchwork comprising elements of different ages and with different original functions. The key features which combine to make up the rural landscapes of the West are very diverse (Figs. 9.5 and 9.6).

Systematic land clearance and agrarian reorganization occurred mainly in the nineteenth century, but with some extensions in the twentieth century and precedents in the eighteenth century. During this period, great areas of communal moorland were divided up and

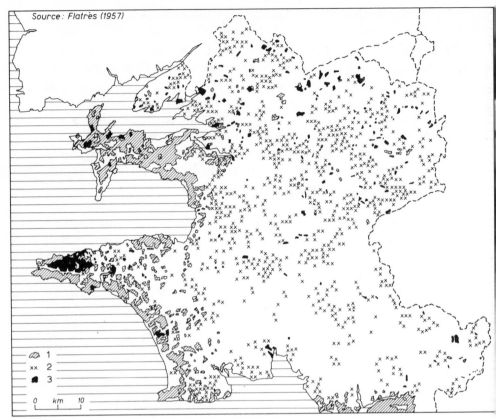

FIG. 9.5. Openfields in southern Finistère. (1) openfields; (2) isolated strip
fields; (3) areas of strip fields. *Source:* old cadaster.

privately-owned wasteland was parcelled out (Figs. 9.7–9.11).
Woodland areas were cleared more rarely, as for example in
Savigny forest in the southern part of Manche *département*. The
pattern of fields and parcels originating from this time is characterized by straight roads and field boundaries. Fields are rectangular and rather squat, but geometrical arrangements in
systematic chequerboard patterns are not very much in evidence.
Variations in shape and distribution are in response to different
sized shares of land and to local differences in the physical
environment. Once the practice of communal grazing on the moorlands had disappeared, further parcels were brought into cultivation in the most recent phases of land clearance, but without any

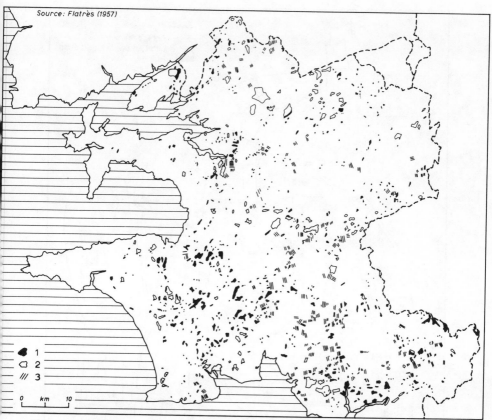

Source: Flatrès (1957)

1
2
3

0   km   10

F IG. 9.6. Enclosures other than of strip fields in southern Finistère. (1) irregular enclosures; (2) enclosed heathland, large irregular pieces; (3) orientated plots. *Source:* old cadaster.

field boundaries being established. 'Neo-openfields' were the
result, in areas such as the moorlands of Saint-Just (Ille-et-
Vilaine) and Saint-Allouestre (Morbihan). But more frequently,
recipients surrounded their newly-acquired parcels of land with
earth banks (*talus*). Generally these were strong enclosures,
veritable ramparts of earth, but on the high moors, where cultivation was not possible, the peasants were content to raise small
banks of earth which were just symbols of ownership.

Similar field patterns are found around *châteaux* and result from
the reorganization of large estates. But this kind of example is rare
and the extent of land redesigned in this way is not extensive (Fig.
9.12). Seigneurial action in modifying field patterns is more often

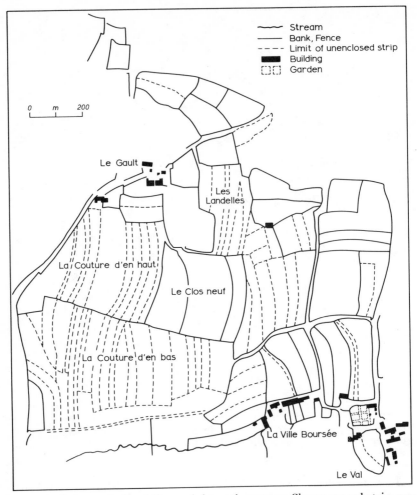

F IG. 9.7. Cadastre de Penthièvre, eighteenth century. Shows curved strip open-fields, recent enclosures (Le Clos Neuf), encroachment on commonland north of the group of farms at Le Gault, also a clachan at La Ville Boursée. *Source: Archives Départementales du Côtes-du-Nord*, Saint Brieuc, Erguy, sheet I.

marked by the creation of *rabines*, straight trackways planted with oaks and leading to isolated manorhouses and *châteaux* in the heart of the country. In general, the *rabines* were superimposed on the earlier agrarian landscape and with total indifference to it. Finally, one must mention the conversion of fields around *châteaux* into woods or parks.

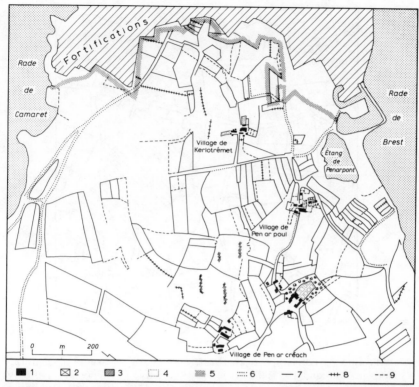

FIG. 9.8. Environs of Quélern Fortifications, Crozon Peninsula, Finistère. (1) building in 1784 and 1840; (2) building in 1784 only; (3) building in 1840 only; (4) gardens; (5) limit of royal property; (6) unenclosed road or lane; (7) fence in 1784 and 1840; (8) fence in 1784 only; fence in 1840 only. *Sources: Archives Départementales du Finistère, Atlas des Ouvrages Extérieures de Brest, 1786* (sheet showing *Retranchements de Quélern*, 1784) and cadastral map of Crozon, 1840.

Probably more ancient features result from the clearance of forest fringes in eastern Brittany and neighbouring regions which have given rise to lines of parallel parcels of land, reminiscent of *Waldhufendörfer* in central Europe or *rangs* in Canada but which are smaller in size and did not result in distinctive settlement patterns.

Many copses and areas of woodland were cleared sporadically by the peasantry through the ages. Written evidence for this kind of operation is lacking, but the patterns produced in the landscape allow an understanding of what had happened.

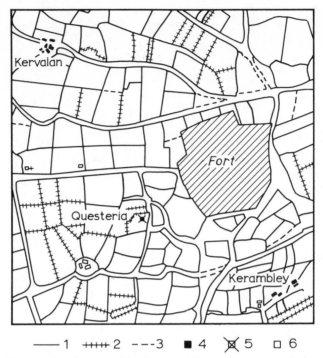

—— 1   +++++ 2   - - -3   ■ 4   ⊠ 5   □ 6

FIG. 9.9. Bocage Landscape near Brest, eighteenth to twentieth centuries.
(1) fence in 1785 and 1949; (2) fence in 1785 only; (3) fence in 1949 only;
(4) building in 1785 and 1949; (5) building in 1785 only; (6) building in
1949 only.

In the uplands and on some granitic plateaux there are groups
of irregular fields, of which some are roughly quadrilateral while
others have curved edges. These fields can only represent the
result of spontaneous clearing operations by individuals to allow
primitive farming in inhospitable areas. Such areas of irregular
fields are rare in western France, by contrast with western Britain
where they cover extensive areas. These fields are surrounded by
dry-stone walls or by earth banks (*talus*).

More frequent are regular fields that have been won by encroachment on the moorland. The pattern of fields on the margins
of existing moorland or of areas that have been recently subdivided
and cleared comprises enclosures that are bounded by earth banks
which follow a convex line along the moorland edge. This pattern

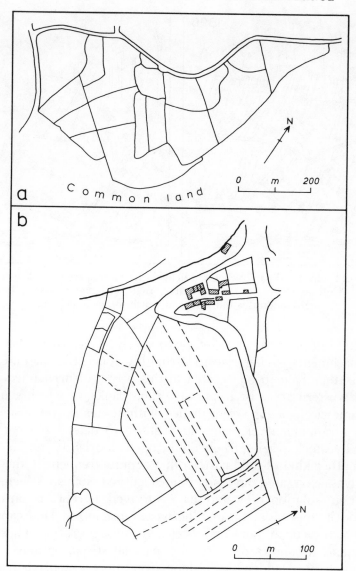

FIG. 9.10. Cadastral Map of Saint-Nic, Finistère, 1808. (a) example of encroachments on the waste resulting in concentric patterns; (b) example of a
clachan with an enclosed area divided into open strips (*méjou, esch*).

in itself is evidence of encroachment, with peasant farmers attempting to enclose the largest amount of land by the shortest possible
length of field boundary. Sometimes the field pattern shows that

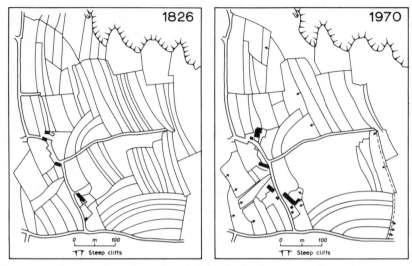

F IG. 9.11. Open and partly-enclosed fields in La Latte, parish of Plevenon now
Fréhel, Côtes-du-Nord. (a) old cadaster, 1826; (b) new cadaster, 1970. An
arrow indicates the parcel to which the bank belongs.

this kind of process has taken place several times, with successive
encroachments giving rise to a roughly concentric arrangement.
Fields that have been created in this way are surrounded in the
most western areas by impressive *talus* banks, of which some are
asymmetrical, being strengthened with stones on only one side.
This arrangement provides an obstacle to defend the enclosure
from livestock grazing freely on the open moorland.

   Another kind of field pattern that is quite frequent in the *bocage*
involves elongated and sometimes curved strips. When these
occur in isolation they may have survived as relics of an earlier
period in the midst of an otherwise reorganized landscape, but
they also occur in more or less clearly defined groups. These may
be squarish bundles of just a few parallel strips, or they may be
arranged in a ladder-like fashion over more extensive areas. In
addition, they may comprise oblong or oval patches, with curved
perimeters that contrast with their internal strip-like arrangement.

   In some places, the small bundles of strips are to be explained
by the fragmentation of fields into two or three parcels following
the sub-division of property. But for large areas and for the most
elongated fields, especially those with S- or reversed S-shaped

FIG. 9.12. Large Irregular Fields around a *Château* and its Home Farm (*Métairie*) at Le Meurtel, Fréhel, Côtes-du-Nord. *Source:* Cadastral map, 1970.

curves, this kind of explanation will not suffice. The pattern of such enclosures is in fact that of former openfields that have been fossilized by old field boundaries without any kind of land reorganization.

Comparison of recent cadastral maps and those drawn in the early nineteenth century shows that some of these elongated and curved enclosures were openfield strips at the beginning of the last century. Similarly an analysis of estate plans shows that this was the case in even earlier periods. Unfortunately there are no medieval documents to show the enclosure of openfields in Brittany, as is the case for Devon and Cornwall, but it is reasonable to think that there were parallel types of change on both sides of the Channel. Indeed, areas of openfield still exist in the Armorican peninsula.

Openfields, either isolated in the midst of the *bocage* or in almost uninterrupted stretches along the coast, form one of the most
distinctive features in the field patterns of western France (Figs.
9.5 & 9.13). They have survived in a few coastal areas in Manche
département, on the islands and along the greater part of the Breton coast, and in some places in the interior of the peninsula. They
seem to be absent from other parts of the West where the only
occurrence of unenclosed land is in the great stretches of meadow-

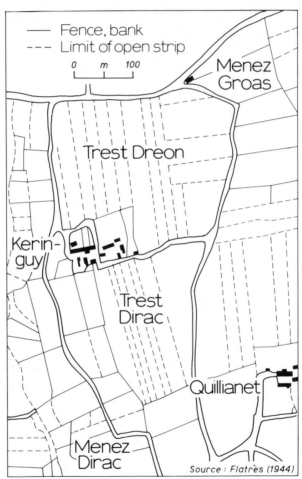

FIG. 9.13. Openfields in Peumerit, Finistère. *Trest* = local name of an area of
openfield; *Dirac* = before, in front of, the clachan; *Dreon* = behind the clachan;
Menez = mountains, and in this case, moorland.

land, that are sometimes subject to flooding, in the damp valleys of Normandy and along the Loire. But nineteenth-century cadastral plans and eighteenth-century estate maps indicate a much more extensive distribution of openfields. They existed in Normandy, especially on the Cotentin peninsula, in Haut-Maine, and in several regions of Brittany from which they have since disappeared completely. If one adds landscape evidence to this information one can conclude that openfields once existed over the greater part of the Armorican massif. However, they appear to have been the dominant feature of the agrarian landscape over only certain clearly determined areas. The existence of names for openfields (such as *champs* and *gaigneraies*) derived from Romance dialects show that they were considered important in past agricultural systems. Breton names, such as *méjou* and *méchou*, are mainly derived from the Welsh terms *mez* or *maes* which represent an old Brythonic word for openfield, which in turn was derived from the Celtic *magos* (Irish *magh*) meaning a cultivated plain.

Although they were created at different times and under different conditions, these openfields display certain common characteristics. Generally there is some kind of collective outer boundary that separates them from the moorland or from the road. Of course when they form patches in the midst of *bocage* they are *ipso facto* surrounded by *talus* banks. Areas delimited in this way vary in size but are never very large. Several tens of hectares is usually the maximum, except on the islands and at some points along the coast, such as Saint-Suliac and la Ville-ès-Nonais on the Rance estuary, where the stretches of openfield are almost reminiscent of the openfields of central Europe.

These openfields are made up of one or of several bundles of strips. Nevertheless, it is difficult to talk of real furlongs (*Gewann*). The strips are sometimes straight, but sometimes curved. Their length and breadth vary enormously and it would be difficult to distinguish the regular and repeated types of measurement that have been recognized for the openfields of central Europe.

The origins of openfields in Armorica are very varied. In the eastern parts of the massif they probably involve small areas that were cleared collectively from the waste and then shared between family groups living in clachans. It seems unlikely that the fields of the Gallo-Roman estates mentioned in the Redon charters, and which appear to have been openfields, would have given rise to the small groups of open strips that were depicted on eighteenth-century maps and emerge from the pattern of the present land-scape.

But the openfields of the West seem to have been one of the basic agrarian structures of Brittany and probably of Cotentin as well. They are often related to old clachans and are surrounded by stone revetted banks of an archaic type. Groups of openfields are sometimes surrounded by banks following a convex line, which suggests a defensive function against the moorlands and their dangers. Undoubtedly they form the most ancient cultivated areas, rather like the *Esch* surrounding the *Drubbel* in north-western Germany.

However some *talus* banks are also very old. Some building techniques, such as stone-revetted banks (similar to those in Cornwall) and banks strengthened by megalithic flagstones, represent continuations of prehistoric building traditions. More-over, true fossil banks dating back to at least Gaulish times have been found beneath sand dunes along the coast (Giot, 1970).[10] Did these banks enclose individual fields or bundles of strips? In any case, coexistence of open strips and fields enclosed by banks seems to be a primitive feature in the agrarian structure of the Armorican far-west.

Conclusion

The present patterns of communication and urban settlement have been superimposed on these diverse rural structures. The former capitals of the Gallo-Roman *civitates* still form the focal points of urban growth over wide areas, including Tours, Angers and Nan-tes on the Loire, Le Mans and Rennes to the north, and Vannes to the west. Capitals of *civitates* which declined, such as Corseul, Jublains and Carhaix, still suffer from weakness in the urban hierarchy. Very small *civitates* in Normandy have only given rise to small episcopal towns, such as Coutances, Avranches, Bayeux and Sées. These towns suffered from serious competition from feudal foundations such as Alençon and Caen. Many villages and market towns were founded during the Middle Ages by the principal *seigneurs* of Brittany, Normandy and Maine. They form a dense network of settlements but many failed to develop beyond the level of small market towns.

The attraction of coastal sites has been extremely important in Brittany and has given rise to two generations of towns. The first of these is medieval in origin and involves sites at the head of rias for example from Dinan to Landerneau and from Quimperlé to Redon. The second generation involves more recent settlements, including expanded towns like Brest and Port Louis, and completely new foundations, such as Lorient.

In western Brittany, Brest and Lorient are the two chief towns; in Basse-Normandie, the chief towns are the feudal foundations of Caen and Alençon and the port of Cherbourg. Elsewhere, the urban network is still dominated by old Gallo-Roman centres, such as Le Mans, Angers, Nantes and Rennes. The pattern of urban settlement in Armorica is diverse, comprising towns of various origins and which have undergone varying degrees of development. But unlike other regions of France, the towns and cities of the West do not completely overshadow the countryside which supports a relatively high density of population and contains rural activities that are still very much alive.

9. Notes

1. Plateaux with deeply incised valleys dominate the interior of western France. Broad alluvial valleys, such as the Loire and the valleys of Normandy, are found only on its margins. Elevated sections of the plateaux are sometimes tree-covered and are generally cultivable. Only in the far west are uplands really mountainous and climatic conditions sufficiently harsh to prevent cultivation.
2. The Pays de Caux also bears a name of Gaulish origin (derived from the Caletes) but that *civitas* lost its autonomy very early.
3. The so-called ZEDE (*zones d'études démographiques et d'emploi*).
4. Very often a ria formed the boundary between two dioceses. A port and its hinterland would therefore be divided between two territorial units, but this problem was resolved when the *départements* were created so that ports and their hinterlands were placed in the same *départements*.
5. See also the work of Fleuriot (1958, 1964).
6. See also the *Atlas Historique de Normandie*, I (1967–72) prepared by the Faculté des Lettres et Sciences Humaines (Caen), especially the maps showing communities of inhabitants of the *généralités* of Rouen, Caen and Alençon 1636–1789.

7. Most modern *bourgs* are the result of spontaneous development (Flatrès, 1960). Nevertheless, during medieval times and especially in Normandy, some seigneurs and dukes accorded burgage privileges to some rural settlements (Musset, 1960). On the concept of the *bourg* examined through time and for several parts of France, see Flatrès-Mury (1972).

8. The forest of Quénécan, on the border between the dioceses of Vannes and Quimper is certainly a frontier forest, but the most important factors explaining its existence relate to the physical environment and the type of feudal domination that operated.

9. The area under wasteland in Finistère *département*, for example, declined from 268,000 ha in 1838, to 229,870 ha in 1882, 173,388 ha in 1920 and 59,221 ha in 1970 (Le Bail, 1925; Ministère de l'Agriculture, 1970; Ogès, 1949).

10. Considerable evidence of Roman centuriation has been found in the Campagne de Caen, but traces are less pronounced in Brittany.

9. References

Adigard des Gautries, J., *Les Noms de personnes scandinaves en Normandie de 911 à 1066, Nomina Germanica*, Uppsala (1954).

Agache, R., 'Détection aérienne des vestiges protohistoriques, gallo-romains et médiévaux dans le bassin de la Somme et ses abords', *Bulletin de la Société Préhistorique du Nord*, numéro hors serie (1970).

Allenou, J., *Histoire féodale des marais, territoire et église de Dol*, Paris (1917).

Bertrand, M., *Bulletin de la Société Lorientaise d'Archéologie*, 41 (1973).

De Boüard, M. (ed.), *Histoire de la Normandie*, Toulouse (1970).

Boussard, J., 'La seigneurie de Bellême au dixième et onzième siècles', in *Mélanges Halphen*, Paris (1951), 43–54.

Brunet, P., 'Problèmes relatifs aux structures agraires de la Basse-Normandie', *Annales de Normandie* (1955), 115–135.

Colbert de Beaulieu, J. B., 'Notices de numismatique armoricaine', *Annales de Bretagne* (1952–66), 59, 81–93, 221–38; 60, 310–35; 61, 184–200; 62, 152–80; 63, 29–54; 64, 24–45; 65, 36–58; 66, 39–62; 67, 76–91; 68, 41–87; 69, 43–73; 70, 37–51; 72, 209–22; 73, 213–18.

Couffon, R., 'Les pagi de la Domnonée au neuvième siècle d'après les hagiographes', *Memoires de la Société d'Histoire et d'Archéologie de Bretagne*, 24 (1944), 1–23.

Couffon, R., 'Toponymie bretonne, la forêt centrale, les Plous', *Memoires de la Société d'Histoire et d'Archéologie de Bretagne*, 26 (1946), 19–34.

Daniel, G. (ed.), *Brittany*, London (1960).

Delumeau, J. (ed.), *Histoire de la Bretagne*, Toulouse (1969).

Delumeau, J. (ed.), *Documents de l'Histoire de la Bretagne*, Toulouse (1971).

Dubois, J., 'La carte des diocèses de France', *Annales Economies, Sociétés, Civilisations,* 20 (1965), 680–91.

Faculté des Lettres et Sciences Humaines de l'Université de Caen, Centre de Recherches d'Histoire Quantitative (1967–72): *Atlas Historique de Normandie,* I.

Falc'hun, F., *L'Histoire de la langue bretonne d'après la géographie linguistique,* Paris (1963).

Falc'hun, F., 'Doctrine de J. Loth sur les origines de la langue bretonne', *Revue de Linguistique Romane* (1966).

Flatrès, P., 'Le pays nord-bigouden', *Annales de Bretagne,* 51 (1944), 158–205.

Flatrès, P., 'Les divisions territoriales de Basse-Bretagne comparées à celles des contrées celtiques d'Outre-Manche', *Annales de Bretagne,* 63 (1956), 1–17.

Flatrès, P., 'La structure rurale de Sud-Finistère d'après les anciens cadastres', *Norois,* 4 (1957), 353–67, 425–53.

Flatrès, P., 'L'étendue des finages villageois en Bretagne', *Norois,* 5 (1958), 181–86.

Flatrès, P., 'Quelques points de géographie des bourgs bas-bretons', *Norois,* 7 (1960), 181–86.

Flatrès, P., 'Les anciennes structures rurales en Bretagne d'après le cartulaire de Redon; le paysage rural et son évolution', *Etudes Rurales,* 41 (1971), 87–93.

Flatrès-Mury, H., 'La notion du bourg en France', in *La Pensée géographique française contemporaine; Mélanges offerts au professeur A. Meynier,* Saint-Brieuc (1972), 563–72.

Fleuriot, L., 'Recherches sur les enclaves romanes anciennes en territoire bretonnant', *Etudes Celtiques,* 8 (1958), 164–78.

Fleuriot, L., *Dictionnaire des gloses en vieux breton,* Paris (1964).

Gautier, M., *Chemins et véhicules de nos campagnes,* Saint-Brieuc (1971).

Giot, P. R., L'Helgouach, J. and Briard, J., *La Bretagne: préhistoire et proto-histoire,* Grenoble (1962).

Giot, P. R., 'De l'antiquité des talus et des dunes armoricaines', *Penn-Ar-Bed,* 60 (1970), 249–56.

Largillière, R., *Les Saints et l'organisation chrétienne primitive de l'Armorique bretonne,* Rennes (1925).

Le Bail, A., *Le Finistère agricole,* Angers (1925).

Longnon, A., *Atlas historique de la France,* Paris (1890).

Loth, J., *L'émigration bretonne en Armorique du cinquième au septième siècle de notre ère,* Rennes (1883a).

Loth, J., *De Vocis Aremoricae forma atque significatione,* Redonibus (1883b).

Merle, L., *La Métairie et l'évolution agraire de la Gâtine poitevine de la fin du Moyen-Age à la Révolution,* Paris (1958).

Merlet, F., 'La formation des diocèses et des paroisses en Bretagne', *Memoires de la Société d'Histoire et d'Archéologie de Bretagne*, 30 (1950), 5–61; 31 (1951), 137–72.

Meynier, A., 'Champs et chemins en Bretagne', *Conferences Universitaires de Bretagne, 1942–43* (1943), 159–78.

Meynier, A., 'Sur de curieux alignements de chemins et de monuments en Bretagne', *Annales de Bretagne*, 51 (1944a), 125–29.

Meynier, A., 'Traces de cadastre romain en Armorique: compte rendu', *Académie des Inscriptions et Belles-Lettres* (1944b), 413–22.

Meynier, A., 'Les ensembles cadastraux circulaires en Bretagne', *Annales de Bretagne*, 52 (1945a), 19–34.

Meynier, A., 'La commune rurale française', *Annales de Géographie*, 54 (1945b), 161–79.

Meynier, A., 'La genèse du parcellaire breton', *Norois*, 13 (1966), 595–610.

Ministère de l'Agriculture, *Recensement général de l'agriculture*, Paris (1970).

Musset, L., 'Recherches sur les bourgs et les bourgs ruraux du bocage normand', *Le Pays Bas-normand* (1960).

Ogès, L., *L'Agriculture dans le Finistère au milieu du dix-neuvième siècle*, Brest (1949).

10

Vernacular Architecture and The Peasant House

GWYN I. MEIRION-JONES

Introduction

Vernacular Architecture and the Historical Geographer

Study of the cultural landscape and its evolution has long been the historical geographer's concern. Field systems and settlement patterns have been examined in detail but most enquiries have stopped short of the dwelling house itself. However, evidence afforded by the house and its ancillary buildings may provide insights into present and past economic conditions which help to elucidate earlier geographies. Establishment of an evolutionary sequence and a chronology of house-types allows the age of buildings to be estimated. Cartographic and documentary coverage varies widely both in time and space and may be very lean before 1800 but by dating buildings it may be possible to show that a site was inhabited perhaps two or three centuries before this can be demonstrated by documentary evidence. Furthermore, the survival of an old house is sufficient to establish continuity of settlement since the time of its earliest datable element. There is also now general recognition, as witnessed by an increasing number of thriving conservation groups, that old buildings form a valuable part of Europe's cultural heritage. The strength of this opinion has led governments to legislate for the protection and preservation of old buildings in various ways. Study of traditional buildings both in town and country creates a body of knowledge and informed opinion upon which to base value judgements that may influence planning decisions.

The Interdisciplinary Approach

Investigation of vernacular architecture in Europe dates largely from the present century, although a few isolated studies in the latter part of the nineteenth century in Britain and the eighteenth century in Germany describe the more picturesque cottages that were then beginning to attract attention. This awareness of older traditions of building was heightened from the end of the nineteenth century when cheap uniform urban house-types became increasingly common in both town and country. Only during the 1920s was 'folk life' given recognition in Britain as a subject for scientific research, and study of vernacular building began.

The earlier studies were made in the countries of north-west Europe rather than France, where the study of vernacular architecture is still at an early stage. The student must turn to the British Isles and Scandinavia for regional and systematic enquiries from which he will learn methods and techniques for studying vernacular buildings and may also gain an insight into the development of the subject. Serious pioneer work in Scandinavia is exemplified by the writings of Erixon (1937, 1938), and Campbell (1937, 1938). Studies of construction techniques in the British Isles by Addy (1898) and Innocent (1916) have become classics, but the first regional study was *The Welsh House* (Peate, 1946), followed by *Monmouthshire Houses* (Fox and Raglan, 1951-4) and a series of enquiries into the lesser domestic buildings of England (Brunskill, 1952, 1963; Marsden, 1958; Wood-Jones, 1963).

Campbell, Erixon, Peate, and later Evans (1940, 1942, 1951 and 1957) saw the peasant house not just as an example of vernacular architecture, but as a structure adapted to family needs which had evolved over the centuries in response to changing economic, social, agricultural and industrial conditions. They studied not only rural buildings but also the folk-ways of the people who inhabited them. The former line of enquiry led to the classification of houses based on building materials, structure and plan, and the establishment of an evolutionary sequence and chronology, whilst the second permitted a much fuller under-standing and interpretation of vernacular buildings.

Architects long neglected the study of the lesser buildings, having been chiefly concerned with the buildings of the upper social classes. The work of Cordingley at Manchester led to a notable series of studies and the development of a systematic recording system. Archaeologists also turned to an examination of vernacular architecture, perhaps partly motivated by the thought that such studies might assist the interpretation of excavated dwellings. The archaeological approach treats the dwelling as an artefact. At its best this approach is exemplified in the work of Fox and Raglan (1951–4) who sought to discover how each style developed, to identify its time range, and to define gaps in the evolutionary record by detailed study of building techniques and house plans. Their work has served as a methodological textbook for many workers, but few would now agree that such an enquiry can be carried out by archaeological methods alone.

Buildings are also historical documents in their own right. Dwellings must be placed in their historical context, and the in-fluence of historical changes may be related to changes in house-type. Inventories of the number and type of farm implements and the disposition of buildings around the farm-yard provide valuable data relating dwellings to the agrarian economy. Barley (1961) and Hoskins (1953) have shown how essential is the need to undertake parallel archive work. Wills, marriage contracts and probate inventories may enable the worker to identify the people who lived in a house, define their social status and work, and dis-cover the number and disposition of rooms, furniture and house-hold goods.

The house must also be seen geographically, and the historical geographer is well equipped to study the peasant house if he can also acquire the relevant skills and the techniques of the architect, archaeologist, and historian. To these he may add his own skills and relate the house to the cultural landscape of which it is the oldest element, for man's first task is to build a dwelling before he clears the woods, ploughs the fields, and sows his crops. Specialists in several disciplines may make distinctive contributions to the study of the peasant house and in so doing demonstrate the value of an interdisciplinary approach.

Destruction and Change

During the present century rural life has been almost completely transformed. Growth of full-time education, changing social consciousness, improvement in living conditions and revolutionizing of private transport have made the countryman more independent and mobile. Rationalization of marketing arrangements has taken away the importance of many local markets. Since 1945 there has been a large-scale abandonment of traditional forms of agricultural labour. This change in the social order, agrarian structure, and economy of rural Europe has been cataclysmic. Many would agree that it has been beneficial, but its effect for the student of Folk Culture has been catastrophic as vast amounts of unrecorded data, both material and oral, have been destroyed.

In England, these changes began at a much earlier date and rural domestic buildings demonstrate gradual modifications over several hundred years. But in parts of continental Europe, and in particular France, it is only since 1945 that the rural economy has changed suddenly from 'medieval' to modern. Massive rural depopulation, abandonment of farmhouses, restructuring of farm holdings, and mechanization have led to completely changed ways of life. Younger people have hastened to the towns leaving an ageing population on the land. As the older generation passes, farms and hamlets have become deserted, particularly in more difficult areas like the Hercynian uplands. In the Breton Monts d'Arrée where hamlets once comprised ten or a dozen small but actively worked farms only one or two may now remain. Houses have either been handed down to a younger generation for use as holiday homes or have been purchased by outsiders. Whole hamlets come to life for only a few weeks in the summer. Until recent times the way of life in parts of France appears to have advanced little beyond that of the Middle Ages, and in parts of the Breton peninsula, for example, life can fairly be said to have remained in a 'proto-historic' phase. But today's countryman is more detached from nature and is increasingly becoming an agricultural operative rather than a *paysan*. The ways and aspirations of the peasant are being replaced by those of the lower middle classes. Some farmhouses are falling into disrepair or lie abandoned, others have been purchased by town dwellers seeking second homes. Resulting restoration and renovation has been all too often disastrous so that original plan and form, and sometimes even the materials, are lost or obscured.

Improvement grants for farmers, provided since the implementation of the Common Agricultural Policy, are also responsible for the destruction and transformation beyond recognition of many peasant dwellings. In the face of the devastating changes that have taken place in rural France in the last fifteen years, the student of vernacular architecture is faced with an urgent task. Little work has been completed compared with that done in the British Isles, Germany and Scandinavia. Valuable evidence is destroyed each year and there is a great need for both regional and systematic studies.

Published Work and Sources

The earliest serious work on the French peasant house dates from the late nineteenth century, but real progress was not made until the interwar period. This interest in the ordinary as distinct from the extraordinary increased further after 1945. With the recent agrarian changes and destruction of farm houses, cottages and buildings has come a realization that the number of true vernacular buildings is diminishing. Acquisition of such houses for use as second homes by town dwellers has undoubtedly led to a greater awareness of rural buildings by a social group that is sufficiently articulate to express concern for the rural heritage and to form organizations for protecting, conserving or converting buildings.

Instituted on 4 March 1964, the *Inventaire Général des Monuments et des Richesses Artistiques de la France* was established to produce a rigorous and homogeneous scientific record for the whole of France. Being intended to cover the full range of French artistic inheritance, it includes some material on the lesser domestic buildings.

The first volumes of the *Inventaire Général* were those for Carhaix-Plouguer *canton* in Finistère, and reports for three other *cantons* have also been published (Ministère des Affaires Culturelles, 1969, 1971a, 1973a, 1973b). The inventories are undertaken essentially from the point of view of art-history and to a certain extent disappoint the student of vernacular architecture. They are largely concerned with buildings of quality and artistic merit and fail to give any idea of the 'typical' house of a region. Indeed they often leave the reader totally ignorant of the nature and structure of the peasant house. Nevertheless, they do include examples of buildings in the manor-house class and are illustrated by a few measured plans and sections. The pre-inventory surveys, available in manuscript at the regional offices of the Commission, are an invaluable source. The *Inventaire Général* extends to two other types of publication, the *Répertoires* and a series of texts dealing with the terminology of art-history. The *Répertoires* are produced on a regional basis, with four having appeared so far (Ministère des Affaires Culturelles, 1970, 1971b, 1972b, 1973c). They list dictionaries, statistical works, catalogues, guides, accounts of travels and journeys, and articles on archaeology, architecture, sculpture, painting and furniture as well as a certain amount of manuscript material. They are of considerable value to the student of vernacular architecture. The most useful publication in the art-history series is the *Vocabulaire de l'Architecture* (Ministère des Affaires Culturelles, 1972a). But whilst it contains descriptions, illustrations and definitions of many technical terms, the absence of terms that are well-known to students of English peasant building forms an obstacle still to be overcome and reflects the fact that so much work remains to be done in France.

Whilst the work of the *Inventaire Général* is non-political, that of the Centre de Recherches sur les Monuments Historiques is concerned, among other things, with the protection and 'listing' of historic buildings of all kinds. A number of valuable publications have resulted for although mostly concerned with great buildings some attention has been paid to detailed study of carpentry of timber roofs and of timber-frame houses. Important among these collections of drawings, with no attempt at analysis or synthesis, are *Charpentes*, *Maisons à Pans de Bois*, and *Beffrois de Charpentes* (Ministère des Affaires Culturelles, Centre de Recherches sur les Monuments Historiques, n.d., 1972).

During the years 1942 to 1948 staff of the Musée des Arts et Traditions Populaires in Paris, no doubt inspired by work being done elsewhere in north-west Europe and aware of the great changes that might follow the end of the war, undertook a study of rural architecture in France, covering almost every *département*.

Their work is unpublished but plans exist to up-date it for publication. Nevertheless the manuscript drawings and notes are available for consultation in the museum. Whilst the collection is not comparable in quality to work then being undertaken in Britain, and far below the standard now to be expected, it contains much valuable evidence recorded before the French rural economy began to change dramatically. The houses that are recorded appear to have been selected subjectively and coverage in both space and time is very uneven. Many important house-types are not even represented. Nevertheless, better work in the Enquête d'Architecture Rurale (E.A.R.) contains plans and sections of houses and farm buildings, and pays attention to construction and carpentry. Each set of drawings is accompanied by a description of the lands and rural economy. Internal arrangements of the house are also often described and those plans which show positions of furniture items are most valuable since they permit an interpretation of the functions of rooms before the old traditions began to give way to new fashions in the post-war years. The quality is variable and some plans are sketchy and superficial, but in spite of shortcomings the survey is invaluable, providing the only known coverage for the whole of France.

Two other surveys deserve brief mention. A two-volume work covers the whole of France by *départements* (Ministère de la Santé Publique, 1939). There is reference to plan and form and descriptions of construction materials but no attempt at study in depth. The emphasis is rather on amenities, water supply and sanitation. Detailed plans are lacking but there is an abundance of photographs and farm houses are plotted in relation to other buildings as is furniture in the houses. Accompanying each chapter is general information on the geography, natural regions, size of farms, and the agricultural regime. This interwar survey may be used in conjunction with the E.A.R. A similar survey containing statistical information was published for Brittany in 1947 (Ministère de la Reconstruction et de l'Urbanisme).

Although concerned mostly with the greater buildings, the Société Française d'Archéologie publishes *Bulletin Monumental* and *Congres*, the emphasis being on art-history and particularly that of stone buildings. These journals contain relatively little material on timber buildings and roof carpentry but there is, nevertheless, a substantial quantity of matter relevant to the study of the lesser buildings. The journals of local archaeological and historical societies occasionally contain articles dealing with houses or groups of houses but rarely contain measured plans and drawings. Founded as an organization to serve the interests of, and provide advice and information to, the growing band of people who own a *résidence secondaire* in the country, the *Maisons Paysannes de France* society has done much to promote interest in the rural house largely through providing advice and guidance on renovation and restoration. Its *Revue* publishes articles on the regional house with photographs and occasionally some plans, but it is in no sense academic. Vernacular architecture has long been neglected in France, in spite of the work of geographers, but there is now evidence that serious research is beginning. The Groupe Habitat Populaire of the School of Architecture at Nantes, has reported on the buildings of the Pays Blanc (Loire-Atlantique) containing plans and sections, and paying attention to carpentry and other details (Groupe Habitat Populaire, 1974). Alongside this work is that of the medieval archaeologists, and with the creation of the journal *Archéologie Médiévale* in 1970 there now exists an outlet for the work of the departments of medieval archaeology at Caen and Aix-en-Provence. A large number of guidebooks and general accounts of the regions listed in the *Répertoires* currently in preparation as part of the *Inventaire Général* of French buildings, contain descriptions of the rural habitat and occasionally also of the interiors of houses (Cambry, 1799). Increased interest in the rural house since 1945 has led to the publication of various books aimed at a general readership. Whilst these are often sketchy in their treatment, they are often illustrated by useful photographs and drawings (Gauthier, n.d., 1959, Fréal and Janneau, 1973; Fréal and Lescroat 1973; Fréal and Quéruel, 1973).

Articles on aspects of peasant building are scattered both in time and space. The greater part of work on French rural buildings is due to the French school of regional geography. Almost simultaneously, Brunhes and Demangeon published the first work attempting to deal with the peasant house throughout France. Brunhes (1920) set out to describe and delimit regional types and produce a map showing the distribution of roof-types, by which he meant roof pitch and roofing material. Beginning with troglodyte dwellings he recognized corbelled structures, and then, basing his classification on building materials, form and, to a certain extent, plan, proceeded to describe selected regional types: in the Pays Basque, Limousin, Rouergue, Brittany, Flanders, Vendée, and Sénonais. Then came a consideration of the two major roof 'types': the steep pitch, slate and flat tile covered northern roof, and the low pitch Roman tile Mediterranean roof. His approach was essentially that of the regional geographer seeking to characterize landscapes and delimit geographical regions.

Demangeon (1920) approached the subject more rigorously and, whilst recognizing strong regional variations, aimed to provide a classification of provincial types based on house and farmyard plan. His work is illustrated by sketch plans and although paying no attention to archaeological evidence provides a model that was greatly to influence subsequent geographical work. Four main classes were recognized: the *maison élémentaire*, claimed to be the most widespread type and found in the Ardennes, Armorica, the Massif Central, eastern France, the Alps and the Pyrenees; the *maison en ordre serré* found from Beauce to Flanders across the Paris basin, Champagne and Picardie; the *maison en ordre lache*, confined to the northern littoral from Manche to Picardie; and the *maison-en-hauteur*, seen essentially as a southern type. Each of these four categories was subdivided into regional varieties. In spite of his early recognition that the importance of plan, disposition of rooms and relation of man, beast and storage was significant, Demangeon's work, like that of Brunhes failed because the house was not studied in depth in all its aspects. The treatment remained essentially superficial and confused house form and farm-yard plan in a manner that made an ordered classification impossible. Nevertheless, his early work of 1920 was developed further (Demangeon, 1925, 1927, 1936, 1937a, 1937b, 1939, 1942, 1947).

The work begun by Brunhes and Demangeon was taken up by others, notably by Robert who produced a series of studies on the houses of the French Alps (1936, 1939a, 1939b, 1942, 1946, 1949a, 1949b, 1954) culminating in a paper on classification and definition (1972). He too is concerned with *maison-types*, that is the most representative dwellings which, in spite of variations in detail, recur throughout a region. His classification falls into four main categories: the exterior appearance of houses; building materials;

agricultural function; plan and the relations between man, beast and storage. This is a much more detailed classification than that offered by Demangeon fifty years earlier, but is clearly in the same tradition, being expanded by virtue of work done in the intervening years.

Later workers have continued in this tradition, notably Vigarié (1969, 1971) who studied the *maison cauchoise* and de Planhol (1968a, 1968b, 1969, 1971) working in Lorraine. More recently, Flatrès-Mury (1970a, 1970b) has studied the contact zone between Brittany, Normandy and Mayenne using a transect running perpendicular to historic boundaries as a sampling frame. Other regional studies include those by Delaruelle (1933) in the Toulouse region, by Chatelard (1930) in the Ariège Pyrenees and by Coque (1956) in the Amiens region. A more detailed, well-illustrated and comprehensive regional survey is that by Salmon (1971) which deals with the constituent elements of plan, doors, barns, dove-cotes, dwellings and farm buildings. These general considerations are followed by detailed descriptions of individual farms.

In a paper dealing with Irish corbelled structures, Henry (1949, 1957) made an important contribution to the study of primitive buildings and included a summary of knowledge of similar structures in France. Local studies of dry-stone and corbelled buildings have also been made by Chemitte (1912), Formigé (1914) and Sartiges (1921). Knowledge of early house forms is increasing as a result of the examination of structures surviving in farmyards but which are of a type used formerly for habitation. Recent work by medieval archaeologists makes it possible to relate such structures to the ground plans of twelfth-century houses (Meirion-Jones, 1976; Bertrand, 1971, 1972–3). Serious studies of French carpentry are few. The outstanding contribution is that of Deneux (1927) who, using examples drawn from the greater buildings of northern France, attempted to establish a chronology for roof construction. This work has been summarized by Hewett (1969), and many of the drawings made by Deneux appear in the collection *Charpentes* (Ministère des Affaires Culturelles, 1972). Two useful studies of the roofs of town houses are those by Quenedey in Rouen (1911) and Annecy (1929). Walton (1960–62) draws attention to the cruck truss in the Dordogne, and Trefois (1937, 1950) includes examples of French timber roofs.

Construction

Building Materials

France is richly endowed with building materials. Choice of materials partly reflects availability, but is also a function of cultural practice and technology. Material was never transported very far for the buildings of common folk. Difficulty and cost of carriage in former times was a major problem. In many places use of building stone was confined to a few km from its outcrop. A rapidly changing lithology is likely to be reflected in equally rapid changes in building materials. All the outcrops suitable for use as building stone in France have been so used for centuries, if not millenia. The fissile limestones of the south were in use for dry-stone corbelled structures from at least the Neolithic period onwards, as were the schists and granites of Armorica. Some limestones, sandstones and granites, for example, allow the mason readily to produce dressed blocks and in areas where stone was abundant and labour plentiful and cheap even the most humble dwellings were constructed of finely cut blocks, as along the Loire Valley between Angers and Saumur. In other areas, the nature of the stone and the difficulty and expense of working it have resulted in a preponderance of buildings with rough rubble walls and finely cut stone being confined to door and window dressings. Where large expanses of drift material obscure the solid geology, or there are extensive unconsolidated deposits, stone gives way to the use of earth and sometimes brick. In France there are still thousands of rural buildings of earth or clay (*pisé, torchis*) prepared by kneading or puddling for an hour or more before use. Such material, when carefully laid, sets as hard as concrete and, provided that it is protected from running water, may last three or four hundred years or more. Farmhouses, cottages and quite large manors are built of it in Brittany and Normandy.

Use of timber is mostly, but not entirely, complementary to that of stone. Undoubtedly, stone has been in continuous use in some parts of France from the pre-historic period but elsewhere it may have superseded timber at an historically recent date. But in eastern and north-eastern France the use of timber has survived. A great deal of work is needed in these areas before any generalizations may be made about the variations in timber-framing. Roofing material shows considerable spatial variation, but the most striking difference is the contrast between the half-cylindrical Roman tiles of the south and the various coverings of much more steeply pitched roofs in the north, where slates and other fissile stones, clay tiles and thatches are widespread. The latter may be of reeds or, more commonly, of wheat or rye straw.

Carpentry

There are few studies of French carpentry to compare with those published in Britain over the last twenty years (Francey and Dimier, 1973). An important exception, however, is the work of Deneux (1927) which examined five hundred roofs between Dunkerque and Loire in great detail and demonstrated that each period was characterized by definite assembly methods. Framing joints and mechanical principles at varying points of time were shown to be different. Evidence for pre-historic roof construction is inadequate but buildings with a central row of posts once had a wide distribution and this form of roof support is probably the oldest known (Childe, 1950a). There are numerous examples from Danubian Neolithic cultures and Iron Age Hallstatt cultures (Childe, 1950b), and it would appear that such buildings continued to be put up in Germany and Denmark well into the eighteenth century. Excavated examples are reported from England and Wales (Smith, 1964) and the type survives widely in France.

At St. Jean-les-Monts an outbuilding with stone walls has its ridge supported by a single row of central posts to which are braced the principal rafters in turn supporting lateral purlins (E.A.R. Vendée).[1] Two admittedly rather primitive houses at Tatforest and Kerspec in Plumelin *commune* (Morbihan) have ridge pieces in part supported by posts rising from ground level. Other examples appear at Hengas (E.A.R., Landes) and at Arcis-le-Ponsart (Marne), where a twelfth-century stone barn has a stone vault supported on a central row of four columns (Francey and Dimier, 1973). The rows of central posts were obviously inconvenient and early builders sought ways of dispensing with them. Improvement seems to have been achieved by using two rows of posts instead of one, thereby creating a nave and aisles effect; or reducing the central post to the much shorter king-post raised on a tie-beam spanning the building; or using crucks, a form of curved principals.

Aisled Hall Construction

In plan the aisled hall is a rectangular structure divided into a nave and aisles by two rows of posts aligned parallel to the axis of the building. The posts are of wood or stone and support a longitudinal and horizontal beam called the arcade-plate. It is upon these arcade-plates that the tie-beams rest, which in turn support the roof-trusses. Occasionally, a stone building will have a stone arcading dividing nave from aisles as in a church, in which case the posts may be stone columns 'joined' together by Gothic or Romanesque arches. In some vernacular houses the 'arcading' may even consist of blank stone walling, pierced only by door-ways. Although there may be considerable variation in detail and in function, there is essentially no difference between an aisled house, an aisled barn and an aisled church.

Aisled houses are now confined to only a few parts of France, but the form survives widely in barns, market halls and churches. Some of the finest examples are the market halls of medieval and early modern date and the barns of religious houses. At Parçay-Meslay (Indre-et-Loire) stands a magnificent early thirteenth-century abbey grange, 56·0 m long and 26·0 m wide with a height of 14·5 m. The vast roof is supported on four rows of posts creating a nave and double aisles (Horn, 1970). At Maubuisson (Seine-et-Oise) another early thirteenth-century barn is somewhat smaller, the nave being divided from the aisles by a stone arcade of circular columns and Gothic arches. An example of an early market hall is that at St. Pierre-sur-Dives (Calvados) probably dating from the late twelfth, early thirteenth-century and still in use (Berger, 1970). Seventeenth-century examples occur at Troussures (Oise), Richelieu (Indre-et-Loire) and Questembert (Morbihan). At Troussures, the barn has stone arcading, whilst at Richelieu and Questembert the market halls are both elaborate wooden structures (Horn, 1970) heavily braced with full king-post trusses. The aisled hall is found elsewhere in France in the form of barns and market halls. It was a common form for large buildings from the thirteenth century right up to the seventeenth century.

The houses of the Landes are also of an aisled form although the 'arcades' are often continuous walls pierced only by doorways. These stone walls frequently rise only to first floor level above which they are continued in timber construction. Many examples have wooden aisle-posts. Such buildings comprise domestic accommodation and provide space for the storage of vehicles and implements, which are normally kept in the nave, the living rooms and other storage occupying the aisles. Many examples survive and in all cases the tie-beam supports a king-post truss on which rests the ridge-piece (Figs. 10.1 and 10.2) (E.A.R., Landes).

FIG. 10.1. An aisled-hall type farmhouse in Les Landes.

FIG. 10.2. An aisled-hall type farmhouse at Marquese, Landes.

The type is further recorded in the Dordogne and in the Basque country. Some Alpine houses, whilst they are not fully developed aisled structures, display a single aisle as at Cret in the Val d'Isère en Tarentaise (E.A.R., Savoie) but there is no suggestion of a developed roof truss. The rafters are supported on rough pine trunks which rest on the gable walls. These buildings are probably to be regarded as degenerate types. The aisled-hall survives widely throughout France and was a common form from the thirteenth century until the seventeenth century. It survives in domestic building in south-west France and occurs in the French Alps in what may be a debased form.

The King-post Roof

The aisled hall was developed to clear the central row of posts from the earlier halls, but aisle posts also came to be regarded as a nuisance. Except for very large buildings, where they remained necessary to roof a wide span, they were superseded by raising the whole aisle truss on to a tie-beam thus clearing the floor completely. Several English examples survive to demonstrate this development (Smith, 1958) but only two French examples are known to the author, at Bray in the Ardennes (E.A.R., Ardennes) and at Annecy in Savoie (Quenedey, 1929). Here the tie-beam supports a pair of posts rising to a collar which in turn supports the king-post. Many more examples may remain to be discovered, but it is likely that this type of truss was never common in France and that the transition from aisled hall to the simple king-post truss may have been a direct one. Alternatively, the king-post roof may have developed directly from the hall with a row of central posts.

The king-post truss is by far the most common type in France and appears to be the sole method of roof support in the vast majority of peasant buildings as well as in larger farm buildings, barns, and churches from the medieval period onwards. It is found at all levels in the social scale from the grandest of *châteaux* and churches to the humblest peasant dwelling and in urban houses as well as in rural buildings. It exists all over France from the Pas-de-Calais to the Pyrenees and from Cotentin to Provence and appears in Brittany where it mingles with the cruck tradition. Two forms are found: the full king-post rising from the tie-beam, and the upper king-post rising from the collar (Cordingley, 1961).[2] The chief variation within these forms is between the long king-post characteristic of northern and western France and the short, stubby king-post associated with the low-pitched roofs of the south.

Whilst the full king-post rising from a tie-beam is most common, a variant in which the post rises from a collar, the upper king-post, is also widespread. It is particularly common in lofts of Breton houses used for the storage of hay or grain as its use clears the loft floor of obstructions. Maget (1953) illustrates examples from the high Alps which show both the full king-post as well as the full length ridge-post from which it has developed. The king-post may be seen by even the most casual observer in countless town buildings and farmhouses and outbuildings across northern France.[3] In Brittany searches have revealed king-posts to be widespread and whilst it is found at the lower social levels, sometimes associated with the upper cruck, houses of the smaller manor house class upwards invariably have this type of roof-truss.[4]

The Coupled-Rafter Roof

At an unknown but apparently early date, a form of roof without a ridge-piece evolved with all the principals of equal scantling. This trussed-rafter roof-type is found in major churches of the twelfth century (Lisieux, Calvados; Puiseaux, Loiret), and in a late twelfth-century house in Dijon. A similar scissors trussed roof, of early thirteenth-century date, is found in the *château* of Blois (Ministère des Affaires Culturelles, 1972, Vol. 1). The relationship, if any, between these types and the other types of roof truss is not yet clear and the coupled-rafter roof may well yet be found to occur more widely than has hitherto been suspected and possibly over a greater social range. Certainly, it is known in the Basque houses of the Basses-Pyrénées where at Arros a coupled rafter roof is braced only by a collar and there is no ridge purlin. Numerous other examples are recorded in the same area. Even where the aisled houses have ridge-pieces supported by king-posts, the absence of principal rafters is noteworthy (E.A.R., Basses-Pyrénées). It is particularly interesting that an apparently early type of roof should have survived in the area where the aisled hall, acknowledged as an early type, has also survived.

The Cruck Truss

Several attempts have been made to define the cruck. Peate (1946) thought of them as

> 'pairs of curved timbers set up in inverted V-form, the timbers crossing at the apex of the triangle thus formed, so forming a fork in which the ridge-piece is fitted. The rafters and purlins are placed on the crucks which therefore bear the whole weight of the roof. The walls of such buildings were therefore of secondary importance and served principally to enclose them: they bore no constructional relationship to the roof' (p. 160).

Raglan (1956) attempting to demonstrate its derivation from the Gothic arch, describes the cruck truss as

> 'composed of two curved or angled pieces of timber called "crucks" or "cruck blades" . . . with convex side outwards and joined at the top in such a way as to support the ridge-piece. In all but the crudest forms, they also directly support the purlins' (p. 101).

The use of the word 'curved' has led to considerable difficulty. Many principal rafters, which are in fact straight, are described correctly as 'crucks' because they perform this function and spring from below the level of the wall-plates. A recent definition of a cruck as 'a single piece of timber stretching from the apex of the roof substantially down the side-walls' (Alcock, 1972, 1973) avoids saying whether it is curved or straight and has the further advantage that it makes no prior assumptions about the relation of the cruck-blades to the rest of the truss.

In its purest form, the cruck-truss should support a roof in its entirety, but it appears to be generally recognized that variations exist in which the walls play a partial load-bearing role. In such cases, the full crucks may support only the ridge-piece, leaving the walls to bear the full weight of the lower ends of the rafters, or the crucks may support lateral purlins thereby taking still more of the roof weight, leaving only the ends of the purlins resting on the wall heads. Two other types occur. The term 'base-cruck' has been applied where

> 'the blades are single baulks of timber which start well below

the eaves and rise to the level of the lowest transverse member. Above this member, here called a tie, the roof may take a variety of forms, including that of another length of timber to continue the blade' (Alcock and Barley, 1972, 133).

The 'upper cruck' has been widely accepted as being related to the full cruck in that the lower parts, the 'legs' of the principals below the tie-beam, are missing. It nevertheless retains a degree of curvature that serves to distinguish it from a straight principal rafter and serves to betray its origin. The example recorded near Tarbes well illustrates the type (Fig. 10.3).

FIG. 10.3. An upper-cruck near Tarbes.

Before discussing the problem further, the evidence for the existence of the cruck in France must be examined. During the course of a long-term survey of the Breton house, numbers of cruck-like structures have been found in Morbihan, Côtes-du-Nord, Finistère and Ille-et-Vilaine, with by far the greatest numbers in Morbihan, the majority being upper-crucks. Full-crucks now appear to be rare in Brittany although there is plenty of oral evidence to suggest that they were formerly more plentiful, surviving in large numbers in field buildings until many of these were swept away during recent agricultural reforms. A particularly good example, however, is to be found near La Roche Bernard in Morbihan (Fig. 10.4). The form of these crucks is not dissimilar to that of the upper-crucks observed and the possibility that they are re-used upper-crucks must not be discounted. Nevertheless, in the present context, they perform the functions of full-crucks, the curvature of the principals coinciding with the wall-head and the relatively short legs being contained almost wholly within the stone walls where they rest on sole-plates set within the wall. A variation on the full cruck-truss is occasionally found in the form of a scarfed- or jointed-cruck, two pieces of wood being shaped and pegged together to form the necessary curved principal.[5] The rather crude example at St. Guyomard, Morbihan (Fig. 10.5) illustrates the type.

The majority of Breton cruck forms are upper-crucks, the blades crossing at the apex to provide a form in which rests the ride-piece and supporting lateral purlins, usually two on each side. Occasionally, the blades are halved and pegged at the apex, the ridge-piece resting in a notch. The cruck-blades are curved, sometimes sharply so, at about the level of the wall-head, at which point they descend vertically, partly or wholly in the thickness of the wall and are tenoned into a tie-beam. This is well shown in Figs. 10.3 and 10.6. At Kervaly, the lateral purlins are either supported on pegs as in the left-hand truss of Fig. 10.6, or notched into the blades as in the right-hand truss. A similar arrangement is present at Meriadec-en-Plumergat (Fig. 10.7) where the ridge-piece is carried in a form and the two pairs of lateral purlins rest on cleats. In the circular structure at Le Parun (Fig. 10.8) the difficulty of distinguishing between straight and curved upper-crucks becomes apparent for there are two trusses, only one of which has curved principals. The use of upper-crucks for circular buildings has been observed elsewhere in Morbihan and must formerly have been much more common.

Fig. 10.4. A cruck barn near La Roche Bernard, Morbihan.

FIG. 10.5a. A scarfed cruck at St. Guyomard, Morbihan.

FIG. 10.5b. Detail of a scarfed cruck at St. Guyomard, Morbihan.

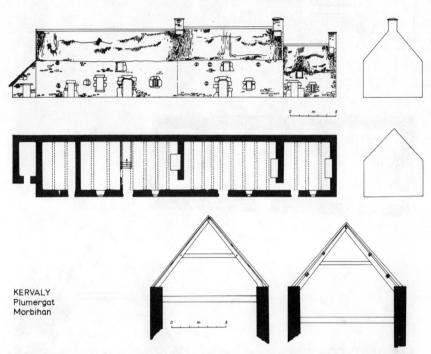

KERVALY
Plumergat
Morbihan

FIG. 10.6. Three conjoined dwellings, from right to left: a single-cell dwelling, a long-house, a second long-house with, additionally, extra accommodation for cows and horses and a lean-to pig-sty beyond. Long-houses of this kind had no physical division between the living-room end (with its hearth and chimney) and the 'lower' end reserved for animals. Entrance was by a common doorway. Wooden partitions, separating the byre, were added later. Internal communication between the three dwellings suggests occupation by kin groups.

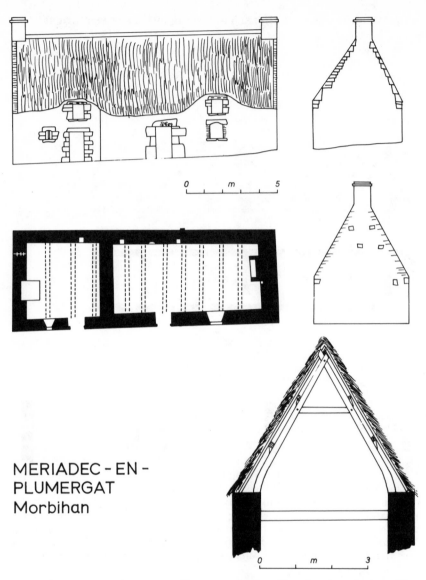

MERIADEC‑EN‑
PLUMERGAT
Morbihan

F IG. 10.7a. Two conjoined dwellings: a single-cell and a long-house. The former byre of the long-house lies to the left of the only doorway, with the living-room to the right. Before the 19th century often there was no partition between accommodation for man and beast, the division of the rectangular space, served by the single doorway, being a functional one only. Door and window elevations and cross-sections show the use of stone and wall thickness. A phallic symbol and date are located over one of the door lintels. The lower drawings show the elevation and section of the simple chimney piece. The chimney hood is of wood construction, corbelled out from the wall. The hearth is of stone blocks.

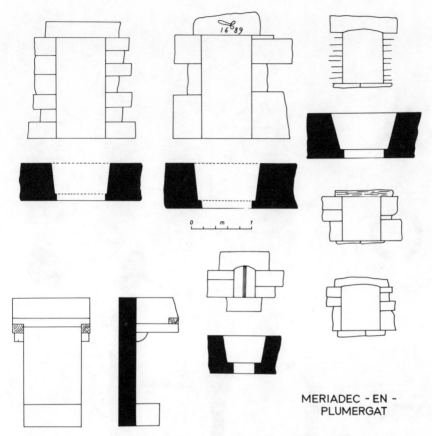

MERIADEC - EN -
PLUMERGAT

FIG. 10.7b. Features of two conjoined dwellings.

The true base-cruck has not so far been found in Brittany, but near Lorient (Morbihan) a structure probably best described as an upper base-cruck is combined with a king-post truss above the collar. This variant is not confined to the Armorican peninsula for it occurs in the Loire valley near Angers (Fig. 10.9).[6] The cruck-truss has also been identified in the Dordogne. Apart from farm sheds with tong-supports, Walton (1960–2) has recorded an unmistakable upper cruck-truss near Gourdon and a scarfed upper cruck-truss near Groslejac, both combined with a king-post rising from a short collar. Interpreting cave paintings in the area in which primitive shelters of Upper Palaeolithic hunters are displayed, Walton suggests that paired couples and a king-post may

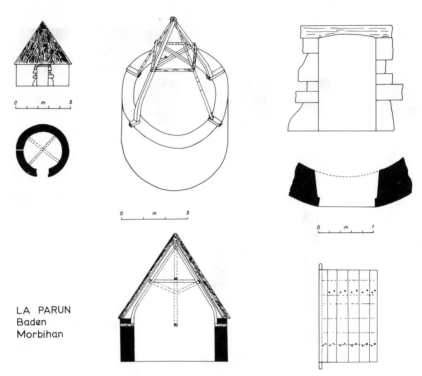

LA PARUN
Baden
Morbihan

FIG. 10.8. This circular building (now used as a pig sty) is of a size and form once more common and widely used, not only for storage and for animals but as a dwelling house as well. Note the upper-cruck construction of the roof. Detailed drawings show: the doorway of partially dressed stone for jambs and wood for lintel; a section across the doorway; and the construction of the door.

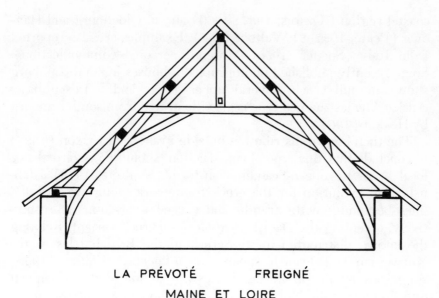

LA PRÉVOTÉ   FREIGNÉ

MAINE ET LOIRE

FIG. 10.9. An upper base-cruck at Freigné, Maine-et-Loire.

have been employed in the Dordogne since Magdalenian times. The upper cruck-truss has also been reported at Argos near Tarbes (Hinton, 1967) (Fig. 10.3).[7] Cruck construction employing a short king-post has a wider distribution in Europe. Trefois (1950) describes an example of a full-cruck combined with king-post at Duclair, west of Rouen. Further examples of crucks and cruck-like structures have been recorded in the Pas-de-Calais (E.A.R.). The cruck tradition can thus be shown unmistakably to be present in north-west France, in the Dordogne, in the Pyrenees foothills, in the lower reaches of the Seine valley and in the north-east.

For an understanding of the origin and development of the type we must now look at the distribution outside France. Large numbers of crucks have been recorded in the British Isles and a recent distribution map shows over 2000 true crucks concentrated in western and northern Britain, with main concentrations in eastern Wales, the Welsh Borders, the middle Thames valley, Leicestershire, the West Riding and north Yorkshire (Alcock, 1973). Undoubted crucks have been identified in the Flanders coastal region (Trefois, 1937; 1960) and in Oldenburg and Hanover (Peate, 1957–8; Walton, 1957). Examples are also reported from Italy (Soeder, 1956; Moreno, personal communication). Some recently published photographs of houses in south Limburg show one full cruck, several upper-crucks and a raised base-cruck.[8] The last-named type is also illustrated from south Limburg by Hekker (1961).

The then known distribution outside France led Erixon (1937) to conclude that this type of construction 'should be regarded as a local West European-Scandinavian form'. Walton (1948) established an evolution for the cruck framework along two parallel lines beginning with straight and curved tong-supports respectively, accepting the Danish *stridsuler* as a cruck variant. Relating the known distribution of the cruck in the British Isles to the Norwegian and Danish spheres of influence, Walton (1954) suggested an origin in the Schleswig region with subsequent diffusion along the North Sea coast to Flanders and across to the Yorkshire coast from where it spread to northern and western Britain. Smith (1964) rejected this hypothesis as unhistorical and by comparing the British distribution with that of surviving Celtic place-name elements and having regard to the continental examples as well as to the slender evidence of excavation, advanced a hypothesis of transmission by the Celtic peoples.

Underlying this discussion is a fundamental disagreement as to whether certain simple structures may be regarded as crucks, and whether the cruck is older than the oldest surviving example. Smith (1964) regards it to be of high antiquity, based primarily on its wide distribution but with supporting archaeological evidence and the analogous *antae* of a stone church in Co. Galway. McCourt (1960–2, 1964–5) has drawn attention to the distribution in Ireland where he regards the cruck as a 'traditional and long-standing feature' belonging in a broad sense to a timber building tradition that embraces much of western and Scandinavian Europe. The archaeological evidence rests on an interpretation of the arrangement of post-holes at sites in Germany (Smith, 1964) and, more recently, at Latimer in Buckinghamshire where inclined post-holes have been interpreted as belonging to a cruck structure of the late fourth or early fifth century (Branigan, 1968). Van Es (1967) has interpreted such evidence at Wijster in the Netherlands and cites further evidence from that country and from north-west Germany. He, too, regards the inner inclined post-holes as former crucks and claims that two roof-types mingle, one demonstrating a new technical device: cruck construction, and goes on to attribute the origin to Westphalia from whence the type spread to the sandy soils of north-west Holland and parts of north-west Germany. There is no proof that the cruck was known in the Hallstatt kingdoms, but it is known in north-west Germany, is strongly represented in surviving buildings in south Limburg and is known all over the Netherlands and Belgium. An origin in the Rhinelands, or in an area south-east of the Rhinelands, in Celtic times and subsequent diffusion in a northerly and westerly direction with the movement of Celtic peoples is highly plausible. The technique could then have spread across the English Channel, later to be displaced by the introduction of other techniques in east and south-east England, and over the whole of France largely to be displaced later by the king-post roof. Alternatively, its diffusion could have been confined to those areas where it has been reported today, along the north coast from Flanders through the Pas-de-Calais to the Seine and then across to Brittany where it survived the Breton invasion of the Dark Ages, invading peoples who may well have reinforced the existing cruck tradition by bringing knowledge of the technique with them.

House Type, Plan and Evolutionary Sequence

Our understanding of origin and cultural significance of plan variations remains very limited. Much recent research on vernacular architecture has been concerned with establishing regional variations in plan leading to important cultural inferences. Aalen (1973) has noted,

'plan serves a useful focus for investigation; it is the main element revealed by archaeological investigation, has direct influence on other structural features of the house and moreover, is the most tenacious element of regional building traditions often exhibiting basic continuity through a succession of changes in building materials and major economic and social developments'.

Early House Forms

Troglodyte dwellings

The earliest type of peasant house for which evidence survives is undoubtedly the cave dwelling, with many formerly inhabited caves existing in drier limestone areas. Brunhes (1920) recorded the current use of *creutes* or *boves* in the rocks along the Aisne, Loire, Loir and Seine valleys and in Périgord and Sénonais immediately after World War I. Sometimes the cave had been abandoned as a dwelling and was used as a cellar or a stable with a new house having being built in front of the cave. Such dwellings may still be found at Langerie-Basse near Les Eyzies and at Brantôme where a whole street of them stands beside the river Dronne. Indeed, they exist along the Loire between Angers and Tours with particular concentrations around Langeais and between Saumur and Candes (Joubert, 1973).

Circular buildings

A tradition of living in circular buildings is known for certainty from the Gallo-Roman period and, in so far as the 'houses of the dead' are modelled on the 'houses of the living' (Crawford, 1953), it seems likely that the circular corbelled dwelling was common in some areas from Megalithic times. Islands off the Breton coast contain remains of circular stone huts attributed to Celtic missionaries. The best preserved is the circular chapel on the Ile Saint-Maudez, with an interior diameter of 2·80 m and walls 0·78 m thick. A door on the south-east side is the only opening. The walls are of granite blocks and the roof vaulted, supported by a pair of ogival ribs. Some 3·00 m to the east lie the remains of a much larger circular cell, with an external diameter of 7·40 m compared with 4·36 m for the chapel. The date of these buildings is not firmly established but Couffon (1938, 1943) attributed them all to the twelfth century, whilst La Borderie (1896) regarded the structures to date from the sixth century with the addition of the ogival vault in the twelfth century. This verdict was accepted by Barbier (1951, 1960). On the neighbouring Ile Lavret the remains of a Celtic monastery of eight circular huts probably also date from the earliest Breton settlements and have been attributed to the sixth century (La Borderie, 1896; Grand, 1958). These buildings are undoubtedly in the tradition of circular 'bee-hive' structures with corbelled stone roofs but, with the exception of the single surviving example on Ile St.-Maudez where the roof has apparently been rebuilt, most Breton examples have been destroyed.

Small circular stone buildings of this kind are distributed widely and are commonly found on rocky coasts or plateaux where schists, slate or fissile limestone is readily obtained, and usually where wood has been scarce or absent in historical times. The surviving distribution shows them to be a feature of remote, economically retarded places where old customs and traditions have survived. They are well-known all over Ireland (Henry, 1949), are reported in Spain and Portugal, and appear to be widely distributed in France. In addition to Brittany, they have been recorded in eastern France as far north as Burgundy (Sartiges, 1921) and along the Rhône valley, in Ardèche, Drôme, Gard and Vaucluse. Stone huts are numerous on the coastal hills of Provence and they appear in the Auvergne, on the arid limestone plateaux of the Causses and in the south-west, notably Périgord. Particularly numerous around Cahors and Figeac, they vary from 2·00 m to 7·00 m in diameter and from 2·00 m to 8·00 m in height (Sartiges, 1921). A typical example is the field hut near Montaléra (Lot) (Fig. 10.10), a dry-stone structure with a single opening, a doorway with roughly dressed jambs and a stone lintel. The asymmetrical corbelled roof is finished with a heavy capstone. Many of these buildings have been observed in the Causses and in Périgord, some being on a square plan and roofed with a circular dome.

Outside France, this type of structure occurs in Dalmatia, Istria, in Crete, in the Caucasus and in various parts of Africa. In Italy *trulli* are still used extensively as dwelling houses around Bari, both in the countryside and in the town of Alberobello (Allen, 1969). Elsewhere, these huts are no longer used as dwellings, but it would appear they continued to be so used in France until the end of the nineteenth century and in several parts of the country there is memory that they were once lived in (Henry, 1957). Most are now used for storage or as tool sheds in vineyards and olive groves.

A full series of constructional types is to be found in Provence, similar to the Irish sequence around Caherciveen-Waterville. Rectangular types occur in several parts of the Vaucluse, particularly around Gordes and Lagnes (Formige, 1914; Chemitte, 1912;

FIG. 10.10. Corbelled field hut near Montcléra, Lot.

Delamarre, 1934). Here, buildings of the Gallarus type are common, in addition to the more usual square and circular huts. Further south other similarities with Irish types occur and circular toolsheds are to be found in gardens around Forcalquier (Basses-Alpes) with conical roofs similar to those of the *trulli* (Figs. 10.11 and 10.12).

Dating these buildings is a problem, since knowledge of the techniques has been handed down for millenia. The circular hut with a corbelled roof was known in western Britain in Neolithic times and there is a close architectural relationship between the corbelled dwellings and the Megalithic monuments of the Mediterranean. The distributions of Megalithic monuments and existing

FIG. 10.11. Corbelled buildings near Gordes, Vaucluse.

FIG. 10.12. Corbelled buildings near Gordes, Vaucluse.

corbelled structures are almost identical and it now seems certain that the technique of corbelled buildings, now surviving in France, spread from the Mediterranean with the migration of the Megalith builders (Ó Ríordáin, 1965; Walton, 1961, 1969). Peasants are still able to build and repair these structures and near Gordes, rectangular corbelled *bori* form a entire village with several buildings bearing seventeenth and eighteenth century dates over the doors (Henry, 1957). Sartiges even suggests that some round and oval huts date from *c.* 1500 B.C. to the Roman conquest. For nearly every important group there are references to finds of Roman or La Tène objects in or near the huts. Henry (1957) suggests that although records are vague, the constant recurrence of round huts in purely local writings is rather impressive, particularly since the buildings are of a traditional type in remote hills and plateaux. Similar huts in Ireland certainly belong to the early Christian period and probably originated much earlier (Henry, 1949; 1957).

Not all circular buildings were corbelled, however, and many must have had thatch roofs supported by wooden poles. A central post rising from the ground to the apex of the conical roof is capable of supporting common rafters resting on top of the wall-head and laid against the apex. At a later stage the full-post, which impeded movement, was abandoned in favour of the tie-beam and king-post. An alternative was a pair of collar trussed rafters, or an upper-cruck truss (Fig. 10.3). These buildings were formerly present in great numbers in Brittany, but the north-facing circular structure at Le Parun (now used as a pig-sty) is one of the few that remains. With an internal diameter of 4·00 m, the rubble walls rise to a height of 2·00 m. There are two trusses but no tie-beams, the feet of the principal rafters resting on wooden blocks set radially in the thickness of the walls. The rafters are trussed by collars and short rough purlins pass on the other sides at the level of the collars. Common rafters rest on these purlins. Thatch is laid over all and the apex is capped with sods of turf. Most of the buildings of this type recorded in Brittany are under 4·00 m in diameter, but one discovered recently in an advanced state of collapse was just over 6·00 m diameter internally. The tradition of circular buildings surviving into the twentieth century has also bequeathed dove-cotes, well-covers (Figs. 10.13 and 10.14), bake-ovens and wind mills to the landscape. The *bordes* of Aquitaine form further exam-

Fig. 10.13a.   Corbelled well near Baden, Morbihan.

ple of circular buildings, being tent-like structures of thatch in use until recently as field huts, byres and sheep shelters (Figs. 10.15 a and b). It is thought that they also served as dwellings before *c.* 1800 (Moniot, 1970).

FIG. 10.13b. Corbelled well near Baden, Morbihan.

The circular building is the easiest to construct. It requires no knowledge of the art of cornering and the circle is the only means of enclosing the maximum area with the minimum of materials. It is unfortunate that having economized on walling materials, the resulting shape is impracticable for many purposes. The internal area is difficult to sub-divide if it is to serve more than one function. This resulted in the building of additional huts, movement from one to the other requiring going into the open air unless the buildings had been conjoined. It is not surprising therefore, that the circular house began to be abandoned in favour of other ground plans.

FIG. 10.14. Circular well-cover at La Croix Havard, Ille-et-Vilaine.

FIG. 10.15. A circular *borde* from the Musée d'Aquitaine.

The oval house

Although the simple rectangular plan has been known since pre-historic times, the oval house, at first sight, seems to represent an evolutionary stage between the circular hut and the rectilinear house. Three types of oval house have been defined: the 'ovate-oblong', with straight sides and true semi-circular ends; the 'elongated circle', resulting from the elongation of a circular hut whether of the corbelled stone roof type or otherwise; and the 'round-rectangular' type whose plan is approximately rectangular but which has rounded corners and sometimes rounded ends (Walton, 1952). Oval houses have been recorded in Africa, India, Italy and the Atlantic fringes of Europe. The use of curvature does not require the knowledge of cornering technique and is well-suited to the construction of roofing techniques using fairly primitive carpentry.

A few oval buildings survive in the French countryside and bear witness to a probable wider existence. The *borde* of Les Landes is such an example, which may occur in either an oval (Fig. 10.16) or a circular form (Fig. 10.15). Walls of clay support a fully hipped thatch roof. The *Enquête d'Architecture Rurale* recorded a

FIG. 10.16. An oval *borde* from the Musée d'Aquitaine.

number of primitive buildings in Brittany and whilst none of these can be said to be oval (indeed they are stone or earth structures with irregular cornering) they all have hipped roofs, which are now rare in the peninsula where gable-ended houses are almost universal. Whether the hipped roof is derived solely from the oval house (Walton, 1952) may be questioned, but it may well be that Breton thatch hipped roofs retain a memory of the oval house. Recent excavations at Pen-er-Malo (Guidel, Morbihan) have uncovered an oval house 11·00 m long and 7·00 m wide at its maximum. The walls, 0·80 m to 1·00 m high and 0·80 m thick at the base, are formed of irregular coursed stonework bounded with vegetable matter. A double hearth was centrally placed. The building has been dated as tenth to twelfth century (Delumeau, 1971). The sides of this structure are anything but straight and it should be regarded as a good example of an elongated circle rather than oval-oblate. The precious example of a farm building at Plumelin (Morbihan) well illustrates the kind of construction that must have risen from these low walls (Meirion-Jones, 1976). The other area where the oval house has survived is the Vendée where the *bourrine* takes several forms, none strictly rectilinear. The oval plan with clay walls and a thatched hipped roof is now becoming rare but was much more common formerly (Perraudeau, 1973).

The Rectilinear House

Circular, oval and rectilinear structures must have co-existed for centuries, indeed millenia, but there appears to have been a gradual transition from a dominance of circular and other curvilinear plans in prehistoric times to a condition in which the curvilinear became an antique exception and rectilinear forms dominated. A square or rectangular space is easier to utilize, sub-divide, alter and extend. However, its creation assumes knowledge of the cornering technique. Where this originated and by which routes it was diffused we do not know, but it seems probable that rectilinear forms developed as a result of using wood. The transition from the oval to the rectilinear plan may have been a consequence of improvement in carpentry and the resulting demands by the carpenter for regular consistent forms. Once the mason had also learned to corner the way was clear for greater symmetry and the hipped roof became a relic of the past. However, as long as the central hearth persisted there was no great demand to do away with the hipped roof, but as soon as the chimney stack came to be built at the gable end hipped roofs could be abandoned and gable walls be erected of stone or wood into which chimney stacks would be set.

The single-cell house is widely distributed in France but is particularly common in the north-west where formerly it represented the home of the lower social classes. It comprises a single room, no more than 6·00 m wide internally and often of no greater length, in which the whole life of the family took place. In the nineteenth century large familes of ten or more children lived in spaces of this size, with the hay lofts providing overspill sleeping accommodation for the children. In Anjou, Brittany and Normandy the hearth is invariably in the gable, entrance being by a doorway at the lower end and light coming from a solitary window. A table, benches, beds and one or two cupboards were the only furniture and, until recently, cooking was done on the open hearth.

Some houses of this kind were detached and set in small areas for vegetable cultivation. Others formed parts of terraces and in some areas of Brittany they are found alongside long-houses in rows of houses associated with the cultivation of former common fields. Elsewhere the single-cell house may be found either at ground or first-floor level conjoined to a larger house (Fig. 10.7), often of 'manorial' status, and serving as a dwelling for a family engaged in the daily life of the manor. At Plurien, Côtes-du-Nord (Fig. 10.17) it is probable that the upper unit was occupied by someone of superior social status, perhaps not greatly inferior to that of the *seigneur*, whilst at ground floor level the single-cell unit could have been lived in by a family of much lower status. It is not uncommon to find single-cell houses tucked away in the corner of a Breton or Norman farmyard and serving to house a land-less day labourer and his family.

The long-house, first identified in Wales and named after the Welsh *tŷ-hir*, is a dwelling in which animals are housed under the family roof itself (Peate, 1946). It is not to be confused with the *maison-en-longeur* and is best expressed in French as *la maison longue*, a precise term already used by some French archaeologists

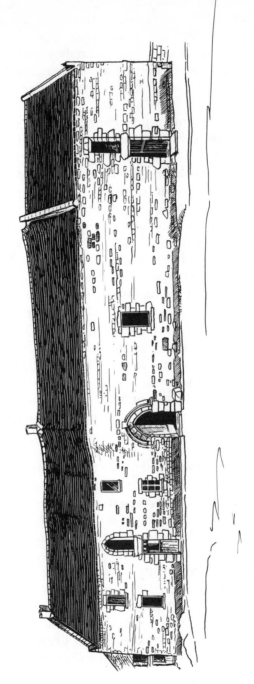

Fig. 10.17. La Salle, Plurien, Côtes-du-Nord.

(Pesez, 1971). The type has been recognized widely in the British Isles and until recently the known distribution of surviving buildings had led to the suggestion that it was 'a late manifestation of Celtic culture, because it is found only in lands of Celtic speech' (Smith, 1963). More recently doubts have been cast on the origin and distribution of the long-house in Britain by Peate (1963, 1964) and by Hurst (1971) who summarizes the evidence for what appears to have been the normal type of dwelling in many deserted medieval villages in England. Current work in Brittany has shown that the house-and-byre type, and particularly the long-house, survives in large numbers, and on the basis of this evidence it has been suggested that the long-house is an earlier west European, rather than a late Celtic, type perhaps being Celtic in the wider sense of having survived from the Gallo-Roman period (Meirion-Jones, 1973a).

Study of the Breton long-house has helped to clarify ideas about the type that appears in a more advanced and sophisticated form in the British Isles. It is now possible to define it as a rectangular or sub-rectangular aisleless dwelling in which man and beast are housed under one roof, at opposite ends, with entry by a common lateral door (Meirion-Jones, 1973b). The type is particularly well illustrated by surviving examples in Morbihan. At Meriadec-en-Plumergat (Fig. 10.7) a long-house is built next to a single-cell dwelling, both being heated by hearths placed against their gable-walls. This example, is now used as a single-cell dwelling but was formerly divided into two cells by a wooden partition. The floors of both the byre and the living room are of *terre battue*. The walls are of stone rubble, roughly coursed and laid with a mortar of *torchis*. Door and windows are dressed with a stone of better quality. Above the lower rooms is a hay loft and the roof is of thatch laid directly on to common rafters. The whole dwelling was admirably suited to a mixed farming economy in which families were too poor to own more than a few animals and where landholdings were small and highly fragmented. There is good reason to believe that the type was once the standard form of dwelling over the whole of Brittany. It occurs in isolation and sometimes in association with a single-cell dwelling, but also in terraces, sometimes of up to a dozen houses. An example with three houses, two of which are long-houses is that at Kervaly in Morbihan (Fig.

10.6). The construction is similar to that of all houses in southern Morbihan, with extensive use of rye thatch over a roof structure that makes use of chestnut poles and is supported on upper-cruck trusses. At Kervaly, the internal communication between each of the three dwellings suggests that the houses were formerly occupied by kin-groups, with perhaps the elderly first generation living in the single cell dwelling, a later addition, at the end. The door and window dressings are finely worked and the walls are of the stone rubble common in the district. Again the plan is of the simplest, living room and byre in both the long-houses, being of roughly equal length. The right-hand long-house may once have had a partition but, as Cambry (1799) observed, there was formerly no internal division in Finistère long-houses and the living room was separated from the byre by a few pieces of furniture. That such arrangements survived in Morbihan until after the Second World War is shown by the plan of a house at Tatforest, Plumelin (E.A.R., Morbihan). The fact that most of the partitions now surviving in Breton long-houses appear to be of nineteenth-century date and are also nailed to convenient beams, suggests that they are later additions made to segregate animals and human beings more effectively. These houses are probably all of seventeenth century date, but only that at Meriadec-en-Plumergat bears a date-stone. The phallic symbol above the date of 1689 more than amply illustrates the late survival of archaic practices, beliefs and superstitions and helps the researcher understand how a relatively early house-type could have survived so long in a form that is much less developed than that in the British Isles, where even in the medieval period long-houses had often acquired a second room.

The long-house has been observed in all five Breton *départements* and can still be found right up to the eastern borders. Casual observation suggests that it also occurs in Normandy and Anjou although doubtlessly in much fewer numbers. Vernacular buildings of northern France from Normandy to the Pas-de-Calais bear strong likenesses to long-house derivatives known in Britain and, if this be so, the long-house tradition may once have been known right up to the Flemish border. A house at Fontaine-les-Hermans (E.A.R., Pas-de-Calais) consists of three *chambres*, the third of which has internal access to the *écurie*. Although not a long-house in its 'pure' form as defined above, it is clearly a derivative.

The *maison cauchoise* illustrated by Vigarié (1969, 1971) (Figs. 10.18 and 10.19) has every indication of being a long-house derivative as do many of the timber-frame houses of Normandy. It would be interesting to see detailed ground plans. Further south, at Cheylade (E.A.R., Cantal) there is a long-house very similar to the Breton type with living room and byre separated by a wooden partition with a communicating door. The house differs from the 'pure' Breton version only by the fact that there is a separate door for access to the byre. This then is a first-order derivative of the long-house. A much larger house at Murat is also a long-house. Again the living room (*salle commune*) is supplemented by a small *salon* (probably formed out of it by sub-division as probably happened also in the previous case), whilst a *chambre des bouviers* has been partitioned off from the byre. The essential internal access from house to byre remains, although once again the form is that of the first derivative rather than the 'pure' long-house. The cattle are provided with two doorways in this very long byre (E.A.R., Cantal).

There seems then to be clear evidence for the long-house tradition in Normandy, more than a suspicion in Mayenne and Anjou, and clear evidence again in the Cantal. The more complex multi-cell houses of the *département* of the Ardennes provide further evidence. In the south-west, the Dordogne contains examples of house and byre under the same roof, but in four examples recorded by the E.A.R., the house is separated from the byre by a *grange*, internal access being maintained in three cases, rather in the manner of the Yorkshire laithe-house. At Nasbinals (E.A.R. Lozère) there is a long-house with *cuisine* and *étable* separated only by a wooden partition, the common doorway leading into the byre. This house is very similar to the pure Breton long-house, but the byre is more elaborately fitted. Further south-west a pure long-house has been recorded in the Pyrénées ariégeoises (Chatelard, 1930). It thus appears that the long-house or its derived forms are strongly represented in Brittany, are in evidence across northern France as far as the Belgian border, occur in the Massif Central in the Cantal and as far south as Lozère and, whilst the Dordogne examples are best left with a question mark at the moment, the type certainly occurs in the Pyrenees. One interesting

FIG. 10.18. Ferme de la Pommerie, Bouville, Seine-Maritime.

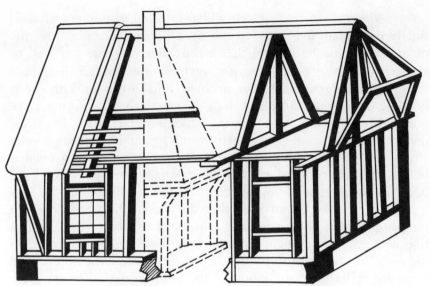

Fɪɢ. 10.19. The timber-frame of *la maison cauchoise* (after Vigarié).

aspect of this distribution is that it accords fairly well with that of
known crucks and cruck-like forms.

Some long-house derivatives If the definition of the long-house
advanced above can be accepted then it follows that the term 'long-
house' must be confined to the 'pure' type in which access for man
and beast is by a common doorway. Where the house is of this
form but evidence of occupation by animals at the lower end is
lacking the term 'long-house form' is to be preferred (Meirion-
Jones, 1973b). By defining the long-house in this way, allowance
is made for the possibility that the house may comprise several
rooms and that the byre-end may likewise be subdivided. The fact
that most Breton long-houses are of the simplest kind must not be
allowed to obscure the fact that more elaborate variations exist,
or existed formerly, in other parts of France. The 'pure' type will
eventually have to be divided into sub-classes but before this can
be done much more field-work is needed, particularly in northern
France.

A long-house built with or altered to provide separate entry to
both dwelling and byre but retaining internal communication may
be regarded as the first derivative. (Once again sub-classes will be
needed eventually to distinguish between plan variations.) The

second derivative is reached when internal communication is finally discarded and entry to the byre is possible only from the outside. It could be argued that a third derivative is required to account for further development when the house and farm buildings have become detached. Other problems make this difficult for it may be that some apparent long-house derivative forms have resulted from gathering separate elements of farm-yard functions under a common roof rather than from a gradual evolution from a single cell occupied by man and beast. Further research is needed before any firm conclusions may be drawn. Meanwhile, great care needs to be taken in attempting classification.

Finally, it must be stressed that the use of the word 'long' in long-house need not necessarily imply any great length. The fact that a range of buildings may appear to be 'long' in the common meaning of the word must not be allowed to mislead the casual observer. Careful examination of the plan is needed to establish the relationship between house and byre before the term 'long-house' may be applied. Likewise the type must not be confused with the great Germanic aisled-house for which the same word has been used in the past. Some French workers have used the term *maison-en-longueur* to describe a variety of forms in which one or more houses and their dependent farm buildings are strung out in a continuous line, either under one continuous roof or under a roof broken at intervals. This expression is used loosely and imprecisely in French writings and must not be assumed to mean more than a row of buildings.

The first-floor house A type of dwelling exists throughout the western margins of Europe in which the principal or common living room (sometimes the only room) is at first-floor level, being built over a cell used as a store, wine cellar or byre. The origin and diffusion of the first-floor dwelling is unknown but it appears in England after the conquest as the Norman first-floor hall (Barley, 1961), survives in the north of England as the bastle, a type of fortified dwelling (Ramm *et al*, 1970), has been reported from Ireland (McCourt, 1970), and is known in both Scotland and Wales. The first-floor dwelling is sometimes entirely detached and sometimes conjoined to another house or to farm buildings. In parts of France it exists both in its single detached form and in the elaborate multi-cellular forms of the Mediterranean areas.

FIG. 10.20. A first-floor house, Keradour, Plougasnou, Finistère.

Various examples have been surveyed in Brittany, some of which stand detached whilst others abut farm buildings or another house. This type is also built adjacent to *petit-manoirs* and was intended to serve as a dwelling for someone of superior social status. At Keradour near Plougasnou (Finistère) such a dwelling stands

between a cart-shed and a long-house. There is no internal communication between the three units at ground floor level. The
buildings are typical of the region being built of granite rubble,
with a finely cut door and window dressings and roofed in slate
(Fig. 10.20). The ground floor room is used for general storage.
The common living room lies at first-floor level and is approached
by an external flight of stone stairs. Dwellings such as these are
not uncommon in Brittany but there is rarely more than one in any
village or hamlet and this suggests that they were formerly the
houses of persons of superior social status. Similar examples occur
in Normandy where they are widely distributed. At Fresnay-le-
Puceux (Calvados) a house almost identical to that at Keradour
stands over a byre with a pigsty built in under the external stairs.
In the Mediterranean region the *maison-à-étage* has a long ancestry
(Demangeon, 1947; Sorre, 1947–52) and the type has probably
been dispersed along the western coastlands from the Mediterranean, being adopted by the upper peasant classes to judge by the
fine examples that survive (Erixon, 1938).

The first-floor dwelling is also adopted at a much higher social
level and is found in the castles and homes of the wealthy during
the Middle Ages as the first-floor hall. Even in those medieval
houses where the common hall is at ground-floor level, it is usual
for the solar (a form of medieval bed-sitter for the senior members
of the household) to be located at first-floor level, This feature
can be found in medieval buildings all over France but a particularly
interesting example occurs near Plurien (Côtes-du-Nord) (Fig.
10.17). The common hall lies to the right of the main doorway.
Immediately to the left are the service rooms above which the solar
lies being approached from the hall by a flight of stone stairs.
Access to the uppermost of these was formerly by an outside stone
stair, now demolished. What makes it likely that the uppermost
of these two single-cell dwellings was for a person of superior
social status is that it shares a common garderobe with the adjacent solar, to which there is no direct communication. It seems
probable that the first-floor dwelling was occupied by a bailiff or
estate manager or even by a senior member of the owner's family.
It is possible that diffusion occurred simultaneously at two different levels, that of the better-off peasant class and that of the
upper end of the social scale.

The aisled house The structural form of the aisled building originated in prehistoric times and can be traced continuously through to the modern period. The type is now widespread in western Europe where it survives most commonly in the form of barns and churches. The aisled house is found in Germany and parts of France and has long been recognized as one of the earliest types of domestic building in England, where it became obsolete before the end of the Middle Ages (Smith, 1955). In France the form is most obvious in great aisled market halls which are found all over the country. The aisled house appears to have survived chiefly in the south-west but there is evidence for its existence in the east and south-east. It achieves its finest development in Les Landes and the Basses-Pyrénées.

(a) *Les Landes* The typical house of Les Landes takes the form of a nave and aisles, sometimes with the addition of an outshot. Construction is sometimes entirely of timber, more often of timber and stone. Three sub-types may be recognized on the basis of construction.

(i) The house in which the outside as well as the nave 'arcades' are built entirely of coursed rubble, the 'arcades' being pierced only by doorways leading to the rooms in the aisles. The nave is of two storeys, a tie-beam resting on wall-plates and supporting a short king-post. A ridge purlin and lateral purlins support a tiled roof which sweeps down over both nave and aisles. Miquellanne in Heugas is a good example in which entry is by doorways placed in the gable walls: a single doorway at the rear and a wide cart entrance at the front (E.A.R. Les Landes). The nave is used for the storage of carts, implements and barrels. The byre occupies the whole of one aisle, the sole entrance being in the front gable. There is no interior access to the byre. The second aisle is divided longitudinally into three rooms, a kitchen, and two *chambres*. Only the former is provided with a hearth and entry is from the nave into the kitchen from which there is access to the other rooms. The living accommodation is entirely at ground-floor level, with the first floor of the nave being used as a granary and hay-loft.

(ii) A house with complete timber frame is found at Métairie Cabanne in Soustous. The roof structure is almost identical to that at Miquellanne but the wall-plates are supported by wooden posts, aisles as well as the nave are divided into two storeys and the roof has a hipped gable at the rear. This timber-frame structure is filled with a roughly coursed stone nogging and differs considerably from the former in functional terms. The rear half is completely sealed off from the front, is not subdivided internally, the arcade posts resting on short stone pillars, and is in use as a byre. The ground floor of the front half is subdivided into seven rooms; the nave and three each in the aisles. Apart from the door in the gable end of the nave, there are also lateral doorways on both sides. A single chimney stack serves two hearths, one in the nave and a second in one of the rooms. A second house in which the aisle structure is wholly of timber stands at Le Grand Lobat in Angresse. Once again the byre occupies the whole of one end. The nave and aisles are strangely divided with four rooms in the four corners of the aisles, the nave and central parts of the aisles being left to form a Greek cross, known as the Grande Salle. Entrance to the house is by two doorways, one in the nave gable, the other in a lateral wall, and both leading into the cross-shaped hall, the only room to be heated. The chimney stack rises through the nave roof.

(iii) The third constructional variation is a hybrid form of (i) and (ii) at Heugas. The nave walls are of stone as far as the floor of the hayloft. From this point they are continued in timber-frame, the spaces being filled with wattle-and-daub. The aisle walls are also of stone and the roof is hipped at the rear. There are again functional differences, particularly as this form has a separate byre. Access is by doorways in the gable walls, that at the front being wide enough for carts. The nave is again divided into three rooms. These buildings whether they be of timber or of stone, or both, have characteristically an elaborate timber-frame front with a recessed entrance porch as shown in Figs. 10.1 and 10.2.

(b) *The Dordogne* is a region of cultural mixing with the aisled house existing alongside long-house derivatives as well as more complex southern forms. Two good aisled houses are Le Denois and L'Hirondelle at Moncaret. In both cases the aisled construction is of timber, the roof is of low pitch with a ridge purlin supported on a short king-post, and the aisles alone are divided into two storeys. Naves are used for storage and one aisle serves as a byre whilst the second is sub-divided into rooms. Apart from the principal gable entrance in the nave, there are numerous doorways giving external access to individual rooms.

(c) *Basses-Pyrénées* The Basque house is still of the classic aisled form but is more complex in its functional sub-division than the aisled houses of the Landes and the Dordogne. Stone-walled and timber-frame walled varieties are found. Whilst examples with two-storeyed nave and aisles exist, as for example at Osses (the *maison lavarraise*) (E.A.R. Basses-Pyrénées), other examples with a full two storeys at Cambo-les-Bains and even three storeys at Sare are well-known as the *maison labourdine*. Plan variations are considerable. At Osses, the aisles and the rear of the nave are divided into seven rooms, two of which serve as stable and byre, one is a cellar. On either side of the front gable entrance are two pairs of rooms consisting of kitchen and *chambre*. The greater part of the nave again serves as a store. There is a strong suggestion of two-family occupation. At Sare the aisles and rear of the nave are given over entirely to the housing of animals and living accommodation is confined to the first floor where again the aisles contain two sets of kitchen and *chambres*. The top storey is for storage. At Cambo-les-Bains, the living quarters are on the ground floor and only one kitchen exists. The byre again occupies the rear of the nave and aisles and the first-floor is used for storage.

(d) *East and South-East France* Numerous structures exist from the Ardennes to the Var which carry strong hints of the aisled-house tradition. This is true at Oppède (E.A.R. Vaucluse) where stone walls rise to give a nave and single aisle effect although there is no semblance of an aisle roof-truss. At Trans-en-Provence a nave supporting a king-post truss is supported by a single and somewhat off-set aisle (E.A.R. Var). The Alpine houses are often complex in plan but, like the Vaucluse and most of the Var houses, lack any roof-truss and consist generally of a well recognizable nave and one or occasionally two aisles, as at Val d'Isère-en-Tarentaise (E.A.R. Savoie). As far north as the Ardennes there are structures which, whilst they cannot be classed as aisled houses in their present form, undoubtedly contain a memory of the aisled house in their timber-work. Thus there is abundant evidence for the survival of the aisled house in south-western France and for its presence along the eastern zone from the Ardennes to Provence.

Other rectilinear forms Study of the French peasant house is still at too early a stage for more than a small number of types to be recognized. Little is known, for example, of the house-types of the Massif Central, the complex rectilinear house-plans of the Mediterranean zone, and the eastern Marchlands of France where Germanic influences are strong. However, several types deserve to be mentioned briefly.

(a) *The medieval 'hall' house* The date at which the hall or common living room, open to the roof and with a centrally placed open hearth, went out of fashion in France is not known. No examples appear to survive, since the chimney came into use much earlier than in England and it seems probably that the open hall had passed out of use by the beginning of the fifteenth century, at least in the homes of the better off. There are signs that in more remote areas the open hearth survived in the homes of poorer groups until recently, as is shown by the house at Tatforest, Plumelin (E.A.R., Morbihan) that was recorded just after World War II. Even after the central hearth had been abandoned, chimneys built and the open halls ceiled over to give an upper storey, the medieval plan remained for some time until the symmetry of the Renaissance began to influence the lesser nobility and the smaller *seigneurs*. The classic medieval plan is illustrated by the *manoir* significantly called La Salle at Plurien (Côtes-du-Nord) (Fig. 10.20). Entry to the hall is by a pair of opposed doorways at the lower end. A single window lights the common living space and heat is provided by a gable hearth located at the upper end. The hall is large, impressive and designed to serve a sizeable household. This plan-type has been observed elsewhere in Brittany, and may well have had a wider distribution in France.

(b) *The symmetrical Renaissance plan house* From the middle of the fifteenth century Renaissance influence spread gradually across France and the new houses of the upper classes began to display that characteristic symmetry of plan. Whilst the pattern of life within the house might go unchanged, it became usual for a house to have two rooms on the ground floor with entry by a central doorway. One such room would still be more important than the other, slightly bigger in size, with a more elaborate chimney-piece and finer window dressings. This would remain functionally the hall. The second room, beyond the cross-passage which long remained a persistent relic of the medieval period, might serve as a kitchen and would almost certainly contain beds. At a lower social

FIG. 10.21. An orthostat-walled house at Tregunc, Finistère.

level the type is illustrated by the orthostat walled house at
Trégunc in south Finistère (Fig. 10.21). The symmetry of plan
gradually spread down the social scale until by the eighteenth and
nineteenth centuries there were many examples of farmhouses and
cottages of two-room plan with a central doorway. In the larger
houses there were often cellars and storage rooms at the rear
approached by a door at the end of the cross passage which led also
in many cases to a circular narrow staircase of wood or stone contained in a tower. Stair-towers are a very persistent feature of the
French countryside.

(c) *Multi-cell houses* One of the characteristics of the peasant
house on the western fringes of the European continent is that it
was traditionally only one room deep and any extension to the rear
took the form of an outshot. Probably this was once the case over
much of the continent, the separate rooms or 'cells' being strung
out in a line. At some unknown date, multi-cellular houses became
known particularly in the Mediterranean lands and along the
eastern borders of France. The *Enquête d'Architecture Rurale* contains many examples, and it must suffice to mention a few. In the
Ardennes, houses exist in which some units (often the stables and
byres) extend the whole width of the house while the building is
sub-divided longitudinally in the living part. In other examples,
the living quarters lie at the front of the house, accommodation
for animals being at the rear. In these houses, rooms have specialized functions (kitchen, dining room, bedroom) unlike western
France where the *salle commune* serves all purposes. In the Rhinelands and further south a similar complex assemblage of cells is
found providing accommodation for animals and human beings as
well as storage for hay, grain, wine and implements.

Conclusions

The rural domestic buildings of France survive in large numbers
from many periods and display great richness and variety of
materials, construction and plan. An evolutionary sequence cannot
yet be established and it may be many years before even the most
tentative suggestions can be advanced. Nevertheless, a number of
important categories of rural domestic building have already been
recognized. Circular houses, corbelled or otherwise, are known, as

are oval and sub-rectangular forms. The long-house is proven in north-western France and can be shown to exist in its pure form in the Ardennes, the South-West and Cantal. Derived forms in other areas indicate that the long-house was probably once the common form of farmhouse across the whole of northern and western France and possibly in parts of the Massif Central, if not the whole of that region as well. Other rectilinear forms are known in great numbers: the single-cell house, the *maison-en-étage* or first floor house, the medieval 'hall' house with hall, service rooms and parlour or solar, the aisled houses with many variations and internal room plan, the symmetrical Renaissance plan house, and the multi-cell houses of the South and South-East. The relationship of these types, if any, and their place in the evolutionary sequence may only be clarified through further work in many parts of France, on both a regional and a systematic basis. Such enquiries should include careful measured drawings and accurate descriptions if they are to be of value and also be accompanied by parallel archive work, particularly into the *Archives des Notaires* with their great store of inventories, marriage contracts and farm leases.

Problems relating to construction are numerous and the serious study of carpentry has scarcely begun save for the work of Deneux, Horn and Berger. Completed work shows that the king-post and upper king-post trusses are widespread. The aisled hall truss, which is found all over the North and West of France in market halls, is known in domestic buildings in the East and South-West. Whether the aisled house was formerly distributed more widely is not yet known. The earlier distribution and consequent diffusion of the cruck truss and rafter roofs are also problematical. Fieldwork on both an intensive and extensive scale is required before the answers to these problems may be found. Such work is vital if light is to be cast not only on the problems of French vernacular architecture but on the classification and development of plan and constructional forms in Western Europe as a whole.

10. Notes

1. Reproduction of the drawings made by the Enquête d'Architecture Rurale is currently forbidden, pending the publication of regional surveys by the Musée des Arts et Traditions Populaires.

2. The late Professor Cordingley's paper provides a classification of roof-types in which terminology is abundantly illustrated.
3. Interesting examples in Rouen and Annecy are given by Quenedey (1911, 1929).
4. Further examples relate to Pontivy, Morbihan (Lisch, 1973), the Abbey of Epau (Prunet, 1973), Limoges (Lebouteux, 1973), and the Vendée (Perrandeau, 1973).
5. See also the description of the Danish *stridsuler* by Innocent (1916).
6. Field work by I. P. Horsey, April 1974. Mr. Horsey is of the opinion that it may well be a very common type in the lower Loire valley.
7. I am grateful to David Hinton for allowing me to produce a line drawing from his photographs.
8. DSM Information Centre (1974), *In Praise of Simplicity*, Heerlen.

10. References

Aalen, F. H. A., 'Vernacular architecture of the British Isles', *Yearbook, Association of Pacific Coast Geographers*, 35 (1973), 27–48.

Addy, S. O., *The Evolution of the English House*, London (1898).

Alcock, N. W., 'Two problems of definition', *Vernacular Architecture*, 3 (1972), 21.

Alcock, N. W., *A Catalogue of Cruck Buildings*, London and Chichester (1973).

Alcock, N. W. and Barley, M. W., 'Medieval roofs with base-crucks and short principals', *Antiquaries Journal*, 52 (1972), 132–68.

Allen, E., *Stone Shelters*, Cambridge Massachusetts and London (1969).

Barbier, P., 'Les vestiges monastiques des îles de l'embouchure du Trieux: l'Ile Saint-Maudez et l'Ile Verte', *Memoires, Société d'Emulation des Côtes-du-Nord*, 80 (1951), 5–40.

Barbier, P., *Le Trégor historique et monumental*, Saint-Brieuc (1960).

Barley, M. W., *The English Farmhouse and Cottage*, London (1961).

Berger, R., 'The potential and limitations of radiocarbon dating in the Middle Ages: the radio chronologist's view', in R. Berger (ed.), *Scientific Methods in Medieval Archaeology*, Berkeley, Los Angeles and London (1970), 89–139.

Bertrand, R., 'Un habitat rustique du XIIe siècle à Pen-er-Malo en Guidel', *Travaux, Société Lorientaise d'Archéologie* (1971).

Bertrand, R., 'Le site médiéval de Pen-er-Malo en Guidel. Bâtiment A: étude du matériel', *Travaux, Société Lorientaise d'Archéologie* (1972–3), 15–17.

Branigan, K., 'The origins of cruck construction—a new clue', *Medieval Archaeology*, 12 (1968), 1–11.

Brunhes, J., *Géographie Humaine de la France*, Paris (1920). (Especially, Types régionaux de maisons et carte générale des toits, vol. 1, 411–44.)

Brunskill, R. B., *Traditional domestic architecture in the Eden valley*, Unpublished M.A. Thesis, University of Manchester (1952).

Brunskill, R. B., *Traditional domestic architecture of the Solway Plain*, Unpublished Ph.D. Thesis, University of Manchester (1963).

Cambry, J. de, *Voyage dans le Finistère: ou état de ce département en 1794 et 1795*, Brest (1799).

Campbell, A., 'Notes on the Irish house'—I, *Folk-Liv*, 1 (1937), 207–34.

Campbell, A., 'Notes on the Irish house'—II, *Folk-Liv*, 2 (1938), 173–96.

Chatelard, M., 'L'habitation dans les Pyrénées ariégeoises', *Revue Géographique des Pyrénées et du Sud-Ouest*, 1 (1930), 306–30.

Chemitte, M., 'Les cabanes en pierres sèches', *Mémoires de l'Académie du Vaucluse* 2e série, 12 (1912), 75.

Childe, V. G., 'Cave men's buildings', *Antiquity*, 24 (1950a), 4–11.

Childe, V. G., *Prehistoric Migrations in Europe*, Oslo (1950b).

Coque, R., 'L'évolution de la maison rurale en Amiénois', *Annales de Géographie*, 65 (1956), 401–17.

Cordingley, R. A., 'British historical roof-types and their members: a classification', *Transactions, Ancient Monuments Society, New Series*, 9 (1961), 73–118.

Couffon, R., Répertoire des églises et chapelles du diocèse de Saint-Brieuc et Treguier, *Mémoires, Société d'Emulation des Côtes-du-Nord*, 70 (1938), 19–27. (This work is continued in the volumes for 1939 and 1947).

Couffon, R., 'Essai sur l'architecture religieuse en Bretagne du Ve au Xe siècle', *Mémoires de la Société d'Histoire et d'Archéologie de Bretagne*, 23 (1943), 1–40.

Crawford, O. G. S., *Archaeology in the Field*, London (1953).

Delamarre, M. J.-B., 'Contributions de l'habitat rudimentaire—les cabanes en pierre sèche des environs de Gordes, Vaucluse', *Comptes Rendus du Congrès International de Géographie de Paris, 1931*, III, Paris (1934), 293–98.

Delaruelle, F., 'La maison élémentaire de la région toulousaine', *Revue Géographique des Pyrénées et du Sud-Ouest*, 4 (1933), 373–83.

Delumeau, J. (ed.), *Documents de l'Histoire de la Bretagne*, Toulouse (1971).

Deneux, H., 'L'évolution des charpentes du XIe au XVIIIe siècle', *L'Architecte* (1927), 19–89.

Demangeon, A., 'L'habitation rurale en France: essai de classification des principaux types', *Annales de Géographie*, 29 (1920), 352–75.

Demangeon, A., 'De l'influence des régimes agraires sur les modes d'habitat dans l'Europe occidentale', *Comptes Rendus du Congrès International de Géographie*, Cairo (1926), IV, 92–97.

Demangeon, A., 'La géographie de l'habitat rural', *Annales de Géographie*, 36 (1927), 1–23, 97–114.

Demangeon, A., *Enquête sur l'habitation rurale en France*, Tours (1936).

Demangeon, A., *Les Maisons des hommes: de la hutte au gratte-ciel*, Paris (1937a).

402 GWYN I. MEIRION-JONES

Demangeon, A., *La Définition et le classement des maisons rurales*, Paris (1937b).

Demangeon, A., 'Maisons rurales de France et musées de plein air', *Folklore Paysan*, 2 (1939), 33–35.

Demangeon, A., 'Essai d'une classification des maisons rurales', in *Problèmes de Géographie Humaine*, Paris (1942), 230–35.

Demangeon, A., *Problèmes de Geographie Humaine*, Pai is (1947), 281–84.

D.S.M. Information Centre. *In Praise of Simplicity*, Heerlen (1974).

Erixon, S., 'Some primitive constructions and types of lay-out, with their relation to European rural building practice', *Folk-Liv*, 1 (1937), 124–55.

Erixon, S., 'West European connections and cultural relations', *Folk-liv*, 2 (1938), 165.

Evans, E. E., 'The Irish peasant house', *Ulster Journal of Archaeology*, 3rd Series, 3 (1940), 165–69.

Evans, E. E., *Irish Heritage*, Dundalk (1942).

Evans, E. E., *Mourne Country*, Dundalk (1951).

Evans, E. E., *Irish Folk Ways*, London (1957).

Flatrès-Mury, H., 'Deux aspects de l'habitat rural: 'cours' et 'plants' sur les confins normands, bretons et manceaux', *Norois*, 17 (1970a), 21–37.

Flatrès-Mury, H., 'Matériaux et techniques de construction rurale dans l'Ouest de la France: l'exemple des confins normands, bretons et manceaux', *Norois*, 17 (1970b), 547–66.

Formigé, J., 'Notes sur les cabanes en pierres sèches de Vaucluse', *Bulletin Monumental*, 78 (1914), 47–57.

Fox, C. F. and Raglan, Lord, *Monmouthshire House*, vols.1–3, Cardiff (1951, 3, 4).

Francey, M. and Dimier, A., 'La grange de Montaon, dépendence d l'abbaye d'Igny', *Bulletin Monumental*, 131 (1973), 367–69.

Fréal, J. and Janneau, G., *Meubles bretons*, Paris (1973).

Fréal, J. and Lescroat, Y., *Maisons de Normandie*, Paris (1973).

Fréal, J. and Quéruel, F., *Maisons de Bretagne*, Paris (1973).

Gauthier, J.-S., *Les Maisons paysannes des vieilles provinces de France*, Paris (n.d.).

Gauthier, J.-S., *Meubles et ensembles bretons*, Paris (1959).

Godfrin, J. and de Planhol, X., 'Découverte d'un type primitif de toit de "tuiles romaines" en Lorraine', *Revue Géographique de l'Est*, 6 (1966), 287–89.

Grand, R., *L'Art roman en Bretagne*, Paris (1958).

Groupe Habitat Populaire, Unité Pédagogique d'Architecture Nantes (1974), *Architecture rurale du Pays Blanc: plaquette de conseils*, Unpublished ms.

Hekker, R. C., 'Fachwerkbau in Südlimburg', *Arbeitskreis für deutsche Hausforschung: Bericht über die Tagung in Aachen, 1961* (1961), 49–74.

Henry, F., 'Early Irish monasteries, boat-shaped oratories and beehive huts', *County Louth Archaeological Journal*, 11 (1949), 296–304.

Henry, F., 'Early monasteries, beehive huts, and dry-stone houses in the neighbourhood of Caherciveen and Waterville: Co. Kerry', *Proceedings Royal Irish Academy*, 58 (1957), Section C, 45–166.

Hewett, C. A., 'The dating of timber roofs by Henri Deneux: an English summary', *Transactions Ancient Monuments Society*, 16 (1969), 89–108.

Hinton, D., 'A cruck house at Lower Radley, Berks., *Oxoniensia*, 32 (1967), 13–33.

Horn, W., 'The potential and limitations of radiocarbon dating in the Middle Ages: an art historian's view', in R. Berger (ed), *Scientific Methods in Medieval Archaeology*, Berkeley, Los Angeles and London (1970), 23–87.

Hoskins, W. G., 'The re-building of rural England, 1570–1640', *Past and Present*, 4 (1953), 44–89.

Hurst, J. G., 'A review of the archaeological research (to 1968)', in M. Beresford and J. G. Hurst (eds.), *Deserted Medieval Villages*, London (1971), 76–144.

Innocent, C. F., *The Development of English Building Construction*, London (1916).

Joubert, G., 'Promenade au départ de Fontevraud', *Les Monuments Historiques de la France*, part 3 (1973), 17–22.

La Borderie, A. Le M. de, and Pocquet, B., *Histoire de Bretagne*, 6 vols., Rennes (1896–1914).

Lebouteux, P., 'La consolidation de l'église Saint-Michel-des-Lions à Limoges', *Les Monuments Historiques de la France*, no. 3 (1973), 23–9.

Lisch, R., 'Le château de Pontivy', *Les Monuments Historiques de la France*, no. 1 (1973), 28–34.

Lucas, M., 'Le site médiéval de Pen-er-Male en Guidel. Les batiments B et C, Travaux', *Société Lorientaise d'Archéologie* (1972–3), 18–20.

Maget, M., 'Ergebnisse neuer Bauernhausuntersuchungen in Frankreich, insbeondere in der Hochalpen', *Arbeitkreis für deutsche Hausforschung*, Monschau (1953), 31–36.

Marsden, T. L., *Minor domestic architecture in the county of Rutland and vicinity*, Unpublished Ph.D. Thesis, University of Manchester (1958).

McCourt, D., 'Cruck trusses in north-west Ireland', *Gwerin*, 3 (1960–2), 165–85.

McCourt, D., 'The cruck-truss in Ireland and its west European connections', *Folk-Liv*, 28–9 (1964–5), 64–78.

McCourt, D., 'The house with bedroom over byre: a long-house derivative?', *Ulster Folklife*, 15–16 (1970), 3–19.

Meirion-Jones, G. I., 'The long-house in Brittany: a provisional assessment', *Post-Medieval Archaeology*, 7 (1973a), 1–19.

Meirion-Jones, G. I., 'The long-house: a definition', *Medieval Archaeology*, 17 (1973b), 135–37.

Meirion-Jones, G. I., 'Some early and primitive building forms in Brittany', *Folk Life*, 14 (1976).

Ministère des Affaires Culturelles, *Finistère, Carhaix-Plouguer*, 2 vols., Paris (1969).

Ministère des Affaires Culturelles, *Répertoire des Inventaires, Limousin*, 2 vols., Paris (1970).

Ministère des Affaires Culturelles, *Haut-Rhin, Guebwiller*, 2 vols., Paris (1971a).

Ministère des Affaires Culturelles, *Répertoire des Inventaires, Région Nord*, 2 vols., Paris (1971b).

Ministère des Affaires Culturelles, *Vocabulaire de l'Architecture*, 2 vols., Paris (1972a).

Ministère des Affaires Culturelles, *Répertoire des Inventaires, Languedoc-Roussillon*, 2 vols., Paris (1972b).

Ministère des Affaires Culturelles, *Landes, Peyrehorade*, 2 vols., Paris (1973a).

Ministère des Affaires Culturelles, *Gard, Aigues-Mortes*, 2 vols., Paris (1973b).

Ministère des Affaires Culturelles, *Répertoires des Inventaires, Lorraine*, 2 vols., Paris (1973c).

Ministère des Affaires Culturelles: Centre de Recherches sur les Monuments Historiques, *Maisons à Pans de Bois*, 8 vols., Paris (n.d.).

Ministère des Affaires Culturelles: Centre de Recherches sur les Monuments Historiques, *Beffrois de Charpentes*, Paris (n.d.).

Ministère des Affaires Culturelles: Centre de Recherches sur les Monuments Historiques, *Charpentes*, 6 vols., Paris (1972).

Ministère de la Reconstruction et de l'Urbanisme, *Résultats Statistiques d'une enquête sur la propriété bâtie dans les communes rurales*, Paris (1947).

Ministère de la Santé Publique et de la Population, *Enquête sur l'habitation rurale en France*, 2 vols., Paris (1939).

Moniot, F., 'Les maisons landaises', *Maisons Paysannes de France*, 2 (1970), 13–18.

Ó Ríordáin, S. P., *Antiquities of the Irish Countryside*, London (1965).

Peate, I. C., *The Welsh House*, 3rd edition, Liverpool (1946).

Peate, I. C., 'The cruck truss', *Man*, 56 (1956), 146–47.

Peate, I. C., 'The cruck truss', *Man*, 57 (1957), 48.

Peate, I. C., 'The cruck truss: a reassessment', *Folk-Liv*, 21–2 (1957–8), 107–13.

Peate, I. C., 'The Welsh long-house: a brief re-appraisal', in I. L. Foster and L. Alcock (eds.), *Culture and Environment*, London, (1963), 439–44.

Peate, I. C., 'The long-house again', *Folk Life*, 2 (1964), 76–79.

Perrandeau, G., 'Bourrines du marais nord-vendéen,' *Cahiers de Maisons Paysannes*, no. 5 (1973).

Pesez, J-M., 'Le village médiéval', *Archéologie Médiévale*, 1 (1971), 307–21.

Planhol, X. de, 'Les limites septentrionales de l'habitat rural de type lorrain', in Jäger, H. *et al.* (eds.), Beiträge zur Genese der Siedlungs- und Agrar-landschaft in Europa, *Geographische Zeitschrift-Beihefte*, Heft 18 (1968a).

Planhol, X. de, *L'Habitat et l'habitation rurale de type lorrain* (1968b), Nancy, 26pp.

Planhol, X. de, 'L'ancienne maison rurale lorraine', *Norois*, 63 (1969), 315–36.

Planhol, X. de, 'Aux origines de l'habitat rural lorrain', in Dussart, F. (ed.) *L'Habitat et les paysages ruraux d'Europe*, Liège (1971).

Prunet, P., 'L'Abbaye de l'Epau', *Les Monuments Historiques de la France*, 1 (1973), 6–27.

Quenedey, R., 'Les combles des maisons du XVIe siècle à Rouen', *Bulletin Monumental*, 75 (1911), 247–64.

Quenedey, R., 'Les combles annéciens', *Revue Savoisienne* (1929), 1–8.

Raglan, Lord, 'The cruck truss', *Man*, 56 (1956), 101–03.

Ramm, H. G., McDowell, R. W. and Mercer, E., *Royal Commission on Historical Monuments (England): Shielings and Bastles*, London (1970).

Robert, J., 'Un habitat de transition: Vallorcine', *Revue de Géographie Alpine*, 24 (1936), 667–700.

Robert, J., *La Maison rurale permanente dans les Alpes françaises du Nord*, Tours (1939a).

Robert, J., *L'Habitat temporaire dans les montagnes pastorales des Alpes françaises du Nord; étude de géographie humaine*, Grenoble (1939b).

Robert, J., 'Habitat temporaire et nomadisme dans les Alpes françaises du Nord', *Information Géographique*, 6 (1942), 1–8.

Robert, J., 'Un habitat temporaire: l'écurie-grange dans les Alpes françaises du Nord', *Annales de Géographie*, 55 (1946), 102–11.

Robert, J., 'La maison rurale et le bois dans les Alpes de Haute-Savoie', *Revue de Bois*, février (1949a), 9–12.

Robert, J., 'Types de maisons rurales dissociées dans le centre de la Gâtine tourangelle', *Travaux de la Section IV, Congrès International de Géographie*, Lisbon (1949b), 133–40.

Robert, J., 'Les montaguettes dans les Alpes françaises du Nord', *Mélanges Géographiques offerts à E. Benevent* (1954), 167–82.

Robert, J., 'La maison agricole: essai de classification et définitions', *Norois*, 19 (1972), 541–48.

Salmon, M-J., *L'Architecture des fermes du Soissonnais: son évolution du XIIIe au XIXe siècle*, Sazeray, Indre (1971).

Sartiges, Vicomte de, 'Les cabanes en pierres sèches du sud de la France', *Bulletin de la Société Préhistorique Française* (1921), 338 et seq.

Smith, J. T., 'Medieval aisled halls and their derivatives', *Archaeological Journal*, 112 (1955), 76–93.

Smith, J. T., 'Medieval roofs, a classification', *Archaeological Journal*, 115 (1958), 120.

Smith, J. T., 'The long-house in Monmouthshire: a reappraisal', in I. Ll. Foster and L. Alcock (eds.), *Culture and Environment*, London (1963), 389–414.

Smith, J. T., 'Cruck construction: a survey of the problems', *Medieval Archaeology*, 8 (1964), 119–51.

Soeder, M., 'Formen und Gefüge Aälterer Hausarten in oberitalien und in Alpenraum', *Tagunsbericht des Arbeitkreises fur deutsche Hausforschung*, Traunstein/Villach (1956), 41–125.

Sorre, M., *Les Fondements de la géographie humaine*, 3 vols., Paris (1947–52).

Trefois, C. V., 'La technique de la construction rurale en bois', *Folk* (1937), 55–72.

Trefois, C. V., *Ontwikkehlings Geschiedenis van onze Landelijke Architectuur*, Antwerp (1950)

Van Es, W. A., 'Wijster: a native village beyond the Imperial frontier, 150–425 A.D.', *Palaeohistoria*, 11 (1967), 386

Vigarié, A., 'Recherche d'une explication de la maison cauchoise', *Norois*, 16 (1969), 177–87.

Vigarié, A., 'Les énigmes de la maison cauchoise', *Annales de Normandie*, 21 (1971), 137–51.

Walton, J., 'The development of the cruck framework', *Antiquity*, 22 (1948), 179–89.

Walton, J., 'The oval house', *Antiquity*, 26 (1952), 135–40.

Walton, J., 'Hogback tombstones and the Anglo-Danish house', *Antiquity*, 28 (1954), 68–77.

Walton, J., 'The cruck truss', *Man*, 57 (1957), 15–16.

Walton, J., 'Cruck trusses in the Dordogne', *Gwerin*, 3 (1960–2), 3–6.

Walton, J., 'Prehistoric corbelled dwellings', *Sonderuck aus dem Berichte über den V. Internationalen Kongress für Vor- und Frühgeschichte, Hamburg, 1958*, Berlin (1961).

Walton, J., 'Megalithic building survivals', in J. G. Jenkins (ed.), *Studies in Folk Life*, London (1969).

Wood-Jones, R. B., *Traditional Domestic Architecture in the Banbury Region*, Manchester (1963).

11
Agricultural Change in The Eighteenth and Nineteenth Centuries

HUGH D. CLOUT

Did France Undergo an 'Agricultural Revolution'?

France, perhaps more than any other West European country, displays a great variety of rural landscapes and farming systems that reflect not only the diversity of her physical geography but also a rich cultural inheritance elaborated over many centuries, indeed, millennia (Goubert, 1970).[1] Even up to 1939 the legacy of the past was strong in respect of many elements of agriculture, including scale of production, limited mechanization, and relative lack of market orientation. Although urban growth and rural depopulation were working vigorously by the second half of the nineteenth century, the French countryside managed to hold the bulk of its population, with the nation's 'rural' dwellers declining only from 23,200,000 in 1831 to 22,100,000 in 1911, whilst those deriving a living from agriculture contracted from 18,700,000 to 15,100,000 over the same period (Hohenberg, 1972).[2] Loss accelerated in both cases after 1860. Many commentators have stressed the eternal order of the fields, with the nineteenth century writer Deslisle (1852) going as far as to claim that agriculture had hardly changed since medieval times, so that a thirteenth century peasant would not feel out of place (Clapham, 1961). Augé-Laribé (1955) insists that such an 'impression of stability and of immobility until recent times is not false. Changes were neither rapid nor very obvious' (p. 2).

Did France therefore share in the major changes in agricultural techniques and customs that marked the appearance of modern agriculture and that is frequently referred to as an agricultural revolution? The question is open to debate. Certainly, fundamental changes in farming were not rapid, extending instead over many years, if not several centuries so that 'nowhere was this gradualness more evident than in France' (Bloch, 1966 p. 197). However the issue must be seen with reference to more sophisticated criteria than speed alone. When due attention is paid to variations in spatial impact through time and the degree of change generated from agricultural innovation it is arguable that a rather more positive view of 'agricultural revolution' may be supported.

The Evidence in Favour

The middle years of the eighteenth century have been selected by many historians as representing the beginnings of such a movement (for example, Augé-Laribé, 1955; Fussell, 1972; Faucher, 1956, 1962; Slicher van Bath, 1969). According to Festy (1947) '. . . one may take 1750 as the date when the "new agriculture" started to demonstrate its existence' (p. 38). It was at this time that a number of processes started to come into convergence and, in turn, began to generate changes in particular areas of French farming (Labrousse, 1970). A new enthusiasm for agriculture developed among

> 'people of more comfortable social status than the peasantry, that is the nobility, rich and poor, and possibly some successful bourgeoisie who were intent on becoming members of that class' (Fussell, 1972, p. 156).

English experiments in agricultural practice were publicised across the Channel in the books and learned journals to which a small proportion of landowners had access. Thus the writings of classical authorities, which had been recognized as the corpus of agricultural advice from medieval times, were gradually superseded by literature from the Low Countries and especially from England. After living in the past the literate minority might begin to sample such works as Jethro Tull's 'Horse Hoeing Husbandry' which appeared in French in 1731 and was publicised by Duhamel du Monceau. Similarly, Didérot's *Encyclopédie* contained a large section on English farming, and Voltaire reported on the activities of Turnip Townshend in Norfolk and of other agronomists (Bourde, 1953, 1958, 1967). Anglomania reigned in this particular stratum of agricultural society and physiocratic principles were proposed. The physiocrats believed that the wealth of any country existed in proportion to the fertility of its territory. They were opposed to the excess and luxury of urban living and the evils of manufacturing; and, instead, defended the virtues of agricultural life. Provincial agricultural societies were set up, first in Rennes (1757) and then in other parts of France, in order to spread the new agricultural gospel of land clearance, new crops, livestock, fertilizers and agricultural implements. A few agricultural schools were established to foster the same objectives but these were hardly realizable so long as communal systems of organization survived.

During the eighteenth century a range of crops, with differing environmental tolerances, came to be cultivated increasingly in a variety of regions (Meuvret, 1971). Buckwheat had been known in Western Europe in medieval times but experienced its first important phase of expansion in the sixteenth century when cereal prices reached unheard of heights. Its cultivation continued to expand during the seventeenth and eighteenth centuries, especially in the less priviliged environments of western and central France, for, as Slicher van Bath (1969) has explained, buckwheat has the advantages of growing on light, sandy soil, does not require direct application of farmyard manure, and has the ability to stifle weeds. But according to Faucher (1962), it was maize and the potato that formed the real 'revolutionary' crops of the eighteenth century.

Maize was being grown in the Basque country, in Bigorre and Gascony in the early seventeenth century, spreading gradually through Guyenne, Quercy, the Terrefort Toulousain and Lauragais then up on to the slopes of the Ségalas on the south-western margins of the Massif Central. The climate of the south-west was most appropriate to this crop, however, and by the second half of the eighteenth century its cultivation had been diffused up the valley of the Rhône on to the plains of the Saône and of Alsace and was also known in the Loire valley and parts of the Paris Basin. Maize was chiefly grown as a fallow crop, which had the effect of gradually modifying the traditional biennial wheat/fallow rotation of the south-west into a wheat/maize rotation. The new crop provided food for man and beast alike and gave yields that were two or three times higher than those from wheat. In addition, it takes less out of the topsoil than the latter, because its roots reach deeper into the ground, however,' maize does require intensive manuring. *Intendants* were instrumental in encouraging land-owners in their *généralités* to experiment with this and with other new crops.[3] Certainly the long-established systems of cultivation were being modified in the south-west during the eighteenth century, so much so that Faucher (1962) was able to claim that one-sixth of French territory that was well-suited to maize pro-duction was already on the way towards achieving its agricultural revolution before the end of the *ancien régime*.

Potatoes were being grown on a garden scale in a range of environments in the second half of the eighteenth century. Like buckwheat, this crop has the advantage of flourishing in damp climatic conditions but to be successful it was necessary for the soil to be dug deeply, dressed with fresh farmyard manure and kept clear of weeds. Potatoes could yield two or three times as much starch per unit area as rye, but had the disadvantage of not keeping well, being difficult to transport, and experiencing great variations in yield from season to season (Slicher van Bath, 1969). The crop was being grown in gardens in Franche-Comté as early as the seventeenth century and gradually spread as a garden crop into other parts of France in the face of opposition from agriculturalists who defended their staple cereals such as rye and, to a smaller extent buckwheat (Dubuc, 1953). Certainly the potato was known and cultivated much more widely in the Low Countries than in France by the middle years of the eighteenth century (Morineau, 1970a). *Intendants*, agricultural societies and monastic estates were important in trying to popularise this crop which was accepted more readily when cereal crops failed and prices rocketed, for example in the 1780s and after 1812–13 (Charra, 1949; Juillard, 1953; Thuillier, 1965, 1974). It had still been unknown in parts of the Massif Central in the 1760s and 1770s but by 1800 the potato had been introduced to virtually all parts of France, admittedly for

differing lengths of time and with varying degrees of intensity. It
was by then firmly established as a field crop in Flanders, Lorraine,
Franche-Comté and Limousin, with less intensive areas of production involving eastern France and parts of the Alps, Massif
Central, Pyrenees and Brittany (Morineau, 1970a) (Fig. 11.1).
This crop was of vital importance in supporting population
growth in the poorer zones of the country.[4] From covering an area
of 560,000 ha in 1817, it increased to 920,000 ha in 1840 and
957,000 ha in 1857 (Block, 1860). For the same dates the annual
yields rose from 47,500,000 hl in 1817 to 102,000,000 hl in both
1840 and 1857. Output was in fact high in each of those years and
the magnitude of variation between years should not be underestimated (Fig. 11.2). The low yields of the late 1840s were
particularly devastating for the rural economies of many areas of
petite culture (Mazières, 1954).

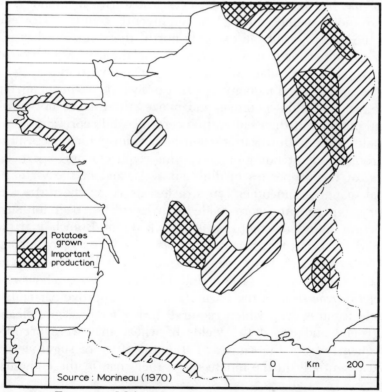

FIG. 11.1. Main potato growing areas *c*.1800.

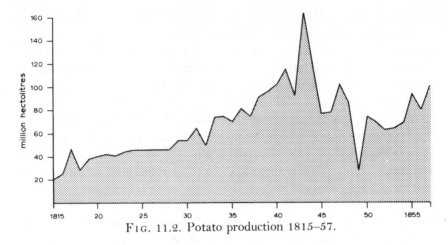

FIG. 11.2. Potato production 1815–57.

Further plant innovations in France included turnips and other crops that had been grown for several centuries in Flanders but spread more widely during the eighteenth century. However, with the exception of the extreme north, these remained largely experimental crops that were produced on the estates of progressive owners. A similar comment would apply to the range of artificial grasses and fodder crops that graced the farms of agronomic experts. Unlike potatoes and maize, these were not 'proletarian' plants, but their cultivation certainly did represent a small start along the path towards scientific farming which necessitated a thorough understanding of the varying requirements of particular plants, of the properties of different soils, and of the virtues of animal manures and other types of fertiliser. At the turn of the century experiments were made with cultivated beet for sugar extraction following the English blockade of French maritime trade which meant that France experienced severe sugar shortages between 1803 and 1810, being cut off from her West Indian sources of cane sugar (Clout and Phillips, 1973). The fertile, stoneless *limon* soils of the Paris Basin were to prove particularly suitable for this crop which required heavy fertilization, cleaned the ground and raised the yields of wheat that were produced subsequently from the same soil. But the story of sugarbeet unfolded essentially in the nineteenth rather than in the eighteenth century.

In the four decades between 1750 and 1789 enlightened estate owners introduced new strains of livestock from England, experimented with enclosure, started to plant up stretches of relatively infertile soils with timber, began to put the principles of agricultural chemistry into practice and made use of new farm implements. In addition, stretches of moorland and marshland were being reclaimed and put into agricultural use.[5] But undoubtedly the real impact of all these changes was very small. For example, Bourde (1953) noted that until 1840–50 the agricultural implements used by the bulk of the French rural population were almost the same as they had been two or three centuries before. A similar comment would apply to each of the other innovations discussed. Indeed most authorities who support the view that France underwent an agricultural revolution after c. 1750 would insist on three essential qualifications relating to time, space and society. Some areas were advanced agriculturally at an early date whilst key changes took a very long time to reach other, essentially isolated, parts of the country. In addition, there were serious social and economic constraints during the *ancien régime,* linked to the feudal system and to the continuing strength of communal agricultural organization, which hindered individualism and innovation in land management (Bloch, 1930).

Slicher van Bath (1969) has identified a complicated history of agricultural development on the Continent in the eighteenth century, with rapid change occurring in some areas, while stagnation or even retrogression affected others. Flanders, Artois and Alsace, along with Catalonia and the Po Valley, were among the leading areas of early agricultural intensification in the seventeenth century from which changes were diffused subsequently. Fallow land gradually disappeared as complicated rotations requiring large inputs of labour and fertiliser were introduced. Fodder crops allowed increased numbers of livestock to be kept and their manure was vital to maintain such demanding systems. The precise character, quality and origins of these intensive practices varied from region to region, however

'. . . in the more densely populated areas of the Continent there was, especially after 1750, a gradual development, a continuation of already existing tendencies' (Slicher van Bath, 1969, p. 179).

Thus, as the record of Arthur Young's Travels in France in 1787–89 and many other sources show, there was tremendous spatial variation in the quality and intensity of agriculture in France at the time of the Revolution. Jacquart's (1974) comments on the lack of unity in the French economic system were just as appropriate to the eighteenth century as to the seventeenth century. The balance of production and consumption varied greatly from one area to another and two contrasting forces operated. Trade links were established between surplus and deficit areas but these natural flows were impeded by regulations, internal customs duties, transport deficiencies and by the fear of famine that affected the population and acted as a brake on commercial exchange, in spite of the chance of profit-making.

Other serious impediments on agricultural specialization and intensification in eighteenth century France included the lack of investments, the surplus of labour on small peasant holdings, special forms of tenancy and feudal dependancy, and the fragmentation of land into tiny parcels often scattered amidst broad fields, and the continuing operation of communal regulations for cropping, grazing, fallowing, and many other practices (Goubert, 1956; Soboul, 1956). Forster (1970) has placed emphasis on the social and cultural restrictions, rather than the technical limitations, that minimized agricultural change during the eighteenth century. Share-croppers, tenants and other peasant farmers were dependant in many ways on their feudal lords and on the communities of which they formed part. Farm leases were short, normally being nine years or less, and such periods were too brief to merit substantial financial input even if communal rules might be manipulated to allow such individualism to occur. Although there were notable exceptions, the majority of large landlords were not willing to risk investing in agriculture. Instead they were obsessed with immediate returns and orientated their financial dealings in accordance with their aspirations for social advancement that might be symbolised by the single word 'Paris'.

'Paris promised much—the marriage market, the money market, the sinecures, offices, preferments and, of course, the magnificent setting, without which to be a gentleman was a poor thing indeed. The land was too often but a means, too often sucked dry, to provide the cream of society the resources to consume' (Forster, 1970, p. 1613).

The argument is, therefore, that poor transport links, tolls, tariffs, taxes and the seigneurial system are less important than is often made out. Instead more attention should be paid to the social aspirations of landowners and the widespread view among peasant farmers that to own and gradually enlarge a subsistence farm as a kind of extension of the family was more important than intensifying productivity and generating surpluses for trade. These attitudes were highly important in contributing towards an understanding of the limited impact of agricultural change during the eighteenth century but, in addition, they continued to exercise influence throughout the nineteenth century. It may even be argued that French agricultural legislation dating from as recently as the 1960s has been hamstrung by deference to peasant traditions and the virtues of the family farm (Wright, 1964).

Nonetheless, the Revolution of 1789 and the legislation that followed it brought the feudal, seigneurial system to an end, attempted to rid the country of the abuses of the *ancien régime*, and stipulated general freedom and the rights of the individual. In the agricultural realm the *Code Rural* spelled out 'the whole territory of France is free, as are the people that inhabit it'. Communal regulations controlling farming behaviour were brought to an end by law, although, in practice, traditions were to die hard. Thus the individual had the right to cultivate his land as he thought fit, without reference to his neighbours or to ancient communal rotations, fallowing, times for sowing and harvesting, collective herds, or systems of stubble grazing. The individual was free to enclose his property if he wished. Each community had the option to divide up and sell areas of common land if the majority so wished. Royal, ecclesiastical and noble estates were expropriated and in many cases were split up and sold off. Farm leases were extended and tithes, taxes and tolls on agricultural produce and on internal trading were abolished. Cultivators were free to grow crops, graze stock, and dispose of their produce as they alone thought fit.

Fundamental though the establishment of these legal rights undoubtedly was—and in particular the ending of the feudal system—it must be recognised that many ancient communal traditions continued to live on into the nineteenth century. Augé-Laribé (1955) stressed how slowly new ideas filtered down to the bulk of the peasantry. In his eyes the 'agricultural revolution' of the late eighteenth century was more of a political revolution than a technical one. The 'new agriculture' that was associated with the physiocratic movement was undoubtedly interesting in the scientific realm but remained restricted in its practical effects, because of the lack of contact between the educated elite and the peasant masses. Its national impact was slight. Bourde (1953) takes a similar view in evaluating the significance of English ideas on French agronomists. It is

'. . . less a fact of economic history than a fact in the history of ideas . . . This may explain why the success of the movement was limited in practice, while very great in theory'.

During the Revolutionary period administrators were more concerned with disseminating political propaganda among the peasantry than with organizing economic progress. Fundamental freedoms had been established, important changes in land owner-ship took place, moorlands were cleared and marshlands drained, and cultivation of the potato and experimental crops, such as sugar-beet, progressed, but the years up to 1815 were disturbed in military terms, with economic advance being subjugated to political survival. Sée (1927) charted the impact of changes in land ownership since 1789, noting that there were significant excep-tions to the general rule of expropriation and also many examples of re-purchasing of land by noble owners. In Cher, Maine, Anjou, Vendée and parts of Loire-Inférieure the distribution of large properties remained much as before. However the grasp of the peasantry and of the bourgeoisie on land ownership was un-doubtedly strengthened nationwide. The first half of the nineteenth century witnessed a continuation of the agricultural changes identi-fied prior to 1800, with the cultivation of artificial grasses and fodder crops making particular progress in the Paris Basin (Vidalenc, 1957, 1970).

In spite of political and economic unification and attempts to improve internal transportation by highway and canal construction, France remained strongly differentiated spatially before the rail-way age.[6] Two pieces of legislation in the 1830s served to reduce those differences. The first was the introduction in 1832 of a system for establishing agricultural committees in each *canton* which, in turn, were concerned with organizing local societies for diffusing information, awarding prizes and generally encouraging agricultural change (Fig. 11.3). The second involved legislation in 1836 which placed the responsibility for maintaining minor roads (but not agricultural tracks) on the local authorities (*communes*) through which they passed. Effects were far from instantaneous, being particularly slow in the remote and impoverished backwoods. Nonetheless, Léonce de Lavergne (1861) could claim, with the wisdom of hindsight, that

'. . . the law of 1836 on local roads has transformed France; farming owes much of the progress achieved in the past quarter-century to it' (p. 442).

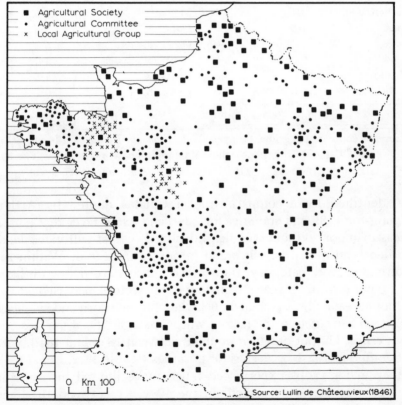

FIG. 11.3. Agricultural societies *c.* 1840.

Rural France on the Eve of the Railway Age

The agricultural enquiry of 1836–38, published in 1840–42 and known widely as the 1840 enquiry, provides a remarkably full set of data on land use, crop yields, prices and livestock for each *arrondissement* in France. This represents a unique and still largely unexploited source that will allow the spatial diversity of French agriculture on the eve of the railway age to be known in detail. Table 11.1 shows the general trends of national land use that may

Table 11.1

Estimated Land Use 1789, 1840, 1859 (million ha)

Main Categories	1789	1840	1859	Cultivated Land	1789	1840	1859
Cultivated Land	25·0	25·7	26·0	Fallow	10·0	6·8	5·0
Gardens and				Wheat	4·0	5·5	6·0
orchards	1·5	1·5	2·0	Oats	2·5	2·8	3·0
Vines	1·5	2·0	2·0	Other cereals	7·0	6·8	6·0
Woodland	9·0	8·8	8·0	Artificial grasses	1·0	1·6	3·0
Meadows	3·0	3·5	4·0	Roots	0·1	1·5	2·0
Moorland	10·0	8·5	8·0	Other crops	0·4	0·7	1·0
TOTAL	50·0	50·0	50·0				

Sources: Léonce de Lavergne, G. (1861): *L'Economie Rurale de la France depuis 1789*, Paris (quoting Arthur Young); and Ministère des Travaux Publics (1840–42): *Statistique Générale de la France*, Paris.

be identified by a comparison of estimates quoted by Arthur Young for 1789 and statistics for 1840 and 1859. Over that period areas of moorland and woodland declined, whilst cultivated land, gardens and orchards, vines and meadows increased. Within the 'cultivated land' category, the surface left as bare fallow declined by 50 per cent in 70 years, whilst all other sectors increased except 'other cereals'. This included buckwheat, mixed corn and rye, each of which retreated in the face of wheat, oats, artificial grasses and root crops. Output of wheat doubled between 1815 and 1840, with a five-fold increase occurring for potatoes (Table 11.2, Fig. 11.2). Other major crops experienced much more limited increases in output over the same period. In the 40 years between 1812 and 1852 numbers of cattle almost doubled as areas under permanent

Table 11.2

Production of Selected Crops, 1815, 1840, 1858 (million hl)

	1815	1840	1858
Wheat	39·5	80·9	109·9
Rye	25·7	30·0	28·8
Barley	14·6	17·0	20·9
Maize	5·6	7·2	7·6
Oats	36·6	48·0	69·9
Potatoes	21·6	102·2	101·4

Source: Block, M. (1860): *Statistique de la France*, Paris.

Table 11.3

Livestock Numbers, 1812, 1829, 1839, 1852 (millions)

	1812	1829	1839	1852
Cattle	6·7	9·1	9·9	12·2
Sheep	35·0	29·1	32·2	33·5

Source: Block, M., (1860), *Statistique de la France*, Paris.

grass and fodder crops advanced (Table 11.3). By contrast the number of sheep actually declined as areas of moorland and fallow that had been used for rough grazing were reclaimed for more intensive forms of agricultural production.

The spatial complexity of French agriculture before the establishment of an effective national system of communication may be demonstrated at a variety of scales and with reference to a wide range of indicators. Maps derived from the statistics of the old cadaster have already been included in Chapter 7 to display basic contrasts in land use at the *département* level. Most *départements* in the Paris Basin had two-thirds or more of their surface under arable use (Fig. 7.2). Permanent grassland was extensive in a distorted 'ring' of *départements* that surrounded the Paris Basin and extended southwards into the Massif Central, whilst wasteland predominated in areas of southern and western France, and extensive stretches of woodland were found in the Basin of Aquitaine and in eastern France. Vines, chestnut trees, almonds, olives and mulberries contributed to the polyculture of the South (Figs.

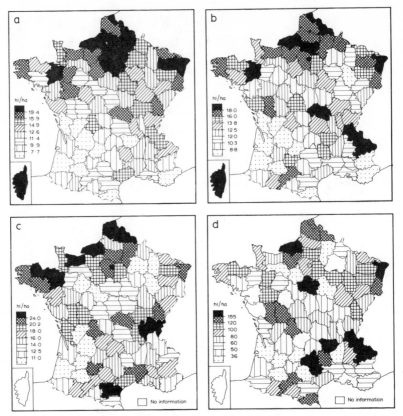

FIG. 11.4. Average yields hl/ha 1835 (octiles by *département*): (a) wheat; (b) rye; (c) oats; (d) potatoes.

7.3 and 7.4). At the same level of generalization, Fig. 11.4 shows striking spatial differences in yields of wheat, rye, oats and potatoes in 1835. The pre-eminence of *départements* in the northern Paris Basin and in Alsace is clear with respect to the first two crops, but for the production of oats and potatoes high-yielding *départements* are much more widespread.

The so-called 1840 enquiry will allow the agricultural complexity of France on the eve of the railway age to be probed more deeply. As Fel has noted in Chapter 7, wheat prices in *arrondissements* in south-eastern France were in excess of 20 *francs*/hl in a 'normal year' in the late 1830s—virtually double what was charged in northern Lorraine (Fig. 11.5). Other high cost areas included

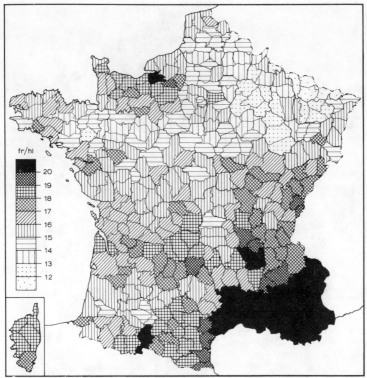

FIG. 11.5. Average price of wheat *c.* 1840 (by *arrondissement*).

Normandy, Corsica, Languedoc-Roussillon, the western *arrondissements* of the Massif Central, the Rhône-Saône axis and Franche-
Comté. Net yields were very high not only in *arrondissements* in
the northern Paris Basin but also in coastal Brittany (Armor),
parts of the Loire valley, the Limagnes of Auvergne, and north-
eastern France (Fig. 11.6). But it must be remembered that the
volume of seed that was applied per ha varied substantially (Fig.
11.7) and as a result, when wheat yields are expressed in relationship to the volume of seed used (rather than in absolute terms),
the productivity of areas beyond the Paris Basin may call for some
reappraisal (Fig. 11.8). Just how these parameters for wheat are
interrelated and how the production of wheat stands in relation to
the wide range of crops recorded in the 1840 enquiry is not yet
known.

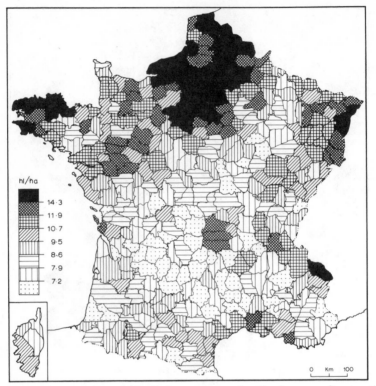

hl/ha

14·3
11·9
10·7
9·5
8·6
7·9
7·2

0   Km   100

FIG. 11.6. Average net yield of wheat *c.* 1840 (octiles by *arrondissement*).

A fairly consistent regional contrast in wheat prices existed between the cheap north-east and the expensive south-east throughout the period from 1797 to 1835, even though absolute values varied from year to year as yields fluctuated (Fig. 11.9). Indeed, Morineau (1969) managed to demonstrate roughly comparable regional differences in wheat prices during the second half of the eighteenth century. Further research is required before agricultural land use, cereal yields and prices, crop combinations, and livestock farming may be depicted in their full complexity for this crucial time in French economic development.

The task of regionalizing French agricultural production on a rigorous basis using the results of the 1840 enquiry remains to be done, however, a number of simple divisions may be derived from the writings of contemporary observers. Lullin de Châteauvieux

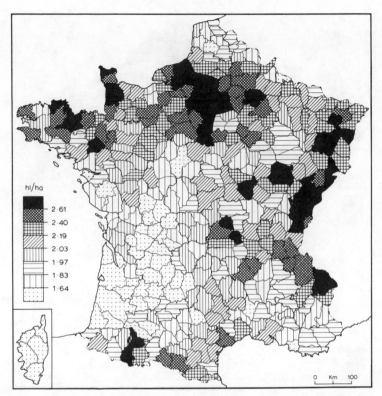

F IG. 11.7. Average volume of wheat seed applied /ha *c.* 1840 (octiles by *arrondissement*).

(1846) recognized eight agricultural regions (Fig. 11.10a). The 'Nord' region was undoubtedly the richest of all parts of rural France, with favourable climatic conditions, good transport, considerable urban development, and benefiting from large financial investments. It was claimed that '. . . it is in this region that most of the improvements in *grande culture* have occurred over the last 40 years' (p. 126). Such changes included new strains of livestock, artificial grasses, sugarbeet and oil crops. The 'Montagnes' region of the Massif Central contained extensive areas of moorland that were considered only worthy of afforestation, whilst the Sud-Ouest had seen a massive extension of maize cultivation. However, it was the 'Région de L'Ouest ou des Ajoncs' that 'presented the most languishing forms of agriculture and offered the greatest

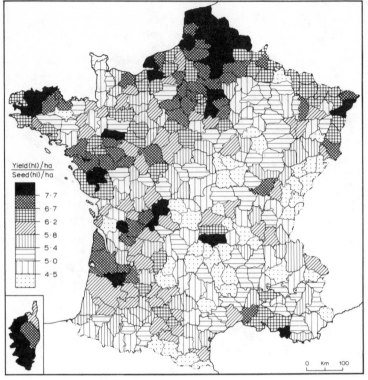

FIG. 11.8. Wheat yield/seed ratio *c.* 1840 (octiles by *arrondissement*).

obstacles to their improvement' (p. 439). In short, '. . . there is
nothing homogeneous about farming in France. This is a fact of
which one must never lose sight' (p. 519). Léonce de Lavergne
(1861) produced a six-fold classification of agricultural regions,
placing the 'Nord-Ouest' in leading position, with the 'Nord-Est'
coming second (Fig. 11.10b). The mountainous 'Centre' region
was considered to be the most backward, with the 'Sud-Ouest'
coming in penultimate position. Just how meaningful these
attempts at regionalization really were and how accurate were the
views of their designers remains to be tested against the numerical
evidence of the 1840 enquiry.

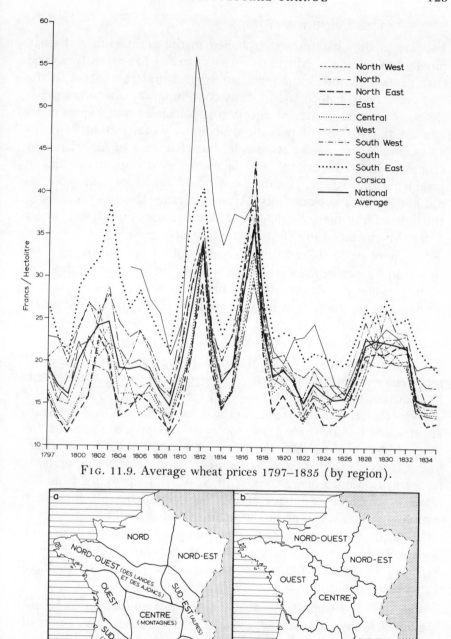

FIG. 11.9. Average wheat prices 1797–1835 (by region).

FIG. 11.10. Agricultural regions according to (a) Lullin de Châteauvieux and (b) Léonce de Lavergne.

The Evidence Against

In spite of the changes accomplished in the eighteenth and early nineteenth centuries, Morineau (1970b and c) has recently argued that France did not experience an agricultural revolution in the 100 years or so before 1840. Many contemporary observers stress the very limited impact of agronomic principles and experiments against the weight of peasant traditions. Total output of crops undoubtedly increased nationwide, but clearance of moorland for cropping and reduction of bare fallows played important roles in producing that result. National seed/yield ratios for major cereals did not increase substantially. After analysing the 1840 returns in the light of fragmentary yield series for a range of estates at earlier dates, Morineau (1969) felt moved to write:

'. . . personally, I doubt the existence of an agricultural revolution in France in the eighteenth century, at least on the basis of the productivity of cereals. The national mean of 1840 remained the same as that noted by Lavoisier in 1788, and of Olivier de Serres c. 1600' (p. 411).

But agriculture involves more than wheat and rye. Changes in the production and productivity of other crops, especially those of *la petite culture*, and of livestock rearing remain to be investigated. In addition, the spatial diversity of France merits a finer mesh of analysis than the *département* level that has been used by Morineau. He stressed the folly of relying too much on national averages, for example by showing that the scatter of wheat yields for a 'normal' year c. 1840 extended from the national average of 9·4 quintals/ha to 5·2 in Lot and Lozère to 20·7 in Nord. But surely the time has come to continue enquiries at the most detailed scale for which nationwide data survive—namely the *arrondissement*?

In spite of reservations about his emphasis on cereals and the scale of enquiry, one may quote the conclusion of Morineau (1970b) as a useful contrast to the variously glowing or qualified views of other authors.

'One has the impression that French agriculture in 1840 remained stagnant, retarded, even primitive in the greater part of the territory . . . Only two *départements*, the Nord and the Pas-de-Calais would sustain a comparison with the pioneering agricultures of England, Belgium and Holland' (p. 179).

The outworking of earlier changes that was captured in 1840 derived from modification in farming practice that had been diffused almost exclusively from Flanders, England and Switzerland. Very little, it is claimed, had come from Mediterranean Europe. Morineau, (1970b) believes 'there is nothing in the 1840 statistics to suggest an agricultural revolution' (p. 180). The Flemish borderland along the Belgian frontier emerges as the only really progressive area and when information for the *département* of the Nord is disaggregated it becomes clear that not only were there important internal contrasts, with some localities being quite backward, but also that the root crops, complicated rotations, intensive stock-rearing and heavy fertilization that characterized agriculture intensification had their origins much earlier than the eighteenth century (Fig. 11.11).[7]

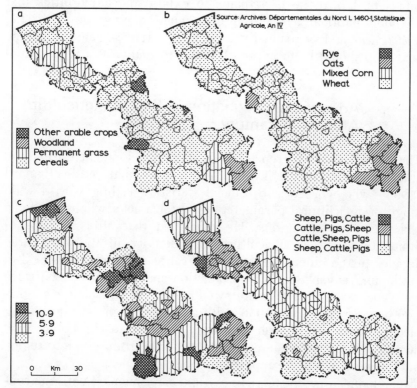

FIG. 11.11. Aspects of agriculture in the Nord *département c.* 1800 (by *canton*): (a) leading aspect of land use, by proportion of land covered; (b) leading cereal crop, in terms of land covered; (c) proportion of land under artificial grasses; (d) livestock combinations in ranked order.

Morineau's work is stimulating in three main respects. First, it questions conventional wisdom about the definition and very existence of an agricultural revolution. Important though indicators of change may be, Morineau insists that it is only the net results—summarized in terms of productivity per unit area—that are significant. Past emphasis on the scientific principles and practical experiments of agronomists, the publication of learned articles by agricultural societies, and even the cultivation of new crops has been misleading since each of these themes involved only the landowning elite, and a small proportion of that, rather than the peasant masses. For Morineau, it is results that count. Second, his publications display a scrupulous and thoroughly innovative analysis of numerical material in both consistent (e.g. the 1840 enquiry) and fragmentary (e.g. estate records of the *ancien régime*) data sets. Third, he is at pains to expose the ambiguities that surround national average figures when moving down to the *département* and occasionally local levels. It is arguable that the next step should be to approach closer to reality at a finer spatial scale.

Advance or Stagnation in French Agriculture After Mid-Century?

The whole issue of French agricultural development during the nineteenth and twentieth centuries has been analysed by Pautard (1965) who worked with official statistics dealing with a wide range of agricultural parameters for France as a whole and for a series of sample regions. He concluded that after a phase of limited advance in agricultural productivity in the first three decades of the nineteenth century, France underwent a period of quickening advance in both production and productivity between 1840 and 1890, which was followed by 60 years of relative stagnation between 1890 and 1950, with a phase of rapid change taking place in the past quarter century. The precise chronology and degree of impact of change varied, of course, from region to region but the general scheme appeared to hold true.

The half century from 1840 to 1890 corresponded with the construction of the national rail network and improved maintenance of all types of road, from the national highways to local roads (Price,

1975). With an increasingly effective system of transport the movement of goods between regions became practical and opened the way for local specialization on products that were most appropriate to the agricultural environment. Thus it was during this period that the milkshed of Paris extended beyond the environs of the city (Dubuc, 1938). Similarly, the capital also drew meat supplies from much more distant regions than had been the case during the *ancien régime* (Vidalenc, 1952). Areas such as the Nivernais, concentrated on advanced livestock farming, whilst the vines spread to the exclusion of subsistence crops in Bas-Languedoc (Thuillier, 1974). Many other examples of specialization have been documented, with the varied agricultural environments of the Paris Basin benefiting from heavy investment of capital expressed, in turn, in labour inputs, fertilizers, mechanization and infrastructural changes, such as drainage and buildings (Brunet, 1960). The precise combination of these modifications varied with both time and space in the component parts of the Paris Basin, with the intensive small farm areas of market gardening around Paris developing differently from the large farm wheatfield landscapes of Beauce or the *limon*-covered northern sections of the Basin where sugarbeet flourished (Pedelaborde, 1961; Philipponeau, 1956) (Fig. 11.12). Rates of agricultural change might in fact be slower in the Paris Basin than in less advanced parts of France, simply because yields were already relatively high and other indices of progress had been established earlier in this favoured northern section of the country. Thus the processes of land clearance and the application of lime to acid soils prior to intensive cultivation were not concentrated in the Paris Basin (Figs. 8.1–8.9). By contrast, modification of already cultivated soils through marling and piped underdraining was, of course, associated with the local availability of marl and the location of damp soils but in each case the relationship between stimulus and response was far from simple (Figs 11.13 and 11.14). The need for change had to be perceived by landowners who also had to be familiar with the technical and agronomic aspects of the soil modification that they were concerned to achieve (Clout and Phillips, 1972).

   To take the single example of piped underdraining, it is surprising that very little land was treated in this way, despite much

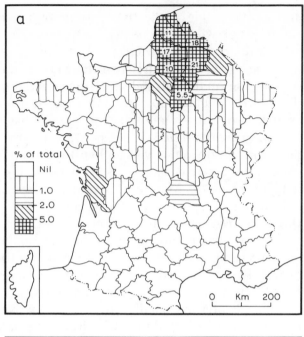

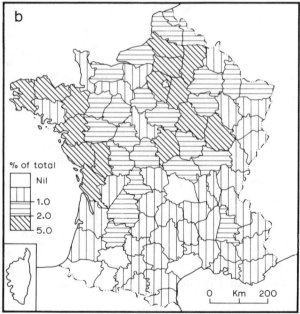

FIG. 11.12. Beet production in 1884 (by *département*): (a) for sugar; (b) for fodder.

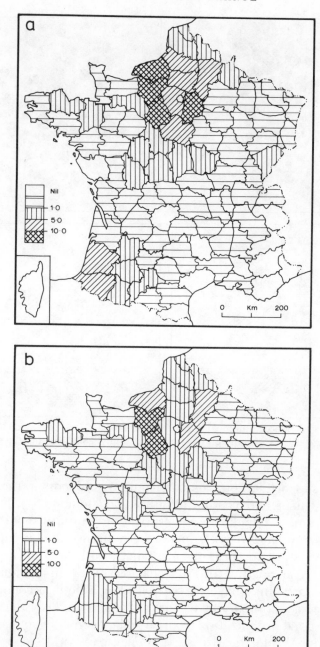

FIG. 11.13. Marling 1852–62 (by *département*): (a) proportion of total land treated; (b) proportion of arable land treated.

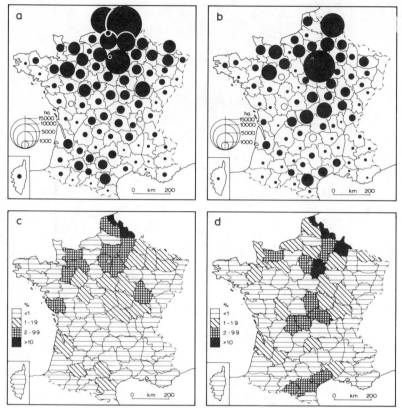

FIG. 11.14. Underdraining (by *département*): (a) land drained 1852–62;
(b) 1882–92; (c) proportion of all underdraining 1852–62; (d) 1882–92.

financial support and propaganda from governments in the second
half of the nineteenth century (Phillips and Clout, 1970). Draining
never became a popular or widespread agricultural modification,
save in a few *départements* in northern France and in the Paris
Basin. Perhaps the peasant mentality, with its inherent con-
servatism and apathy towards change, noted in contemporary
official reports, may have played a leading role in accounting for
the limited adoption of this technical change. Similarly the absence
of interest and organization from large landowners may have been
significant. While the British draining loans of 1846 and 1850
were quickly used by landowners, the French loan of 1856 was
neglected, despite the fact that it was based on similar principles

to the British loan. Reasons for the relative failure of piped under-draining as a significant modification in French agriculture may be sought in the physical, technical, financial, economic and structural realms. In particular, the structure of much of French farming did not encourage the spread of draining. The lack of long leases was thought a drawback to the acceptance of draining by many farmers. In inner parts of the Paris Basin where leases ran from 9 to 18 years, farmers were willing to pay interest on draining outlay. But in western *départements*, where leases ran for 9 years or less, it was recorded that farmers disliked paying extra rents for draining. Perhaps more important in hindering the adoption of draining was the small size and highly fragmented nature of holdings in most parts of the country. A great number of official reports recorded that such farm structures were not conducive to widespread drain-ing. A further reason was suggested in the poorer agricultural *départements*. In parts of the south-west, the expense of draining was too great to be borne and the technique was therefore not adopted. It proved to be useful only in areas of agricultural prosperity, where 'high farming' techniques were pursued—and with few exceptions that meant the Paris Basin. (Fig. 11.15)

Although detailed analysis remains to be done of the impact of biological progress (in the form of new crop strains and livestock breeds), of farm machinery of all kinds and of the use of non-traditional fertilizers, one suspects that many forms of agricultural change failed to be adopted by the bulk of French farmers during the second half of the nineteenth century. That is not to belittle the achievements of land reclamation and liming in the west and centre of France or to underplay the effect of national systems of transport to gradually permit regions to specialize on those branches of farming for which they were best prepared in terms of physical endowment. But it is undeniable that a mass of conditions, even 'obstacles', interacted to retard the pace of change in French farming.

Checks and Balances in French Farming

Perhaps two groups of 'obstacles' need to be emphasized. The first involved the general psychology of peasant farming and land-ownership which had, of course, been strengthened by the events

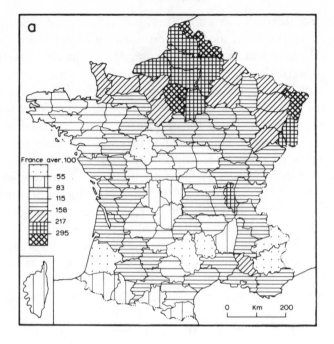

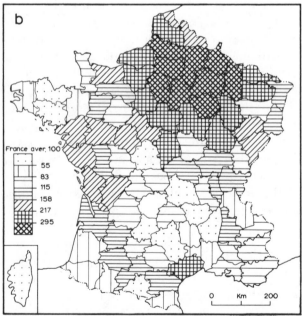

FIG. 11.15. Value of crop production (by *département*): (a) per cultivated ha
1852; (b) per agricultural worker 1862 (francs).

of the Revolution of 1789. Although there were some marked exceptions to the rule, it would not be wrong to observe that division of common lands and property held by the Crown, Church and nobility served to fragment land ownership and to strengthen the grasp of a vast number of small and medium owners on land resources. Many authors would argue that the firmly entrenched system of peasant farming determined the nature of French agriculture after 1789 and slowed down the impact of agricultural advance and intensification. According to Sée (1927) this was the ransom that had to be paid for the Revolution. Legislation for dividing up common land was complemented by further laws ensuring that each heir obtained a share of the family farm and that agrarian individualism should be strengthened.[8] The end result was to produce an extremely numerous class of small landowners and sustained many farms that were semi-subsistent in character. Under such a system, profits were normally devoted to purchasing extra plots of land rather than buying equipment or fertilizers. Even as late as 1929 France still contained 2,950,000 farms of more than 1 ha apiece, compared with 3,200,000 in 1862 and as many as 3,650,000 in 1882. Linked to this importance of peasant land ownership is the fact that communal traditions of agricultural management, indeed the organization of much of rural life, did not disappear overnight. Revolutionary legislation had declared the rights of the individual in farming as in other sectors but centuries of learned behaviour were not to be swept away, especially in the remoter regions where rates of literacy were low and the impact of primary schooling and more particularly agricultural education was slow indeed.

Hohenberg (1972) has recently reappraised the long-held view of 'obstacles' preventing agricultural change and has instead offered a more refined argument which identifies powerful counterbalances to the weak processes of change that operated in the nineteenth century. He maintains that the outward appearance of immutability was misleading, arguing:

> 'through the nineteenth century, rural France underwent more change than appears on the surface . . . it is more appropriate to describe French rural life as "flux, conflict, diversity" than as "stability, simplicity, homogeneity"' (p. 239).

Hohenberg does not favour interpretations that allowed French agriculture to remain 'isolated' from forces of change associated with urban development, industrialization, trade, political processes and the creation of transport networks. Instead he believes that

'. . . rural France was not static, but rather the seat of mechanisms working to offset, limit and tame the strong impulses for change that accompanied European modernization in the nineteenth century' (p. 219).

It is argued, first, that rural elites failed to perform leadership roles to stimulate agricultural change. Second, early industrialization in France generated surprisingly weak responses in the form of requiring labour to move from countryside to town and as a result feedback effects which might be expected to stimulate change in rural areas were of limited impact (Crouzet, 1967). Third, the family farming system, with its emphasis on near self-sufficiency in food and investing profits in land, was reluctant to commit itself to labour- and skill-intensive forms of production for urban markets.

The other essential condition that served to slow down the spread of agricultural change in France was the erection of a protectionist trade barrier after 1880 which cushioned French peasant farmers from the powerful challenges of agricultural producers in the New World that were able to transport supplies of grain and meat relatively cheaply in steel-hulled steamships (Tracy, 1964). Free trade encouraged agricultural modernization and specialization in many parts of Western Europe, with the case of Denmark being particularly striking. By contrast, French domestic producers, peasant and progressive alike, were enjoying protection and French agriculture was entering the phase of relative stagnation between 1890 and 1950 that was identified so clearly by Pautard (1965).

Retrospect and Prospect

At the end of the nineteenth century many sectors of French farming were certainly very different from what they had been 100 years earlier. Areas of bare fallow had declined from c. 10,000,000

ha to 3,600,000 ha in 1882 and were to fall to 1,300,000 ha at the
end of World War I. Clover, sainfoin, trefoil and other fodder
crops were gradually accepted as valuable replacements for the old
fallows, particularly in the more progressive northern areas. Rich
fields of cereals and sleek well-fed livestock in the Paris Basin
contrasted with much less impressive specimens in parts of the
centre, west and south where, of course, the use of machinery was
rare. Peasant systems of land management predominated and contributed towards blocking change. Although much of the past
remained in French agriculture and the number of rural dwellers
had declined only slightly during the nineteenth century (still
representing 60 per cent of the national population in 1901), there
were important regional differences in rural population change.
Already by the mid-nineteenth century the local economies of
parts of the Massif Central and elsewhere in the area of *petite
culture* had been shattered beyond repair in response to the famine
conditions of the late 1840s and the disruption of craft activities.
Out-migration took on new dimensions, becoming permanent
rather than just seasonal and hardening with the passage of the
years as the construction of the railway network further weakened
the spatial 'insulation' that such areas had experienced in the past,
reduced their viability, and, of course, made travelling a much
easier proposition. Young people with drive and initiative left,
gradually lessening the propensity of such communities to replace
themselves and leaving land management to the often less dynamic
who remained. In some respects out-migration served to reduce
population pressure on land resources and allowed farms to be
enlarged through purchase and more especially through leasing.
But the end results were normally fragmented into a large number
of dispersed parcels and in any case peasant traditions of agricultural organization remained powerfully in operation.

   Three areas of enquiry relating to agricultural change in nineteenth-century France may be identified as worthy of further
investigation. The first two are essentially practical in character,
while the third is conceptual. To begin with, much more attention
needs to be paid to the various statistical sources which relate to
French agriculture in the nineteenth century and which may be
exploited in order to determine the precise, detailed and complex
pattern of agricultural production throughout the country for a

range of dates. The 1840 enquiry is particularly inviting as a source but successive decennial returns (1852, 1862, 1882, 1892) and other enquiries also offer great possibilities (Désert, 1975; Gandilhon, 1969; Garrier, 1967). Cross sections may then be compared and a measure of net change be derived therefrom. It is then essential to tackle complementary data sources in order to test and expand the impressions derived from statistical comparisons. Pautard (1965) has already made an important start along this line of enquiry, but vast topics and sources of documentation remain virtually untouched.[9]

The second area of investigation involves the origin, spread and influence of agricultural innovations, which may be in the realms of mechanization, of fertilization techniques, of livestock or of crop strains. Information on such themes may be gathered haphazardly from regional studies but it is arguable that these issues demand attention both in their own right and for the contribution they make to a more critical understanding of the temporal and spatial impact of change in French agriculture during the critical period of lagged modernization.

The third area of enquiry involves raising very basic questions about the concept of 'agricultural improvement' which is all too often assumed to take place but is rarely defined and demonstrated.[10] On inspection of accessible material on eighteenth- and nineteenth-century agricultural change in France it is clear that the simple and relatively unqualified list of technical changes was considered an adequate alternative to a critical discussion of the practice of agricultural improvement. Definitions of the concept were rarely encountered and the roles of specific processes in the general dynamic 'model' of agricultural advance, which might be applied to temporal and spatial contexts other than those of France in the eighteenth and nineteenth centuries were not normally discussed or demonstrated. The work of Morineau (1968, 1969, 1970a,b,c) is perhaps the most meaningful example of a questioning approach.

To Abbé Nicholas Baudeau writing in 1767 the objective of *l'amélioration de la terre* involved the use of techniques

> '. . . on a particular soil, to make it easier to cultivate, more abundant in better crops, and easier to harvest' (quoted in Cepède & Valluis, 1969, p. 62).

Already the complexity of the idea of 'improvement' has been introduced. The soil has to be rendered more easily cultivable. This would involve physical and chemical changes as well as modifications in soil-moisture conditions. Harvests from a defined area should increase not only in quantity but also in quality. A variety of viewpoints and lines of argument, both of a theoretical and pragmatic nature, might be adopted in trying to arrive at a working definition of 'agricultural improvement' in an historic context. Some of these will be considered below.

Changes in agricultural productivity through time might be seen as a fundamental starting point. Simple concern with increases in volume for any given crop produced from the defined area proves unsatisfactory, since, as Morineau (1970b) argues, the volume of seed applied may also have increased. Seed/yield ratios therefore need to be calculated. Another problem involved conditions in which the quality of the crop harvested might be judged to have increased but not the total quantity involved. Thus, a crop innovation for a particular locality (e.g. wheat) might replace a traditional product (e.g. buckwheat or rye) and precise and direct comparison would be precluded. In such a situation it might be argued that 'change' rather than 'improvement' is all that might be demonstrated, for in order for the researcher to make the necessary value judgement to confirm that an 'improvement' had taken place he would need more than the subject of opinions of contemporary writers and would require a reliable series of statistics on yields, capital and labour inputs, prices and a variety of ancillary points of information, both for the area within which the 'improvement' was suspected and for other areas which need to be used as controls. In spite of the existence of valuable statistical sources, reliable and detailed information of such a character is rarely available for nineteenth-century France.

The general absence of input/output information which might be sought from detailed estate accounts makes economic definitions of 'improvement', such as a farmer making a profit rather than a loss or a greater profit than before, very difficult to substantiate. Given the relatively closed, peasant farming economies of many parts of France in the nineteenth century, a case for 'improvement' argued rigorously on economic criteria would be almost impossible to sustain. A similar conclusion might arise from discussions of social change in the countryside, for one might argue that the agricultural labouring classes should necessarily enjoy 'better' conditions if 'improvement' had taken place. The conceptual problem surrounding such an issue and the absence of suitable quantifiable information are major difficulties.

At a more practical level, considerations of the diffusion of technical innovations and the more widespread use of existing techniques have been viewed as short-cut methods of presenting 'improvements'. The writers of the county reports submitted to the Board of Agriculture provide convenient listings for early nineteenth-century Britain (Marshall, 1818). Under-draining later came to be viewed as 'the great improvement of the age' (Mingay, 1968). French writers in the eighteenth and nineteenth centuries and the agricultural statistics that were collected from c. 1840 onwards emphasized a number of specific processes. Thus the statistics of 1852, 1860 and 1862 singled out marling, liming, surface- and under-draining, and land clearance (*défrichement*) as *améliorations agricoles* worthy of particular mention. Unless the situation before and after marling or under-draining, for example, may be known with great precision and the economic or productive characteristics of the latter be shown to demonstrate an advance on the former, it would be erroneous, although extremely convenient, to speak automatically of agricultural 'improvement'.

In the modern world, land reform, either in an organizational or a spatial sense, is sometimes equated with the beginnings of agricultural advance. The trend towards individualism encouraged by immediately post-Revolution legislation has been claimed by contemporary agronomists and by historians working with the wisdom of hindsight as an important stimulus in encouraging agricultural advance (Bloch, 1930). It is clear, however, that humbler members of French agrarian society viewed associated developments, such as the abolition of communal grazing and the division of areas of communal land, in quite different terms and envisaged financial ruin rather than betterment (Bloch, 1966). A truly meaningful use of the term 'agricultural improvement' in historical geography should involve investigating the assumptions and subjective decisions made by individuals in sections of society in the past. It might be argued that while such value judgements might be accepted for one place and for a specified period, they should not be transferred automatically to all spatial, social and economic contexts. After rigorous testing, however, specific aspects of such value judgements might be found relevant to other places and periods.

Following through this point it is clear that in practice many historical geographers have tended to assume that the reclamation of wild and watery lands may be equated directly with 'improvement' and that this is necessarily a progressive process involving the intensification of land use. This point would be hard to demonstrate, even if methods for measuring varying intensities of differing forms of historic land use were available. Widely divergent anticipations of the results of reclamation by peasant farmers and agronomists confirm that 'improvements' are not facts for mass consumption but are often the appraisals expressed by the higher, literate members of agrarian society, whose writings have formed the fodder which later agricultural researchers have devoured (Grigg, 1967).

The task remains for hypotheses regarding the definition of agricultural 'improvement' to be set up and tested against available statistical material on agricultural change. Modifications in legal conditions, transformation of the 'physical environment', improved transportation, changes in commodity prices, and varying perceptions of regional opportunities for agricultural intensification each need to be examined scrupulously before 'improvement' (as opposed to 'changes') are recognized. Perhaps too many ideas on agricultural conditions in eighteenth- and nineteenth-century France have been fabricated from the writings of travellers and 'experts' who possessed limited knowledge of local problems but whose powers of literacy have contributed to the distorted impressions held by later workers. As Sauer (1941) stated, the historical geographer

'. . . needs the ability to see the land with the eyes of its former inhabitants, from the standpoint of their needs and capacities. This is about the most difficult task in all human geography . . . to place oneself in the position of a member of the cultural group and time being studied' (p. 10).[11]

In short, the term 'agricultural improvement' should be used sparingly. 'Improvement' needs to be defined, hypotheses need to be built and tested, and 'improvement' actually proved, otherwise the more accurate and innocuous term 'agricultural change' is to be preferred.[12]

11. Notes

1. See chapter 5 and Duby and Wallon (eds) (1975–76).
2. The formal definition of 'rural' *communes* involves units with fewer than 2000 residents in the central settlement.
3. Perez (1944) includes a case study of the role of the *intendant* D'Etigny in stimulating agricultural changes (e.g. enclosure, land clearance, cultivation of maize and tree crops) in the area that was to become Gers *département*.
4. See chapter 7 by André Fel.
5. See chapter 8 by Keith Sutton.
6. Transport changes are discussed in chapter 12.
7. The origins of intensive farming in Flanders are open to debate. However the triennial rotation system with bare fallows, which still operated in much of northern France in the eighteenth century, had disappeared from the Flemish Plain since the late Middle Ages when the foundations of the 'new farming were laid to be built upon during the seventeenth century and the first half of the eighteenth century. See Slicher van Bath (1963) and Braure (1932).
8. There were, in fact, some parts of France where the 'equal shares' rules for dividing up landed proportions were circumvented.
9. See Appendix I for some further thoughts on this issue.
10. The term 'agricultural improvement' has been studiously avoided in earlier sections of the present chapter for that reason.
11. An interesting example of differences in economic appraisal in a Thai village is presented by Moerman (1968), especially chapter 7 'Choice in farming', which compares the villager's perspective with the outsider's perspective. Chayanov (1966) presents a range of evaluations of economic opportunities by peasant families, see especially p. xvi. Brookfield (1969) provides essential critical discussion on varying perceptions of environmental resources, while Heathcote (1965) offers a useful exemplification from semi-arid Australia.
12. Hypotheses regarding the chronology, location, character and significance of features of agricultural change may be derived from studies of specific areas in the past carried out by practitioners of a wide range of 'human

sciences' or from cautious considerations of 'modernization' in developing parts of the world in the second half of the twentieth century, for example, Soja (1968).

11. References

Augé-Laribé, M., *La Révolution Agricole*, Paris (1955).

Baudeau, N., *Première Introduction à la philosophie économique au analyse des états policés*, Paris (1767).

Bloch, M., 'La lutte pour l'individualisme agraire dans la France du XVIIIe siècle', *Annales d'Histoire Economique et Sociale*, 2 (1930), 329–81 and 511–56.

Bloch, M., *French Rural History*, London (1966).

Block, M., *Statistique de la France*, Paris, 2 vols (1860).

Bourde, A. J., *The Influence of England on the French Agronomes, 1750–1789*, Cambridge (1953).

Bourde, A. J., 'L'agriculture à l'anglaise en Normandie au XVIIIe siècle', *Annales de Normandie* (1958), 215–33.

Bourde, A. J., *Agronomie et Agronomes en France au XVIIIe siècle*, Paris, 3 vols (1967).

Braure, M., *Lille et la Flandre Wallonne au XVIIIe siècle*, Lille, 2 vols (1932).

Brookfield, H. C., 'On the environment as perceived', *Progress in Geography*, 1 (1969), 51–80.

Brunet, P., *Structure agraire et économie rurale des plateaux tertiaires entre la Seine et l'Oise*, Caen (1960).

Cepède, M. and Valluis, B. W., *La Pensée agronomique en France, 1510–1930*, Paris (1969).

Charra, W., 'Notes sur l'évolution des Causses de Quercy au cours du XIXe siècle', *Revue Géographique des Pyrénées et du Sud-Ouest*, 20 (1949), 175–221.

Chayanov, A. V., *The Theory of Peasant Economy*, (eds) D. Thorner, B. Kerblay and R. E. F. Smith. Homewood, Illinois (1966).

Clapham, J. H., *Economic Development of France and Germany, 1815–1914*, Cambridge, 4th edition (1961).

Clout, H. D. & Phillips, A. D. M., 'Fertilisants minéraux en France au XIXe siècle', *Etudes Rurales*, 45 (1972), 9–28.

Clout, H. D. & Phillips, A. D. M., 'Sugar-beet production in the Nord département of France during the nineteenth century', *Erdkunde*, 27 (1973), 105–19.

Crouzet, F., 'Agriculture et révolution industrielle', *Cahiers d'Histoire*, 241 (1967), 67–86.

Désert, G., 'Viande et poisson dans l'alimentation des Français au milieu du XIXe siècle', *Annales, Economies, Sociétés, Civilisations,* 30 (1975), 519–30.

Deslisle, L., *La Classe Agricole en Normandie au moyen âge,* Paris (1852).

Dubuc, R., 'L'approvisionnement de Paris en lait', *Annales de Géographie,* 47 (1938), 257–66.

Dubuc, R., 'La culture de la pomme de terre en Normandie avant et depuis Parmentier', *Annales de Normandie* (1953), 53–68.

Duby, G. and Wallon, E., *Histoire de la France Rurale,* Paris, 4 vols (1975–6).

Faucher, D., 'La révolution agricole du XVIIIe–XIXe siècle', *Bulletin de la Société d'Histoire Moderne,* 20 (1956), 2–11.

Faucher, D., *La Vie Rurale vue par un géographe,* Toulouse (1962).

Festy, O., *L'Agriculture pendant la Révolution française,* Paris (1947).

Forster, R., 'Obstacles to agricultural growth in eighteenth century France', *American Historical Review,* 75 (1970), 1600–15.

Fussell, G. E., *The Classical Tradition in West European Farming,* Newton-Abbot (1972).

Gandilhon, R., 'La série M (administration générale) des archives départementales', *Revue Historique,* 241 (1969), 147–62.

Garrier, G., 'Les enquêtes agricoles du XIXe siècle: une source contestée', *Cahiers d'Histoire,* 241 (1967), 105–113.

Goubert, P., 'The French peasantry in the seventeenth century', *Past and Present,* 10 (1956), 55–77.

Goubert, P., 'Les campagnes françaises', in F. Braudel and E. Labrousse (eds) *Histoire Economique et Sociale de la France,* II (1970), 87–160.

Grigg, D. B., 'The changing agricultural geography of England: a commentary on the sources available for the reconstruction of the agricultural geography of England, 1770–1850', *Transactions of the Institute of British Geographers,* 41 (1967), 73–98.

Heathcote, R. L., *Back of Bourke: a study of land appraisal and settlement in semi-arid Australia,* Melbourne (1965).

Hohenberg, P., 'Change in rural France in the period of industrialization, 1830–1914', *Journal of Economic History,* 32 (1972), 219–40.

Jacquart, J., 'French agriculture in the seventeenth century', in P. Earle (ed) *Essays in European Economic History, 1500–1800,* Oxford (1974).

Juillard, E., *La Vie Rurale en Basse-Alsace,* Paris and Strasbourg (1953).

Labrousse, E., 'Les bons prix agricoles du XVIIIe siècle: l'expansion agricole', in F. Braudel and E. Labrousse (eds.) *Histoire Economique et Sociale de la France,* II (1970), 367–565.

Léonce de Lavergne, G., *Economie rurale de la France depuis 1789,* Paris (1861).

Lullin de Châteauvieux, F., *Voyages agronomiques en France,* Paris, 2 vols (1846).

Marshall, W., *Review and Abstract of the County Reports to the Board of Agriculture,* London, 4 vols (1818).

Mazières, B., 'Etude géographique de l'alimentation dans le Lot entre 1840 et 1880', *Revue Géographique des Pyrénées et du Sud-Ouest*, 25 (1954), 293–312.

Meuvret, J., *Etudes d' Histoire Economique*, Paris (1971).

Mingay, G. E., Introduction to the second edition of Caird, J., *English Agriculture in 1850–51*, London (1968).

Moerman, M., *Agricultural Change and Peasant Choice in a Thai Village*, Berkley and Los Angeles (1968).

Morineau, M., 'Y a-t-il eu une révolution agricole en France au XVIIIe siècle?' *Revue Historique*, 486 (1968), 299–326.

Morineau, M., 'Prix et 'révolution agricole', *Annales, Economies, Sociétés, Civilisations*, 24 (1969), 403–23.

Morineau, M., 'La pomme de terre au XVIIIe siècle', *Annales, Economies, Sociétés, Civilisations*, 25 (1970a), 1767–85.

Morineau, M., 'Was there an agricultural revolution in eighteenth century France?' in R. E. Cameron (ed) *Essays in French Economic History*, Homewood, Illinois (1970b), 170–182.

Morineau, M., *Les Faux-semblants d'un démarrage économique en France au XVIIIe siècle*, Paris (1970c).

Pautard, J., *Les Disparités régionales dans la croissance de l'agriculture française*, Paris (1965).

Pedelaborde, P., *L'Agriculture dans les plaines alluviales de la presqu'île de Saint-Germain-en-laye*, Paris (1961).

Perez, O., 'La révolution agricole du XVIIIe siècle en Gascogne gersoise', *Revue Géographique des Pyrénées et du Sud-Ouest*, 15 (1944), 56–105.

Phillips, A. D. M. and Clout, H. D., 'Underdrainage in France during the second half of the nineteenth century', *Transactions of the Institute of British Geographers*, 51 (1970), 71–94.

Phlipponeau, M., *La Vie rurale de la banlieue parisienne*, Paris (1956).

Price, R., *The Economic Modernization of France, 1730–1880*, London (1975).

Sauer, C. O., 'Foreword to historical geography', *Annals of the Association of American Geographers*, 31 (1941), 1–24.

Sée, H., *La Vie économique de la France sous la monarchie censitaire, 1815–1848*, Paris (1927).

Slicher van Bath, B. H., *An Agrarian History of Western Europe, A.D. 500–1850*, London (1963).

Slicher van Bath, B. H., 'Eighteenth century agriculture on the continent of Europe: evolution or revolution?' *Agricultural History*, 43 (1969), 169–79.

Soboul, A., 'The French rural community in the eighteenth and nineteenth centuries', *Past and Present*, 10 (1956), 78–95.

Soja, E. W., *The Geography of Modernization in Kenya*, Syracuse (1968).

Thuillier, A., *Economie et Société Nivernaises au début du XIXe siècle*, Paris (1974).

Thuillier, G., 'L'alimentation en Nivernais au XIXe siècle', *Annales, Economies, Sociétés, Civilisations*, 20 (1965), 1163–84.

Tracy, M. A., *Agriculture in Western Europe: crisis and adaptation since 1880*, London (1964).

Vidalenc, J., 'L'approvisionnement de Paris en viande sous l'ancien régime', *Revue d'Histoire Economique et Sociale*, 30 (1952), 116–32.

Vidalenc, J., 'L'agriculture dans les départements normands à la fin du Premier Empire', *Annales de Normandie* (1957), 179–201.

Vidalenc, J., *Le Peuple des Campagnes, 1815–1848*, Paris (1970).

Wright, G., *Rural Revolution in France*, London (1964).

12

Industrial Development in The Eighteenth and Nineteenth Centuries

HUGH D. CLOUT

Introduction

Whether or not France underwent an 'industrial revolution' has proved a major challenge in definition and interpretation for several generations of economic historians. Some authorities have recognized the existence of such a 'revolution', although having done so are far from being in agreement on its chronology (Dunham, 1958; Fohlen, 1970, 1973; Henderson, 1967; Rioux, 1971). Duby and Mandrou (1964) express some reservations about economic and demographic revolution in the eighteenth century but are generally in favour of the idea.

> 'Revolution? Perhaps the word is a little too strong, in these areas where there are no sudden changes or violent convulsions. But it alone has the force to indicate the scope of a movement which is equalled only . . . by the other Revolution, that of 1789, which, although its importance has not been overrated, cannot alone explain everything' (p. 350).

For Fohlen (1970) the appropriateness of the term 'industrial revolution' is open to debate but, provided that it is interpreted in a fairly loose way, it may be seen that the industrial revolution in France covers a period of approximately a century, from 1750 or 1770 to 1870. In the course of these years the use of coal was generalized, steam triumphed as a source of energy, and work was mechanized in such sectors as metallurgy, chemicals and textiles (p. 203). Milward and Saul (1973) offer a similar interpretation.

'By the 1850s . . . France already had much of the apparatus of an industrial society. Whether or not the concept of an 'industrial revolution' is thought to have any meaning, the vital changes in the French economy took place before the 1850s, and the first of them, particularly those in the cotton goods industry, took place before 1815' (p. 256).

Change was protracted in the extreme in this country where factory-based production developed much more slowly than in Great Britain, Belgium, Germany or the United States, and where establishing turning points is a delicate matter (Crouzet, 1967, p. 68). Price (1975) has argued recently that:

'. . . if a terminal point has to be assigned to the economic *ancien régime*, perhaps this would be the period 1850–80 rather than 1789' (p. ii)

for by then the railway network had begun to forge the country into one economic system rather than a series of variously isolated units that had been characterized by varying degrees of fiscal juridical separation prior to 1789. In short, there is little agreement on the chronology of an industrial revolution in France, but many would echo the words of David Landes (1969):

' "France" wrote Clapham "never went through an industrial revolution". She did, but it was muffled' (p. 236).[1]

This essay will attempt to chart elements of continuity and change in French industrial production in the eighteenth and nineteenth centuries. During that period different branches of manufacturing and different parts of the country adopted technical innovations with varying degrees of enthusiasm. Far from being able to identify a clear cut 'revolution' one is instead confronted by a complicated array of local conditions and differing rates of change in specific sectors. In general terms, France had become unified territorially by the end of the seventeenth century but continued to be divided into 'trade zones reflecting the gradual accretion that had built the nation state. And these formal barriers were complicated by a network of informal boundaries defining markets and zones of supply for goods, like grain or wood or salt, that were vital to local survival' (Landes, 1969, p. 127).

The Revolution of 1789 and the mass of subsequent legislation established the formal basis of equality and of economic, fiscal and juridical liberty but it must be recognized that functional changes were not instantaneous. It was to take many decades for national economic unity to be achieved and not before new modes of transportation, particularly the railway, had begun to master the discipline of distance.

As Fohlen (1970) has shown, the period 1790 to 1810 introduced an impressive list of laws and decrees which modified the foundations of economic life in France. Internal tolls and taxes were abolished as were the dues that had been levied on goods entering towns. A uniform metric system of weights and measures was introduced. The principle of free competition among producers was established, with all craft gilds being abolished in 1791, and coalitions between workers or between producers were also forbidden. Finally, and in fact in breach of the general rights of the individual, mines might be operated only with State concessions in order to ensure efficient exploitation of the nation's mineral wealth. These measures were crucially important in providing the legal basis for a new economic system which was not however created instantaneously. Changes were gradual in every respect and it was probably not until after the mid-nineteenth century that the lines of the newly laid railways began to weld France into a single economic nation and to solidify the gamut of diverse modifications that had occurred in individual industrial branches during the preceding 100 years. For this reason the present essay will concentrate first on the 'traditional' industrial pattern, will then examine the emergence of a national system of communications by the middle years of the nineteenth century, and will finally depict industrial France between 1850 and 1900, by which time even the most cautious commentators would agree that fundamental changes in the location and scale of manufacturing had occurred.

The 'Traditional' Industrial Pattern

Spatial dispersion, smallness of scale, integration with other
sectors of local economies, and use of local sources of energy and
also usually of raw materials were critical themes in the industrial
geography of France prior to the age of the steam engine and of
the economic territorial unity that accompanied it. In earlier times
each settlement or at least each small area had to manufacture a
basic range of goods for its own use. Few, if any, villages throughout the nation were without wood turners, clock makers and a host
of other workshop trades (Fig. 12.1). Commercial exchanges over

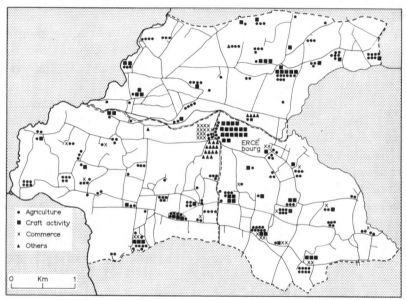

FIG. 12.1. Employment categories of heads of households in Ercé *commune*,
Ille-et-Vilaine, 1856.

defective networks of communication were difficult and expensive,
being rendered even more unattractive by the internal dues and
tolls that existed prior to 1789. The power of human muscle was of
prime importance, with all the spatial freedom that such a mobile
source would allow. Then came wind, water and wood into the
energy story. It is hardly surprising that the traditional industrial
pattern was far from what we are accustomed to expect from our
own acquaintance with coalfields, ports and capital cities. Even by

the late seventeenth century the pattern and character of most branches of French industry was still 'medieval', although high quality manufactures were concentrated in some urban centres (Léon, 1970). Gilds were mainly restricted to large towns, whereas free master craftsmen and artisans were found in small towns and villages (Kellenbenz, 1974). Certainly, gilds in France never acquired the degree of importance they generated in the Netherlands or in Germany. During the eighteenth century rural crafts flourished increasingly and the gilds declined, being supressed by Turgot in 1776, then being re-established, only to be abolished at the Revolution.

Most kinds of textiles, metal goods and even luxury goods were produced in the countryside. Industrial scenes were rural. Chimneys were few and far between. In the eighteenth century the most 'industrial' landscapes in France involved the countryside around Lille and Rouen (Milward and Saul, 1973). Many 'industrially employed' workers were in fact peasants who did not own enough land to live from the fruits of the soil and had to turn their hand to craftwork or to mining for part of the year. When such trades were concerned with extracting or processing local raw materials Kellenbenz (1974) maintains that dual activity workers had every chance of succeeding, but industries that involved imported raw materials (e.g. silk, cotton) were more likely to be 'organized' along stricter lines and might well be in the hands of contractors from the towns, the nobility or the church who could command the necessary capital for such operations. For example, as early as the sixteenth century entrepreneurs were distributing raw materials and collecting thread or cloth from outworkers living in villages over wide areas in Normandy, Picardy, Touraine, Poitou and Languedoc (Zeller, 1970). The silk industry of the Lyonnais was a prime example of dependence on urban merchant-manufacturers.

As Fischer (1973) has argued, there seems to be agreement that domestic industries settled in the sixteenth to eighteenth centuries mainly in regions, and within the regions in locations, with a landless or virtually landless population which often was undergoing rapid increase (p. 160). After due consideration of crucial factors such as raw materials, markets and transport costs, contractors

'looked for cheap labour and therefore planted the new industries where a rural proletariat already existed, or where small-holdings which did not support a family throughout a year prevailed, or where the soil was poor and difficult to work as was mostly the case in mountainous regions. Certainly the economic structure of the villages in question played a part in the beginning and this economic structure was affected by such different conditions as soil fertility, microclimate, and laws or customs of inheritance' (Fischer, 1973, p. 161).

Put more bluntly, 'poor soil and division of holdings were the parents of rural industry' (Landes, 1969, p. 198).

In addition to the almost 'automatic' local industries and those organized by contractors the traditional industrial pattern contained a third element that had been introduced by the State in order to reduce reliance on imported products, especially luxury goods, and thereby cut back the flow of precious metals leaving the country. Accordingly, special Royal *manufactures* were set up to make tapestries (that had previously been imported from the Low Countries), high quality glassware in the Venetian style, carpets and many other products (Zeller, 1970). The key phase for this form of industrial stimulation was the reign of Henri IV (1589–1610) since only eight of the 48 *manufactures* existing in 1610 had predated his coming to power. The first *manufactures* were located around Paris, in the Ile-de-France, and on the banks of the Loire, but more distant locations around Lyons and other parts of France were selected as this policy continued to operate during the remainder of the seventeenth century, particularly under the guidance of Colbert and with the help of provincial *intendants* during the eighteenth century (Léon, 1970).

Admittedly there were a number of privileged zones of industrial development by the second half of the eighteenth century in areas where good communications, high densities of population or very fertile soils provided added incentives for manufacturing to flourish, but it would still be true to maintain that dispersal was the main spatial characteristic (Woronoff, 1970). The survey of the iron industry undertaken by the Bureau de Commerce in 1788–89 showed that iron production was very widespread, involving small and technologically simple hearths, furnaces and forges that relied on wind, water and charcoal and was sited on small deposits of iron ore (Gille, 1966; Levainville, 1932). Such works were small enough to be shifted should supplies of ore or charcoal run out. Shortages of charcoal were certainly becoming serious during the eighteenth century and complaints proliferated in the *cahiers de doléances* and elsewhere about the ruthless exploitation of timber reserves by iron-makers, glass-workers and others without due attention to the problem of replanting. Figure 12.2 shows the

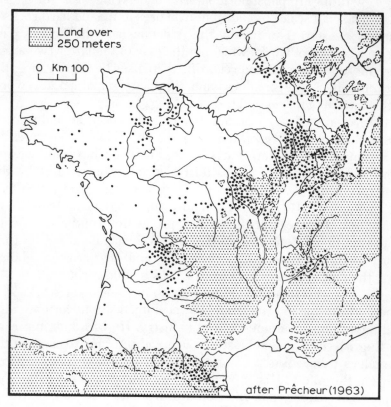

FIG. 12.2. Ironworks in France at the time of the Revolution.

pattern of ironworks in France at the time of the Revolution (Gille, 1960; Pounds, 1957; Pounds and Parker, 1957; Prêcheur, 1963). With the exception of a couple of works in Alsace and Lorraine, each of these establishments was very small. Ores were exploited in mountain areas of the eastern Pyrenees, where workings dated back to the thirteenth century, and in Dauphiné where high quality ores could only be worked in more clement summer conditions (Armengaud, 1953). The secondary rocks (Oolites, middle and upper Lias) of the eastern and southern margins of the Paris Basin gave rise to a rash of iron-working districts from Lorraine to Périgord whose economic 'health' in the eighteenth century was closely linked to the availability of charcoal and water (Pijassou, 1956). Lorraine was not an exceptional producing area at this stage, with highly phosphoric *minette* underlying ores being used only on a small scale. In addition, iron ores in the old hard rocks of Brittany, western Normandy, the Ardennes and the Vosges gave rise to a scatter of works which, in the case of the latter two areas, were more specialized and scientific than elsewhere in France. But in every other case smallness and simplicity remained key words in the pattern of forges and furnaces (Fig. 12.3a.).

The volume of cast iron and bar iron produced annually in the 1780s is shown by *généralité* in Fig. 12.3b. This demonstrates the importance of the eastern Paris Basin, Franche-Comté and western Normandy in the national pattern of production. In fact by that time quantities of semi-processed iron were being imported from Germany, Spain, Russia and especially from England and Sweden for finishing in France. But the bulk of production continued to come from traditional domestic sources and was manufactured by time-worn methods. Innovations were few and far between. Gabriel Jars, the *ingénieur des mines* from Lyons had been charged in 1756 by the French Government to visit mines and iron works elsewhere in Europe in order to make recommendations for extending and improving the domestic iron industry. He was duly impressed by English coke-fuelled blast furnaces and returned to suggest that a modern iron works *à l'anglaise* should be established at Montcénis in Burgundy. His experiment was started in 1776 using local supplies of coal for coke and iron ores from the Morvan. It was not a success but the Montcénis–Le Creusot site was to be revived in 1836.

Other ore deposits, such as lead and copper, gave rise to refining works in the Beaujolais, Lyonnais and in many other areas. Metal tools, arms and equipment were produced in workshops in numerous parts of the country from the knife-makers of Thiers (Auvergne) and the lock-makers of Vimeu (Picardy) to the specialist weapon-makers and cutlers of Saint-Etienne and the

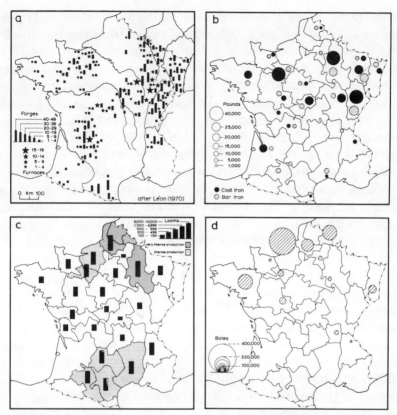

Fɪɢ. 12.3. Aspects of industrial activity during the *ancien régime* I: (a) number of forges and furnaces 1789 (by site); (b) annual production of cast iron and bar iron in the 1780s (by *généralité*); (c) distribution of looms, 1703–08 (by *généralité*); (d) production of linen cloth, 1785–6 (by *généralité*).

Forez who imported bar iron from Berry to supplement their own meagre supplies of ore. Glassworks proliferated on great estates with initially large but increasingly depleted timber reserves and local supplies of sand in the Champagne, Normandy, Nevers, Forez, upper Poitou, Auvergne, Languedoc and Guyenne (Dion, 1938; Dubois, 1974). Salt works on the Atlantic coast, in Provence and in Languedoc also made call on the declining woodland resources.

Textile manufacturing formed the second major branch of industry in France prior to the age of the steam engine and like iron working was also spatially dispersed. Some branches were concentrated in particular regions and towns such as Amiens, Beauvais, Lyons, Rheims, Rouen, Tours and Troyes cornered certain quality textile markets but nonetheless, cloth was being produced very widely. France supported great flocks of sheep, amounting to perhaps 20,000,000 in 1789 with important concentrations in Berry, Champagne, Languedoc, Nivernais and Picardy. Even so wool had to be imported from Spain, Portugal, the Levant, Germany and even the Baltic region to supply French spinning wheels and weaving looms. During the second half of the eighteenth century particular efforts were made to increase the number of fleeces produced in France and the experimental breeding of Spanish merinos at Rambouillet and elsewhere was undertaken to this end. *Généralités* in the outer Paris Basin and in Languedoc were particularly important producers of woollen goods (Marres, 1935) (Fig. 12.3c). Linen and canvas were made to meet purely local needs in virtually every part of France but large quantities of linen were manufactured from local supplies of flax in Normandy, Picardy, Brittany and the Nord (Fig. 12.3d). As far as these branches of cloth-making were concerned the concept of the 'industrial region' was almost totally alien; all provinces contained looms by the hundreds; and virtually every village had its flock of sheep and its hemp garden. Working the land and 'industrial work' intermingled as individuals took whatever job came up according to the changing seasons and changing opportunities (Léon, 1970, p. 219). But even so, water was an important localizing factor for driving simple machinery and for washing textiles and paper (Fig. 12.4a).

By the late eighteenth century silk yarn was being twisted and spun in country areas of Touraine, Bas-Languedoc, the Nîmes region, Provence, Vivarais and especially around Lyons. Links with urban merchants were essential for obtaining raw materials (sometimes from Italy or Spain) and disposing of the finished or semi-finished product. But it was the cotton industry above all other that was being 'organized' during the eighteenth century, with certain branches becoming mechanized. This activity, of course, depended on imported raw materials from the Levant, America, Guadeloupe and San Domingo, and the pattern of major cotton producing centres in the 1780s should be interpreted with that fact in mind (Fig. 12.4b). In the second half of the eighteenth century machinery imported from England such as the Crompton

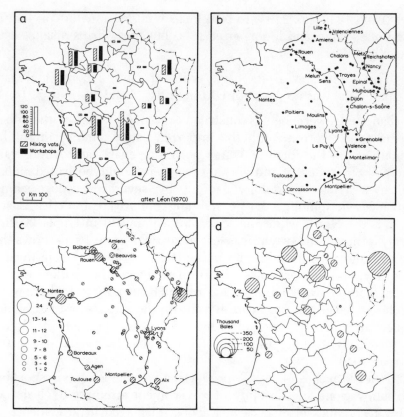

FIG. 12.4. Aspects of industrial activity during the *ancien régime* II: (a) paper-works, 1789 (by *généralité*); (b) main cotton producing centres 1785–89; (c) number of firms producing printed cotton cloth 1770–89; (d) volume of printed cotton cloth produced 1786–89 (by *généralité*).

mule-jennies coming in 1782, had been tried out in the cotton areas of Rouen, Paris, Picardy, Alsace and Dauphiné but these were simply experiments. However, mechanized printing and dyeing of cotton goods was being developed in Switzerland and although prohibited in France until 1785 because of opposition from old established textile gilds spread to the Republic of Mulhouse that was not incorporated into the French realm until 1798. The two dozen enterprises in Mulhouse (Fig. 12.4c) and the large volume of production coming from Alsace (Fig. 12.4d) are to be explained in this way. In addition, mechanized spinning had become established in Normandy, Alsace, Picardy and Paris before 1800 and as Fohlen (1970) remarks, 'went through its revolution between

1800 and 1830' (p. 218). In fact, Paris was still a major concentration of spindles and looms after 1800 but these firms disappeared quickly following 1815.

'The capital, with its high costs of land, labour, and raw materials, was no place for cotton mills' (Landes, 1969, p. 159).

Urban mills were being constructed at many sites in the other areas where cotton might be imported easily, energy might be obtained (in the form of water power or coal), and where vast support brigades of outworking weavers could be called upon, since weaving technology lagged by several decades behind advances in spinning. Large spinning mills were built in Alsace and in the Nord, while the scale of development in Upper Normandy although important was less majestic. Figure 12.5a shows the wide range of craft industries in the latter region in the eighteenth century, and, in particular, the rural weavers who worked thread from water-powered mills in and around Rouen. By 1823 there were to be no fewer than 121 cotton mills on the watercourses of Seine-Inférieure *département*, of which 95 were located in Rouen *arrondissement* along the Robec, Cailly and Sainte–Austreberthe streams (Sion, 1909).

Other branches of textile production were much less responsive to innovations and, in spite of government attempts to 'learn' of new techniques elsewhere in Europe, displayed little evidence of moving from the 'traditional' phase by the end of the eighteenth century. As Fohlen (1970) remarks,

'. . . new processes, whether English, German or Austrian, were seen as oddities and not as normal and safe techniques' (p. 202).

The essentially traditional pattern of industrial location in France is shown in Fig. 12.6 derived from the statistics of the old cadaster which spanned three decades prior to 1840. Windmills and watermills were distributed widely, reflecting the features of a largely rural craft manufacturing base (Fig. 12.6a). Windmills were particularly numerous along sections of the west coast, whilst watermills lined streams that flowed from elevated areas such as the Massif Central. The pattern of forges and furnaces reflected the distribution of ores, charcoal and running water, especially on the northern and eastern margins of the Paris Basin

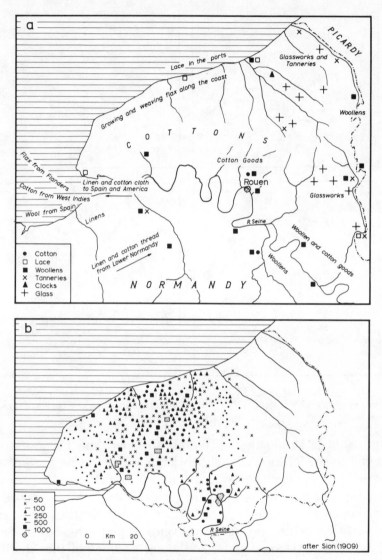

FIG. 12.5. Industry in Upper Normandy (a) craft activities in the eighteenth century; (b) cotton workers in Seine-Inférieure 1863 (by *commune*).

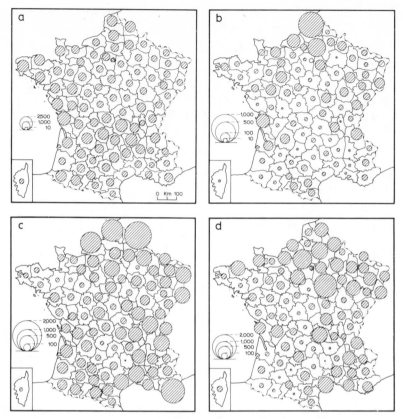

FIG. 12.6. Industrial plant at the time of the old cadaster (by *département*):
(a) windmills and watermills; (b) forges and furnaces; (c) factories; (d) other
industrial buildings.

(Fig. 12.6b). Production of metals for maritime purposes contributed to the location of such works in Atlantic *départements* that
contained important ports. Nascent industrial regions emerge
from Fig. 12.6c which shows factories (*usines*)—as opposed to
workshops—that were engaged in producing textiles and other
commodities, with very large concentration in the Nord, Seine
Valley, Paris, Alsace, Lyons, and along sections of the Mediterranean coast. Remaining types of industrial building were located
in close relation to the general distribution of population, with
large numbers being found in the more densely peopled northern
third of the country (Fig. 12.6d). These maps capture patterns
which were to be modified substantially after mid-century, as the

countryside slowly lost many of its manufacturing functions to the benefit of emerging urban centres which strengthened their grasp on French industrial production and on the nation's human geography.

Advances in Transport and the Emergence of a National Economic System

The improvement and integration of the national economy formed an important challenge for a succession of French monarchs and administrators during the seventeenth, eighteenth and later centuries. Extensive and efficient systems of internal communication by both land and water were essential prerequisites for these objectives to be met. Important progress was achieved in the two centuries prior to the Revolution and the impact of improved communications was undoubtedly great along particular routes and in particular areas of France. However, vast sections of the country remained in relative isolation with the physical problems associated with moving goods over poor roads or along treacherous waterways being compounded by the numerous dues and tolls that had to be paid at internal custom posts during the *ancien régime*.

In spite of serious deficiencies many stretches of new road were constructed, old roads were maintained and canals were dug between 1599 and 1789. The first date is important since it marks the reorganization by Henri IV of the *Service des Ponts et Chaussées* as a centralized body. In the early seventeenth century Sully was appointed Surveyor General, at the end of the century Colbert created the post of Highways Commissioner, and in 1716 the Highways Department became an autonomous unit. The *Ecole des Ponts et Chaussées* that was founded in 1747 was to survive all the later political upheavals and continued to train engineers to implement plans for a system of Royal or national highways that was to link Paris with each of the provinces of France. Many of these highways were characterized by straightness, not only because of the direct inheritance or more subtle influence of Roman roads but because a decree of 1705 had stipulated that main highways should be made in straight sections, ignoring land holdings and relief.

The 'great spiderweb around Paris, upon which the macadamed network of the nineteenth century is traced', was constructed gradually and deliberately as monarchs and administrators were fully conscious that they were reinforcing the administrative, commercial, and intellectual primacy of Paris (Duby and Mandrou, 1964, p. 366). But even when due allowances are made for the technical processes of surveying and paving,

> '. . . this gigantic work was executed less by an extraordinary financial effort than by the affliction of the French peasant. Between 1726 and 1738, there was gradually and cautiously instituted a Royal *corvée* which lasted until 1776 despite unanimous complaints and protests' (Duby and Mandrou, 1964, p. 367).

Peasants were required to supply each year between 10 and 30 days of labour along with digging tools, wagons, and beasts of burden, for the specific task of road construction. On the basis of this inequitable system an estimated 25,000 km of main roads had been built or restored between 1740 and 1780 to establish a network of which even Arthur Young was envious. Provincial *intendants* vied with each other to put centrally conceived programmes into practice, with the Breton system constructed during the

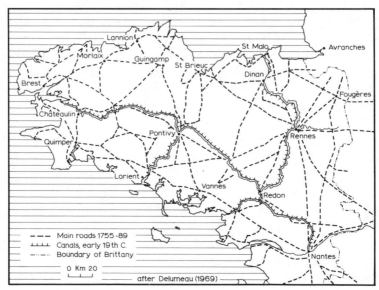

FIG. 12.7. New highways and canals in Brittany during the eighteenth and early nineteenth centuries.

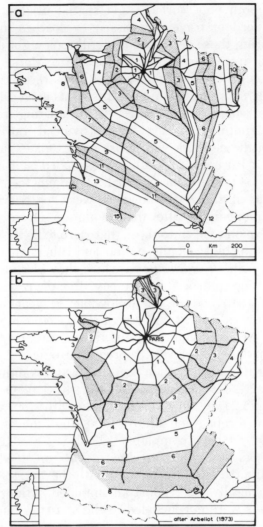

FIG. 12.8. Approximate time taken to travel between Paris and the provinces
in (a) 1765 and (b) 1780.

administration of the Duc d'Aiguillon being particularly worthy of
mention. At first the capital of the *généralité* (Rennes) was linked to
major towns such as Vitré, Brest, Saint-Malo, Nantes and Vannes,
and then after 1755 these towns were linked one to another (Fig.
12.7). However, in spite of important achievements in the second
half of the eighteenth century, the system of Royal highways

exemplified both poor surfaces and spatial incompleteness. The maximum speed of travel by passenger coaches increased substantially during those decades but it still took eight days to travel by fast coach from Paris to Toulouse or to Marseilles in 1780, admittedly by contrast with 15 and 12 days respectively in 1765 (Arbellot, 1973) (Fig. 12.8). Peasants' carts moved along sections of the network much more slowly. Axes radiating from capital to province did nothing to ease inter-provincial journeys and the filling out of the network with cross routes for example between Bordeaux, La Rochelle, and other ocean ports and interior cities formed a major task for the first half of the nineteenth century.

Main roads of military importance were constructed especially in the West immediately after the Revolution. Decrees in 1811 and 1813 divided main roads into those that were to be the financial and practical responsibility of the nation and others that were to be maintained by the *départements* in which they were located. Road improvement recommenced vigorously after the restoration of the Bourbons in 1815 and in the following 30 years 7000 km of national highways and 22,000 km of *département* highways were constructed (Milward and Saul, 1973) (Fig. 12.9). Nonetheless, 'Royal' or 'national' highways represented only 4·03 per cent of the total length of French main road and water communications in 1837 (Ministère des Travaux Publics, 1840–42). Only 3134 km were paved and 21,582 km were surfaced with stones. Substantial stretches needed repair and almost 4000 km of the 34,511 km network had not yet been completed (Table 12.1). Highways that were the responsibility of the *départements* involved 36,578 km but were of limited extent compared with the 771,458 km of local roads that generally were poorly maintained. Minor rural roads and farm roads were not included in the statistics but such tracks were in a deplorable state almost universally. Legislation of 21st May 1836 made the maintenance of local roads the compulsory responsibility of local authorities but this was slow to come into effective operation and should be seen more as a declaration of intent. It was only from the 1850s that substantial progress was made in reducing the isolation of rural *communes*, with further achievements being made after legislation in 1868 which granted financial aid to rural communities that could not afford to pay for essential road improvements (Price, 1975).

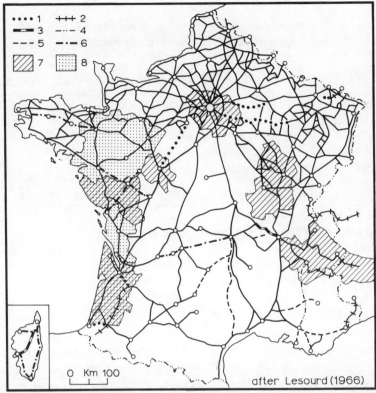

FIG. 12.9. Development of the network of main roads 1780–1850. Route (1) improved, (2) built during the reign of Napoleon I; (3) improved, (4) built during the Restoration of 1814–15; (5) improved, (6) built during the July Monarchy 1830–48; (7) *départements* where programmes of road building were accelerated during the reign of Napoleon I; (8) *départements* recognized in the order of 12 November 1838 as being in particular need of strategic highways.

In addition to 842,545 km of roads and highways (Table 12.1), France contained 8966 km of navigable rivers and 3699 km of canals in 1837. The Seine, Loire, Garonne and Rhône were navigable over considerable distances, although sailing was often difficult for ocean-going vessels having to cope with vagaries of tide, wind and shifting shoals. To gain mastery of these water-courses proved an ongoing challenge over the centuries, as Roger Dion (1934) has demonstrated so eloquently for the Val de Loire. However, differing perceptions of management problems along these watercourses and the often conflicting views of farmers, merchants and sailors meant that navigation conditions were far

Table 12.1

Roads and Navigable Waterways (1837)
according to the Statistique Générale

	Length (km)	% of total	In good condition	In need of repair	Still to be completed
Royal Highways	34,509	4·04	24,716	5851	3942
Département Highways	36,578	4·27	22,228	5214	9136
Local Roads	771,458	90·20			
Navigable Rivers	8966	1·05			
Canals	3699	0·43			
TOTAL	855,210	100·00			

Royal Highways in good condition:
paved 3134 km, with surface of stones 21,582 km;
in need of repair:
paved 746 km, with surface of stones 5105 km;
still to be paved 175 km, still to be surfaced with stones 3767 km.

from ideal. Small vessels made use of many other rivers but they were, of course, significant lacunae in the pattern of natural water-courses. From the early years of the sevnteenth century this was being complemented by canals which were cut across intervening watersheds. The first was excavated south of the Loing valley from 1604 to 1643 and allowed small vessels to move between the Loing and Seine navigation systems. Thus, for example, timber was carried on rafts or simple barges from the upper Loing basin to Paris where these 'vessels' (as well as their cargoes) were dismantled and used for construction purposes or as firewood, since this was easier and cheaper than attempting to convey them back upstream (Fig. 12.10). In the second half of the seventeenth century the Canal du Midi (1666–87) connected the Garonne with the Mediterranean and during the eighteenth century a number of other short junction canals were excavated to give a total of 1000 km in use on the eve of the Revolution.[2] Progress was slow until the Restoration but in the years 1815–48 the length of canals in France was extended from *c.* 1100 km to more than 4000 km (Fig. 12.11).[3]

As well as traversing watersheds, canals were being dug to run parallel to stretches of river that were particularly difficult to

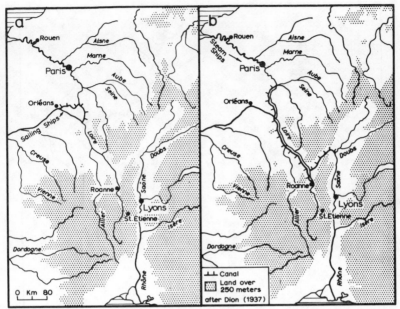

FIG. 12.10. Canal links between the basins of the Loire and the Seine
(a) c. 1700; (b) 1838.

navigate. For example, the decision was taken in 1807 for a lateral
canal to be dug alongside the Loire between Digoin and Briare but
work was not ordered to begin until the law of 14th August 1822
and was completed in 1838 (Dion, 1937). By that time the rail
link had been constructed from the mines of Saint Etienne to
Roanne via Andrézieux and the new lateral canal allowed an easier
movement of coal from central France to the capital city (Fig.
12.10).

It was indeed central France, and more precisely the area of
Saint Etienne/Rive-de-Gier, that formed the cradle for French railways. The first concession was granted in 1823 for horsedrawn
coal-wagons to operate on rails over a distance of 21 km between
Saint Etienne and Andrézieux on the Loire. This line came into
operation in 1827 and was followed by another between Saint
Etienne, Givors and Lyons which was authorized in 1826 and completed in 1832 (Fig. 12.12). It operated steam locomotives and
carried passengers as well as goods. In fact, steam traction had been
first used on a part of that line in 1830. During the following 10

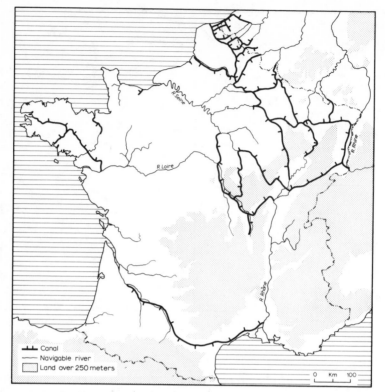

Fᴵɢ. 12.11. Canals and navigable waterways in the late nineteenth century.

years a series of local lines linking mines, canals and rivers, were constructed, for example between Andrézieux and Roanne in 1833 (running parallel to the shallow and hazardous Loire) and between Alès and Beaucaire. The highly influential line between Paris and Saint Germain was built in 1837, contributing to a total of 573 km of track by 1841. These sections were fragmented achievements and had been constructed without any 'grand design' and in the face of powerful opposition from canal operators and from many industrialists. A national system of trunk lines had been in fact conceived by Legrand, head of the Highways Department, as early as 1830 but his plan was not to receive formal approval until the decisive law of 1842 which provided for 3600 km of lines between Paris and six provincial destinations, and from Lyons to Mulhouse via Dijon, and from Bordeaux to Marseilles via Toulouse.[4] The Paris–Orléans and Paris–Rouen lines were opened in 1843 but the

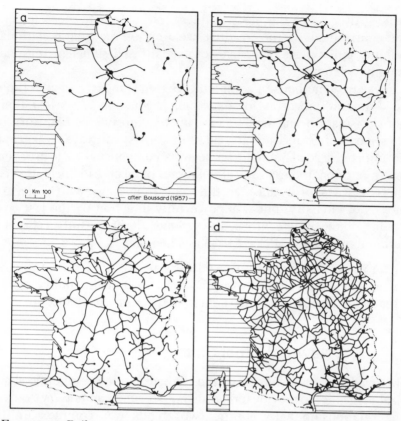

FIG. 12.12. Railway network in (a) 1840; (b) 1850; (c) 1860; (d) 1870.

execution of the plan did not come until the Second Empire after great debate on the precise routes to be followed.[5] Six great regional companies were created by 1859 and the rail network grew from 3554 km in 1851 to 8681 km in 1858, 17,440 km in 1870 and 19,600 km in 1875. The Freycinet Plan was approved in 1878 to join by rail every *préfecture* and *sous-préfecture* to Paris and accordingly the network increased from 26,327 km in 1882 to 36,800 km in 1900 and 43,731 km in 1910.

In addition, local narrow-gauge lines (*chemins de fer d'intérêt local*) were constructed from early times to reach 1800 km in 1881 and 9331 km in 1911. Trains reached towns high in the mountains and villages deep in the heart of the country but the centrality of Paris in the mainline system was undeniable with east–west cross-links being much more slow and complicated than journeys to

Paris.[6] After 1844 the electric telegraph added another element that contributed to the gradual welding of the single national economy in the place of a series of partially self-sufficient regional economic systems.

These new methods of communication in some cases had a rapid and dramatic impact as for example, production areas lost their historic isolation and had to face up to vigorous competitors in other parts of France or abroad. But canals, railways, telegraph and improved roads should be seen as components in a broader, slower but nonetheless radical amalgam of changes which affected different parts of France at different times and with differing degrees of intensity, but was powerfully in action by the last two decades of the nineteenth century. One might usefully echo the caution expressed by Price (1975) as he noted:

'. . . the responsiveness of producers and consumers to the new situation should not be exaggerated . . . it seems unlikely . . . that a genuine national market existed before the 1880s' (p. 37).

A New Industrial State?

The gradual establishment of the unified national economic space paralleled the more widespread use of steam as an energy source. The relationship between the two trends was complex in the extreme, with causes and consequences becoming interdigitated in a seemingly inextricable fashion. Generation of steam to drive industrial machinery required massive imports of primary energy in the form of coal and it is indeed the coalfield landscapes of France that bear some of the most persistent 'scars' of nineteenth-century development. In fact, coal consumption in France outstripped production throughout the century so that the proportion supplied from domestic mines varied from 15 per cent to 75 per cent of the volume consumed. On the eve of the Revolution 600,000 tons were being mined each year, with over two-thirds coming from areas around Valenciennes and Saint Etienne. A further 240,000 tons were imported, with 180,000 tons from Britain and 50,000 tons from Belgium (Léon, 1970). Steam engines were not as yet in use in France but coal had been employed as a fuel since the 1730s in branches of the metallurgical, chemical, textile and sugar refining industries of Alsace and by the 1870s was also popular in these sectors in other progressive areas around Rouen and Saint Etienne. In the 110 years after 1789 domestic coal production was to rise to 33,000,000 tons annually, with the speed of growth accelerating markedly after mid-century (Table 12.2).

Table 12.2

French Coal Production and Steam Engines

Coal Production (million tons)				Number of Steam Engines	
1789	0·60	1860	8·30	1818	150–200
1815	0·88	1862	10·00	1830	570
1820	1·00	1867	12·70	1839	2,450
1824	1·10	1869	13·40	1848	6,000
1830	1·86	1886	20·00	1870	28,000
1840	3·00	1897	30·00	1900	84,000
1850	4·40	1899	33·00		

The first prototype steam engine in France had been experimented with in 1779 for pumping water from the Seine and it was not until 1811 that steam engines were applied to textile production (Fohlen, 1970). But from 1815 numbers increased rapidly, reaching 6000 by mid-century and 84,000 by 1900 (Table 12.2). Admittedly, the start was slow since old-established water-powered industries in hilly areas attempted to develop their existing technology to a higher degree of perfection rather than turn to steam and coal.

The folded and faulted coal deposits of the long, narrow trough of Saint Etienne/Rive de Gier had been mined on a small scale since the fourteenth century and during the seventeenth and eighteenth centuries this was the most productive coal area of France, with 20,000 tons being mined in 1715 and c. 300,000 tons at the end of the century (Gille, 1947) (Fig. 12.13). Environmental conditions in this mountainous watershed were harsh and moving coal to the Loire and Rhône river systems required hazardous journeys by wagon or muleback (Pounds and Parker, 1957). Saint Etienne also supplied coal to Paris via the valley of Loing and the early canals cut through the Loire/Loing interfluve. But the journey was difficult and it was customary to wait until the

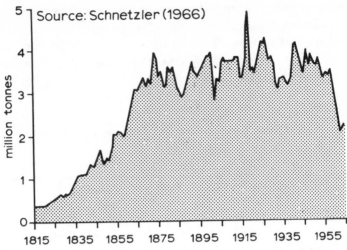

F IG. 12.13. Coal output from the Saint-Etienne/Rive-de-Gier field, 1815–1966.

river level was at its highest before making the journey down-stream. Construction of the early railways and the canal alongside the Loire opened the mines of Saint Etienne to a much wider market, with output rising from *c.* 500,000 tons in 1824 to 1,000,000 in 1835 and 1,640,000 tons in 1852. Annual production doubled during the remainder of the century but stabilized at be-tween 3–4,000,000 tons, with an all-time peak of 4,918,000 tons being recorded in 1918 (Perrin, 1937; Schnetzler, 1966). Saint Etienne undoubtedly lost ground and markets to the Nord/Pas-de-Calais coalfield but the mines of central France had the locational advantage of being distant from the vulnerable northern and north-eastern frontiers and as a result experienced short-lived periods of recovery during wartime when production was dis-rupted in coalfields further north.[7] In fact, Saint Etienne was one of the mushrooming palaeotechnic wonders of the nineteenth century, supporting a range of industries that included armaments, glass, machinery, metallurgy and textiles, and a population that grew in the coalfield *communes* alone from 56,000 in 1806 to 264,000 in 1881.[8] Further north, lie the coal deposits of the Blanzy/Le Creusot depression which is furrowed by the Canal de Bourgogne and has access to the Saône, to the Loire, and also to Paris. Mining began in the sixteenth century but it was not until the Schneider family recommenced coal-fired metallurgical production at Le

Creusot in 1836 that the coal basin entered a real growth phase. It produced about one-tenth of national output each year for the remainder of the century.[9]

However it was in the *départements* of the Nord and the Pas-de-Calais that the real success story of French coal-mining was enacted during the nineteenth century (Trénard, 1972). This forms the westernmost section of the chain of coal deposits from the Ruhr, through Aachen and Wallonia to northern France (Wrigley, 1961). Belgian coal miners, and associated industrial workers had traditions of production extending back to medieval times, whereas coal-mining in northern France was much more recent (Geiger, 1974). Poor quality coal had been discovered near Valenciennes in 1720 with useful deposits being found at Anzin, near that city, in 1734. Rights of exploitation were claimed by the *Compagnie des Mines d'Anzin* that was founded early in the century, but the real start began in 1757 when the reorganized company in the hands of the 'pit barons' firmly established its rights to control mining. On the eve of the Revolution it was already employing 4000 workers in 37 pits and was producing 300,000 tons—half of the national output. As Gillet (1969) explains, the period between Revolution and Restoration was one of stagnation for the northern coalfield.

'When the coming and going of the armies had stopped, the annexation of Belgium seems to have delayed . . . development; free entry of Belgian coal and certainty of being able to count on the important resources of the Liège, Charleroi and Mons fields, did not encourage the development and extension of a field only beginning its convalescence. Output at Anzin stagnated' (p. 180).

But this period served as one of consolidation and extension of concessions for Anzin. By 1830 the company owned about a quarter of French coal output and had a virtual monopoly of production in the north. With 5000 workers it was probably the largest centralized industrial organization in France, and its owners included some of the greatest names in French and Belgian commerce, politics and society. Casimir Perier, first minister after the July Revolution (1830), was the leading figure in the company during the 1820s.[10]

Prospecting fever reached new heights between 1834 and 1839, with large investments and important scientific enquiries taking place not only in northern France but elsewhere in the country and in southern Belgium.

In fact, the north was producing only about one quarter of French coal output in 1846–47, being surpassed by Saint Etienne/ Rive de Gier. Nevertheless, by then the potential for take-off in northern coalmining was becoming stronger. The urban monster of Paris was hungry for coal, as were the new railways and steam engines; the Saint Quentin Canal, begun in 1810 was completed by 1830 and gave access to the Oise waterway; and, above all else, in 1847 the concealed coal deposits of the Pas de Calais were discovered to extend westwards beyond Douai. Pits, railways, roads and *corons* obliterated sections of the richly-farmed landscapes and interdigitated with the fields that remained.[11] From an output of 1,000,000 tons of coal at mid-century, the yields of the Nord/Pas-de-Calais rose to 20,000,000 in 1891 out of a national total of 33,000,000 tons, with the northern share galloping from 24 per cent in 1850 to 30 per cent in the 1860s, 44 per cent in 1880, 54 per cent in 1890 and 61 per cent in 1899 (Table 12.3). Within the

Table 12.3

Coal Production in the Nord/Pas-de-Calais 1872–1913 (million tons)

	Nord	Pas-de-Calais	Regional Total
1872	3·2	2·6	5·8
1880	3·7	4·8	8·5
1900	5·7	14·6	20·3
1913	6·8	20·6	27·4

north the share from the concealed coalfield of the Pas-de-Calais gained ever-increasing dominance after 1880. The 'Black Country' of the coalfield flourished along with the textile cities of Lille-Roubaix-Tourcoing-Armentières and the metallurgical towns in the Schelde and Sambre valleys as the third component of the northern conurbation. The coal companies in this region continued to draw the major part of their shareholders and directors from the bourgeoisie of Cambrai, Valenciennes and Lille-Roubaix-Tourcoing. As Gillet (1969) explains:

'. . . it was under the banner of liberalism that the coalmining companies of the Nord and the Pas-de-Calais developed, although certain important decisions, especially about transport and wages, were made collectively by all the companies, or by the most powerful companies of the fields' (p. 200).

By comparison with trends of manufacturing location in Britain, Belgium and Germany, the coalfields of France were surprisingly unattractive for key industrial sectors, such as textiles and metallurgy, and the earlier the period one examined in the nineteenth century, the more appropriate that statement would be (Fig. 12.14). For the greater part of the first half of the century the

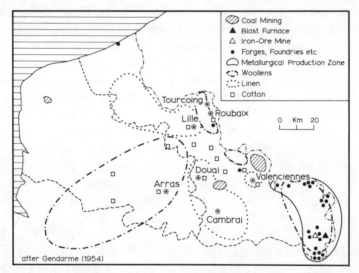

FIG. 12.14. Industrial locations in the Nord/Pas-de-Calais in the early nineteenth century.

traditional systems of technology and the old locations of the iron industry were indubitably dominant. Most deposits of iron ore were not close to coal supplies so that, with high transport costs and the firmly entrenched belief that charcoal iron was superior to coke-produced metal, the site features of the *ancien régime* retained their importance into the nineteenth century (Chollat-Varagnac, 1969). Indeed, the number of charcoal furnaces continued to increase to reach a peak of 433 in 1837 (Fohlen, 1970). Pounds and Parker (1957) recognized the survival of the ancient order until mid-century, although from the 1830s onwards this pattern began to diminish in importance as experiments with coke-fired smelting took place at Hayange (c. 1820), Le Creusot (1836), and later at Valenciennes, Anzin, Saint Etienne, and at other places. Rocketing demands for rails and iron for building wagons and locomotives after 1852 generated very rapid expansion in coke-smelting and at approximately the same time new techniques of cheap steel production were being perfected. Thus, in 1856 Bessemer obtained a patent for his converter and started production at Imphy in Nièvre *département*. This necessitated high quality iron ore being imported from Spain and in like fashion, rich ores were needed for open-hearth acid steel-making and were shipped from Cumberland, North Africa and Sweden as well as from Spain. New steel-making locations in this 'coastal phase' included Boulogne, Calais, Marseilles, the Gironde and the Loire estuary (Pounds and Parker, 1957). The years between 1878 and 1914 witnessed yet another major shift in industrial location as the 'orefield phase' of steel-making became firmly established in Lorraine (truncated by the post-Franco–Prussian war frontier of 1871) and to a lesser extent in western Normandy. The Gilchrist-Thomas basic method of steel-making was perfected in 1878 and allowed phosphorus to be removed from the thin *minette* ores of Lorraine (Clapham, 1961; Martin, 1957; Prêcheur, 1963). National output of iron ore rose enormously, from 714,000 tons in 1833, to 1,250,000 in 1845, 4,000,000 tons in 1870, 7,000,000 tons in 1904, and 22,000,000 tons in 1913. In that fateful year, on the eve of the Great War 20,000,000 tons came from the *département* of Meurthe-et-Moselle, mainly from the north-eastern corner between Briey and Longwy. To quote Clapham (1961):

'One understands why the German industrial expansions of 1915 wanted to retain that north-east corner. They would have crippled the French iron industry, in all probability for ever, and guaranteed their own supplies of raw material' (p. 239).

By this time, traditional metallurgical locations had disappeared, albeit, after a lingering death, so that the lineaments of modern patterns of production were clearly in evidence (Prêcheur, 1963).

However, rather than metallurgy it was the textile industries of

France that were the driving force in the industrialization and development of the country for the most of the period 1815–70 and cotton was by far the most progressive sector (Milward and Saul, 1973, p. 316). In several parts of France the manufacture of cotton cloth spread into the countryside, replacing traditional fabrics such as linen and wool in the rural workshops of Picardy, Flanders and Brittany. Annual imports of raw cotton increased from 19,000 tons c. 1820 to 86,000 tons c. 1870, with the United States emerging as the dominant source of supply in the place of the Mediterranean countries and Brazil, which had been important early in the century.[12] Le Havre emerged as the cotton port *par excellence* and ensured that raw cotton was available more cheaply in Upper Normandy than around Mulhouse in Alsace. Nonetheless, Alsace was undoubtedly the more technologically advanced area and raw cotton was available at more moderate prices following the construction of the railway to Mulhouse in 1852. Widespread adoption of steam-powered machinery in cotton spinning led to important locational shifts as water-powered sites were abandoned in favour of points where supplies of coal were readily available. Thus, in north-eastern France, the main centres of cotton-spinning shifted from the upper valleys of the Vosges to lower areas in Alsace where costs of coal supply had been reduced by the opening of the Rhône–Rhine Canal in 1832, which gave access to Le Creusot and Blanzy, and of the Marne–Rhine Canal in 1854, which enabled Saarland coal to arrive by water. Already, by the late 1830s the largest manufacturing enterprises on the Continent (after the Cockerill metallurgical works in Belgium) were the cotton mills of Alsace.

The cotton industry of Upper Normandy demonstrated very clearly the contrasting rates of technological adaptation in the spinning and weaving sectors. Mechanization of spinning through the use of water and later of steam power had the effect of strengthening, albeit temporarily, the weaving economy of the villages of the Pays de Caux, since that sector had not yet been mechanized. Sion (1909) reports the recruitment of workers from other parts of northern France to swell the army of 30–50,000 handloom weavers that could be found in the countryside north of Rouen in the 1830s and 40s. However, mechanized looms had begun to make their appearance in Seine-Inférieure in the late 1820s, so that by mid-century rural weaving was seriously threatened. Considerable numbers of Cauchois weavers survived for a couple more decades (Fig. 12.5b) but by the end of the century very few remained, and as a result a massive flood of rural out-migrants was unleashed in the direction of urban areas surrounding Rouen. Mechanization of the woollen and linen industries were slower than in the cotton sector, but by the final quarter of the century cloth-making, in all its branches, had become a mechanized largely urban activity (Crouzet, 1970). The loss of Alsace (and in particular of Mulhouse) following the Franco–Prussian war, reduced the 5,300,000 spindles of the French cotton industry by 1,500,000 and strengthened the relative hold of the north and of the towns around Roanne in the national picture (Forrester, 1921). In spite of changes in location, the urban nature of textile production and most other elements of manufacturing was undeniable (Fig. 12.15).

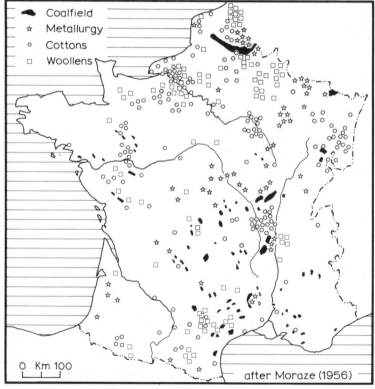

Coalfield
Metallurgy
Cottons
Woollens

0 Km 100

after Moraze (1956)

FIG. 12.15. Distribution of leading aspects of manufacturing c. 1880.

The half-century from 1850 to 1900 contained,

'the great turning point . . . when the steam engine, stationary
or mobile, begins to supply men with an energy whose returns
are quite superior to the energy of running water, men or
horses; in this time, iron, cast-iron and steel, make a growing
place for themselves in architecture as well as in domestic life . . .
this is the birth of contemporary France, whose towns expand
and rural areas begin to become brutally depopulated, where
Paris and the Seine valley acquire 1,000,000 people every 25
years and build more than 150,000 houses at the same rate'
(Duby and Mandrou, 1964, pp. 479–81).

To the observer of *fin de siècle* Lille, Lyons, Rouen, Saint Etienne,
or especially certain parts of Paris, amidst townscapes dominated
by chimneys, factories and artisans' dwellings, it might seem that
France had indeed become a new industrial state (Hudson, 1971).
But these examples, for all their importance, were exceptions to
the rule and Armengaud (1972) warns that the link between
industrialization and urban concentration is far from being as close
and simple as one might believe (p. 189). France remained a profoundly rural nation, a land of peasants with an uneven veneer of
urban-industrial life that made her greatly different from her West
European neighbours (Geiger, 1974). One can do no better than
echo the words of Fohlen (1970).

'France, a country of small and medium peasant proprietors,
reinforced by the Revolution of 1789, did not have a labour
force as abundant and, apparently, as miserable as England. A
continental country, it lacked adequate transportation for a long
time. A country of landowners, it was reluctant to use its capital
in low profit enterprises. The slowness of the French Industrial
Revolution before 1850, and its acceleration after 1850, can thus
be explained. The term "revolution" is ill-suited to a phenomenon that occurred over such a long period of time' (p. 225).

12. Notes

1. The reasons for this 'muffling' are examined critically by Fohlen (1970).
2. These include the Loing Canal 1733; the Somme Lateral Canal 1724–35;
   the Crozat Canal between Saint-Quentin and Chauny 1738; the Neuffossé

Canal between the rivers Lys and Aa 1774; and the Central or Charolais Canal 1783–92.

3. These include the Saint-Quentin Canal (to Cambrai) 1810; the Rhône–Rhine Canal 1790–1832; the Berry Canal 1835; and later in the century the Marne–Rhine Canal 1854; the Canal de l'Est (canalized Meuse) 1878; the Burgundy Canal 1883; the Coalfield, or Saar, Canal 1886; and the Sambre–Oise Canal 1889.

4. Lines radiated from Paris to Valenciennes via Lille; to Le Havre via Rouen; to Strasbourg via Nancy; to Marseilles via Lyons; to Bayonne via Tours and Bordeaux; and to Bourges.

5. For example, Paris–Lyon–Méditerranée 1856; Paris–Bordeaux 1853; Paris–Strasbourg 1853; Paris–Belfort 1858.

6. The location of the mountainous Massif Central made east-west links between Lyons and the west coast ports an expensive and technically difficult problem.

7. The small coalfields of the Massif Central, such as Albi, Brassac, Carmaux and Langéac, also shared in comparable wartime booms.

8. See the discussion in Chapter 13 of urban growth around Saint-Etienne during the nineteenth century.

9. Development of the nascent coalfield of northern Lorraine accelerated after the mid-1840s as railways were constructed and demands for coal and coke increased (Haby, 1965). However, the area passed out of French control as a result of the Treaty of Frankfurt (1871) after the Franco–Prussian War.

10. The technical, financial and organizational changes of the company during the period 1800–33 are discussed in detail by Geiger (1974).

11. Some of the landscape implications of nineteenth-century mining and manufacturing are reviewed in Chapter 13.

12. The American Civil War, of course, brought serious disruptions to the pattern of supply.

12. References

Arbellot, G., La grande mutation des routes de France au milieu du XVIIIe siècle, *Annales, Economies, Sociétés, Civilisations*, 28, (1973), 765–91.

Armengaud, A., La fin des forges catalanes dans les Pyrénées ariégoises, *Annales, Economies, Sociétés, Civilisations*, 8, (1953), 62–6.

Armengaud, A., 'Industrialisation et démographie dans la France du XIXe siècle', in P. Léon et al. (eds), *L'Industrialisation en Europe au XIXe siècle*, Paris, (1972), 187–200.

Boussard, J., *Atlas Historique et Culturel de la France*, Paris (1957).

Chollot-Varagnac, M., 'La mort de la forge de village', *Annales, Economies, Sociétés, Civilisations*, 24, (1969), 391–402.

Clapham, J. H., *Economic Development of France and Germany, 1815–1914*, 4th edition, Cambridge (1961).

Crouzet, F., 'Agriculture et révolution industrielle', *Cahiers d'Histoire*, 241, (1967), 67–86.

Crouzet, F., 'Essai de construction d'un indice de la production industrielle française au XIXe siècle', *Annales, Economies, Sociétés, Civilisations*, 25, (1970), 56–99.

Delumeau, J. (ed), *Historie de la Bretagne*, Toulouse (1969).

Dion, R., *Le Val de Loire*, Tours (1934).

Dion, R., 'A propos du Canal de Briare', *Etudes Rhodaniennes*, 13, (1937), 161–174.

Dion, R., 'Usines et forêts: conséquences de l'ancien emploi du bois comme combustible industriel', *Revue des Eaux et Forêts*, 76, (1938), 771–82.

Dubois, J. J., 'La forêt d'Eu: un cas de permanence des frontières provinciales', *L'Espace Géographique*, 3, (1974), 19–28.

Duby, G. and Mandrou, R., *A History of French Civilisation*, London (1964).

Dunham, A. L., *The Industrial Revolution in France*, New York (1958).

Fischer, W., 'Rural industrialization and population change', *Comparative Studies in Society and History*, 15, (1973), 158–70.

Fohlen, C., 'The industrial revolution in France', in R. E. Cameron (ed) *Essays in French Economic History*, Homewood (1970), 201–225.

Fohlen, C., 'The industrial revolution in France 1700–1914', in C. M. Cipolla (ed) *The Fontana Economic History of Europe: the emergence of industrial societies*—I, London (1973), 7–75.

Forrester, R. B., *The Cotton Industry in France*, Manchester (1921).

Geiger, R. G., *The Anzin Coal Company, 1800–1833*, Newark (1974).

Gendarme, R., *La Région du Nord: essai d'analyse économique*, Paris (1954).

Gille, B., *Les Origines de la grande industrie métallurgique en France*, Paris (1947).

Gille, B., *Les Forges françaises en 1772*, Paris (1960).

Gille, B., *Histoire de la métallurgie*, Paris (1966).

Gillet, M., 'The coal age and the rise of the coalfields in the North and the Pas-de-Calais', in F. Crouzet *et al.* (eds) *Essays in European Economic History 1789–1914*, London (1969), 179–202.

Gillet, M., *Les Charbonnages du Nord de la France au XIXe siècle: étude économique et sociale*, Paris (1973).

Haby, R., *Les Houillères Lorraines et leur région*, Paris (1965).

Henderson, W. O., *The Industrial Revolution on the Continent*, 2nd edition, London (1967).

Hudson, K., *A Guide to the Industrial Archaeology of Europe*, Bath (1971).

Kellenbenz, H., 'Rural industries in the west from the end of the middle ages to the eighteenth century', in P. Earle (ed) *Essays in European Economic History, 1500–1800*, Oxford (1974), 45–88.

Landes, D. S., *The Unbound Prometheus: technological change and industrial development in Western Europe from 1750 to the present*, Cambridge (1969).

Léon, P., 'La réponse de l'industrie', in F. Braudel and E. Labrousse (eds) *Histoire Economique et Sociale de la France*, II (1970), 217–265.

Lesourd, J. A., *Atlas Historique de la France Contemporaine, 1800–1965*, Paris (1966).

Levainville, J., *L'Industrie du fer en France*, Paris (1932).

Marres, P., *Les Grands Causses*, Tours (1935).

Martin, J., 'Location factors in the Lorraine iron and steel industry', (1957), *Transactions of the Institute of British Geographers*, 23, 191–213.

Milward, A. S. and Saul, S. B., *The Economic Development of Continental Europe, 1780–1870*, London (1973).

Ministère des Travaux Publics, *Statistique Générale de la France*, Paris (1840–42).

Moraze, C., *Les Français et la République*, Paris (1956).

Palmade, G., *French Capitalism in the Nineteenth Century* (1962), trans. G. M. Holmes, Newton Abbot (1972).

Perrin, M., *Saint-Etienne et sa région économique*, Tours (1937).

Pijassou, R., 'L'ancienne industrie du fer dans le Périgord septentrional', *Revue Géographique de Pyrénées et du Sud-Ouest*, 27 (1956), 243–68.

Pounds, N. J. G., 'Historical geography of the iron and steel industry of France', *Annals of the Association of American Geographers*, 47 (1957), 3–14.

Pounds, N. J. G. and Parker, W. N., *Coal and Steel in Western Europe*, London (1957).

Prêcheur, C., *La Sidérurgie française*, Paris (1963).

Price, R., *The Economic Modernization of France, 1730–1880*, London (1975).

Rioux, J-P., *La Révolution industrielle: 1780–1880*, Paris (1971).

Schnetzler, J., 'Le basin houillier de la Loire', *Information Géographique*, 30, (1966), 110–118.

Sion, J., *Les Paysans de la Normandie Occidentale*, Paris (1909).

Trénard, L. (ed), *Histoire des Pays-Bas français*, Toulouse (1972).

Woronoff, D., 'Vers une géographie industrielle de la France de l'ancien régime', *Annales, Economies, Sociétés, Civilisations*, 25 (1970), 127–30.

Wrigley, E. A., *Industrial Growth and Population Change: a regional study of the coalfield areas of north-west Europe in the late nineteenth century*, Cambridge (1961).

Zeller, G., 'Industry in France before Colbert', in R. E. Cameron (ed) *Essays in French Economic History*, Homewood (1970), 128–139.

13
Urban Growth, 1500-1900

HUGH D. CLOUT

Introduction

During the final quarter of the eighteenth century and throughout the nineteenth century France experienced important advances in economic development, albeit in a less impressive fashion than in Britain or Germany. Urban growth and rural-urban migration were vital aspects of the complex process of modernization. The proportion of the French population that lived in urban settlements is estimated to have increased from about 10 per cent in the late seventeenth century, to 20 per cent at the Revolution, 25 per cent in 1851, and 40 per cent in 1901 (Dupeux, 1970, 1976). The final figure was lower than those recorded in Britain and Germany where more than half of the total population was living in towns and cities at the beginning of the twentieth century. But the pattern as well as the pace of urban growth was different in France from what was occurring elsewhere in Western Europe. Centralization of French administrative, economic and political decision-making in Paris concentrated power and people in Paris so that by 1901 the capital contained 10 per cent of the national population and was five times more populous than Marseilles, the largest provincial city. France lacked cities and conurbations of a magnitude comparable to those that had developed along the coasts and in coal-based industrial regions of Britain and Germany. In provincial France urban power continued to reside in old-established, medium-sized cities and in smaller market towns.

The establishment of new towns, rural/urban migration, conditions of urban life, and changes in morphology between 1500 and

1800 form guiding themes in the first part of this chapter. This is followed by a consideration of the increasing urban population of nineteenth-century France, the replanning of inner Paris before and during the regime of Prefect Haussmann, the rise of Parisian suburbia, and the growth of administrative and industrial cities in the French provinces.

Urban Growth, 1500–1800

Foundation of New Towns

By far the greater part of French urban growth between 1500 and 1800 involved the expansion of existing towns and cities. However four types of new town were created: ports, fortress towns, settlements close to royal or noble residences, and towns for housing industrial workers.

The rulers of France sought to strengthen the nation's commercial role during this period of overseas expansion. Additional ports and harbours were therefore needed to accommodate larger fleets of naval and commercial vessels. The first example of modern urban creation in France dates from 1516 when François I agreed to the requests of Rouennais citizens that a site for a new harbour should be prospected at the mouth of the Seine to replace the silted port of Harfleur (Jarry, 1953). Excavation for Le Hâvre-de-Grace began in the following year and three years later the project was extended to include a walled town as well as the harbour (Fig. 13.1). In the first half of the seventeenth century Cardinal Richelieu attempted to create another commercial port, this time in southern Brittany. The venture failed but in 1666 the French East India Company selected a site on the Blavet estuary nearby for a new port. At first, Lorient was no more than a modest collection of shacks but within 50 years it had attracted over 7000 inhabitants (Lemée, 1936). Other foundations in the 1660s established new towns and harbours at Brest, Rochefort and Sète on the western and southern coasts of France.

The sixteenth century saw the construction of new fortress towns at Rocroi and Villefranche-sur-Meuse (near Stenay), together with Vitry-le-François (1545) which was built to replace Vitry-en-Perthois which had been burned down. The following century was not only a time of French commercial expansion but

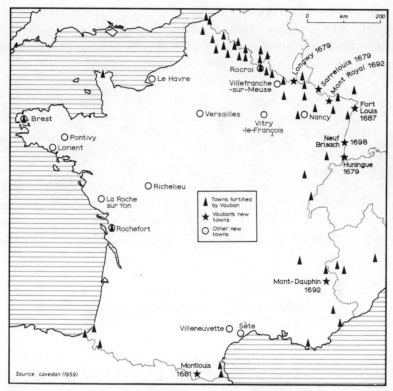

FIG. 13.1. New towns and fortified towns.

also one of territorial aggrandizement. Eight regularly-planned fortress towns were built along national frontiers by Vauban and the morphology of about 50 existing settlements was modified drastically by the construction of moats, walls and other elaborate defences (Decoville-Faller, 1961) (Fig. 13.1).

Settlements established close to castles or palaces formed the third type of new town in France but these were few in number by comparison with their proliferation in the German lands (Lavedan, 1959). The new town of Nancy was founded by the Dukes of Lorraine after the German invasion of 1587 and in 1603 the new town of Charleville was established on the northern frontier. Thirty years later Cardinal Richelieu obtained royal permission to construct a town close to his *château* in Poitou (Stewart, 1952). Migrants were granted privileges such as temporary exemption from taxation in order to encourage them to settle in this new town. The creation of Versailles in 1671 beyond the gates of Louis XIV's palace south-west of Paris provides undoubtedly the best-known example of a residential new town in France which was emulated in many other parts of Europe (Foncin, 1919) (Fig. 13.2).

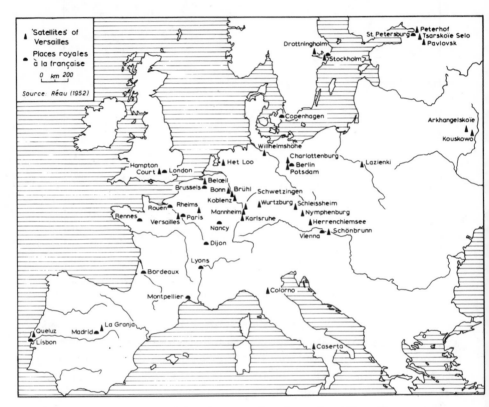

FIG. 13.2. Urban features after the style of Versailles.

Prior to the 'industrial revolution' very few settlements were founded in France with the special purpose of housing industrial workers. However some examples date back to the seventeenth century. Thus in 1666 Colbert established the settlement of la Glacière close to Cherbourg in order to house the employees of a glassworks, and eleven years later permission was granted for a small walled town to be created for Cévenol weavers at Villeneuvette near Clermont-l'Hérault. But these industrial settlements were not a success.

No more than a score of new towns was built in France between 1500 and 1800. Some, such as Brest and Le Havre, later flourished as important ports and provincial centres, but the majority remained small and functioned simply as local market towns. Vauban's town of Mont-Royal on the river Moselle formed an exception, since it survived only five years before being destroyed in 1697. The really significant aspects of urban growth in France between 1500 and 1800 involved the expansion of existing towns and cities as the number of town dwellers increased as a result of migration from the countryside. Towns were not only enlarged to accommodate them but were also embellished, for example, by the construction of *places royales* which were also implanted in other parts of Europe (Fig. 13.2).

Rural/Urban Migration and the Quality of Urban Life

Little is known of rural/urban migration in France before official census-taking began in 1801. However, two basic propositions may be made. First, the larger and more dynamic the urban centre the broader the migration field it would control (Croix, 1974). Thus during the eighteenth century Paris exercised a 'blanketing effect' over migration for up to 300 km from the city. Provincial cities controlled migration fields that were less than half that size (Henry and Courgeau, 1971). This point is illustrated by Fig. 13.3 which depicts migration to Bordeaux for two short periods in the eighteenth century. Second, the volume of migration was inversely related to distance from each attractive urban centre. However the 'concentric rings' of such a simple distance-decay model were distorted into sectors of varying attractiveness because of the unequal distribution of routeways which provided access to the city and the existence of rural areas with differing agricultural systems and population pressures. Outmigration was particularly strong from impoverished, overpopulated areas.[1] Thus, in the 1780s the exceptionally large volume of migrants moving to Bordeaux from the Limousin uplands and from the Pyrenees may have resulted for this reason (Fig. 13.3).

Traditions of temporary or seasonal migration from rural areas with limited local resources also help to explain irregularities in

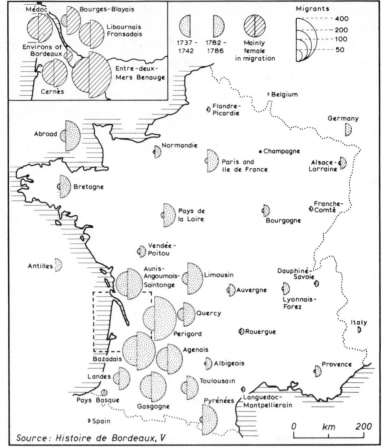

F IG. 13.3. Migration to Bordeaux, 1737–42 and 1782–86.

the distance-decay model of migration. As Fel has already shown
in chapter 7 many peasant farmers moved during the summer
months from the Limousin to work as builders' labourers in Paris
and in other large cities to supplement thereby the meagre returns
derived from working their upland farms. 'Migration systems' of
this kind also operated from the Alps, the Pyrenees and many
other poor rural areas in France (Beteille, 1970). The range of
temporary employment held by rural migrants was large. Figure
7.7 shows the types of job that were taken by migrants from the
Auvergne province of the Massif Central during the summer
months or, in some cases, for periods of a few years (Poitrineau,

1962). Most Auvergnats moved to Paris but some villages dispatched their temporary migrants as far afield as Spain. Recognition of the existence of such historic 'migration systems' and of the diffusion of urban information into the countryside that resulted from their operation helps elucidate the pattern of migration fields that may be defined with more precision for the nineteenth century (Poussou, 1970).

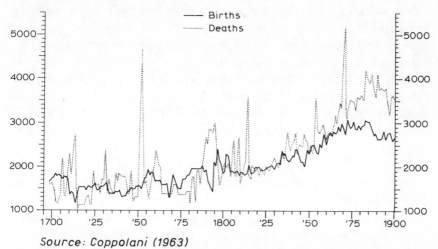

Source: Coppolani (1963)

FIG. 13.4. Natural change in Toulouse, 1700–1900.

Migration from the countryside was essential to simply maintain population numbers in French cities during the eighteenth century. Housing, hygiene and other aspects of urban living were poor throughout the country and the experience of Toulouse where deaths exceeded births for 43 years during the century was not exceptional (Fig. 13.4) (Coppolani, 1963). Crude death rates were high and fluctuating in all French cities, ranging in the case of Toulouse from 27·0 per thous. (1750) to 47·4 per thous. (1790). Infant mortality rates were catastrophic, with averages between 1750 and 1763 varying from 345·0 per thous. in the affluent Toulousain parish of la Dalbade to 639·0 per thous. in the poor parish of Saint-Nicolas. Death rates of all types were grossly inflated during famines and epidemics. Absolute figures and chronological details obviously varied from town to town but Jean-Jacques Rousseau was correct when he observed that '. . . les villes sont le tombeau de l'espèce humaine' (Coppolani, 1963).

Precise causes of migration from the countryside to urban hot-beds of disease are difficult to determine. Undoubtedly town life was perceived as 'attractive' in both social and economic terms. Workshop industrialization before the steam-based 'industrial revolution' offered urban sources of employment but the majority of city workers received meagre wages and had to endure living and working in miserably squalid conditions. Towns existed as places of refuge for the peasantry whose numbers were growing too rapidly in some parts of France to be supported by local agricultural resources. Additional workshops were opened in Toulouse and in other cities during the eighteenth century to employ work forces that had been repelled from the countryside rather than attracted to the town. Sizeable 'floating populations' moved into cities during famines and other agricultural crises only to migrate back to the land when farming conditions returned to normal.

In spite of the atrocious conditions experienced by all but the most affluent, the proportion of town dwellers in France doubled during the eighteenth century from about one-tenth to one-fifth of the total population, which grew from 19 millions to 26 millions over the same period. In absolute terms the number of French townsfolk increased from less than 2 millions to about 5.7 millions. But even so, France was reported to be less urbanized than other West European countries. The English traveller Arthur Young (1931) noted that during the 1780s

> '. . . less than one fourth of the people inhabit towns; a very remarkable circumstance because it is commonly observed that in flourishing countries the half of the nation is found in towns.'

His comment was based on experience of England, Holland and Lombardy which he considered to be more than 50 per cent urbanized.

The distinction between 'urban' settlements and 'rural' ones was a matter of debate in the eighteenth century as at other times.[2] For example, large settlements in Alsace that were commonly recognized as 'towns' contained sizeable groups of farmers and vinegrowers as well as craftsmen and traders (Rochefort, 1960). Thus, in 1756 a statistical enquiry had registered 30 per cent of the province's population as 'urban' but up to half the inhabitants of

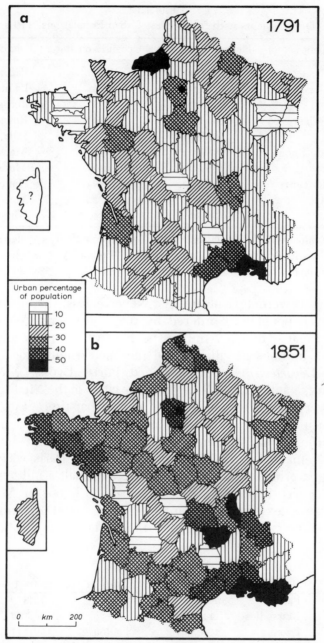

FIG. 13.5. Urban population 1791 and 1851, by *département*.

Table 13.1
Départements with the Largest Urban Populations, 1791

Département	Urban Population	Urban Percentage	Leading City
Seine	556,800	77	Paris
Rhône-et-Loire	215,400	32	Lyons
Gironde	200,000	33	Bordeaux
Seine-Inférieure	184,550	41	Rouen
Nord	168,800	30	Lille
Bouches-du-Rhône	163,200	51	Marseilles
Hérault	108,700	41	Montpellier
Loire-Inférieure	108,100	21	Nantes
Seine-et-Oise	105,900	33	Versailles
Gard	100,700	45	Nîmes

Source: Evaluation of Population des Villes et des Bourgs ordered by the Constituent Assembly 1791, quoted in Young, A. (1931), *Voyages en France en 1787, 1788, 1789*, Paris, trans. H. Sée, p. 858–859.

some towns were agriculturalists. Nevertheless, the evaluation of the French population ordered by the Constituent Assembly in 1791 estimated that 5·7 million people lived in *villes* and *bourgs* and 20·5 millions in villages and the open countryside (Young, 1931). *Départements* that contained Paris, Lyons, Marseilles, Bordeaux, Nantes, Lille, Rouen and the cities of the Mediterranean South were by far the most urbanized at that time (Fig. 13.5a). Too much emphasis should not be placed on the precise numbers included in the Constituent Assembly's evaluation but the general pattern remains valid (Table 13.1). By 1801 Paris was the un-challenged primate city of France with over half a million inhabitants. As such it was five times as large as Lyons or Marseilles which came next in the hierarchy with over 100,000 inhabitants apiece (Garden, 1970) (Table 13.2, Fig. 13.6). They were

Table 13.2
Population of the Ten Largest Cities in France, 1801

Paris	547,736	Nantes	73,879
Marseilles	111,130	Lille	54,756
Lyons	109,500	Toulouse	50,171
Bordeaux	90,992	Strasbourg	49,056
Rouen	87,000	Amiens	40,289

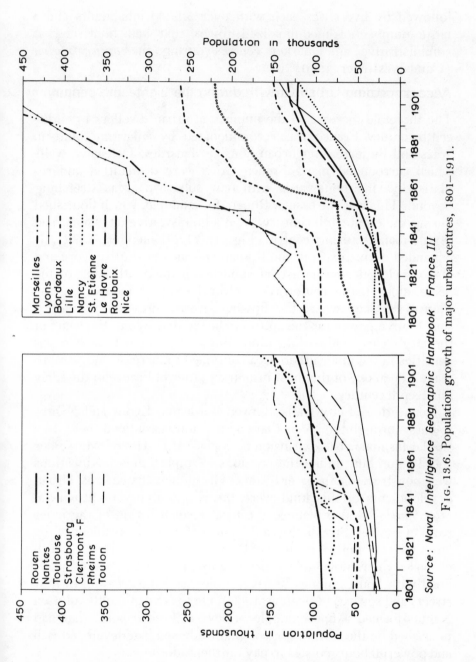

Source: *Naval Intelligence Geographic Handbook France, III*

FIG. 13.6. Population growth of major urban centres, 1801–1911.

followed by five cities each with over 50,000 inhabitants and a large number of medium-sized towns that had flourished as administrative and market centres during the *ancien régime* (Combès-Monier, 1970).

Accommodating Urban Growth during the Eighteenth century

The threefold increase in the number of urban dwellers in eighteenth-century France was accommodated by enlarging built-up areas and by increasing urban housing densities. Defensive walls which surrounded many French cities were dismantled and replaced by ring boulevards with new suburban areas stretching beyond. This was the case at Rouen, for example, which flourished during the eighteenth century as an administrative city, port, and textile-manufacturing centre (Fig. 13.7) (Boulenger, 1936). It expanded outwards from the Roman and medieval urban core and also developed new industrial suburbs on the south bank of the Seine, along major routeways, and in the valleys incised into the Plateau de Caux where fast-flowing streams provided the necessary motive power for the cotton industry that was at the heart of the city's early industrialization. But at the same time housing densities in the inner urban area continued to increase and were to make Rouen one of the most insanitary cities of France in the early nineteenth century.

Demolition of city walls allowed Bordeaux, Lyons and Nantes to burst through the bonds that had previously confined them. In a similar fashion urban expansion took place at Le Havre, Marseilles and Toulon but, unlike the previous examples, new fortifications were constructed at greater distances from their city centres. Urban developments of this kind were the responsibility of provincial *intendants* who also planned the total reconstruction of the inner parts of Rennes, Strasbourg and Nantes. The embellishment of the latter city stemmed from the Plan du Ceineray (1761) which proposed the removal of the city's ramparts, construction of quays lined with houses along the river Loire, and the creation of new streets and squares (Cabanne, 1967). On the eve of the Revolution Nantes formed a fine example of several French ports that had flourished on the fortunes of colonial trade and had developed rich and powerful bourgeoisies to pay for their adornment.

Paris took its full share of the urban remodelling that took place

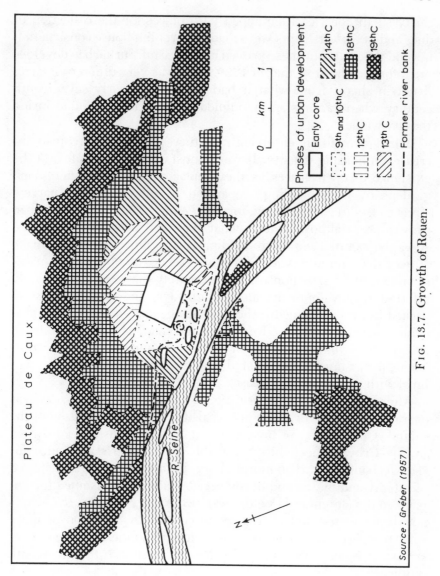

FIG. 13.7. Growth of Rouen.

in France prior to 1789 (Hautecoeur, 1961). Two rings of walls were constructed in less than two centuries, with one being built during the reign of Louis XIII and the walls of the *Fermiers Généraux* dating from 1785–87 (Lavedan, 1959). This latter wall was 23 km long and was pierced by seventeen large gates and thirty small ones, each equipped with offices for the collection of dues and taxes. Attempts were made to prohibit house construction beyond the walls but these proved unsuccessful. Surburban development forged ahead so that in 1789 Paris was very different in size, if not in shape, from what it had been in the early seventeenth century when gardens and ploughed fields were still found inside the city walls.

Urban growth in eighteenth century Paris also involved increases in housing density. It was almost as if Parisians feared the existence of open spaces as they replaced courtyards, fields and gardens by high buildings separated by alleyways and narrow streets. Eighteenth-century formulae for accommodating urban growth were almost exactly what they had been in the Middle Ages. Not until 1783 were building restrictions imposed to make 30 feet the minimum width for new streets and 60 feet the maximum height for new houses. Unfortunately these regulations only referred to developments along highways, and so tall, densely-packed houses continued to be built in the spaces which remained behind street frontages. However some changes took place in the urban plan of inner Paris prior to the Revolution. The Ile-Saint-Louis, for example, was created from two smaller islands and was lined with new quays and houses.

After the fall of the *ancien régime* the *Comité des Artistes* was charged in 1793 to draw up proposals for the transformation of the capital. Confiscation of property that had previously been owned by the Crown, the nobility and the clergy offered a chance for radical changes in urban morphology. In fact the land was disposed of rapidly and by the end of the decade had been consumed for unplanned development (Poète, 1941–45). The *Plan des Aristes* was not implemented and all that resulted was the addition of more suburbs much as had been done before. Significant plans to restructure the city were not to come until well into the nineteenth century.

Urban Growth in the Nineteenth Century

Increases in Urban Population

The first official census of population for the whole of France was conducted in 1801. This heralded quinquennial collections of data which, with a few exceptions, were to operate throughout the century. As a result of these censuses, natural changes, rural/urban migration, and increases in the number of town residents may be quantified more reliably than for earlier times. The fundamental problem of distinguishing 'urban' centres from villages and other forms of 'rural' settlement was not resolved administratively until 1846 when *communes* with more than 2000 inhabitants in their chief settlements (*chefs-lieux*) were recognized as being 'urban'. The pattern of urbanization at mid-century captured a situation when a quarter of the nation lived in towns and cities. The administrative definition of 'urban' necessarily varied from what had been used in the estimates of 1791, but *départements* containing Paris, Lyons, Marseilles, Toulon and the small towns of the eastern section of the Massif Central were more than half urbanized by 1851 (Fig. 13.5). Other very significant areas of urban development existed close to the Belgian frontier, in the inner Paris Basin, along the Rhône corridor, in the Midi, and in parts of Brittany.

Living conditions remained poor throughout the nineteenth century for the greater proportion of the French urban population which was housed in crowded centres of old provincial cities and in rapidly-growing industrial towns. Deaths continued to outnumber births during the first half of the century at Caen, Orléans, Rennes, Rouen, Strasbourg, Toulon and Toulouse (Pouthas, 1956). Amiens, Lyons, Marseilles and Nancy experienced short but insignificant periods of natural increase.[3] French towns and cities continued to devour population as they had done in the past. In Coppolani's words, urban centres were simply '. . . les villes mangeuses des hommes' (1963, p. 37).

Conditions were particularly poor in industrial communities such as Rouen where crude death rates ranged from 33·0 per thous. to 37·0 per thous. even during the second half of the century (Sion, 1909). They were thus far ahead of average rates in Paris (26·0 per thous.) over the same period. Two-fifths of the children born in Rouen died before they reached three years of age. Tuberculosis was rampant in all the cotton manufacturing towns of the Basse Seine, resulting from a combination of long hours of factory work in poor conditions, low wages which restricted the quality and range of diet, and sadly inadequate housing. Densities of up to ten people per room were reported in the gravely-overcrowded

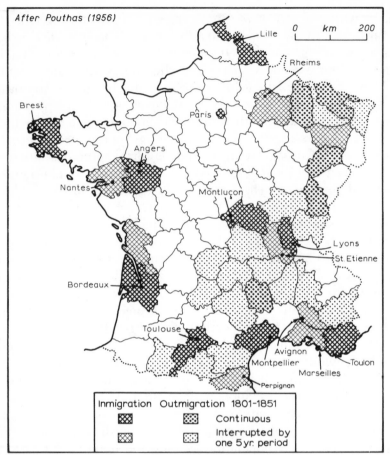

FIG. 13.8. Trends of internal migration 1801–51 (by *département*).

quarters of Rouen along the Robec valley and between the cathedral
and the church of Saint-Maclou. Living conditions in the city and
its surrounding communities were amongst the worst in France,
being surpassed only by the textile-producing towns of Lille,
Roubaix and Tourcoing which formed 'a human ants' nest' next to
the Belgian border (Blanchard, 1906).

Increases in urban population continued to be produced by
immigration rather than by natural gain but the average diameter
of migration fields increased as the century progressed. Quickening
urban industrialization and city reconstruction demanded ever-
growing supplies of labour which the cities were unable to produce.

As in previous centuries, rural/urban migration continued to provide the solution. Railway construction not only furnished another source of employment for rural workers but as construction progressed also moved gangs of labourers from their home villages to new environments. When completed, the railways allowed speedy and efficient transportation of goods and people and thereby provided a mechanism to aid the diffusion of urban ideas and attitudes into the countryside.

Five *départements* experienced continuous net migratory loss during each quinquennial intercensal period between 1801 and 1851 (Fig. 13.8). In sixteen others net migratory gains were registered for only one five-year period. Population-exporting *départements* were widespread in regions of high population pressure but limited local resources in the Alps, Massif Central, Pyrenees and north-eastern France (Hohenberg, 1974). Over the same period ten *départements*, each containing at least one large city, had experienced continuous net migratory gain. Gains were interrupted during only one period in eight other areas. Conditions in the remaining *départements* were more complicated with periods of migratory loss alternating with phases of gain (Pitié, 1971).

Important differences existed in the size of migratory fields around French cities in the first half of the century (Pouthas, 1956). Many northern centres drew their migrants almost entirely from within radii of 50–60 km, in other words from their home *départements* (Fig. 13.9). By contrast, southern cities attracted migrants from much larger regions which embraced not only their immediate environs but also impoverished mountain zones from which human beings were the most important export commodities. The capital dominated an even larger migration field.

In the first half of the century Paris drew the majority of its new inhabitants from within a 300 km radius which corresponded, in general terms, to the outer rim of the Paris Basin. An investigation into the birthplaces of immigrants living in Seine *département* (greater Paris) in 1833 confirmed that each *département* dispatching more than 2·0 per cent of the capital's migrants was found in the Paris Basin (Fig. 13.10a), with 18 per cent coming from the neighbouring *départements* of Oise, Seine-et-Oise, and Seine-et-Marne (Chevalier, 1950). However long-distance migration to

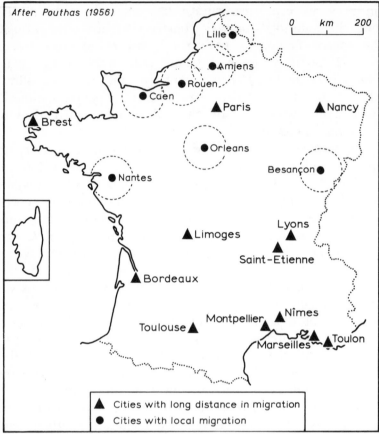

F I G. 13.9. Local and long-distance migration to French cities during the nineteenth century.

the capital operated at this early stage from the western *départements* of the Massif Central (Fig. 10b). A second enquiry fifteen years later showed that a very similar pattern still existed at the beginning of the railway era, albeit with a larger number of migrants resident in Paris (Fig. 13.11).

By the final decade of the century the capital's migration field had expanded to cover a much broader section of France. A vast Y-shaped zone of attraction extended not only into the Massif Central but also into Brittany and north-eastern France (Fig. 13.10 c & d). Only 9·5 per cent of migrants came from the three *départements* closest to the city, by contrast with double that pro-

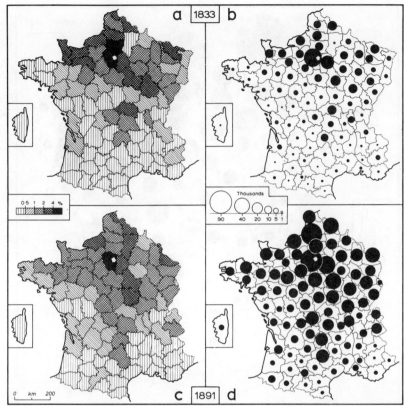

After Chevalier (1950)

FIG. 13.10. Residents of Paris born in other parts of France. (a) proportion of total in 1833; (b) numbers involved; (c) proportion of total in 1891; (d) numbers involved.

portion 60 years previously. The most distant south-eastern and south-western parts of the country sent relatively few migrants to the capital since rural/urban migration in those regions was directed predominantly to Marseilles, Montpellier, Toulouse, and Bordeaux. Even after the loss of much of the economic vitality that the latter city had enjoyed in the eighteenth century, the flood of rural migrants continued (Guillaume, 1966).

Coppolani's (1963) work on the birthplaces of Toulousains in 1872 provides a detailed case study of provincial migration. Half of the city's inhabitants had been born there. A further 22 per cent came from the surrounding *département* of Haute-Garonne, 3 per cent from abroad, and the remainder from other parts of France

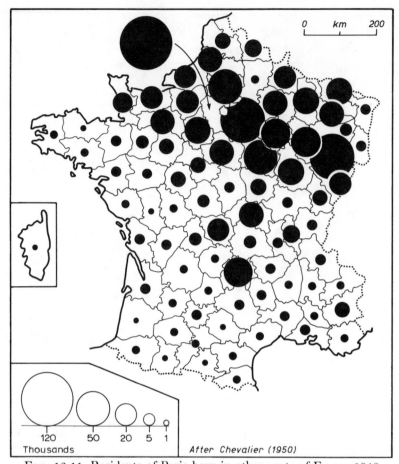

FIG. 13.11. Residents of Paris born in other parts of France 1848.

Table 13.3
Birth Places of Migrants Resident in Toulouse in 1872 (Per Cent)

Département	(per cent)				
Ariège	21·0	Seine	2·8	Lot-et-Garonne	1·5
Tarn	16·0	Aveyron	2·6	Pyrénées-Orientales	1·1
Tarn-et-Garonne	7·9	Basses-Pyrénées	2·2	Cantal	0·8
Aude	7·7	Hérault	2·1	Gard	0·7
Gers	7·0	Gironde	1·9	Dordogne	0·7
Hautes-Pyrénées	3·3	Lot	1·7	Other places	18·8

(Relates to 24,459 residents born outside Haute-Garonne).
Source: Coppolani, J., *Toulouse au XXᵉ siècle*, Toulouse (1963), p. 46.

(Table 13.3). *Départements* which furnished more than 0·5 per cent of the city's migrant population were located in the south-western corner of the country with Paris forming a single exception which was partly explained by the migration of Parisian civil servants and professionals to take up posts in Toulouse (Fig. 13.12a). A similar regional migration field was defined around Saint-Etienne (Perrin, 1937). At the end of the nineteenth century 53 per cent of the city's residents had been born in the city. Almost one-third came from Loire (20 per cent) and Haute-Loire (9 per cent) *départements*. The remaining 18 per cent came predominantly from other parts of the Massif Central but long-distance migrations drew miners and factory workers from northern and north-eastern France to the city's dynamic industrial environment (Fig. 13.12b).

Long-distance migratory movements to Paris from Brittany, the Massif Central, and north-eastern France displayed differing internal characteristics. Migration from the Massif Central was well-established as a result of seasonal and temporary movements to the capital's builders'-yards (Chatelain, 1967). Until the 1840s migration had been on foot or by wagon but thereafter most migrants travelled by rail (Pinkney, 1953). As communications became easier temporary movements were gradually replaced by permanent outmigration. Most migrants went straight from their home villages to the capital at an early age. Electoral registers indicated that two-thirds of the migrants were aged between 20 and 25 when they first arrived in Paris. However Louis Chevalier (1950) has expressed doubts about such information since other sources showed that many migrants were teenagers. Migrants returned home for occasional visits and also diffused information by letter so that the Parisian *milieu* became almost as well known to some residents of the Massif Central as the villages in which they lived. Towards the end of the century outmigration had deprived some parts of the Massif of virtually all their young men. Working the land was left to women and elderly men. In some areas harvesting could only be completed with the help of paid labour brought in from other parts of the Massif. Auvergnat migrants found employment easily enough in Paris among relatives and friends who had migrated earlier. They worked in cafés, hotels, restaurants and stables and acquired both notoriety and fame as coalmen, wood sellers, and peddlars in the capital.

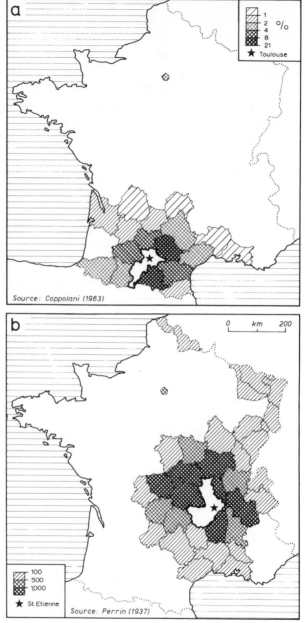

FIG. 13.12. Migration fields of two provincial cities. (a) Proportion of residents of Toulouse born in *départements* other than Haute-Garonne, 1872; (b) number of residents of Saint-Étienne born in *départements* other than Loire and Haute-Loire.

Migration from north-eastern France was a more complex process, frequently involving step-like movements from villages to local towns and then to Paris (Chevalier, 1950). For this reason migrants from Alsace and Lorraine were generally older than their counterparts from the Massif Central. The movement of Bretons to Paris was relatively unimportant until after 1875. On average migrants were older than those from the Massif Central but like them they moved directly from the countryside to the capital. The existence of the railway network facilitated migration but some Parisian industrialists went out into the Breton countryside in search of labour and transported workers in wagons to the factories and workshops of Paris.

Communities of Auvergnats, Bretons and other provincial migrants developed around the appropriate railway termini in the rapidly-changing heart of Paris as well as in the outer suburbs (Beteille, 1974). Some of these new Parisians lived in considerable hardship. Thus Abbé Gautier, a Breton priest in Paris, testified to the plight of members of his flock.

'. . . The Breton takes on jobs in factories, workshops and building sites that nobody else wants. Anything is good enough for him. He just lives from day to day, often with a wife and four, five, or even six children left behind. Hence he takes even the harshest and dirtiest jobs. He is really the pariah of Paris' (Chevalier, 1950, p. 210).

Until mid-century approximately half of the capital's population had been born in the city. Thereafter the proportion fell drastically. In 1861 only 10 per cent of the total French population resided outside the *département* where it had been born (Mauco, 1935). But in the capital things were different with two-thirds of all 'Parisians' having been born beyond the city. About 90 per cent of the capital's increased population throughout the century resulted from inmigration, with peaks occurring when labour was needed for the great exhibitions (1851, 1878, 1889, 1900), for urban-redevelopment schemes during the Second Empire, and for the excavation of the underground railway at the end of the century.

Paris before Baron Haussmann

The *département* of the Seine increased its population six fold from 632,000 to 3·8 millions during the nineteenth century. But after the 1850s the capital spread beyond the limits of the *département* to include new suburbs in Seine-et-Marne and Seine-et-Oise. Thus the population of all three areas increased from 1·3 millions to 4·9 millions over the century and the built-up surface of greater Paris grew dramatically (Fig. 13.13). Expansion on the urban periphery was complemented by important modifications in the urban morphology of inner Paris between 1800 and 1900.

During the *ancien régime* the French monarchy had feared the Parisian mob and Louis XIV's creation of Versailles represented an attempt to separate the centres of political and economic power. The Revolution brought this period of dissociation to an end. Thereafter more power and people were concentrated in Paris than ever before and the inadequacies of the capital's utilities became all the more apparent.

The first half of the nineteenth century represented a transition between unstructured urban growth in eighteenth-century Paris and planned urbanization that was to follow after 1850. In Lavedan's (1952) words:

'. . . the Napoleonic urbanists spoke a language that used the vocabulary of Louis XIV's time but their ideas were already those that Haussmann was to implement later' (p. 7).

Napoleon was concerned with the planning of Paris for social reasons as well as for matters of prestige. He sought to create a city of 3 or 4 million people but this was not to come until the middle years of the century. Urban development was envisaged as a way of avoiding discontent, opposition and unemployment. Financial constraints prevented the implementation of the *Plan des Artistes* but key features from it were selected for improving urban amenities. Napoleon considered that new roads and city squares were of secondary importance to better water supplies, sewers, abattoirs and markets. The prefects of the Seine *département* who preceeded the famed Baron Haussmann put this interpretation of city planning into practice.

Paris' water supply had been drawn from the river Seine and

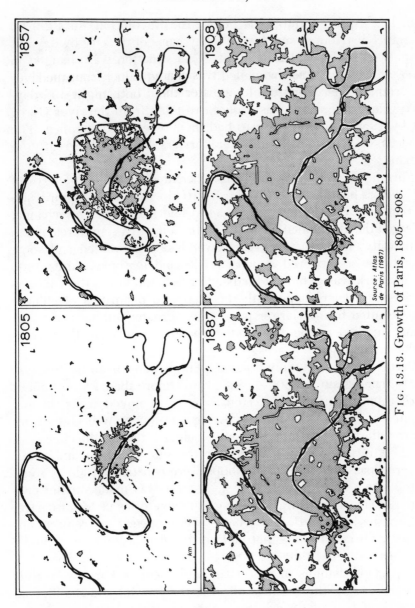

Fig. 13.13. Growth of Paris, 1805–1908.

Source: Atlas de Paris (1967)

from local springs and wells before the Revolution. In 1799 60 fountains distributed supplies to many parts of the city by day but water was not provided at night. This situation was changed in 1806 when water was channelled by open aqueduct from the river Beuvronne. Thereafter the fountains flowed both night and day. Two years later water was brought to Paris from the river Ourcq but by 1850 only 5300 houses had their own piped supplies. The services of Paris' 20,000 water carriers were still greatly in demand.

Turning from water supply to efficient disposal, the length of city sewers had been increased from 10 km 1650 to 35 km in 1800 (Urbanisme et Architecture, 1954). The main collector channel followed the abandoned meander of the Seine in a semi-circle north of the city. In 1740 the great sewer had been walled and some stretches were covered in with bricks and masonry. After 1800 the network was extended further to reach 155 km in the 1830s as engineers tried to cope with the increased quantities of effluent that resulted from a larger population, greater volumes of water being supplied to the city, and increased runoff from the streets of the expanding urban area.

Paris had been severely flooded by high water from the Seine in 1801–2 and again in 1806–7. As a result more than 4 km of quays were rebuilt immediately. Houses were removed from the old bridges of Paris to facilitate crossing and four new bridges were built. Other urban improvements included the establishment of five abattoirs and new markets for the sale of wheat and wine. Covered passages lined with shops were constructed along some of the city's main thoroughfares. A start was made on the provision of street lighting, and the great cemeteries of Montmartre, Montparnasse and Père Lachaise were opened to replace unhygienic burial grounds that had proliferated around the capital's churches (Auzelle, 1953).

Important changes in the urban equipment of Paris were thus achieved during the regimes of prefects Chabriol and Rambuteau in the first half of the century. Nevertheless, Paris remained a congested and unhealthy city. The IVth and VIIth *arrondissements* had average densities of 850 and 960 inhabitants per ha at mid-century (Lavedan, 1953). In some quarters densities exceeded 1000/ha. The insurrections of 1830 and 1848 which led to the overthrow of the Bourbons and of Louis-Philippe had originated in these slum areas. The same quarters endured the most atrocious sanitary conditions. Building regulations had limited the height of houses fronting on to highways but buildings with six or seven storeys continued to be built in the inner cores between streets. Small courtyards between the houses served as latrines as well as access points. Not surprisingly these quarters experienced high mortality during epidemics such as the cholera outbreak of 1848–9. In the words of De Marguerittes (1855):

> '. . . poverty is apparent. It scowls at you. It sits doggedly at the doors of its wretched, broken-down houses . . . Numerous ragged and half-naked children, with uncombed hair, clatter by you in wooden clogs . . . The men . . . stand in groups at the corners of dark, damp alleys into which the sun has never penetrated' (p. 266).

Baron Haussmann and the Renewal of Inner Paris during the Second Empire

Conditions such as these faced Haussmann in 1853 when he was appointed prefect of the Seine *département* by Napoleon III (Pinkney, 1957, 1958). The Emperor reiterated the aims of his predecessor Napoleon I as he sought to destroy unhealthy quarters and make Paris the most beautiful city in the world. He had spent years in exile across the Channel and was familiar with English techniques of urban development. The Emperor himself formulated many of the ideas that Haussmann and his assistants were to put into operation (Chastel, 1964).

The need to maintain law and order loomed large in Haussmann's plans for the 'new Paris'. Broad, straight avenues were to be laid out to facilitate the movement of cavalry (Fig. 13.14). Civil disturbances after 1830 had been most pronounced on the Ile-de-la-Cité and along the east/west *Croisée* through the innermost section of the right bank. Massive expropriation and demolition programmes erased housing from the Ile-de-la-Cité (Foncin, 1931). In its place an assemblage of public buildings was laid out around the cathedral of Notre-Dame. The island's resident population fell from 15,000 to under 5000 (Lavedan, 1952). Three main

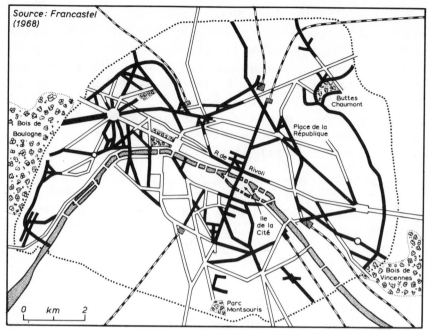

F IG. 13.14. Features of the street plan of central Paris dating from the plans of Haussmann.

highways ran north/south across the island and outside Notre-Dame a great open space (200 m × 150 m) was created that could serve as an assembly point for soldiers from the neighbouring barracks (Chapman, 1953, 1954). Extensive areas of slum housing on the right bank were demolished along the line of the *croisée de Paris* as the rue de Rivoli was reconstructed and extended eastwards to the Bastille.[4]

North/south boulevards were to be laid out and this necessitated more demolition. Paris—the city of insurrection—was 'disembowelled'. Highways were also constructed around the city as well as through it. The outer ring of boulevards marked the former limit of Paris before its enlargement by the annexation of additional *communes* in 1859. *Grands boulevards* were created closer to the city centre with their *pièce de résistance* being formed by the place du Château-d'Eau (later to become the Place de la République), which served as a military assembly point close to the Prince Eugène barracks from which broad, straight avenues fanned out into eastern Paris. By 1869 Paris contained 155 km of roadway of which one-fifth represented the realization of the projects of Napoleon III and Haussmann.

The Emperor had been impressed by Hyde Park and other parks during his exile in England (Réau, 1953). Such parks were adopted as models for the Bois de Boulogne and the Bois de Vincennes that were laid out beyond the limits of the Ville de Paris (Fig. 13.14). Open spaces were also created in the inner city at the Buttes-Chaumont (1864) and at the Parc Montsouris (1867). In spite of achievements of this kind, Haussmann's schemes involved the disappearance of rather more open space than was created as private parks and gardens were smothered by bricks and mortar (Lavedan, 1952).

The central markets of the capital were also reorganized in this great period of urban rebuilding. Plans for a great market hall had been proposed in 1811 but were not implemented (Kerhervé, 1959). As the population of Paris grew during the first half of the century so the marketing system in the city centre became pro-gressively more chaotic with a series of specialized markets proliferating on the right bank (Fig. 13.15a). Proposals for im-provement were suggested in the 1840s and in 1851 Louis Napoleon Bonaparte laid the first stone of a new marketing hall. The resulting building was an architectural disaster, resembling a military *Blockhaus* rather than a market hall. After a public outcry this *Fort de la Halle* was demolished by order of the Emperor.

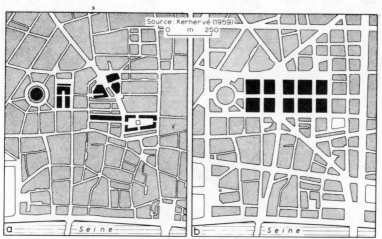

FIG. 13.15. Les Halles (a) before and (b) after Haussmann.

Napoleon III had been enchanted by cast-iron and glass architecture of mid-nineteenth century England. He was also impressed
by the roofwork of the Gare de l'Est and sketched out his ideas for
'glass umbrellas' to cover the projected market. The design was
shown to Haussmann who in turn showed it to Victor Baltard who
had been responsible for the disastrous *Fort*. The Emperor wanted
buildings with 'iron, iron, nothing but iron' (Hugueney, 1968).
Baltard worked from designs for municipal markets in English
cities and produced an anonymous scheme that met with Imperial
approval.

Various sites on the Ile de la Cité and on the right bank were
suggested for the new market buildings (Fig. 13.16). An area
north of the rue de Rivoli and west of the boulevard de Sebastopol
was selected and demolition was begun, reducing the population
of the Halles quarter from 11,000 in 1841 to less than 5000 in the
1850s. Six great cast-iron and glass pavilions were installed in
1857 to be followed by four more ten years later (Fig. 13.15a and
b). Broad highways replaced tortuous streets to give market
traffic improved access from the boulevards (Fig. 13.14). The

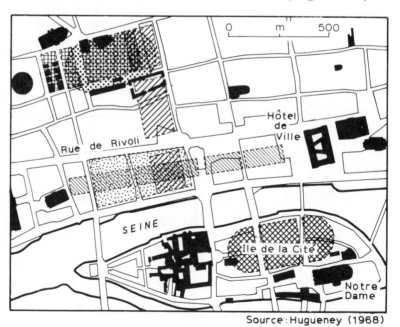

Source: Hugueney (1968)

FIG. 13.16. Sites proposed for the reconstruction of Les Halles.

new streets were lined with modern buildings but blocks of poor housing survived behind the elegant facades to function as reception areas for impoverished migrants who continued to settle in this quarter later in the century.

Water supplies and sewerage facilities were further improved by the engineer Belgrand under the direction of Haussmann (Anon., 1953a). In spite of improvements earlier in the century, water supplies were still far from adequate in the early 1850s. In the following two decades water was piped distances of up to 170 km from the Eure, Marne and Yonne. New artesian wells were bored beneath the city and vast storage reservoirs constructed. Additional mains facilitated the distribution of water throughout the city. Effluent disposal was made more efficient by extending the sewer network to 560 km in 1869 and enlarging the diameter of channels. Only 15 km of old narrow sewers remained in use in 1869. Untreated effluent was still fed into the river Seine, since the first sewage works were not to be established until the 1890s at Achères and Gennevilliers (Urbanisme et Architecture, 1954).

Public-transport facilities were improved along with many other aspects of capital-city living in the second half of the century. Concessions for operating horse-drawn trams had been granted in the Ville de Paris after 1828. These were reorganized under a single authority in 1854 when a tramway service started operation between Sèvres and Vincennes (Anon, 1953b). Omnibus and tramway services proliferated and, together with the surface railway, contributed to the growth of Parisian suburbia during the remainder of the century. The *métro* did not start operations until 1900, 37 years after the first underground services in London and 28 years after the opening of New York's subway system. Even then the *métro* was built by the Ville de Paris for the Ville de Paris and did not extend into the suburban areas beyond the city limits where very rapid growth of housing and population was taking place.

The public works masterminded by Haussmann and Napoleon III undoubtedly brought significant functional and visual improvements to the inner city of Paris during the Second Empire. But errors were also committed. 'Surgical urbanism' erased not only slums from the townscape but also churches and other historic monuments. Redevelopment of the Ile-de-la-Cité surrounded

Notre-Dame and the Sainte-Chapelle by dreary municipal buildings and has been seen by some as Haussmann's greatest error of
judgement. Urban renewal in central Paris necessitated a substantial removal of the poor population to ill-built suburbs beyond
the city limits that were growing rapidly without planned provision of utilities. Two cities were developing: the planned
modern city for the rich, and the inner slums and outer suburbs for
the poor (Chapman, 1957).

Many of Haussmann's schemes included strong spatial in-
equalities. Daily supplies of piped water had certainly been increased in the city from 112,000 m³ in 1852 to 430,000 m³ in 1869
but supplies were not evenly distributed between neighbourhoods.
New boulevards improved main communication links but streets
that had not been remodelled became even more crowded as
vehicles poured on to them from the new highways. Increased
flows of traffic moved to the new central markets and intensified
the congestion of horse-drawn vehicles on boulevards and side
streets alike. Workshop industries proliferated in inner quarters
such as the Marais after fashionable residents had departed to
newly-built urban areas in western Paris. Industrialization in inner
Paris intensified the flow of raw materials and manufactured goods
to and from the heart of the city and caused further congestion.
Other aspects of street planning were neglected or miscalculated.
Thus, for example, Paris' new railway termini were not adequately
served by the new boulevards with only the Gare de l'Est being
provided with a direct access route to the city centre (Fig. 13.14).

All the schemes undertaken at Haussmann's command may be
criticized by virtue of their scale. City planning in nineteenth
century Paris was conceived inside the framework of the Ville de
Paris in spite of the fact that suburbanization was already the most
dynamic aspect of urban growth. It was, almost as if Haussmann
had forgotten that he was prefect of the Seine *département* and not
simply mayor of the Ville de Paris (Lavedan, 1952). The development of Parisian suburbia was left to the devices of private
developers who implanted their piecemeal schemes without the
control of public authorities. Suburban Paris became an

'. . . unspeakable collection of rabbit hutches of which any other
capital city would be ashamed' (Réau, 1953).

Suburban Paris in the Nineteenth Century

The population of the Ville de Paris rose from 550,000 to 1·17 millions during the first half of the nineteenth century but growth was not distributed evenly (Fig. 13.17). The innermost IVth and VIIth *arrondissements* experienced moderate growth until 1846 but declined thereafter, with the IVth *arrondissement* undergoing a net

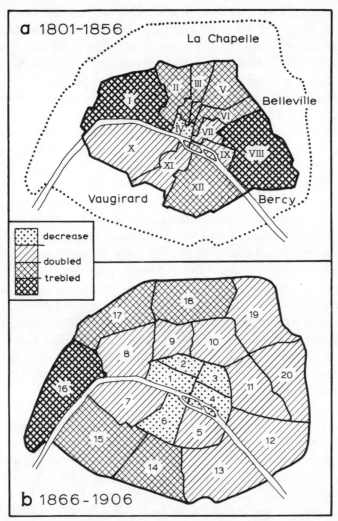

FIG. 13.17. Population change in Paris, 1801–56 and 1866–1906.

loss of population between 1801 and 1856. Population growth inevitably occurred where new housing estates had been developed under prefect Rambuteau prior to 1830. Such areas included the quarters of Europe, François Ier, Grenelle, the Plaine de Passy, and Saint-Vincent-de-Paul (Rouleau, 1967; Atlas de Paris, 1967). The largest scheme involved the purchase of 105 ha of cultivated land by the entrepreneur J-B. Violet from the property of the *château* of Grenelle. The new housing estate included twelve streets, a neighbourhood church, and a central square. Plans for the Europe estate were not completed because of the implantation of the Saint-Lazare railway terminus but further to the east the Saint-Vincent-de-Paul scheme prevented the Gares du Nord and de l'Est being located side by side as had been planned.

In spite of such additions to its townscape, Paris was not greatly different in the 1830s from what it had been at the time of the Revolution. By contrast, Paris in the 1860s included many of the essential features of the present city. In the early decades of the century the city had been almost completely contained inside the walls of the *Fermiers-Généraux*. Eighteen highways fanned out from it towards major provincial cities and linear suburbanization along some of these arteries had taken place for short distances beyond the city walls. Limited extra-mural expansion had been stimulated by the availability of relatively cheap housing for the urban poor who moved from the city centre, and for rural migrants in search of work in the capital's factories, workshops, and service industries. Six railway termini were built between 1837 and 1849 to replace the former makeshift platforms and by 1855 nine railway lines converged on the capital (Francastel, 1968). But trains were infrequent at this early stage of development, fares were high, and stations few and far between. They did not serve the rural zone on the immediate periphery of the built-up area.

A new ring of fortifications was built between 1840 and 1844 and thereby increased the *intra-muros* area by one third (Fig. 13.17). Nevertheless, the environs of Paris retained much the same appearance as before. Forests that had been the hunting reserves of the nobility and of the sovereigns of France remained largely unchanged. The city was ringed by the ancient towns of Corbeil, Pontoise and Saint-Denis together with the *châteaux* that had been constructed after 1600 (Lucet-Vivier, 1955). Villages in the inner Paris Basin were populous but still predominantly agricultural communities supporting mean population densities of over 100/km², double the national average at this period (Demangeon, 1948). Frédéric Le Play's description of rich market gardens that covered areas of damp soil in a band 3 to 10 km from central Paris in 1855 evoked the pattern captured by Roussel's survey of 1731 (Dupuy, 1900; Lavedan, 1952).

Much of this changed in the 30 years after 1855. Railway stations in and around Paris doubled in number to reach 200 at the end of this period. Fares became more reasonably-priced and stopping trains more frequent. Commuting to employment in central Paris from outer *arrondissements* still inside the 1840 fortifications, from *communes* outside the walls and from even more distant settlements became quite feasible.

Farmland was replaced by housing estates. Small lots proliferated close to 'suburban' railway stations for the piecemeal construction of houses as fragments of agricultural land were disposed of in a chaotic fashion (Bastié, 1964). Parkland around the *châteaux* was consumed by housing. Woodland was felled.[5] Communities such as Auteuil, Belleville, Bercy, la Chapelle Saint-Denis and Vaugirard which had supported farmers, market gardeners and vinegrowers as well as containing the weekend and seasonal homes of affluent Parisians, became integral parts of the rapidly-growing capital (Fig. 13.17a).[6]

Inner *arrondissements* continued to lose population throughout the second half of the nineteenth century but outer areas grew rapidly (Fig. 13.17b). Communities in Seine and Seine-et-Oise *départements* beyond the Ville de Paris also increased their population dramatically, with seven suburban towns experiencing growth coefficients above five between 1851 and 1901 (Fig. 13.18).

The chronology of development and details in the spatial pattern of suburbanization varied between communities but the general trends were clear (Bourget, 1954; George, 1964; Leheu, 1954; Leloup, 1954; Ruy, 1953). Agricultural villages and stretches of riverside that had attracted Parisians for their Sunday recreation and had been captured in the works of the impressionist painters disappeared beneath the tide of suburban development. Their place was taken by a chaotic mixture of factories, gasworks, housing, railway yards, sewage works, and other urban utilities. Fertile

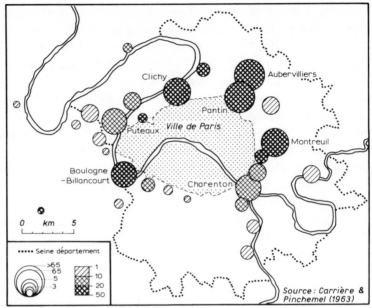

FIG. 13.18. Coefficients of population growth of towns in Seine *département*,
1851–1901.

market gardens which had formerly flourished in these areas were
relocated at greater distances from the city centre. The relentless
march of unplanned suburbanization had begun with a vengeance.
Small administrative units that had been suitable for the management of agricultural villages became increasingly unable to meet
the demands of growing numbers of suburbanites in search of their
share of the good life that they believed the city offered them. The
seeds had been sown that were to give rise to a suburban dilemma
of crisis proportions in the 1920s and 1930s (Bastié, 1964).

Urban Growth in Provincial France

Planning schemes in provincial cities could not be compared in
scale or grandeur with the changes that took place in Paris during
the nineteenth century. That was a sign of the times. The provinces were simply 'the provinces'. Provincial capitals that had
flourished as important administrative centres before the Revolution were demoted to much less significant *chefs-lieux* of *départements* under the tighter centralized grip of Parisian administration.

Only two completely new towns were created. These were constructed as civil and military 'colonies' in Brittany and the Vendée
where administrators were established alongside the military to
diffuse republican points of view from Paris into unresponsive
parts of the nation. Pontivy was constructed on a modest grid
pattern alongside the canal du Blavet in central Brittany and la
Roche-sur-Yon was built at a central situation to administer the
Vendée from a site that had been selected by Napoleon I (Figs.
13.1 and 13.19).

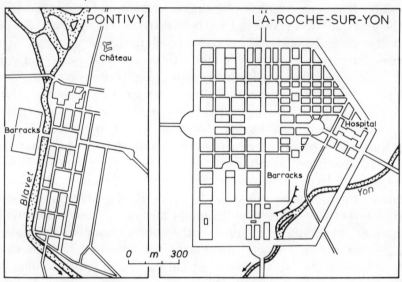

Source: Lavedan (1952)

FIG. 13.19. Pontivy and La Roche-sur-Yon.

Provincial cities experienced modifications in their ground plans
and townscapes in the early years of the nineteenth century as new
bridges and streets were built and minor improvements to harbour
facilities were undertaken. In the second half of the century
'Haussmannization' spread from Paris to other parts of France and
indeed to cities elsewhere in the world (Réau, 1953). Imperial
highways were laid out in Avignon, Lyons, Marseilles and
Toulouse. The creation of the rue de l'Impératrice (later rue
Jeanne d'Arc) in Rouen involved demolition of 500 houses and two
churches and was particularly reminiscent of the straight north/
south boulevards through central Paris. Lyons too was 'Hauss-
mannized' by prefect Vaisse between 1853 and 1864. One of his

major concerns was to rebuild a city centre in which future civil disturbances, such as those that had occurred in 1831 and 1834, might be speedily controlled by military force (Gallois, 1925). The rue Impériale and other broad straight streets were constructed in response to this concern for strategy. Haussmann's aesthetic aims were not forgotten when the Parc de la Tête d'Or (1856) was created alongside the river Rhône in emulation of the Bois de Boulogne.

French entry into the coal-based industrial age earlier in the century had been paralleled by the construction of steam railways. The first line was opened in 1830 between Saint-Etienne and Givors on the river Rhône and was extended to Lyons in 1832. Ten years later the decision was taken to create a star-like network of main lines linking Paris to Lille, Le Havre, Nantes, Bordeaux, Marseilles and Strasbourg. The greater mobility which the railways afforded accelerated rural/urban migration to existing cities and promoted suburban development. It also permitted the establishment of resort towns both inland and on the coast and assisted the transformation of mining and manufacturing settlements into large industrial cities. Other settlements developed railway-maintenance towns such as la Roche-Migenne exactly midway between Paris and Dijon (Pinchemel, 1969). Deauville provides an example of nineteenth-century resort development (Lavedan, 1952). The settlement was sited in the midst of dunes and marshland on the Normandy coast but contained only 100 inhabitants in 1859. In that year 200 ha of land were purchased by a financier and a fashionable doctor. A casino was constructed and within five years the resort had been created. Twenty years later a similar development took place on the Picardy coast at Paris-Plage on to which the resort of Le Touquet was grafted at the turn of the century. Biarritz on the Franco–Spanish frontier formed another example of a resort town which experienced dramatic growth after 1851 (Fig. 13.20). Spas such as Vichy also greatly increased their population, but even more important rates of growth were taking place in the textile-producing cities, in mining towns on the coalfields of northern and eastern France, and at major ports such as Calais, Le Havre and Saint-Nazaire.

Textile-producing towns had experienced rapid growth after 1770 with the Alsatian city of Mulhouse, for example, growing

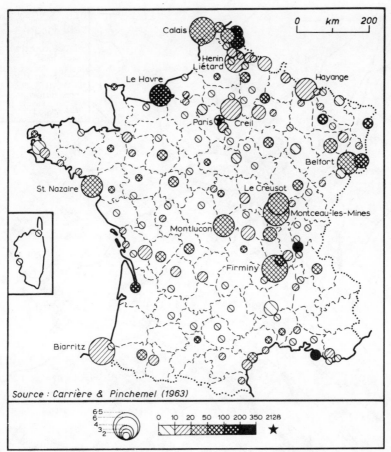

FIG. 13.20. Coefficients of population growth in provincial cities, 1851–1901.

from 10,000 to 36,000 between 1812 and 1836. Cities close to the Belgian border also rapidly increased in size. Thus Tourcoing grew from 12,000 to 81,670 (+ 580 per cent) during the nineteenth century and its neighbour Roubaix expanded from 8700 to 121,000 (+ 1300 per cent) at a fairly steady rate throughout the century (Fig. 13.21) (Bruyelle, 1965). Much of this growth was due to immigration from Belgium. Thus in 1876 55 per cent of the population at Roubaix was Belgian-born. The cotton-manufacturing city of Rouen had experienced prodigious growth during the eighteenth century but thereafter its population remained fairly stable but expansions were taking place vigorously in surrounding communities beyond the city limits.

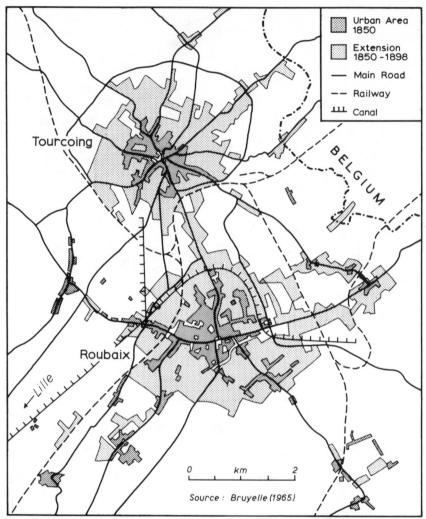

FIG. 13.21. Roubaix and Tourcoing: nineteenth-century urban growth.

Saint-Etienne increased its population from 16,000 to 150,000 during the course of the century from a rich industrial base of coal mining as well as textile and metallurgical manufacture (Fig. 13.6). The inclusion of figures for surrounding communities raised the total population of this industrial 'black country' from 56,000 to 300,000 over the same span of years (Perrin, 1937). Le Creusot, located similarly on the eastern edge of the Massif Central, also grew dramatically from 2700 to 24,000 in the 30 years after 1836 when the Schneider family opened its foundry. Major ports, industrial centres, coal-mining and metallurgical towns thus formed the real 'boom towns' of France during the nineteenth century, by contrast with old administrative cities such as Nantes and Clermont-Ferrand which experienced more modest rates of growth (Fig. 13.6).

The increasingly numerous working-class population was often housed in conditions of almost indescribable squalor in the industrial cities of France. The textile centre of Lille formed one of the worst examples. Three thousand workers lived in cellars 2 m or 3 m below ground level in the Saint-Sauveur quarter at mid-century (Gossez, 1904). Access from the street was by staircases down which water poured on rainy days to flood the earth floors of the cellars. Not surprisingly, the impact of cholera and other epidemics was disastrous in such conditions.

Newly-constructed accommodation in the northern cities was often scarcely better than that provided in cellars and other old buildings. The built-up area of Roubaix and Tourcoing expanded four-fold during the second half of the century (Fig. 13.21). Sometimes the new industrial workforce was housed in small industrial cottages on estates constructed by the millowners. The so-called *forts* that were built in Roubaix after 1830 were of this type, with each housing over 100 families in single-storeyed terraced houses (Bruyelle, 1965). But many industrial workers were accommodated in cramped courtyards where conditions were much worse.

Courtyard dwellings in central Lille had existed as far back as the mid-sixteenth century but most were constructed during the seventeenth and eighteenth centuries. By contrast, courtyards in suburban Lille and in Roubaix and Tourcoing were mostly built between 1850 and 1900 (Fig. 13.22). Before the development of public transport systems in the final years of the nineteenth century workers had to be housed within walking distance of their workshops (Pinchemel, 1954). Patches of arable land, meadow and gardens that had remained undeveloped behind lines of housing inside the walls of Lille were gradually consumed for building and tiny cottages were laid out in courtyard blocks (Fig. 13.23). Access was provided by passageways that had served the agricultural holdings or had been pierced specially through the house-fronts. The courtyard system offered several advantages to

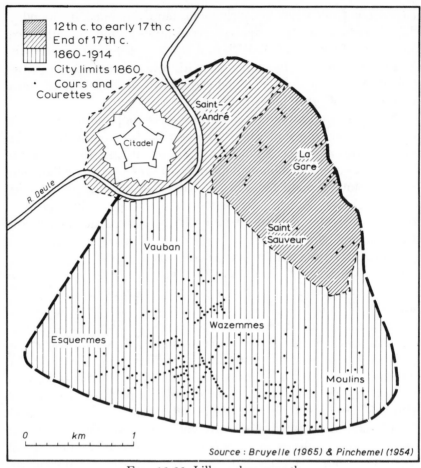

FIG. 13.22. Lille: urban growth.

landowners and developers. Land behind the housefronts was cheaper to purchase than that fronting directly on to the street. The expense of installing pavements and new sewers was not incurred when courtyard infilling took place. Neither were there restrictions on housing density or minimum standards of construction to be adhered to since city regulations did not apply to construction behind the streetlines.

The net result was the construction of 170 courtyards in Lille and many more in Roubaix and Tourcoing. Their morphology varied in response to the pre-existing agrarian structure but each

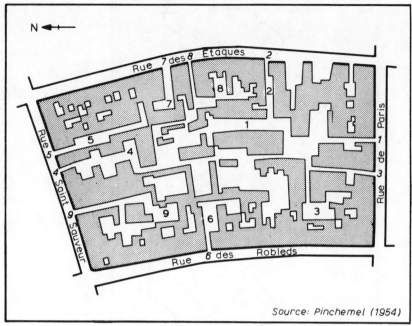

N ◄—+——

Rue 7 des 8 Étaques 2
Rue 5 Saint 9 Sauveur
Rue 6 des Robleds
Rue de Paris

Source: Pinchemel (1954)

FIG. 13.23. Lille: an example of courtyard dwellings. (Numerals indicate the entrance to and location of a court).

housed between 50 and 100 households apiece.[7] The accommodation which they provided ranged from bad to atrocious. Some courtyards were floored with bricks or cement but many were simply pounded earth. Communal pumps and latrines were in the yards. Effluent disposal was primitive and channels blocked easily. Rising damp formed a particularly serious problem especially for cottages that were so orientated that they received no direct sunlight. The health conditions of courtyard dwellers were extremely poor and epidemics of cholera, influenza, typhoid and typhus ran riot. Infantile mortality rates were appalling. Two-thirds of children born in the courtyards during the second half of the nineteenth century died before they reached five years of age.

Other forms of industrial housing were constructed by factory owners elsewhere in France. Accommodation on such estates was normally better than in the courtyards of the northern textile towns. Thus by 1860 the Schneider family had housed 3000 persons in various grades of dwelling allocated by rank to office staff, foreman and workmen in the company town of Le Creusot close to the

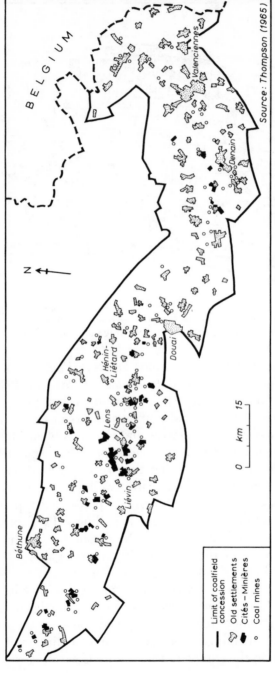

F IG. 13.24. Settlements on the Nord/Pas-de-Calais coalfield in the late
nineteenth century.

pitheads for their employees. This type of housing had become widespread in the coalfield of Nord *département* by the late nineteenth century (Fig. 13.24). Practically everywhere in the area the *corons* were restricted in size relative to the established urban centres. The essential features were simplicity of house type, rectangular street plan, location close to the mines, and total disregard in their siting for proximity to existing towns (Thompson, 1965). Similar estates grew up around other coal-mining, metallurgical, and textile-producing towns and in spite of numerous urban renovation schemes nineteenth-century working-class housing still characterizes large sections of the townscapes of Lille, Lyons, Metz, Nantes, Saint-Etienne, Strasbourg and other French industrial cities (Leow, 1971; Nonn, 1965).

The Legacy of Nineteenth-Century Urbanization

During the nineteenth century the urban population of France almost tripled, rising from 5·7 millions to 15·9 millions (+ 180 per cent). This rate of increse was far ahead of the 48 per cent growth rate registered for the total population. The proportion of the workforce engaged in 'rural' pursuits, such as farming and forestry, fell from 64·4 per cent (14·3 millions) to 41·8 per cent (8·2 millions) between 1851 and 1901 (Fig. 13.25) (Caheu, 1953). By contrast, employment in manufacturing, transport, commerce, and other 'urban' activities rose from 35·6 per cent (7·9 millions) to 58·2 per cent (11·5 millions). Numbers would have been even greater had the provinces of Alsace and Lorraine not been lost as a result of the Franco–Prussian War. However 60 per cent of the French population still lived in the countryside at the end of the century and the proportion was not to fall below half until 1926, coming 75 years after a comparable situation had been reached in England and Wales.

In general terms the largest cities in France grew much faster than their smaller counterparts during the nineteenth century. In 1801 1·69 million people had lived in the thirty largest cities and represented 6·4 per cent of the national population. By 1901 the figure had risen to 9·26 millions which involved 23·8 per cent of

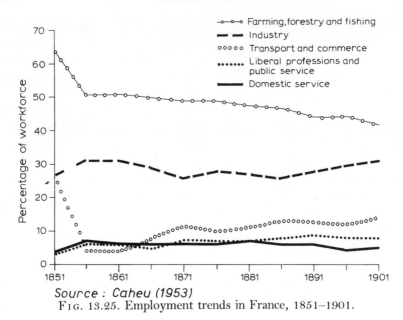

Source : Caheu (1953)
FIG. 13.25. Employment trends in France, 1851–1901.

all French citizens. The thirty largest cities increased their share
of the total urban population from 29·8 to 58·2 per cent.

There were however fundamental differences in the pace of
urban growth during the two halves of the century. From 1801 to
1851 the urban population of France grew by 60 per cent whilst the
national population increased by 36 per cent. Nevertheless the rate
of urban growth was probably slower than before the Revolution
(Dupeux, 1970). During the second half of the nineteenth century
the pace of change was quite different. Urban dwellers increased in
number by 75 per cent but the national population rose by only
9 per cent. The total population of the thirty largest cities more
than tripled, rising from 2·9 millions in 1851 to 9·2 millions in
1901. The second half of the nineteenth century might well be
characterized as a period of 'urban revolution' which was most
recognizable amongst the higher-order centres of the urban hierarchy (Carrière and Pinchemel, 1963). Ratios between growth
rates recorded in the two halves of the century varied in detail but
rates of expansion between 1851 and 1901 for twenty-nine of the
thirty most populous cities were greatly in advance of what they
had been in the first half of the century (Fig. 13.26).

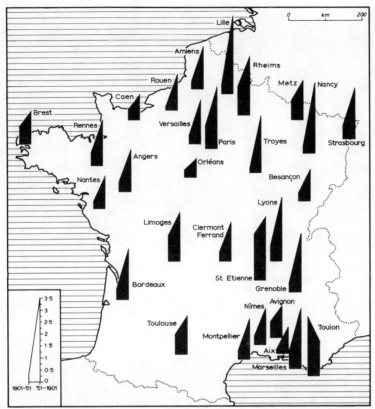

F I G. 13.26. Population growth in French cities, 1801–51 compared with 1851–1901. (Index 1 = 100 per cent growth, i.e. doubling; 2 = 200 per cent growth).

Between 1801 and 1851 the most rapid increases in urban population were recorded in industrial cities (Saint-Etienne, Rheims, Metz, Limoges), ports (Brest and Toulon), and in bi-functional cities combining regional administration with port activities (Marseilles) or with industrial growth (Toulouse) (Fig. 13.27). Paris experienced an above-average but not exceptional rate of growth ($+$ 92·5 per cent). However the absolute figures involved were much greater than for any other French city since the capital grew by almost half a million people from 550,000 to 1,053,000. Six of the eight largest provincial cities, which had contained 50,000 to 111,000 inhabitants apiece in 1801, demonstrated unexceptional growth rates. Increases inside the city limits of Nantes and Rouen were slow by comparison with the

FIG. 13.27. Population increase in major French cities, 1801–51 (%).

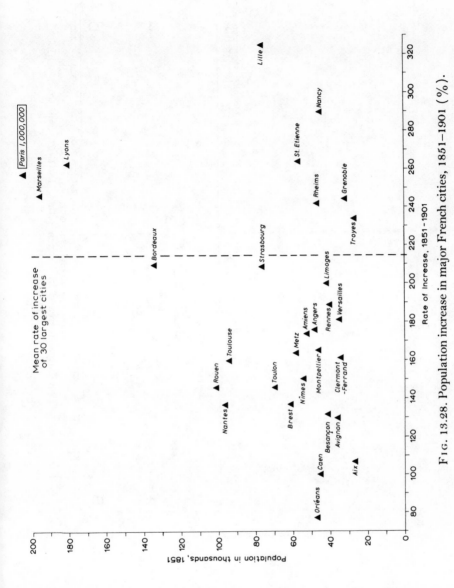

FIG. 13.28. Population increase in major French cities, 1851–1901 (%).

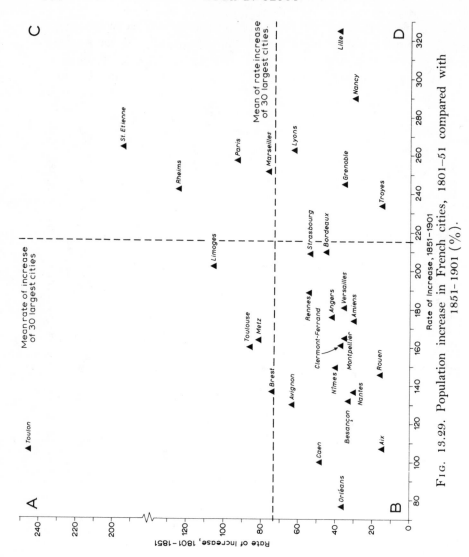

Fig. 13.29. Population increase in French cities, 1801–51 compared with 1851–1901 (%).

growth of other large cities. Rates of urban increase were much higher in the second half of the century than they had been in the first, with particularly rapid growth taking place at Lille, Nancy, Saint-Etienne, Lyons and Paris (Fig. 13.28). Most cities containing 25,000 to 70,000 inhabitants in 1851 experienced below-average rates of growth during the remainder of the century.

Five of the thirty major cities experienced precocious growth in the first half of the nineteenth century but then slowed down (Fig. 13.29, Category A). Five others grew exceptionally fast between 1851 and 1901 (Category D). By contrast, Marseilles, Paris, Rheims and Saint-Etienne experienced above-average growth rates in both halves of the century (Category C). These continuously dynamic cities were all located in the eastern half of the country (Fig. 13.30). The remaining sixteen of the thirty

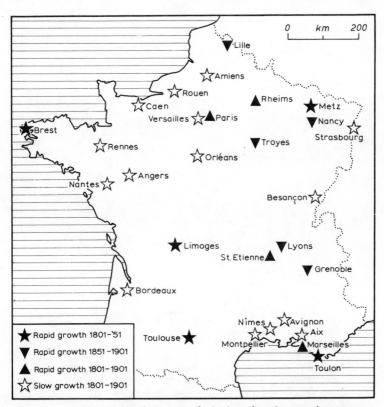

FIG. 13.30. Rates of urban growth during the nineteenth century.

major cities exhibited below-average rates of growth during both halves of the century (Category B). These slow-growing cities were found mainly in southern and western France. Using the evidence of nineteenth-century urban growth, a clear distinction may be drawn between the rapidly-urbanizing, economically dynamic North and East of France and the less urbanized, economically backward South, Centre and West. Such a division corresponds closely to the two fold economic regionalization of contemporary France that has been suggested by economists and geographers since World War II.

In general terms, the largest French cities in 1801 exhibited above-average rates of growth throughout the century (Fig. 13.31). This was true not only of Paris—the classic example of a

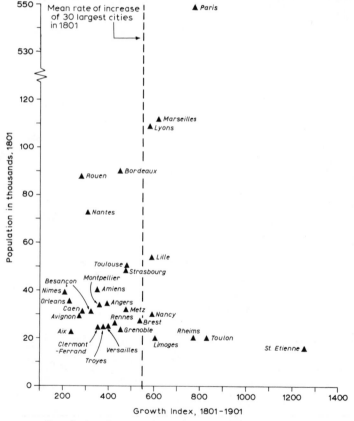

FIG. 13.31. Population increase in major French cities, 1801–1901 (%).

'primate city'—but also of Lyons and Marseilles which rivalled each other for second place in the urban hierarchy. Both contained over 100,000 inhabitants in 1801 and more than 600,000 100 years later. A small number of cities which had contained between 20,000 and 60,000 inhabitants at the beginning of the century experienced rates of population growth that were above average for the thirty cities. These included the port of Toulon and four other cities which combined administrative roles with industrial development (Lille, Limoges, Nancy and Rheims). However the best example of a nineteenth century 'boom town' was provided by Saint-Etienne which rose from a mere 16,000 in 1801 to over 200,000 in 1901.

The spatial patterns that resulted from industrial development and rapid urbanization in France during the second half of the nineteenth century lie at the heart of modern problems of regional management. Paris grew to such an extent that it dominated not only the urban hierarchy but also the whole of national life (Gille, 1962). With just over half a million inhabitants it had contained 2 per cent of the national population in 1801. Fifty years later the proportion had only risen to 3 per cent but in 1901 greater Paris (Seine *département*) contained 10 per cent of the inhabitants of France. Overdeveloped Paris stood in marked contrast with the underdeveloped 'French desert' (Gravier, 1947). At a slightly more sophisticated level of regionalization, contrasts might be recognized between eastern and western France, separated along a line running from Normandy to the east of the Massif Central and then southwards to the mouth of the river Rhône. At an even finer level of distinction, most of the major cities that were to be selected as *métropoles d'équilibre* for purposes of regional organization in the 1960s and 1970s had already occupied the top places in the urban hierarchy in 1801 (Fig. 13.27).

Paris and the large provincial cities owe much of their present visual attractiveness to the outcome of urban planning in the eighteenth and nineteenth centuries. But they, together with the coal-based industrial zones, have also bequeathed a legacy of over-crowded slum-housing and urban congestion that had demanded action similar to the 'surgical urbanism' practised by Haussmann and by the provincial prefects (Lavedan, 1953), Haussmann's 'new Paris' delights the tourists but his wide *boulevards* have become far from adequate for dealing with the growing flood of Parisian traffic. In recent years the capital's food markets have been relocated on the margins of the city and Victor Baltard's glass and cast-iron pavilions have been demolished in the name of progress. Suburban development continues to give rise to enormous social and economic problems in the planned era of the second half of the twentieth century just as it did in the age of speculative building from 1850 until World War II. The third quarter of the twentieth century, with its rising rates of car ownership and its powerful mass media of communication, has permitted the spread of urbanism as a way of life to the remotest areas of France. Urbanization has become far more diffuse than could have been imagined before 1900. However the fundamental problem remains of remodelling an out-dated urban framework that has been inherited from the past in order to meet the needs of today and to try to anticipate those of tomorrow.

13. Notes

1. The analysis by Gascon (1970) of migration to Lyons between 1529 and 1563 gives similar conclusions. The volume of migration was greatest from poor agricultural environments close to the city, namely the regions of Bresse, Savoie, Dauphiné, Lyonnais, Beaujolais and Forez. About two-thirds of the migrants were rural in origin but an important flow of people to Lyons derived from the cities of the lower Seine valley, including Paris.
2. See, for example, the discussion in Pouthas (1956), p. 67.
3. Pouthas (1956) gives a detailed description of rates of natural change in major French cities, but note the criticisms of Spagnoli (1971) regarding the statistical imprecision of some parts of Pouthas' work.
4. Other detailed studies of the urban morphology of parts of inner Paris are contained in Sutcliffe (1970) and Zunz (1970).
5. A fascinating and eminently readable discussion of forest and woodland, of the roads to Paris and of the river Seine at the end of the eighteenth century is provided by Cobb (1975).
6. Demangeon (1948) vol. II provides descriptions of these settlements in the eighteenth century and early nineteenth century before suburbanization took place.

7. Another study of the relationship between agrarian structures and subsequent urban patterning is provided by Prêcheur (1953). An interesting view of nineteenth-century suburban development south of Strasbourg is found in Rimbert (1967).

13. References

Anon., 'Les eaux de Paris', *La Vie Urbaine* (1953a), 291–297.

Anon., 'Les transports publics parisiens', *La Vie Urbaine* (1953b), 298–301.

Atlas de Paris et de la région parisienne, Paris (1967).

Auzelle, R., 'Haussmann et les cimetières', *La Vie Urbaine* (1953), 284–290.

Bastié, J., *La Croissance de la banlieue parisienne*, Paris (1964).

Beteille, R., 'Les migrations saisonnières en France sous le Premier Empire: essai de synthèse', *Revue d'Histoire Moderne et Contemporaine*, 17 (1970), 424–41.

Beteille, R., *Les Aveyronnais*, Poitiers (1974).

Blanchard, R., *La Flandre*, Lille (1906).

Boulenger, P., 'L'industrialisation régionale rouennaise', *La Vie Urbaine*, 31 (1936), 19–49; 32 (1936), 89–134; 33 (1936), 177–204.

Bourget, J., 'Prolétarisation d'une commune de l'agglomération parisienne: Colombes', *La Vie Urbaine* (1954), 185–194.

Bruyelle, P., 'Lille, Roubaix, Tourcoing', *La Documentation Française, Notes et Etudes Documentaires*, 3206 (1965), 1–112.

Cabanne, C., 'Nantes, Saint-Nazaire', *La Documentation Française, Notes et Etudes Documentaires*, 3362 (1967), 1–46.

Caheu, L., 'Evolution de la population active en France depuis cent ans d'après les dénombrements quinquennaux', *Etudes et Conjoncture*, 8 (1953), 230–288.

Carrière, F. and Pinchemel, P., *Le Fait urbain en France*, Paris (1963).

Chapman, B., 'Baron Haussmann and the planning of Paris', *Town Planning Review*, 24 (1953–4), 177–192.

Chapman, J. M. and Chapman, B., *The Life and Times of Baron Haussmann: Paris in the Second Empire*, London (1957).

Châtelain, A., 'Les migrations temporaires françaises au XIXe siècle; problèmes, méthodes, documentation', *Annales de Démographie Historique* (1967), 9–28.

Chastel, A., 'Du Paris de Haussmann au Paris d'aujourd' hui', in Michaud, G. ed., *Paris: présent et avenir d'une capitale* (1964), Paris, 1–28.

Chevalier, L., *La Formation de la population parisienne*, Paris (1950).

Cobb, R., *Paris and its Provinces 1792–1802*, Oxford (1975).

Combès-Monier, J., 'L'origine géographique des Versaillais en 1792', *Annales de Démographie Historique* (1970), 237–50.

Coppolani, J., *Toulouse au XXᵉ siècle*, Toulouse (1963).

Croix, A., *Nantes et le pays nantais au XVIe siècle: étude démographique*, Paris (1974).

Demangeon, A., *La France, économique et humaine*, Paris (1948).

Decoville-Faller, M., 'La région de Neuf-Brisach: les étapes du peuplement, la vie de relation et ses problèmes', *Revue Géographique de l'Est*, 1 (1961), 343–62.

Dupeux, G., *La Société française*, Paris (1970).

Dupeux, G., *French Society 1789–1970*, London (1976).

Dupuy, P., 'Le sol et la croissance de Paris', *Annales de Géographie*, 9 (1900), 340–358.

Foncin, M., 'Versailles: étude de géographie historique', *Annales de Géographie*, 28 (1919), 321–341.

Foncin, M., 'La Cité', *Annales de Géographie*, 40 (1931), 479–503.

Francastel, P., 'Paris: un héritage culturel et monumental', *La Documentation Française: Notes et Etudes Documentaires*, 3483 (1968), 1–60.

Gallois, L., 'Le site et la croissance de Lyon', *Annales de Géographie*, 34 (1925), 495–509.

Garden, M., 'L'attraction de Lyon à la fin de l'Ancien Régime', *Annales de Démographie Historique* (1970), 205–22.

Gascon, R., 'Immigration et croissance au XVIᵉ siècle: l'exemple de Lyon', *Annales, Economies, Sociétés, Civilisations*, 25 (1970), 988–1001.

George, P., 'L'accroissement géographique et démographique du Paris contemporain', in Michaud, G. ed. *Paris: présent et avenir d'une capitale*, Paris (1964), 29–54.

Gille, B., 'Fonctions économiques de Paris', in Michaud, G. ed. *Paris: fonctions d'une capitale*, Paris (1962).

Gossez, M., *Le département du Nord sous la IIᵉ République*, Lille (1904).

Gravier, J.-F., *Paris et le désert français*, Paris (1947).

Gréber, J., 'Le projet d'aménagement et la reconstruction de Rouen', *La Vie Urbaine* (1957), 161–217.

Guillaume, P., 'La population d'une grande cité de province au XIXᵉ siècle: essai sur les sources et leur interprétation d'après l'exemple de Bordeaux', *Annales de Démographie* (1966), 23–36.

Hautecoeur, L., 'L'urbanisme à Paris de la renaissance à la monarchie de juillet', in Michaud, G. ed. *Paris: croissance d'une capitale*, Paris (1961), 97–133.

Henry, L. and Courgeau D., 'Deux analyses de l'immigration à Paris au XVIIIᵉ siècle', *Population*, 26 (1971), 1073–1092.

Hohenberg, P., 'Migrations et fluctuations démographiques dans la France rurale, 1836–1901', *Annales, Economies, Sociétés, Civilisations*, 29 (1974), 461–97.

Hugueney, J., 'Les Halles centrales de Paris au XIXe siècle', *La Vie Urbaine*, (1968), 81–130.

Jarry, D., 'La reconstruction du Havre', *La Vie Urbaine* (1953), 81–129.

Kerhervé, J., 'Le quartier des Halles à Paris', *La Vie Urbaine* (1959), 111–150.

Lavedan, P., *Histoire de l'urbanisme: époque contemporaine*, Paris (1952).

Lavedan, P., 'Le nouveau Paris, *La Vie Urbaine* (1953), 180–240, 302–317.

Lavedan, P., *Histoire de l'urbanisme; renaissance et temps modernes*, Paris (1959).

Leheu, P., 'Le développement d'une banlieue: Argenteuil', *La Vie Urbaine* (1954), 195–220.

Leloup, Y., 'Un faubourg industriel: Boulogne-Billancourt', *La Vie Urbaine* (1954), 167–184.

Lemée, G., 'Lorient: une ville née d'un chantier de constructions navales', *La Vie Urbaine*, 35 (1936), 321–336.

Loew, G., 'Le centre de Metz', *Mosella*, 1 (1971), 36–58.

Lucet-Vivier, F., 'Asnières et son château', *La Vie Urbaine* (1955), 15–32.

Marguerittes, J. de, *Ins and Outs of Paris*, Philadelphia (1855).

Mauco, G., 'Remarques sur le mouvement de la population en France depuis le début du XIXe siècle', *Annales de Géographie*, 44 (1935), 371–384.

Nonn, H., *Strasbourg: des densités aux structures urbaines*, Paris (1965).

Perrin, M., *Saint-Etienne et sa région économique*, Tours (1937).

Pinchemel, G., 'Cours et courettes lilloises', *La Vie Urbaine* (1954), 9–37.

Pinchemel, P., *France: a geographical survey*, London (1969).

Pinkney, D. H., 'Migrations to Paris in the Second Empire', *Journal of Modern History*, 25 (1953), 1–12.

Pinkney, D. H., 'The Imperial Plan: Haussmann and the Paris of Napoleon III', *Landscape*, 7 (1957), 15–20.

Pinkney, D. H., *Napoleon III and the Rebuilding of Paris*, Princeton (1958).

Pitié, J., *Exode rural et migrations intérieures en France*, Poitiers (1971).

Poete, M. (1941–45), 'Paris: son évolution créatrice', *La Vie Urbaine* (1941–45), 41, 275–318; 42, 359–374; 43, 21–43; 44, 79–109.

Poitrineau, A., 'Aspects de l'émigration temporaire et saisonnière en Auvergne à la fin du XVIIIe et au début du XIXe siècle', *Revue d'Histoire Moderne et Contemporaine* (1962), 1–25.

Poussou, J. P., 'Les mouvements migratoires en France et à partir de la France de la fin du XVe siècle au début du XIXe siècle: approches pour une synthèse', *Annales de Démographie Historique* (1970), 11–78.

Pouthas, C. H., *La Population française pendant la première moitié du XIXe siècle*, Paris (1956).

Prêcheur, C., 'Nancy: rapports de l'actuelle structure urbaine et de l'ancienne structure agraire', *Bulletin de l'Association de Géographes Français*, 235–6 (1953), 106–116.

Réau, L., 'Le nouveau Paris', *La Vie Urbaine* (1953), 165–179.

Réau, L., *L'Europe française au siècle des Lumières*, Paris (1938).

Rimbert, S., *La banlieue résidentielle du sud de Strasbourg; genèse d'un paysage suburbain*, Paris and Strasbourg (1967).

Rochefort, M., *L'Organisation urbaine de l'Alsace*, Paris (1960).

Rouleau, B., *Le Tracé des rues de Paris*, Paris (1967).

Ruy, P., 'Trois communes de la banlieue est de Paris', *La Vie Urbaine* (1953), 130–148.

Sion, J., *Les Paysans de la Normandie orientale*, Paris (1909).

Spagnoli, P. G., 'The demographic work of Charles Pouthas', *Historical Methods Newsletter*, 14 (1971), 126–140.

Stewart, C., *A Prospect of Cities*, London (1952).

Sutcliffe, A., *The Autumn of Central Paris*, London (1970).

Thompson, I. B., 'A review of problems of economic and urban development in the northern coalfield of France', *Southampton Research Series in Geography*, 1 (1965), 31–60.

Urbanisme et Architecture, *Etudes en l'honneur de Pierre Lavedan*, Paris (1954).

Young, A., *Voyages en France en 1787, 1788, 1789*, trans. H. Sée, Paris (1931).

Zunz, O., 'Le quartier du Gros Caillou à Paris', *Annales, Economies, Sociétés, Civilisations*, 25 (1970), 1024–1085.

Appendix I

Some Sources For The Historical Geography of Rural France in The Eighteenth and Nineteenth Centuries

HUGH D. CLOUT

Introduction

Source material for investigating the historical geography of France, as any long-settled country, is both voluminous and varied. The pages that follow are not intended to form a comprehensive guide to information that may be derived from sources as diverse as the controversial findings of archaeology, anthropology or toponomy. Rather they are a much more restricted commentary on manuscript and printed sources housed in archival repositories and which relate to rural conditions in eighteenth- and nineteenth-century France. Maps will be considered as well as literary and statistical sources.

The French archival system reflects the administrative hierarchy of *commune*, *département* and nation. Each *commune* contains documentary collections relating to population change, land ownership and other local affairs. These materials are housed in the mayor's office. Information is mainly related to post-1789 conditions, but earlier papers may also be found. The material condition and storage of these documents varies enormously, depending on the zeal of successive mayors' secretaries, prices offered for 'waste' paper, and mundane problems such as mice and rising damp. In some *communes* early papers have been removed for safe keeping to the second-order repositories, the *archives départementales*.

These are found in the chief town of each *département* and contain rich and often well-catalogued collections of documentary material from medieval times through to the immediate past, since modern administrative papers are deposited in these archives when they are no longer needed for everyday use. Source material relates to administrative units located within the boundaries of the post-Revolutionary *départements*, with material from the *ancien régime* relating to approximately the same areas. *Archives départementales* also contain important library collections of printed statistics, published results of historical research, regional periodicals, and historical maps.

Finally, there are the *archives nationales* in Paris which contain a wide collection of documents over a time span similar to that for the *archives départementales*. Papers relate either to individual localities or to the whole country, for example in the form of results of enquiries undertaken in administrative areas throughout France. Specialized archives of individual ministries are also found in Paris. Valuable information on source material in the *archives nationales* of interest to geographers is contained in inventories drawn up by Demangeon (1905a) and Schmidt (1902, 1907). In addition, the commentary by Gille (1964) on the value of enquiries undertaken between the seventeenth century and 1870 as sources for the history of France is an essential guide for historical geographers working at either the national or the *département* level. Similarly, the article by Soboul (1947) on source material for local studies affords much assistance.

Eighteenth-Century Sources

Population Data

Perhaps the most fascinating set of eighteenth-century archival sources is provided by the parish registers drawn up before the *commune* system was instituted following the Revolution. Details of marriages, births and deaths were recorded chronologically in each parish. This body of data forms the basic raw material from which French historical demographers have produced local and regional case studies of demographic change (Henry, 1953). Numerous aspects of rural life have been elucidated by painstakingly assembling, coding and analysing these data.

Local and regional conditions varied considerably but completed case studies have been summarized by Henry (1972 p. 49) in the following way. The broad demographic characteristics of the French peasantry in the eighteenth century included late marriage (an average age of 25 for women and 27–28 for men); a low proportion of older unmarried people; high marital fertility (4 or 5 children per marriage on average, but 6 or 7 children for marriages of completed fertility); low total sterility; average interval between births in the order of 2·0–2·5 years while the women were fairly young; low illegitimate birth rates; and variable frequency of premarital conception according to region. Birth control was practised in rural areas during the eighteenth century and had probably existed as early as the latter years of the seventeenth century in some areas of France. Rates of infantile mortality were generally high, varying between 20 and 25 per cent. This was largely due to diseases which affected the newly-born. Mortality rates for children under 10 years of age were also high. Less than two-thirds of those born survived to 15 years of age. Mean expectancy of life was about 30 years, including infant and juvenile mortality in this calculation, of course.

Comprehensive census taking was not to take place in France until the beginning of the nineteenth century, but there were several important estimates of population during the eighteenth century, such as the enquiry undertaken at the behest of Orry in 1745 (de Dainville, 1952). Such estimates must be viewed with caution but they are full of interest for historical geographers, showing important contrasts in population density, with particularly populous areas being found in the extreme North of France, around Lyons and in the southern part of the Massif Central (Morineau, 1971) (Fig. 7.5). The national population rose from 19,660,000 in 1700, according to the *intendants'* estimates, to 21,670,000 in 1763 (Messance) and 24,680,000 in 1783 (Neckar).

Provincial Enquiries

The eighteenth century formed a period of statistical enquiry in many other respects, with provincial *intendants* gathering local information on numerous aspects of social and economic life at the behest of the Crown. But with the exception of parish registers and various taxation documents there were virtually no accurate statistics that might be used as a base for determining provincial conditions. The first official census and detailed enquiries on land taxation, land use, and agricultural and industrial activities were not undertaken until the nineteenth century. For this reason eighteenth-century enquiries could be no more than the informed guesswork of local administrators. They were not accurate representations of reality. Nevertheless they convey important impressions of contemporary conditions, as is the case in Fig. A.1

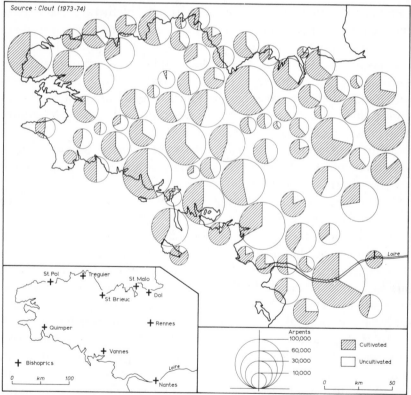

FIG. A.1. Cultivated land and waste in Brittany, 1733 (by *subdélégation*).

which displays the distribution of cultivated land and waste for each *subdélégation* in Brittany in 1733 (Sée, 1906). Enquiries were undertaken on many other themes between 1750 and 1789 including the practice of stubble-grazing on fallows and the extent of enclosed land in the kingdom. Results of these enquiries reveal the extent to which traditional communal systems of agricultural organization were still being pursued (Bloch, 1930).

Cartographic Evidence

A start was also made on the preparation of cartographic surveys, covering areas larger than individual towns or estates. One of the finest series of such maps comprises the *plans d'intendance* for the *généralité* of Paris which were drawn up between 1776 and 1789 to aid the estimation of taxation (Bloch, 1943). Major land-use categories were depicted in colour on each parish map, which was accompanied by a brief numerical summary expressed in standard royal *arpents* rather than in the various local forms of areal measure that pre-dated the introduction of the metric system after the Revolution. These maps are particularly valuable since they allow a cartographic reconstruction of land-use features, of which some have now disappeared from the landscape. Thus, vines covered sunny hillslopes south and east of Beauvais city in the 1780s (Fig. A.2) but no traces remain today. Similarly, the communal wastelands of Bray have been replaced by areas of permanent pasture. The vineyards around Paris were much more extensive standing in contrast with cider country to the west (Fig. A.3) (Fourquin, 1964).

At approximately the same time as the *plans d'intendance* were being prepared members of the Cassini family were undertaking a survey of the whole kingdom. Work was started in 1744 but was not finished until 1793. The whole of France was depicted at a scale of 1:86,400 on 182 sheets (88 × 55·5 cm), of which the last was published in 1818. These maps provide an unparalleled picture of settlements and road networks in the second half of the eighteenth century, and also indicate outlines of blocks of marsh, moorland, wood and vines. Thus, for example, the distribution of wasteland and marsh in Brittany, suggested by contemporary writings and official enquiries may be appreciated with more geographical precision from the Cassini maps (Clout, 1973–4) (Fig. A.4). In

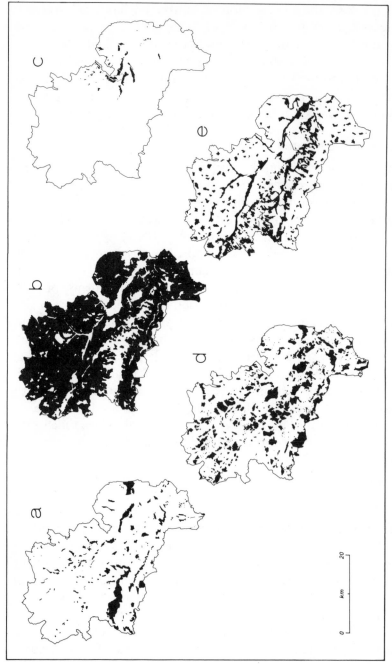

FIG. A.2. Land use around Beauvais in the 1780s: (a) wasteland; (b) arable;
(c) vineyards; (d) woodland; (e) meadows.

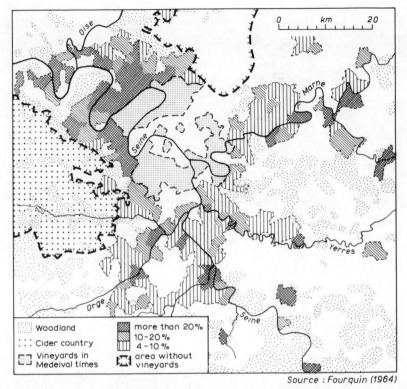

FIG. A.3. Vine growing in the inner Paris Basin in the 1780s.

addition to the maps themselves, detailed volumes of surveyors'
notes have survived and provide a valuable source which might be
exploited to great advantage by historical geographers (de
Dainville, 1955; Lerat, 1957).

Contemporary Journals

The writings of contemporary travellers contain fascinating but
often biased views of French life in the second half of the eighteenth
century. Arthur Young's journal, kept during his travels in
France in 1787, 1788 and 1789, is undoubtedly the best-known
source of this kind, presenting vivid descriptions of provincial
conditions and comparing the deficiencies of France, and especially
its agriculture, with the merits of England. Whilst admitting
Young's prejudices, his writings nevertheless contain much
valuable information by virtue of the fact that he travelled so

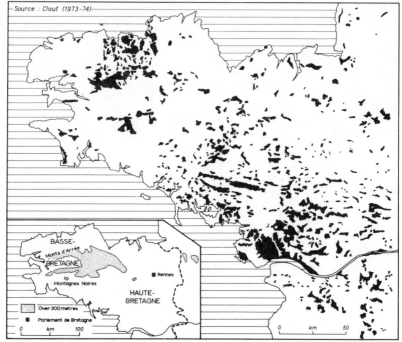

FIG. A.4. Major areas of wasteland and marsh in Brittany, after the Cassini maps.

widely in the country, wrote so much, and took the same set of pre-conceived ideas with him wherever he went (Fig. A.5). In spite of the fact that he travelled an average of *c.* 30 km each day and sometimes missed local subtleties, his appraisal of conditions is more readily comprehensible than the opinions of a score of local experts, each with his own prejudices. Young's recognition of soil types (Fig. A.5) predated geological surveys and his descriptions of local farming practices provided valuable starting points for retrospective study by such scholars as Dion (1934), Morineau (1968; 1971) and Pautard (1965).

Revolutionary Enquiries

The disturbed years surrounding the French Revolution provoked a flurry of enquiries and reports which contain information of interest to historical geographers. Only two of the many bodies of data drawn up at this time have been selected for discussion here. First, the *cahiers de doléances* which were drawn up in 1789 by

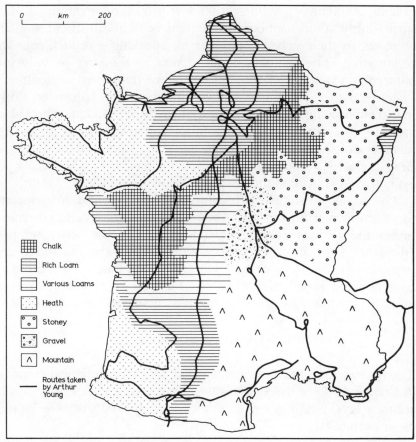

0 km 200

Chalk

Rich Loam

Various Loams

Heath

Stoney

Gravel

Mountain

Routes taken
by Arthur
Young

FIG. A.5. Arthur Young's travels in France and his appraisal of soil types.

members of each community throughout France to present their grievances to the Crown. The contents of these *cahiers* exemplify the diversity of French life during the second half of the eighteenth century and the wide range of views held by the population regarding social and economic matters as well as political affairs. To take a single example, opinions varied enormously on the utility of communal wastelands in Brittany (Sée and Lesort, 1909–1912). Members of urban communities frequently argued that moorlands should be cleared, enclosed, and used for permanent cultivation or converted to improved pasture. On the other hand, many small peasant farmers in rural communities insisted that this valuable resource should remain unenclosed and be used for communal grazing and temporary cultivation as it had been for centuries. But surprisingly some members of peasant communities held similar opinions to their urban counterparts, speaking out in favour of reclamation. The contents of the *cahiers de doléances* provide innumerable examples of the deficiencies of traditional agricultural systems, with, for example, soil erosion from bare fallows on sloping ground being graphically described (Vogt, 1953). They also indicate the nature of perception of topographical features by members of the peasantry. Thus the scarp slopes of the Pays de Bray appeared 'mountainous' to local inhabitants who rarely, if ever, travelled beyond the nearest market town (Clout, 1969b).

The second example of Revolutionary documentation, selected for discussion from the many enquiries that were ordered, comprises the agricultural enquiry undertaken at the behest of the Minister of the Interior, François de Neufchâteau, in the years immediately following 1797. Details of agricultural conditions, land use and population were recorded for local administrative units. Many manuscripts have survived in *archives départementales*.

Nineteenth-Century Sources

The nineteenth century formed a great period of statistical enquiry in France. In some cases this was undertaken at a very refined and accurate level but in others estimates and approximations were the order of the day.

The Census

The first official census took place in 1801. This was followed by a number of estimates which projected from these figures. But after the first quarter century census-taking operated on a quinquennial basis with the regular pattern of enquiry being interrupted only during the troubled times of the Franco–Prussian War when the census was postponed until 1872. Trials and errors were manifold in the early enquiries but the quality of census-taking improved with the passage of years (Châtelain, 1954). The regular quinquennial collection of figures provides a useful complement to the chronological registration of births, deaths and marriages in every *commune*. By making use of the census data and the *commune* registers of vital events, net volumes of migratory change may be calculated and plotted, as well as rather more obvious parameters of population change.

In addition to such purely quantitative data censuses after 1836 included enumeration lists (*listes nominatives*) in which the sex, exployment and other details were recorded for each inhabitant (Pinchemel, 1957). Such sources offer great potential for determining differences in the social and economic structure of villages and examining these differences in the context of varying rates of population change, proximity to urban centres and highways, and a range of other variables.

The Cadaster

The second major nineteenth-century source is the cadastral land survey.[1] With the fall of the *ancien régime* old systems of taxation were abolished and replaced by a land tax calculated on the amount and quality of property held by each landowner. Early post-Revolutionary attempts failed to operate these reforms in an equitable fashion. However a series of maps was prepared between 1790 and 1807 which showed the major categories of land use on *commune* base maps. It was intended that the fiscal contribution of each *commune* should be calculated from such maps but the method was open to abuse and maps were completed for only a few *communes* when the scheme was abandoned and replaced by a detailed ground survey of land parcels in each *commune* in France (the *ancien cadastre parcellaire*).

This survey began in 1807 and seven years later 9000 *communes* had been investigated and mapped. The fall of the First Empire slowed down operations until 1821, but by mid-century the whole of metropolitan France had been covered. Naturally the documents became out of date and had to be revised in the present century. Changes in land ownership had, however, been noted throughout the nineteenth century but the cadastral maps were not altered. In addition to twentieth-century revisions, two other evaluations of land revenues had emanated from legislation in 1850 and 1879. These were simply generalized statements produced by taxation officials, but in spite of less rigorous methods of enquiry, statistics from these surveys provide further impressions of economic conditions during this important period of agricultural change.

The main cadastral documents were produced in duplicate, one copy being held by the appropriate *commune* authorities and the other being deposited at the headquarters of the relevant taxation area. Sometimes the nineteenth-century material has been deposited in the *département* archives, but more recent information remains in the local tax offices since it is in everyday use. The 1850 and 1879 estimates appear to have survived for only a limited number of areas, and in such instances they are housed either in the *archives départementales* or in the archives of the *Direction Départementale des Contributions Directes*.

Early cadastral maps (*plans par masses de cultures*) showed areas of similar land use by tints or literal symbols. They appeared at several scales and covered only a few *communes* in each *arrondissement*. However, they provide a clear sample of the face of the country in the early nineteenth century. By contrast with other French cadastral surveys they do not provide a national coverage or show individual landholdings, nor are they accompanied by detailed landownership inventories. Their existence is rarely appreciated and their discovery is simply good fortune.

The *ancien cadastre parcellaire* of the early nineteenth century consisted of the following documents: maps (*plans parcellaires* and *tableaux d'assemblage*); geographical inventories of landholdings by *sections of communes* (*états de sections*); and alphabetical registers of landholders (*matrices*). There were two major categories of map. Master *plans* (*tableaux d'assemblage*) presented the division of each *commune* into *sections* and, if necessary, indicated the further subdivision of the *sections* into sheets. *Commune* boundaries, major lines of communication, watercourses, state properties, and main settlement features were indicated by various colours, but the methods were not standardized.

The second type of map was the *plan parcellaire* which was produced by detailed ground survey. These maps indicated each land unit or parcel, which was defined according to areal contiguity; location in the same place-name area (*lieu-dit*); uniformity of land use; and possession by a single owner. Each parcel of land was indicated on the map by a number for the relevant *section* into which it fell. This facilitated cross checking of material between documents. The *sections* were derived from local appreciation of subdivisions within individual *communes* and were used to speed consultation of detailed plans and avoid using long numerical series in the land register where each parcel was recorded. The enumeration was simply related to each individual *section*. These detailed plans were constructed on paper of a uniform size (105 × 75 cm) and therefore had to be at different scales according to the size of the area depicted and the degree of division of landholdings. Outlines of landownership units were shown but no indication of land use was provided, except for the distinction between buildings and non-built areas. Unfortunately the importance of colouring systems used, for example, for buildings, was reduced by lack of standardization. However, physical boundaries, such as hedgerows, were often shown by different types of symbol from unmarked divisions in areas of openfield.

Geographical inventory books (*états de sections*) were laid out according to the order of the predetermined *sections*. Details of ownership, location, surface covered, land use, land quality, and amount of tax to be levied were given for each parcel in the *section*. Each entry was placed on a separate line and fully described the ownership unit at the date of the original survey. Summaries were given for each page and were totalled at the end of the register. Final pages totalled areas under the various categories of land use, their quality, and the sums that were to be levied. Areas that were exempt from taxation, such as the state domain, were also noted.

Land ownership books (*matrices*) form the third major document of the old cadaster. Each landowner was entered on a separate page where all units in his possession at the time of the survey were listed and described. Landownership registers were further subdivided, providing one for built-up tracts and another for rural areas. Both registers were kept up to date between major revisions in contrast with the maps which were not modified.

Information from the less exacting enquiries of 1850 and 1879 gave a wide range of statistical details for each *commune*. Tables of estimated land use together with calculated revenues were drawn up, of which the first part formed a brief geographical monograph discussing situation, topography, soils, types of cultivation, land ownership, commerce, industries, means of communications, markets and population. In addition, original cadastral information was listed in summary form in the 1850 and 1879 documents permitting comparisons to be made.

More recent surveys supply varying quantities of data. The 1907 revaluation simply reconstructed the register of landholders at that date. No new maps or geographical inventories were drawn up, but summaries of land use were included. The *cadastre renové* instituted in 1930 involved drawing new detailed plans to show landholdings. Master plans were also produced. The cadastral revision now in progress throughout France is producing a range of documents very similar to the *cadastre renové*.

These cadastral documents present both advantages and disadvantages for a study of the historical geography of France. Perhaps the major drawback is the time span involved in the construction of the old cadaster so that an exact cross section in time may not be achieved for more than limited groups of contiguous *communes*, that were surveyed at approximately the same time. A second complication is related to the nature of taxation units. No indication of farm holdings is given, since all the information relates to land-ownership units. A third problem comes from the fiscal nature of the land-use classification, accentuated by the use of local terminology.

However, a number of advantages counterbalance these limitations. Precision of ground survey and methods of recording in the old cadaster are unrivalled in eighteenth-century enquiries and later agricultural surveys and estimates during the nineteenth century. Old cadaster plans were superior to other contemporary topographical maps and indeed were used to help in the compilation of the 1:80,000 *Carte d'Etat Major*. The documents provide useful material at various scales from the parcel, to the *section*, *commune*, or group of *communes*. A functional advantage stems from collective conservation of the material at departmental tax offices or local archives, which allows the researcher to work through a vast amount of bulky material. Further advantages will become apparent from the following sections concerning the use and potential of these documents.

The main aims of the cadaster were to establish and codify land-ownership, and this source has been used extensively in studying the impact of landowners resident in towns upon the ownership of properties located in the countryside. This important aspect of town/country relations has been studied in detail for the Toulouse region, Bas-Languedoc and Haute-Normandie (Brunet, 1965;

Dugrand, 1963, Elhaï, 1965).

In contrast with such abstract studies of landownership, much cadastral work has been completed on visible aspects of the rural scene. The classic example is found in the *Atlas de France* (1937) where Dion indicated a variety of settlement morphologies that were derived from cadastral maps. Work undertaken in Brittany further exemplifies the importance of large-scale cadastral maps in historico-geographical research. Using the old cadaster Flatrès (1957) plotted areas of openfield that punctuated the early nineteenth-century landscape of southern Finistère which has now largely been covered by enclosures. The wealth of detail contained in cadastral maps may also be used in studying ground plans of rural buildings. Research by Pinchemel (1944) and Coque (1956) has shown the dynamism of individual farmsteads on the Picardy Plain. Demangeon (1905b) had long recognized enclosed court-yard farms as traditional features of this area, but scrupulous analysis of old maps demonstrated that this form developed by infilling of spaces between earlier individual farm buildings. Changes in the distribution of settlement through time may also be appreciated from cadastral plans. For example, Flatrès (1957) derived his classification of agglomerated rural settlements in Brittany by comparing details from the old cadaster with the modern landscape.

Perhaps the most elaborate use of the cadaster has been concerned with the study of land use, both in terms of mapping distributions for defined cross-sections but also for indicating changes between survey periods. Re-creation of land-use details for isolated *communes*, as at Brouckerque on the Flanders Plain (Fig. A.6), has been attempted by many researchers. Land-use information in the *états de sections* may be transferred on to the base of the *plans parcellaires* to show complete regional patterns for the early nineteenth century. Thus Fig. A.7 depicts the precocious development of grassland farming in the western section of the Pays de Bray, which stands in contrast with the openfield arable of the surrounding plateaux of Upper Normandy (Clout 1969a). Although constructing such maps is an extremely laborious task, the precise results obtained avoid problems involved in statistical generalizations at the *commune* level.

Perpillou (1940) made extensive use of such *commune* land-use

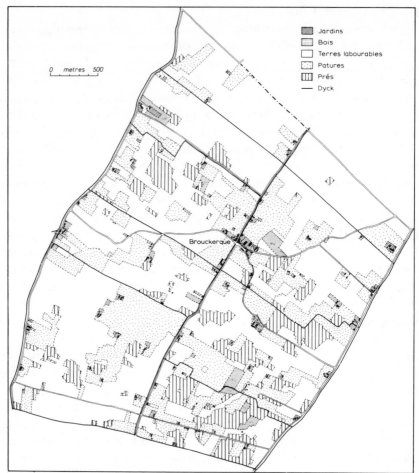

FIG. A.6. Land use in Brouckerque *commune*, after the old cadaster.

totals in the Limousin region, which he studied from the documents
of the old cadaster and the 1907 revision. In spite of the limitation
of working within the administrative framework of *commune*
boundaries, major land-use characteristics and their sub-regional
variations do emerge and may be considered in conjunction with
other forms of evidence in undertaking historical regional geography. Figure 7.2 takes the operation one stage further and
summarizes at the *département* level major land-use categories from
the old cadaster for the whole country. Perpillou extended his

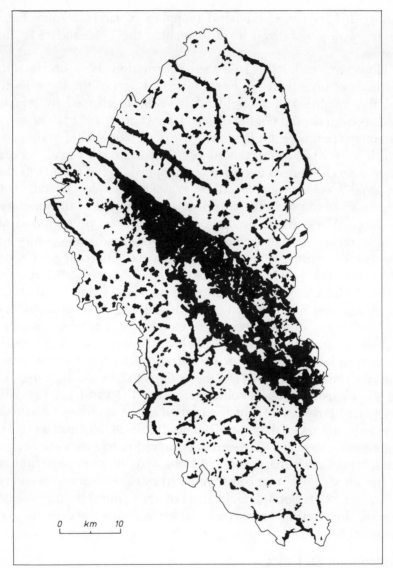

FIG. A.7. Permanent grass in the Western Section of the Pays de Bray, after the old cadaster.

commune by *commune* analysis to cover each region of France and it is to be hoped that eventually synthetic maps will be produced showing dominant land-use characteristics for the early nineteenth century and 1907, as well as the modern period. As Sutton has shown in Chapter 8, cadastral mapping of land use may be extended at a generalized level to include the 1850 and 1879 summaries.

However, cadastral land-use information is open to other methods of investigation. For the central part of the Pays de Bray the five qualities of ploughland have been mapped by *commune sections* from the data of the old cadaster (Clout, 1971). The results demonstrate the generally poor quality of ploughland in this zone, which was later converted to permanent grass. Fiscal revenues themselves have been analysed and mapped by Fel (1962) to show regional specialization of either grassland or ploughland, in the highlands of the Massif Central in the early part of the nineteenth century. Work in the Sologne has shown that presentation of a simple series of land-use cross sections through the century may conceal complicated, intervening processes of change (Sutton, 1969 and 1971). Thus statistics in the 1850 and 1879 revisions showed that areas of wasteland were not always converted directly to wood, since an intervening ploughland stage was often involved.

A variety of other aspects of economic life in rural areas may be considered from the evidence of cadastral documents. A generalized pattern of industrial enterprises throughout France at the time of the old cadaster has already been depicted in Chapter 12 (Fig. 12.6). Industrial details contained in the 1850 and 1879 revisions are particularly useful, but the limited survival of these documents prevents any more than localized study. Basic information on road communications in nineteenth-century France may be derived from topographic maps, but additional data on road conditions and seasonality of use may be obtained from the cadastral revisions of 1850 and 1879. Commercialization of agricultural products may be studied in relation to markets which are described in the same sources.

Agricultural Statistics

Agricultural statistics were not collected in a particularly rigorous fashion in France before 1929. The first nineteenth-century agricultural enquiry was conducted in 1814. Unfortunately the national cover is incomplete but the fragmentary information that remains in national and *département* archives has been collated and published (La Statistique Agricole de 1814, 1914). This enquiry was undertaken at a stage when the metric system was still an innovation and the cadastral land survey had only just started. As a result, numerical information in the 1814 returns must be treated only as a guide providing a rough order of magnitude.

Preparations for the next agricultural enquiry were started in 1835. Questionnaires were sent to *commune* mayors who were instructed to make local enquiries and then fill in statistics on such topics as the amount of land devoted to specified crops, yields obtained, fallows, other aspects of land use, and livestock numbers, (Gille, 1964). Results were gathered between 1836 and 1839. Again they were only rough estimates, since the cadaster was still incomplete and metric measures were not fully understood. In addition, it was not always clear if average yields were being recorded, as required, or whether those for the individual survey year were noted. However the local returns were collated and 'controlled' by members of special *département* agricultural commissions to give a final result that seemed reasonable to local experts. Some detailed *commune* questionnaires have survived in *archives départementales* but results were collected and published at the *département* level (Statistique de la France, Agriculture, 1840). Data from this source on cereal yields have been used to advantage by Morineau (1968, 1971) in his stimulating essays asking 'Was there an agricultural revolution in France in the eighteenth century?'

In the remainder of the nineteenth century so-called decennial agricultural enquiries were undertaken in 1852, 1862, 1882 and 1892, with the events of the Franco-Prussian war preventing an enquiry being held in 1872. The method of investigation was roughly similar to that undertaken in the 1830s, comprising detailed questionnaires to *commune* mayors, with *département* commissions controlling the results. The quality of the statistics improved with the passage of time, as the land surface of each *commune* was known precisely from the old cadaster, use of the metric system became commonplace, and officials grew accustomed to making detailed investigations, reading enquiry forms and answering the precise questions that were asked. Detailed documentary fragments of many of these enquiries are still to be found in national and departmental archives but the results from each survey have been published in summary form. As well as providing

data on crops, yields, prices, and livestock, these agricultural
statistics provide information on farm holdings, implements, crop
rotations, the agricultural labour force, rates of pay, fertilisers, and
land improvements. The nation-wide picture of underdraining,
marling, and other aspects of agricultural change may be depicted
from these sources (Phillips and Clout, 1970; Clout and Phillips,
1972.)

Two other main sets of agricultural information were collected
and printed during the nineteenth century. The first of these
followed a parliamentary decree in 1866 and involved completion
of a detailed 161-item questionnaire and submission of reports
from local agricultural experts, farmers, and landowners. The
country was divided into survey areas for purposes of the enquiry
and many of the statistical and literary reports submitted to the 28
agricultural committees were published in full or part in a 10-
volume survey (Ministère de l'Agriculture, Enquête Agricole,
1867–72). The quality and detail of the results varied from area to
area, and as a result it is not easy to obtain a precise nationwide
picture of particular themes from these volumes. They do, however, provide very detailed material for regional studies. The final
set of published statistical information is contained in the Statistique
Internationale de l'Agriculture (1876). This has two particular
merits for research; it partially fills the gap created by the absence
of a decennial enquiry in 1872, and also allows ready comparison
with agricultural conditions from a number of other countries.

Other Statistical Sources

Three other types of statistical source are of particular value to
historical geographers working on rural France during the nineteenth century. The first of these involves the *mercuriales* which
recorded cereal prices and yields, and the cost of livestock at local
markets throughout France. These manuscript details have been
conserved in many *archives départementales* and allow trends of
prices and yields to be investigated with precision. Secondly, many
départements produced statistical yearbooks which included not only
detailed lists of figures but also analytical essays on local agricultural conditions, industrial production, and many other topics.
Finally, the specialized publications of provincial agricultural
societies provide useful insights into farming conditions. Many

such societies had been established in the second half of the eight-eenth century, when local landowners and agronomists wrote learned treatises on the need for agricultural advance and the various means that might be employed to achieve it. After the period of Revolutionary disruption many of these societies were reconstituted and their subsequent publications include not only theoretical statements on agricultural improvement but also practical advice and factual reports on local agricultural conditions. The latter information allows local changes in land use and agri-cultural production to be investigated in some detail (Clout, 1972–3).

In the twentieth century new techniques of analysis, such as computerized data handling, have come to aid research in historical geography. But in addition new 'documents' have been created. Aerial photography and the results of what has been called

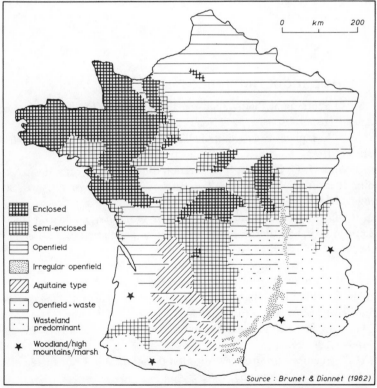

0   km   200

Enclosed

Semi-enclosed

Openfield

Irregular openfield

Aquitaine type

Openfield + waste

Wasteland predominant

Woodland/high mountains/marsh

Source : Brunet & Dionnet (1962)

FIG. A.8. Types of rural landscape in modern France.

'archaeology from the air' offer new insights. For example, detailed analysis of modern air-photograph coverage has been combined with the findings of geographers and historians to produce a nationwide map of field patterns (Fig. A.8) as they exist in the modern landscape (Brunet and Dionnet, 1962). It may be claimed that to a large extent the field patterns of past centuries are still recognizable. Air photography has also been of vital importance in the recognition of relict features such as deserted settlements (Chevallier, 1965), former field patterns (Chevallier, 1963) and earlier road patterns.

Appendix Note

1. I am indebted to Keith Sutton for allowing me to incorporate the substance of an earlier joint publication on this theme into the present discussion.

Appendix References

Bloch, M., 'La lutte pour l'individualisme agraire dans la France du 18e siècle', *Annales d'Histoire Economique et Sociale*, 2 (1930), 329–81, 511–56.

Bloch, M., 'Les plans cadastraux de l'ancien régime', *Mélanges d'Histoire Sociale*, 3 (1943), 55–70.

Brunet, P. and M. C. Dionnet, 'Presentation d'une essai de carte des paysages ruraux de la France', *Bulletin de l'Association de Géographes Français*, 305–6 (1962), 98–103.

Brunet, R., *Les Campagnes toulousaines: étude géographique*, Toulouse (1965).

Châtelain, A., 'Valeur des recensements de la population française au 19e siècle', *Revue de Géographie de Lyon*, 4 (1954), 273–80.

Chevallier, R., 'Un document fondamental pour l'histoire et la géographie agraire: la photographie aérienne', *Etudes Rurales*, I (1963), 70–80.

Chevallier, R., 'Photographie aérienne et villages désertés', in *Villages désertés et histoire économique*, Paris (1965), 63–81.

Clout, H., 'The increase in the grassland area of the Pays de Bray., *Erdkunde*, 23 (1969a), 20–29.

Clout, H., 'Structures agraires et utilisation du sol dans le Bray au 18e siècle', *Acta Geographica*, 76 (1969b), 13–22.

Clout, H., 'L'évolution du paysage rural dans la partie occidentale du Pays de

Bray, d'après les documents de l'ancien cadastre (début du 19e siècle)', *Norois*, 71 (1971), 510–20.

Clout, H., 'Agricultural progress and environmental degradation in Pyrénées–Orientales during the nineteenth century'. *Bulletin de la Société Royale de Géographie d'Anvers*, 83 (1972–3), 31–53.

Clout, H., 'Reclamation of wasteland in Brittany, 1750–1900', *Bulletin de la Société Royale de Géographie d'Anvers*, 84 (1973–4), 29–60.

Clout, H. and Phillips, A. D. M., 'Fertilisants minéraux en France au 19e siècle', *Etudes Rurales*, 45 (1972), 9–28.

Coque, R., 'L'évolution de la maison rurale en Amiénois', *Annales de Géographie*, 65 (1956), 401–17.

de Dainville, F., 'Un denombrement inédit au 18e siècle: enquête du controleur général Orry 1745', *Population*, 7 (1952), 49–68.

de Dainville, F., 'La carte de Cassini et son intérêt géographique', *Bulletin de l'Association de Géographes Français*, 251–2 (1955), 138–47.

Demangeon, A., *Les Sources de la géographie de la France aux archives nationales*, Paris (1905a).

Demangeon, A., *La Picardie*, Paris (1905b).

Dion, R., *Essai sur la formation du paysage rural français*, Tours (1934).

Dion, R., 'Types de terroirs ruraux', in *Atlas de France*, Paris, Planche 37 (1937).

Dugrand, R., *Villes et campagnes en Bas-Languedoc: le reseau urbain du Bas-Languedoc méditerranéen*, Paris (1963).

Elhaï, H., *Recherches sur la propriété foncière des citadins en Haute-Normandie*, Paris (1965).

Fel, A., *Les Hautes terres du Massif Central: économie agricole et tradition paysanne*, Paris and Clermont-Ferrand (1962).

Flatrès, P., 'La structure rurale du Sud-Finistère d'après les anciens cadastres', *Norois*, 4 (1957), 353–67, 425–53.

Fourquin, G., *Les Campagnes de la région parisienne à la fin du moyen âge: du milieu du 13e siècle au début du 16e siècle*, Paris (1964).

Gille, B., *Les Sources statistiques de l'histoire de France des enquêtes du 17e siècle à 1870*, Paris (1964).

Henry, L., 'Une richesse démographique en France: les registres paroissiaux', *Population*, 8 (1953), 281–90.

Henry, L., 'Historical demography', in Glass, D. V. and Revelle R. (eds.), *Population and Social Change*, London (1972), 43–54.

Lerat, S., 'Les pays de l'Adour à la fin du 18e siècle, d'après la carte de Cassini', *Revue Géographique des Pyrénées et du Sud-Ouest*, 28 (1957), 373–87.

Ministère de l'Agriculture, *Enquête agricole*, 10 vols., Paris (1867–72).

Morineau, M., 'Y a-t-il eu une révolution agricole en France au 18e siècle?' *Revue Historique*, 486 (1968), 299–326.

Morineau, M., *Les Faux-semblants d'un demarrage économique*, Paris (1971).

Pautard, J., *Les Disparités régionales dans la croissance de l'agriculture française*, Paris (1965).

Perpillou, A., *Cartographie du paysage rural limousin*, Chartres (1940).

Phillips, A. D. M. and Clout, H. D., 'Underdraining in France during the second half of the nineteenth century', *Transactions, Institute of British Geographers*, 51 (1970), 71–94.

Pinchemel, P., 'Habitation rurale et maisons rurales en Picardie', *Bulletin de l'Association de Géographes Français*, 165 (1944), 102–08.

Pinchemel, P., *Structures sociales et dépopulation rurale dans les campagnes picardes de 1836 à 1936*, Paris (1957).

Schmidt, C., 'Les sources de l'histoire d'un département aux archives nationales', *La Révolution Française*, 47 (1902), 1–12.

Schmidt, C., *Les Sources de l'histoire de France depuis 1789 aux archives nationales*, Paris (1907).

Sée, H., *Les classes rurales en Bretagne du 16e siècle à la Révolution*, Paris (1906).

Sée, H. and Lesort, A. (eds.), *Cahiers de doléances de la sénéchaussée de Rennes*, 4 vols, Paris (1909–1912).

Soboul, M., 'Esquisse d'un plan de recherches par une mongraphie de communauté rurale', *La Pensée*, 13 (1947), 34–50.

Statistique de la France, Agriculture, Paris (1840).

Statistique Internationale de l'Agriculture 1873, Paris (1876).

Sutton, K., 'La triste Sologne: l'utilisation du sol dans une région française à l'abandon au début du 19e siècle', *Norois*, 61 (1969), 7–30.

Sutton, K., 'The reduction of wasteland in the Sologne: nineteenth-century French regional improvement', *Transactions Institute of British Geographers*, 52 (1971), 129–44.

Vogt, J., 'Erosion des sols et techniques de culture en climat tempéré maritime de transition: France et Allemagne', *Revue de Géomorphologie Dynamique*, 4 (1953), 157–83.

Young, A., *Voyages en France en 1787, 1788, 1789*, trans. Sée, H., 3 vols, Paris (1931).

Appendix II
Additional Reading on Themes in The Historical Geography of France

HUGH D. CLOUT

Material of relevance to studying the historical geography of France is found in a very wide range of books and journals. The following list, which is far from exhaustive, presents items that have not been mentioned in the chapters of the present book.

Allix, A., 'Le trafic en Dauphiné à la fin du moyen-âge', *Revue de Géographie Alpine*, 11 (1923) 373–420.

Allix, A., *L'Oisans au moyen-âge: étude de géographie historique en haute-montagne*, Paris (1929).

Allix, A., 'Anciennes émigrations dauphinoises', *Revue de Géographie Alpine*, 20 (1932), 119–126.

Arbos, P., 'Migrations ouvrières en France au début du 19e siècle', *Revue de Géographie Alpine*, 20 (1932), 614–618.

Aries, P., 'Sur les origines de la contraception en France', *Population*, 8 (1953), 465–72.

Armengaud, A., 'Mariages et naissances sous le Consulat et l'Empire', *Revue d'Histoire Moderne et Contemporaine*, 17 (1970), 373–89.

Armengaud, A., *La Population française au XIXe siècle*, Paris (1971).

Arque, P., 'La conquête du sol en Périgord méridional', in *Melanges Daniel Faucher*, 1 (1948), 12–26.

Audin, A., 'Sur la géographie de Lyon romain', *Revue de Géographie de Lyon*, 27 (1952), 133–40.

Baehrel, R., *La Basse-Provence rurale*, Paris (1961).

Baker, A. R. H., 'Etablissements ruraux sur la marge sud-ouest du Bassin Parisien dans les premières années du XIXe siècle', *Norois*, 15 (1968), 481–92.

Baker, A. R. H., 'Adjustments to distance between farmstead and field: some findings from the southwestern Paris Basin in the early nineteenth century', *Canadian Geographer*, 17 (1973), 259–75.

Baker, A. R. H., 'A nation of peasants', *Geographical Magazine*, 48 (1975), 24–30.

Baratier, E. (ed.), *Histoire de Marseille*, Toulouse (1973).

Barrère, P., 'Le paysage girondin autour de Bordeaux', *Revue Géographique des Pyrénées et du Sud-Ouest*, 20 (1949), 222–252.

Bautier, R. H., 'The fairs of Champagne', in Cameron, R. (ed.) *op. cit.* (1970), 42–63.

Bertrand, A. J. C., 'L'activité des tanneries et des mégisseries du Vivarais vers la fin du 18e siècle', *Revue de Géographie Alpine*, 26 (1938), 401–416.

Beteille, R., 'Les Rouergats à Paris, XIXe et XXe siècles: un phénomène socio-réligieux mal connu, le rôle du clergé dans l'émigration', *Etudes de la Région Parisienne* (1972), 46 (33) 9–18 and 46 (34) 12–20.

Bethemont, J., *Le thème de l'eau dans la vallée du Rhône: essai sur la genèse d'un espace hydraulique*, Saint-Etienne (1972).

Billinge, M., 'Technological resistance', *Geographical Magazine*, 48 (1976), 349–53.

Biraben, J. N., 'Inventaire des listes nominatives de recensement en France', *Population*, 18, (1963), 305–28.

Biraben, J. N., 'La statistique de population sous le Consulat et l'Empire', *Revue d'Histoire Moderne et Contemporaine*, 17, (1970), 359–72.

Blache, J., 'Les trappeurs du Vercors au moyen âge', *Revue de Géographie Alpine*, 10 (1922), 305–310.

Blache, J., 'L'essartage, ancienne pratique culturale dans les Alpes dauphinoises', *Revue de Géographie Alpine*, 11 (1923), 553–575.

Blache, J., Carcel, C. and Rey, M. 'Le troupeau bovin dans les Alpes du Dauphiné et de Savoie au milieu du 18e siècle', *Revue de Géographie Alpine*, 21 (1933), 419–431.

Blanchard, M., 'L'enquête de 1811 sur le roulage', *Revue de Géographie Alpine*, 8 (1920), 585–626.

Blanchard, M., 'Note sur le premier projet de chemin de fer dauphinois, 1828–29', *Revue de Géographie Alpine*, 14 (1926), 215–218.

Blanchard, M., 'Quelques points de l'histoire des chemins de fer autour de Lyon, 1830–1853', *Revue de Géographie Alpine*, 20 (1932), 199–236.

Blanchard, M., 'Routes et roulage en Savoie, 1815–59', *Revue de Géographie Alpine*, 22 (1934), 611–621.

Blanchard, M., 'Textes relatifs à l'économie savoyarde 17–18e siècles', *Revue de Géographie Alpine*, 25 (1937), 211–223.

Blanchard, R., *Grenoble: étude de géographie urbaine*, Paris (1912).

Blanchard, R., 'Les routes des Alpes occidentales à l'époque napoléonienne, 1796–1815', *Revue de Géographie Alpine*, 9 (1921), 312–321.

Bloch, M., *The Ile-de-France*, London (trans. J. E. Anderson) (1971).

Bonnamour, J., 'Paysages agraires aux confins du Morvan et de l'Auxois', *Bulletin de l'Association de Géographes Français* (1960), 294–5, 156–68.

Bouhier, A., 'Gaigneries et terroirs de hameaux dans le sud-ouest vendéen', *Norois*, 4 (1957), 455–68.

Bourgeois-Pichat, J., 'Evolution générale de la population française depuis le XVIIIe siècle', *Population*, 6 (1951), 635–62.

Boutruche, R., 'Les courants de peuplement dans l'Entre-Deux-Mers: étude sur le brassage de la population rurale', *Annales d'Histoire Economique et Sociale*, 7 (1935), 13–37 and 124–54.

Boutruche, R., 'La dévastation des campagnes pendant la guerre de cent ans et la reconstruction agricole de la France', *Publications de la Faculté des Lettres de Strasbourg* (1945), 106.

Boutruche, R., 'La crise d'une société: seigneurs et paysans du Bordelais pendant la guerre de cent ans', *Annales, Economies, Sociétés, Civilisations*, 2 (1947), 336–38.

Brillet, A., 'Une petite ville bretonne: Quimperlé en 1815', *Norois*, 15 (1968), 493–501.

Brunet, R., 'Les recherches sur la propriété rurale des citadins et l'exemple de Toulouse', *Bulletin de l'Association de Géographes Français*, 265 (1957), 66–75.

Cameron, R. (ed.), *Essays in French Economic History*, Homewood (1970).

Canal, S., 'Quelques aspects de l'économie agricole du Tarn-et-Garonne vers le milieu de 19e siècle, d'après l'enquête de 1866', *Revue Géographique des Pyrénées et du Sud-Ouest*, 5 (1934), 57–84.

Caput, J., 'La vie rurale dans la vallée sous-pyrénéenne du Gave de Pau', *Revue Géographique des Pyrénées et du Sud-Ouest*, 21 (1950), 258–282.

Caput, J., 'La formation des paysages agraires béarnais: observations et problèmes', *Revue Géographique des Pyrénées et du Sud-Ouest*, 27 (1956), 219–242.

Cavaillé, A., 'Cent cinquante ans de vie rurale à Saint-Projet; Tarn-et-Garonne', *Revue Géographique des Pyrénées et du Sud-Ouest*, 21 (1950), 127–159.

Cavaillès, H., *La Vie pastorale et agricole dans les Pyrénées des Gaves de l'Adour et des Nestes*, Paris (1931).

Cavaillès, H., 'La transhumance dans les Basses-Pyrénées', *Revue Géographique des Pyrénées et du Sud-Ouest*, 4 (1933), 490–498.

Cavaillès, H., 'Les accès de Bordeaux', *Revue Géographique des Pyrénées et du Sud-Ouest*, 14 (1943), 150–168.

Champier, L., 'Recherches sur les origines du terroir et de l'habitat en Mâconnais et en Châlonnais', *Etudes Rhodaniennes*, 22 (1947), 206–238.

Champier, L., 'A la frontière des terroirs: le problème de l'assolement à Bragny-sur-Saône à la fin du 18e siècle', *Revue de Géographie de Lyon*, 24 (1949), 227–245.

Champier, L., 'Le défrichement de la Forêt de Bièvre (Bas-Dauphiné), essai d'interpretation d'un type de terroir méridional', *Revue de Géographie de Lyon*, 27 (1952), 436–450.

Champier, L., 'Mise au point sur quelques questions agraires', *Revue de Géographie de Lyon*, 29 (1954), 211–220.

Charaud, A. M., 'Bocage et plaine dans l'ouest de la France', *Annales de Géographie*, 58 (1949), 113–25.

Châtelain, A., 'Les migrations temporaires anciennes à Lyon et dans les pays environnants', *Revue de Géographie de Lyon*, 24 (1949), 37–50.

Châtelain, A., 'Problèmes ruraux en Bugey au milieu du 19e siècle', *Revue de Géographie de Lyon*, 27 (1952), 155–164.

Châtelain, A., 'La formation de la population lyonnaise: l'apport italien, seconde moitié du 19e siècle, début du 20e siècle', *Revue de Géographie de Lyon*, 27 (1952), 317–326.

Châtelain, A., 'Notes sur la population d'un village bugiste, Belmont, 17e–19e siècles', *Revue de Géographie de Lyon*, 28 (1953), 113–120.

Châtelain, A., 'La formation de la population lyonnaise; apport d'origine montagnarde (18e–19e siècles)', *Revue de Géographie de Lyon*, 29 (1954), 91–116.

Châtelain, A., 'Les usines-internats et les migrations dans la région lyonnaise; seconde moitié du XIXe et début XXe siècle', *Revue d'Histoire Economique et Sociale*, 48 (1970), 373–94.

Châtelain, A., 'Complexité des migrations temporaires et definitives à Paris et dans le Bassin Parisien (XVIIe–XXe siècles)', *Etudes de la Région Parisienne*, 44 (27) (1970), 27–39.

Châtelain, A., 'Les migrations temporaires de détente et de loisirs des Parisiens (XVIIe–XXe siècles)', *Etudes de la Région Parisienne*, 44 (1970), 27–32 and 45 (1971), 31–8.

Châtelain, A., 'L'attraction des trois plus grandes agglomérations françaises: Paris, Lyon, Marseille en 1891', *Annales de Démographie Historique* (1971), 27–41.

Chevalier, B., 'Bailleurs et preneurs en Touraine après la guerre de cent ans', *Etudes Rurales*, 16 (1965), 117–24.

Chevalier, L., *Labouring Classes and Dangerous Classes in Paris during the first half of the nineteenth century*, London (trans. F. Jellinck) (1973).

Chevalier, M., 'L'habitat rural dans la région de Nérac', *Revue Géographique des Pyrénées et du Sud-Ouest*, 13 (1942), 60–100.

Chevalier, M., 'Les caractères de la vie pastorale dans le bassin supérieur de l'Ariège', *Revue Géographique des Pyrénées et du Sud-Ouest*, 20 (1949), 5–84.

Chevallier, R., *Les Voies romaines*, Paris (1972).

Cholley, A., *Les Préalpes de Savoie*, Paris (1925).

Chombard de Lauwe, J., *Bretagne et Pays de la Garonne: évolution agricole comparée depuis un siècle*, Paris (1946).

Clos-Arceduc, I. C. G., 'Sur la destruction du bocage', *Etudes Rurales*, 2 (1961), 99–101.

Clout, H. D., 'Timeless rural France', *Geographical Magazine*, 48 (1975), 151–55.

Coppolani, J., 'Physionomie et répartition fonctionnelle des quartiers de Toulouse', *Revue Géographique des Pyrénées et du Sud-Ouest*, 13 (1942), 17–59.

Corbin, A., 'Migrations temporaires et société rurale au XIXe siècle: le cas du Limousin', *Revue Historique*, 246 (1971), 293–334.

Crubellier, M., 'Le Briançonnais à la fin de l'ancien régime', *Revue de Géographie Alpine*, 36 (1948), 259–299, 335–371.

de Dainville, F., *Le Langage des géographes: termes, signes, couleurs des cartes anciennes, 1500–1800*, Paris (1964).

de Dainville, F., 'Les bases d'une cartographie industrielle de l'Europe au XIXe siècle', in P. Léon, *et al.* (eds) *op. cit.* (1972), 15–33.

Daveau, S., 'Une communauté jurassienne au 18e siècle, les Foncine', *Revue de Géographie de Lyon*, 29 (1954), 117–130.

Deffontaines, P., 'Sur la géographie préhistorique', *Annales de Géographie*, 33 (1924), 19–29.

Delaruelle, F., 'La maison élémentaire de la région toulousaine', *Revue Géographique des Pyrénées et du Sud-Ouest*, 4 (1933), 373–383.

Delaspre, J., 'La naissance d'un paysage rural au 18e siècle sur les hauts plateaux de l'est du Cantal et du nord de la Margeride', *Revue de Géographie Alpine*, 40 (1952), 493–499.

Delasselle, C., 'Les enfants abandonnés à Paris au 18e siècle', *Annales, Economies, Sociétés, Civilisations*, 30 (1975), 187–218.

Dellozcour, M., 'La répartition des vestiges préhistoriques dans les Alpes françaises et à leurs abords', *Revue de Géographie Alpine*, 12 (1924), 189–246.

Demolins, E., *Comment la route crée le type sociale: les routes de l'antiquité*, Paris (1901).

Demontzey, P., *Traité pratique de reboisement et du gazonnement des montagnes*, Paris (1882).

Deniau, J., 'La vigne et le vin à Lyon au XVe siècle', *Etudes Rhodaniennes*, 6 (1930), 263–76.

Deniaud, A., 'Champs ouverts à la lisière de la forêt de Paimpont', *Norois*, 8 (1961), 153–65.

Delisle, L., *Etude sur la condition de la vie agricole et l'état de l'agriculture en Normandie au moyen âge*, Paris (1851).

Desert, G., 'Aperçu sur l'exode rural en Basse-Normandie à la fin du 19e siècle', *Revue Historique*, 250 (1973), 107–118.

Devailly, G., *Le Berry du Xe siècle au milieu de XIIIe*, Paris. (1973).

Devèze, M., 'Forêts françaises et forêts allemandes', *Revue Historique*, 236 (1966), 347–380; and 47–68.

Deyon, P., *Amiens, capitale provinciale: étude sur la société urbaine au XVIIe siècle*, Paris (1967).

Dion, R., 'Orléans et l'ancienne navigation de la Loire', *Annales de Géographie*, 47 (1938), 128–54.

Dion, R., *Les Frontières de la France*, Paris (1947).

Dion, R., 'Reflexions du méthode à propos de "La Grande Limagne" de Max Derruau', *Annales de Géographie*, 60 (1951), 25–33.

Dion, R., 'L'ancien privilège de Bordeaux', *Revue Géographique des Pyrénées et du Sud-Ouest*, 26 (1955), 223–236.

Dion, R., 'Les origines de la Rochelle et l'essor du commerce atlantique aux XIIe et XIIIe siècle', *Norois*, 3, (1956), 35–50.

Dion, R., 'Les voies romaines du Nord de la France étudiées sur les cartes', *Publications de la Société de Géographie de Lille*, (1944–5), 5–35.

Dion-Salitot, M. and Dion, M. *La crise d'une société villageoise*, Paris (1972).

Donkin, R. A., 'The growth and distribution of the Cistercian order in medieval Europe', *Studia Monastica*, 9 (1967), 276–86.

Dupâquier, J., 'Des rôles de tailles à la démographie historique; l'exemple du Vexin français', *Annales de Démographie Historique* (1965), 31–42.

Dupâquier, J., 'Sur la population française au 17e et au 18e siècle', *Revue Historique*, 239 (1968), 43–79.

Febvre, L., *La Terre et l'évolution humaine: introduction géographique à l'histoire*, Paris (1922). (Translated into English as 'A Geographical Introduction to History', London (1925).

Fénelon, P., 'Saint-Mayme de Péreyrol: étude de structure agraire', *Revue Géographique des Pyrénées et du Sud-Ouest*, 18–19 (1947–8), 17–44.

Fénelon, P., 'Quelques terroirs périgourdins', *Norois*, 2 (1955), 399–406.

Fénelon, P., 'Structure agraire d'un finage périgourdin', *Norois*, 5 (1958), 21–40.

Festy, O., *L'Agriculture pendant la Révolution française: les conditions de production et de récolte des céréales*, Paris (1947).

Feuchère, P., 'Dans le nord de la France: la permanence des cadres territoriaux,' *Annales, Economies, Sociétés, Civilisations*, 9 (1954), 94–100.

Flatrès, P., 'Le rentier de Saint-Dominique de Morlaix; étude de géographie historique', *Bulletin de la Société Archéologique du Finistère* 82 (1956), 150–59.

Font-Réaulx, J. de, 'Note sur certaines statistiques et dénombrements ordonnés au 18e siècle par les Intendants du Dauphiné', *Revue de Géographie Alpine*, 10 (1922), 429–444.

Font-Réaulx, J. de, 'Où en est l'atlas historique du Dauphiné?' *Revue de Géographie Alpine*, 38 (1950), 525–533.

Francastel, P., 'Versailles et l'architecture urbaine au 17e siècle', *Annales, Economies, Sociétés, Civilisations*, 10 (1955), 465–479.

Gachon, L., 'Un siècle d'histoire des sols de France: dégradation et refection', *Revue de Géographie de Lyon*, 2 (1950), 81–89.

Gadoud, M., 'Note sur une statistique des forêts du 18e siècle à nos jours', *Revue de Géographie Alpine*, 8 (1920), 141–145.

Galibert, G., 'Introduction à l'étude de la géographie humaine du plateau d'Anglès', *Revue Géographique des Pyrénées et du Sud-Ouest*, 21 (1950), 160–177.

Galliano, P., 'La mortalité infantile dans la banlieue sud de Paris à la fin du 18e siècle, 1774–1794', *Annales de Démographie Historique* (1966), 139–180.

Gallois, L., 'Les Dombes', *Annales de Géographie*, 1 (1891–2), 121–31.

Gallois, L., *Régions naturelles et noms de pays*, Paris (1908).

Galy, G., 'La mise en place de l'habitat dans les Pyrénées-Orientales', *Etudes Rurales*, 22 (1966), 82–98.

Galy, G., 'Origine de quelques types d'habitations rurales en France', *Etudes Rurales*, 31 (1968), 113–22.

Gamblin, A., 'Le pays de Lalleu', *Publications de la Société de Géographie de Lille* (1944–5), 36–94.

Gascon, R., 'Structure et géographie d'une maison de marchand de soie à Lyon au 16e siècle', *Revue de Géographie de Lyon*, 27 (1952), 145–154.

Gascon, R., *Grand commerce et vie urbaine au XVIe siècle: Lyon et ses marchands*, Paris, 2 vols (1971).

Gautier, M., 'La forêt de Loudéac et ses abords depuis le milieu du XVIIe siècle: contribution à l'étude des défrichements récents dans l'intérieur de la Bretagne', *Annales de Bretagne*, 45 (1938), 72–88.

Gautier, M., 'Remarques sur la structure des champs bretons', *Annales de Bretagne*, 48 (1941), 387–94.

Gautier, M., 'Quelques remarques sur la terminologie agraire en Bretagne', *Annales de Bretagne*, 53 (1946), 136–39.

Gautier, M., 'Une tentative de défrichement et de chaulage dans la Bretagne intérieure au XVIIe siècle', *Annales de Bretagne*, 46 (1939), 53–65.

Gautier, M., *La Bretagne centrale: étude géographique*, La Roche-sur-Yon (1947).

Gautier, M., 'La Roche-sur-Yon: géographie urbaine', *Annales de Bretagne*, 55 (1948), 209–17.

Gautier, M., 'Les chemins morts dans la France de l'Ouest', *Annales de Bretagne*, 57 (1950), 216–28.

Gay, F., 'Les communaux en Berry', *Acta Geographica*, 48 (1963), 17–24.

George, P., 'Anciennes et nouvelles forêts en région méditerranéenne', *Etudes Rhodaniennes*, 9 (1933), 85–129.

Gibert, A., 'Notes au sujet de l'ancien flottage du bois sur le Doubs', *Revue de Géographie Alpine*, 21 (1933), 433–446.

Giner, J., 'Contribution historique à l'étude de la greffe du noyer au Dauphiné', *Revue de Géographie Alpine*, 19 (1931), 187–198.

Giot, P. R., *Armoricains et Bretons*, Rennes (1951).

Glass, D. V. and Eversley, D. E. C. (eds.), *Population in History*, London (1965).

Glass, D. V. and Revelle, R. (eds.), *Population and Social Change*, London (1972).

Gomez-Ibañez, D. A., *The Western Pyrenees*, Oxford (1975).

Goron, L., 'Les migrations saisonnières dans les départements pyrénéens au début du 19e siècle', *Revue Géographique des Pyrénées et du Sud-Ouest*, 4 (1933), 230–272.

Goubert, P., *Familles marchandes sous l'ancien régime: les Danse et les Motte de Beauvais*, Paris (1959).

Goubert, P., *Beauvais et le Beauvaisis de 1600 à 1730*, Paris (1960).

Goubert, P., 'Registres paroissiaux et démographie dans la France du 16e siècle', *Annales de Démographie Historique* (1965), 43–48.

Goubert, P., *Cent Mille provinciaux au XVIIᵉ siècle*, Paris (1968).

Goubert, P., 'Legitimate fertility and infant mortality in France during the eighteenth century', in Glass, D. V. and Revelle, R. (eds.), *op. cit.* (1972), 321–30.

Gras, J., 'Problèmes de contact entre structures agraires en Anjou du nord-est', *Norois*, 13 (1966), 473–90.

Grenier, A., *Manuel d'archéologie gallo-romaine*, Paris (1934).

Grosdidier de Matons, M., 'La Châtaigneraie cantalienne', *Revue de Géographie Alpine*, 15 (1927), 249–277.

Guichonnet, P., 'Le cadastre savoyard de 1738 et son utilisation pour les recherches d'histoire et de géographie sociale', *Revue de Géographie Alpine*, 43 (1955), 255–93.

Guichonnet, P., 'Les biens communaux et les partages révolutionnaires dans l'ancien département du Léman', *Etudes Rurales*, 36 (1969), 7–36.

Guilcher, A., 'Points de vue nouveaux sur la structure agraire de la Bretagne', *Information Géographique*, 10 (1946), 9–15.

Guilcher, A., 'Le finage des champs dans le cartulaire de Redon', *Annales de Bretagne*, 53 (1946), 140–44.

Guillaume, P., *La Population de Bordeaux au XIXᵉ siècle*, Paris (1972).

Gulley, J. L. M., 'Le marnage dans le bassin parisien', *Revue de Géomorphologie Dynamique*, 13 (1962), 26–30.

Hanotaux, G., *La France en 1614*, Paris (1913).

Hemmings, F. W. J., *Culture and Society in France, 1848–1898*, London (1971).

Henry, L. and Levy, C., 'Quelques données sur la région autour de Paris au XVIIIᵉ siècle', *Population*, 17 (1962), 295–326.

Higonnet, P., *Pont-de-Montvert: social structure and politics in a French village, 1700–1914*, Cambridge, Mass. (1971).

Higounet, C., 'Une carte agricole de l'Albigeois vers 1260', *Annales du Midi*, 65 (1958), 65–72.

Higounet, C., 'La géohistoire', in Samaran, C. (ed.), 'L'Histoire et ses méthodes', Paris (1961), 68–91.

Higounet, C. (ed.), *L'Histoire de l'Aquitaine*, Toulouse (1971).

Ho, J., 'Les origines des Parisiens d'adoption au début du XIXᵉ siècle', *Population*, 25 (1970), 1287–89.

Imberdis, F., 'Une route Lyon–Bordeaux à travers les monts d'Auvergne, antérieure au 18e siècle', *Revue de Géographie Alpine*, 16 (1928), 169–177.

Jacquemet, G., 'Les porteurs d'eau de Paris au XIXᵉ siècle', *Etudes de la Région Parisienne* (1971), 45 (29) 1–4 (30) 11–17 (31) 8–17 (32) 12–21.

Jacquemet, G., 'Belleville aux 19e et 20e siècles: une méthode d' analyse de la croissance urbaine à Paris', *Annales, Economies, Sociétés, Civilisations*, 30 (1975), 819–843.

James, M. K., 'Fluctuations in the Anglo-Gascon wine trade in the fourteenth century', *Economic History Review*, 4 (1951–2), 170–96.

Jarry, E., *Formation de l'unité française*, Paris (1942).

Jarry, E., *Monographies provinciales*, 2 vols., Paris (1943 and 1948).

Judt, A., 'A society in stagnation', *Geographical Magazine*, 48 (1976), 236–40.

Juillard, E. and Angrand, J. P., 'L'utilisation du sol dans les départements de l'Est de la France du XIXᵉ au XXᵉ siècle', *Revue Géographique de l'Est*, 1 (1961), 14–40.

Kreisel, W., 'Structures agraires de Waldhufendorf dans le Jura', *Revue de Géographie de Lyon*, 44 (1969), 85–113.

Lambert, E., 'Le livre de Saint Jacques et les routes du pèlerinage de Compostelle', *Revue Géographique des Pyrénées et du Sud-Ouest*, 14 (1943), 5–33.

Latouche, R., 'La fruitière jurasienne au 18e siècle', *Revue de Géographie Alpine*, 26 (1938), 773–791.

Lebrun, F., 'Registres paroissiaux et démographie en Anjou au 16e siècle', *Annales de Démographie Historique* (1965), 49–50.

Lefebvre, T., 'La transhumance dans les Basses-Pyrénées', *Annales de Géographie*, 37 (1928), 35–60.

Lefebvre, T., *Modes de vie dans les Pyrénées Atlantiques Orientales*, Paris (1933).

Le Névanic, M., 'L'agriculture en Ille-et-Vilaine 1815–1870', *Annales de Bretagne*, 25 (1910), 624–29.

Lenoble, F., 'La légende du déboisement des Alpes', *Revue de Géographie Alpine*, 11 (1923), 5–116.

Léon, P., 'Deux siècles d'activité : l'usine d'Allevard, 1675–1870', *Revue de Géographie Alpine*, 36 (1948), 215–258.

Léon, P., 'La naissance de la grande industrie en Dauphiné, fin du 18e siècle-1869', *Revue de Géographie Alpine*, 40 (1952), 601–613.

Léon, P., 'Vie et mort d'un grand marché international, la Foire de Beaucaire (18–19e siècles)', *Revue de Géographie de Lyon*, 28 (1953), 309–328.

Lerat, S., 'Les coteaux de Jurançon et de Monein ; problèmes d'habitat et de structure agraire', *Revue Géographique des Pyrénées et du Sud-Ouest*, 27 (1956), 356–384.

Le Roy Ladurie, E., *Le Territoire de l'historien*, Paris (1973).

Letonnelier, G., 'Les origines de la culture intensive du noyer dans le Bas-Grésivaudan', *Revue de Géographie Alpine*, 18 (1930), 306–325.

Livet, G., 'La Double', *Revue Géographique des Pyrénées et du Sud-Ouest*, 13 (1942), 170–260.

Livet, R., 'Quelques origines de l'habitat rural dispersé en Provence', *Annales, Economies, Sociétés, Civilisations*, 9 (1954), 101–105.

Longnon, A., *Géographie de la Gaule au VIe siècle*, Paris (1878).

Longnon, A., *Atlas historique de la France*, Paris (1885).

Longnon, A., *La Formation de l'unité française*, Paris (1922).

Loubergé, J., 'Villages et maisons rurales dans la vallée moyenne de Gave de Pau', *Revue Géographique des Pyrénées et du Sud-Ouest*, 29 (1958), 20–50.

Lovie, J., 'Les ressources forestières de la Savoie pendant les premières années du régime français, 1860–1875', *Revue de Géographie Alpine*, 49 (1961), 741–759.

Malet, H., *Le Baron Haussmann et la rénovation de Paris*, Paris (1973).

Mandrou, R., 'Littérature de colportage et mentalités paysannes, XVIIe et XVIIIe siècles', *Etudes Rurales*, 15 (1964), 72–85.

Marcilhacy, C., 'Emile Zola "historien" des paysans beaucerons', *Annales, Economies, Sociétés, Civilisations*, 12 (1957), 573–586.

Markovitch, T. J., 'L'industrie française de 1789 à 1964 : histoire quantitative de l'économie française', *Cahiers de l'Institut des Sciences Economiques Appliquées*, série AF (1965–6), 4–7.

Markovitch, T. J., 'L'industrie française au XVIIIe siècle. L'industrie lainière à la fin du règne de Louis XIV et sous la Régence', *Cahiers de L'Institut des Sciences Economiques Appliquées* (1968), 11.

Marsh, G. P., *The Earth as modified by human action*, London (1874).

Martin, D., 'La Grande Rue de la Guillotière, étude géographique d'une voie lyonnaise', *Revue de Géographie de Lyon*, 25 (1950), 169–214.

Mauco, G., *Les migrations ouvrières en France au début du XIXe siècle, d'après les rapports des préfets de l'Empire de 1808 à 1813*, Paris (1932).

Maureille, P., 'Histoire agricole, toponymie et cadastre. L'exemple de la commune de Neuvic-en-Corrèze', *Etudes Rurales*, 32 (1968), 72.

Maury, L. F. A., *Les Forêts de la France dans l'antiquité et au moyen âge*, Paris (1866).

Maury, L. F. A., *Forêts de la Gaule et de l'ancienne France*, Paris (1867).

Merle, L., 'La métairie de la Gâtine poitevine sous l'ancien régime', *Norois*, 1 (1954), 241–66.

Merle, L., 'Origines et évolution d'un bocage, l'exemple de la Gâtine poitevine', *Annales, Economies, Sociétés, Civilisations*, 12 (1957), 613–18.

Meyer, J. (ed.), *Histoire de Rennes*, Toulouse (1972).

Meyer, J., 'L'histoire des provinces françaises et la rénovation des études régionales', *Revue Historique*, 246 (1971), 39–58.

Meynier, A., *A Travers le Massif Central: Ségalas, Levézou, Châtaigneraie*, Aurillac (1931).

Meynier, A., 'Les plans parcellaires: les sources d'erreur dans le cadastre français', *Annales d'Histoire Economique et Sociale*, 5 (1933), 150.

Meynier, A., 'La commune rurale française', *Annales de Géographie*, 54 (1945), 161–79.

Meynier, A., 'Enigmes d'histoire rurale en Bretagne', *Annales Economies, Sociétés, Civilisations*, 4 (1949), 259–67.

Meynier, A. and Guilcher, A. (1949), 'La 31e excursion géographique interuniversitaire: paysage rural et structure agraire', *Annales de Géographie*, 58 (1949), 8–12.

Meynier, A., 'Les champs ouverts du sud-ouest du Limousin', in *Melanges Géographiques offerts à P. Arbos*, vol. 1 (1953), 137–48.

Meynier, A., 'Les idées de M. Champier sur le bocage', *Norois*, 1 (1954), 5–13.

Meynier, A., 'La carte instrument de recherche: les communes de France', *Annales, Economies, Sociétés, Civilisations*, 13 (1958), 447–81.

Michelet, J., *L'Histoire de la France*, 19 vols., Paris (1833–67).

Miège, J., *La Vie rurale du sillon alpin: étude géographique*, Paris (1961).

Moguelet, J., 'Les pratiques communautaires dans la plaine vendéenne au 19e siècle', *Annales, Economies, Sociétés, Civilisations*, 18 (1963), 666–676.

Mollat, M. (ed.), *Histoire de l'Ile-de-France et de Paris*, Toulouse (1971).

Moreau, J. P., 'Questions agricoles en Basse-Bourgogne au 18e siècle', *Annales de Géographie*, 59 (1950), 346–353.

Moreau, J. P., 'Une cause de transformation du paysage agraire en Bourgogne: la dislocation de la communauté rurale', *Revue de Géographie de Lyon*, 35 (1960), 175–181.

Mougin, P., 'La question du déboisement des Alpes', *Revue de Géographie Alpine*, 12 (1924), 497–545.

Mouralis, D., 'Les phénomènes d'habitat dans le massif des Baronnies, Pré-Alpes du sud', *Revue de Géographie Alpine*, 12 (1924), 547–644.

Musset, R., 'A propos de la maison normande: du Pays de Caux au bocage normand', *Annales de Normandie* (1955), 271–79.

Musset, R., 'Le nom et l'ancienne ceinture forestière du Pays de Caux: les villages des défrichements médiévaux', *Norois*, 8 (1961), 321–27.

Nicod, J., 'Problèmes de structure agraire en Lorraine', *Annales de Géographie*, 60 (1951), 337–48.

Nougier, L. R., 'Essai sur le peuplement préhistorique de la France', *Population*, 9 (1954), 241–74.

Nougier, L. R., 'Le peuplement préhistorique de la France', *Acta Geographica*, 30 (1958), 13–17.

Ogden, P., 'Expression spatiale des contacts humains et changement de la société; l'exemple de l'Ardèche, 1860–1970', *Revue de Géographie de Lyon*, 49 (1974), 191–209.

Ogden, P. E., 'Empty France', *Geographical Magazine*, 48 (1975), 93–97.

Papy, L., 'Les marais salants de l'ouest', *Revue Géographique des Pyrénées et du Sud-Ouest*, 2 (1931), 121–161.

Papy, L., 'Brouage et ses marais', *Revue Géographique des Pyrénées et du Sud-Ouest*, 6 (1935), 281–323.

Papy, L., 'L'ancienne vie pastorale dans la Grande Lande', *Revue Géographique des Pyrénées et du Sud-Ouest*, 18–19 (1947–8), 5–16.

Pavard-Charraud, A. M., 'Bocage et plaine dans l'Ouest de la France', *Annales de Géographie*, 58 (1949), 113–25.

Perpillou, A. V., 'Essai d'établissement d'une carte de l'utilisation du sol en France', *Acta Geographica*, 18 (1952), 110–15.

Perpillou, A. V., 'Paysages ruraux du sud du Poitou', *Norois*, 1 (1954), 391–406.

Perpillou, A. V., 'L'évolution de l'utilisation du sol par l'agriculture dans huit départements du midi de la France', *Centre National de la Recherche Scientifique: Centre de Documentation Cartographique et Géographique*, 7 (1960), 19–34.

Perpillou, A. V., 'L'utilisation agricole du sol dans quelques terroirs des plaines champenoises', *Acta Geographica Lovaniensia*, 3 (1964), 257–76.

Perpillou, A. V., 'L'évolution du paysage rural de la Normandie depuis le début du XIXe siècle', in Dussart, F. (ed.), *L'Habitat et les paysages ruraux de Europe*, Liège (1971), 340–64.

Perpillou, A. V. and Dacharry, M., 'L'utilisation agricole du sol dans les Alpes françaises du Nord', *Acta Geographica* (1961), 2–9.

Perrier, A., 'Quelques noms du vocabulaire de géographie agraire du Limousin', *Revue Géographique des Pyrénées et du Sud-Ouest*, 33 (1962), 255–266.

Piel, E., 'Etapes du peuplement et géographie humaine du Marais de Dol', *Annales de Bretagne*, 56 (1949), 165–74.

Pijassou, R., 'Structures agraires traditionnelles et révolution agricole dans les campagnes périgourdines', *Revue Géographique des Pyrénées et du Sud-Ouest*, 37 (1966), 233–262.

Pirenne, H., 'Le vin et l'histoire française', *Annales d'Histoire Economique et Sociale*, 5 (1933), 225–43.

Plaisance, G., 'La toponymie des défrichements et déboisements', *Revue Géographique de l'Est*, 2 (1962), 221–32.

Plaisse, A., *L'Evolution de la structure agraire dans la Campagne du Neubourg*, Paris (1964).

Plandé, R., 'La propriété foncière à Rieux-Minervois, Aude, de 1667 à 1932', *Revue Géographique des Pyrénées et du Sud-Ouest*, 4 (1933), 384–395.

Poitrineau, A., 'L'alimentation populaire en Auvergne, au 18e siècle', *Annales, Economies, Sociétés, Civilisations*, 17 (1962), 323–331.

Pounds, N. J. G., *An Historical Geography of Europe, 450 B.C.– A.D. 1330*, Cambridge (1973).

Pounds, N. J. G. and Roome, C. C., 'Population density in fifteenth century France and the Low Countries', *Annals of the Association of American Geographers*, 61 (1971), 116–30.

Prince, H. C., 'Some reflections on the origin of hollows in Norfolk compared with those in the Paris region', *Revue de Géomorphologie Dynamique*, 12 (1961), 110–17.

Raison, J. P., 'Conditions et rythmes d'évolution de l'activité agricole dans les Bas-Boulonnais et la plaine maritime flamande', *Acta Geographica* (1962), 10–29.

Rascol, P., 'Albi: étude géographique', *Revue Géographique des Pyrénées et du Sud-Ouest*, 4 (1933), 145–199.

Raveau, P., *L'Agriculture et les classes paysannes: la transformation de la propriété dans le Haut-Poitou au XVIe siècle*, Paris (1926).

Réau, L., 'Le rayonnement de Versailles', *Revue d'Histoire Moderne et Contemporaine*, 1 (1954), 25–47.

Reed, J. L., *Forests of France*, London (1954).

Reinhard, M., 'La population des villes: sa mesure sous la Révolution et l'Empire', *Population*, 9 (1954), 279–88.

Renard, J., 'Problèmes agraires du nord-est de la Vendée', *Norois*, 14 (1967), 373–97.

Renouard, Y., 'The wine trade of Gascony in the middle ages', in Cameron, R. (ed.) *op. cit.* (1970), 64–90.

Reynier, E., 'La vie rurale dans la région privadoise vers 1600', *Revue de Géographie Alpine*, 28 (1940), 73–88.

Rives, J., 'L'évolution démographique de Toulouse au XVIIIe siècle', *Bulletin d'Histoire Économique et Sociale de la Révolution Française* (1968), 85–146.

Robert-Muller, C. and Allix, A., 'Un type d'émigration alpine:

les colporteurs de l'Oisans', *Revue de Géographie Alpine*, 11 (1923), 585–634.

Rochefort, M., 'La pénétration des capitaux bourgeois dans la campagne autunoise: ses conséquences sur l'habitat et la structure agraire', *Revue de Géographie de Lyon*, 25 (1950), 249–266.

Rollet, C., 'L'effet des crises économiques du début du XIXe siècle sur la population', *Revue d'Histoire Moderne et Contemporaine*, 17 (1970), 391–410.

Roupnel, G., *La Ville et la campagne au XVIIe siècle: étude sur les populations du pays dijonnais*, Paris (1955).

Roux, S., 'L'habitat urbain au moyen âge: le quartier de l'université de Paris', *Annales, Economies, Sociétés, Civilisations*, 24 (1969), 1196–1219.

Russell, J. C., 'The metropolitan city region of the middle ages', *Journal of Regional Science*, 2 (1960), 55–70.

Sachet, M., 'Les problemes de changement d'échelle dans la réprésentation cartographique de l'utilisation du sol', *Acta Geographica (Paris)*, 3 (1975), 3–13.

Saint-Jacob, P. de, 'Mutations économiques et sociales dans les campagnes bourguignonnes à la fin du XVIe siècle', *Etudes Rurales*, 1 (1961), 34–49.

Sanfaçon, R., *Défrichements, peuplement et institutions seigneuriales en Haut-Poitou du Xe au XIIIe siècle*, Quebec (1967).

Savouret, G., 'La structure agraire et l'habitat rural dans les Hautes-Vosges', *Publications de la Société de Géographie de Lille* (1942), 5–62.

Sclafert, T., *Le Haut-Dauphiné au moyen âge*, Paris (1926).

Sclafert, T., 'L'industrie du fer dans la région d'Allevard au moyen âge', *Revue de Géographie Alpine*, 14 (1926), 239–355.

Sclafert, T., 'A propos du déboisement des Alpes du sud', *Annales de Géographie*, 42 (1933), 266–277, 350–360.

Sclafert, T., 'A propos du déboisement des Alpes du sud: le rôle des troupeaux', *Annales de Géographie*, 43 (1934), 126–145.

Sclafert, T., 'Les monts de Vaucluse: l'exploitation des bois du 13e à la fin du 18e siècle', *Revue de Géographie Alpine*, 39 (1961), 673–707.

Sée, H., 'The economic and social origins of the French revolution', *Economic History Review*, 3 (1931), 1–15.

Sée, H., 'Les classes rurales en Bretagne du XVIᵉ siècle à la Révolution', *Revue d'Histoire Moderne et Contemporaine*, 6 (1904–5), 309–34.

Sée, H., 'Landes, biens communaux et défrichements en Haute-Bretagne dans la première moitié du XIXᵉ siècle', *Memoires de la Société d'Histoire de Bretagne*, 7–8 (1926–7), 179–201.

Sée, H., *Histoire économique de la France*, Paris, 2 vols (1948 and 1951).

Sentou, J., 'Les facteurs de la révolution agricole dans le Narbonnais', *Revue Géographique des Pyrénées et du Sud-Ouest*, 18 (1947), 89–104.

Siegfried, A., *Tableau politique de la France de l'Ouest sous la Troisième République*, Paris (1913).

Soulas, J., 'Les étapes de l'évolution du Havre de 1789 à nos jours', *Annales de Géographie*, 40 (1949), 205–213.

Soyer, J., *La conservation de la forme circulaire dans le parcellaire français*, Paris (1970).

Specklin, R., 'Etudes sundgoviennes: les origines de l'habitat rural', *Revue Géographique de l'Est*, 3 (1963), 211–40.

Sutcliffe, A., 'A nation of reluctant townsfolk', *Geographical Magazine*, 48 (1976), 290–96.

Taillefer, F., 'Etudes sur les paysages ruraux du Sud-Ouest', *Revue Géographique des Pyrénées et du Sud-Ouest'* (1950), 21, 96–126 and 234–57.

Tilly, C., *The Vendée*, London (1964).

Tinthoin, R., 'Essai de géographie urbaine historique', *Revue de Géographie Alpine*, 60 (1972), 341–58.

Tomas, F., 'Quelques traits de la géographie et de l'histoire agraires de la plaine du Forez', *Revue de Géographie de Lyon*, 38 (1963), 131–61.

Toutant, H., 'La vie économique dans le Vercors méridional et ses abords, d'après le cartulaire de l'abbaye de Léoncel, 1137–1790', *Revue de Géographie Alpine*, 10 (1922), 549–607.

Trénard, L., 'Structure agraire dans le Bas-Bugey', *Revue de Géographie de Lyon*, 24 (1949), 331–340.

Tresse, R., 'Le développement de la fabrication des faux en France de 1786 à 1827, ses conséquences sur la pratique des moissons', *Annales, Economies, Sociétés, Civilisations*, 10 (1955), 341–358.

Vacher, A., *Le Berry: contribution géographique d'une région française*, Paris (1908).

Vallaux, C., *Géographie sociale: la mer*, Paris (1908).

Vallaux, C., *Géographie sociale: le sol et l'état*, Paris (1911).

Vidal de la Blache, P., 'Les conditions géographiques des faits sociaux', *Annales de Géographie*, 11 (1902), 13–23.

Vidal de la Blache, P., *La France de l'Est*, Paris (1920).

Vidal, C., 'Les documents du moyen âge relatifs à la géographie de la région lyonnaise: Fond de Malte', *Revue de Géographie de Lyon*, 27 (1952), 141–144.

Vince, M., 'La Brière: origine des marais, son habitat, temoin d'un genre de vie abandonné', *Norois*, 8 (1961), 332–36.

Vogt, J., 'Notes agraires rhénanes: l'ancienneté de l'assolement biennal alsacien', *Revue Géographique de l'Est*, 3 (1963), 241–43.

Walle, E. Van de and Preston, S. H., 'Mortinatalité de l'enfance au XIXe siècle à Paris et dans le département de la Seine', *Population*, 29 (1974), 89–107.

Wolff, P., 'Villes et campagnes dans le Midi français mediéval', *Revue Géographique des Pyrénées et du Sud-Ouest*, 19 (1948), 125–132.

Wolff, P. (ed.), *Histoire du Languedoc*, Toulouse (1967).

Index